# THE
# VOYAGES
# OF THE
# DISCOVERY

Ann Savours is a distinguished polar historian. Educated at London University and the Sorbonne, she worked for many years at the Scott Polar Research Institute in Cambridge and then at the National Maritime Museum at Greenwich, where she was in charge of the Arctic Gallery and closely involved with the shipboard *Discovery* exhibition in Dundee.

She is a long standing Fellow of the Royal Geographical Society, a council member of the Hakluyt Society, and is a former Honorary Secretary of the Society for Nautical Research. Ann Savours is married, with two grown-up sons, and lives with her husband Laurie in a peg-tiled house in Kent.

Her previous books include *The* Discovery *Diary of Edward Wilson 1901–4* and *Scott's Last Voyage*.

# THE VOYAGES
## OF THE
# DISCOVERY
### THE ILLUSTRATED HISTORY OF SCOTT'S SHIP

Ann Savours

*Foreword by HRH The Duke of Edinburgh*

*Preface by the late Sir Peter Scott*

*To all 'Discoverers',
past and present*

*This edition first published in Great Britain in 1994 by*
Virgin Books
an imprint of Virgin Publishing Ltd
338 Ladbroke Grove
London W10 5AH

*First published by Virgin Books 1992*

Copyright © Ann Savours 1992

The moral right of the author has been asserted

A catalogue record for this book is available from the British Library

ISBN 0 86369 811 5

Maps and charts drawn by Vera Brice and Leslie Robinson

*Typeset by*
TW Typesetting, Plymouth

*Printed and bound in Great Britain by*
Butler & Tanner Ltd,
Frome, Somerset

# CONTENTS

# ILLUSTRATIONS

# COLOUR PLATES

# MAPS AND DIAGRAMS

To seafarers, every ship has a personality of its own. Some live out their lives in modest obscurity, others achieve varying degrees of fame or notoriety.

Several ships have borne the name 'Discovery' and, as might be expected, many of them have been associated with famous explorers. Hudson, Baffin, Cook, Vancouver and Nares commanded a 'Discovery ' at some time in their careers, but it is the 'Discovery', built at Dundee and launched in 1901, that is probably the best known of them all.

Designed and built for Antarctic exploration, she was commanded by Commander R.F. Scott RN on her first expedition to the south seas. She came to be known as Scott's 'Discovery', although she was not involved in Scott's second, more famous and tragic, expedition to the Antarctic.

She will always be associated with Antarctic exploration, but until she was honourably retired in 1931, 'Discovery' also enjoyed a varied and adventurous career in other employment. She was a familiar sight on the Thames until 1979 when she was moved to St Katharine's Dock for a few years and then back home to Dundee to be carefully restored and opened to the public.

Ann Savours has pieced together a fascinating and detailed 'biography' of this famous ship. Her scholarly record is the result of much patient research and I am sure that it will make very interesting reading to both the expert and the uninitiated.

# PREFACE

BY THE LATE SIR PETER SCOTT

I am delighted to have been asked to contribute this preface to an enthralling and scholarly book about the ship used by my father on his first expedition to the Antarctic from 1901 to 1904.

This *Discovery* was built in Dundee at the very beginning of the twentieth century—one of the last wooden three-masted sailing ships to be built in Britain. It was the type of vessel that took Columbus to discover the New World and was modelled on the lines of the old Scottish whalers for use in the ice. She was at least the sixth ship to be called *Discovery*. Down the ages the name has been linked with great explorers—Baffin, Cook, Vancouver and Nares—and the name is still alive today on one of the space shuttles.

*Discovery* was almost continually in use during her active life and had strong Commonwealth connections, with Canada, Australia and New Zealand. Her three Antarctic voyages were different in aim and character. Thus, in her working life, her span stretched from the heroic age of exploration to the modern era of research using radio and aircraft.

She was one of the last annual supply ships of the Hudson's Bay Company, sailing across the Atlantic from London through the ice of the Davis and Hudson Straits, into Hudson Bay, as her predecessors had done since the 1670s. She survived two world wars and even saw service during the Russian Civil War.

From 1925 to 1927, *Discovery* worked as a research ship for the scientific study of oceanography and of the great whales. This research in the Southern Ocean was part of a series later known as '*Discovery* Investigations' and laid the foundations of our knowledge of the food chains dependent on krill—work which is very relevant today.

The British, Australian and New Zealand Antarctic Research Expedition (BANZARE) from 1929 to 1931 represented *Discovery*'s final work in the Antarctic. Thereafter, she became familiar to Londoners, lying in a berth on the Embankment, and acting as a base for the Sea Scouts. It was during that period that all of my children were christened in the *Discovery*'s ship's bell. Later still, because of the enormous cost of unshipping the masts in order to go under the Thames bridges for refits, she was reberthed in St Katharine's Dock, below Tower Bridge. In 1986, *Discovery* went 'home', to Dundee.

I am very glad to have this opportunity of wishing Ann Savours's book every success.

# AUTHOR'S NOTE AND ACKNOWLEDGEMENTS

Writing this book has been something of a voyage of discovery in itself. I undertook the task at the suggestion of Dr Basil Greenhill, CB, CMG, then Director of the National Maritime Museum, Greenwich. This was in 1979, when the Maritime Trust (London) had taken the *Discovery* over from the Admiralty and when the museum had agreed to organise displays in the hold, illustrating her history. Some years later, on the strength of the first draft, a publisher was found by my literary agent, Bruce Hunter of David Higham Associates. It was at this point that Gill Gibbins of Columbus Books became involved and she fortunately stayed with the project, despite subsequent company takeovers, which caused inevitable delays. Frustrating as these were, they enabled me to work in 1989 on the papers of Captain John King Davis in the State Library of Victoria, Melbourne. These had only that year been made available to scholars. Sadly, however, the delay has meant that some of the older people who helped me have died. I think particularly of the late Sir Alister Hardy, FRS, whom it was an inspiration to visit and whose promised 'tailpiece' about the joys of sailing in the old *Discovery* was never written. Both Sir Alister and the late Sir George Deacon, FRS, were kind enough to read the draft of the 1925–7 chapters. I am similarly indebted to Captain A. R. Williamson, DSC, who sailed in the *Discovery* to Hudson Bay in 1911 (and even earlier to South Russia) and whom again it was a pleasure and privilege to meet; and to Dr D. Dilwyn John, of the 1925–7 voyage, who maintained his interest in the book, despite all the delays. Mr John Bentley and Mr George Gourlay kindly allowed me to quote from their 1925–7 papers.

The Colbeck family have a special connection with the *Discovery*. Captain William Colbeck was master of the *Morning* and commander of the relief expeditions during the National Antarctic Expedition, 1901–4. His son, Captain W. R. Colbeck, was Navigating Officer of the *Discovery* during Mawson's BANZARE Expedition, 1929–31. Captain Colbeck has died, but his widow and family, as well as his brother, Mr Mark Colbeck, CBE, have continued to encourage and help.

Other *Discovery* families and individuals have been similarly kind, namely Charles and Peggy Longstaff, Mrs Evelyn Forbes (*née* Farrar) and Lord Kennet (1901–4 expedition); Commodore and Mrs E. S. Baker (1906–11); Lord Shackleton, Ethel Burton and Nancy Rycroft (1916); Dr Mavis Gunther, Mrs Ros Marsden and Dr N. Gunther,

Mrs Margaret Marshall, Mrs Patricia Mantell and Mr Michael Hardy (1925–7); Captain K. M. MacKenzie, Mrs E. Riley and Mr C. B. Child (1929–31).

The Trans-Antarctic Association has made a generous award towards the cost of illustrations.

I am particularly indebted to Mrs Shirlee Anne Smith, until recently Keeper of the Hudson's Bay Company Archives, Provincial Archives of Manitoba. She kindly transcribed some logs when time ran out for me during two visits to Winnipeg. It was from her home that I visited Lower Fort Garry on the Red River and flew with the Rupertsland Record Society to Churchill and York Factory on Hudson Bay in 1988.

'A ship is a secret society,' John Keegan once said. I have to thank Mr M. R. C. (Tim) Parr and Mr Alan Viner for casting a critical eye over certain chapters, likewise Dr Charles Swithinbank; Mr S. G. Brown; Mrs Christine Kelly; Professor Glyndwr Williams; Dr P. G. Law, AO, CBE; Dr G. de Q. Robin; Dr Haakon Mosby; Mr David Lyon; Mr A. W. H. Pearsall, ISO; Mr John Silverlight; Professor Arnold Wolfendale, FRS; Dr Terence Armstrong and Professor Bryan Ranft for critical reviews of parts of the ms. Needless to say, any nautical or other errors must lie at my door. I remain grateful to the late G. P. B. Naish for the chance to crew in his old pilot cutter *Dolphin* years ago and more recently to the Sail Training Association and to Mariners International for the chance to sail 'before the mast' in their tall ships, *Sir Winston Churchill* and *Astrid*; also to the Australian Antarctic Division (ANARE) for my visit to Macquarie Island in the *Magga Dan*.

The staff of the sadly defunct Mawson Institute, University of Adelaide, were immensely helpful and I have to thank Dr Fred Jacka, Mrs Edna Sawyer, Mrs Heather Duff, Mr Richard Ferguson and Dr André Phillips. At the Royal Geographical Society, Mrs Christine Kelly, Mr David Wileman and Mr Ted Hatch were similarly kind and at the National Maritime Museum, thanks are due to Mrs Trisha Palmer (who transcribed Captain MacKenzie's diary), Ms Geraldine Charles, Mrs Marilla Fletcher, Miss C. MacLeod, Miss Lindsay MacFarlane (who mounted the *Discovery* photograph albums), Mr John Munday, Mr Michael Dandridge, Dr Roger Morriss, Dr Kristen Lippincott, Mr Robert Baldwin, Mr H. D. Howse, MBE, DSC, Mr A. N. Stimson, MVO, Miss Clare Towers, Mrs Elizabeth Wiggans, and Mr Neville Upham. I thank too Vice-Admiral Sir Patrick Bayly, KBE, CB, DSC; Wing Commander K. P. Lucas, MNI, RAF; Mr Rick Hogben and Mrs Janet Hales of the Maritime Trust; Mrs Dorothy Norman (British Museum, Natural History); Dr Nicholas Rodger (Public Record Office); Miss Pat Mugliston (Aberdeen University Library); Mr Arthur Credland (Town Docks Museum, Hull); Mr David Henderson (Dundee Museums); Ms Jo-Anne Smith (Canterbury Museum, Christchurch, NZ); Miss Anne Morton and Mr Alex Ross (Hudson's Bay Company Archives); Mr H. G. R. King, Mrs Sylva Gethin, Mr William Mills, Dr Bernard Stonehouse and Mr R. K. Headland (Scott Polar Research Institute, Cambridge); Lieut.-Com. A. C. F. David, RN, and Captain Richard Campbell, RN (MOD Hydrographic Office); Mrs Pauline Simpson and Dr A. L. Rice (Institute of Oceanographic

Sciences, Deacon Laboratory); Dr John Heap, CMG, and Dr Geoffrey Hattersley-Smith (Polar Regions Section, Foreign and Commonwealth Office); Madame Jacqueline Carpine-Lancre (Musée Océanographique, Monaco); the librarian and staff of the Royal Society; the staff of the Imperial War Museum; the Merchant Trading Company (Metco); the Mitchell Library, State Library of New South Wales; Ms Mary Maciorowski (Agassiz Galleries, Winnipeg); Mrs Jane Lovelock (Templeman Library, University of Kent at Canterbury); Mrs Margaret Slythe (Dulwich College); Mr S. D. Robertson (Department of Trade and Industry); Mons. P. Henwood (Service Historique de la Marine à Brest); Mme A. Henwood (Archives Municipales, Brest); Prof. C. Meriot (Université de Bordeaux); Mr Tony Marshall and Ms R. Newton (State Library of Victoria); Mr D. Harrowfield (formerly Christchurch Museum, NZ); Mr Jonathan Bryant and Mr Alan White of Dundee Industrial Heritage Trust; and Scottish Enterprise, Tayside.

I acknowledge with particular indebtedness the kindness of HRH the Prince Philip, Duke of Edinburgh and of the late Sir Peter Scott in writing the foreword and preface to the book; of the late Captain R. E. D. Ryder, VC, RN, and Mr Duncan Carse for their reminiscences of James Holland Martin; and of former Sea Scouts Dr John Nash, Mr Peter Hollins, RIBA, and Lieut.-Com. J. Dawkins, VRD, RNR. I am also grateful for help from the late Professor Charles Elton, FRS; Mrs Valentina Ward; the late Dr Walter Kenyon; Mr Ivo Meisner; Mr John Massey Stewart; Dr Willem Hackmann; Miss Margaret Deacon (Mrs Seward); Mr David Geddes; Professor W. Barr; Mr Peter Lawrence; Mrs A. Houstoun Stewart; Dr K. F. Perachie; Mr Eric W. Morse; and to those who have nobly typed the ms., Mrs Doreen Brown, Mrs Ann Goldsworthy, Mrs Pamela Skrine and Mrs Karen MacLellan also Trish and Alfie Jarvis. I acknowledge those associated with the book's production, Ms Sally Holloway, Mr Paul Forty, Mr Nick Law, Miss Vera Brice and Mr Douglas Matthews. Lastly I thank my husband, Laurie, who despite being something of a bibliophobe, put up with all the piles of books and papers about the house and helped in many practical ways. (I should perhaps add that many of these books came from the polar or maritime booksellers Maggs Bros., Bluntisham, Mainmast, P. J. Walcot, High Latitude, Anthony Simmonds, Gaston Renard, F. et R. Chamonal and Colin Bull, whose catalogues I have perused with pleasure and profit.)

Thirteen years is a long time to have a work on the stocks and I apologise to anyone or any institution I have inadvertently omitted to mention here.

Ann Savours
Little Bridge Place
near Canterbury, Kent

August 1992

# PART I

# THE NATIONAL ANTARCTIC EXPEDITION, 1901–4

# ONE

## The Origins of the National Antarctic Expedition and the Building of the *Discovery*

### THE ORIGINS OF THE NATIONAL ANTARCTIC EXPEDITION

'Gentlemen.'

On a late November day in 1893, Dr John Murray was beginning his address to the Fellows of the Royal Geographical Society. It is difficult to believe that a century ago Antarctica, the ice-bound continent at the bottom of the world, was almost unknown. Sightings of land had been made from sailing ships in a number of places but whether these, when linked, formed the coastline of a continent or were merely groups of islands remained to be seen. Because of the continental types of rocks dredged from the bottom of the sea and because some shallow soundings appeared to indicate a continental shelf, it was suspected that a continent might well lie inside the Antarctic Circle. However, this all had to be proved. In 1893, the interior was almost as much *terra incognita* as in Captain Cook's day.

'What', Dr Murray asked, 'is the nature of the snow- and ice-covered land observed at so many points towards the South Pole? Is there a sixth continent within the Antarctic Circle, or is the land nucleus, on which the massive ice-cap rests, merely a range of lofty volcanic hills?'[1] Murray was a famous man of science and had taken part in the *Challenger* deep-sea expedition of 1872–6. He had recently been in touch with geographers and scientists in many parts of the world and found among them complete unanimity on the question of South Pole exploration to

determine the nature and extent of the Antarctic Continent; to penetrate into the interior; to ascertain the depth and nature of the ice-cap; to take magnetical and meteorological observations both at sea and on land; to observe the temperature of the ocean at all depths and seasons of the year; to take pendulum observations on land, and possibly also to make gravity observations at great depths in the ocean; to bore through the deposits on the floor of the ocean at certain points to ascertain the condition of the deeper layers; to sound, trawl and dredge; and study the character and distribution of marine organisms . . .

Only by these investigations, he said, could many general scientific problems concerning the Ice Age, the form and make-up of the Earth, the circulation of the oceans and of the atmosphere, and the origins of the flora and fauna of both land and sea be solved. 'This country has frequently sent forth expeditions, the primary object of which was the acquisition of new knowledge—such were the expeditions of Cook, Ross and the *Challenger*: and the nation as a whole has always approved such action, and has been proud of the results, although they yielded no immediate return. Shall it be said that there is to be no successor to these great expeditions?'

Murray saw the exploration being undertaken by two small ships of the Royal Navy, landing two wintering parties, one near Mount Erebus, the active volcano sighted in the 1840s from the Ross Sea, and the other in Graham Land, discovered by John Biscoe in the 1830s, part of what is now known to be the Antarctic Peninsula. The ships would not be frozen in but should return northwards to the open sea, making observations along the edge of the pack-ice during two winter seasons. The land parties might be largely non-naval—and one or two civilians might be attached to each ship, as in the *Challenger*. He called for a 'good workable scheme' to be drawn up and had little doubt that a 'Minister will be found sufficiently alive to the spirit of the times, and with sufficient courage to add a few thousand pounds to the navy vote for three successive years' in order to fund what he saw as the greatest scientific challenge of the day, 'a steady, continuous, laborious and systematic exploration of the whole southern region with all the appliances of the modern investigator'.

In the discussion that followed Murray's paper, there was general approval of his proposals. Among the speakers was the aged botanist, Sir Joseph Hooker, who had sailed with Ross during the great Antarctic exploring and scientific voyage of 1839–43 that resulted in the discovery of the Ross Sea, Mount Erebus and of Victoria Land, named after the Queen and 'surely the whitest if not the brightest jewel in her crown'. After other eminent Fellows had spoken in support, the President of the RGS, Sir Clements Markham, brought the meeting to a close by saying that he considered Dr Murray's paper should mark a fresh start in the campaign for the renewal of Antarctic discovery. He then announced that the Council of the Society had appointed an Antarctic Committee to report on the best way to carry out 'a task from which I, for one, will never swerve until it is completed'. He went on:

> We are, of course, devoted to geographical research and to the interests of science, and we look upon those objects as a chief reason for despatching an expedition. But as an Englishman I feel that the greatest result of all will be the encouragement of that spirit of maritime enterprise which has ever distinguished the people of this country, and the keeping alive of our glorious naval traditions.

Sir Clements Markham, KCB, FRS,[2] when formerly Secretary of the Royal Geographical Society, had played a considerable part in the despatch of the Arctic Expedition of 1875–6, led by Sir George Nares; in his youth, he had sailed in HMS *Assistance* (Captain

Ommanney) on one of the Arctic expeditions searching for Sir John Franklin in 1850–1. Now he thanked Admiral Sir Erasmus Ommanney and the Committee of the British Association for their endeavours during the previous decade, and referred also to the zeal which had inspired Baron von Mueller, Captain Pasco 'and our other friends in Australia'.[3] Markham was a forceful character, not easily thwarted in his resolve, and he had determined in his own mind that an Antarctic expedition should be organised, confident that once public support was demonstrated, the government would be sure to concur. The way forward, however, proved slower and stormier than he had foreseen.

The keel of the *Discovery* was laid at the old Stephen's Yard of the Dundee Shipbuilders Company in March 1900. She was launched with some ceremony on 21 March 1901, numbering among her predecessors of the same name Hudson's and Baffin's small vessel of 55 tons, Captain Cook's former Whitby collier, Vancouver's sloop of war and Sir George Nares's auxiliary barque, on whose lines Scott's *Discovery* was designed 'to sail the high seas and push forcefully through the looser ice packs'.[4] That the *Discovery* was built at all was due to three men: Sir John Murray, the great oceanographer, Sir Clements Markham, President of the Royal Geographical Society and 'Father' of the National Antarctic Expedition, and Mr Llewellyn Longstaff, whose donation of £25,000 at a critical juncture bridged the gap between Markham's plans and their execution.

The pages of this book tell the story of the design and construction of one very special wooden ship and of her three Antarctic voyages, each different in origin, purpose and area of operation. They reveal the *Discovery*'s life as a merchant vessel in the ownership of the Hudson's Bay Company, not only as a supply ship for the fur trade, but also as a small cargo carrier in the First World War working between the French Atlantic ports, Archangel and south Russia.

Laid down in the last years of Queen Victoria's reign, when wooden shipbuilding was becoming obsolete, she would witness echo-sounding and cosmic ray research pioneered during her later voyages and carry a sea-plane on her decks for use in exploration. The *Discovery*'s career is recounted often in the words of her captains, officers, scientists and crew, and others such as the Sea Scouts and RNVR, who lived or trained aboard, during her long years in London beside the Thames Embankment. Finally her most recent—and perhaps last—voyage, from London to Dundee, where now she lies is celebrated. The perils and dangers to which the *Discovery* was subjected during her active life were very many. She was by no means perfect—and had her faults as well as her virtues.

Her first and most famous captain was Robert Falcon Scott, commander of the National Antarctic Expedition of 1901–4. The *Discovery* was built for this expedition; his first voyage south was therefore her maiden voyage. Scott and his company were bound to her with very special ties. Towards the end of the expedition, early in 1904, the *Discovery* still lay gripped in the ice of McMurdo Sound, with miles of ice between her and open water. The Admiralty had ordered that she should be abandoned if she were not freed by the breakup of the ice. It was when recollecting this fearful possibility, anathema to any sailor, that Scott would write of the ties binding them to the *Discovery* as 'very far beyond the ordinary'. Sir Douglas Mawson and other later explorers, scientists and seafarers expressed a similar affection or appreciation (but sometimes exasperation) for her.

The meeting of the Sixth International Geographical Congress in London during the summer of 1895 was an important milestone. Sir Clements Markham was its Chairman, as President of the Royal Geographical Society. A memorable paper, 'Ueber Südpolar-forschung', was delivered in German and English by Dr Georg von Neumayer, the kindly, distinguished and courtly director of the Marine Observatory (Deutsche Seewarte) in Hamburg.[5] He forcefully advocated the renewal of south polar exploration, one of the great passions of his life. Neumayer was strongly supported in this by Dr John Murray and Sir Joseph Hooker. Markham appointed him chairman of a committee charged with drawing up a resolution later passed by the Congress on the future of Antarctic discovery. This stated that 'the exploration of the Antarctic regions' was 'the greatest piece of geographical exploration still to be undertaken'. In view of the increased knowledge that would accrue 'in almost every branch of science' from such exploration, learned societies world-wide were recommended to urge that 'this work should be undertaken before the close of the century'.[6]

Despite what he called his 'advanced age', two years later Neumayer accepted the Royal Society's invitation to attend a meeting held on 24 February 1898, at which Dr John Murray spoke of 'The scientific advantages of an Antarctic expedition'.[7] In the discussion that followed, Neumayer referred to Sir James Clark Ross, whose 'exceedingly well executed' work in the Antarctic ceased fifty-five years before. Since that time, he said, it had never been prosecuted in any way that could compare with 'the glorious scientific and nautical spirit manifested' by Ross. 'It is in view of this fact that we all look to the British nation as the one destined to carry on the exploration of the South Polar regions and it was to assist this' object' as much as he could, as well as to do homage to Ross's memory, that he had come from Germany to the meeting. Other eminent scientists and geographers of the day spoke in favour of sending an expedition to carry out work in their particular fields. The meeting ended with an enigmatic remark by Professor D'Arcy Thompson that 'the Antarctic holds for us innumerable problems of which we can foresee neither statement nor solution, as well as the solution of those that we can in some measure foresee'.

The great scientific circumnavigation of HMS *Challenger* (1872–6) and the Arctic expedition of 1875–6 in HM Ships *Alert* and *Discovery* had both been financed by the Government. Markham anticipated that the proposed Antarctic expedition would also be an official one. He therefore appealed directly to the First Lord of the Admiralty, George Goschen, 'pointing out the advantages that would be derived from a further knowledge of the South Polar Regions—the verification of the dimensions of the vast Antarctic Continent and the invaluable scientific work that would be accomplished. Nor did he omit to mention the enormous benefit that would accrue to the Navy, by the practical training of officers in a school where courage, self reliance, and other qualities so essential to a seaman, would be developed.'[8]

Markham received the following reply from the First Lord of the Admiralty, dated 9 November 1895:[9]

> Your reference to my action in the case of the Challenger expedition is a guarantee to me that you will not ascribe what I am about to write to any want of appreciation on my part of the value of scientific exploration and discovery, the first importance of which I most fully recognise.
>
>   But at the present moment I must frankly and clearly state that I should not on any representations which might be sent to me, however influential the quarter might be from which they proceeded—be prepared to commit the Admiralty to the fitting out of an Antarctic expedition. . . .

Sir Clements responded, saying that 'under present circumstances', he was 'not altogether unprepared' for such an answer. 'We may have to look on', he continued, 'while other nations do the work which was once specially our own: but on the other hand it is possible that it may still be done by us when happier times arrive, and when this country is again able to take its old place in the van of exploration.'[10] Times had changed. As Dr Rodger has pointed out, in the 'placid naval world of the 1870s', the Navy 'looked forward to war in much the same way as the Church of England looked forward to the Second Coming; it was the theoretical goal of all its activities, but it scarcely affected its practical life at all'.[11] But by the 1880s and 1890s, when Markham was advocating the despatch of a naval expedition to the Antarctic, there was a new feeling in the air stimulated by 'social Darwinism and the victory of Prussian discipline and preparedness' over France, which, 'among other factors taught people to value naval strength and worry about naval unpreparedness'.[12] Public pressure led to the rapid expansion of the Navy, while at the same time, the service was changing fast, following the introduction of new types of ships and weapons.[13] The long decades of *Pax Britannica* after the Napoleonic Wars were coming to an end. The Admiralty was preoccupied with the growth of the fleet and the changing technology in the last years of the nineteenth century. It was not inclined towards geographical and scientific exploration, as had been the case in the middle years after 1815.[14]

The Council of the Royal Geographical Society eventually agreed to Murray's suggestion and Markham's proposal of December 1895 that a private expedition should be undertaken. In April 1897, it resolved to subscribe and raise funds. In February of the following year, the President and Council of the Royal Society, the scientific adviser to the government, consented to join the Royal Geographical Society and organise a joint expedition.[15] Markham had meanwhile been campaigning to interest the public and persuade subscribers. He had raised only £14,000 by March 1899, including a donation of £5,000 from Mr Harmsworth the newspaper magnate, when a Mr Llewellyn Longstaff of Wimbledon enquired whether £25,000 would enable the expedition to start.[16] Explaining to Sir Clements that he had always been interested in scientific matters, Longstaff (a Fellow of the Royal Geographical Society for nearly 30 years) paid this princely sum to the credit of the National Antarctic Expedition. The gift, he said, gave him 'peculiar pleasure to be able thus to contribute towards the advancement of our knowledge of the planet on which we live'.[17] Not only would the donation enable the Societies 'to equip an efficient expedition consisting of one vessel', Markham was reported to have said on its acceptance, but it would enable them 'to co-operate with the Germans in the scientific exploration of the Antarctic regions'.

A paint manufacturer, born in 1841, the son of a founder of the Chemical Society, Longstaff was no mere Croesus, but a keen traveller, philanthropist and supporter of the Red Cross. He rose to be Lieut.-Col. of the first Volunteer Battalion of the East Yorkshire Regiment, retiring in 1880 with the Long Service Medal. An enlightened employer, he pioneered profit-sharing and pensions for his employees, and gave generously and without ostentation to many causes. He continued to take a great interest in the National Antarctic Expedition, making further donations to it and later to Scott's last expedition in the *Terra Nova*, 1910–13, and died in November 1918.[18] Both Markham and Scott felt that he should have been knighted.[19] 'In appearance he might easily be taken for an explorer', reported the *Evening News*[20] of Longstaff, 'as he has the close cut beard and bronze complexion of a naval captain, and shrewdness and energy are written all over his face.' At a monthly house dinner of the Royal Societies' Club, in replying to Sir Clements Markham's kind words, Mr Longstaff said that he had long wished to do something for science. His sons had given him a book on Antarctic voyages for his birthday, and this perhaps had directed his attention to the subject.[21] As Markham's biographer has pointed out, Longstaff's munificence

> . . . justified Markham, having now nearly £40,000 in his possession, to approach the Government with confidence and ask for monetary assistance. Mr Longstaff's noble and patriotic gift altered the whole position of affairs and led to important results. Mr Balfour consented to receive a deputation, and to cut a long story short, the Prime Minister cordially announced that the Government would contribute the sum of £45,000 on condition that an equal amount was forthcoming from other sources.
> . . . Only £3,000 was required to make up the amount necessary to secure the Government grant and on Markham's appeal to the Council of the Royal Geographical Society, that enlightened body unanimously consented to subscribe the money required. Another appeal was made to the public and in August 1900, he had the satisfaction of announcing that the total subscribed to the fund amounted to £93,000.[22]

Thus the National Antarctic Expedition came into being, financed from both public and private funds. In contrast, the German South Polar Expedition was very largely a state enterprise to be endowed with an imperial grant-in-aid of 12,000,000 marks (£60,000) in five yearly instalments, according to a report in the *Standard* of 16 May 1899 from Berlin. This same report gave the reason for despatch of the German expedition as being the lack of progress in Antarctic exploration since the voyage of Sir James Clark Ross in the 1840s. Scientific work would also be undertaken and the expedition would depart in the autumn of 1901 in a wooden ship. Dr E. von Drygalski, Professor of the University of Berlin, had been appointed leader. Although to some extent rivalry between Great Britain and Germany helped to realise the Antarctic projects of either nation, the aim of both expedition committees was co-operation in science and non-duplication of the areas of geographical exploration. The British were to follow Ross into the Ross Sea and the Germans the American explorer Wilkes towards his 'Termination Land' of the 1840s, to the south of Kerguelen. In the event, what has been called a 'great international campaign of scientific discovery . . . a peaceful and unobtruding campaign, devoid of glamour and thrilling glory' was mounted against the Antarctic, not only by Germany and England, but also by Scotland, Sweden and France between 1901 and 1905.[23]

Sir Clements Markham now had to convert or build a ship, appoint a leader and staff, and decide on a geographical and scientific programme for the National Antarctic Expedition. A joint Antarctic Committee was formed from the two societies, its chairman being the president of the Royal Society, Lord Lister, and its vice-chairman, Sir Clements Markham. Markham's diary refers to some of the later meetings of the Joint Committee as 'miserable', 'as usual, a regular bear garden' full of what he considered were noisy and troublesome professors, some of whom he pronounced to be 'howling cads'.[24]

The main bone of contention between Markham and the 'wild professors on the warpath' was the conduct of the expedition and the respective responsibilities of the leader and the scientific director. He had managed to persuade Mr Goschen, First Lord of the Admiralty, to allow a naval officer to captain the ship, with another as his chief assistant, plus two or three officers from the Royal Naval Reserve. The Admirals on the RGS side and Markham maintained that the naval commander should be in overall charge of the expedition, as had been so in the case of the great Antarctic voyage of HM Ships *Erebus* and *Terror* under Sir James Clark Ross in the 1840s. Professor J. W. Gregory had been appointed Scientific Director. He was an eminent geologist and had done field work in various parts of the world, including East Africa and Spitsbergen. Markham described him as a 'little man with a very low voice, always nervously pulling his moustache'.[25] He was a versatile man of great talent, beloved by his colleagues and students. Besides numerous geographical and geological works, he had (at this time) already written *The Great Rift Valley* after his explorations of 1892–3, and was later to publish two other travel books, *The dead heart of Australia* and *To the Alps of Chinese Tibet*. His undoubted scientific ability made his resignation over differences with Markham regarding his role and the scientific work of the expedition a cause for regret.

A more regrettable and earlier casualty still was Sir John Murray. He had wished the expedition to be a largely oceanographic one, succeeding HMS *Challenger*'s great voyage of 1872–6, while Markham believed the main object should be geographical exploration in high latitudes, with 'dredging when practicable'. Sir Clements had written to his cousin, Admiral A. H. Markham, from Norway, 'Do not let that overbearing fellow Murray meddle more than is necessary. Of course he cannot have things like the "Challenger"; and dredging will be a very secondary part of the work.'[26]

Markham likewise strongly disagreed with the proposal of the Biological Sub-Committee 'to turn the Antarctic Expedition into a mud-larking cruise in accessible seas'. Another point of contention was Murray's insistence that the scientific work should be directed solely by an eminent scientist. To this, Markham could not agree. In the same letter to his cousin, he wrote that 'These mud larkers must not be allowed to appropriate the title of "Scientific Staff". The captain and executive are the real "Scientific Staff" for geography, magnetism, meteorology, deep sea soundings and dredging, etc. etc.'

Dr H. R. Mill, Librarian of the RGS and historian of the Antarctic, described Murray's resignation:

> From his association with the *Challenger* Sir John Murray was the natural organiser of a purely scientific expedition. He, like Markham, believed in employing naval officers and men, but, unlike Markham, he insisted on the scientific work being under the sole direction of an eminent man of science. He also held that if the expedition had to be got up privately, a sum of money amply sufficient to meet all contingencies should be in sight before any expenditure was made. In a conversation between Murray and Markham in the Upper Library [of the Royal Geographical Society's house] at Savile Row, these points were debated with deadly earnestness. Markham maintained that as soon as the money needed to equip one ship was ready the expedition should go, as he believed that the force of public opinion would eventually compel the Government to provide a second ship to act as tender to the first. Agreement was impossible; Murray, the greatest British physical geographer withdrew, and took no further part in the arrangements.[27]

Although Markham had left the Navy after six years as a cadet and midshipman, he retained a great love for the service. He was able to keep in touch through his cousin, Albert (later Admiral Sir Albert Hastings Markham). The story of how Sir Clements acted as Fate or a *deus ex machina* in Captain Scott's life has often been told, leading to Scott's being given command of the National Antarctic Expedition and culminating in his death in the tent on the Barrier during the return from the South Pole in 1912.[28] Markham had picked Scott out as future leader at the age of 18 when he won a boat race in the West Indies in 1887. Twelve years later, he still favoured Scott, observing to his cousin that of the ten men under consideration, Scott was 'by far the best if Egerton recommends him'.[29] In a frank private account of the origins of the National Antarctic

Expedition, Markham described his ideal commander: 'He must be a *naval officer*, he must be *in the regular line* and not in the surveying branch and he must be *young*. These are essentials. Such a commander should be a good *sailor* with some experience of ships under sail, a *navigator* with a knowledge of *surveying*, and he should be of *a scientific turn of mind*. He must have *imagination* and be capable of *enthusiasm*. His temperament must be *cool*, he must be *calm, yet quick and decisive* in action, *a man of resource, tactful* and *sympathetic*.'[30]

Markham gave the news of the anticipated appointment of Robert Falcon Scott (confirmed at a meeting of the Joint Committee on 25 May 1900) and of Royds as his chief assistant to Mr Llewellyn Longstaff in a letter dated 6 April 1900.

Lieut. Scott is now serving under Captain Egerton, than whom there is no one better qualified to advise us. For he combines Arctic experience with a wide knowledge of the rising generation of naval officers when in active service at sea. So I asked his opinion of Scott. He replied—'You certainly could not do better than put Scott in command. He is just the fellow for it, strong, steady, as keen as possible, genial, scientific, a good head on his shoulders and a very good officer. I am in hopes he will get his promotion in June. He thoroughly deserves it.' His age is 30. He will have about a year to make himself thoroughly acquainted with Antarctic questions and superintend all the work.

Royds is a splendid young fellow, aged 23; nephew of Sir Wm. Rawson, the Commander-in-Chief in the Channel. He was working last year, in charge of a 'destroyer' at the mouth of the Thames, manoeuvring at the rate of 30 knots: and won the approval of de Robeck, the very smart Commander of the flotilla. Just the same nerve and quickness of decision is needed for work in the ice. I think with the Admiralty and Capt$^n$. Egerton that these are the very men for us.[31]

Markham gave a faithful rendering of Captain Egerton's letter about Scott and Royds. The letter, and Egerton's formal certificate of Scott's qualifications, are in the archives of the Royal Geographical Society. The testimonial reads as follows:

Lieutenant Robert F. Scott the Torpedo Lieutenant of H.M. Ship under my command is in my opinion a very worthy candidate for the Command of the Antarctic Expedition and no officer having previous knowledge of Arctic or Antarctic work being forthcoming I am at a loss to name any officer who is likely to be more suitable. Lieut. Scott is an officer of great capabilities and possesses a large amount of tact and common sense, he is of strong physique and robust health—a scientist and an expert in electricity, very keen, zealous, of a cheerful disposition full of resource and a first rate comrade. He has had considerable experience in square rigged ships and writes a clear and concise report. I therefore have much pleasure in recommending him to the Committee of Selection.[32]

Captain Egerton had heard that Scott's selection was hanging in the balance and reinforced his view of Scott's suitability as commander of the Antarctic expedition in a letter to Sir Leopold McClintock, one of the old 'Arctic Officers' of the previous century and now closely concerned with the expedition: 'I feel sure we may rely upon his upholding the honour and traditions of the service as an explorer. I have a very high opinion of him as my predecessor Prince Louis of Battenburg had and I feel sure that there is nothing in the way of Magnetic or Astronomical observations that he would not readily pick up, besides what I have said of him in the enclosed sheet. Hoping that what I have said may strengthen your hand in securing his appointment as I firmly believe Scott to be a good man for the work.'[33]

Scott was officially made commander of the National Antarctic Expedition in June 1900. At the end of that month he was promoted to the rank of Commander, Royal Navy, soon relinquishing his duties as First Lieutenant of the *Majestic*, flagship of the Channel Squadron. He could then give his whole attention to the affairs of the expedition.

## THE BUILDING OF THE *DISCOVERY*

Markham visited Norway in the early days of planning the expedition (probably 1898) to inspect a number of steam vessels specially built for ice navigation, in the company of Dr Fridtjof Nansen, the great Norwegian explorer, who had recently returned from his voyage in the *Fram*.[34] None of them was apparently suitable. The available Scots wooden whalers were also considered but rejected for the same reason as the Norwegian vessels; the materials of their construction would make magnetic observations almost valueless and thus nullify a very important aspect of the scientific programme.[35] Once the expedition stood on a firmer financial footing (on receipt of Mr Longstaff's donation), a Ship Committee was formed, under the chairmanship of Sir Leopold McClintock, which first met in April 1899.[36] Before the building of a new ship was decided upon, Markham enquired of the Admiralty as to the condition and availability of the former steam whaler *Bloodhound*, which (as HMS *Discovery*) had wintered in the far north with the Nares expedition of 1875–6. Markham had been encouraged in this by Admiral Sir Anthony Hoskins, a former First Sea Lord.[37] Hoskins sat on the Ship Committee of the expedition and was disappointed when the old *Discovery* was pronounced to be hopeless by the Admiralty in a letter to Markham written by Admiral Sir Arthur Wilson on 12 April 1899:

On account of the age and known condition of the *Discovery*, the Admiralty would incur a grave responsibility if they allowed her to be used for such rough service as an Antarctic expedition. She was surveyed last year and in the report it was decided that she was only fit to be used in her present comparatively easy service until a new vessel could be provided. Your best plan will be to build a new vessel on similar lines. We can let you have the drawings for that purpose if you apply for them.[38]

Markham also consulted the Director of Naval Construction, Sir William White, as to the building of a wooden vessel for the expedition. After remarking that a supply of properly seasoned timber 'of the appropriate curved form' would have to be collected from many sources, since 'wood shipbuilding is almost dead', White went on to suggest in his letter of 25 March 1899 that Markham appoint W. E. Smith, then Chief Constructor at the Admiralty and one of White's principal assistants, as his technical adviser. Not the least of Smith's qualifications was 'that he had been brought up as a wood ship-builder'.[39]

White wrote again to Markham on 4 April 1899. He hoped that Markham would reconsider a proposal to have the vessel built in Norway by Colin Archer of Larvik, the builder of Nansen's *Fram*, which had been specially designed to be squeezed out of very heavy ice pressure, while beset in the Arctic Ocean. Sir William White considered that 'it would be a matter for great regret that a ship to carry a British Antarctic Expedition should be built outside these Islands', and went on to remark, 'We have only a few wood-ship builders left, but they are quite capable of doing all you want.'[40] No doubt Markham had thought of building the ship in Norway during his visit to Norwegian ports with Nansen.[41]

Markham heeded White's advice and the new *Discovery* was constructed in the British Isles—one of the last three-masted wooden ships and the first built purely for scientific research since Halley's *Paramore*, of 1694. Mr W. E. Smith was given permission to design the vessel, while similar leave was given to Engineer Commander P. Marrack, RN, of the engineering branch of the Controller's Department to prepare plans for the engines, boilers and stern gear, 'with the advice and assistance of Mr Wootton (retired Inspector of Machinery), whose experience in the use of the screw propeller in ice navigation was extremely valuable'.[42] Chief Inspector James Wootton had gained this experience as one of the engineer officers during the Arctic expedition of 1875–6 in the *Alert* and *Discovery*.

The *Discovery*'s designer, Mr W. E. (later Sir William) Smith, CB, was born in Portsmouth in 1850. He began work at the age of ten in the dockyard rope-house. Through private study and public examinations, he became a shipwright apprentice and was one of four apprentices selected to train in the Royal School of Naval Architecture, from which he passed out first in his year, with a rare First Class Fellowship in April 1873. He made his career in the design branch of the Admiralty, becoming Chief Constructor in 1894 and Superintendent of Contract Work in 1902 (a new post), arising (according to the obituary) from his having to deal with 'such questions as the improvement of armour and the best methods of testing its qualities, and also the relations between the Admiralty and the warship contractors'. This post he held with 'great distinction' for a decade. He also taught at the Royal Naval College, Greenwich, for many years, being appointed Instructor of Naval Architecture in 1881.

Smith was recommended to the Ship Committee as having been trained in wooden shipbuilding and one wonders with what nostalgia he may have turned from the construction of mighty ironclads to the design of a sailing vessel not unrelated to the old 'wooden walls' of these islands. In the 1920s, towards the end of his distinguished career, he was associated with the restoration of the most famous of the fighting ships, HMS *Victory*, to her Trafalgar condition by the Society for Nautical Research.[43]

Admiral Sir Leopold McClintock was particularly well qualified to chair the Ship Committee. Besides his Arctic experience during the search for Sir John Franklin in the 1850s, when he became noted for his sledge travelling, he had been Admiral Superintendent of Portsmouth Dockyard at the time of the Arctic expedition led by Sir George Nares, who (together with other Arctic officers) was also a member of the committee.[44]

The new vessel was to be called *Discovery* as the latest in a long line of exploring vessels of that name commanded in the seventeenth and eighteenth centuries by captains such as William Baffin, Captain Cook and George Vancouver. Mr W. E. Smith gave a paper in 1905 after the return of the National Antarctic Expedition on 'The design of the Antarctic Exploration Vessel, *Discovery*', at a meeting of the Institution of Naval Architects.[45] The published version of this paper includes an account of the evolution of the design, together with folding drawings and specification details enough 'to enable the naval architect to construct a similar vessel or to make improvements thereon'. The first formal meeting of the Ship Committee at which were present Sir Clements Markham, Admiral Sir Leopold McClintock, Admiral Sir George Nares, Admiral Sir Albert Markham, Vice-Admiral Pelham Aldrich, Rear-Admiral G. le C. Egerton and Mr W. E. Smith was productive. According to Markham, the full Ship Committee consisted of the above plus Captain E. W. Creak, at that time Superintendent of Compasses of the Admiralty Hydrographic Department, Captain W. H. May, Admiral Sir Richard Vesey Hamilton, Admiral Sir Anthony Hoskins and (occasionally) Rear-Admiral Sir William Wharton, then Hydrographer of the Navy.[46]

'As a starting point,' wrote Smith, 'the drawings of the old *Discovery*, that went into the Arctic Regions in 1875–76 with the expedition of Sir George Nares, were considered, and it was, as a first measure, directed that the new vessel should be built of wood and should follow as closely as possible on the general lines of the old *Discovery* as regards dimensions, lines, sail area, etc., leaving special features as regards strengthening, details of accommodation, etc., to be improved upon as might prove practicable.' The lines of the old *Discovery* were to be copied because she was thought to be the ultimate development of the nineteenth-century steam whalers of Dundee, whose overhanging stem enabled her to force a passage more easily through the pack-ice. 'On account of the great success of the *Fram*,' continued Mr Smith, 'it came under consideration whether it would not be well for the new vessel to have a midship section shaped as in that vessel, of a pronounced "peg-top" character, so as to promote lifting out of danger when exposed to a heavy crushing pressure of ice, but after full consideration, it was decided that, having regard to the many thousands of miles of tempestuous seas the new vessel would have to traverse both outwards and homewards, it would be better to have an ordinary ship-shaped section, as being more conducive to general goodness of behaviour under trying sea-going conditions.[47]

A laboratory, similar to that of the *Challenger*, and accommodation for a complement of 43 souls were to be provided, together with stowage for two years' provisions. The power would be not less than 400 i.h.p., and the coal-carrying capacity greater than the old *Discovery*'s 190 tons. 'Modern merchant practice as regards double topsail yards etc ... so as to facilitate the efficient working of the sails by a small complement', was another of the Committee's requirements. In addition, a two-bladed lifting screw was to be fitted to be readily shipped and unshipped, while a similar ease of shipping and unshipping the rudder was also specified. While the naval architect was busy producing plans to these instructions, the magnetic work of the expedition was also considered: a wholly non-magnetic ship with engines was an impossibility and the final compromise required the exclusion of iron and steel from within a radius of 30 feet from the magnetic observatory, which was to be situated on the upper deck. Among the far-reaching effects of this condition, said Mr Smith, was that hemp cordage had to be used for the main shrouds, which were 'set up by hemp lanyards rove through the old-fashioned wood dead-eyes', once so familiar to older members of the profession. In order to provide accommodation for the commanding officer less isolated than that in the old *Discovery* (the space in the counter abaft the engine-room) and for other reasons specified by Mr Smith, the new vessel was to be lengthened by ten feet. One of the advantages was that the power could be increased to 450 i.h.p. The Ship Committee on 30 June 1899 discussed these features fully, and accepted the increase in length, although aware that small size had proved an advantage in previous exploring vessels. Earlier vessels employed for polar exploration had been merely adapted for the purpose. Captain Cook's ships were, for example, Whitby colliers, others in the eighteenth and nineteenth centuries were bomb vessels and yet others merchant or naval vessels.[48]

An innovation by the designer of the *Discovery* was her rounded overhanging form of stern,[49] which contrasted with that of earlier exploring vessels and whalers, which had 'the old wooden frigate form of square counter stern, so long current in the British Royal Navy'. It was 'evidently of great advantage in ice work ... as it gave much better protection to the rudder, rudderpost and screw'. The new form of stern would also prove its worth, reasoned the designer, when sailing in heavy seas and since the helmsman 'had of necessity to be right aft in order that he might keep his eye on the sails', he would 'be drier ... and less likely to be exposed to a green sea in heavy Antarctic gales, than in a vessel with the old form of stern'. This proved to be the case, although, as Mr Smith pointed out, 'a corresponding disadvantage' was that 'in a heavy sea with no way on, there is much more noise set up by the falling of the stern on a wave than ... with the older form . . .'. Mr Smith went on to remark that he had been fortified in his advocacy of the rounded overhanging stern 'by the fact that Nansen had, in a somewhat less pronounced degree, adopted it in the *Fram* in conference with his naval architect—our old friend Mr. Colin Archer'.

It is interesting to note that the Ship Committee discussed the question of bilge keels, which it recognised would add to the comfort of those on board by decreasing the rolling of the vessel. However, 'after full consideration, it was decided that, as bilge keels would very much add to the risk of the vessel getting entangled in ice, and to the danger of her remaining fixed in it, if she were once entangled, they should not be fitted'. The designer's remarks, which are quoted below, are also interesting, in view of the fact that bilge keels were eventually fitted to the *Discovery* during her 1925–7 Antarctic expedition and that her propensity to roll was a constant feature of logs and diaries until then, and even afterwards. Mr Smith wondered (after the experience of the National Antarctic Expedition) 'whether it is not practicable to fit bilge keels in some easily detachable and attachable manner, so as to secure greater comfort when out of the way of ice and no danger of entanglement when in the ice'.[50]

A thoughtful feature of the design was the provision of two water ballast tanks in the port and starboard bunkers able to hold about 60 tons of water. 'It was recognised', wrote Mr Smith, 'that the vessel might have to come back from the Antarctic regions over long distances in stormy seas with little or no stores in her holds, and with correspondingly diminished stability to stand up under her canvas, and, as the possibility of obtaining solid ballast could not be relied upon, it was decided to fit a water ballast tank . . .'. These tanks strengthened the vessel 'and did not diminish to any appreciable extent the coal carrying capacity . . . as on the outward voyage this ballast tank was to be filled with coal'.[51] The ballast tanks did, however, make coaling ship an unpleasant task and they, together with the beams, made it difficult to trim the coal.[52] A spare rudder was carried on deck, which was in fact used later. The rudder and the propeller lifted up through the deck for easy replacement. The lifting propeller, for which, unusually, there was no banjo frame, was fitted with 'bolt-on' blades, enabling spares to be carried. Seven watertight transverse bulkheads and the centre line bulkhead so subdivided the hull as to make the vessel virtually unsinkable.[53]

On 29 November 1899, Admiral McClintock, Chairman of the Ship Committee, described the future *Discovery* as follows. This summary of her design is so concise and was so little modified in practice that it is quoted here in full:

The Ship will be 172 feet long, 33 feet extreme beam and will be 1570 tons displacement. She will be built of oak and elm, with an ice casing of green heart. Though somewhat larger, her general lines will be similar to those of Discovery. Her bows will be sharp and overhanging, like Discovery, and they will be specially strengthened for forcing her way through the ice. The thickness of her sides amidships at the water line, will be 25 inches. The stern and counters will be so shaped as to afford protection to the screw and rudder, both of which will be fitted so as to be raised quickly out of the water.

The consumption of coal is approximately, as follows:

| Speed (in knots) | 6 | 7 | 8 |
|---|---|---|---|
| Tons per *diem* | 4¹/₂ | 6¹/₂ | 9 |
| Distance for 240 tons (of coal) | 7,700 | 6,200 | 5,100 |

This does not include the amount of coal that will be required for warming, dredging and sounding purposes. It is possible however, that some 20 or 30 tons of coal can be stowed elsewhere in the ship, either on the upper deck, or in unoccupied spaces below. The full power speed of the ship will be about 8 knots, somewhat in excess of the speed of [the old] Discovery. In order to fall in with magnetic requirements, the engine and boilers will be situated aft. The horse power will be 450, and the ship will stow, in bunkers, 240 tons of coal. She will be fitted with masts and sails, and barque rigged, so that fuel can be economised while making a voyage, and advantage can be taken of favourable winds, even when navigating in the pack. The Magnetic Observatory, 8 feet by 6 ft. 6 in. will be on the bridge before the mainmast, and no iron work will be permitted within 30 feet of it. [It was in fact fitted on the upper deck.] For biological work there will be two houses, properly fitted on deck, and a laboratory 10 ft. by 7 ft. forward on the lower deck. There will be an auxiliary engine, and special arrangements for sounding to a depth of 4,000 fathoms, and also for dredging up operations. All other details have been carefully designed for ice navigation, for promoting warmth and dryness below, and for facilitating scientific investigations. The cabin accommodation includes a sitting and sleeping cabin for the captain, one for the navigator with places in it for the chronometers and with facilities for drawings &c. The other cabins for the other executive officers, and one for the engineer, and three for scientific civilians, of whom one, or more, ought to be surgeons, one to be in medical charge of the ship. Extra cabin space can be found for two or more scientific civilians, but only by encroaching on the space now set apart for the health and comfort of the crew.

The Ship Sub-Committee are much indebted to Mr. W. E. Smith for the skill and ability he has devoted to the design and details of the ship, and also to Mr. Marrack for his work connected with the engines and boilers, and the protection of the propeller. They congratulate themselves on the fact that the plans and designs approved are those of a vessel which will be, by far, the best adapted for severe weather and ice navigation, as well as for scientific investigations, that has ever entered the polar regions.

They are of opinion that the total complement of this vessel should not exceed 48 to 50 souls.[54]

The precise specification 'for building and equipping the hull of a single screw wood ship to be engaged in Antarctic exploration' is to be found as an Appendix to the architect's paper of 1905.[55] Alterations to the original specification are usefully shown in italics. These were made chiefly on the grounds of economy.

Tenders were invited for the construction of the vessel. A letter from Mr W. E. Smith to Sir Clements Markham of 14 December 1899[56] informed the president of the RGS that there had been only two tenders. As Scott remarked in his narrative of the expedition, by the end of the nineteenth century the adze and the wood-plane were giving way to the puncher and the riveter used in steel shipbuilding.[57] Of these two, that of the Dundee Shipbuilders Company was very much the lower, but still higher than the Committee was in a position to accept. (The other was from Vickers of Barrow-in-Furness.) In discussion with the technical representative of the company, Mr Smith had been able to lower the price of the hull, through certain omissions, from £50,650 to £33,700. The naval architect pointed out to Sir Clements that the existing circumstances of the shipbuilding industry were unique in that the Admiralty was pressing its shipbuilding policy to the utmost. Because of the demand for vessels generated by the Boer War in South Africa, he continued, shipowners could almost obtain their own terms. He concluded that the Dundee tender could not be bettered and it was accepted on 16 December 1899[58] on condition that the original beam design of 33 feet be retained and that separate tenders for the auxiliary machinery could be invited. In the end, the tender of the Dundee Shipbuilders for the engines was also accepted rather than that of the Caledon Shipbuilding and Engineering Company.[59] These were designed by Engineer Commander P. Marrack, RN, and were triple expansion, developing 450 hp at about 90 revolutions per minute. Appendix B of Mr Smith's paper of 1905 includes a specification by Marrack of the main machinery and boilers, which were manufactured extremely well by Messrs Gourlay of Dundee. Owing to Marrack's 'enthusiasm and great skill', testified Mr Smith, 'the *Discovery* was fitted with engines and boilers which within the limits of weight and power permissible were, with respect to all good qualities, second to no engines that have ever been built'. Sadly they would be sent for scrap during the Second World War. In view of later criticism of the work of the Dundee Shipbuilders (particularly concerning the 'Dundee leak'), it seems only fair to quote her architect's last words regarding the building of the *Discovery*.

> It is proper to state here that the Dundee Shipbuilders' Company has very great experience in what is necessary for vessels to be engaged in Polar work. They went with great spirit into the question of the alterations of the specification that might be accepted, and I am much indebted to them for their valuable assistance in this matter. They not only freely placed their experience at my disposal for the information of the Committee . . . and, on the order being definitely placed with them, they prosecuted the work with vigour, and completed it so that the Expedition was enabled to start in good time for the arduous task before them.[60]

The vessel was to be barque-rigged (i.e. square-rigged on the foremast and mainmast with fore-and-aft rig on the mizzen). 'The ship was under-masted', wrote Captain Scott after the voyage; 'the mainmast from truck to keelson was only 112 feet, and this is extremely short for such a vessel, while comparatively speaking for this height of mast, the yards were square (i.e. long), the mainyard being 60 feet in length.' He concluded that she 'could have carried a much larger sail area with advantage', especially in light winds, when she was 'an extremely sluggish sailer'.[61] The barque's sailing qualities were further hindered by the incorrect positioning of the masts, which should, according to Scott, have been placed further forward.[62] Messrs Baxter Brothers of Dundee supplied the sail cloth for the *Discovery* and on the return of the expedition, Scott wrote to inform the firm of his satisfaction with their product.[63] The problem with the masts was remedied in the vessel's refit of 1924. Her architect's paper and drawings of 1905 and suggestions for further improvements in the light of the experience gained during the National Antarctic Expedition are set out in the *Transactions of the Institution of Naval Architects*.

It is interesting to note in contrast that the *Gauss*, built at the same time as the *Discovery*, for the German South Polar Expedition of 1900–3, was designed, broadly speaking, on the lines of the *Fram*. The Ship Committee of the National Antarctic Expedition had chosen to follow the lines of the Scottish whalers, built to push through the ice, rather than remain fast in it, considering also the need of the *Discovery* to make the long ocean passages to the other side of the world. However, the *Discovery* would spend two winters in the ice (albeit in a sheltered bay), while the *Gauss* was beset (as was the *Fram* under Nansen) in the open sea. A decade later, the *Fram* was to carry Amundsen's South Polar expedition of 1910–12 to the Ross Sea and to circumnavigate the globe twice, covering a distance of 54,000 nautical miles.[64]

An account of the *Gauss* and her construction can be found in Drygalski's narrative, *Zum Kontinent des eisigen Südens*. The German expedition's leader pronounced his auxiliary barquentine to be 'the best polar ship there has ever been',[65] a claim also made for the *Discovery* and, of course, for the *Fram*. It is worth quoting Amundsen, for whom the *Fram* was converted in rig to a topsail schooner and given diesel engines, on her sailing qualities. These were tested in the first real gale met south of the Cape in 1910.

> . . . A single one of these gigantic waves would have cleared our decks in an instant, if it had come on board, but the *Fram* did not permit any such impertinence. When they came up behind the vessel, and we might expect at any moment to see them break over the low after-deck, she just raised herself with an elegant movement, and the wave had to be content with slipping underneath. An albatross could not have managed the situation better. It is said that the *Fram* was built for the ice, and that cannot, of course, be denied; but at the same time it is certain that when Colin Archer created his famous masterpiece of an ice-boat, she was just as much a masterpiece of a sea boat . . .[66]

By February 1900, Mr Smith had concluded it was time to appoint an overseer for the hull of the *Discovery* on behalf of the Royal Geographical Society. The post was offered on his recommendation to Mr E. Bate, retired Inspector of Shipwrights, formerly of Portsmouth Dockyard, who was said to be thoroughly experienced in wooden shipbuilding.[67] Mr Bate must have needed all his experience in view of the complex structure of the hull and its different woods. Captain Scott described the side of the *Discovery* as follows, after pointing out that the side of a modern steel ship is less than an inch in thickness.

> The frames, which were placed very close together, were eleven inches thick and of solid English oak; inside the frames came the inner lining, a solid planking four inches thick; whilst the outside was covered with two layers of planking, respectively six and five inches thick, so that, in most places, to bore a hole in the side one would have had to get through twenty-six inches of solid wood.

Various woods were suitably placed to make up the side and tiers of beams stiffened the frame.

> The inner lining was of Riga fir, the frames of English oak, the inner skin, according to its position, of pitch pine, Honduras mahogany, or oak, whilst the outer skin in the same way was of English elm or greenheart. The massive side structure was stiffened and strengthened by three tiers of beams running from side to side, and at intervals with stout transverse wooden bulkheads; the beams in the lower tiers were especially solid, being eleven inches by eleven inches in section, and they were placed at intervals of something less than three feet.

Strong as the sides were, the bows were yet stronger. Here a 'network of solid oak stiffeners', continued Scott, 'gave to this portion of the vessel a strength which almost amounted to solidity'. The keel 'at the fore end of the ship gradually grew thicker till it rose in the enormous mass of solid wood which constituted the stem'. The bow and stem were protected by steel plates for some four feet on both sides, in preparation for the icebreaking for which her overhanging stem was designed.[68] The construction by the Dundee Shipbuilders was undertaken for £34,050 plus £10,322 for the engines. The keel was laid on 16 March 1900.[69]

The *Discovery* was launched a year later on 21 March 1901. Pressure of work at the Admiralty was such that her designer found it impossible to be there.[70] Sir Clements and his wife Minna, Lady Markham, reached Dundee the day before and were met at the station by Mr Low (the chairman of Dundee Shipbuilders), Mr Paterson (the Manager) and Lieut. Royds. Markham's diary recorded the day of the launch.

> *March 21st.* At twelve I went down to the dock and went over the 'Discovery' with Mr. Paterson, Mr. Bate our Inspector, Scott, Armitage and Royds . . . at 3 Mrs.

Low and Minna called for us to go to the launch, at the Dockyd. After waiting a short time in the office, Minna was conducted by Mr. Low to the platform before the stem of the *Discovery*. I followed and there were also Mr. Paterson, the other Directors, Scott, Armitage, Royds and Koettlitz, Mr. Bate, Keltie, Mill etc. Minna was presented with a pair of gold scissors, and at a signal she cut a ribbon. The bottle of wine was smashed against the bows, there was a pause of two minutes and then the good ship 'Discovery' glided into the sea—a beautiful sight—amidst tremendous cheers: the strongest ship ever launched, and the first built specially for exploring work, in this country. Minna was presented with the gold scissors in a morocco case with an inscription.[71]

The *Dundee Advertiser* next day gave full coverage to the launching ceremony, quoting the speeches at length. Among these was an interesting letter from the *Discovery*'s designer, which was read by Mr Bate. In the letter, Mr Smith wished success to the builders and continued, 'The building of the *Discovery* is of so unique a character that much more than usual interest attaches to her.' As the *Discovery*'s designer, he had 'sometimes been exacting', but had always been 'handsomely met'. There was 'no firm in the country', he concluded, 'having a greater knowledge of what is necessary in these particulars for this type of vessel than the Dundee Shipbuilders Company'. Then followed a banquet at the Queen's Hotel during which there were toasts to the *Discovery* and to her builders. 'It all went off without a hitch,' concluded Markham.

The meetings of the joint committee of the Royal Society and the Royal Geographical Society did not proceed with similar ease. On 16 February 1901, Mr Kempe, Treasurer of the Royal Society, 'a sensible, friendly man', came to see Sir Clements 'about a *modus vivendi* with that troublesome body'.[72] The solution lay in the establishment of a small Executive Committee, which resolved the difficulties and finally drafted the Instructions, leaving much to the discretion of the Commander.

# TWO

## Plans, Preparations, the Outward Voyage to the Ross Sea

### PLANS AND PREPARATIONS

WHICH REGION OF THE ANTARCTIC should the expedition explore? Both the Hydrographer (Rear-Admiral Sir William Wharton) and Sir George Nares wished the expedition to avoid Victoria Land as a place of operations for several reasons. One was that it had been recently visited by the private expedition in the *Southern Cross* of 1898–1900, financed by Sir George Newnes and led by C. E. Borchgrevink (incidentally, much to Markham's annoyance at thereby being forestalled into the Ross Sea).[1] Sir Clements however opted for the overall advantages of 'McMurdo Bay' (now McMurdo Sound), Victoria Land, as the 'best place for winter quarters, in full view of the great burning volcano', Mount Erebus. A better climate might be found there than at Cape Adare, where Borchgrevink had wintered; travelling parties could explore inland. 'A journey due south would enable researches to be made along the edge of the ice-cap, while a journey westward into the interior would be of equal importance, and would possibly effect co-operation with the Germans working in from the west.' This route, he maintained, offered the best prospect of successfully carrying out the objects of the expedition with the minimum of risk. Victoria Land was to be Scott's goal.[2]

The Instructions to the Commander of the Expedition attained what Sir Clements called their 'final' version on 20 May 1901.[3] Even these had to be adapted following Professor Gregory's resignation, when the Instructions to the Director of the Civilian Scientific Staff and certain paragraphs in Scott's Instructions became as a consequence null and void. Scott quoted the 'principal paragraphs' of his Instructions in his narrative as

... The objects of the expedition are (*a*) to determine, as far as possible, the nature, condition, and extent of that portion of the South Polar lands which is included in the scope of your expedition; and (*b*) to make a magnetic survey in the southern regions to the south of the 40th parallel, and to carry on meteorological, oceanographic, geological, biological, and physical investigations and researches. Neither of these objects is to be sacrificed to the other.

... We, therefore, impress upon you that the greatest importance is attached to the series of magnetic observations to be taken under your superintendence, and we desire that you will spare no pains to ensure their accuracy and continuity. The base station for your magnetic work will be at Melbourne or at Christchurch, New Zealand. A secondary base station is to be established by you, if possible, in Victoria Land. You should endeavour to carry the magnetic survey from the Cape to your primary base station south of the 40th parallel, and from the same station across the Pacific to the meridian of Greenwich. It is also desired that you should observe along the tracks of Ross, in order to ascertain the magnetic changes that have taken place in the interval between the two voyages.

. . . It is desired that the extent of land should be ascertained by following the coastlines; that the depth and nature of the ice-cap should be investigated, as well as the nature of the volcanic region, of the mountain ranges, and especially of any fossiliferous rocks.

. . . You will see that the meteorological observations are regularly taken every two hours. . . . It is very desirable that there should, if possible, be a series of meteorological observations to the south of the 74th parallel.

As regards magnetic work and meteorological observations generally, you will follow the programme arranged between the German and British Committees, with the terms of which you are acquainted.

Whenever it is possible, while at sea, deep-sea soundings should be taken with serial temperatures, and samples of sea-water at various depths are to be obtained for physical and chemical analysis. Dredging operations are to be carried on as frequently as possible, and all opportunities are to be taken for making biological and geological collections.

. . . The chief points of geographical interest are as follows:—To explore the ice-barrier of Sir James Ross to its eastern extremity; to discover the land which was believed by Ross to flank the barrier to the eastward, or to ascertain that it does not exist, and generally to endeavour to solve the very important physical and geographical questions connected with this remarkable ice-formation.

Owing to our very imperfect knowledge of the conditions which prevail in the Antarctic seas, we cannot pronounce definitely whether it will be necessary for the ship to make her way out of the ice before the winter sets in, or whether she should winter in the Antarctic Regions. It is for you to decide on this important question after a careful examination of the local conditions.

If you should decide to winter in the ice . . . your efforts as regards geographical exploration should be directed to three objects, namely—an advance into the western mountains, an advance to the south, and an exploration of the volcanic region.

. . . In an enterprise of this nature, much must be left to the discretion and judgement of the commanding officer, and we fully confide in your combined energy and prudence for the successful issue of a voyage which will command the attention of all persons interested in navigation and science throughout the civilised world. At the same time, we desire you constantly to bear in mind our anxiety for the health, comfort and safety of all entrusted to your care.[4]

Reference was also made to the 'complete details respecting sledge work both by men and dogs'[5] provided by Sir Leopold McClintock and Dr Nansen, as well as to Armitage's previous polar experience in taking scientific observations, sledge travelling and 'the driving and management of dogs'. Records should be deposited during the voyage by pre-arrangement whenever possible. The final paragraph (No. 27) read:

The *Discovery* is the first ship that has ever been built expressly for scientific purposes in these kingdoms. It is an honour to receive the command of her; but we are impressed with the difficulty of the enterprise which has been entrusted to you, and with the serious character of your responsibilities. The Expedition is an undertaking of national importance; and science cannot fail to benefit from the efforts of those engaged in it. You may rely on our support on all occasions, and we feel assured that all on board the *Discovery* will do their utmost to further the objects of the Expedition.[6]

The British had played a long and honourable part in polar exploration, beginning with the Cabots, Frobisher and Hudson in the Arctic, and extending to the Antarctic with Captain Cook, Biscoe, Balleny, Ross and *Challenger*. However, by 1900, although several of the nineteenth-century 'Arctic Officers' had relevant experience, the most up-to-date expertise regarding food and equipment was available mainly in Norway, gained from Nansen's crossing of the Greenland ice-cap and his voyage in the *Fram* of 1893–6. Captain Scott visited Norway in October 1900 and received practical help from the great Norwegian explorer. He travelled on from Norway to Berlin, where he met the leader of the German South Polar Expedition, Professor Erich von Drygalski, who was also planning to leave the following summer; the two expeditions were to co-operate in the field.

The National Antarctic Expedition was organised from its headquarters at Burlington House in London. The indefatigable Secretary, Cyril Longhurst, and the officers, as appointed, took up their duties in London, Kew, Dundee and elsewhere. Scott wrote, 'It would not be possible for me to describe half the work that went on in this office; suffice to say that it kept me extremely busy for six days in the week. My room soon became a veritable museum of curiosities: sledges, ski, fur clothing and boots were crowded into the corners, whilst tables and shelves were littered with correspondence and innumerable samples of tinned foods. In the midst of this confusion I worked steadily on with all the ups and downs that such occasions will bring, sometimes in high hope that all was going well, and sometimes with the dreary feeling that by no possibility could we be ready to start at the required date.' Provision lists for three years were drawn up and ordered;

clothing, both tropical and polar, had to be provided; sledges, tents, furs and other equipment had to be thought of and selected with care. Besides these, since the party was to be completely cut off from civilisation, were the boatswain's stores, the carpenter's stores, the engineer's stores, equipment for use in ice—including explosives for destroying the ice and fireworks for signalling. 'There were tobacco, soap, glass, crockery, furniture, mattresses,' continued Scott, 'and all such requisites for personal comfort; oil lamps and candles for lighting, and stoves for heating; medicines and medical comforts; a photographic outfit; a library of many hundred volumes; also a balloon equipment; canvas boats of various kinds, huts for our shore station, instruments of many descriptions; and so on, almost *ad infinitum*.'[7]

Many commercial firms supplied their goods free. The total sum available of £92,000 was diminished by the cost of the ship at £51,000, while more than £25,000 was reserved for wages and the expenses of the voyage. The remainder was sufficient to equip the expedition thoroughly as befitted a national enterprise. On 3 June 1901, the *Discovery* berthed in the East India Dock on the Thames and the two busiest months of preparation and loading began, interspersed with numerous dinners and social entertainments during the first hot Edwardian summer following the death of the old Queen early in the year.

The *Discovery* sailed from London on the last glorious day of July 1901, to be greeted from the *Worcester* (training ship) and every passing craft as she sailed down river with 'flags and hooters and sirens' making an 'immense noise'. Crowds were everywhere.[8] The vessel was 'swung' for the adjustment of her compasses at Spithead and then moored in Cowes Harbour during the celebrated yachting week. Here King Edward VII and Queen Alexandra came aboard on 5 August. Edward Wilson, the young second surgeon and zoologist, who kept a beautifully illustrated diary of the voyage, described their visit.

> We were fully busy the whole morning, nigh on till 11.30 when the King and Queen came on board, clearing up and tidying and putting our smartest bits of apparatus and our prettiest coloured solutions in prominent positions. Microscopes were set out, water bottles, thermometers, everything arranged and tidied up . . . The King shook hands with us all round when he came on board, and again when he left. The Queen also. The King gave the Victorian Order of the Fourth Class to Captain Scott before leaving, having with great difficulty fished it out of his tail-coat pocket, which was a long way round on the wrong side of his stout figure. He gave us a few words of royal encouragement, was shown all over the ship and then left.[9]

Besides Sir Clements Markham, Sir Leopold McClintock and Sir Allen Young (both of Arctic fame) were on board, as were Captain Scott's mother and Dr Hugh Robert Mill of the Royal Geographical Society. The expedition's chief benefactor, Mr Llewellyn Longstaff, was also present. The preceding May he had anonymously donated a further £5,000, which Markham hoped would 'have the effect of completing the subscriptions, and ensuring the despatch of the *Discovery*'s tender' (i.e. a relief ship). In his letter of thanks, Markham told Longstaff that the King had consented to become Patron of the expedition. His Majesty also wished the White Ensign to be flown 'if consent can be got from The Admiralty'.[10] Captain Scott, who looked 'paler and more tired and worried than before' according to Longstaff, had sent a steam-launch for the expedition's benefactor, who was presented to the King before the officers were. The King 'spoke to me in a very complimentary way,' wrote Longstaff, 'but I don't recollect very much of what I said'.[11] The royal party expressed an interest in the practical side of life in the Antarctic and Queen Alexandra even tested the softness of the mattresses in the bunks.[12]

The *Discovery* made her departure from England next day on 6 August 1901. Having wished them all Godspeed, Sir Clements Markham wrote confidently in his diary that night,

> I believe all the executives possess the qualities to make good polar officers, and that they will work well and harmoniously together, which is the main thing.

> > 'By mutual confidence and mutual aid,
> > Great deeds are done and great discoveries made,
> > The wise new prudence from the wise acquire
> > And one brave hero fans another's fire.'[13]

The men who composed the National Antarctic Expedition are named below in a list which includes not only those who sailed from Cowes, but those who joined or left later. The abbreviation MN after a seaman or stoker's name means that he belonged to the Merchant Navy; RMLI stands for Royal Marine Light Infantry. The list is taken from that given by Scott and amended from Erskine's article in the *Naval Review*.[14]

## THE SHIP'S COMPANY

OFFICERS
Robert Falcon Scott, Captain, RN
Albert B. Armitage, Lieut. RNR, Navigator and Second-in-Command
Charles W. R. Royds, Lieut. RN, First Lieutenant
Michael Barne, Lieut. RN
*Ernest H. Shackleton, Sub-Lieut. RNR
*George F. A. Mulock, Lieut. RN
Reginald W. Skelton, Engineer Lieut. RN, Chief Engineer
Reginald Koettlitz, Surgeon and botanist
Edward A. Wilson, Surgeon, zoologist and artist
Thomas V. Hodgson, Marine biologist
Hartley T. Ferrar, Geologist
Louis C. Bernacchi, Physicist

WARRANT-OFFICERS, RN†
Thomas A. Feather, Acting Boatswain
James H. Dellbridge, Second Engineer
Fred. E. Dailey, Carpenter
Charles R. Ford, Ship's Steward

PETTY OFFICERS, RN
Jacob Cross
Edgar Evans
William Smythe
David Allan
Thomas Kennar
*W. MacFarlane

MARINES
Gilbert Scott, Private, RMLI
A. H. Blissett, L/Cpl. RMLI

CIVILIANS
Charles Clarke, Cook
*Clarence Hare, Assistant Steward
*H. C. Buckridge, Laboratory Attendant

SEAMEN
Arthur Pilbeam (RN)
William L. Heald (RN)
James Dell (RN)
Frank Wild (RN)
Thomas Williamson (RN)
George B. Croucher (RN)
Ernest E. Joyce (RN)
Thomas Crean (RN)
Jesse Handsley (RN)
William J. Weller (MN) Dog handler
*W. Peters (RN)
*J. Walker (MN)
*J. Duncan (MN) Shipwright
*H. R. Brett (MN) Cook
G. T. Vince (RN) Died March 1902
Charles Bonner (RN) Died December 1901

STOKERS
William Lashly (RN)
Arthur L. Quartley (RN)
Thomas Whitfield (RN)
Frank Plumley (RN)
*W. Page (RN)
*William Hubert (MN) Donkeyman

*Wintered for one season only
†Erskine tells us that these were given acting rank in 1901 for the expedition only,
  but Dailey and Feather attained WO rank during it.

## THE VOYAGE TO CAPE TOWN

The *Discovery* anchored off Funchal a week after leaving Cowes. Here Captain Scott despatched the first of his official 'Letters of Proceedings' to the presidents of the Royal Society and the Royal Geographical Society. He also wrote more personally to Markham, already concerned by the *Discovery*'s slow speed.[15] This slow progress proved a serious drawback in that it meant there was little chance to try out the deep-sea sounding and dredging gear on passage to New Zealand before reaching more tempestuous seas. The *Discovery* had to arrive in the Antipodes in time to proceed to the Antarctic at the beginning of the southern summer, 1901–2, so as to have a full season in the Ross Sea after penetrating the pack-ice to the north.

Captain Scott's overall satisfaction was shown nevertheless in a letter to Admiral Markham's wife, written on passage after leaving England. 'Tell the Admiral', he wrote, 'that . . . we have left very little behind, that the scientific people are no trouble and quite willing to put their hands to the work of the ship, that the ship leaks a good bit, but quite accountably.' He was finding that there were advantages in a long journey before entering the 'regions of our real work', presumably from shaking down together and because this was the *Discovery*'s maiden voyage. 'We are all extremely comfortable and happy,' he continued, 'the men are first class and the scientific people are as eager as everyone else to bear a hand in the general work of the ship.' He thanked her for offering to keep in touch with the wives; only four men were married and Sir Clements had their addresses. He thanked her too for the bunches of white heather, which he had distributed. His own sprig was pinned just over his desk.[16]

Much has been written since then about the man who sat at that desk, and how he came to be appointed as leader of the expedition at the age of thirty-three, joining from HMS *Majestic*, Channel Squadron. After considerable earlier experience under sail, he had learned about surveying, surveying instruments, electricity and magnetism as a 'Torpedo Lieutenant', as Markham called him. In appearance, wrote one of the *Discovery*'s scientists, Scott was 'a fair, well-built man of medium height with true-blue eyes. . . . He had a pleasant voice, a pleasant smile and a crisp and charming manner.' He was to take a tremendous interest in the scientific work, frequently making original suggestions to the scientists. His predominant trait, thought the same expedition member, was 'his sense of right and justice. He had a terrible sense of justice. Truth and right and justice were his gods.' This sense seems to have come from an inward rather than a specifically religious conviction. A pipe-smoker and great reader, as is shown by the literary quality of his writing, he was not fond of drink, perhaps from lack of money to indulge. He was almost the sole support of his widowed mother and four sisters. He could be irritable and impatient, and prone to 'occasional moods of silence and contemplation' owing to laziness, in contrast to hard work carried out 'swiftly and clearly' at other times. Scott was to show considerable solicitude for and sympathy with his men, particularly the naval 'blue jackets', and in his published narrative would later refer to the 'loyalty and devotion' of those he called his 'sailor friends'.[17] Being 'sensitive and highly strung', he would hate driving the sledge dogs to death and having to kill the seals. Perhaps one of his most important qualities as commander of the Antarctic expedition of 1901–4 was his 'deep and reverent attitude towards nature and a most genuine love of science'.[18]

As the *Discovery* approached the Equator on 30 August, 'a loud voice from forward hailed the ship', wrote Shackleton (later to become famous as leader of his own Antarctic expeditions in the *Nimrod*, the *Endurance* and the *Quest*), 'and bade us back the main yard, for Neptune's messenger was coming on board. In a moment or two, an old man was seen on the foc'sle head, who in a loud voice demanded the name of the ship: "The good ship *Discovery*", answered the officer of the watch. At this answer, the Triton moved down the ladder towards the bridge and mounted the upper bridge where the Captain and officer of the watch were standing' to enquire about the candidates for baptism. Next day at 2 p.m., 'Neptune and his consort and court, hailed the ship and came on board', continued Shackleton. 'After a go of grog they quickly proceeded to business amidships, where a platform about 12 feet high had been erected on which the victim's chair or stool was placed fastened by a rope, so that when he was pushed in the bath below, the chair would not go with him; a large sail full of sea-water made the bath, and in it our Tritons disported themselves. There stood Neptune and his consort on the platform with the doctor and his greasy soapy pill, the barber and his foaming tallow lather and huge razor. After the victim had been interviewed, he was handed over to the tender mercies of the Tritons, and it was generally a gasping, almost breathless creature that emerged from the other end of the bath.' Because the chair slipped, Wilson, the junior surgeon, escaped lathering, shaving and the pill and got away with a mere ducking. Ferrar, the geologist, objected to his treatment and received a double dose on the platform as a result. He 'struggled a lot in the bath, not knowing that under the disguise of wigs and oilskins were hidden the strongest men in the ship'. Shackleton concluded that 'the whole affair went off well, though the men got a bit rough towards the end'.[19]

The members of the expedition came to know each other on the voyage south. Some acquired nicknames, including the marine biologist, Thomas Vere Hodgson, who became known as 'Muggins', after rushing out from his cabin one day exclaiming that he had found a 'Muggins' or some such in course of doing a dissection.[20] Aged thirty-seven, short, moustached and bald-headed, Hodgson was one of the two oldest members of the expedition. Captain Scott tells us that he escaped from having to earn a living in business to work at the Plymouth Biological Laboratory and later became curator of the Plymouth Museum. Three years older than Hodgson was Dr Reginald Koettlitz, the senior surgeon and botanist. He had trained at Guy's Hospital and was tall, lean and bespectacled, with a shock of curly hair and whiskers. Captain Scott tells us that the surgeon's father, a minister of the Lutheran Church, had settled in Dover and married an Englishwoman. Koettlitz, with Armitage, the navigator and second-in-command, had taken part in the Jackson–Harmsworth Expedition to Franz-Josef Land (Zemlya Frantsa-Iosifa), a group of islands to the north of Russia, in the 1890s. There they had witnessed the excitement of Nansen's arrival after leaving the *Fram* in an attempt to sledge to the North Pole. Armitage was trained as a boy in the *Worcester* and had experience in sail before joining the Peninsular and Oriental (P. & O.) Steam Navigation Company, of which he was eventually to become Commodore.[21]

The First Lieutenant, Charles Royds, had been a *Conway* cadet, passing into the *Britannia* in 1890. He joined the expedition from HMS *Crescent*. His uncle, Wyatt Rawson, was an officer of the Arctic expedition of 1875–6. 'He had all to do with the work of the men and the internal economy of the ship', wrote Scott. He was also responsible for the meteorological observations, a routine, tedious and time-consuming task.[22] He was to do much to make the *Discovery* a happy ship, being regarded with affection and respect by officers and men, whose welfare he had at heart. Michael Barne, the other naval lieutenant, had only recently been promoted. He came from HMS *Majestic*, where Scott had picked him out as being 'especially fitted for a voyage where there were elements of danger and difficulty'. During the expedition he was assistant magnetic observer, and also in charge of the sounding apparatus. Scott later described how Barne would disappear from winter quarters for the day with a packed lunch and the 'Flying Scud', a sledge rigged with sails, on which sat a sounding machine for use through holes in the ice.[23] Another man from the *Majestic* (where he had been senior engineer) was the *Discovery*'s chief engineer, Reginald Skelton. He was to assist the scientific work in many ways and also, as photographer, took what Scott called 'the most excellent pictures that have ever been obtained by a polar expedition'.[24]

The remaining sea officer was Ernest Shackleton. He had been educated at Dulwich College in south-east London and was with the Union-Castle Line's *Carisbrooke Castle* when appointed to the *Discovery*. Sir Clements Markham got him made a Sub-Lieutenant in the Royal Naval Reserve. Much has been written about Shackleton, who was to find fame through polar exploration, his one year in the *Discovery* being the first step on the ladder. One of the scientists wrote of him,

> Just as he had been in his former ships, Shackleton was the life and soul of *Discovery*. His mind was alert, his good humour inexhaustible. Besides being in charge of the holds and the stores, he carried out his ordinary duties as an executive officer. He was a fine self-reliant seaman, fearless and dominant, with a stern regard for detail and discipline. He permitted no liberties from those under his command, and could be brutally truculent if such occasion arose. But he was singularly sympathetic and understanding, sentimental to the verge of tears when expressing his own feelings or spouting lines from his favourite poets. In his deep Irish voice he could wheedle and coax; successfully if he required something, which he generally did.[25]

The geologist who replaced Professor Gregory was Hartley T. Ferrar. Born in Dublin, brought up in South Africa and educated in England, he had graduated in Natural Sciences from Sidney Sussex College, Cambridge, only the June before the expedition departed. A keen oarsman, we are told that he heard of his appointment to the *Discovery* after rowing in a race at Henley.[26]

The junior surgeon and naturalist of the expedition was Dr Edward Adrian Wilson, a graduate of Gonville and Caius College, Cambridge. He trained at St George's Hospital, London, and was appointed, despite a poisoned arm, to the expedition by Scott, and allowed three months' convalescence in January 1901 by the Admiralty Medical Board. He was able to return to London in March when he worked under Mr George Murray, Keeper of Botany at the British Museum (Natural History). Here he learned how to skin birds and how to identify the southern birds and seals. His great talent lay in watercolours and drawing and he loved the birds, trees and flowers of the English countryside. Captain Scott was to develop a very great respect and affection for Wilson and persuaded him to go south again in the *Terra Nova* in 1910 as chief of the scientific staff. As they lay dying in the tent on the 'Barrier' in 1912, Scott wrote of him to Mrs Wilson

> His eyes have a comfortable blue look of hope and his mind is peaceful with the satisfaction of his faith regarding himself as part of the great scheme of the Almighty. I can do no more to comfort you than to tell you that he died as he lived, a brave, true man—the best of comrades and the staunchest of friends.

Wilson was to keep a very full diary of the *Discovery* expedition of 1901–4 and his paintings and drawings illustrate Scott's and Armitage's narratives of the expendition, as well as the volumes of scientific results and the expedition's magazine, *The South Polar Times*.[27]

The four warrant officers were important members of the expedition and Scott was greatly pleased with his choice of Thomas Feather as boatswain, Frederick Dailey as carpenter, J. H. Dellbridge as second engineer and C. R. Ford as ship's steward. The crew consisted partly of merchant seamen, two of whom came from Dundee, and 'British blue jackets', naval ratings who were selected by Scott's friends in various ships of the Channel Squadron from other volunteers.[28]

The engines were well tested in the Atlantic. Thirty-three days were spent under steam, at an average daily consumption of just over 7 tons of coal, greater than had been hoped. From 24 to 30 August, the engines pushed against head winds in the tropics. Being new, they 'required more than ordinary care and adjustment', wrote Scott, during this 'unexpectedly long period of steaming'. He praised the engine-room staff, 'who worked day and night to avoid a breakdown' despite a temperature in the stokehold while in the tropics of 140°F.[29]

The *Discovery* called briefly at the uninhabited tropical island of South Trinidad off Brazil and entered Table Bay on 3 October 1901. Here at Cape Town the bunkers were refilled with coal and then the *Discovery*, rolling through an angle of 90°, made a short passage to the naval station at Simon's Bay, where she was refitted, thanks to the kindness of Sir Arthur Moore, the Commander-in-Chief, despite the exigencies of the Boer War. The ship's magnetic instruments had carefully to be compared with those at the Cape in order to ensure an accurate survey between South Africa and New Zealand. Armitage, who was responsible for the magnetic work as far as New Zealand, wrote to Sir Clements Markham on 14 October 1901 impressing upon him the necessity of spare magnets and needles for the instruments, especially as the Germans were 'doing their utmost, with no expense spared'.[30] On a separate page of his letter, he added incidentally 'I like Captain Scott better than ever.' The Hydrographer of the Navy, Sir William Wharton, wrote to Sir Clements on 14 December 1901, saying that his department would help if at all possible. However, with eight instruments of four different types, he could not guarantee that new needles would fit without careful adjustment.[31] It was Wharton, as Hydrographer, who had supplied most of the expedition's scientific instruments.[32] The magnetic programme had been arranged by Captain E. W. Creak, Director of the Admiralty Compass Observatory. He remarked to Markham in a letter concerning Armitage's request that he knew 'of no ship which has had such equipment as the *Discovery*'; in fact she was 'better equipped by far than the *Challenger*, which for months and even years used her Fox Circles without damage'. Indeed, the *Discovery* had 'duplicate instruments where the *Challenger* had only one'.[33]

Four crew members were discharged at the Cape. They were replaced by volunteers from the fleet, Vince, Plumley and Joyce, the last of whom was later to become well known as one of Shackleton's men. R. Sinclair, a merchant seaman, also joined together with Horace Buckridge, domestic and laboratory assistant. Buckridge was an educated man, who had served throughout the Boer War as a sergeant with a unit of Australian Bushmen. He volunteered to come without pay. Scott thought this undesirable and he was given £5 a month.[34] Mr George Murray of the British Museum, who had accompanied the expedition as temporary Director of the Civilian Scientific Staff, also left the ship at Cape Town. Scott had found him excellent as a mess-mate and director, but '*entre nous* most unpractical in his ideas for working deep-sea tackle'.[35] It was Murray who had edited the authoritative *Antarctic Manual*, a handbook published by the Royal Geographical Society in July 1901 for the National Antarctic Expedition.

## CAPE TOWN TO NEW ZEALAND

The *Discovery* suffered a succession of gales after leaving the Cape from 27 October to 3 November 1901. Skelton noted a record run of 217 miles under sail alone on 27 October, at an average 9 knots, which he thought was 'as much as she will ever do for any time'. The amount of fresh water distilled daily from the sea during the gale was reduced to eight tons, from the ten produced when the ship was steady. Skelton thought it spoke 'very well for the seaworthiness of the ship that a sea hasn't even wetted her name yet' given the 'tremendous sea' running. The record was again broken on 31 October, with 223 miles made under sail.[36] 'As this spell of bad weather may be accounted the first real test of the ship's seaworthy qualities,' wrote Scott, 'it is pleasing to record that she proves entirely satisfactory from this important point of view. She rises easily and lightly to the heaviest seas, is wonderfully stiff under canvas and surprisingly dry. I had expected the possibility of shipping seas over the stern when running before heavy weather and consequently some risk of "broaching to" and am agreeably surprised to find that no such danger exists—the ship, in fact, proves in all respects a wonderfully good sea-boat to the great credit of her designer, as the point might have been easily overlooked in an attempt to follow the lines of modern polar ships and in forgetfulness of the extreme difference of sea conditions in these Southern latitudes to those experienced in the waterways of the North. I attribute the ease with which she rises to heavy following seas, entirely to the rounded shape of the stern, which I think will also give us a great advantage in the ice . . . A good sea-boat is usually what seamen call "lively" and the *Discovery* proves anything but an exception to this rule: she is tossed about like a cork on the big seas and we have recorded rolls up to 47°.' He added that while the heavy motion did not cause discomfort, it added to the difficulties of much of the work, especially the magnetic observations.[37] Armitage was in charge of these, while Royds took on meteorology, Shackleton sea-water sampling and Barne the sounding machines, deep-sea thermometers, etc.

Lyttelton, New Zealand, was to be their next port of call but a detour was made to the south of 40°S. for the sake of the magnetic survey, 'far out of the track of ships and into the regions of ice'.[38] The 60th parallel was crossed on 15 November, and next day the *Discovery* received what Scott called 'her baptism of ice'. Towards nightfall 'we became closely surrounded by the pack, which consisted of comparatively small pieces of ice from two or three feet in thickness and much worn at their edges by the constant movement of the swell . . . the grinding of the floes against the ship's side was mingled with the more subdued hush of their rise and fall on the long swell and for the first time we felt something of the solemnity of these great southern solitudes'.[39] By the evening of 17 November, the vessel was stopped by heavy ice. It was one solid mass of ice as far as the eye could see. 'A Grand Sight', wrote one of the seamen, a Dundee man.[40] The opportunity was taken while in these latitudes to capture specimens of the birds to be found in the pack: the Southern fulmar, the Antarctic petrel, the snow petrel, and the prions or whale-birds. Skelton admired Wilson's splendid sketches of them and thought these should be very useful in correcting the British Museum catalogues, where 'the descriptions of the birds, colouring, beaks, feet etc.' were 'all wrong'. Skelton also recorded four rather unsuccessful attempts to sound between 15 and 21 November. The line 'kinked and broke' and everything was lost on the first occasion. On the second, the wire broke again. Skelton remarked that this meant that a total of 4,000 fathoms of wire plus 'three or four driver tubes, one thermometer and sundries' had been lost in four soundings. A further 900 fathoms of wire were lost on 21 November when Skelton observed, 'the game is getting rather expensive'.[41]

The sub-Antarctic island of Macquarie, an isolated speck of land about half-way between Australia and the Antarctic continent, was visited briefly on 22 November 1901. It is green with tussock grass and other plants in summer and has no ice-cap, unlike South Georgia and the other islands south of the Antarctic Convergence. It is a haven for thousands of penguins, for hundreds of elephant seals and the nesting place of albatrosses, cormorants, petrels, skuas and other sea birds. It also has an interesting flora.[42] For many years in the nineteenth century, Fur seals were exploited and practically exterminated by the sealers, who later turned to boiling down Sea elephants and even penguins for their oil. The interesting story of the island has been written by Dr J. S. Cumpston.[43] The *Discovery* anchored off the east coast in Lusitania Bay. The scientists were put ashore through the fringe of thick kelp (a gigantic seaweed) and were soon busy collecting specimens, including eggs and young from the penguin rookeries, which cover a considerable area of ground. 'The novelty of the situation, of our first view of the penguins and of so many other strange sights put us all into the highest spirits and aroused the enthusiasm of the collectors to fever heat,' wrote Scott in his diary.[44] His Aberdeen terrier was much pleased and excited with his run on shore, 'until he came to the penguins, when he was most obviously and comically divided between a desire to run away and a feeling that he ought to appear bold in such strange company. The result was a series of short rushes, made with suppressed growls and every hair bristling, but ending at a safe distance.'[45]

Following their visit to the island, penguin was served for dinner and penguin eggs for breakfast. 'Must own to a weak stomach in these matters,' wrote Scott afterwards, 'but am much rejoiced to see the excellent spirit shewn by the crew—they all eat and most pronounced favourably, where I rather expected a kicking against the pricks in a matter where they are usually so pig-headed and obstinate.'[46]

The *Discovery* berthed in Lyttelton Harbour on 29 November 1901. Here Scott must have received a letter dated 29 October 1901, from 'your affectionate friends', the President of the Royal Society and the President of the Royal Geographical Society. While acknowledging Scott's heavy responsibilities, they wrote '. . . we have full confidence in your ability, judgement and skill, and that you possess those higher qualities which fit you to lead men in times of hardship and peril, and to secure such a measure of success as the powers of nature arrayed against you may render possible. We ask no more.' They also reminded him that efforts were being made to despatch a relief ship next season.[47]

The expedition received enormous kindness, both public and private, in New Zealand. The *Discovery*'s rigging was overhauled and refitted with the help of men from HMS *Ringarooma*. Her stores were restowed and in part replaced, after being damaged by a persistent leak. Here Shackleton, the merchant seaman, came into his own. 'His interest and enthusiasm, combined with shrewd common sense and experience in cargo work has proved invaluable,' wrote Scott, 'and I am sure no ship ever left on such an expedition with a more accurate knowledge of her resources or the exact position of every comestible she carried.'[48] The coal bunkers were refilled with 285 tons, while 45 tons were later taken on as deck cargo.[49] In an endeavour to stop the leak, the vessel was twice docked. The second time, the heavy steel plates protecting her bows were removed and 'every inch of the bottom examined'. It was all in vain and the leak persisted.[50] Captain Scott decided that it must be put up with and the water pumped out daily. Writing later of this, the *Discovery*'s architect concluded of her construction that 'The work generally was done well. One careless man would account for the whole of the really important defects that were discovered.'[51]

The magnetic survey was one of the main aims of the expedition. For this, a base was needed in the southern hemisphere, such as Hobart had been sixty years earlier for Sir James Clark Ross.[52] It was important to make the 'necessary absolute and relative magnetic observations with the instruments on board the *Discovery*', the Societies' presidents had written in advance to the director of the Christchurch Observatory, Mr Coleridge Farr, and to establish 'as complete a base station as your resources will permit'.[53] In Christchurch, simultaneous observations could be made on 'term days' in accordance with those of the Antarctic expeditions and in international co-operation. The arrival of L. C. Bernacchi, the physicist, by fast steamer, the last officer to join *Discovery*, meant that this base could be set up.

Louis Bernacchi came from a family originating in northern Italy. His father, a brilliant scholar, was the owner of Maria Island, Tasmania, where young Bernacchi had been brought up in 'wild but enchanting surroundings'. He spent several years at the Melbourne Magnetic Observatory, where he qualified as Astronomer, Meteorologist and Magnetician.[54] He joined Borchgrevink's *Southern Cross* expedition as Physicist. His book, *To the south polar regions*, was published in the year he joined the National Antarctic Expedition. He was later to write a life of L. E. G. Oates and a history of the *Discovery*.

The popular appeal of the *Discovery* was such that she was viewed or seen off by thousands of people, some brought to Lyttelton by special excursion trains. 'We had a visit from the Moirie Ladies', wrote Duncan, shipwright from Dundee, '. . . some of them were riged up in thare own style of dress and they looked splendid. They were served with lunch on board and getting a Photo of the Ship signed by the Officers, departed wishing every success to the Discovery Captain and Crew.'[55] Despite the 'flocks of curious visitors', the ship was at last ready to sail, very deeply laden, from Lyttelton on 21 December 1901.

> Below, every hold and stowage space was packed to the brim—even the cabins were invaded with odd cases for which no corner could be found. But the scene on deck was more extraordinary. Here, again, were numerous packing-cases for which no more convenient resting-place could be found, the after-part of the deck was occupied by a terrified flock of forty-five sheep, a last and most welcome present from the farmers of New Zealand. Amidst this constantly stampeding body stood the helmsman at the wheel; further forward were sacks of food, and what space remained was occupied by our twenty-three howling dogs in a wild state of excitement. Above the deck, the skid-beams, fitted for the carriage of our boats, were in addition piled high with the woodwork of our huts, adding, we estimated, a weight of some thirty tons, and therefore requiring to be secured with many lashings and much care.[56]

No doubt, during the short farewell service conducted by the Bishop of Christchurch, there were many prayers said silently for fine weather during the passage across the Southern Ocean. The expedition enjoyed a great 'send-off' from those packing the wharves and quays, while two warships, the *Ringarooma* and the *Lizard*, steamed slowly

THE VOYAGES OF THE DISCOVERY

ahead of the *Discovery* and her escort of 'five gaily-dressed steamers, crowded with passengers, and with bands playing and whistles hooting . . .'.[57] In the excitement of departure, a young seaman named Bonner had climbed above the crow's nest to the top of the mainmast, from which he hurtled with a wild cry to his death on the corner of an iron deckhouse. The loss of this 'smart young seaman' was greatly felt, wrote Scott. He was buried with naval honours at Port Chalmers.[58] Bonner was replaced by Able Seaman Jesse Handsley, who volunteered from HMS *Ringarooma*, as did AB Thomas Crean. Crean must have replaced AB Robert Sinclair, who deserted in New Zealand, being very depressed since his shipmate's death and 'imagining himself in some sort responsible'. Scott took no steps to apprehend him.[59]

Commander A. R. Ellis, the editor of Lashly's diaries, has remarked that 'this accident brought together the two men [Lashly and Crean] whose names were later to be linked in one of the greatest Antarctic stories on Scott's second and last expedition in the *Terra Nova*, 1910–13'. This was the perilous return journey of 750 miles to base of Scott's 'Last Supporting Party' from the polar plateau in January and February 1912. Lieut. E. R. G. R. Evans (later Lord Mountevans) had been overcome by scurvy. He was first nursed on skis and then, for the last 80 miles, hauled on the sledge by his two stout but struggling companions, Lashly and Crean. 'It would be difficult to imagine two more different types', continues Ellis. 'Lashly was a man of very few words who went about his work humming quietly to himself with a contented smile on his face. Crean described himself as the "wild man from Borneo". He came from County Kerry and, like Lashly, was a strong, healthy utterly dependable sort of man with a great zest for life.'[60]

After taking on the deck coal at Port Chalmers (the port of Dunedin), the *Discovery* took a final departure on the morning of Christmas Eve 1901, as HMS *Ringarooma* manned ship and cheered her again. By the evening, under steam and sail in the open sea, the 'last view of civilisation, the last sight of fields, and trees and flowers, had come and gone,' wrote Scott, 'and as the night fell, the blue outline of friendly New Zealand was lost to us in the northern twilight'.[61]

## FROM NEW ZEALAND TO THE ANTARCTIC

The Antarctic continent is bounded by the Southern Ocean, one of the stormiest seas in the world. In the nineteenth century, the square-rigged fast sailing ships would there run their easting down, blown by the westerly gales of the forties and fifties on Great Circle courses, which shortened the voyage to Australia, New Zealand and the Far East. Captain Cook's great circumnavigation of the globe of 1772–5 in high southern latitudes disproved the existence of the theoretical geographers' supposed fertile continent of *Terra Australis* and showed that if land existed nearer the South Pole, it would be 'doomed by nature to everlasting frigidness and never once to feel the warmth of the sun's rays, whose horrible and savage aspect I have no way to describe'.[62] British and American sealers followed in the wake of the *Resolution* and *Adventure*, decimating the Fur seals, but discovering new lands as well. The three national expeditions of the early 1840s (French, American and British) charted portions of the coast of Antarctica, while one of these, commanded by Sir James Clark Ross in HM Ships *Erebus* and *Terror*, penetrated the belt of summer pack-ice that surrounds the continent to discover the Ross Sea, the 'icy barrier' of the Ross Ice Shelf (which borders the Ross Sea to the south) and the volcanic peaks, Mount Erebus and Mount Terror adjoining McMurdo Sound, the area to which Scott was directed to sail in the *Discovery*.

Only one ship had previously wintered in the Antarctic, the *Belgica* of the Belgian expedition of 1897–9 led by Adrien de Gerlache which was beset in the pack of the Bellingshausen Sea to the west of the Antarctic Peninsula for several months; and only one expedition had wintered on the continent, the party landed at Cape Adare from the *Southern Cross*, in February 1899, led by C. E. Borchgrevink. The *Southern Cross* had skirted the cliffs of the Ross Ice Shelf, finding that it had retreated since Ross's day. A sledging party had briefly landed to make a short journey to a record 78°50′ S.[63] The *Southern Cross* had been preceded into the Ross Sea and at Cape Adare by a pioneer Norwegian whaling voyage in the *Antarctic* of 1894–5, led by H. J. Bull and financed by Svend Foyn of Tønsberg, who invented the explosive whaling harpoon operated from the bow of a whale catcher, not from small boats. Borchgrevink had been a member of this expedition, which made what was claimed to be the first landing on the Antarctic continent at Cape Adare and first discovered plant life there.[64]

Fine weather enabled the *Discovery* to traverse the stormy seas south of New Zealand largely under sail, without losing any deck cargo. New Year's Day saw the first 24 hours of daylight. The first iceberg was sighted on 2 January 1902, when approaching the Antarctic Circle. Soon, 17 of these flat-topped tabular bergs were counted, none more than 100 feet high.[65] These had calved from the ice shelf and were small in comparison with those sometimes reported with a length of fifty or more miles. 'Several we passed close to', wrote Wilson, 'and enjoyed the blue depths and the pure whiteness of the flat tops and the caves and grottos, into which the spray dashed and rose sometimes to 80 or 90 feet. It was a fine sight.'[66] The Antarctic Circle was crossed on 3 January and soon, wrote Scott, the *Discovery* 'encountered the first of the scattered fragments of sea ice which form the outriders of the pack . . . . Slight shocks' were felt as her 'ironclad prow forced a way through the honey-combed floes'.[67] Lieut. A. B. Armitage, RNR of the P. & O. Company, had been appointed by Sir Clements Markham as the navigator and second-in-command because of his Arctic experience with F. G. Jackson in the *Windward*.[68] He found the southern sea ice much more level than that in the north.[69] Known as the 'Pilot', Armitage navigated the *Discovery* in the realms of ice, and was fascinated by the problems they posed.

Perched aloft, almost at the very summit of the main mast, snugly ensconced in the crow's nest (which, with its hood and seat, is more comfortable than the casual

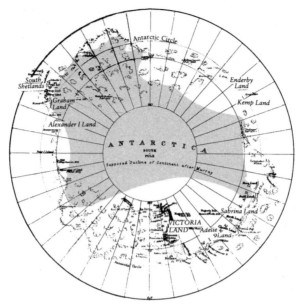

Map of Antarctica south of latitude 60°S. showing the 'supposed outline of the continent after Murray'. From a series of maps by J. G. Bartholomew, illustrating Dr John Murray's address of 1893, in the *Geographical Journal*, Vol. III, No. 1, January 1894

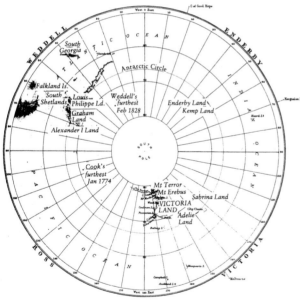

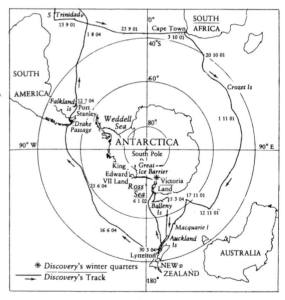

The Antarctic regions from latitude 50° S., *c* 1900, reduced from a coloured map in the pamphlet printed by William Clowes, London 1901, entitled 'Plan of Operations for the National Antarctic Expedition'

The track of the *Discovery* in the southern hemisphere during the National Antarctic Expedition 1901-4, from the map by D. E. G. Cole in E. A. Wilson's *Discovery Diary*, Blandford, London 1966 observer would believe) and with a powerful telescope . . . the look-out man enjoys a form of *sport* that would appeal to many if they once came under its spell.

It always seemed to me that I had more absolute control of the ship when I was in that situation than in any other. . . . Ahead and all around is a vast, illimitable field of ice, which in the farthest distance appears to be absolutely impervious to attack. Somewhat closer are . . . thin black-looking streaks of water, and still closer to the ship, the weak places in the line of defence . . . and one is able to guide the ship from one lead to the other by the least line of resistance.

For some distance ahead the pilot in the crow's nest can estimate the respective mass of each ice-piece, and so can tell which one to avoid, and which it is safe to pass over. Long, cruel-looking spurs extend far under water from some of them, and others are quite smooth-sided.

The officers at the engine room telegraph and in the engine room, as well as the men at the wheel, are kept busily employed during this kind of navigation, for on their quickness in obeying the orders from the nest often depends the issue: whether the good ship glides safely by a dangerous mass of ice, or is brought up against it, quivering in every timber. At times, the only way to get from one lead of water to another is to face a passage, and then, as with full way on, the gallant craft charges the obstruction, the man in the nest involuntarily grasps the pole as she mounts upon and breaks down the neck of ice which bars her way to freedom.[70]

Under sail and steam, the *Discovery* made an easy passage through the 270-mile belt of pack-ice in five days, emerging from the 'grinding floes'[71] on 8 January 1902. Time had been spent celebrating both a belated Christmas and their entry into the Antarctic regions, many of the afterguard trying skis for the first time. The ship was watered from the ice and seals captured as specimens and for food. Seal meat was cooked and served regularly, meeting with general approval. Scott himself owned to some squeamishness in the matter, but found the steaks and joints much more palatable than penguin. 'The men like their ration,' he wrote, 'except Walker, who having been a whaler is evidently influenced by the time-honoured prejudice of his class.'[72] Tow-netting was carried out for the microscopic flora and fauna on the surface of the sea. The sheep were slaughtered and the joints of mutton hung in the rigging to be roasted as a special treat on Sundays. Scott vividly describes the bird life of the pack: the Southern fulmars, the Antarctic petrels, the skuas, the giant petrels and the dainty snow petrels.[73] Penguins were abundant, wrote Scott.

The squawk of the penguin was constantly heard, at first far off and often long before the birds were seen; curiosity drew them to the ship . . . As the ship forced her way onward, these merry little companions would again and again leap into the water, journeying from floe to floe in their effort to find out what it all meant. Some of the sailors grew very expert in imitating their call, and could not only attract them from a long distance, but would visibly add to their astonishment when they approached.[74]

A sounding of 1,480 fathoms was made at the southern edge of the pack and temperatures of the sea water obtained at various depths. Land was seen on entering open water and at midnight, the sun shone on Mount Sabine,[75] one of the high peaks of Victoria Land. The *Discovery* anchored in Robertson Bay and parties landed at the site of Borchgrevink's winter quarters near Cape Adare. Bernacchi and Armitage took instruments ashore to determine dip and total force, while others examined the hut and the large rookery of Adélie penguins, despite its pungent odour. The naturalists sought specimens and in the evening Bernacchi led a pilgrimage to visit the high and lonely grave of his former comrade in the *Southern Cross*, Nikolai Hanson. Scott described this first smiling glimpse of Antarctica.

> The scene in the bay after we had returned for our late evening meal was very beautiful; the surface was calm and placid, beyond it the sunlight fell on the bold peaks and splendid glaciers of the Admiralty Range, the sharp summits of Mounts Minto and Adam were well defined against a clear sky, while the lofty peak of Sabine was lost in a mystery of fleecy cloud. The placid, deep shadowed sea was dotted with streams of brilliantly white pack-ice, whilst here and there a table-topped iceberg showed the sharpest contrast of light and shadow as the sun fell on its smooth, steep sides. The tide was making out of the bay with considerable strength, and now and again bore past us a floe alive with busy, chattering penguins.[76]

The hut and some of the stores were found in good condition. Duncan, as a wooden shipwright, took a particular interest in the hut and found it a well-constructed log cabin, rather superior to the one they were carrying.[77] Despatches and letters were left in the hut, later to be picked up by the relief ship *Morning*.

The *Discovery* now stood to the south, against adverse winds, generally using a single boiler along the mountainous and mainly ice-bound coast of Victoria Land. Armitage records that the auxiliary barque had her first real test in ice when steaming away from Robertson Bay, when heavy close pack was being brought in on the tide. 'Well did she justify our faith in her powers', he wrote, 'and, with Skelton in the engine-room to encourage her, she answered her helm as though endowed with life, and by dint of charging here and boring there, emerged from the ordeal triumphant.' Armitage had been woken by Captain Scott to con the ship from the main top, at a time when the pack seemed likely to sweep her 'against one of the huge grounded bergs or heap us up on shore'.[78] She rode out a storm in the lee of Coulman Island,[79] where winds of 90 m.p.h. made her almost unmanageable. They left a written record of proceedings, protected by a cylinder, attached to a tall red-painted pole, conspicuous from the sea.[80] Hodgson, the biologist, was delighted with his best haul of marine life so far. Thirty-one seals were killed on the coast nearby, records Duncan, 'for use during the Winter Months as fresh meat'.[81] Those skins thought earlier to be worth preserving as specimens had been flensed of their layer of blubber and stored in barrels containing brine.[82] 'It seemed a terrible desecration', wrote Scott, 'to come to this quiet spot only to murder its innocent inhabitants and stain the white snow with blood; but necessities are often hideous, and man must live.'[83] The meat was hung in the rigging.

The ship gradually worked her way from Lady Newnes Bay to Wood Bay. 'The atmosphere was exceedingly clear', wrote Armitage, observing that they 'could plainly see Coulman Island and Mount Erebus at the same time, although they are 240 miles distant from one another'. This clarity could prove very deceptive, as Scott had found when approaching Coulman Island. He remarks how distant objects later seen on sledging journeys could assume 'extraordinary false appearances', and ascribed the errors made sometimes by earlier explorers to this fact.[84] Heavy ice blocked Wood Bay, making it impossible to leave a record there. 'From here', wrote Scott, 'the solitary volcanic cone of Mount Melbourne could be admired in its grandeur, constituting the most magnificent landmark on the coast.'[85] They were by then south of the magnetic pole, towards which the south-seeking end of the compass still pointed, so that although they were still travelling south, they appeared to be travelling north.

It was time to begin a search for secure winter quarters. A possible site was found in an inlet later named Granite Harbour, where a large party bounded ashore, leaping from floe to floe. In this sunny sheltered spot, tinkling brooks meandered over the stones, bordered by moss 'of almost luxuriant growth'. McMurdo Sound proved too full of ice to penetrate far beyond lat. 77°30′S. A plain seemed to be 'stretching directly south', Scott was pleased to note. There was no sign of the 'Parry Mountains' charted by Ross. A cone-shaped hill was named Mount Discovery and the western mountains, the Royal Society Range.[86] On 21 January, the *Discovery* turned east to follow Ross's 'Great Ice Barrier'.


## ALONG THE ICE SHELF: CAPE CROZIER TO EDWARD VII LAND

The expedition was later to ascertain that Mount Erebus and Mount Terror form Ross Island, a triangle whose extremities are Cape Armitage to the south, Cape Bird to the north and Cape Crozier to the south-east. The existence of the active volcano, Mount Erebus, in these icy regions was one of the more remarkable discoveries made by Sir James Clark Ross. Its white slopes rising to nearly 14,000 feet, crowned by a plume of smoke or an orange glow in winter, have become familiar to those interested in the Antarctic from H. G. Ponting's splendid photographs (taken during Scott's *Terra Nova* expedition) and from Edward Wilson's watercolours. The *Discovery* rounded the northern corner at Cape Bird, between it and off-lying Beaufort Island. A whaleboat managed to land through the surf at Cape Crozier, where Bernacchi and Barne made magnetic observations and where the important task was completed of setting up another post and record cylinder on the mountain-side, in the midst of an extensive penguin rookery whose members objected strongly to this intrusion.[87] From the summit of a nearby volcanic cone, Scott, Royds and Wilson were able to look down on Ross's other remarkable discovery, the 'Great Ice Barrier', off whose cliffs for 400 miles had sailed *Erebus* and *Terror* sixty years before, and later, the *Southern Cross*.

> Now for the first time this extraordinary ice-formation was seen from above. The sea to the north lay clear and blue, save where it was dotted by snowy-white bergs; the barrier edge, in shadow, looked like a long narrowing black ribbon as it ran with slight windings to the eastern horizon. South of this line, to the S.E. of our position, a vast plain extended indefinitely, whilst faint shadows on its blue-grey surface seemed to indicate some slight inequality in level; further yet to the south, the sun faced us, and the plain was lost in the glitter of its reflection. It was an impressive sight, and the very vastness of what lay at our feet seemed to add to our sense of mystery.[88]

On 23 January, the *Discovery* began to steam eastward along the Barrier. The officers surveyed the undulating heights of the sheer ice cliffs, finding that they ranged roughly from 50 to 240 feet. The ship was stopped three times in every 24 hours to make a sounding. The use of steam gave the *Discovery* a great advantage over the *Erebus* and *Terror*, which had relied on sail alone and therefore could not approach too near to the ice front. It was found that the ice had receded since the 1840s and that the *Discovery*'s course was south of the Barrier as charted by Ross. By 29 January, she was not only south but east of Ross's farthest venture of 1842, from which he had seen a strong appearance of land to the south-east. The character of the ice shelf soon changed; behind an ice front of some 10 to 20 feet above the sea, 'the snow surface rose in long undulating slopes to rounded ridges whose height we could only estimate'. A sounding of 100 fathoms confirmed that this was indeed land. Fog hindered exploration on the next day but in the evening it cleared sufficiently to reveal (at a height of some 2,000 feet) patches of 'real live rock, the actual substance of our newly discovered land'. As Ross had named his South Victoria Land after the young Queen Victoria, so Scott called that discovered by the National Antarctic Expedition King Edward VII Land after her son and recent successor. The *Discovery* reached her farthest south of 78°36'S. on 26 January 1902, the fourth day along the Barrier.[89]

By 31 January, shallow soundings alone indicated the nearness of land. The fog lifted to reveal numerous grounded icebergs round which lay heavy pack of great extent. 'Under a dark and threatening sky', wrote Scott, ever alive to an impressive scene, 'the pack-ice showed intensely white in an inky sea, whilst the towering walls of the icebergs frowned over us, shaded from the palest to the most intense blue.'[90] Emperor penguins (the largest and most stately of the penguin species) were seen that day, three of which were killed as specimens. In the evening from the crow's nest, Edward Wilson saw some thousands of them in groups of a hundred or more through the big telescope, while much smaller groups were dotted everywhere on the ice floes. He concluded that 'these were the Emperor's rookeries, which no one has found before', but since they were 'five miles inland across floe ice all fast to land', and new ice was forming on the sea where the ship lay, 'our only chance was to keep moving and the journey to these Emperors was out of the question'.[91]

On 1 February, Scott decided it was time to return westward to establish winter quarters, also bearing in mind the coal supply. Wilson's sketches, made in between skinning birds in an empty coal bunker, depict the new land that had been discovered. The highest part of the Barrier had been found to be 280 feet. It was noted that at least in some places it was afloat. On the return voyage to McMurdo Sound, a bight about three miles long in the ice shelf was investigated. The ship was able to lie alongside the ice front and balloon ascents were made by Scott and Shackleton to 700 feet from which height no land could be seen. Accounts are confused as to who else, if anybody, ascended. Armitage, Bernacchi and four men sledged south to examine the undulating surface of the Barrier. They spent a cramped night in their tent ashore and the southernmost point they reached was lat. 79°03'.5S. in long. 194°55'.25E.[92] Borchgrevink had landed and reached lat. 78°34'S. on 16 February 1900 from the same or a similar natural harbour in the Barrier, probably that later named 'Bay of Whales' by Shackleton in 1908.[93] What Scott called 'Balloon Bight' seems to have been renamed Discovery Inlet, later probably merging into the Bay of Whales through changes in the Ross Ice Shelf. The return along the Barrier was made as quickly as possible. By 8 February 1902, the *Discovery* was once more in McMurdo Sound, which was clear of ice where earlier there had been ice floes, some twelve feet thick.[94]

# THREE

## Winter Quarters, McMurdo Sound, First Wintering, 1902

## WINTER QUARTERS

A LIKELY SITE FOR WINTER QUARTERS was found in a little ice-filled bay, later known as Winter Harbour at the head of McMurdo Sound, near the southern tip of Ross Island. It was protected to the west by a small rocky promontory, which became known as Hut Point, and on the other side by Cape Armitage, named after the *Discovery*'s navigator.[1] It appeared sheltered from ice pressure and shallow enough for there to be no danger from icebergs. 'From the point of view of travelling', wrote Scott at the time, 'no part could be more seemingly excellent; to the SSE as far as the eye can reach, all is smooth and even, and indeed everything points to a continuation of the Great Barrier in this direction. We should be within easy distance for the exploration of the mainland, and apparently should have little difficulty in effecting a land communication with our post office at Cape Crozier.[2]

The *Discovery* was secured by ice anchors, but sudden squalls would cause the ship to uproot these from time to time and it was found necessary to keep the fires alight, so as to get up steam at short notice. She was also carried into 'awkward positions with regard to the ice-foot or the shallow bank which lay immediately off it' by the tide and swell,[3] sometimes parting her cables. 'When close in to the ice foot,' wrote Wilson, 'she bumped and groaned and squeaked and grunted like nothing I have heard before, and as my bunk had only a few feet of timber separating it from the point of contact, I had disturbed nights for a bit. The noise was perfectly amazing—long low musical notes rising to a perfect shriek or dying away in a long low groan.'[4] Scott used gun cotton to blow up some of the ice ahead of the ship to edge her further in.[5] The vessel was eventually frozen into 'the most perfect little natural harbour imaginable', wrote Wilson on 8 February 1902.

We all realized our extreme good fortune in being led to such a winter quarter as this, safe for the ship, with perfect shelter from all ice pressure from the north and south and west, a low shore and ice foot on the east where the huts could be satisfactorily built on rock, sheltered from the S.E. prevailing winds by a range of hills from five to seven and ten hundred feet high, and all within sight of not only Erebus and its column of smoke, and Terror, but of an immense and splendid range of mountains, hitherto unknown, which caught and reflected the pink glow of the sun with its wonderful violets night and morning, and away to the south a new island 2,000 ft. high on a plain of ice, the back of the Great Ice Barrier, our field of sledging work next year. Nothing was wanting, and our hopes ran very high that night.[6]

A further advantage, noted by both Scott and Wilson, was the abundance of Weddell seals—a 'wholesome sight to us', wrote Wilson, 'because it practically puts scurvy out of the question if we can get fresh meat regularly to eat'.[7]

Captain Scott had earlier outlined the three-year programme of work. In Wilson's words, this was:

Make straight for McMurdo Bay; find good winter quarters and get settled into them as far south as possible. Spend the winter there. Give up next summer chiefly to sledging in three directions. One party to go due south from winter quarters. The ship to wait for its return. Other smaller parties and excursions to make out the immediate neighbourhood of McMurdo Bay and Erebus and Terror, and to come back to the ship. By this time the relief ship will have found our letters at Cape Crozier and will come to us in McMurdo Bay. The relief ship will now take Armitage and a party to Wood Bay to go inland, for the Magnetic Pole, and wait for them till their return when they and the relief ship will return to Lyttelton. Meanwhile, the *Discovery* will have collected its sledge parties and will go up by Cape Adare and by Cape North to see if anything can be made out of Wilkes Land, and when the season comes to an end, run straight up to Lyttelton, arriving there about the end of March 1903. Here we spend the winter months refitting, and then in December '03 we start south again to get further information about this east end of the Barrier where we found our new land. We go straight for this part and spend the whole summer working it out and then run up in March, out of the ice, and home round Cape Horn without going again to New Zealand at all.[8]

*Man proposes and God disposes.* Scott's plans were modified in the event.

Having found a sheltered harbour, free from danger to the ship, Scott decided to winter the *Discovery* there and to use her for the expedition's living quarters. A prefabricated hut had been brought south, which Armitage tells us was made in Australia from a design by Professor Gregory 'more suitable for a colonial shooting lodge, than for a polar dwelling place'. It was erected with some difficulty and several picks were broken in excavating holes in the iron-like frozen ground for the corner posts.[9] The weather was kind and not a day was missed while the outer building was being constructed between 15 and 26 February, although it was 'a cold job', thought Duncan, 'working on House top in this Latitude, with Temperature at Zero'. The indoor work could be done in bad weather.[10]

The two observation huts were erected with less trouble, at a distance from the ship. Armitage describes them as being made of 'skeletons of wood which were filled in with double walls and roofs of asbestos sheets—a German invention'.[11] That the crew (or at least some of them) were interested in the scientific work is shown by Duncan's description of the instruments written on 27 February 1902, the date the magnetic hut was completed.

> Observation Hut is now finished thare is some very fine Instruments inside it fitted on A Bench is A machine for Resting [i.e. registering] Magnatic Elements its rather A curio as thare is only 3 of this particular kind made. one hear and 1 with the German ship and one in Hamburg. The other instrument is Earthquake regester its fitted on A large stone Pipe let into the Earth so as to recieve any shock. This is the only connection we have with the outside World. Another one is for testing the amount of Electry [Electricity] in the Air. Mr. Bernachie has charge of these.[12]

Penguins and seals were butchered to provide fresh food for the winter to supplement the tinned and other provisions. Kennels were made for the dogs on shore, although these proved a waste of time, as their owners preferred to curl up outside in the snow.[13]

The young geologist, Hartley Ferrar, had been the first to climb one of the nearby hills (Observation Hill) and to realise that they were on an island (Ross Island). He built a cairn to mark the event.[14] Gradually, the area surrounding winter quarters was explored on foot or on skis and the local landmarks given names, which have become familiar to others over the years: Arrival Bay, Crater Heights, Pram Point, Castle Rock and the Gap. 'Repeated walks are taken to the hill tops in the immediate vicinity,' wrote Scott at this time, 'and eyes are turned towards the South—the land of promise.'[15] By mid-February 1902, the long Antarctic summer's day showed signs of coming to an end.

> The sun is now very near dipping at midnight and will soon give us an appreciable night. In the evening and morning it is therefore low and gives all the effects of sunset and sunrise for many hours together. The scene is wonderfully beautiful, dressed in soft tones. The most characteristic feature is a wonderful violet light that tinges the snowslopes and icefoot and fades into the purple outline of the distant mountains. Here and there a high peak is radiantly gilded by a shaft of sunlight and the cirrus clouds that usually hang about some of the slopes and valleys are thrown in striking contrasts of brilliant light and deep shadow.[16]

Here Scott was painting in words the scene depicted in watercolours by Dr Wilson.

The 'blue jackets' found a football pitch on the fast ice and the officers joined in, beating the men in a match by one goal.[17] Skiing proved popular, but not without accidents. Some splendid runs had been found near the ship and practice led to astonishing progress. Skis were unknown to the old British Arctic expeditions and were a novelty on this one. Scott found skiing 'a most pleasurable and delightful exercise'. As far as travelling was concerned, his initial reaction was that they would probably be of little use when dragging sledges, despite being helpful on level snow and magnificent down a slight slope. What he called a 'light screw shoe' needed devising during the winter.[18]

As they settled down to life and work beneath the great smoking volcano, the Antarctic took its toll: Seaman Vince slid down an icy slope in murky weather to drown in the sea on 11 March. Miraculously, another shipmate, young Hare, found his way back to the ship unharmed after getting lost and then falling asleep in the snow for thirty-six hours. They had both been members of a sledge party sent to deposit a record at Cape Crozier for the relief ship, directing her to winter quarters. Everyone was overjoyed at Hare's return. Wilson felt he would never forget the effect of Hare's appearance on some members of the expedition, 'notably, the Skipper, who looked as though he thought the dead was really walking in'.[19] Scott was heard to remark 'Thank God, one of my Boys has returned.'[20] The ship's siren was sounded during the search for the missing men and later on, more steam was raised and the *Discovery* rounded Hut Point to leave no shadow of doubt as to Vince's fate. A boat party under Shackleton had previously searched the area. 'Life was a bright thing' to Vince, wrote Captain Scott, 'and it is something to think that death must have come quickly in the grip of that icy sea'.[21] A number of lessons were learned from this sad episode and from other early sledging journeys that autumn, as to the harshness of Antarctica, the fickleness of the climate and as regards travel and equipment. Scott considered Hare's survival a great tribute to the clothing with which the expedition had been provided. It was at this time too that Seaman Wild's powers of leadership were shown in bringing his companions to the ship and safety.[22]

The *Discovery* was still not properly frozen in by the end of March. Young ice (making communication difficult in the boats with the shore) kept forming and then dispersing, posing Scott with a dilemma. He was anxious about the ship's vulnerability to gales until she was well frozen in, as they had extinguished the boilers to save coal; he was also unwilling to commit a large party ashore because the men would be needed if the ship were driven from the ice. On the other hand, there was a lot to be done before the winter really set in.[23]

However, the ship gradually became frozen in from astern, and by 28 March the sea ice appeared to have come to stay. On Easter Sunday (30 March), ice flowers sprang up on the surface of the frozen sea, as if specially perfected for that day. 'This is the season of flowers', wrote Scott. These Easter lilies of the far south were 'very beautiful ice-flowers, waxen white in the shadow, but radiant with prismatic colours where the sun rays light on their delicate petals . . . clear-cut and perfect in form.'[24] Meanwhile preparations for the winter progressed. The meteorological screen was erected ashore about 60 yards astern of the ship and an anemometer (to measure wind speed) on the mizzen cross trees. Tide poles were set up and a windmill briefly operated on board to generate electric light.

The *Discovery* was covered with an awning of waggon cloth (as had been the Arctic ships wintering in years gone by). Scott had gone to some trouble to acquire this material, but thought in fact that ordinary canvas would have been stronger and better. The boats had been earlier landed on the ice to make room for the awning to be spread.

## THE DARK WINTER

Shackleton provides a good picture of the routine of a winter's day and indeed of the long winter nights on board the *Discovery* during the months of darkness, when the sun disappeared below the horizon, from April to August.[25]

At six o'clock the quartermaster whose night watch it is calls the cook. He immediately gets up and lights the fire. Then, at seven o'clock, the men and officers turn out, and a working party of men proceed with their sledge to a small glacier, which is about a hundred yards from the ship, and there, with pick and shovel, break up the ice, put it into a big box on the sledge and cart it back to the ship. Another party on board puts this supply of ice into the melter over the galley stove, and the first party comes back for a fresh supply. In two journeys we could get enough ice to supply the whole ship for the day.

Then the ward-room servants and other men pick out of the ice-box whatever they want for themselves or for the officers, and melt down their ice in other receptacles. At eight o'clock all hands go to breakfast, which consists of porridge, seal meat, bread and butter and jam and tea and coffee or cocoa. At nine o'clock the Captain reads prayers on the mess deck, and after that the men are told off to their various jobs. Some are employed making sleeping bags for sledging, others repairing the weather cloth that covers the whole ship, which occasionally gets holes in it owing to the blizzards and the weight of snow which settles on it. Another party starts shovelling the thick snow off the vessel, for tons of drift accumulate on and around the ship. We never minded the vessel's sides being piled up with snow, for this kept us warm inside, but it would not have done to have had too great a weight of snow actually on the ship.

Other men would be told off to assist the officers in their various duties, some helping to skin and stuff the birds and seals, which will be used as specimens in the museums when the ship comes back. Others would go out with the officers who had charge of the soundings. They might be away perhaps three or four hours from the ship, getting the depth of water all round within three or four miles. A couple more men would help Mr. Hodgson, the biologist, whose work it was to obtain as many marine specimens as possible. He was extremely fortunate in obtaining over five hundred new kinds of marine animals, spiders and shrimps, star and shell-fish, and various other things that live and swim in the sea. It was only owing to his energy in working right through the long winter in the dark and cold that he was enabled to make such a good collection.

In order to clean the skulls of the seals all we had to do was to give them to the biologist. He put them down the hole where he drew his fish nets, and in about two days the shrimps, of which there were millions, had completely cleaned all the flesh away from the bone. The head was put in a pillow-case with holes in it, or in a net, which gave free access to the shrimps. Another party of men would assist the officer who had charge of the stores to get up the necessary rations for the day, and yet another couple of men would be told off to assist the geologist who roamed around collecting rock specimens. He unfortunately was unable to get very many interesting specimens as the land at our winter quarters was almost entirely volcanic, and therefore there were no fossils to be obtained.

At one o'clock comes dinner for the men, the officers' dinner not coming on until six. The men prefer a good meal in the middle of the day, and then they take an afternoon sleep. At eight o'clock at night the officer for the day makes an inspection of the ship and reports to the captain. Then the time for play begins. Our hut—which was not used, as nothing happened to the ship—was converted into the 'Royal Terror Theatre', and there all sorts of plays and concerts and minstrel shows were given. Lieutenant Barne was manager, as he had a great gift for writing and localising plays. We generally had a show once a month. Cards were in great demand, and not only the officers, but the warrant officers and blue-jackets became adept at bridge. Some of the blue-jackets could remember every card that was playing in a 'no trump' hand.

Our paper, the *South Polar Times*, which was published in the winter came out once a month, and was contributed to by officers and men alike. I hope to have this published shortly in England. We had a semi-scientific article in every issue, and the lighter side of the expedition was also touched on. The offices of the *South Polar Times* were situated in one of the food stores, and it was just as impossible to get to the editorial sanctum there as it is to reach the same sanctum of any of the London papers. Dr. Wilson's beautiful illustrations are the feature of the book, and Captain Scott's articles, both humorous and serious, are of great interest.[26]

Though it was impossible for plants to grow outside, we made a brave attempt to have a garden in our ward room, and had the pleasure of seeing on Good Friday two crocuses blooming in our little box of earth which we had brought with us from civilisation. We did not dare to disturb the box by taking it down, so a rug was spread on the table, and everybody who wanted to have a look came in and got on top, and had a view of the flowers. Those two blossoms were the only things we had seen in the way of flowers since the end of 1901. We also had a vegetable garden of mustard and cress, and there was sufficient when the crop was grown to give a mouthful to half-a-dozen people. The happy recipients were a party of officers and men who had just returned from a sledge journey, to whom the green stuff was especially acceptable. We were able to keep warmth enough in the ward-room for the plants to grow, for we had two good stoves, and we could easily regulate the temperature, which was kept at a mean of fifty-five so you see we were never very uncomfortable on board, though if you put your hand out in your bunk you could feel a lump of ice on the bolt that penetrated the cabin from the outside of the ship. It was there and on the board overhead in one's cabin that all the moisture froze.

The officers took turns in staying up all night to take meteorological readings. This had to be done every two hours whether it was blowing a blizzard or calm, and sometimes an officer would come down to the ward-room after his ten minutes' encounter with the weather absolutely white with snow and his face white with frost-bites. We used to console ourselves during these nights when we had to be up by making special little suppers for ourselves, using a frying pan in the ward-room, and the delicious smell of cooking would penetrate to the other officers' cabins between one and two in the morning, and if it did not bring out a boot thrown by way of protest, it generally brought out two or three pyjama-clad sleepless men to partake of the supper.

All was brightness and light within the ship and the noise of the howling wind outside could hardly be heard, but what a change it was to open the door and go on deck. The swirling snow got into your eyes and into every crevice of your clothes and the cold air quite took one's breath away. But the weather was not always like this. Sometimes a full moon rode high in the sky and the whole country was bathed in glorious light, and on those clear nights we sometimes saw a gleam of light away in the Northward, which was a sign that still there was a Sun, though he had hidden his face from us. I cannot imagine anything more wonderful and awe-inspiring than this great white plain, the huge mountains rising away in the distance beyond; and that great volcano with its heavy pall of smoke hanging over our little camp day and night. There we were, forty-eight men, with a Continent to ourselves.

I pick out of my diary a note of a typical day in the winter:

*Thursday 19 June, 1902—Went up Crater Hill with Wilson. It was snowing, misty and blowing, with heavy drifts and as black as Hades. The temperature at the time was minus forty-six F. Wilson got his nose frost-bitten. We killed a couple of seals later on, which curiously enough came out on the floe though they did not usually in this sort of weather. I find I can handle ropes and even pull up the fishing line without having to put my gloves on for at least two minutes. Hodgson went in tonight to the mess deck with a bottle of his spiders and shrimps to explain to the men the anatomy of the beasts, their method of getting food, and their general habits.*

*We are making a point of taking turns once a week to give the men a general idea of our scientific work, and they are very keen on it. We have just taught the warrant officers bridge. The temperature in the ward-room was allowed to get above sixty somehow or another tonight, with the result that the ice in my cabin has melted, and half my socks have to be dried, as the water ran into one of the drawers containing my clothes.*

When the sun came back on August 22nd, all hands were out on the floe to see the truant. Unless one has gone through the experience of the absence of the sun one cannot realise what the return means. There was magic in the colouring of the sky. Everything and everyone seemed to pick up and gain a new life. The very clouds were iridescent with rainbow hues and warm, rich colouring. Then the change from twilight into night, which, in its turn, was lit by a crescent moon, was weirdly beautiful.

Bread and cakes were fresh baked continually, seal meat was eaten three times weekly, tinned meat also three times (in pies, etc.) and the New Zealand mutton saved for Sundays. There was ample butter, milk, cheese, jam and bottled fruits. Wilson examined every tin as it was opened in the mornings. Officers and men ate the same food. The cook shipped in New Zealand had to be clapped in irons for a short time to bring him to his senses on arrival in winter quarters. He proved a great trial, his tall stories being evidently more extensive than his culinary powers. Once the fires were let out, the wardroom and officers' cabins became very cold, there being no insulation between them and the icy bunker below. Scott records having to sit in his cabin with his feet in a box of hay to keep them warm. Each week had its routine and the captain made sure that every member of the ship's company had sufficient exercise and fresh air. There was ample tobacco for the smokers.

Bernacchi was the only one of them who had already spent a winter in the Antarctic and he makes an interesting comparison between life in the *Discovery* and that in the hut at Cape Adare, where 'officers and men, living together in so restricted a space, ten of us in all, had found tempers wearing thin' long before the winter ended. In contrast, in the *Discovery*, 'each officer had his own sanctum, and the men in their quarters could enjoy their leisure in their own way. The friction of conflicting tastes was eliminated from the beginning.' He also found that the 'comparative formality of meals . . . helped to preserve an atmosphere of civilised tolerance . . . seldom found in polar exploration'. Likewise, in day-to-day living, he considered 'the traditions of the naval service' to have been 'of infinite benefit'.[27]

The diary kept by James Duncan provides a continuous record of the first winter as experienced on the lower deck. He took plenty of exercise on foot or on skis during the long winter darkness by the light of the aurora, the stars and the moon, sometimes going for a run before breakfast. The dog of which he was put in charge was called Maggie. On 20 April 1902, he writes of the day being one of 'Fine weather looking just like a winter morning at Home. A very desiloute look around never the less we are quite Happy.'[28] He describes the beauty of the moonlight on the high peaks and glaciers. The sailors slept in hammocks. One of his only three complaints was about the 'heart breaking' French salamander stoves.

Our heating Stoves on the Mess Deck is A complete fraud they wont do anything but smoke and our Sleeping Place is sufficating and full of sulfar. The Gentleman that accepted them for heating had very little idea of what was wanted. Just now the After stove is in use and the fore one has a Coat of White Frost all over it 15 ft. apart so that may give some idea of our Comfort.[29]

He began a scrap album of magazine cuttings and a half model of the *Discovery*. A draughts tournament was won by Wild. His second grumble (on 9 June) was that although a theatrical party was under way

we have had nothing in the way of Amusement since 1st May so things are very slack with our Officers. They were to work wonders during the Winter but have not started yet and the Winter is nearly half gone and only 1 Consert. We made inquiries about Classes being formed but no move was made by the After Guards. We don't have any idea of what has been done in the Scientific work, as they don't give any information. It's rather hard on the lower Deck Hands.[30]

Scott gathered the impression with regard to the messdeck 'that the regular organisation of lectures and entertainments would disturb rather than add to the comfort of the community'.[31]

A lecture was in fact given by the biologist, Mr Hodgson, about his catches on 2 July, records Duncan. 'It was very interesting showing some of his Speciments [sic] & gave the Mess Deck great satisfaction.'[32] Duncan had to make a blackboard for the lectures, later that month. Ferrar, the geologist, next talked about his work. He was followed by Armitage in August, who gave a lantern lecture on his experiences during the *Windward* Arctic expedition. The last lecture of the winter was by the captain, who spoke about sledging, sledging gear and its care. The hut on shore (icy cold as it was) turned into the Royal Terror Theatre for a play and a minstrel show, the audience having walked home to the ship through the drifting snow, said Duncan, as all carriages were engaged![33]

'Christmas' was celebrated at midwinter, some of the hands having turned out the main hold to get at the Christmas puddings and cakes. Coloured paper was issued with which to decorate each mess. Bloaters were served for breakfast on 23 June, which was 'Christmas morning with us', wrote Duncan.

All hands were busy Dressing there Mess and there is some splendid Designs. 12.30 the Captain and officers walked around the Mess Deck and was very much pleased with our work. We each recieved A small Present which Mrs. Royds had sent on Board also Mrs. Wilson. We gave 3 Cheers for them. Dinner Served 1 PM consisting of Real Turtle Soup Boiled Ham Kiddney Beans and Potatoes, Desert Plum Pudding and brandy Sauce. Small Bottle of Bass it was A success. We had a sleep after that. Tea Cakes and Sweets. Grog served out at Night finishing up with A Consert. 12.30

a.m. Some had not got enough to drink and approched the Captain in the way of putting A Strand in the Main Brace but he was not having any telling them to go to Bed.[34]

As the sun began to return, with only a little twilight at first, preparations were started for the spring and summer sledging journeys. This involved furs, sleeping bags, tents, provision bags, boxes for the stores, handles for ice-axes and runners for the sledges. Duncan in addition began to make a cross of English oak in memory of George Vince.[35] It was found that the boats had almost sunk through the ice and much time was spent over several weeks by the sailors in trying to dig them out.

# FOUR

## SLEDGE JOURNEYS, 1902–3 SEASON, SCOTT'S SOUTHERN JOURNEY

### SLEDGING JOURNEYS, SUMMER 1902

IN HIS NARRATIVE OF THE EXPEDITION, Scott went into some detail concerning the first sledging journeys made soon after the *Discovery*'s arrival in Winter Harbour, 'partly because they show how much we learnt by our failures and partly because it is necessary to realise that sledging is not such an easy matter as might be imagined'. He found 'the errors were patent; food, clothing, everything was wrong, the whole system was bad'; but that their experience was put to good use at least, in that 'the general sledging work of the second summer was vastly superior to that of the first'.[1] He also describes the routine, 'charm and fascination' of sledging, as well as its 'hardships and trials', distinguishing between the chilly spring journeys and the warmer summer ones, each having its own 'drawbacks and difficulties', hunger being the worst on summer explorations, because of their length. In concluding, he drew attention to sledging as 'an occupation for men'.

> Sledging draws men into a closer companionship than can any other mode of life. In its light the fraud must be quickly exposed, but . . . the true man stands out in all his natural strength. Sledging therefore is a sure test of a man's character, and daily calls for the highest qualities of which he is possessed. Throughout my sledging experience it has been my lot to observe innumerable instances of self-sacrifice, of devotion to duty, and of cheerfulness under adversity, such qualities appeared naturally in my comrades because they were demanded by the life.[2]

On 11 September 1902, Armitage left with Ferrar and four men with a sledge, all on skis, to cross the sea ice to the west in order to find a way through the mountain range and on to the inland ice. The occasional reference occurs to this party's object as being the South Magnetic Pole, the aim sixty years earlier of Sir James Clark Ross. Doubtless geographical considerations caused the modification of this earlier proposal. Royds was to travel south-west to search (unsuccessfully) for another route inland. Scott, Barne and Shackleton began an abortive southern reconnaissance with two dog teams on 17

September and had to make a fresh departure on 24 September, with the boatswain, Feather, replacing Barne whose fingers had been badly frostbitten. A depot (marked with a black flag) was laid near the end of the Bluff, which Scott described as a long peninsula thrust out into the great ice sheet and which was later named Minna Bluff, after Lady Markham. 'Beyond the Bluff', wrote Scott, 'our eyes rested searchingly on the new country that rose above our snowy horizon.' They found this land curved sharply westwards, but were most impressed with the immensity of the 'great snow plain' on which they were travelling.[3]

The dogs brought them swiftly home to the comfort of the ship on 3 October 1902, where it was possible to bath, change and creep into bed 'without the usual accompaniment of ice' and where 'the greatest delight of all' was 'to possess the sledging appetite in the midst of plenty'.[4] However, all was not well aboard the *Discovery*: Armitage's western reconnaissance party had returned with scurvy, the dreaded deficiency disease of long sea voyages caused by lack of vitamin C. This was first proved in 1907, but not generally accepted for another ten years. There were also signs of scurvy in other members of the expedition. Scott was puzzled as to how this had come about.

> Of course there is no good blinking our eyes to the fact that this is neither more nor less than scurvy, but whence it has come, or why it has come with all the precautions that have been taken, is beyond our ability to explain. The evil having come, the great thing now is to banish it. In my absence, Armitage, in consultation with the doctors, has already taken steps to remedy matters by serving out fresh meat regularly and by increasing the allowance of bottled fruits, and he has done an even greater service by taking the cook in hand. I don't know whether he threatened to hang him at the yardarm or used more persuasive measures, but whatever it was, there is a marked improvement in the cooking.[5]

The cause of the outbreak remained in doubt, because of the state of medical knowledge at the time, and appeared to Scott and his advisers to have been caused by the tinned food, which was all of the best quality and which was always tested on opening by one of the doctors. It was nevertheless known that fresh food would keep the disease at bay and fresh seal meat had been provided three times a week, with frozen mutton on Sundays. More sealing parties were sent out after the advent of the disease and enough fresh meat was brought in to enable Scott to ban tinned food altogether and to pronounce the outbreak of scurvy at an end by 20 October 1902. Wilson noted his own recovery 'without recourse to lime juice', which disagreed with him. This was available on board, but not made compulsory.[6,7] Fine crops of mustard and cress were grown by Koettlitz in boxes of Antarctic soil.

One of the priorities of the sledging season was to place a record of the expedition's whereabouts in the cylinder at Cape Crozier. Royds, Skelton and their party left to do this on 4 October 1902, the doctors having pronounced them to be in good shape. They returned on 24 October, safe and well, having successfully sledged across the ice skirting the southern slopes of Mounts Erebus and Terror on Ross Island to reach the record pole among the Adélie penguins to the north. However, this was not all that they had accomplished: they bore the joyful news of a remarkable discovery in the realm of natural history—the breeding-place of the Emperor penguin, first seen by Skelton from the tall cliffs at Cape Crozier. Skelton's diary of 12 October 1902 relates how he, Quartley and Wild, 'equipped with lunch, 1/2 plate camera, alpine rope, crampons etc.', were trying to find a way down the cliffs to the sea ice, below the snow slopes of Mount Terror. From the bare rocky cliff they looked down 'into a bay formed between the junction of the Barrier and the land' where the sea ice appeared to have remained fast all winter. 'In the corner of the bay', continued Skelton, 'a large number of Emperor Penguins were huddled together; from the discolouration of the ice it looked as if they had been there some time. They were mostly . . . in a space not more than 100 yards square, with a few outlying stragglers.' The party counted between 250 and 300 birds in sight and Skelton took some photographs.

On 18 October, the party moved camp to a lower level after being confined for five days during a very fierce blizzard. Skelton, Quartley and Evans set off to cross the hard hummocky ice ridges and crevasses (with the aid of sharp crampons, ice-axes and a climbing rope), which lay for some miles between their camp and the ice front. 'Arriving at the edge of the Barrier', wrote Skelton, 'we looked directly down on what we at once realised was an Emperor Penguin rookery, as several dead youngsters could be seen.' At this spot, the ice cliff was only some 25 feet high and they were able to find an easy route down to the sea ice, arriving at the rookery in time to stay for most of the afternoon. Skelton noted the behaviour of the penguins in great detail.[8] Sir Clements Markham had characterised the engineering lieutenant as a 'stirling [sic] able and zealous officer, thoroughly acquainted with the scientific and practical branches of the profession and a man of inventive genius'. His prediction that Skelton would prove an invaluable member of the expedition was further borne out by these observations.[9]

## THE SOUTHERN JOURNEY, SUMMER 1902–3

Captain Scott chose Dr Wilson and Lieut. Shackleton to accompany him on this sledge journey across the Great Ice Barrier (now more prosaically known as the Ross Ice Shelf). They set off on Sunday 2 November 1902, an overcast, cold and windy day, with nineteen dogs, five sledges and many eager helpers. 'Can anyone, I wonder,' wrote Wilson in his diary beforehand, 'realise exactly what it is, leaving the ship and all one's companions, except two, for three months in this desolate region to walk down into the absolutely unknown south, where as far as one can see, nothing awaits one but an icy desert and one literally carries one's little all on a sledge! It's a funny game, because one has got so very attached to the ship as a home and the whole bay here and hut as a sort of estate.

One's cabin moreover is full of one's home associations, a small sanctuary for happy recollections, lamp soot and general comfort.'[10]

Leaving behind the bulkier volumes of his expedition journal, Captain Scott used a soft-covered sketch book as his diary of the southern journey. Its pages confirm his talent

*Weights on Leaving 'A'*

|  | lbs. |
|---|---|
| Dog-food | 400 |
| Tank | 8 |
| Sledge | 35 |
| Bamboo | 4 |
| Tomahawk | 3 |
|  | 450 |

|  | |
|---|---|
| Dog-food | 400 |
| Tank | 8 |
| Sledge | 35 |
| Bamboo | 3 |
|  | 446 |

|  | |
|---|---|
| Ready provision bag | 16 |
| Kit bag | 20 |
| Spare foot-gear bag | 10 |
| Five biscuit cases | 217 |
| Tent | 29 |
| Ice-axe, shovel, and dog pickets | 10 |
| Three blouses | 15 |
| Sledge | 35 |
| Bamboo and straps | 5 |
|  | 357 |

|  | |
|---|---|
| Three sleeping-bags | 45 |
| Tank | 6 |
| Contents 9 provision bags | 227 |
| Seal-meat | 70 |
| Alpine rope | 5 |
| All ski on top | 30 |
| Sledge | 35 |
| Bamboo and straps | 4 |
|  | 422 |

|  | |
|---|---|
| Repair bag | 12 |
| Instrument box | 40 |
| Cooker, Primus, &c. | 34 |
| Oil | 60 |
| Sledge | 28 |
| Securings | 3 |
|  | 177 |
|  | 1,852 |

The dotted lines show plans of sledges and straps.

for vivid and descriptive writing, although the supposed quotations from it in the published narrative have generally been extended, and couched in a more polished and literary style, like those taken from his other diaries.

The weights pulled on leaving the first depot, together with the equipment of the sledges, are illustrated on the previous page.[11]

In the faith that the ice shelf would continue southwards, snowshoes, crampons and other items useful in rough climbing were omitted. The bamboo was to mark depots and the seal meat was meant to ensure the party's good health. Despite Scott's earlier prediction, skis were used.[12]

A sledge meter, like a bicycle wheel, made by the engine-room staff of the *Discovery*, recorded the distances actually pulled. A prismatic compass was taken, but Scott, as navigator, in fact 'depended for all bearings on the compass attached to our small theodolite, which possessed a simple light needle and seemed to give a greater accuracy'.[13]

The expedition's Siberian sledge dogs (twenty dogs and three bitches) had been obtained by a Russian named Alexander Ivanovitch Trontheim. They were of three different types and came to the Antarctic via Archangel, the London Zoo and Lyttelton. This mixed team joined the *Discovery* 'unnamed and unknown; we had not a scrap of their history, nor could we tell within a thousand miles whence they came'.[14] However, by the beginning of the southern journey, each could answer to his own new English name.[15] The king dog, Nigger, 'ruler of our pack[,] had held the same high office', wrote Scott,[16] 'when he had travelled among 400 of his kind' (also bought in Russia for another expedition).

In peace he was gentle and dignified, but in war, as we knew to our cost, he was swift and terrible . . . He was a black dog with some tawny markings, and possessed the most magnificient head and chest, though falling off a little in the hinder quarters. A more perfect sledge dog could scarcely be imagined; he chose his place naturally as the leader, and if put into any other position would make himself so unpleasant to his neighbours, and generally behave so ill, that he was very quickly shifted. In the happy times before sickness fell on our team, it was a delight to watch 'Nigger' at his work: he seemed to know the meaning of every move. He would lie still as a graven image till he saw the snow being shovelled from the skirting of the tent, when he would spring and pace to and fro at his picket, giving out a low throaty bark of welcome as any of us approached, and now and again turning towards his neighbours to express his opinion of them in the most blood-thirsty snarl. A few minutes later, as the leading man came to uproot his picket, his keen eye would watch each movement, and a slow wagging of his tail would quite obviously signify approval; then as the word came to start, he would push affectionately against the leader, as much as to say, 'Now, come along', and brace his powerful chest to the harness. At the evening halt after a long day he would drop straight in his tracks and remain perfectly still with his great head resting on his paws; other dogs might clamour for food, but 'Nigger' knew perfectly well that the tent had to be put up first. Afterwards, however, when one of us approached with the dog-food, above the howling chorus that arose one could always distinguish the deep bell-like note of the leading dog, and knew that if disturbance was to be avoided, it was well to go to the front end of the trace first.

Captain Scott also characterised the other dogs and some of these almost come alive in his accounts.[17]

'Lewis' was a big, thick-coated, brindled dog, a very powerful but not a consistent puller; always noisily affectionate and hopelessly clumsy, he would prance at one and generally all but succeed in bowling one over with boisterous affection. . . . 'Jim' was a sleek, lazy, greedy villain, up to all the tricks of the trade; he could pull splendidly when he chose, but generally preferred to pretend to pull, and at this he was extraordinarily cunning. . . .

The general opinion of 'Spud' was that he was daft—there was something wanting in the upper storey. In the middle of a long and monotonous march he would suddenly whimper and begin to prance about in his traces; in dog-language this is a signal that there is something in sight, and it always had an electrical effect on the others, however tired they might be. . . .

'Kid' and 'Bismarck' were the only two dogs of the team that bore an outward resemblance, both being short-legged animals with long, fleecy, black-and-white, coats. But the likeness was only superficial. Inwardly they differed much, for whereas 'Bismarck' was counted amongst the lazy eye-servers, 'Kid' was the most indefatigable worker in the team; from morn to night he would set forth his best effort. The whip was never applied to his panting little form, and when he stopped it was to die from exhaustion. With all our efforts we could never quite tame 'Birdie', who had evidently been treated with scant respect in his youth. At the ship he would retire into his kennel and growl at all except those who brought him food, and to the end he remained distrustful and suspicious of all attempts to pet him. He was a large, reddish-brown dog, very wolfish in appearance, but a powerful puller when he got to understand what was required of him . . .

'Wolf' was the most hopelessly ill-tempered animal; his character seemed to possess no redeeming virtue. Every advance was met with the same sullen, irreconcilable humour, and the whip alone was capable of reducing him to subjection. . . . To the effort to swell the numbers of our team Bernacchi had sacrificed his own property, 'Joe', and poor 'Joe' had a history. He had been born in the Antarctic Regions at Cape Adare; later in life he had learnt to behave himself with proper decorum in a London drawing-room; and now he had returned, no doubt much against his will, to finish his career in the land of his birth. He was a very light dog, with a deceptively thick coat; much pulling could not be expected from his weight, and he certainly gave but little . . .

The high land discovered on the southern journey, described below by Shackleton in a popular magazine,[18] is now known as the range of Western Mountains that lie between the Ross Ice Shelf and the high inland ice sheet. They form part of what are now called the Transantarctic Mountains linking the Ross and Weddell Seas on either side of the continent.

This journey lasted ninety-four days, and a great part of the time we used to march fifteen miles a day, and only get five miles to the South because our dogs began to die when we were a fortnight out from the ship, and we had to pull half our sledges for five miles—I am speaking of geographical miles—then walk back five miles and pull the other half of the sledges up five. This sort of work went on for a month, and then we reached as near to the high land as possible (it was unsafe to leave our stores on the level ice, as we might not have found them, whereas the high peaks are good guides), so we made a depot of the provisions we did not need, and with the remaining few dogs pushed straight South.

When we found our dogs dying we shortened our food ration, which was already pretty scanty; and to economise our stock of oil, only lit the stove twice a day. So we used to have a cold lunch as we marched, consisting of seven lumps of sugar, a little bit of dry seal meat, and a biscuit and a half. This was slung on a little bag attached to our coats, and as we marched we ate. We never knew whether it was sugar, biscuit or seal meat we were putting into our mouths until we tasted it, the poor dogs always looking up to us hoping for a stray crumb to drop; but we were short ourselves, so, their food having gone bad, we were forced to throw it away, and at the end of a day's march had generally to kill one of the dogs to feed the others.

We had to warm our aluminium pannikins over the stove, otherwise the cold vessels would have damaged our lips. It was a trial, every time we had meals, to get our food into our mouths, though, indeed, we would gladly have suffered more of these trials, if we could have had more food to put into our hungry bodies. At the end of the day's march, we were sometimes so tired that we had to lift first one leg, then the other with our hands in order to get into the tent.

As the days went on we got more and more hungry, and then we began to dream of food, which is a thing that often happens when men are very hungry. I dreamt that three-cornered jam tarts were always flying by me. I used to reach my hand out to catch them, but they always disappeared. Dr Wilson, one of my companions, used to dream that he was cutting up sandwiches for a school treat—he never got a share of those sandwiches himself. The Captain—my other companion—used to dream he was feeding, but he was just as hungry when he woke up. And so we went on, day after day, all through November, all through December, and on the 31st December we reached our furthest South and here the British flag was hoisted.

Besides being leader of the party, Captain Scott was navigator and to some extent surveyor, taking sights and rounds of angles to ascertain their own position (checked by the dead reckoning of the sledge meter) and that of the mountains and headlands seen to the west. On 25 November, he described the joy of passing latitude 80°S., aware that none of their charts showed any details other than a plain white space beyond that parallel.[19]

The published version of his diary for 27 November recorded the sickening work of driving southwards the weary, miserable, ill-nourished dogs.

> It was my turn to drive today; Shackleton led and Wilson pulled at the side. The whole proceedings would have been laughable enough but for the grim sickness that holds so tight a grip on our poor team . . . Luckily, the turn for doing the actual driving only comes once in three days, but even thus it is almost as bad to witness the driving as to have to do it.[20]

Two days later they observed a splendid display of mock suns.

> Shortly after four o'clock today we observed the most striking atmospheric phenomenon we have yet seen in these regions. We were enveloped in a light, thin stratus cloud of small ice-crystals; it could not have extended to any height, as the sun was only lightly veiled. From these drifting crystals above, the sun's rays were reflected in such an extraordinary manner that the whole arch of the heavens was traced with circles and lines of brilliant prismatic or white light. The coloured circles of a bright double halo were touched or intersected by one which ran about us parallel to the horizon; above this, again, a gorgeous prismatic ring encircled the zenith; away from the sun was a white fog-bow, with two bright mock suns, where it intersected the horizon circle. The whole effect was almost bewildering and its beauty is far beyond the descriptive powers of my sledging pencil.[21]

On 4 December, Scott described beauty in miniature—snow crystals falling on a calm, cool night:

> Suddenly and apparently from nowhere, a small shimmering body floats gently down in front of one and sits lightly as thistledown on the white surface below. If one stoops to examine it . . . one finds that it is a six-pointed feathery star, quite flat and smooth on either side . . . it is only on looking closely that one discovers the intricate and delicate beauty of their design.
>
> The effect of these *en masse* is equally wonderful. They rest in all positions and therefore receive the sun's rays at all angles, and in breaking them up reflect in turn each colour of the spectrum. As one plods along towards the midnight sun, one's eyes naturally fall on the plain ahead, and one realises that the simile of a gem-strewn

carpet could never be more aptly employed than in describing the radiant path of the sun on the snowy surface. It sparkles with a myriad points of brilliant light, comprehensive of every colour the rainbow can show, and is so realistic and near that it often seems one has but to stoop to pick up some glistening jewel.[22]

Despite troubles with the dogs, constant gnawing hunger and symptoms of scurvy, the party experienced the great joy of discovering and recording new land each day, as the splendid chain of the Western Mountains unfolded. The daily grind, the hopes and fears, delights and aversions and the discoveries recorded in Scott's narrative and Wilson's diary ring very true. Scott had made the course slightly to the east of south rather than due south, so as to be nearer to the new land at the edge of the ice shelf. One of the most impressive features of this strange and lifeless landscape was the existence of the coastline to their right. The relatively level surface of the 'Barrier' over which they were travelling seemed to take the place of the sea. The coast itself was indented; its many bays were bordered by 'white snow slopes, glaciers and broken ice-cascades', contrasting here and there with conspicuous 'black rocky headlands and precipitous uncovered cliffs'.[23]

At the end of a fine day, Dr Wilson would sketch with astonishing accuracy the great line of the Western Mountains. This caused him snowblindness at times, making his eyes very painful. On the day after a particularly bad attack he went blindfold on ski.

> Luckily the surface was smooth and I only fell twice. I had the strangest thoughts or day dreams as I went along, all suggested by the intense heat of the sun, I think. Sometimes I was in beech woods, sometimes in fir woods, sometimes in the Birdlip woods, all sorts of places connected in my mind with a hot sun. And the swish-swish of the ski was as though one's feet were brushing through dead leaves, or cranberry undergrowth or heather or juicy bluebells.[24]

Entries in Scott's manuscript diary say much about difficulties and delays caused by the weakness of the dogs. He concluded that their ration of dried fish, which may have putrefied in the tropics, was poisoning them. They also suffered from the heat of the sun and struggled in the soft snow. By 10 December, when Snatcher died from inflammation of the bowels, the party had to face the possibility of losing all the dogs and so failing to attain a high latitude. The animals improved when fed on the remains of their dead comrade, raising Scott's hopes that, 'dieted on themselves', they would do better, 'but the whole thing is very disappointing—we could so easily have taken seal meat or biscuit and avoided this trouble'. On 14 December, they made good a mere two miles, despite strenuous exertions.[25] However, the unfolding of the chain of Western Mountains buoyed up the party's spirits, despite the realisation that the land was further off than had appeared, having been thrown up by a mirage.

Christmas Day saw them coming up to 82°S. Wilson read Holy Communion in his sleeping bag, before turning out, and his diary that day records the naming of a snow peak abreast of their camp as 'Christmas Height'.[26]

Scott describes the advance towards the inlet later named after Shackleton, which was to be their turning point and their furthest south.

> *December 27* We have had a most interesting day from the spectacular point of view. I observed a gap in the coast line two days ago behind which there appeared to be no hills ... Today we altered the bearing rapidly and as it rolled back it revealed to sight a magnificent mountain peak which must be of very exceptional height ... The coast runs in in a very deep inlet, quite a fjord, to the base of the range and it has been like the opening out of a new panorama ...

He began to think that their discovery of 'so much new land and so much new matter for discussion' might find their trip 'a corner in polar history', and that if so, their 'hard work and short commons' would be repaid.

The published version of Scott's sledging diary for 27 December, quoted below, is far more literary and dramatic.

> Yesterday I noticed that we were approaching what appeared to be a deeper bay than usual, and this afternoon this opening developed in the most interesting manner.
>
> On the near side is a bold rocky snow covered cape, and all day we have been drawing abreast of this; as we rapidly altered its bearing this afternoon it seemed to roll back like some vast sliding gate, and gradually there stood revealed one of the most glorious mountain scenes we have yet witnessed ... It was with some excitement I noticed that new mountain ridges were appearing as high as anything we had seen to the north, but, to my surprise, as we advanced the ridges grew still higher, as no doubt did my tones. Then, instead of a downward turn in the distant outline came a steep upward line; Pelion was heaped on Ossa, and it can be imagined that we pressed the pace to see what would happen next, till the end came in a gloriously sharp double peak covered with a few flecks of cirrus cloud.

Their thoughts in camp that night turned to the 'splendid twin-peaked mountain' (some 12,000 feet), a monster of unsurpassed eminence and dignity. Here at last they decided they had found something fit to honour the 'father of the expedition' and Mount Markham it became.[27]

The next day they pitched their farthest camp, gaining a breathtaking view of the landscape. To the south they made out a striking cape, beyond which rose a mountain of some 10,000 feet—Mount Longstaff, named after the expedition's greatest benefactor. Scott concluded that mountainous country must continue beyond Mount Longstaff for some fifty miles and that the direction of the coastline for at least a degree of latitude must be S.17°E. He remarked on their good fortune in having glorious weather in which to view the magnificent scene and in which to sketch and take angles. A blizzard followed by fog prevented their seeing much more from slightly further south and they turned for home between lat. 82°16′S. and 82°17′S., the dogs being too exhausted to notice the change. Unfortunately, a great chasm in the ice prevented the party from actually reaching the land from the ice shelf, and no specimens of its rock were brought back.

Scott had hoped to reach a more southerly latitude, but could not, because of the failure of the dogs, which one after another tragically 'left their bones on the great southern plains'.[28] He had realised that a number of the weaker dogs would have to be sacrificed to the stronger, but had hoped 'that a remnant of the larger and stronger beasts would survive to enjoy again a life of luxury and ease'.[29] The reason they did not was that the dog-food, Norwegian dried 'stock fish', contained no vitamins and may have gone bad in the tropics.[30] By New Year's Day 1903, the state of the dog team had become pitiable, only a few being able to pull. Some had to be held on their feet at the beginning of the march before their limbs became stiff enough to support them. 'Poor "Spud" fell in his tracks today,' wrote Scott, 'we carried him for a long way on the sledge and then tried him once more, but he fell again, and had to be carried for the rest of the journey tucked away inside the canvas tank ... Towards the end of our day's march it had always been possible to get a semblance of spirit into our poor animals by saying "Up for supper". They learnt early what the words meant, and it has generally been "Spud" who gave the first responsive whimper. This afternoon it was most pathetic; the cheering shout for the last half mile was raised as usual, but there was no response, until suddenly from the interior of the sledge-tank came the muffled ghost of a whimper. It was "Spud's" last effort: on halting we carried him back to his place, but in an hour he was dead.'[31]

A sail improvised from the floorcloth of the tent helped the remaining two sledges along while the wind blew from the south. By 7 January, the remaining dogs merely walked alongside the sledges. Scott admitted to his moral cowardice in allowing Wilson and Shackleton to do his share in the dirty work of killing the animals, which they all three hated.[32]

On 13 January they picked up depot B and were able to have a really filling and nourishing 'hoosh'. A medical examination the next day revealed more symptoms of scurvy, especially in Shackleton whose throat seemed congested, causing him to cough and occasionally to spit blood. Everything had to be sacrificed (including a closer look at the northern coast) in the efforts to reach the next depot and keep Shackleton on his feet. He was to do little pulling and no camp duties. He wrote afterwards:

Well, we eventually found our depot, after which I broke down and haemorrhage started. Then everything we did not absolutely need was thrown away, and all the weight of the pulling devolved on my two companions, and it was only owing to their care of me and kindness during this trying period that I was enabled to reach the ship, for I could do no pulling and could only just struggle on ahead of the sledges. Captain Scott and Dr. Wilson were at one time pulling 270 lb. each, and they were not in good, robust health, having signs of scurvy and being weak from want of food, yet their thoughts and care was always for me, and no man ever had the good fortune to have better, stronger, and more self-denying friends than I had at that time.[33]

Scott decided to retain the instruments (a heavy item), but, with great sadness, to sacrifice the last two dogs, thus lightening the sledges of the animals' food. On 15 January, he wrote: 'This morning "Nigger" and "Jim" were taken a short distance from the camp and killed. This was the saddest scene of all; I think we could all have wept. And so this is the last of our dog team, the finale to a tale of tragedy; I scarcely like to write of it. Through our most troublous time we always looked forward to getting some of our animals home. At first it was to have been nine, then seven, then five, and at the last we thought that surely we should be able to bring back these two.'[34]

An increase in the ration of seal meat helped slightly to lessen the party's symptoms of scurvy. Over changing snow surfaces, they made their way to the north, greeting familiar landmarks such as the plume of Mount Erebus with joy. They reached depot A on 28 January, so ending short rations. Shackleton kept going on skis, but he and his companions were far from well, knowing that scurvy was still advancing with rapid strides. The southern journey ended with the home-coming to the *Discovery* on 3 February 1903. Wilson's diary records their arrival at the ship.

Made an early start, the Captain and I pulling, Shackleton going on ski. The day began rather overcast, dead calm but very close and warm. Moderately good surface, and all the home landmarks well in sight, though Observation Hill and Cape Armitage of course cover the ship from our view. After marching 2 or 3 hours however, we saw ahead of us what we thought was a seal at the edge of the old Barrier ice. It turned out to be the remains of our last year's depot, and before we reached it, we had the greater pleasure of seeing two figures hurrying towards us on ski. Just 6 miles from the ship we met them—Skelton and Bernacchi, clean tidy looking people they were. And imagine our joy on hearing that the relief ship *Morning* had arrived a week or more before and that all our mails and parcels were waiting for us in our cabins. All the news was good about everything, except that there were still eight miles of ice floe to go out before we should be free to leave our winter quarters. However, that didn't trouble us much.

We camped and had a good lunch and then these two pulled our sledges in for us. Our flags of course were flying and we had a very gay march in, listening to scraps of the world's news, and scraps of our own little world's news, the news of the ship. We had been doubly cut off for three months from any news but what we had brought ourselves from the unknown south. Three miles from the ship we were met also by Sub. Lieut. Mulock, one of the *Morning*'s officers, a very nice young fellow who is to join up with us on the *Discovery*. He is an R.N. Officer of the Survey Department. Next we were met by Koettlitz, Royds and all the rest, and a crowd of men. It was a great home coming, and as we turned Cape Armitage we saw the ship decorated from top to toe with flags and all the ship's company up the rigging round the gangway ready to cheer us, which they did most lustily as we came on board. They were all most enthusiastic and everyone shook us by the hand all round, it was a most delightful welcome . . . A lot of photographs were taken and indeed we must have been worth photographing. I began to realize then *how* filthy we were—long sooty hair, black greasy clothes, faces and noses all peeling and sore, lips all raw, everything either sunburnt or bleached, even our sledges and the harness—things one didn't realize before, and our faces the colour of brown boots, except where the lamp soot made them black.

Then came the time for a bath, and clothes came off that had been on since November the second of the year before, and then a huge dinner. Captain Colbeck, Engineer Morrison, Lieuts. Doorly and Mulock were all there, and a long and tiring evening followed. But instead of drink and noise and songs and strangers, I know I was longing to lie down on my bunk and have a long quiet yarn with Charles Royds. I was in no hurry at all to spring at my letters, for I felt an absolute confidence that everything was well with all that I cared for most at home . . . Such was our homecoming after an absence of over thirteen weeks.[35]

Scott described the joy of rounding the Cape, of seeing 'our beloved ship', which was still held fast in her icy prison, but trim and neat. 'She was fully prepared to face again the open seas, and the freshly painted side glistened in the sunlight. A fairer sight could scarcely meet our snow-tried eyes; and to mark the especial nature of the occasion a brave display of bunting floated gently in the breeze, while, as we approached, the side and rigging were thronged with our cheering comrades.'[36] He goes on to tell of the great welcome the party received and how they revelled in the 'unwonted luxury of clean raiment', which clothed them 'at a feast which realised the glories of our day-dreams'.

Gerald Doorly, an officer of the relief expedition in the *Morning*, was present at the welcome-home feast and slept afterwards on board the *Discovery*. He described how the southern party's hunger remained unappeased, despite the banquet. Shackleton and Wilson enjoyed the feast in their cabins. Afterwards, Captain Scott kept them surreptitiously supplied with more food from the pantry. Doorly relates that he had not been asleep for more than an hour, when he heard Scott 'rousing Shackleton, whose cabin was next door. "Shackles", I heard him call, "I say, Shackles, how would you fancy some sardines on toast?" In a little while the smell of toasting bread at the wardroom fire permeated the place, and a few minutes later I heard Wilson thanking the captain for the luxury! This continued at intervals during the early hours and struck me as being at once humorous and pathetic.' The extract is interesting in that it does away with the idea of any estrangement between Scott and Shackleton during the journey.[37] The last entry in Scott's sledging diary on 9 February 1903, some days after their return, recorded that all three were recovering from the strain. He ended by saying, 'There is every reason to think however that our return was none too soon.'[38]

In concluding his account of the southern journey, Scott wrote,

And so our southern sledge journey came to an end on February 3, 1903, when for ninety-three days we had plodded with ever-varying fortune over a vast snowfield and slept beneath the fluttering canvas of a tent. During that time we had covered 960 statute miles, with a combination of success and failure in our objects, which I have endeavoured to set forth in these pages. If we had not achieved such great results as at one time we had hoped for, we knew at least that we had striven and endured with all our might.[39]

This modest appraisal cloaks the achievements of Scott, Shackleton and Wilson. They had in fact made the first extended journey into the interior of the unknown southern continent, not merely making a bee-line towards the Pole, but altering course so as to approach the coastline and the Western Mountains, thus enabling these to be surveyed and sketched.[40] The recovery of geological specimens had to be left to later comers, since a great chasm blocked the way from the ice sheet to the coast. All in all, and considering the state of dietary knowledge and their lack of previous experience, this was an effort of which they could be proud.

During the absence of the southern party, much had been going on. The most remarkable achievement was the fine pioneering sledge journey made by Armitage, Skelton and party through the mountains west of the *Discovery* and on to the Antarctic ice sheet, to an altitude of nearly 9,000 feet, by way of the glacier later named after the geologist, H. T. Ferrar. Rock specimens and photographs taken in this region gave evidence of the geology of the continent.[41] Armitage recounted the journey in his book *Two Years in the Antarctic*, and it was summarised and praised by Scott in his narrative. Scott would follow and improve upon their route going beyond their farthest west during the next sledging season, and penetrating a long way into the interior over the high plateau of ice beyond the mountain range.

The *Discovery* had been made ready for sea (no mean task) and the boats had been recovered from their icy prisons after a great struggle. Shorter journeys to investigate Ross Island and the region adjoining winter quarters had been made in the captain's absence by Koettlitz, Ferrar, Hodgson and Bernacchi. Royds (who was in charge of the ship) made another visit to Cape Crozier, where he was disappointed and surprised to find that the young Emperor penguins were no longer there. However, the Adélie penguins were back for the summer and were busy nesting. Royds's party gathered enough eggs for those on board the *Discovery* and brought back one very special egg—an Emperor penguin's—found by Blissett, half buried in the snow. Royds's diary recorded these remarkable discoveries on 8 November 1902.

10.30 Arrived on Penguin ground. Saw all the penguins, but not a sign of a live young one anywhere. After putting the whole pack of about 120 on the run (by the cliffs) went off to another pack which we saw about $1^1/_2$ miles away. Put them on the run and caught and felt several but no luck. At 1.0 started off for the sea edge as we saw several packs there. Walked about 3 miles out, put two large packs of about 100 in each on the run but still no luck. We were now on the edge of new ice and no sign of penguins in sight further out . . . There is not much doubt that the youngsters have made for the water. We counted 30 dead ones, of which we brought back 12. Seals were numerous, two youngsters, one very lately born, and one dead young one. Only one dead big Emperor was seen. 5 Skuas were seen and were busy eating the dead penguins. A large number of snow petrels were also seen flying about the cliffs. We walked all along the edge of the new ice to the cliffs putting another pack of about 20 Emperors on the run, and then back for about 4 miles along the cliffs to the barrier edge. Seals were lying all along the crack against the cliffs, all bulls.

5.0 Arrived back at the barrier edge, and commenced searching for eggs or parts of the shell . . . just as I had said we would return, Blissett called my attention to a round thing which on being pricked out with an ice-axe turned out to be a complete Emperor's egg, with a crack down the middle . . . It has been a great disappointment not finding the young birds, but the egg makes up for a lot . . . Coming back with the egg was an anxious time, and nothing could have been treated with such care and consideration . . .[42]

A sports day had been held on 8 November 1902 in honour of King Edward VII's birthday. The programme stated that 'Prices of Admission to the Floe Football Ground' would be

Members of the Antarctic Athletic Club, Free.
To Public. One Emperor Penguin's Egg.
Children not admitted at any price.

The general arrangements made by C. R. Ford, Hon. Secretary, included: starts by watch and flag to be made by Lieut. Armitage, the Committee (Messrs Cross, Quartley, Whitfield and Wild) to be on hand to assist, and 'cooling drinks to be supplied at the Ice-foot during the day' free to members of the Antarctic Athletic Club, on presentation of their membership cards.

The day proved to be a fine one. The *Discovery* was dressed with flags and a great silken Union Jack hoisted at Hut Point, 'the first time we have hoisted our colours in the Antarctic', remarked Duncan. The competitions were toboggan races, sledge-pulling, putting the weight, tug of war, ski-running and rifle-shooting. Skelton, Walker and Duncan came first, second and third in the exciting ski-running competition and Duncan was awarded a delightful watercolour by Edward Wilson of the *Discovery* in winter quarters.[43] The day concluded with a show of lantern slides by Koettlitz, Hodgson and Skelton, followed by songs by Wild, Bernacchi, Heald, Armitage, Pilbeam, Ferrar, Croucher and Allan. Prizes won in the sports were distributed by 'Her Royal Highness, Princess Lobodon Carcinophagus, attended by Lord Hyperoodon Planifrons and Countess Pagodroma Nivea, prominent members of the local nobility.' A special treat afterwards at supper were sandwiches of mustard and cress grown by Dr Koettlitz in the wardroom skylight. The men were so delighted with this taste of green food that they gathered at the wardroom door to give him three hearty cheers.[44]

# FIVE

## First Relief Expedition of the *Morning*, 1902–3

### 'JOY COMETH IN THE MORNING': THE FIRST RELIEF EXPEDITION
### 1902–3

IN LONDON, the indefatigable Sir Clements Markham had set about what he called 'the wearisome work' of 'writing to rich people to subscribe to the relief ship'. He found at first that the rich buttoned up their pockets and that the Government was unwilling to help.[1] However, with the interest and support of the King and the Prince of Wales (later King George V), the money (some £22,000) was collected, of which Mr Longstaff subscribed a further £5,000 and Mr Edgar Speyer a like amount.

It had been suggested to Sir Clements that a relief ship might be found among the Navy's obsolete gunboats. The Hudson's Bay Company's marine adviser, Captain Inglis, recommended that one of these should be bought from the Admiralty, since he himself had recently bought the *Pelican* for the company and found her a good vessel for ice. However, when Sir Clements's cousin, Admiral Markham, went to see about the gunboats at the Admiralty, he brought back such a bad report that the Relief Ship Committee resolved to buy the small wooden whaler, *Morgen*, from Norway.[2]

Markham's 'History of the Morning', in the archives of the Royal Geographical Society, tells in his spidery hand, with characteristic attention to detail, of the necessity for a relief ship, how funds were raised and how the *Morgen* was purchased, renamed, refitted and equipped. It also includes biographical notices of her officers and men.[3]

He had early dismissed the available Scottish whalers as unsuitable and expensive and turned therefore to Norway, where the wooden whaler *Morgen*, 31 years old, headed the list as 'the strongest steamer in the Norwegian whaling fleet'. With his old friend, Captain Bonnevie of Lerwick, a surveyor for the Norwegian *Veritas* (the Norwegian equivalent of Lloyd's) since 1894 (according to Markham), and a good seaman with immense experience of sealers and whalers, Markham visited Tønsberg, the whaling port on the Oslofjord, on 18 September 1901. 'We came to the conclusion', wrote Markham, 'that the *Morgen* was the only wooden ship that would suit our purpose.' Mr William Colbeck, RNR, Chief Officer of the *Montebello* (Wilson Line), also accompanied him.

'The *Morgen* was built specially for strength', wrote Markham, 'by old Svend Foyn of Tønsberg, the well-known Commodore of the Norwegian Whaling fleet. When he died, the property came to his nephew, Mr. J. Bull, and his ships were for sale.' The party was met at the station by Mr Bull, whom Markham unkindly described with his usual frankness as 'a horrid looking creature in high hat, frock coat and patent leather boots'. Mr Bull's price had come down since 1897 when Markham first considered the purchase and he agreed to take £3,880. Examination confirmed the strength and soundness of the vessel. Her engines were 'old fashioned, but extraordinarily strong', likewise the boilers. A new iron boiler bed was required. Mr Colbeck and Mr Walker, chief engineer of the *Montebello*, examined the engines three weeks later and reported satisfactorily. A special meeting of the Council of the Royal Geographical Society on 2 October 1901 resolved that the Society should own the ship, with the President as managing owner. Fearing delay, Markham accepted the price on his own responsibility and the Relief Ship Committee approved the purchase next day (24 October 1901).

The *Morgen* was brought to Sheerness by a Norwegian crew, having been repainted black with a white ribbon, says Markham, at Sandefjord, with her new English name *Morning* in white. She was towed up river to be refitted by Messrs Green of Blackwall on 4 January 1902 and while she was in the East India Dock, Markham heard the sad news of Captain Bonnevie's death, whom he described as a man who 'knew his business thoroughly and was an honourable, diligent and faithful Agent'. The *Morning* became classed as a yacht in March 1902, through Markham's election as Honorary Member of the Royal Corinthian Yacht Club, whose Commodore presented the ship with two ensigns and five burgees. The vessel's dimensions are given by Markham as length 140 feet, breadth 31 feet 4", depth 16$\frac{1}{2}$ feet, registered tonnage 297. The whale oil tanks were taken out and sold and the *Morning* was refitted with a large store-room, a wardroom with six side cabins, a galley, petty officers' mess with eight bunks, sick-bay and chart-room (aft on upper deck). She was given new fore- and mainmasts, bow sheathing, spare rudder and propeller, the new boiler bed, new shaft pumps and ballast tanks (these at Mr Longstaff's special request and expense).

At a meeting of the Relief Ship Committee (which 'dear old Sir Leopold McClintock' attended) on 20 November 1901, Captain William Colbeck of Hull was proposed as Commander of the relief expedition.[4] He had been a member of the *Southern Cross* expedition, specialising in magnetism, had an Extra Master's certificate and was also a Sub-Lieutenant in the Royal Naval Reserve. He was serving at the time in the ships of the Wilson Line, Hull,[5] whose Captain Pepper recommended him as 'a thorough seaman, a first-class scientific and practical navigator, a good disciplinarian and a born leader of men, imparting enthusiasm and respect'.[6] Colbeck accepted the appointment on 30 December 1901 and took charge of the ship on 10 February 1902.

The Admiralty allowed two naval officers to volunteer: these were Sub-Lieutenant G. F. A. Mulock, RN, Fourth Officer, and Lieutenant E. R. G. Evans, RN, whom Markham described as 'an uncommonly strenuous young person', later in life to find fame as Evans of the *Broke*.[7] Mr R. G. England was Chief Officer, Dr G. A. Davidson, Surgeon, and Mr J. D. Morrison, Chief Engineer. There were two midshipmen and a ship's company of twenty-nine.

The third officer was Mr Gerald Doorly, RNR, like Evans, a former cadet in the *Worcester* training ship. He was later to write a book about the *Morning*'s Antarctic voyages. He described in this how he came to join the *Morning* in the East India Docks. He found her 'ridiculously insignificant' after the splendid P. & O. liners in which he had been serving. 'It was only too true', he wrote, 'that this small barque-rigged vessel of 290 tons with a quaint little yellow funnel in the after-end, and a strange-looking tub at the mainmast head, was the steam yacht *Morning* in course of preparation for her adventurous voyages.' His former 'chum' of *Worcester* days popped his head out from the 'one absurd little hatch' and said, 'Welcome to the *Dreadnought*.'[8] She departed from the East India Docks on 9 July 1902, amid a 'bravery of bunting', ringing cheers and whistles of good luck, a last-minute item in her equipment being a piano, presented by Sir Clements at Evans's request, which Doorly described as arriving in a van 'hurriedly alongside with the jangling of harness and the panting of horses'.[9]

The tale of the brave little *Morning*, 'a record of difficulties overcome by sturdy perseverance', was alas never told in print by Captain Colbeck and it was not until 1916 that Gerald Doorly's lively account appeared. However, through the kindness of Captain W. R. Colbeck in making his father's letters available, it has been possible to remedy this to some extent. The *Morning* arrived at Lyttelton, New Zealand, without touching at the Cape, on 16 November 1902, where she was generously treated, as the *Discovery* had been. The following account of the first Antarctic expedition of the *Morning* is based on Captain William Colbeck's letter to his fiancée of March 1903.[10]

The *Morning*, dressed over all, departed from Lyttelton on 6 December 1902, being given a good send-off from New Zealand with bands playing amid cheering crowds and steamers firing off volleys of signal rockets. Colbeck's hopes of eating a Christmas dinner with Scott and his crew were ruled out by the contrary winds and bad weather experienced right down to the edge of the pack-ice. They were very deep laden and Colbeck ruefully observed that the carcasses of mutton in the foretopmast rigging really put the finishing touch to the beauty of his ship. On 13 December they lost a whaleboat and on 22 December the first iceberg was sighted. The *Morning* struck out on a new track east of all previous explorers in 178°–180°E. Colbeck was justified in this venture by being able to continue further south in open water.

He enjoyed a very special present on Christmas Day—the discovery of two unknown islands in lat. 67°24′.50S. long. 179°55′.50W., one of which was later named after Captain Scott. 'It was my idea', wrote Colbeck regarding the naming of the islands, 'to suggest to Sir Clements Markham that the larger island should be called Markham Island and the other Haggitt's Pillar' (after his own brother), 'but as Scott wants to leave Sir Clements' name on the land in farthest south, I have waived the point and have written fully to Sir Clements Markham leaving the matter to him and suggesting that it be called

Scott Island unless he thinks the funds of the expedition would be augmented by naming it after one of the generous donors to the Relief Ship Fund'. A landing was effected with difficulty and specimens obtained of the many thousands of birds nesting on the north side, chiefly petrels. Colbeck felt his islands had 'nothing very special about them, no vegetation and apparently all one kind of rock, excepting the small island which has a peculiar cone at the top'. The next day while making a sketch survey of the coast, they 'bumped on a rock' and later encountered the pack-ice and some huge icebergs, which (in thick weather) looked like more undiscovered islands.

From Christmas Eve (while navigating through the ice) until they reached the *Discovery*, Colbeck lay down 'all standing' (i.e. without undressing) so as to be always on call. Even in bed he was on the qui vive, with 'the constant hurry and scurry of feet over one's head and the voice of the officer of the watch constantly striking on one's ear with the order to "hard up" or "hard down" the helm, which can only mean . . . that he is trying to clear a 'berg or heavy piece of ice'. There was little rest for the 'Captain of a Polar Mail Steamer', as he described himself. Bad or foggy weather sometimes resulted in his being called on deck fifty times a day. On 28 December he went below for a cup of tea at 4.30 p.m. but was called on deck to find the ship very close to a large iceberg. Despite the engines going full speed astern, the *Morning* hit the iceberg and lost her bobstay; Lieut. Mulock had put the ship on full speed when the captain had left the deck and (says Colbeck) he could not get over what he had done for the rest of the evening. However, when a boat was sent out to examine the bow plates, everything was found to be all right and the ship had started nothing. A strong appearance of land was observed to the east, which was in fact King Edward VII Land, sighted by the *Discovery* during her outward voyage.

On one fine day, 55 miles were made through the pack to the south-west but in thick foggy weather, through close pack, only 15 or 18. On these days, '. . . one had to practically feel one's way from one floe to the other and suddenly go full speed astern or turn sharp round in order to avoid a 'berg or get out of a cul-de-sac into which we had blindly groped our way'.

Later on, he tells us, Colbeck grew wiser and stopped and waited for clear weather once a fog came down. During the first week of the new year (1–6 January 1903), they encountered a strong ESE gale and blizzard. Heavy blocks of ice and broken icebergs were strewn around in all directions, giving the *Morning* some very nasty knocks, 'but the old ship took them like a brick and came up smiling'. On 8 January 1903, they landed at Cape Adare (where Borchgrevink and his *Southern Cross* party—Colbeck among them—had wintered in 1899) and picked up the record left by the *Discovery*. The little *Morning* had penetrated the pack earlier than any of her predecessors, wrote Colbeck, beating the *Discovery* by more than 42 hours. Proceeding south, they found no records of the main party, but left their own on Possession and Franklin islands.

On 18 January 1903, Colbeck and a small party landed on Cape Crozier. Dr Davidson spotted the post erected by Scott's people. 'You can imagine my delight and relief', wrote

Colbeck to Edith, his fiancée, 'when I opened the cylinders and found that the Discoverys were in McMurdo Bay and wintering in 77°50′S.' Heavy ice and a contrary current caused the *Morning* to make only slow progress towards the Point, being made to 'bide the Ice King's time'. They found open water off Cape Bird in the early evening of 23 January and were able to proceed until the masts of the *Discovery* were sighted just before midnight, at which time in these latitudes it is still daylight. 'I had the pleasure of first seeing her', wrote Colbeck in the same letter, '—saw her masts above a spit of land running out from the Nor'ard of her winter quarters. We fired off rockets and dressed ship, everyone on board at the highest pitch of excitement, simply bubbling over with it.' However, the *Morning* was stopped in her gallop by a field of fast ice extending unbroken over ten solid miles to the *Discovery*. 'The "Discoverys" soon saw us. We saw a figure on Hut Point waving arms in windmill fashion for a few minutes and then bolt wildly back to his ship to spread the news.'

Colbeck learned later that Armitage (in command during Scott's absence in the south) was the only one who took things at all quietly. He refused to lose his night's sleep, saying, 'Yes, all right. Call me if she comes along-side.' Bernacchi wanted to start off straight away over the ice for his letters and he and the others were believed to have been much annoyed by the old Pilot's indifference; Armitage did not leave until after breakfast, as he had arranged. A jolly evening (a good dinner followed by singing) finished about midnight aboard the *Morning* when everyone 'found a soft plank to sleep on'.

The next morning (26 January), Skelton, Bernacchi and Hodgson left with a sledge loaded with letters and parcels, meat and vegetables. Armitage and the others returned on the 29th. Mulock accompanied them to help Armitage work up his observations. Colbeck tried in vain to get Armitage to start cutting and blasting the ice to complement the efforts of the *Morning*'s people. The 'Discoverys' were confident that the ice would go out. When Colbeck told them that this was a fatal mistake, he was only laughed at for his pains. He was under the orders of the commander of the expedition on joining forces and so had to 'lie low and say nothing', as he put it.

On 3 February he decided to try to get some scheme afoot for releasing the *Discovery*. As luck would have it, he reached the ship only to find that Scott had arrived on board about half an hour before and that 'Everyone was too excited to do anything but talk of the Southern journey and congratulate the three men, Wilson, Shackleton and the "Skipper" on their reaching Farthest South.' Colbeck joined the celebrations and returned the next day to his own ship, since Scott was too busy with his letters and 'imbued with the same hope as the other chaps that the ice would break up in its own sweet time and let them get away at the end of the month'.

Colbeck trudged over to the *Discovery* again on 10 February, getting caught in a gale *en route*. After a discussion with Scott, it was decided to transfer stores from the relief ship as quickly as possible, to enable the *Morning* to depart at the end of the month. Then, if the ice broke up, the *Discovery* could follow and if not they would be prepared for another season. 'This was the best I could do', wrote Colbeck, 'as they all firmly believed that the ice would break away and were betting ten to one that they would get to New Zealand before us.' From 12 to 23 February, the stores were sledged over the ice from the *Morning* to the *Discovery*. Then the *Morning* went alongside a glacier snout and discharged twenty tons of coal for the *Discovery* to pick up on her release from the ice. The *Morning* also watered ship from the glacier.

Ten officers and twenty-two men from the *Discovery* came over to the *Morning* to see her off. A big dinner party on the eve of departure was held in the small wardroom, seventeen sitting down at table. The next day (2 March), wrote Colbeck, 'everyone's spirits were at dead low water and a general depression prevailed'. At 1.30 p.m. the sledges were put over to the ice and loaded up for the return journey to the still-imprisoned *Discovery*. 'Everyone had their own particular "loot" to attend to from photographic plates and medical gear to tooth powder and sponges' and at 2 p.m., 'the last of the party went over the bows and our last adieus had been said'. The *Morning* weighed anchor and backed astern and as she turned round, 'cheer after cheer was given by both parties and messages of good cheer were shouted across the water to those we were leaving behind until we were well out of hearing'.

The *Morning* departed carrying a number of men discharged by Captain Scott from the *Discovery*. The most senior of these was Shackleton, replaced by Sub-Lieut. Mulock, RN, who was to do some good work as surveyor and map-maker to the expedition. Shackleton had been a zealous, talented, cheerful and lively officer and his departure, much against his will, was greatly regretted by his comrades. Scott reported

> This gentleman has performed his work in a highly satisfactory manner but unfortunately his constitution has proved unequal to the rigours of a polar climate. It is with great reluctance that I order his return and trust that it will be made evident that I do so solely on account of his health and that his future prospects may not suffer.[11]

It has sometimes been said that Scott used the *Morning*'s departure to send home the men of the Merchant service so as to make the *Discovery* virtually a naval vessel. In actual fact, one petty officer, RN, one leading stoker, RN, and one able seaman, RN, were discharged from the *Discovery*, the first (W. MacFarlane) for reasons of health, whom Scott recommended 'on his return to H.M. Service as a thoroughly good man under ordinary conditions'. Scott was unable however to recommend the other two on their return to the service. Of Duncan, Carpenter's mate, and James D. Walker, a whaler, he wrote: 'These men have done their work well on the whole, but are of no exceptional use and have been a source of disturbance on the mess deck.' Nevertheless he recommended that their bonuses should be paid. Young Clarence Hare (Domestic), who so miraculously survived a period of lengthy exposure early in the expedition, was allowed 'to return to N. Zealand at his own request. He has done his work well', reported Scott. Neither William Herbert (Donkeyman) nor Horace Buckridge (Domestic) was recommended for a bonus, nor was the ship's cook (Brett), whom Scott considered 'a continual source of trouble and . . . unpopular throughout the ship'.[12] Captain Scott explained the position in a letter to Admiral Markham:

> I found it was a mistake to try and mix the merchant service and naval element on the messdeck—they have never pulled well together though both excellent in their way. I am therefore sending most of them and one or two naval people away and have given all the rest a chance of going. The men that remain are therefore the best. They have all behaved splendidly and mean to stick by the ship.[13]

Scott's published diary entry remarking that the names of the eight volunteers to return were 'precisely those which I should have placed there had I undertaken the selection myself' (despite his earlier mention of only 'one or two undesirables') was unfortunate.[14] That, and the omission of those who departed in the *Morning* (except Shackleton) from the list of expedition members at the beginning of Scott's narrative, must have caused some heart burning and needless hurt on its publication.

Captain Colbeck felt the poignancy of the *Morning*'s departure. The men being left behind to face another Antarctic winter, he thought, looked such a forlorn and wretched little group, as they stood on the edge of the ice, five miles away from their ship, but at least they had received letters and had been able to reply to them. Writing a few days later, he confessed that he got the blues whenever he thought of the poor beggars, 'as I last saw them starting back to camp dragging two heavily laden sledges behind them'. The expedition's health was a matter of great concern to him, because every one of them had suffered from scurvy, some more severely than others. Scott had wisely, he thought, said very little about the disease in his reports. The *Morning* had spared all the fruits and vegetables possible, a risky gesture, reflected Colbeck, since they were left with only six months' tinned provisions on board the *Morning*, and would at one point be in danger of having to winter themselves in the pack off Beaufort Island.

Scott had given the commander of the relief expedition all his official reports unsealed, so that Colbeck could read them on the way north to see what had been said about the *Discovery*'s position and also because he might like to know of their doings in the Antarctic. Colbeck commented to his fiancée that 'they have done *very, very well* indeed and accomplished far more than was ever expected of them and that is saying much'. Of Colbeck's own work, Scott had written to Sir Clements Markham

> The course taken by Captain Colbeck and his conduct of the *Morning* seems to me to reflect the greatest possible credit on him. No better officer could have been chosen for the work, and since his arrival here no effort has been spared by himself, his officers or men in furthering our interests and hastening the despatch of stores.

The *Morning* found some difficulty in navigating through young ice which was 'screwing'

An album of Mulock's charts was published after the expedition's return by the Royal Geographical Society, with an accompanying pamphlet also by Mulock. It is interesting to note his conclusion as to the 'Parry Mountains' sighted by Sir James Clark Ross on 28 January 1841 and proved by the *Discovery* to be non-existent. Mulock believed these to have been the summits of Minna Bluff, White Island and Black Island, which the *Discovery* also sighted on 23 January 1902 'to the southward over the barrier surface', when 'just to the eastward of Ross island'.[4] Mulock's 'new chart of the Barrier . . . taking in the whole length from Cape Crozier to the limit of the land which we found to the eastward' caused much discussion in the wardroom on its completion, recorded Wilson on 1 August 1903. It showed that the ice front had receded some five to fifteen miles south since Ross's voyage of sixty years previously. After noting various other points of interest, Wilson concluded that 'we seem at last to have probed the mystery of this Great Barrier to some purpose', while he anticipated that the next summer's sledging should 'help still more to unravel the question'.[5]

Wilson gives a detailed description of the routine of the second Antarctic winter in the *Discovery*. His work was indoors, 'drawing or reading or writing', with an hour or more in the fresh air, morning or afternoon.[6] By the end of June he had completed 'the last long sheet of southern sledge journey'.[7] Scott's thoughts meanwhile were with the next season's sledging, and by early July, the various journeys were more or less decided. Wilson summarised the plans as at 1 July 1903.

All sledging except my own journey to Cape Crozier will be over by December 15th and every man and officer will then be put on to the [ice] saws, working in sets which will carry on night and day. There will be various short journeys, chiefly depot parties, in October and November and two or three main parties, two, I believe, in November and December. Barne will take Mulock to the southwest and explore one of the straits we saw last year, with seven men. The Captain with Skelton and seven men will go west, up the mountains on to the inland ice. Royds comes with me to Cape Crozier, and spends the summer till the middle of December on the ship's work and meteorology. Ferrar goes with the Captain and Skelton to the west. Koettlitz will again go on a short trip or two, and I shall have three journeys altogether to Cape Crozier.[8]

In the event, it was Armitage who stayed in charge of the ship and of the sawing camp—a 'sore disappointment' to him, for he had set his heart 'on sledging over the barrier to the south'.[9] Wilson felt that Captain Scott had 'quite rightly' refused Armitage's request to 'try and get further south than we did last year', without dogs.

The end of their 'second long polar night', which Scott recalled as having passed quietly and pleasantly, came on 21 August 1903, when the sun's rim could just be seen above the northern horizon. 'I climbed Arrival Heights', wrote Scott, 'and got a view of the golden half-disc.' He was much cheered by the sight of the sun's rays that were 'gilding our surrounding hills'.[10] Preparations for the coming sledging season had been going on and almost all of the gear had to be thoroughly repaired.[11] One day, wrote Wilson, the wardroom became a 'mountain of finnesko and sennegraes', for the selection of the soft Lapp footware for sledging.[12] Two days later, on 19 August 1903, he inspected the provisions for his Cape Crozier journey.

> All the food for each journey is now prepared, weighed out and packed in linen bags, and labelled, and each lot of bags for one week for one tent, i.e. three men, is in a larger bag, known as a weekly bag. For a journey of three weeks one takes three weekly bags for a party of three men, and each weekly bag contains about a dozen smaller bags containing pemmican, oatmeal, peameal, cocoa, chocolate, red ration, sugar, milk, tinned milk, frozen and cut into small cubes, pepper, salt, onion powder, and a tin of tea.[13]

## SLEDGING JOURNEYS, 1903

Two main supported parties were planned towards the west and south-west. The captain's western party aimed to study the geology of what was later called the Ferrar Glacier and by it to reach and explore the inland ice sheet that Armitage had attained the previous year. The second supported party, led by Barne and Mulock, was to examine one of the 'extraordinary straits', which had appeared (to the previous year's southern party from a distance of some 20 or 30 miles) 'to run through the mountain ranges without rising in level'. A third (unsupported) party led by Royds and Bernacchi was to sledge across the ice shelf in a south-easterly direction to see (at Bernacchi's suggestion) whether the 'barrier surface continued on a level to the eastward'. A number of 'periodic visits' was to be made by Wilson to the Emperor penguin rookery, where it was hoped that he 'would be able to observe the habits of these extraordinary creatures from the commencement of their breeding season'.[14]

The day before the start of the new sledging season, with the departure of Wilson and Royds to Cape Crozier on 7 September 1903, the *Discovery* was 'in a state of bustle', wrote Scott, with 'people flying to and fro, packing sledges, weighing loads, and inspecting each detail of equipment'. He added that there had been no sign of scurvy in the ship during the winter and that judging 'by the laughter and excitement we might be boys escaping from school'.[15]

The object of Scott's own depot-laying party, which left on 9 September, was a reconnaissance of the lower reaches of the New Harbour (later Ferrar) Glacier, round which Armitage had skirted the previous season, by crossing the adjoining hills and descending onto the glacier higher up its course. A route was in fact found by Scott's party on the glacier's northern and smoother side (where there is less melting in summer), which seemed likely to cut down the time to reach Cathedral Rocks, the site of their

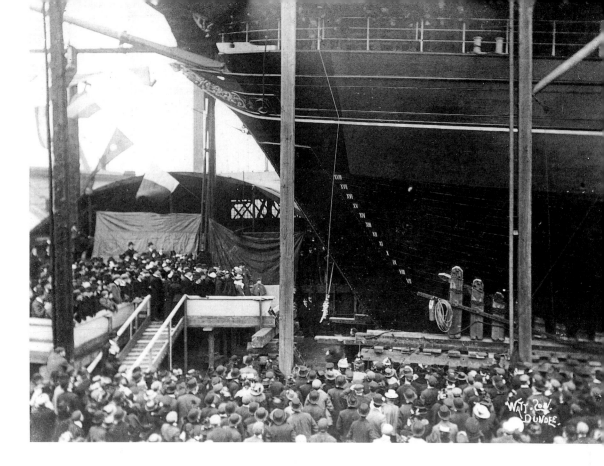

*Above:* The launch of the *Discovery* in Dundee, on 21 March 1901

*Far left:* Advertisement for the Dundee Shipbuilders' Company from the *Discovery* exhibition catalogue, Bond Street, London, 1904

*Left:* The *Discovery*'s triple expansion engine

*Top left:* Aboard the *Discovery* at Cowes, 5 August 1901. *Left to right:* Skelton, Scott, Sir Clements Markham, Sir Leopold McClintock, Mr Longstaff, Hodgson, Admiral Markham, Ferrar.

*Left:* Captain Scott seeing off the Royal party from the *Discovery*, Cowes, 5 August 1901

*Below:* Midwinter 'Christmas' dinner on the lower deck of the *Discovery*, 21 June 1902

*Above:* Section of the panorama drawn by Dr E. A. Wilson of the mountains bordering the Great Ice Barrier entitled 'New Land. Southern sledge journey 28 Dec. 1902'. Pencil, much reduced

*Below:* The *Discovery* in winter quarters, McMurdo Sound, during the National Antarctic Expedition, 1901-4

*Left:* Able Seaman James Dell and his team of six dogs born during the first winter in the Antarctic, 1902

*Below:* The southern sledge party on departure, November 1902. *Left to right*: Shackleton, Scott, Wilson

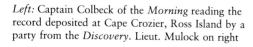

*Left:* Captain Colbeck of the *Morning* reading the record deposited at Cape Crozier, Ross Island by a party from the *Discovery*. Lieut. Mulock on right

*Bottom left:* Shackleton aboard the *Morning* on arrival in Lyttelton, New Zealand, March 1903, having been invalided home

*Below:* Captain Colbeck *(at left)* and Captain Scott aboard the *Morning*, January 1904

*Above:* Captain Harry MacKay, Master of the *Terra Nova*, with the crew during the voyage to relieve the *Discovery*, 1903-4

*Right:* The relief ships *Morning* (nearest the camera) and *Terra Nova* at the edge of the sea ice, twenty miles from the *Discovery*, January 1904

*Below:* The *Morning* and *Terra Nova* reach the *Discovery* in winter quarters, 14 February 1904, after six weeks of blasting and charging the sea ice

*Left:* Captain J. G. Ford, Master of the *Discovery*, during her voyages to Hudson Bay, 1906-11

*Below:* Hudson's Bay Company, Charlton Island depot, James Bay, photographed *c* 1910. The company's arms can be seen, also the jetty set up for the summer

*Bottom:* York Factory, Hudson's Bay Company post, photographed *c* 1910

*Top left:* The port of Brest *c* 1912

*Above:* The icebreaker *Canada*, Archangel, February 1919

*Left:* Captain James Fairweather (holding the ship's cat) and the officers of the *Discovery* during the Shackleton relief voyage, 1916

*Below:* The *Discovery* being refitted at Devonport for her voyage to rescue Shackleton's men on Elephant Island, 1916

depot, from three weeks (over the hills) to a few days. Very low temperatures, each night in the minus fifties Fahrenheit, were met, and the party marched home to 'our snug ship' across the fifty miles of frozen sea in record time. Barne's depot-laying party to White Island had met even severer temperatures, well below minus 67.7°F at which the thermometer broke. Joyce's foot had been saved by the 'officers taking it in turns to nurse the frozen member in their breasts', an incident that Joyce himself and the rest of the party regarded with hilarity.[16]

Wilson's visit to the Emperor penguin rookery at Cape Crozier was his first. The party had set out as early as possible after the return of the sun, in order to try to observe the penguins still incubating their eggs. Using crampons, they were able to reach the fast bay ice, 'streaked and splashed in every direction by the droppings of the birds that breed here'. They found that a large group of the birds had been scared away by the fall of a big portion of the Barrier, when 'huddled together here brooding on their eggs'. The party picked up sixteen of these deserted eggs, some of them unbroken. The main colony of about a thousand birds was standing a little way away under the ice cliff. Wilson was greatly surprised to find not brooding birds, but parents 'already nursing chicks apparently every bit as old as those were that Royds and Skelton brought home the year before', but five weeks later.[17] He was driven to conclude that the eggs were laid and the chicks hatched in the depths of the Antarctic winter, in temperatures as low as the minus sixties Fahrenheit. The extraordinary life cycle of the Emperor penguin was not in fact confirmed until Wilson, Cherry-Garrard and Bowers made their famous winter journey to the rookery during Scott's *Terra Nova* expedition of 1910–13.

The party had a tricky climb back to camp, seeing 'nothing of the risky ice ridges we were crossing, except what was just under foot', wrote Wilson. 'Royds led with the ice axe carrying nothing. I followed with a satchel containing all the unbroken eggs, about eight, each as big as a swan's, and in my blouse I had about 15 frozen Emperor chickens, so that I was fairly cumbersome. Cross came after with a net bag of cracked eggs and chicks and a ski pole.'[18] This strange little procession of three reached camp safely to be joined later by Whitfield, Williamson and Blissett, who had been to the deserted Adélie penguin rookery to look for specimens of dead chicks. The whole party started for home next day with a valuable cargo of eggs and chicks, the eggs being packed in an empty biscuit box lashed to the sledge. With temperatures in the minus sixties at night, camping became immensely uncomfortable, but the men's 'constant jokes and humbug' made light of all difficulties. 'One's clothes, being all wet at night and frozen all day', wrote Wilson, 'became so board-like that one can neither do up nor undo any buttons. The burberry suit of overalls, which one wears from crown to heel are wet and frozen, so that every movement crackles them like a suit of tin armour, and one must stand rigidly still to hear one's neighbour speak.' After three painful nights in the tents, they returned to the ship, with flags flying. Wilson and Royds relished the 'roaring fire in the ward-room and a full feed of hot buttered toast and tea'.[19]

Wilson spent some time on his return painting and cataloguing his specimens, blowing the eggs and feeding the surviving chick, which proved useful to the artist for illustrating the attitudes the species assumed in life.

> He is a regular caution, frightfully wayward and obstinate, and very vicious, losing his temper and grizzling in the most human fashion, pecking as hard as possible if he isn't allowed to do exactly as he wishes. He has me out of bed regularly twice every night, chirruping in the most ear-piercing way till I feed him with chewed seal meat, and then he insists on being fed full every four hours throughout the day. He likes sitting up late to look at the candle and gets frightfully angry, struggling and chirruping in his box if I put him to bed early. He is covered with the softest silky grey down and his head is made of black and white velvet in beautiful contrast. Only his figure is shockingly aldermanic, just about as ugly as can be.[20]

Wilson was to make a second journey to Cape Crozier in October 1903, the anniversary of Skelton's visit, and found the chicks bigger, but still in down. He took with him a record of proceedings to fix to the post at the Adélie penguin rookery, where the birds were just beginning to return after the winter to nest. A week later these had the last laugh on Wilson, Whitfield and Cross, for not an egg had yet been laid. As the disappointed egg-seekers sat by a rock eating their dry cheese and biscuit, the Adélies 'made love to one another all around us and stole each other's nesting stones and stood bolt upright with their heads in the air chortling to themselves, as they slowly waggled their flippers. For they knew they had sold us a pup, as fair a pup as was ever sold to anyone in the Antarctic up till now, and we knew that in a day or two the ground would be literally strewn with eggs and we could have filled a cart.'[21]

Scott's western journey, which was the great bonus to the expedition resulting from the unexpected second year in the Antarctic, was the most important made in the southern spring of 1903. He had been somewhat diffident about the achievements of the southern journey in the previous sledging season, but with regard to the western journey, he confessed to 'some pride' at having successfully overcome the 'immense difficulties, such as would have brought us hopelessly to grief in the previous year ... and when all circumstances are considered, the extreme severity of the climate and the obstacles that stood in our path, I cannot but believe we came near the limit of possible performance'.[22]

Armitage and his party had earlier 'reached the inland ice-cap and could claim to be the first to set foot on the interior of Victoria Land'. However, although they 'appeared to have been on a lofty plateau', they had only been able to sledge a short distance over it to the west. This meant, wrote Scott, that 'the nature of the interior of this great country was therefore still wrapped in mystery'.[23] Armitage's western journey had also shown the very great interest of the region from a geological point of view. His rock samples pointed to the likelihood of there being sedimentary deposits, 'which alone', in Scott's words, 'could serve to reveal the geological history of this great southern continent'.[24]

It took the explorations of this century (in which the *Discovery* played her part) to show that Antarctica is indeed a great continent and not a number of smaller land masses overlain by ice which covers all but one per cent of the underlying rock to an average depth of 8,000 feet. In the words of H. G. R. King, 'the ice free slopes of mountain ranges, the exposed tips of buried peaks or *nunataks*, and the rare iceless valleys form, as it were, windows into the structure of the continent itself', scarcity greatly increasing their importance.[25] In the absence of Professor J. W. Gregory, who had resigned as chief of the scientific staff, it fell to the young Cambridge graduate, Hartley Ferrar, to be the first to examine one of these exciting areas—the 600 square miles of new territory in the region of the valley glacier that now bears his name.[26]

A party of twelve left the *Discovery* on 12 October 1903. First came Scott's carefully selected advance party, which consisted of Scott, Skelton, Feather, Evans, Lashly and Handsley, then Ferrar's party of three and, thirdly, the supporting party of three led by Dailey, the carpenter. The original plan of all twelve ascending to the inland ice sheet (via the Ferrar Glacier) had to be abandoned, when it was discovered on 18 October, at a height of 6,000 feet near the Solitary Rocks, that only one of the four sledges was sound: the runners of the other three, made of German silver, had been pretty well 'split to ribbons' and the wood underneath 'deeply scored'.

Scott found this region 'very beautiful and interesting', no doubt doubly so to him after the monotony of his previous long journey over the Ross Ice Shelf.[27]

> Tonight it is difficult to imagine oneself in a polar region ... We are in a deep gorge, not narrow, as the glacier here is probably four or five miles across, but the cliffs on either side are so majestic and lofty that the broad surface of the glacier is wholly dwarfed by them.
>
> We are on the south side of the valley, and towering precipitously between three and four thousand feet above our heads are the high sunlit pinnacles of the Cathedral Rocks; they were well named by Armitage, for their lofty peaks might well be the spires of some mighty edifice. ... On the further side of our valley the hills rise almost as abruptly as on this; reddish brown is the predominant colour there also, but where the sunlight falls on the steeper cliffs it is lightened almost to a brick red.[28]

Their camp on the evening of 16 October was in the medial moraine, a long line of scattered boulders, varied in shape and colour. This line could be seen 'winding down with graceful curves over the blue surface of the glacier', towards the distant, pearl grey, ice-covered sea. Looking upwards, towards the west, whither they were bound, the 'highway of boulders' followed the curving slopes of the glacier, which here wore 'a formidable aspect', having in its centre an 'immense cascade'. This appeared like a 'river which had been suddenly frozen in its course, with the cascade to show where its waters had been dashing wild over a rocky shallow ...' Its 'gleaming white waves and deep blue shadows' would have to be circumvented next day on the upward journey. 'The upper valley', continued Scott, 'is perhaps our most beautiful view; the dark cliffs form a broad V and frame the cascading glacier, and above it the distant solitary peak of the Knob Head Mountain and a patch of crimson sky.'[29]

By the following evening they were encamped in a great ice basin looking down on the gorge by which they had entered. From the camp they could see the white slopes of Mount Lister culminating in an ice-free summit, 11,000 feet above them. Scott records the feast of colour that must have been particularly welcome to eyes dulled by the gloom of a second Antarctic night. The steep, bare hillsides surrounding their camp had a basic colour scheme of russet brown, shading from bright red to dull grey with an occasional vivid yellow, the whole forming a 'glorious combination of autumn tints', which few forests could excel. The horizontal layers of the hills were also of great interest to the geologist.

It was from the camp at the Solitary Rocks that the party was forced to return to the ship next day. The sound sledge was left with the spare food and the party almost flew back to the ship, covering 87 miles in three days—another record march.[30] From various broken sledges at winter quarters the carpenter was able to produce two sound ones: an eleven-footer for the plateau party and a seven-footer for Ferrar's geological party. On 26 October, the reduced party of nine started westward again.

They were back again at their depot above the 'Vale of Winds' on 1 November 1903. The lid of the instrument box left there had blown open in a gale; Skelton's goggles had disappeared and Scott found to his horror that his *Hints to Travellers* was gone. This was a serious matter, since he was depending on the data in this R.G.S. publication to work out his sights and fix the party's position with accuracy on the polar plateau, when beyond the mountains. Determined not to return to the ship a second time, Scott consulted his companions and was 'fortified by their willing consent to take the risks of pushing on', despite 'the risk of marching away into the unknown without exactly knowing where we were or how to get back'.[31]

With the use of the crampons made by Skelton, and the skill of Lashly and Skelton in repairing the sledge runners, the party passed gradually from the hard abrasive ice to snow, then onto ice again in the upper reaches of the glacier, against a bitter head wind and driving snow on 2 and 3 November 1903. By the evening of 3 November they had reached 7,000 feet where (in Scott's words) 'the masses of dark, bare rock were becoming detached and isolated, whilst the widening snowfields were creeping upward with the ever-increasing threat to engulf all beneath their white mantle'.[32] Despite being laid up in their tents during a week of continual blizzards between 4 and 11 November 1903 at 'Desolation Camp', they reached 8,900 feet above sea level, on 13 November 1903, having 'at length won our fight and reached the summit' with nearly five weeks' provisions still in hand. They found themselves 'on a great snow-plain, with a level horizon all about'. However, 'to the south-east, Mount Lister and the higher peaks of the Royal Society Range still showed well above our level', enabling Scott on a clear day to fix their latitude by bearings and to note the features which would act as signposts on their return to the glacier. Scott also improvised a method of determining the daily change in the sun's declination to allow him to find the party's latitude with reasonable accuracy when out of sight of land.[33] Ferrar, Kennar and Weller (the geological party) had separated from the plateau party on 11 November 1903, leaving Scott, Skelton, Feather, Evans, Lashly and Handsley to push on, facing a bitter wind at high altitude, westward across what Scott called the vast and lifeless plateau. They turned their backs 'upon the last mountain peak' that could remind them of home, and stood fascinated at the threshold of the unknown.[34]

On 22 November, Scott reluctantly resolved to divide the party, sending back Skelton with Handsley and the boatswain (after whom the mountain at the head of the glacier was later named Mount Feather), all 'lion hearted people' who had been forced through 'sheer incapacity' to pull less hard than Evans, Lashly and Scott himself; these three consequently pressed on at a faster pace still farther to the west. The temperature fell each night to the minus forties and during the day it hardly rose above −25°F, with a constant wind which cracked and cut their faces and hands. It made the taking of observations with the theodolite a punishing task and even jokes in the tent at night were not encouraged since laughing had become so painful. The plateau was uneven and was found to rise and fall, its surface varying from smooth on the summits and eastern faces to heavy, sharp *sastrugi* (snow waves) in the hollows and on western faces. 'We were like a small boat at sea,' wrote Scott, 'at one moment appearing to stand still to climb some wave, and at the next diving down into a hollow.' The sledge capsized quite often, causing a small loss each time of precious cooking oil.[35]

Scott considered these three weeks of sledge-pulling as the toughest physical exercise he had ever experienced but he looked back on it with great satisfaction. He did not think they could have accomplished any more, given 'the splendid qualities and physique' of his two chosen companions, Evans and Lashly. 'Evans', he wrote, 'was a man of Herculean strength, very long in the arm and with splendidly developed muscles. He had been a gymnastic instructor in the Navy and had always been an easy winner in all our sports which involved tests of strength.' He was chosen again by Scott to travel over this same inland ice sheet south to the Pole, some ten years later during the *Terra Nova* expedition of 1910–13 and was to die during the tragic return. Scott described Lashly as 'not above the ordinary height', nor 'more than ordinarily broad, and yet he weighed 13st. 8lbs. and had one of the largest chest measurements in the ship. He had been a teetotaller and non-smoker all his life and was never in anything but the hardest condition . . . With these two men behind me', wrote Scott, 'our sledge seemed to become a living thing, and the days of slow progress were numbered. We took the rough and the smooth alike, working patiently on through the long hours with scarce a word and never a halt between meal and meal. Troubles and discomforts were many, and we could only guess at the progress we made, but we knew that by sticking to our task we should have our reward when our observations came to be worked out on board the ship.'[36]

Commenting on Scott's remark that 'There is no class of men so eminently adapted by training to cope with the troubles and tricks of sledging life as sailors', Commander Ellis, the editor of Lashly's diaries, compares Scott's experience with that of Nansen in 1895 in the north. While Nansen found his 'sailor companion' Johansen unable to give him 'any sort of intellectual companionship', Ellis reckoned that Scott 'would not have chosen Lashly and Evans only for their practical value. Being a naval officer to the core he had more in common with his sailors than Nansen the scientist had. Even so, the social and educational gulf between senior officer and lower deck was very great.' Commander Ellis has also pointed out that 'In all his accounts of events on this journey, Scott never used the word *I*; it is always *we*. They even shared a three-man sleeping bag.' He concluded that Scott, 'who was a thinking man, found the companionship of Lashly and Evans stimulating and congenial. A very real bond of affection and loyalty existed between the three men.'[37]

On 30 November they thankfully finished the westward march in long. 146°33′ E. Travelling up the last slope, Scott hoped against hope to find a different view—perhaps some distant mountains, but all they saw was 'a further expanse of our terrible plateau'.

> Here, then to-night we have reached the end of our tether, and all we have done is to show the immensity of this vast plain. This scene about us is the same as we have seen for many a day, and shall see for many a day to come—a scene so wildly and awfully desolate that it cannot fail to impress one with gloomy thoughts. . . .
>
> Luckily, the gloom of the outer world has not been allowed to enter the door of our tent. My companions spare no time for solemn thought; they are invariably cheerful and busy. Few of our camping hours go by without a laugh from Evans and a song from Lashly. I have not quite penetrated the latter yet; there is only one verse which is about the plucking of a rose. It can scarcely be called a finished musical performance, but I should miss it much if it ceased.[38]

They wondered at supper whether future explorers would travel further over this inhospitable country. Evans remarked, recorded Scott, 'that if they did "they would have to leg it", and indeed I think they would'.[39] Far beyond the reach of human help, the little party in their rather threadbare tent had the great ice sheet to themselves. They were not to know that in the future, men would explore Antarctica from the air. Even the under-ice topography would be ascertained by instruments carried in aircraft high above the land surface. The next parties to 'leg it' over 'South Victoria Land' were making for the South Magnetic Pole: David, Mawson and Mackay, during Shackleton's *Nimrod* expedition of 1907–9 and Bage, Webb and Hurley during Mawson's Australasian Antarctic Expedition of 1911–14. To Scott, the month spent on the high plateau remained 'as some vivid and evil dream', a 'continuous strain on mind and body lightened only by the unfailing courage and cheerfulness of my companions'.[40] They began the 300-mile journey back to the *Discovery* on 1 December 1903.

The biting wind was now at their backs while marching, but still plagued them at camp sites. An overcast sky caused them to lie up for a time on 2 December, because they could not see the surface in the dark. The likelihood of further delay led Scott to think they might soon land in 'Queer Street', trying to make long marches on reduced rations. Nevertheless, at the end of the day, he wrote, 'my companions are undefeatable. However tiresome our day's march or however gloomy the outlook, they always find something to jest about. In the evenings we have long arguments about naval matters, and generally agree that we could rule that Service a great deal better than any Board of Admiralty. Incidentally, I learn a great deal about lower-deck life—more than I could hope to have done under ordinary conditions.'[41] A gritty snow surface like sand and a southerly wind cut the pace to one mile an hour on 9 December. Scott's anxiety grew as they approached the edge of the plateau. Evans sighted land on the afternoon of 10 December, which was cheering. However, navigating 'by rule of thumb', there was no certainty that they would hit their own glacier first, when so many others flowed down through the mountains from the plateau. Overcast weather hid the tops of the mountains which should have been their landmarks. Ten hours' daily pulling on a heavy surface reduced them to ghosts of their former selves, yet they remained fit, despite acute hunger pains and numerous frost-bites, particularly to Evans's nose. Pushing on steadily eastward on 13 December, they began to descend.

Next day, they rocketed down an ice fall on what all three agreed to have been 'the most adventurous day in our lives'. In the morning, the clouds still covered the mountain tops, so they continued their eastward march, soon coming across a rough area, which they were unable to circumvent. Preferring the dangers of pressing on in the whirling snow to trying to sit out a blizzard, they threaded their way round hummocks and across crevasses onto a smoother, steeper surface for which they donned crampons, Captain Scott guiding the sledge in front with the two men holding it back in the rear.

Suddenly Lashly slipped, and in an instant he was sliding downward on his back; directly the strain came on Evans, he too was thrown off his feet. It all happened in a moment, and before I had time to look the sledge and the two men hurtled past me; I braced myself to stop them, but might as well have attempted to hold an express train. With the first jerk I was whipped off my legs, and we all three lay sprawling on our backs and flying downward with an ever-increasing velocity.

For some reason the first thought that flashed into my mind was that someone would break a limb if he attempted to stop our mad career, and I shouted something to this effect, but might as well have saved my breath. Then there came a sort of vague wonder as to what would happen next, and in the midst of this I was conscious that we had ceased to slide smoothly and were now bounding over a rougher incline sometimes leaving it for several yards at a time; my thoughts flew to broken limbs again, for I felt we could not stand much of such bumping. At length we gave a huge leap into the air, and yet we travelled with such velocity that I had not time to think before we came down with tremendous force on a gradual incline of rough, hard, wind-swept snow. Its irregularities brought us to rest in a moment or two, and I staggered to my feet in a dazed fashion, wondering what had happened.[42]

He found the others rising to their feet, bruised and shaken like himself, but sound in limb. They had descended some 300 feet of the highest of the 'ice cascades' of the glacier that they had been seeking. At this lower level, away from the driven snow, they perceived many familiar features of the landscape including distant Mount Erebus with its plume of smoke. After nearly a month without seeing any landmarks, their rule-of-thumb navigation methods had none the less proved to be astonishingly accurate. They packed their scattered belongings and scanty food to march farther down the glacier, descending the second ice fall carefully and without accident, when, some five miles from the depot, 'All of a sudden,' wrote Lashly, 'the Captain and Evans disappeared down a crevasse . . . leaving me on top. It was now my duty to try and get them up again.'[43] He managed to secure the damaged sledge, supported by two skis, above the crevasse while holding on to it—and Scott and Evans dangling below. Scott was in the better position to move first.

As a first step I took off my goggles; I then discovered that Evans was hanging just above me. I asked him if he was all right, and received a reassuring reply in his usual calm, matter-of-fact tones. Meanwhile, I groped about on every side with my cramponed feet, only to find everywhere the same slippery smooth wall. But my struggles had set me swinging, and at one end of a swing my leg suddenly struck a projection. In a moment I had turned, and saw at a glance that by raising myself I could get foothold on it; with the next swing I clutched it with my steel-shod feet, and after a short struggle succeeded in partly transferring my weight to it. In this position, with my feet firmly planted and my balance maintained by my harness, I could look about me.

I found myself standing on a thin shaft of ice which was wedged between the walls of the chasm—how it came there I cannot imagine, but its position was wholly providential; to the right or left, above or below, there was not the vestige of another such support—nothing, in fact, but the smooth walls of ice. My next step was to get Evans into the same position as myself, and when he had slipped his harness well up under his arms I found I could pilot his feet to the bridge.

All this had occupied some time and it was only now that I realised what had happened above us, for there, some twelve feet over our heads, was the outline of the broken sledge. I saw at once what a frail support remained, and shouted to Lashly to ask what he could do, and then I knew the value of such a level-headed companion; for while he held on grimly to the sledge and us with one hand, his other was busily employed in withdrawing our ski. . . .

There remained no other course for Evans and me but to climb out by our own unaided efforts, and I saw that one of us would have to make the attempt without delay, for the chill of the crevasse was already attacking us and our faces and fingers were on the verge of freezing. After a word with Evans I decided to try the first climb myself, but I must confess I never expected to reach the top. . . . It is some time since I swarmed a rope, and to have to do so in thick clothing and heavy crampons and with frost-bitten fingers seemed to me in the nature of the impossible. But it was no use thinking about it, so I slung my mits over my shoulders, grasped the rope, and swung off the bridge. I don't know how long I took to climb or how I did it . . .

. . . With two of us on top and one below, things had assumed a very different aspect, and I was able to unhitch my own harness and lower it once more for Evans; then with our united efforts he also was landed on the surface, where he arrived in the same frost-bitten condition as I had. For a minute or two we could only look at one another, then Evans said, 'Well I'm blowed'; it was the first sign of astonishment he had shown.[44]

They wasted no time in the chill wind discussing their escape, but trudged on pulling the broken sledge, keeping a sharp look-out for crevasses and harnessed so that only one of them could disappear at a time. Early in the evening they reached the depot where there was enough food to carry them on to the main depot some miles down the glacier. There was not only food, but sunshine, calm, rest and peace. The steam from their cooking rose straight upward in the still warm air. Scott wrote that 'Evans's astonishment at the events of the day seemed to grow ever deeper, and was exhibited in the most pleasing manner. With his sock half on he would . . . say suddenly, "Well, sir, but what about that snow bridge?" or if so-and-so hadn't happened "where should we be now?" and then the soliloquy would end with "My word, but it was a close call!" '[45] Scott felt this indeed to be true.

They were further cheered during their descent of the glacier by finding notes at various pre-arranged points containing good news of Skelton's and Ferrar's parties. Before making for the ship, Scott, Lashly and Evans spent a long day on 17 December 1903 exploring the north arm of the Ferrar Glacier, later to become known as the Taylor Glacier, after the geologist of the *Terra Nova* expedition. They made the remarkable discovery that the glacier was withering away. It did not discharge its ice as icebergs into the sea, but ended tamely in a strange steep snow-free valley, where there were frozen lakes and long muddy moraines. They lunched on a sandy spot next to a stream, Scott thinking how it was almost impossible to believe that they could be less than a hundred miles from that terrible plateau.[46]

They then climbed to a vantage point of some 700 feet but failed to see the sea which was shut out from their view by the steep winding gorges. However, the height enabled them to take in the wild beauty of the valley. By the time they returned to their camp and supper, they had spent fourteen hours walking and climbing over very rough country. Scott reflected on their discovery,

I cannot but think that this valley is a very wonderful place. We have seen today all the indications of colossal ice action and considerable water action, and yet neither of these agents is now at work. It is worthy of record, too, that we have seen no living thing, not even a moss or lichen; all that we did find, far inland among the moraine heaps, was the skeleton of a Weddell seal, and how that came there is beyond guessing. It is certainly a valley of the dead: even the great glacier which once pushed through it has withered away.[47]

The valley is one of three forming the McMurdo oasis, the most extensive area of ice-free land in Antarctica. The valley is called the Taylor Dry Valley and has been studied not only by Griffith Taylor, after whom it is named, but by modern geologists, naturalists and limnologists.[48]

On the home-ward journey, the travellers were dismayed to find the ice in McMurdo Sound as fast as ever. Late on Christmas Eve they saw the masts of the *Discovery* and were welcomed by Koettlitz, Ford, Handsley and Quartley—the only four on board. 'And so', wrote Scott, 'we spent our Christmas Day in the snug security of our home quarters, and tasted once again those delights of civilised existence to which we had so long been strangers.' He was later able to work out his observations quietly at his desk and was relieved to find that his watch was accurate, for on its accuracy depended their longitudes on the plateau.[49] Scott had calculated that during the western journey, he, Evans and Lashly had averaged 15.4 miles a day over the 81 days' absence, during which time they had sledged 1,098 miles and climbed heights totalling 19,800 feet.

During their absence, a number of other journeys had been accomplished, while Skelton and Ferrar had returned before them from the west. Skelton had used the half-plate camera to good effect.[50] Ferrar's observations showed that the Royal Society Range had a simple geological structure, the rocks comprising mainly thick horizontal layers of sandstone. Ferrar named this formation Beacon Sandstone. Basalt and granite were also present. He was delighted to find some seams of coal running through the sandstone from which he collected specimens. The importance of these in yielding fossils of the fern *Glossopteris* and a gymnospermous wood was not truly demonstrated until 1928, although 'Fossil found here by Mr. Ferrar' is marked on the map showing sledge journeys from winter quarters in Scott's narrative. The presence of coal indicated that in earlier geological times the climate of Antarctica must have been warm, with abundant trees and plants.[51]

Scott soon learnt about the other sledge journeys. Barne and Mulock had only been able to reach the entrance (Barne Inlet) of what was later called the Byrd Glacier, owing to southerly gales. Here they found progress so impeded by crevasses and ice ridges that they were compelled to return without exploring the glacier itself. Mulock was tireless in surveying this area of Victoria Land. He used his theodolite to good effect and was able to ascertain the positions and heights of some two hundred peaks. They also accidentally discovered that Depot A, on the ice sheet of the Great Barrier (the Ross Ice

Shelf) off Minna Bluff, had moved over 600 yards in just over a year. They had realised earlier on in the expedition that the Barrier was not only afloat, but moving—the vast pressure ridges against the slopes of Mount Terror and elsewhere giving evidence of this. Barne and Mulock returned to the ship after 68 days out.

Royds, Bernacchi and party were 31 days out, sledging to the south-east over what Scott called 'the same unutterably wearisome plain' of the Great Barrier, and accomplishing 'an exceedingly fine journey'. Bernacchi described the journey in an earlier history of the *Discovery*.[52] He also gives a light-hearted account of sledging in the Antarctic, when the explorer is 'harnessed to a cycle of things—chiefly unpleasant—which there is no avoiding, starting with the struggle, amounting at times to a fight, with the erection of the tent . . .'. He is one of the few writers of the time who refers to the 'daily hygienic ceremony', which he calls 'one of the nightmares of sledging in Antarctica'.

> On turning out of the tent in the early morning, heavily clad, for it is usually blowing with varying intensity and a temperature below zero, you are haunted by a vague trouble which you realise must be faced. There are no facilities within the tiny tent; latrines are impossible. They take too long to build and in any case are useless since they fill in immediately with drifting snow. Temporary shelters are merely places for whirling drift, and so there remains the open snow spaces.
>
> Feeling like a ham in a sack, you go through various preparatory antics of loosening garments—preferably within the tent, and prowl around some distance away facing always the biting wind, and watchfully awaiting a temporary lull. The rest is a matter of speed and dexterity, but invariably the nether garments are filled instantly with masses of surface-drifting snow, which you must take along with you and suffer the discomforts of extreme wetness for hours.[53]

Bernacchi and his party achieved their main objective in discovering that the Barrier continued level to the south-east. Bernacchi made many observations with a Barrow dip circle in perfect conditions free of magnetic interference and these were an important contribution to building up a picture of the region's magnetic conditions. Armitage, Wilson and Heald examined and surveyed the Koettlitz Glacier during this second sledging season. Wilson made a third visit to the Emperor penguin rookery at Cape Crozier, where he solved the mystery of the chicks who had vanished while still in down (and unable to swim) the previous year, with the discovery that batches of young and old birds sailed out to sea on ice floes released in the spring. Wilson, Hodgson and Croucher later investigated the strand crack between land ice and floating ice on the south side of Ross Island, a matter which had an important bearing on the question of whether the ice shelf was afloat or aground.[54]

The journeys accomplished during this second fortuitous summer in the Antarctic added a great deal to knowledge of the continent, both in geography and in science. Scott concluded his review of the 1903 sledging work and wrote that

When all things are considered, it must be conceded that no polar ship ever wintered in a more interesting spot than the 'Discovery'. . . . from the first we saw what great possibilities lay before us, and determined that no effort should be spared to take advantage of our opportunities. During one long season we had laboured hard to this end, but yet its finish found us with many important gaps in our knowledge. Then fortune decided that we should be given another season to complete our work . . . and I trust it will be agreed that after the close of our second sledging season we were justified in considering that the main part of our work was done.[55]

# SEVEN

## Second Relief Expedition of the *Morning* with the *Terra Nova*, 1903–4, Release of the *Discovery* from the Ice

### ARRIVAL OF THE RELIEF SHIPS

AFTER RECUPERATING AND FEASTING for a few days on board the snow-bound *Discovery*, a dyspeptic Scott with Lashly and Evans, both visibly gaining weight on Ford's savoury dishes (culled from Mrs Beeton), went north over the sea ice to the sawing camp. This had been set up by Armitage on Scott's order to saw through the fast sea ice of the strait between the *Discovery* and the open sea. Scott found the thirty men there in good condition and high spirits. They looked like tramps in tattered clothing, with faces burnt brown by the sun and enormous appetites, which the cooks, using penguins, seal meat and supplies brought by dog team from the ship, found hard to satisfy. The main party slept in turns in a large tent near the Dellbridge Islands. Scott was pleased to be with his men again and declared New Year's Day 1904 a holiday. He lay awake that night listening to the strange noises around them.

> The Weddell seal is a great musician and can produce any note from a shrill piping whistle to a deep moan, between whiles he grunts and gurgles and complains in the weirdest fashion. As there were some hundreds of these animals on the ice, there was a chorus of sounds like the tuning of many instruments. To this was added the harsh, angry cawing of the skua gulls as they quarrelled over their food, and now and again one of the dogs would yap in his dreams, whilst from the main tent came the more familiar snores of humanity. At first I missed one sound from this Antarctic concert, but it came at last when the squawk of a penguin was borne from afar on the still air; then the orchestra was completed.[1]

A visit to the edge of the sea ice next day confirmed the depressing news that twenty miles of ice lay between the *Discovery* and open water. Scott watched the team of officers, scientists and men sawing through seven feet of ice to make a channel for the ship. Astonished at the small result of ten days of effort and convinced of the futility of the work, he ordered it to stop. Ice saws had been used during the British naval expeditions to the Arctic of the nineteenth century and this occasion must have been one of the last, if not *the* last, that such a cumbersome, back-breaking apparatus was employed.[2] Aware of the likelihood that the expedition would have to remain for a third year in the Antarctic, Scott told off four men to lay in a stock of penguins for the winter to vary the usual diet of seal meat. He and Wilson made their way to the north, Scott to watch for the break-up of the ice and Wilson to study the wildlife. This was to be an outing with no hard sledging. They saw many Adélie penguins busy about their own affairs and were surprised to discover a rookery on the rocks at Cape Royds near which they pitched their tent on the sand.

They later walked to the north side of the cape, where a lazy sea was lapping the sandy beach. Scott was delighted to look at the sea again and wished that the *Discovery* could be lifted up and deposited twenty miles to the north. After a wash in a small stream near the tent and a supper of penguins' liver and seal kidneys eaten from the frying pan, he con- cluded that 'life in the Antarctic Regions can be very pleasant'.[3] Wilson wrote a touching note to Lieut. Royds, forgetting, when he dated it, that the year was by then 1904.[4]

Penguin Rookery Camp                                          Jan 5, 1903
Cape Royds, McMurdo Strait.

My dear Charles,

This is as perfect a camping ground as I have yet struck. We are on fine hard gravel, on a small height which overlooks the open sea, the edge of the fast ice, the pack moving in and out, a beautiful little rookery of Adélies, scores of Skuas with eggs and young, streams of water, sandy beaches; Erebus is in full view and so is the whole Strait, to the very end. Miles of rock and earth to wander over, whales to watch, etc. etc.

Yours, truly in Antarctic clover,
Ted Wilson

This idyll was soon to be disturbed. He and Scott were writing in their tent, when Scott saw the *Morning* barely three miles from them. They talked over their plans and when they looked again 'lo and behold, there before us lay a second ship like the first. We were dumbfounded . . .' They set off for the two ships after instructing the other men to inform the *Discovery* and organise a party to fetch off the mails.[5]

The *Morning* under Captain Colbeck, and a second relief ship, the Scottish steam whaler *Terra Nova*, skippered by Captain Henry MacKay, an experienced master with the Dundee whaling fleet, had arrived on 5 January 1904.[6] 'It was a thrilling moment approaching the ships,' wrote Wilson. 'No one was expected and everyone was below. The watchman funnily enough never saw us till we were quite close up and then each ship thought we were stragglers from the other ship.' Eventually four Scots whaling men realised they were strangers, but spoke 'such perfect Dundee' that Scott and Wilson found them hard to understand. However, the two gathered that the Government had stepped in with the *Terra Nova*. After shaking hands all round, the commander of the National Antarctic Expedition and its second surgeon, almost unrecognisable—'sun scorched, unwashed, unshaven and in rags'[7]—boarded the *Morning* and were made very welcome.

They learned of the state of affairs in London regarding the expedition, both through Captain Colbeck and through the orders and letters he carried. The two Societies, unable to raise the funds themselves for a second relief voyage, had been obliged to appeal to the Government. An Admiralty Committee had been formed which despatched the *Morning* and the more powerful *Terra Nova* to relieve Scott, whose orders left no doubt (on the grounds of expense) that he must abandon the *Discovery*, rather than spend another year in the Antarctic. This mandate left him in 'a very cruel position'. Even under ordinary conditions, Scott maintained, no sailor could lightly abandon his ship. 'But the ties which bound us to the *Discovery*', he wrote later, 'were very far beyond the ordinary; they involved a depth of sentiment which cannot be surprising, when it is remembered what we had been through in her and what a comfortable home she had proved in all the rigours of this Southern region'.

The *Terra Nova* had been quickly and well equipped by the Government for the voyage to the Antarctic. Because of the need for haste, she was towed through the Suez Canal by a relay of cruisers at a speed (thought Scott) that must have surprised the barnacles on her stout wooden sides.[8] By the end of November 1903 she lay off Hobart, Tasmania, to be joined by the *Morning*, which had wintered in Lyttelton. The two ships departed from Sandy Bay on 6 December 1903 on a wearying voyage to the south. Colbeck had given MacKay written instructions as to his future movements, telling him to abide by those rather than the earlier (Admiralty) ones. He also altered their track further to the east and acted independently as regards the stores, coal, gun cotton etc., informing the Admiralty Committee in writing afterwards of what he had done. Colbeck found the faster vessel's 'asinine tactics' of running rings round the slower *Morning* a hindrance at sea, although occasionally amusing.

The relief ships had met their first iceberg on 23 December and entered the pack early on 26 December in lat. 62°35′ S. long. 179°W. MacKay and some of his officers came on board the *Morning* for Christmas dinner. Earlier on Christmas Day, the *Morning*'s doctor (Davidson), who was making a representative collection of birds from the trip, added to these a number from an iceberg nearby. Many toasts were drunk in the evening to those at home and the master of the *Terra Nova* was evidently keen to make a night of it. 'Poor old MacKay!' wrote Colbeck, 'I thought he was never going back to his ship that night. He didn't, as a matter of fact. He did not leave us until about 3 a.m. Boxing Day! having told the Second Mate to keep a good look-out during his absence and that he would be back before dark. *N.B. It did not get dark until Feby. 22nd.*'[9]

Captain Colbeck attributed the ships' good run through the pack to his decision to follow the easterly course and to his experience during the previous voyage. They reached the open water of the Ross Sea in lat. 70°22′ S., resulting in a happy New Year's Day 1904, after less than four-and-a-half days' actual steaming, a week earlier, he reckoned, than any previous expedition. They passed a hundred miles east of Cape Adare, giving the land a wide berth until Franklin Island, where a party landed to search for a record from the *Discovery*. None was found. On 4 January they left the island and steered for McMurdo Sound, through open water as far as Beaufort Island, where they worked through loose pack for eighteen hours. They then proceeded at full speed through open water to the edge of the fast ice, eighteen miles north of the *Discovery*, which they sighted at 12.40 p.m. on 5 January, nearly three weeks earlier than the previous voyage.

Sledge parties transported mails, meat and vegetables across to the *Discovery* from the relief ships, which experienced considerable difficulty at the ice edge in McMurdo Sound with sudden gales and oncoming icebergs. Killer whales were also a menace, and badly frightened at least one of the party on their way to the *Discovery*, swimming underneath and cracking the ice that he was walking on.[10]

On 13 January 1904, Captain Scott wrote to Captain Colbeck, telling him that the sawing work of the *Discovery* team was a waste of time, that there was a lot of equipment to be transferred if the *Discovery* were abandoned and that the prospect seemed increasingly likely. He planned to begin the transfer as soon as possible and to use the main camp on the sea ice as an entrepôt for the sledging parties. The various articles would be sent in order: scientific collections and note books, instruments, scientific library and books of value, and finally private effects. Royds and two men would be sent to try to clear ice with explosives at the *Morning*'s end and Captain MacKay of the *Terra Nova* would be asked to help. Scott ended this letter by saying, 'I hope your throat is better. It is dismal work looking to the North and contemplating the prospect.'[11] There were still nearly 20 miles of ice between the *Discovery* and the open sea.

On 15 January, blasting began at the ice edge with qualified success only, the ice going out or not, almost of its own accord. The scientific records and collections were sledged over a poor ice surface to the *Morning* and *Terra Nova* and Scott became increasingly pessimistic about freeing the *Discovery*. On 11 February, Captain Colbeck received a copy of Scott's arrangements for abandoning the *Discovery*, although the ice was by then going out consistently.[12] Colbeck was optimistic about her chances and Scott went to see him the following day when there were still two and a half miles of solid ice between the two ships. With only three weeks to go before their orders would oblige them to leave her, it was a question simply of whether the ice would break up faster than the season would close in. The ice was eight feet thick, no easy task to bore. The two relief ships were still nearly two miles from the *Discovery* on 13 February 1904 but the next day, amazingly, saw the excitement of her release, as recorded by Captain Colbeck.

## THE RELEASE OF THE *DISCOVERY*

Feby. 14th was the *day of days*. We had a strong ENE wind and light NW swell, the best of conditions for our work. We dislodged about 600 yds. before noon and had the pleasure of seeing it drift Northwards and leave a clear ice face for the swell to act on. In the afternoon the ice broke away as quickly as we could fire the charges and by 4.30 we had crossed the bridge of 8 foot ice and were working in 3 to 4 feet thick. ... I began to think we might possibly reach the *Discovery* before midnight.

I shall never forget that last two hours ... Slowly and steadily we worked towards them, inch by inch, one might almost say, but always getting nearer, and then that burst of enthusiasm, that fanatical yell, and that cheer after cheer that went up on all sides, when we forced the last piece and the Union Jack was unfurled at Hut Point, rings in my ears yet ... My own hat came off and I yelled as hard as anyone, not that I wanted to, but simply because I had to. I had to shout or do something to ease my feelings. I had caught the fever as bad as any of them. Scott was terribly excited. He came on board as soon as I got alongside the ice face and could scarcely speak. It meant all the difference of complete and comparative success to him and there was not a happier man living than Scott on that night.

Colbeck's elation was mirrored in the *Discovery*. It was while dinner was being eaten on board earlier that same day that the excitement began with a shout down the hatchway, 'The ships are coming, Sir!' to Scott.

There was no more dinner, and in one minute we were racing for Hut Point, where a glorious sight met our view. The ice was breaking up right across the strait, and with a rapidity we had not thought possible. No sooner was one great floe borne away than a dark streak cut its way into the solid sheet that remained and carved out another, to feed the broad stream of pack which was hurrying away to the north-west.

... Meanwhile our small community in their nondescript, tattered garments stood breathlessly watching this wonderful scene. For long intervals we remained almost spell-bound, and then a burst of frenzied cheering broke out ... By eleven o'clock all the thick ice had vanished ... a few minutes later the *Terra Nova* forged ahead and came crashing into the open, to be followed almost immediately by her stout little companion, and soon both ships were firmly anchored to all that remains of the *Discovery*'s prison, the wedge that still holds in our small bay.[13]

The ice that encased her was finally cracked by explosive charges some two days later. The last one shook the ship from stem to stern. The cracks widened, there was a gurgle of water and a creaking aft. The *Discovery*'s stern 'rose with a jump as the keel was freed from the ice that had held it down. Then, as the great mass of ice on our port hand slowly glided out to sea, our good ship swung gently round and lay peacefully riding to her anchors with the blue water lapping against her sides.'[14]

Scott concluded his account of these memorable days by writing

Thus it was that after she had afforded us shelter and comfort for two full years, and after we had borne a heavy anxiety on her behalf, our good ship was spared to take us homeward. On February 16, 1904, the *Discovery* came to her own again—the right to ride the high seas.[15]

That evening, the ship's company landed at Hut Point and assembled round the cross erected earlier to the memory of their shipmate, George Vince. Captain Scott read the prayers, while all stood bare-headed. He thought the cross should endure for centuries in a climate where nothing decays; he was not to know that nine years later, another cross to his own and his companions' memories would stand nearby, in full view of *Discovery*'s winter quarters.[16]

# EIGHT

## Homeward Voyage, Homecoming, Expedition Results

### HOMEWARD BOUND, 1904

THE ANTARCTIC DID NOT PART LIGHTLY with the *Discovery*. Steam was raised on 17 February just in time to prevent her striking the ice-foot broadside on, after dragging her anchor. In attempting to round Hut Point the same morning in a gale, the ship crashed head foremost onto a shoal and stopped dead with her masts quivering. Scott wrote, 'We took the shore thus at about 11 a.m., and the hours that followed were truly the most dreadful I have ever spent. Each moment the ship came down with a sickening thud which shook her from stem to stern, and each thud seemed to show more plainly that, strong as was her build, she could not long survive such awful blows.'[1] An attempt to force her over ended in failure. The engines were pronounced useless, as their inlets were choked. By 3 p.m. Scott decided that nothing more could be done until the gale abated. Their situation was horrifying.

During a dreary and almost silent evening meal, with the ship aground below the summit of Hut Point, on which they could all see the cross erected to Vince, the officer of the watch burst in and reported her working astern. The current had turned and was running strongly in the opposite direction. The inlets were free again, the engines began to revolve and the *Discovery* slipped free. That comparatively little damage was sustained proved the solid structure of the ship. Their little bay had indeed tendered, as Scott remarked, a treacherous farewell.

The *Discovery* coaled only 50 tons from the *Terra Nova*, although it had been previously agreed that MacKay would transfer 100. Colbeck unselfishly spared twenty-five tons, an action much appreciated by Scott. It meant that before making for New Zealand, the *Discovery* could try to venture to the west of Cape North and the Balleny Islands, in the event sailing over land reported in 1840 by Lieut. Charles Wilkes, commander of the United States Exploring Expedition.[2] The little *Morning* was obliged to return north alone under sail, facing very severe gales from the north-west, dead ahead of her for days on end.

The three ships had a rendezvous at the Aucklands, a group of uninhabited islands south of New Zealand. The *Discovery* arrived first on 15 March 1904, with only ten tons of coal remaining. She was followed some days later by the *Terra Nova* (from which more coal was obtained) and only twenty-four hours later still by the *Morning*. Here the ships' companies were able to enjoy the beauty of the green earth after the desolation of the Antarctic. Off Cape Adare, the *Discovery* had been obliged to ship her spare rudder, the other having been shattered somehow. Scott remarked that despite the facilities afforded by the rudder-well, the task was no easy one, both rudder and fittings being very ponderous. On departing from McMurdo Sound, all hands, officers and men, had had to labour extremely hard to get the ship coaled, watered and into sea trim. A scare was caused by the failure of the pumps. Scott was able ruefully to contrast his own ship's continual heavy rolling with the steadier *Terra Nova*, which followed in her wake with scarcely a movement. Wilson provided more specific detail writing that 'A roll of 48° to starboard rather upset things at dinner. There were wonderful crashes. I saw one man's lap receive a bowl of brown sugar, a plate of stewed plums, a glass of port and a cup of coffee.'[3]

The three ships proceeded in company from the Auckland Islands to Lyttelton, New Zealand, where they received a tremendous welcome on Good Friday, 1 April 1904. The *Discovery* completed her circumnavigation by sailing east from New Zealand largely in the latitude of the fifties south, finishing her magnetic survey in the Falkland Islands and searching for the non-existent 'Dogherty Islands' *en route*. The first high-latitude soundings were taken in the South Pacific Ocean, showing an average depth of over 2,000 fathoms. The *Morning* arrived while they were anchored in Port Stanley. She had rounded the Horn (unlike the *Discovery* which sailed through the Straits of Magellan) and was said to have burst her old engine's high-pressure cylinder.[4]

Edward Wilson's diary entry on 26 July 1904 in the South Atlantic, some days out of Port Stanley, provides a vivid description of the gale experienced that day and is also a fine tribute to the *Discovery* (and her makers) on the homeward leg of her maiden voyage.

In some of the squalls it blew as hard as we have ever had it, up to a hurricane force, and the seas were forty and fifty feet, immense as only the South Atlantic can make them. Every minute or two came a vivid flare of blue lightning that dazzled one, like splashes of flame all round and then the most pitchy blackness for a second and then the sails and masts and rigging came out again, like an indian ink drawing on a grey background, and the shriek and the roar of the storm in the rigging even drowned every scrap of the thunder. ... There is nothing made by man more wonderful than a sailing ship and to realise this fully one must spend some hours at night under more sail than appears quite safe in a sou' westerly gale in the roaring forties with squalls of force 10 and 11 by Beaufort's scale. And then, one must spend eight hours bumping and grinding the very soul out of her on the rocks, in the ice and the fury of the Antarctic southerly blizzard. One may see her gripped in ice and half buried in snow drift and she waits patiently, one may see her smiling fresh with new paint in the tropics and she looks beautiful, one may have felt her punching her way in the face of head winds when all else fails, by steam, or rolling till she creaks and groans again in a flat calm on a long and heavy swell. She may look obstinate, she may be trying, but wait till you see her tried to the utmost and when she has to bend or break she is like a really perfect human being and she bends double first. Then you can realise how instinct with life and therefore lovable is the work of man, if only he has done his best.[5]

## HOMECOMING AND EXPEDITION RESULTS

Both vessels made slow passages to the north, that of the *Discovery* in the tropics doubtless being particularly felt because of the presence of a decomposing specimen of sea elephant carried on the skid beams.[6] A more pleasant feature of the return voyage was a visit to the Prince of Monaco's yacht, *Princesse Alice*, in the Azores. The *Discovery* arrived at Spithead on 10 September to a hearty welcome from Sir Clements Markham, Sir Allen Young and cheers from all the men-of-war. Markham sailed round in the *Discovery* to the Thames, where she berthed in the East India Dock on 15 September. Shackleton was there and when everyone else had gone off with friends, Scott, Markham and Shackleton dined together and had 'a very jolly evening'.[7] The indomitable *Morning* eventually arrived in Plymouth towards the end of the month, her engines and boilers in a wretched state. She was towed to Devonport to await instructions, a tiny vessel among a great fleet of battleships and cruisers.

The members of the National Antarctic Expedition including those of the *Morning* were reunited on 7 November 1904, when a nervous Captain Scott gave a memorable lecture at the Royal Albert Hall to a full house. Medals were awarded to Scott and a special presentation was made to Captain Colbeck of a silver loving-cup in the form of a globe supported by three seals, showing the tracks of the *Morning*. Sir Clements Markham received a silver sledge (later mounted on a stand of *Discovery* oak) from the officers and men of the *Discovery*, a gift that he valued immensely and is depicted beside him in the portrait that hangs in the Royal Geographical Society.[8]

## HOME

The *Discovery* had completed a rewarding first voyage and the expedition she carried made a splendid contribution to Antarctic geography and science. The interior of the unknown southern continent had been explored for the first time, while some questions had been answered and others posed in relation to its nature and to the life of the creatures round its coasts. Scott's narrative of *The Voyage of the 'Discovery'* published in 1905 was a notable addition to polar literature, as were the two delightful volumes of the

*South Polar Times*, reproduced in facsimile in 1907. Bernacchi's summary of the achievements of the National Antarctic Expedition is a fair evaluation.

> The expedition had returned after more than three years' absence with the richest results, geographical and scientific ever brought from high southern latitudes. A vast new land (King Edward VII Land) had been discovered. Many hundreds of miles of unknown coast, with ranges of mountains of great height and immense glaciers emptying into the Ice Barrier, had been seen and plotted. The Antarctic Plateau, averaging nearly 10,000 feet in height, had been found and partly traversed where, subsequently, the South Pole itself was found to be situated, proving that the Antarctic Continent was almost all under ice without vegetation or animal life of any kind. Never had a polar expedition come home with so great a harvest of original research work . . .
>
> The specialists of *Discovery* were lone-handed and were confronted with many unknown difficult problems. Hodgson always must be regarded as the pioneer of Antarctic marine biology . . . Ferrar is the pioneer of Antarctic geology. The extensive physical work, part of an international programme, for which I was responsible, was one of the principal objects of the expedition. It was completed. In due time the scientific work was reduced, discussed and published in many large volumes by the Royal Society.[9]

Comparisons are always difficult to make and it is open to question whether indeed the *Discovery*'s findings surpassed those of Cook in 1772–5 which in Scott's words 'defined the Antarctic region', or those of Ross in 1839–43, which 'discovered it'.[10] However, there is no doubt that members of the National Antarctic Expedition of 1901–4 stood squarely on the shoulders of these giants and were the first to look far into the continent itself. It was not long before Shackleton and Scott himself were to return and continue the work of the *Discovery* in the Ross Sea area of the Antarctic, the scene of what was later called by one who served with both of them 'the heroic age of Antarctic exploration'.[11]

Sir John Murray paid the expedition a fine tribute, given his disagreement with Sir Clements Markham early in its history. In February 1905, after hearing Captain Scott's paper on the geographical results, he generously expressed his 'very high appreciation of the manner in which the work of this expedition has been carried out, and the large additions to knowledge which it has furnished', particularly the evidence, from the observations of the *Discovery*, for the existence of an Antarctic continent. He would 'yield to no-one in the appreciation . . . of the most excellent work . . . done by this expedition, and the great contribution to human knowledge which it has furnished'.[12]

# NINE

## PURCHASE BY THE HUDSON'S BAY COMPANY, 1905, VOYAGES 1905 AND 1906

*Many great merchant expeditions set out in the last four centuries from the shores of these Islands and materially altered the lands to which they sailed. Of these, none was more prominent than the Hudson's Bay Company. Its resounding title, 'The Adventurers of England Trading into Hudson's Bay', aptly conveys the spirit which has imbued it from its Royal origins in the 17th century to the present day. Its interests have swelled from the early trading posts, where furs were the principal article of trade, to the vast commercial undertakings of the 20th century, when the Company is active in so many spheres of exploration and development in every province of Canada.*[1]

Sir Winston Churchill

TO THE NORTH OF THE MAINLAND of North America is an archipelago of Arctic islands, extending to within 200 miles of the Pole. The discovery of a sea route or north-west passage from Atlantic to Pacific, through the maze of often ice-bound waterways surrounding the Arctic islands, was the objective of a number of British naval expeditions in the first half of the nineteenth century, an aim eventually achieved only with tragic loss of men and ships. Today these channels are being considered again as shipping routes for companies interested in the exploitation of the natural gas, oil and mineral reserves of the far north. The improved design of icebreakers and ice-strengthened ships, more detailed charts and greater knowledge of ice and its distribution, have enabled modern vessels to operate in certain of these ice-infested and hazardous waters for longer seasons and in higher latitudes than ever before.

## THE HUDSON'S BAY COMPANY

The icy waters of one passage north of 60° were, however, navigated yearly by wooden sailing ships for two centuries and a half, beginning with the *Nonsuch* in 1668 and ending with the *Discovery*. This was Hudson Strait, which leads into the great basin of Hudson Bay, both first entered and explored in 1610–11 by Henry Hudson in an earlier

*Discovery*. The successful voyage of the *Nonsuch* opened up a sea route to trade in furs with the American Indians and led to the incorporation of the Hudson's Bay Company by royal charter in 1670. On 2 May of that year King Charles II granted a charter under the Great Seal of England to the eighteen Adventurers or supporters of the voyages, granting them, under the governorship of Prince Rupert, the 'sole Trade and Commerce of all those Seas Streightes Bayes Rivers Lakes Creekes and Soundes in whatsoever Latitude they shall bee that lye within the entrance of the Streightes commonly called Hudson's Streightes together with all the Landes and Territorys upon the Countryes Coastes and confynes of the Seas Bayes Lakes Rivers Creekes and Soundes aforesaid that are not actually possessed by or granted to any of our subjectes or possessed by the Subjectes of any other Christian Prince or State'. They were to be the 'true and absolute Lordes and Proprietors' of this vast territory, to be known as Rupert's Land.[2] The Adventurers were effectively given the modern provinces of Ontario and Quebec north of the Laurentian watershed and west of the Labrador boundary, Manitoba, most of Saskatchewan, the southern half of Alberta, and much of the Northwest Territories, an area of 1,486,000 square miles comprising 38.7 per cent of modern Canada.[3]

The fur trade proved profitable in the early years of the Company and three wooden forts were built on James Bay (the southern arm of Hudson Bay). These were Fort Charles (later called Fort Rupert River and Rupert's House), Moose and Albany, all established before 1685. Wars in Europe against the French had their repercussions in the Bay, where there was at least one naval engagement. By the late eighteenth century none the less many lengthy inland journeys had been made by such men as Kelsey, Stewart, Henday and Hearne, with the aim of stimulating peaceful trade with the Indians. British rivalry with the French continued until the conquest of French Canada in 1759, that *annus mirabilis* or year of victories. Ten years later, the North West Company, based in Montreal, began to emerge as a competitor, until by 1776 it had become a power in the land. The Hudson's Bay Company's rivalry with the Northwesters, whom Washington Irving called the Lords of the Lakes and Forests, was based on the competition of two routes—Hudson Bay versus the St Lawrence River—for the trade of the fur regions to the north. Each side established posts in the interior and endeavoured to wrest the fur trade from the other. The two companies eventually began to unite in 1821 after years of 'violence, bloodshed, and a bewildering flood of seizures, warrants, arrests and court actions', under the name of the senior enterprise.[4]

A great period followed in the history of the enlarged and reorganised Hudson's Bay Company. In 1821 parliament confirmed the charter which gave the right of exclusive trade which was extended to the rest of the Northwest Territories, north to the Arctic Ocean and west to the Pacific on condition that it assumed responsibility for law and order and acknowledged its duties towards the Indians.[5] For half a century the Company 'had control of a truly continental domain ... where it traded with the many natives in the vast area—from the boundary of Labrador to the Pacific and from the lower reaches of the Mackenzie River to the American passes over the Rockies—practically in unbroken peace, while from time to time wars almost of extermination broke out south of the border'.[6]

The officers (chief factors and chief traders, often known as wintering partners) were given a share in the annual profits of the fur trade. For forty years after the merger, the power and efficiency of Sir George Simpson, the Governor-in-Chief—as he became formally known in 1839—dominated this fur empire. Known as the 'little Emperor', this short, tough, illegitimate Scot not only ruled, but travelled the length and breadth of Rupert's Land and the north-west. The officers of the Company were men of integrity, with a tremendous sense of duty in their relations with the Indians and with others in the Company's employ. They 'were more than fur traders; they were the builders of a nation'.[7] Many of their names are well known in the history of Arctic exploration: Samuel Hearne (who travelled with the Indians to the mouth of the Coppermine River), Dease and Simpson (who explored much of the north coast of America) and Dr John Rae (who found the first relics of the lost Franklin expedition of 1845–8). Adventure books for boys by R. M. Ballantyne (himself a former Company man), such as *The young fur traders*, *Hudson Bay* and *Ungava*, and those by James Fenimore Cooper, kept not only young readers but many an older one spellbound.

By the mid-nineteenth century, the need for change became apparent, as immigrants from Britain and Europe wished to settle in the west. With the Deed of Surrender of 1869 (given royal assent in 1870), the General Court of the Company gave back to Queen Victoria the lands given by Charles II to their forebears. The Company left 'a record of achievement which facilitated the task of the new Government. Peace had been maintained in the wilderness, trading had been conducted without violence, principles of justice had been established and the exploration successfully accomplished has continued to be of the utmost service, even in modern times.'[8]

The transformation from monopoly to open competition in the new Dominion of Canada established in 1867, a land of pioneering settlements and migrating peoples, was on the whole successfully made by the old Company. The fur trade continued, but assumed a lesser importance and a chain of large retail stores was set up in the cities to meet the needs of the settlers and to diversify the Company's interests. Many of the old wintering partners were not happy with the changes involving the abolition of commissions and the consequent breakdown of the long-standing promotion ladder. The *métis* (half-breeds of the Red River area) were also apprehensive of the change and it can be argued that the new arrangement was of little advantage to the native peoples. With the opening of the north to free traders, trappers and adventurers, the Indians became demoralised, while game herds and to some extent fur bearers were destroyed. 'It is an unquestionable fact', wrote a former HBC man (Philip Godsell, who joined in 1906 and who served the Company for twenty years), 'that so long as the Hudson's Bay Company enjoyed a monopoly in the North, the fur trade followed an orderly existence, while the Indians were on the whole fairly happy and contented. This of course was in no small measure due to the upright character and fine loyalty of the employees at the posts. . . .

For the soul-searing solitudes of the isolated posts bred an unflinching honor, an undeniable zeal, and a spirit of sacrifice in those who carried on the wilderness trade. These men, most of whom came out as lads from Scotland and spent their entire lives in the service, knew one interest only and that was "The Company". .... Forty years after the surrender of the charter, this feeling and undeviating loyalty still remained a dominating influence in all the older districts, and it was from traders of this type that we younger men received our training.'[9]

The years that *Discovery* was in the Company's service in the north (1905–11 and 1918) were among the last before the railways, motor transport, aeroplanes and radio shortened both time and distance there. As Charles Camsell pointed out in his introduction to *Arctic trader*, Godsell joined the service when the lifestyle of Post managers at many of the northern trading posts had hardly changed over a hundred years. Summer transport and communication were by York boat and birch bark canoe; in winter by the carriole and dog sled. Post managers were obliged by their isolation to depend on themselves and their own resourcefulness for their very survival. The Fur Lords to some extent still ruled the north. At the proper season, the annual visit of 'the ship from England' was awaited eagerly by the posts on the shores of Hudson Bay. From 1905 to 1911 that ship was the *Discovery*. She has the distinction of being one of the last of a line of wooden sailing ships, which for well over two centuries had made the stormy transatlantic voyage from London, through the ice-infested and uncharted waters of Hudson Strait and Bay, to the Company posts at the mouth of the Churchill, Hayes, Albany, Moose and Rupert rivers in the southern portion of the Bay.

## THE *DISCOVERY* IN HUDSON'S BAY COMPANY OWNERSHIP

The Honourable Company became the owner of the *Discovery* in January 1905. There had been hopes that she would continue as an exploring ship after the return of the National Antarctic Expedition in 1904 or even as a government vessel pursuing fishery investigations in the North Sea in conjunction with the International Council for the Exploration of the Sea.[10] These hopes were dashed when it was announced in the Press that the Joint Committee of the Expedition had been forced to sell a vessel which cost £50,000 to the Hudson's Bay Company for £10,000, despite Captain Scott's claim that she was a better ship than when she was launched. 'But it is hoped', reported the *Morning Post*, 'that her special equipment as a scientific ship will not be entirely removed and that the board of the Hudson's Bay Company will permit her to be used, as occasion may present itself, for subsidiary scientific work in the Arctic regions.'[11] Had she passed to the whaling fleet, it would have been necessary to gut her entirely for conversion to a whaler.

Late in 1904, the Company was seeking a replacement for the *Stork*, which had been forced by ice to winter off Charlton Island, James Bay, from October 1904 to August

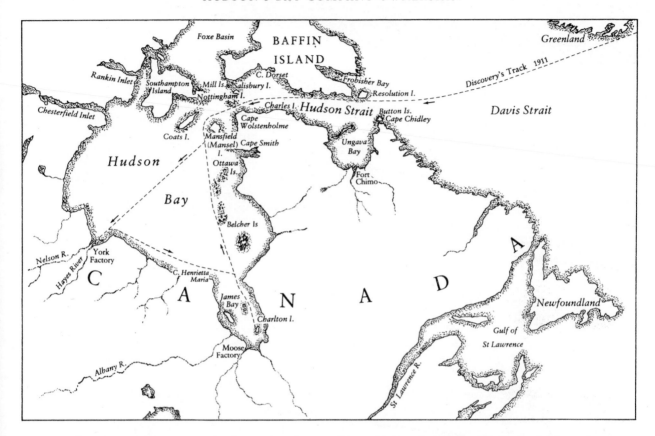

The *Discovery*'s voyages to Hudson Bay and James Bay, 1905-11 and 1918-19, with the track of the 1911 voyage to York Factory and Charlton Island approximately plotted

1905, arriving in London only on 4 October 1905, and thus missing a year's shipment or 'outfit'.[12]

Messrs Williams and Sage, Engineering and Nautical Experts, Licensed Valuers and Arbitrators of Bishopsgate in the City of London, recommended on 31 December 1904 the purchase of the *Discovery* as a steamer (auxiliary), which might be adapted for the Company's service.[13] They had heard the previous day that the French Geological Society and others had surveyed the ship with a view to buying her and had therefore to move quickly. After further discussion about the depth of water at Charlton Island in relation to the *Discovery*, Messrs Williams and Sage were authorised to take formal possession of her on 17 January 1905 for the Hudson's Bay Company.[14]

These marine superintendents placed her in a graving dock (Messrs Glengale Iron-works' dry dock) the following week so that she could swiftly be examined, repaired, refitted and adapted more cheaply than afloat at a distance. Messrs Williams and Sage considered the lifting propeller in the banjo frame 'a most objectionable style and not necessary for your trade'. To dispense with this, only a new tail shaft would be required, since both the working and spare propellers ought to be adaptable to the new shaft. A more radical change had been made in the case of the *Pelican*, another HBC ship, also with a lifting propeller when bought.[15] The *Discovery*'s windlass, winding engine, galley stove, skylight, ladders, gun metal and brass were sold as scrap or for reuse, being unserviceable for the HBC trade. An anchor crane was supplied by Messrs W. and E. Moore, who had bought the windlass and winding engine. By mid-April 1905 the vessel was ready to be undocked and placed in the Company's berth in the West India Docks (London); the necessary alterations and additions were nearly complete. Only the painting, graining, cleaning and varnishing, reeving the rigging, bending the sails etc. had still to be done.[16] Messrs Williams and Sage thought carefully about the *Discovery*'s precise coal requirements, given that she had also to carry a considerable amount of cargo. They calculated that 180 tons of 'special double screened Welsh steam coals' would be sufficient for the 30 days' steaming to make the journey down the river Thames (and across the Atlantic under sail alone) and through the Hudson Strait to Charlton and back depending on ice conditions.[17]

The *Discovery* had effectively been converted from a scientific and exploring ship to a cargo vessel for the Hudson's Bay Company. There seems to have been no attempt to retain her scientific gear. The magnetic and dredging laboratories at the sides of the vessel had been extended to accommodate the officers below the bridge. The wardroom and other accommodation between decks had been removed to provide space for the holds. The crew had quarters in the forecastle, and there was one small passenger cabin with four berths. A steam windlass had been erected on the forecastle head and the stiffening taken out of the ship to give a clear hold—the cross timbers and bulkheads being cleared out for cargo. The clear hold space between the collision bulkhead and the boiler room bulkhead permitted the maximum possible carrying capacity.[18]

The ship was to continue in the Hudson's Bay Company's ownership for the next eighteen years. The years 1905 to 1911 were spent on the yearly run from London across the Atlantic to Hudson Strait in northern Canada, then westwards through the ice-infested Strait into Hudson Bay and south to James Bay to unload at Charlton Island. Here the 'returns' (mainly furs) were shipped and a few passengers taken on board for the home-ward voyage. These voyages of the *Discovery* have been called dull and routine,[19] but this is untrue: the navigation of Davis Strait, Hudson Strait and Hudson Bay was neither. The strength of the *Discovery*'s bow and the power of her engine were much needed during this passage.

Happily, the very extensive records of the two greatest chartered companies, the East India Company and the Hudson's Bay Company, survive to this day. The records of the former are in London; those of the latter, after some three centuries in London, moved in 1974 to Winnipeg, where the Company's headquarters now are. Among the many historic and fascinating documents in the archives is one especially remarkable for its continuity. This is a large vellum-bound book of ships' movements, covering the years 1719 to 1929, an epitome of the maritime history of the Honourable Company.[20] Under each different route are listed the name of a vessel, her master, and the dates of her call at various posts—or of her passing certain headlands outward and homeward. The collection of ships' logs includes those of the *Discovery* commanded by Captain Ford, for the years 1906 to 1908 and 1910 to 1911.


## 1905 HBC VOYAGE

No log for the 1905 voyage has yet been found and details are scarce. The command of the *Discovery* was given to Captain Alexander Gray of Peterhead (aged 65), Master of the *Pelican* (because Captain Ford in the *Stork* was beset in the ice), with A. Cleveland Smith as Mate.[21] It was agreed that the following year (1906), Captain Ford would relieve Captain Gray of the command of the *Discovery*, who would then resume command of the *Pelican* (until 1908, when he presumably retired).[22] During this first voyage in the Company's ownership, the *Discovery* left the West India Dock on 15 June 1905, called at Aberdeen from 21 to 22 June, where the carpenter and two Able Seamen deserted and for whom replacements were signed on.

She anchored at Charlton Island (James Bay) on 27 August and started her return trip on 8 September, passing the Lizard in Cornwall on 1 November and berthing in the West India Dock two days later.[23] The *Pelican*, commanded by G. F. Lovegrove, the other supply ship that year, departed from London on 17 June. She visited the posts on the Labrador coast, then York Factory and Churchill (on the west coast of Hudson Bay), and returned via Fort Chimo (on Ungava Bay).[24]

Captain Gray was an experienced sailor in polar seas and a 'tall grey-haired man with a leonine head, a weatherbeaten countenance and an extremely gruff voice'.[25] Sadly, one of the substitute Able Seamen lost his life in lat. 60°54′N. An entry in the official log (copied from the now missing mate's log) shows that 'The watch went aloft to secure the weather clew of the Main upper topsail. At this time it was blowing very hard and the ship labouring very heavily, A. Curley A.B. lost his hold on the yard and fell into the sea and was drowned. The night was very dark and a tremendous sea running—it was impossible to render any assistance. This sad event has cast a gloom over the ship as Curley was a smart sailor and general favourite.' It was noted that the Articles were in a 'dilapidated condition through having been soaked with sea water for several days in bad weather during the voyage'. The scale of provisions for the crew per man is the remaining item of interest from the Crew List and Official Log.[26]

Beef: 1$^1/_2$ lbs. Sunday Tuesday Thursday Saturday
Pork: 1$^1/_4$ lbs. Monday Wednesday Friday

Flour: $^1/_2$ lb. Saturday Tuesday Thursday
Peas: $^1/_3$ lb. Monday Wednesday Friday
Rice: $^1/_2$ lb. Saturday
Water: 3 quarts daily
Bread: 1 oz. daily
Tea: $^1/_8$ oz. daily
Coffee: $^1/_2$ oz. daily
Sugar: 2 ozs. daily
No spirits allowed
Substitutes at Master's option.

## 1906 HBC VOYAGE

Captain John Graham Ford (1849–1925) took command of the *Discovery* in 1906 and remained her master until 1911. Born at Torryburn, near Dunfermline, Fife, he had earlier commanded the barque *Lady Head* on the London–James Bay run from 1891 until 1903, the year she was stranded on Gasket Shoal, thirty miles north of Charlton Island, and abandoned on 25 September.[27] Captain Ford's 1900 voyage of only three months and twenty days in the *Lady Head* was noted in red ink in the 'Book of ships' movements' (HBC Archives) as 'The quickest on record'.

The log of the 1906 *Discovery* voyage to Hudson Bay was kept by G. F. Lovegrove, Chief Officer, who had commanded the *Pelican* the previous year. The *Discovery* cast off from the West India Dock at 5.30 a.m. on 14 June 1906, proceeding with a pilot under steam down the busy river towards the sea. The crew were mustered and found all on board. At noon she arrived at Gravesend, and anchored at the Powder Ground. After being inspected by the Government Inspector, the Powder Barge came alongside and 85 barrels and kegs and two cases of gunpowder were taken on board. A Channel pilot relieved the river pilot, the anchor was weighed and the ship proceeded at full speed. The Channel pilot must have been dropped that evening. Sea watches were kept and regulation lights strictly attended to. The pages of the log were now headed 'Discovery from London to Peterhead'. This port in the north-east of Scotland was reached on 18 June. Some 'fowels' (chickens presumably) were taken on board as stores. The ship proceeded next day out of Peterhead with the engine at full speed.

The pages of the log were now headed 'Discovery from London towards Hudson Bay'. On 20 June, she made 118 nautical miles; on the 21st, 119 nautical miles and on the 23rd, 123 nautical miles. The engines were then stopped for good to make the passage of the North Atlantic under sail alone, no doubt to the joy of Captain Ford, who was a sailor of the old school and no lover of noisy machinery. Next day, the latitude by account was given as 60°02′ N. and observed, 60°14′ N.; longitude by account was given as 18°31′ W. and by chronometer 18°56′ W. The *Discovery* was by then due west of Shetland

and to the south of Iceland. The winds and weather were variable and the daily distance travelled varied accordingly. Gales in early July produced a heavy cross sea, causing the ship to labour and strain heavily, sometimes shipping a quantity of water. The clip hooks of the main fore topgallant sail sheet carried away at 7.45 p.m. on 8 July, causing the sail to split. The following day the gale continued strong, with hard squalls and heavy rain. Seas were shipped fore and aft, washing away the starboard light screen. The position on 9 July was given as latitude (by account) 57°36′N., (by observation) 57°28′N. and longitude (by account) 33°42′W., (by chronometer) 34°21′W. well to the south of Greenland. Foggy weather on 10 July gave way to clearer weather, the ship rolling and straining heavily, with decks continually awash. On 13 July a hard gale in gusts and squalls caused the clew iron of the foresail to carry away. The *Pelican* had, of course, also met gales in the North Atlantic; Philip Godsell, one of the new apprentice clerks on board, described what must have been a similar experience for those in the *Discovery*. 'The sky became a dull leaden colour, the wind rose until it shrieked through the rigging, the sea became black as ink, while the rolling of the boat was terrific, and she creaked and groaned as though in pain. Yet, hour after hour, the lookout for'ard answered the bells with the inevitable cry of "All's well".'[28]

Steam was ordered in the *Discovery* on 16 July and all sail furled in latitude (by account) 58°29′N., (by observation) 58°26′N., and longitude (by account) 36°22′W., (by chronometer) 36°11′W., i.e. to the south-east of Cape Farewell (Kap Farvel), the southern tip of Greenland. All fore- and aft-sails were set for some hours during the evening of 17 July. Several pieces of ice were seen next day, the temperature of the air being 39°F and of the water 43°F. Next day the pack-ice was skirted in foggy weather, and later, all square sail was set, with engines slow. Oil bags were hung over each bow to prevent the sea breaking on board in a strong gale on 19 July. The main topgallant and foresail were handed (furled) during the day. The gale moderated on 20 July, but the ship continued to take heavy seas on board at times. The upper fore- and main topsails and jib were set.

The south cape of Greenland was rounded and a passage made to the north and west under sail or steam, occasionally skirting sea ice, as the ship crossed the 700 miles width of Davis Strait, named after John Davis, who first navigated it in 1585 in two wooden sailing ships, the *Sunneshine* and *Mooneshine*. The 'Land of Resolution' (Resolution Island) was sighted at the entrance to Hudson Strait, which is some 400 miles long and 100 wide, on 26 July. Several icebergs were sighted in the afternoon, no doubt carried south by the Labrador current. The ship was able to work slowly to the west through heavy pack-ice, with steam and sails as required. Occasionally she was beset. At times she was able to forge ahead through open pack. Twelve large icebergs were visible on 29 July and several were passed. The ship became beset and no open water could be seen next morning from the crow's nest. The ice opened out later however and the freshwater tanks were filled from the pools on the floe, the ship being moored to the ice.

By 31 July the *Discovery* was roughly half-way through the Strait. The *Pelican* (bound for York Factory) was sighted that evening about eight miles to the NNE. The following evening, she was bearing west-by-north about eight miles. Viewed from the deck of the *Pelican*, the *Discovery* 'appeared as a mirage, riding in the sky'.[29] The south-east end of Salisbury Island (at the western end of the Strait) bore north-by-east on 2 August in the forenoon. Cape Wolstenholme was sighted at 4 p.m. and the west end of Digges Island at 8 p.m., marking the entrance to Hudson Bay.

Cape Pembroke, Coats Island, was sighted the following afternoon, as the ship proceeded south in the shallow waters of the Bay, steaming through scattered pack-ice, among some heavy floes, on 6 August. During the afternoon of 7 August the ship was stopped several times and soundings of 10 fathoms, 12 fathoms and 100 fathoms were made, until at 4 p.m. Cape Henrietta Maria (marking the western entrance to James Bay) bore west-by-north, six miles away. This cape was named in 1631 after King Charles I's Queen by Captain Thomas James in the *Henrietta Maria*. At 6 p.m. a sounding of 17 fathoms was made, at 8 p.m. the lead was cast in 20 fathoms and at 11.40 p.m. in 23 fathoms. Another shallow sounding of 25 fathoms was made at 2 a.m. next day to the north of Bear Island. Towards noon a strong gale got up with rough choppy sea. By 8 p.m. the sea was subsiding and the ship was stopped and a sounding made in 22 fathoms. On 9 August at 6 a.m. the lead was cast in 30 fathoms. Four hours later the south end of Western Island bore east-by-south. In the afternoon, soundings of 20 fathoms and 10 fathoms were made and by 5.30 p.m. Lisbon Rock was abeam, five miles distant. A hand at the lead took soundings of from 10 to $8^1/_2$ fathoms between 7.30 p.m. and 9.25 p.m. when the ship dropped anchor off Charlton Island, her destination at the southern end of James Bay.

Next morning at six, the anchor was weighed and the *Discovery* proceeded at half speed towards the bar, a hand at the lead sounding in. She anchored near the bar buoy in 10 fathoms at 8.45 a.m. to await the tide. The crew worked at rigging cargo gear and making ready for moving alongside the wharf. About 11 a.m. Mr McKenzie arrived. He was manager of the Hudson's Bay Company post of Moose Factory, first established in 1673 on the mainland to the south of Charlton Island. The manager and his staff travelled in the *Inenew*, a small vessel used to transport goods in James Bay. The *Inenew* steamed away again at noon, taking with her to Moose a Mrs Cockram [*sic*] and her child, who had been passengers from London in the *Discovery*, as well as the Second Engineer, Joseph Love, who was to join the *Inenew* in place of her chief engineer on 15 August. Amid rain, lightning and thunder, with Mr W. L. Miller (who was in charge of the Charlton depot) acting as pilot on board, the *Discovery* anchored abreast the wharf at Charlton Island in 40 fathoms to wait for the tide. The night watch was set. The following morning (11 August), the anchor was hove up and she steamed closer in, anchoring in 60 fathoms.

All hands worked at mooring ship, which was hove alongside the wharf and moored ahead and astern by noon. The main hatches were taken off and the bulk of the cargo broken. The crew were at work in rainy, unsettled weather, washing the decks, cleaning the ship and pumping her out. Her draught on arrival was found to be 17 feet 2 inches fore and 16 feet aft. Just over 104 tons of coal or patent fuel had been used for the 58-day outward passage, leaving nearly 76 tons in the bunkers. No work was done the next day, Sunday, which was instead spent ashore exploring the low sandy wooded island.

## CHARLTON ISLAND AND ITS HISTORY

A modern visitor to Charlton Island, Dr W. A. Kenyon of the Royal Ontario Museum, Toronto, has described this uninhabited island with great charm. He tells us that it is some eighteen miles long, dotted with small shallow lakes, much of it open parkland and meadows, sprinkled with the occasional evergreen. There are fairly dense stands of spruce round most of the ponds and along many of the streams. Two short ridges rise to about one hundred feet, but otherwise the island is a low, undulating, sandy plain. Extensive reefs and shoals extend from its shores.

> Wandering inland from the old Hudson's Bay Company depot, you find that the parkland . . . and indeed the whole island, is composed of a fine, white sand, covered with a thick spongy carpet of caribou-moss. Blueberries and strawberries are scattered about with incredible profusion; cranberries and saskatoon berries . . . are quite plentiful. It is an odd sensation . . . to stretch out on the moss on a warm, sunny afternoon and be enveloped with the sweet, sticky smell of crushed berries. As you lie there you suddenly realise that Charlton Island is a strangely muted place. The geese and ducks that nest all over it are quiet and unobtrusive, as though they were reluctant to announce their presence till their young ones are old enough to fly. The loons are a bit more boisterous, but only if they are well off-shore. At home, they too are silent. Beaver are plentiful on the ponds and streams, but they go quietly and industriously about their business. On bare patches of sand or along the beach, the tracks of foxes and lynx will frequently appear, though the animals themselves are neither seen nor heard. There is nothing to mark their passing but the line of their footprints. If you follow their tracks, you find that they never deviate from their fixed path. Never do they stop to see if there might be some tasty or intriguing object lurking behind a boulder, or beneath a fallen log. They clearly have some urgent and personal matters to attend to on the other side of the island.
>
> As you continue your explorations, your impressions gradually sort themselves out. You reach a point, finally, where you are no longer bothered by the apparent contradiction between the feelings of silence and solitude on the one hand, and the richness and vitality of the living things on the other. For you know that in some distant valley, near the beginning of time, another explorer must have felt the same way as he set out one evening to stroll through *his* garden, thoughtfully munching an apple.[30]

A compelling, fiercer impression of Northern Canada is given by P. G. Downes:

The lashing, screaming wind and the sudden vengeful bursts of cold rain mocked and intensified a consuming restlessness with which every one in the North seems sooner or later to become obsessed. It is as if he were in self-protection forced to share the unseen movement and the rhythm of the natural world about him. It is almost as if he felt that should he remain inactive for even a few hours the deadening grey impact of the world of raw nature would crush him. He is constantly fleeing an unknown, a subconscious enemy. Once he surrenders, he is lost; he is engulfed in a gripping prison of apathy, the space, the crushing power of a world of nature too big to struggle against; it breaks the spirit, it leaves his body to be swallowed up in the immensity. This world of insatiable relentless movement seems to possess everything in the Barrens and lastly it is communicated to man himself. The living world, the animals, the birds, the very winds, storms, and lastly the ground itself, seems in a constant state of flux and movement. The caribou are ever wandering over the country, day and night. The wolves, the foxes, even the tiny lemming roam and migrate and pass, it seems, never resting. The birds migrate and change, are here today and silently gone tomorrow. The fish appear and disappear, ever migrating, moving from the lakes up the rivers and back again. The weather is never constant for a day—sunshine, storms, and always the winds are blowing and herding the distraught clouds across the sky. The grey rocks crack and crumble; the land flows and creeps; the greater the depth into the earth the slower the rhythm and the movement but always it is there, inexorable, mighty and timeless. The coasts are slowly emerging from the sea, but the evidence is perceptible; the great glaciers far to the north grind down to the ocean. The lakes are retreating, and the trees and muskeg follow them. The rivers eat and groan in their labours as they devour the banks and with their moving boulders grind away at their rapids and falls. In this macrocosm of change and flux is man. He too must catch the strange beat or perish . . .[31]

Charlton Island is not without its history. It was here that Captain Thomas James of Bristol (after whom James Bay is named) wintered in 1631–2, during his 'strange and dangerous voyage' in the *Henrietta Maria* (70 tons), searching for a north-west passage into the South Sea. Forced to winter there by the ice, the party built a 'mansion house, wherein we did all lye together', a second house 'to dresse our victuall' and the third for a storehouse. The *Henrietta Maria* was deliberately holed and sunk in shallow water offshore, presumably to avoid being carried out to sea or crushed by heavy ice in deep water. Three men died during the winter and one fell through the sea ice; three stone tombs and a cross were erected on the island. On the cross, wrapped in lead, were fastened pictures of Charles I and his Queen, after whom the ship had been named. Underneath these were the royal arms, and then the arms of the city of Bristol. Captain James fastened a letter to the cross on 1 or 2 July 1632 when they were about to leave as a testimonial to the party's efforts and in case 'God should take us into his heavenly Kingdome' during the perilous voyage home.[32]

The island was visited in 1672 by the men who were establishing the fur trading post of Rupert House near the mouth of Rupert River. Because of the difficult access by ship to the posts at Rupert, Moose and Albany, it was decided in 1679 to build warehouses on Charlton Island to store furs in the spring and in turn to receive cargo from London. A two-and-a-half-storey house built in 1681 has been excavated there.[33] The island was vulnerable to attack and the depot was taken by the French in 1686, who also captured the three posts on James Bay. These were re-established, but Charlton Island appears to have remained deserted apart from its brief capture in 1803–7 by one of the two north-west companies existing at the time,[34] and apart from an equally brief attempt to combine cattle-farming with timber operations towards the end of the Napoleonic Wars.[35] In 1839 a beaver colony was established on the island;[36] by the turn of the century, it was yielding 100 to 150 beaver skins yearly to the Rupert's House Post without seriously depleting the stock.[37]

At the turn of the century in less troubled times, Charlton Island again became the Company's entrepôt in James Bay and continued to be used until the railway from the south reached Moosonee in 1932. The warehouse was built at what is now known as House Point, opposite Danby Island. The manager's house and the staff house still stand.[38]

Moose Factory, at the southern end of James Bay, had been the earlier port of entry for the London ships. A large establishment was maintained in the nineteenth century at Moose, mainly because of the numbers required when the ship from England had to be first unloaded and her cargo afterwards distributed to the other James Bay posts of Albany, Rupert's House, Fort George and Whale River in smaller craft. Moose Factory was poorly situated though, mainly because of the difficulties of local navigation. Dr Alexander Milne, Inspecting Officer of the Hudson's Bay Company, reported in 1900 on the complicated transport system there and advised the re-adoption of Charlton Island as a port of arrival and depot, setting out its various advantages over Moose.[39]

The *Discovery* was to carry a much larger cargo than previously sent to Charlton in one vessel (estimated at 850 to 900 tons). With a draught of 16 to 17 feet, she would draw more water than the *Lady Head* (15 feet 6 inches), which had occasionally touched bottom when at the wharf at low tide. It was thought that the *Discovery*'s bilges might be damaged if this ever happened to her. There was no permanent jetty at Charlton Island: the structure had to be wholly removed each winter because of the ice. Spars and planks were therefore sent out in the ship with which to build an additional length of jetty, so allowing the vessel to moor in at least 20 feet of water. The officer in charge of the James Bay District was in fact able to extend the wharf before the *Discovery*'s arrival. He reported on 10 September 1905 that she was 'unloaded in $5^{1}/_{2}$ days, re-loaded and ballasted in $2^{1}/_{2}$ days, eight days in all'.[40]

From 13 to 17 August, the crew discharged cargo and tarred down the rigging and backstays; the Company's small steam vessel *Inenew* was loaded during the week. On the afternoon of the 17th, the crew began shifting patent fuel from the fore lower hold into the bunkers aft and also put five tons of coal from the shore into the bunkers. Twenty-six casks of whale oil were taken on board that day. The thermometer registered 80°F, having been 58°F three days before. The hours worked by the crew were from 6 a.m. to 6 p.m. On the Saturday, besides moving the patent fuel, they cleared the 'tween decks rigging gear for taking in ballast and got logs on board for shifting boards, also taking a further five tons of coal from the shore, all by 9 a.m.

The ship's moorings were then slacked up and she was hove off from the wharf. The moorings were hove taut and from 10.30 a.m. till 5.45 p.m., 72 tons of ballast were taken on board. This was often of sand, which could be sold in London and was needed because the return cargo (largely of furs) was light. Part of the crew were sent away to get fresh water on the Monday and Tuesday (20 and 21 August 1906) and more ballast was taken on board, making 160 tons in all. All the cargo was taken in and stowed by noon on the Tuesday, comprising 102 bales, 69 cases, 26 casks of oil, 45 bags of feathers, 30 packs, 2 kegs, 2 casks and 16 private packages. Four tons of patent fuel were shifted out of the after trunking into the bunkers. The vessel was shifted on Wednesday 22 August and anchored again away from the wharf in 45 fathoms. The crew were occupied as well in trimming ballast, getting fresh water from the shore and clearing up. All the fresh-water tanks were filled.

The following morning, the HBC barque *Stork*, commanded by Captain N. E. Freakley, was in sight off the bar. She had departed from the West India Dock on 12 June.[41] The *Discovery*'s crew were at work that day bending sails, trimming ballast and making ready for sea. The main hatch was battened down and after the ship was cleared up generally, the anchor was weighed and she proceeded at half speed down river to the bar, Mr Miller acting as pilot. At 3 p.m. the ship stopped and anchored in 8 fathoms of water close to the *Stork*. The boat was lowered to take the pilot on board the *Stork*, being afterwards placed in chocks on the main hatch of the *Discovery*.

On Friday 24 August 1906, after new wire wheel ropes had been rove (the old ones being partly stranded), the anchor was weighed and the ship steamed at full speed to the WSW, courses being various to the master's orders. At noon, when in sight of Lisbon Rock, all square sail was set, with a moderate breeze and clear weather. The ship's log (now headed 'Discovery from Charlton towards London') records the home-ward voyage until her arrival on 5 October 1906 off London's South West India Dock, awaiting tide. She entered the dock at 1.30 a.m. and was hauled into the basin. The ship was moored and the crew discharged at 2.30 a.m., her draught being 12 feet 8 inches forward and 15 feet 6 inches aft. G. F. Lovegrove, Chief Officer and keeper of the log, made his last entry: 'This ends this log.'

CHAPTER

# TEN

## Voyages 1907–11

### 1907 HBC VOYAGE

LOVEGROVE TOOK UP HIS PEN AGAIN the following year on 20 June 1907, noting the *Discovery*'s draught on leaving London as 15 feet 6 inches forward and 18 feet 2 inches aft. The crew were mustered as the ship steamed down river out of the West India Dock when it was found that one man had failed to join. 68 kegs and 4 boxes of gunpowder were loaded before leaving the Thames. On 24 June at Peterhead, 5 cases of cargo from London, some stores, 4 dozen 'fowels', beef and mutton were taken on board. The course followed was again north of the British Isles and westward across the North Atlantic, giving the southern tip of Greenland a wide berth, as before. The crew worked as usual at their various tasks, for example on 18 July in lat. 57°N. long. 50°44′ W., when to the south-west of Cape Farewell (Kap Farvel), they were occupied making a canvas screen for the engine-room and canvas cask covers for the stores, while the carpenters decked over the 'boats skidds' on the starboard side.

After crossing Davis Strait, between Greenland and northern Canada, 'Cape Resolution' was sighted on 24 July and the *Discovery* entered the eastern entrance to Hudson Strait, meeting pack-ice the next day. The crow's nest of a polar ship in those days was a barrel (entered from a trap door below) situated high above the decks on the fore- or mainmast, from which the ship could be navigated through ice. The observer at such a height could make out the most promising leads for the ship to enter between the ice floes. It was invented by Captain William Scoresby, senior, the whaling captain, in the late eighteenth century. A modern ship has a more sophisticated version of the old barrel—the masthead conning position, sometimes called the 'spotting top'. By 31 July, Cape Wolstenholme at the western end of the Hudson Strait was in sight (a speedy passage) and on 9 August at 3 p.m. the *Discovery* was hove alongside the jetty at Charlton Island and moored ahead and astern with offshore and onshore moorings.

The crew were at work at 6 a.m. the next day rigging cargo gear, hauling the ship's boat up on shore etc. and at 7.30 a.m. they began discharging and landing cargo. Two hands were filling up fresh water from the shore, while one hand helped the carpenter

*119*

in caulking, paying and painting the new half-round abreast the engine-room. No work was done on the following day, a Sunday. Monday 12 August was spent tarring the rigging, filling up with fresh water and landing cargo. All the cargo was out of the 'tween decks by 8 a.m. next morning. The carpenter and a couple of hands had earlier been busy taking down the powder magazine in the 'tween decks. The crew next turned to getting the flour out of the coal bunker into the 'tween decks ready for landing. Discharging and landing cargo continued until 6 p.m. This went on too during 14 August, the carpenter fitting up shelves in the steward's store-room, while some of the crew filled up the fresh-water tank from shore and tarred down rigging and backstays at the fore and main. Work continued as before all day.

During the afternoon the SS *Inenew* arrived and went out to tow the *Stork* (which had been reported on 13 August) to anchor close to the Company post. By 8 a.m. on 16 August, all cargo was out of the *Discovery*'s main hold. The cargo was afterwards got up out of the port after store-room and landed, thus completing the landing and discharge of all the cargo. The gear was then shifted and at noon coaling the bunkers began, part of the crew clearing up the hold. Heavy rain stopped work, but by 6 p.m. seventeen tons had been taken on board. Rain partly stopped work again next day, but 54 tons of patent fuel was taken on for the bunkers. On the Sunday no work was done. Coaling finished by 11 a.m. next day to a total quantity of 80 tons. In the afternoon, 54 tons of ballast were loaded, shifting boards having been lashed up in the lower hold. The carpenter was meanwhile occupied in repairing the jolly boat.

During 20 August the crew continued to take in and trim the sand ballast. The SS *Inenew* came alongside at 10 a.m. and discharged twelve barrels of oil, skins, and 48 bales, as well as seven tons of stone ballast by 11.30 a.m. when the taking in of sand ballast was resumed. The carpenter was at work repairing the 'tween deck fore and aft of the main hatch. Part of the crew stowed the oil and bales. Ballasting finished by 8 a.m. next day, by which time 8 tons of stone and 140 of sand had been loaded. Between 9 and 11 a.m., the home-ward cargo was taken aboard. This consisted of 74 bales and 29 cases of fur and one keg, as well as seven cases of missionary goods. The carpenter was afterwards at work repairing the bridge deck, while the crew trimmed the ballast and took on a further 200 gallons of fresh water till 6 p.m.

On 22 August, the *Discovery* was unmoored and her anchor hove. The *Stork* was then taken in tow and dropped down the tide to an anchorage close to the wharf. More fresh water was taken on next day. New main topgallant clew lines (26 fathoms each of 2-inch manila) and new jib halyards (38 fathoms, 2-inch manila) were rove, while the fore topgallant clew lines were turned. More water was obtained on Saturday 24 August 1907, the crew being sent away in the large boat with a tank and pumping gear. At 11 a.m., the SS *Inenew* came alongside from Rupert House, with the Reverend J. E. Woodall the Anglican minister, Mrs Woodall and their two children, doubtless the owners of the seven cases of missionary goods already loaded. They brought with them, as passengers, a further five packages. Nine cases of fur and five bales were unloaded from the *Inenew*, which steamed away at 12.30. The cargo was stowed and a further 450 gallons of fresh water taken on board the *Discovery*, the tank then being stowed in the after 'tween decks. The main hatches were put on and battened down, while the cargo gear was sent down, the ship cleared up and made ready for sea by 5 p.m.

A third Sunday was passed at Charlton Island, as usual without work being done on the sabbath. In a moderate gale next day, the crew washed the decks and cleared up the after store-rooms, fore peak etc. A new weather cloth was made for the bridge.[1] The anchor was weighed at 5 a.m. on 27 August and the home-ward voyage begun. Cape Wolstenholme was rounded on 2 September. Three days later, icebergs surrounded the ship in Hudson Strait. The lifeboats and gear were overhauled and cleaned by the crew on 9 September, as the *Discovery* (rolling and lurching heavily at times) proceeded towards London. She passed the SS *Hungarian* (red funnel, white band and black top) a few days later in lat. 53°58′ N. long. 34°27′ W. During the passage, the crew painted the bridge, cleaned the ship, scraped the pins and rail etc. and put anchors over the bows. They also worked at scraping the masts, oiling them and painting. The *Discovery* proceeded up the English Channel in late September and berthed in the South West India Dock on the 27th, her draught being 12 feet 6 inches forward and 14 feet aft. Clearing up was done and the crew discharged by 5 p.m. Mr Lovegrove, Chief Officer, ended the log after a home-ward voyage of 32 days.

## 1908 HBC VOYAGE

The mate wrote the first entry for the next voyage in the *Discovery* (still commanded by Captain Ford) on 13 June 1908, when the ship was ready to depart from the West India Dock, her draught of water being 16 feet 4 inches forward and 18 feet 6 inches aft. The customary call was made to take on gunpowder down river. The ship anchored in Peterhead Bay and took on stores on 17 June. From 20 June, 'Daylight all night' was entered at the bottom of each page, as the *Discovery* proceeded north and west on her usual course south of Cape Farewell (Kap Farvel) towards Davis Strait and Hudson Strait. On 23 June a hard gale in lat. 61°23′ N. long. 17°09′ W. caused her to labour and strain heavily as she took heavy lee seas on board. The Boatswain, Mr Cawdrey, was thrown against the deck water tank and hurt his ribs. The pumps were 'strictly attended to' each day, an entry not previously made in the logs. These were obviously necessary as the decks flooded fore and aft in the high cross seas, heavy rain and hard squalls experienced during the gales.

On 12 July, in lat. 61°16′ N. long. 62°12′ W., when nearing Hudson Strait, the *Discovery* entered open pack, the engines turning at 'slow ahead'. Several icebergs were in sight. Solid pack stretched across the entrance to the strait and several large bergs were around as the ship approached 'Cape Resolution' and 'Hattons Head'. 1908 proved to be a particularly bad year for ice and the passage through Hudson Strait took 28 days from 13 July to 10 August. It was due to the ice that the *Stork* was detained and lost that season. Typical extracts from the *Discovery*'s log read:

*15 July* 4 a.m. Fog clearing. No open water visible from crow's nest.

*21 July* 2 a.m. Ice closed in all round. Put the 2 anchors out on large floe and moored ship to it. Lat. ob. 61°38′ N. Long. chron. 67°54′ W.

*22 July* p.m. Crew at work filling up fresh water tanks again. By observation ship has drifted 8 miles to the E. since noon. [They were trying to work westwards.] 5.30 p.m. Ordered steam, ice opening out to the N.W. took the anchors in and at 6 p.m. slow ahead and half speed working through the pack. 11.30 p.m. Stopped, ice close and heavy. Moored with 2 anchors again.

*2 August 1908* Wind freshens in gusts . . . ice close all round. 5 a.m. Ice opening out and ship driving to the south . . . half speed ahead. Hard gale with rain. Ship not able to make headway. Made fast to a large flow with 2 anchors. At 9 a.m. stopped engines, keeping steam ready in case of breaking adrift. Noon. Hard gale with snow. p.m. ditto . . . ice anchors breaking adrift. Slow ahead engine, put anchor in again and stopped engine.

*7 August* a.m. Working the ship through heavy pack ice at various speeds. No open water visible from crow's nest, ice appears to be blocking the Straits from land to land. 6.30 Jammed in the pack. Stopped engines.

*10 August* 8 a.m. Cape Moses Oats S. by W. 15′ heavy scattered ice pack all round. 4 p.m. Cape Wolsternholm [*sic*] W. by N.1/4 N. 10 p.m. Open water, clear of the pack.

Passing between Digges Island and Nottingham Island next day through ridges of scattered ice, they were clear of the pack by noon and able to advance 123 nautical miles by midday next day into Hudson Bay. Pack-ice and fog were still encountered to the southward at times. The usual cautious approach with the lead was made to Charlton Island and at 6.50 p.m. on 19 August, and with Mr Miller again on board as pilot, the *Discovery* anchored off the Post.[2]

A fortnight was spent at Charlton Island unloading cargo (including a boiler which had to be slung over the side into a specially prepared boat), coaling the bunkers, obtaining fresh water and ballast. One hundred bags of flour were put on board the schooner *Pride*. The SS *Inenew* came alongside, as usual, being loaded from the shore across the *Discovery*'s deck, leaving afterwards for Rupert's House. The homeward cargo consisted of 21 casks of oil, 90 bales, 26 cases, 25 bags of feathers, 25 packs, 2 kegs, 2 boxes and 3 bundles. The passengers this year were Mr and Mrs Donald Gillies and three children. The ship began her homeward voyage on 3 September. Oil bags were again used on occasion during gales to prevent the sea breaking on board. She proceeded up the English Channel in early October and berthed in the South West India Dock later on 7 October.

No log survives for the next year's voyage in 1909. However, we know that Captain

Ford was still her master. The *Discovery* left the West India Dock on 19 June and arrived at Charlton Island on 12 August. She departed from the island on 25 August, berthing on 2 October at the West India Dock.


## 1910 HBC VOYAGE

Captain Ford again commanded the *Discovery* with G. F. Lovegrove as Chief Officer and keeper of the log, whose relatively descriptive entries (for a log) supply much of the available information for these voyages. The ship unmoored from the South West India Dock on 21 June 1910, all crew being on board. She again took on gunpowder before proceeding north to Peterhead, where she anchored from 25 to 27 June. The customary gales were endured during the outward passage. A sudden shift of wind for instance at 1 a.m. on 5 July in lat. 58°45′ N. long. 25°15′ W., increased to a violent gale, and brought all hands on deck to reduce sail, to lower topsails and foresail. The upper fore topsail and inner jib were split and deck cargo was washed adrift. The 'Land of Resolution' and 'Hattons Head' were sighted on 21 July, when the crow's nest was sent aloft, ice anchors brought on deck and a ladder rigged to the fore top to reach the crow's nest. The ship was able to work with much less difficulty than two years previously through the ice of Hudson Strait and she moored at Charlton Island on 4 August.

The *Discovery* spent some three weeks at Charlton, not departing until 28 August. Another boiler was lifted out of the hold on to the deck soon after arrival. The crew discharged cargo on to trolleys on the jetty. The usual repairs to rigging were made, water taken on board etc. The fore peak was pumped out and the carpenter payed the seams of the bridge deck with putty to make it more waterproof; much of the cargo had been damaged by salt water when heavy seas flooded the decks in bad weather. The crew coaled the cross bunker from the lower main hold (28 tons) on 12 August. The limber boards were then taken up and examined and the gear shifted for taking on ballast.

The carpenter worked on the schooner *Pride* on 15 August, cutting away her main deck to make room for taking the boiler, which was lowered during the afternoon into the schooner's hold. Cargo, consisting of 18 casks of oil and 71 packages, bales, etc., was taken on board the *Discovery* from the *Inenew*. Eight tons of coal were put on board her from the shore, as well as the funnel smoke box and boiler gear. The *Inenew* was discharged and loaded a second time, across the *Discovery*'s deck, on 22 and 23 August. More water and ballast were obtained for the *Discovery*.

Unloading and loading were complicated this season. The *Discovery* had cargo for the HBC post of York Factory, all of which had to be first landed on shore so that the boiler could be removed, and then restowed on board afterwards. Four canoes had also been landed for the same reason and were restowed and stored on the skids the same day (23 August). A total of 236 cases, bales and packs were taken on board from the shore for London, as well as 73 from the *Inenew*, plus 18 barrels of oil.

The *Mooswa*, a small steam vessel of 80 tons, had to be taken in tow by the *Discovery* to York Factory. On 24 August, she was hauled alongside, her deck gear unrigged and stowed away. Twenty tons of coal were put into her hold and bunkers, plus a spare propeller, boiler tubes and ten gallons of oil. Her hatches were battened down and her boat taken aboard the *Discovery*, as well as one ton of coal for her bunker and a case of gear. The following day, she was made secure for towing and all made ready for sea. The *Inenew* arrived from Rupert's House to deliver a further 14 packs of fur. More preparations for sea were made on 26 and 27 August, including the making of rope fenders by the crew, to put between the ship's side and the *Mooswa*. Anchor was weighed at 5.50 a.m. on the 28th, full speed ahead out of the sound. 'Tulaloak' was pilot on board while a hand was at the lead, ready to sound. The pilot was discharged at 7 a.m. and the *Mooswa* passed astern with the tow-lines secured.

On 30 August at about 9 a.m. the ship was under sail some miles off Cape Henrietta Maria when the steel tow-line of the *Mooswa* parted. Two tow-lines were resecured, but parted again almost immediately: the deteriorating weather prevented another attempt and the *Mooswa* drifted away. At daylight next day, she was nowhere to be seen. The wind increased to a hard gale with a confused heavy sea, the *Discovery* rolling heavily and filling her deck at times. At 10 a.m. the spanker split up the leech and across the cloths. The lead was cast and in the afternoon the squalls rose to hurricane force in dark gloomy weather, the ship labouring and straining heavily and filling the deck with sea. The *Mooswa* was not in sight at dawn next morning (1 September) by which time the wind had moderated to a fresh breeze. Some scattered ice was to be seen. Steam was ordered at 5.30 a.m. and an hour later the ship steered to the east-north-east in search of the missing vessel in a strong breeze and ugly sea with heavy north-westerly swell and overcast sky. At 9.30, the *Discovery* came up to the *Mooswa*, dodging close to her until the sea moderated. This was in lat. 55°18′ N. long. 80°38′ W. The log reads:

> p.m. At 1 p.m. all hands on deck, swung the port life boat out and asked for volunteers to man the boat, but only 3 men offered, so the Master ordered the boat to be swung in and landed on the skidds [*sic*] again until the sea subsided. At 4 p.m. all hands called on deck and the Master said he would give a gratuity of £1 per man if they succeeded in getting the *Mooswa* to York; at 4.30 p.m. the port life boat was swung out and manned by a crew in charge of the Mate, and the perilous task was performed without any accident. Got two hawsers made fast to the 'Mooswa' and then pulled for the ship, and got the Life Boat hoisted up and placed on the skidds and secured. Adjusted the towing hawsers and at 6.30 p.m. engines half speed ahead, kept ship on her course, NW. Secured the canoes and at 7 p.m. sent all hands to supper.

The next three days were trouble free, apart from occasional dense fog, during which the lead was cast. Land was made out mid-morning on 6 September and a cautious approach was made, still casting the lead. The *Discovery* anchored in 7 fathoms at 5.30 p.m. in a strong breeze with choppy sea and NE swell. It was found impossible to keep the *Mooswa* clear of the ship, as the wind was across the tide and it was dangerous for her to be alongside. The anchor was therefore hove up and the ship steamed round to make a lee side. Three men got on board the *Mooswa*, and the tow-lines cleared. She was anchored with a 3$^1$/$_2$-inch wire hawser astern of the *Discovery* (the men having been taken on board the ship again), for fear she would be smashed up alongside on account of wind and sea. 'After all the risk and work', wrote Lovegrove in the log, 'managed to steam clear of her to a safe distance, stopped and anchored in 7 fthms. water . . . by 8 p.m. All hands being on deck.' Three rockets were fired from the roadstead to signal the ship's arrival to the York Factory Post some twenty miles away, it being impossible to approach much nearer, owing to the extensive mud banks at the mouths of the Hayes and Nelson rivers, which empty into Hudson Bay. For the watching traders at the fort in the wilderness, the sight of the rockets meant that 'at last, the long looked for annual ship had arrived with supplies and letters from the outside world'.[3] She lay at anchor all day on 7 September in a north-westerly swell and rough sea. At 6 p.m. the beacon of York was made out to the south-west. A further three rockets were sent up from *Discovery* to signal the Post, which answered, and the ship answered again late in the evening. At 5 next morning, four coast boats were in sight sailing from York Post.

The log keeper does not report the arrival of the officer in charge of York Factory in the first boat, but in Philip Godsell's day, he scrambled up the rope ladder followed by three 'hilarious young Scotsmen', apprentice clerks like Godsell himself, who had just returned 'with their Indian crews from their distant trading posts, where during the past nine months, they had seen no white men and rarely spoken English. Now, during their brief stay at the erstwhile capital of fur land, they were making up in riotous fun for their enforced solitude of the winter, ere returning to their lonely trading posts.'[4]

The *Discovery*'s crew cleared the canoes and jolly boat from the main hatch and rigged cargo gear for both sides of the ship. One cargo boat from York Factory came alongside and was loaded and away by 10 a.m. The second was half loaded, when it had to leave the ship's side on account of wind and sea. By midday, the three remaining coast boats had to seek shelter, as the wind increased to a gale. On board the *Discovery*, the hatches were put on and the hauling lines, deck gear etc. cleared. At 5 p.m. in a strong south-westerly gale, with heavy squalls, the *Mooswa* was found to be dragging her anchor. She drove past the *Discovery* and brought up suddenly 200 yards astern of her. Much of the next day was spent manoeuvring the two vessels so that they did not smash against each other and Chief Officer Lovegrove noted that he had spent all night on deck watching the *Mooswa*.

By 12 September, wind and sea had moderated sufficiently for the *Mooswa* to be towed further inshore towards the York Factory beacon, a hand at the lead sounding. Four boats from Fort York were loaded next day. The *Mooswa* was hove alongside the *Discovery* and twelve tons of coal taken out of her into the ship's bunkers. Her hold was cleaned and loaded with cargo. Five men from the Post, the second engineer, a fireman and a hand to steer were put on board the *Mooswa*. She finally cast off from the ship at 7 p.m. and steamed away to the Post in a fresh breeze, no doubt much to Captain Ford's relief. The boats and the *Mooswa* were loaded again in the next couple of days, the *Mooswa* taking on board 450 bags of flour and five cases. A hard gale early on 17 September caused the *Discovery* to pitch and strain at her windlass. The engines were put slow ahead at 2.30 a.m. to ease the strain. The ship rolled heavily when across the tide, putting her bulwarks under and flooding the deck, while the crew had to secure all movable gear and cargo about the deck. The starboard anchor next day was hove up and its flukes found to be fouled by the port cable. The port anchor was also foul and was cleared. Some cargo in the 'tween decks broke adrift, because of the heavy lurching and rolling.

At 8 p.m. on 20 September two rockets were sent up to signal the Post for boats and at 2.30 a.m. the lights of the *Mooswa* were seen in the distance. The hands were turned out when she arrived alongside the *Discovery* at 4 a.m.; by 7 a.m. she steamed away for the Post with 348 packages of general cargo on board. Four hours later, three boats had also come alongside and been loaded, thus emptying the *Discovery* of her YF (York Factory) cargo. A Mr Moir, passenger for London, joined the ship with his luggage and two boxes were taken on board for a Mrs Campbell. Mr Moir may have been the Harry Moir, 'a tall, fair-haired chap' and 'a good hunter', who shot a polar bear found helping itself to seal meat stores in the blubber house. His stories of hunting and adventure kept young Godsell awake until far into the night.[5]

At 6 a.m. the following day, all hands were at work taking the Charlton cargo out of the lower hold and re-stowing it in the 'tween decks. In the afternoon, the crew painted the combings of the main hatch and 'tween deck hatch, stowing away hauling lines, warps, fenders etc. Repairs had already been made to the service on the jib guy and bowsprit shroud, while the best upper fore topsail, best foresail and best spanker were bent for the home-ward voyage in place of worn sails. The main hatch was battened down. The jolly boat was put in the chocks on the hatch and secured. All cargo gear was sent down and the ship made generally ready for sea at 6 p.m. Snow was falling as the night watch was set.

The Second Engineer (Harold Morgan from Swansea) and two hands away in the *Mooswa* kept the *Discovery* waiting that day and the next for their return from York Factory, for no obvious reason. They arrived at last by boat at 6.30 a.m. on Saturday 24 September and an hour later the ship steamed at full speed ahead out of the bay, homeward bound towards London. The second engineer and two hands would no doubt have told their shipmates about their visit to the Post in the wilderness, which had once been the 'busily throbbing heart of the Hudson's Bay Company's inland trade'[6] although they left no account of it. Perhaps young Morgan was entertained to meals in the large mess room in the officers' quarters, the walls of which were adorned with oil paintings of Lord Nelson and the Battle of Trafalgar.[7] Godsell, who had first arrived there four years earlier in the *Pelican*, recalled that 'very dusky, but comely, Cree squaws, gaudy in their bright tartan dresses and embroidered moccasins, waited upon us and moved silently about the room'. He may, as did Godsell before him, have congregated with the other young men 'under the dim light of a coal-oil lamp in the garish, yellow-painted Bachelors' Hall, the walls of which were hung with a picturesque assortment of beaded shot-pouches, powder horns, moose-skin capotes, guns, snow-shoes, moccasins and brightly coloured sashes'. Here yarns were swapped or the gramophone played while fancy biscuits and tinned fruit were consumed. In those days, the Company was a powerful force in the area and its old traditions still prevailed. Godsell describes how the flag was raised to the top of the eighty-foot flag-pole in the centre of the fort, while the cannons roared, for the visit of Chief Factor McTavish that 'mighty potentate'.[8]

Sir John Franklin, who died in 1847 off King William Island during the British naval expedition searching for the north-west passage in HM Ships *Erebus* and *Terror*, was landed at York Factory from the HBC Ship *Prince of Wales* on 30 August 1819 at the beginning of his overland journey to the Arctic Ocean. He described the Post in detail.

> York Factory, the principal depot of the Hudson's Bay Company, stands on the west bank of the Hayes River, about five miles above its mouth, on the marshy peninsula which separates the Hayes and Nelson Rivers. The surrounding country is flat and swampy and covered with willows, poplar, larch, spruce and birch trees; but the requisition for fuel has expended all the wood in the vicinity of the fort, and the residents have now to send for it to a considerable distance . . . Though the bank of the river is elevated about twenty feet, it is frequently overflown by the spring floods, and large portions are annually carried away by the disruption of the ice, which grounding in the stream, have formed several muddy islands. These interruptions, together with the various collections of stones that are hid at high water, render the navigation of the river difficult, but vessels of two hundred tons burthen may be brought through the proper channels as high as the Factory.
>
> The principal buildings are placed in the form of a square, having an octagonal court in the centre; they are two stories in height, and have flat roofs covered with lead. The officers dwell in one portion of this square, and in the other parts the articles of merchandise are kept: the workshops, storehouses for furs, and the servants' houses are ranged on the outside of the square, and the whole is surrounded by a stockade twenty feet high. A platform is laid from the house to the pier on the bank for the convenience of transporting the stores and furs, which is the only promenade the residents have on this marshy spot during the summer season. The few Indians who now frequent this establishment belong to the *Swampy Crees*. There were several of them encamped on the outside of the stockade . . . .[9]

The waterways of the vast hinterland to the west and north-west of York Factory had rung in the summer months for most of the nineteenth century and earlier with the songs of the 'voyageurs' transporting either furs to the east for shipment to England or supplies to the west. The ultimate logistics of the Hudson's Bay Company from York Factory (closely paralleled by those of the North West Company from Montreal before their union in 1821) are succinctly outlined by Eric W. Morse.[10]

> The object was to get furs from the vast Mackenzie District on board sea-going vessels at York Factory, and the trade goods back—impossible for a return run within the ice-free months. The solution was a neat one. Furs from everywhere west of Lake Superior were collected at Norway House' and taken down by a large brigade of York Boats in August in time to catch the ship at York Factory. This brigade neither wintered there nor returned with empty boats: the new shipment of trade goods was picked up and carried to Norway House, to be stored and sorted over winter. Taking the Fort Garry shipment only, the brigade then went south on Lake Winnipeg to winter around the Forks of the Red and Assiniboine. In early June, by which time Lake Winnipeg was free of ice, the La Loche Brigade started off with nearly empty York Boats for Norway House. The whole of the year's 'Outfit' for the Mackenzie River, dropped off the previous autumn, was picked up and transported by the familiar Cumberland–Churchill River route all the way to Methye Portage twelve miles overland. The boats were left at the portage landing, but the tons of supplies were transported eight miles to The Rendez-vous at the little lake here to be picked up by the Mackenzie Brigade, whose boats were waiting at the north end of the Methye Portage. No voyageur returned unloaded over the portage, for the previous year's collection of Mackenzie furs had to be carried east to York Factory.

The transport system, with York Factory as its focal point, was in part superseded by the St Paul–Red River route in the 1860s and by 1870 the importance of York Factory had greatly waned.[11]

The *Discovery*'s passage to London from York Road, Nelson Bay, is recorded in the log with familiar entries regarding the gales, the oil bags and the ship 'labouring and straining heavily and flooding her deck'. On this return voyage there was trouble with the steering gear. Despite fall tackles having been put on the tiller to check the heavy strain on the wheel the day before (in lat. 53°12′ N. long. 31°31′ W., both by account), on 13 October in a hard gale when under lower topsail, reefed courses and mizzen and fore topgallant staysail, the big cogwheel of the steering purchase on the bridge broke in two with the heavy jerking strain of the rudder. The rudder was secured by tackles and steering tackles were got on the wires, enabling the ship to be steered, until the engineers could repair the broken parts of the wheel by the following evening. The SS *Pelican* was sighted on 27 October to the south-west in lat. 50°53′ N. long. 17°37′ W. She was under lower topsail and fore topgallant staysail, but immediately set upper topgallant half courses and main topgallant sail and went away out of sight to the south-east. The *Discovery* was moored to the quay and the crew discharged at the West India Dock by 3.30 p.m. on 5 November 1910. 'This ends the log' wrote Lovegrove, who had been off duty sick for two days in mid-October, as had the bos'n for a day in November. Pasted at the end of this particular log book is a sworn Protest by John Graham Ford (master of the *Discovery*) 'for all losses, costs and damages' caused by the cables having parted at York Roads, when the *Mooswa* was in tow, dated and signed at Dunfermline in the county of Fife on 27 January 1911.

## 1911 HBC VOYAGE

The last voyage of the *Discovery* of this series from London to the Bay in 1911 may have been Captain Ford's last command, since he was by then 62 years old. G. F. Lovegrove, Chief Officer from 1905 to 1910, was replaced by G. R. Redfearn, who (as Mate) kept the log. This voyage differed from the others in that the ship called first at York Factory (from 5 to 8 August) and then at Charlton Island (from 14 August to 12 September). The SS *Beothic* of about 3,000 tons displacement, a steel-built sealer from St John's, NF, was chartered this season by the Company to deliver supplies to York Factory from 1 to 5 August and to Charlton Island from 8 to 22 August. The *Beothic* sailed from St John's on 30 June and returned there on 30 August. She presumably took on the supplies at Montreal, where she was in port from 4 to 19 July.[12]

The *Discovery* departed from the West India Dock (despite a seamen's strike) on 17 June 1911 to steam down river, making the usual calls at the Powder Ground off Gravesend and at Peterhead (21 June). A first-hand account of this voyage was written by Captain A. R. Williamson, DSC, who sailed before the mast as an Able Seaman.[13] Each seaman bought his straw-filled mattress and pillow (a 'donkey's breakfast') at a ship's chandlers outside the dock gates, which were delivered on board by the chandler's boy, pushing a hand-cart. After the port and starboard watches had been picked from the crew by the two mates, these mattresses, plus blankets, were spread by each man in his chosen bunk (the starboard watch installed in the starboard six bunks and the port watch on the port side of the forecastle. A regular ship routine of watch and watch (four hours on deck and four below) was established.

After all square sails and fore and afters had been set on 2 July, the engine was stopped, the boiler fires drawn and the *Discovery* proceeded under sail alone, being then some 500 miles east of Cape Farewell, with the Denmark Strait between Greenland and Iceland open to the north. The usual 'fair winds and foul, moderate seas and rough' were encountered, 'all the chances and changes to be met with in any ocean passage'. The seamen went about their duties happy and contented, remembering the four and a half golden sovereigns piling up month by month, while the voyage lasted. Captain Williamson writes that

The happiest man on board was Captain John Ford. He had been in command of the Company's ships for more than twenty years and was thus experienced in all the difficulties and hazards to be met with during a Hudson's Bay voyage. As this was his sixth voyage in the *Discovery*, he was also wise to the barque's peculiarities. He was a *sailor of the sail* of the old school and with the main engine stopped, the bridge engine room telegraph hidden from sight under a canvas cover and the engine room staff sitting on buckets playing cards beside their silent engine, our Old Jock was in his proper element. While at the wheel, it was pleasant to see him strutting to and fro, casting glances aloft at every turn to study the set of the sails and when he ordered us to man the braces to trim the yards to a shift of wind, we were intrigued by the way in which he chanted his orders in an old fashioned manner, no longer heard in modern windjammers—'*Well, the main yard!* Be-e-lay there; Oh, be-e-lay!'

By 19 July, the *Discovery* was some 140 miles from Resolution Island (at the eastern entrance to Hudson Strait), during a day of fog patches, rain showers and moderate winds. The previous day, the cables had been shackled to the bower anchors, ready for instant use. Able Seaman Williamson was sent up aloft at midnight with three other members of the starboard watch to furl the fore and main topgallant sails:

At eight bells the helmsman was relieved, the port watch went below and the Second Mate ordered his watch *Aloft and furl!* I mounted the fore rigging followed by Clifford, while the other two members of the starboard watch went up to furl the main topgallant sail. Up on the fore t'gallant yard Clifford and I hauled the sail up on the yard and while passing the gaskets, I was conscious of a continuous murmuring, which seemed to come out of the fog on the port side. We were making fast the last gaskets, when we were startled by a sudden short shout from the Captain on the bridge below: *Hang on, aloft! Hang on!* Clifford and I braced ourselves on the footropes and looking down, saw emerging from the fog ahead the edge of a large sheet of ice right athwart the bows. Even as we saw it, the advancing ship crashed into it, the bows lifted and the foremast whipped under the impact. It was as well that we had received that timely warning to hang on, but our barque had been designed to cope with ice and after the initial check, she gathered way and her stout raking stem, sheathed with iron plating, charging into the ice floe, forced it aside and it slithered aft along the starboard side to vanish in the murk astern. At the same time, the source of the murmuring noise was revealed—the fog to port had receded a little and at its base appeared a line of surf—a slight swell breaking along the edge of the pack ice, extending fore and aft as far as was visible.[14]

Captain Williamson explains how the secret of entrance into Hudson Strait is to keep to the north, where a branch of the Labrador current turns west (instead of continuing south towards Labrador and Newfoundland). The *Discovery*'s auxiliary engines and Captain Ford's skill in ice navigation enabled her to follow leads among the ice floes and bergs to within ten miles of the southern point of Resolution Island. Here the westward-flowing current carried the barque, together with polar pack-ice and bergs from the north, in the right direction. Once past Resolution Island they worked their way towards the centre of the Strait where thinner one-season ice provided easier going. Accompanied by a 'continual noise of crashing, grinding and bumping', the ship made her way by dead reckoning under gloomy skies, every change of course and distance run having to be recorded. When the ice was too heavily packed, the barque was 'manoeuvred alongside the adjacent floe to await a favourable lead opening up, rope ladders were put over the side and we descended on the ice armed with long iron rods with chiselled off ends. With these implements we dug holes in the ice opposite the bow and stern into which ice anchors were inserted. These were short pieces of round iron bent to form a shallow hook, with a hawser attached which was hove taut on board and made fast, thus securely mooring the vessel until we were able to proceed.' It was on these occasions that the opportunity was taken to water ship from the pools of fresh water in hollows on the floes.

Captain Williamson's account provides many interesting insights into these voyages to Hudson Bay, complementing the more formal and matter-of-fact writing of the mate. He noted the wildlife of the region, its peace no doubt disturbed by the 'bumping and crashing' of the *Discovery*'s stem thrusting aside the loose pieces of ice in the leads.[15]

> Parties of seals were frequently seen basking in the sun on the floes while the occasional walrus would watch us pass on our way. On one occasion a lone walrus was observed enjoying a siesta on a large piece of ice in mid-channel ahead of us. The helmsman was directed to steer for the icy raft and we gathered to see the outcome. Our noisy approach woke the sleeper and he stared in astonishment at the approaching monster but just in time he heaved his great bulk into the water just before the stem struck his icy bed which tilted and capsized under the impact while the late occupant was belting along at his utmost speed to gain the shelter of a small inlet in the side of the adjacent floe. As we were steaming past we were amused to see the face of a very startled walrus, with one flipper on a ledge of ice, peering round the corner to watch the monstrous invader pass. His round eyes and tusks gave him the comical appearance of an elderly gentleman with drooping mustaches; but the most impressive of the local fauna were the half dozen polar bears which were sighted, at various times, moving over the floes. One splendid specimen stood motionless about half a mile away to watch us pass—a magnificent and unforgettable sight.

More difficult ice conditions were met south of Big Island, where the Strait narrows to 60 miles and the Labrador current peters out. Far heavier ice was traversed when navigating through 'Charles' Patch', relates Captain Williamson, where the hardened ice of several seasons is carried into Hudson Strait towards Charles Island, diagonally across the track of an inward-bound vessel making for Hudson Bay. By 29 July they were passing Cape Wolstenholme at the western end of the Strait. The next day, with open water ahead, the officer of the watch was able to descend from the foretop to his usual position on the bridge. Passing between Coats Island and Mansel ('Mansfield' in the logs) Island, the barque proceeded south-west towards York Factory, off which she anchored on 4 August 1911.

A launch came to take Captain Ford ashore and the crew (apart from the night-watchman) enjoyed a good night's rest after seven weeks of watch-and-watch. The *Mooswa* brought lighters alongside (the log calls them three sail boats) and a clerk from the Post to receive the 45 tons of cargo, which was unloaded by 8 August; a small shipment of furs was taken on board for London. Captain Ford was in good form after a spell ashore and his barque once more under sail, chanting his orders cheerfully to the crew. The *Discovery* anchored off Charlton Island at 8 p.m. on Sunday 13 August, at the end of her outward voyage.

Captain Williamson describes the last Sunday evening on Charlton Island (Sunday 10 September 1911). He and his watchmate, Clifford, had paddled over to Danby Island in a borrowed canoe:

The light was beginning to fade as we . . . strolled back through the woods, enjoying the ripe wild strawberries growing there in profusion. It was a beautiful evening, calm and peaceful, as we embarked the canoe and dug in our paddles. Midway across the strait, without a word being said, we ceased paddling, drew the paddles across our knees and sat quietly, breathing in the pure, unpolluted air and admiring the scene which we would never forget. Ahead of us the black hull of our ship was becoming indistinguishable from the dark woods behind, while above the trees the masts, yards and rigging were sharply etched against the pearly light of the sky, now fast fading into the darkness of the coming night. As we sat and gazed a flickering light appeared ahead which soon turned into a blaze and as we resumed paddling the sound of singing came across the waters. Having reached the shore and securely moored the canoe, we walked along the beach to join our shipmates and the stevedores who, having lit a camp fire, were spending a farewell evening of yarning and singing. There was no 'flowing bowl' to enliven the proceedings but there was good fellowship in plenty. Our Welsh shipmate, Taffy Jones, possessed a good voice and at our request he gave us 'Rio Grande', 'Spanish Ladies', 'Rolling Home' and other capstan and topsail halliard shanties to which we roared out the choruses. In return the Canadians sang some of the haunting songs of the 'voyageurs'. When the fire died down it was carefully extinguished and we walked back to the pier where the stevedores bade us farewell before they returned to the bunkhouse.

The following day, the barque was made ready for sea and a small black bear arrived by boat in a rough cage and was embarked as a passenger and placed in the large hen-coop, not apparently unduly perturbed. The *Discovery* sailed for home on 13 September, berthing in the West India Dock on Sunday 29 October. The bear was taken to the London Zoo, full of life and in good shape after his rough passage. The crew received their wages in golden sovereigns the following Tuesday, watched by Captain Ford who, in his smart dark suit, could have passed for a 'City gent ... but we, his erstwhile shipmates knew him for what he really was—a Master of the Sea, a prime seaman, wise and experienced in commanding and handling a ship in all the hazards and dangers of navigation in northern latitudes'.[16]

# PART III

# THE FIRST WORLD WAR
# AND ITS AFTERMATH,
# 1915–20

# ELEVEN

## To New York and Archangel, 1915

### THE GREAT WAR

In 1912, the *Discovery* and the *Pelican* were replaced as supply ships by a steamer newly constructed for Arctic navigation, in which the Hudson's Bay Company had a majority interest. This was the legendary *Nascopie* (2,600 tons), which was to make 36 voyages through Hudson Strait before sinking off Baffin Island during her last one in 1947. In October 1913, the Company agreed to sell the *Discovery* for £9,500 to an Antarctic expedition that never sailed. Its leader was a J. Foster Stackhouse, Fellow of the Royal and Royal Scottish Geographical Societies, who paid £1,000 deposit on the purchase. The expedition's writing paper was headed at first with a logo showing the *Discovery* in the ice and then with a map of the world illustrating the proposed track of the expedition. It started as the 'British Antarctic Expedition 1914' and in 1915 became the 'British Antarctic and Oceanographical Expedition'. Its offices were in London and it had the support of Sir Clements Markham. The aim was to survey as much of the Antarctic coastline as possible 'to determine what lands are insular and what lands are continental'. Winter quarters were to be established firstly in Graham Land and afterwards in King Edward VII Land. Stackhouse was unable though to raise enough money to pay the other instalments on the ship. He died in 1915 aboard the torpedoed *Lusitania*, apparently returning from a fund-raising visit to North America. The £1,000 deposit was kept by the Company which maintained that the expenses involved in retaining the steamer at the expedition's disposal in the South West India Dock amounted to more than that sum.[1]

The *Discovery* was to play a small part in the great conflict that brought to an end on 4 August 1914 that *Pax Britannica* which had existed since the defeat of Napoleon a century before. She was one of a merchant fleet of some three hundred, purchased and financed by the Hudson's Bay Company, acting as agents for the French Government. Managed by the specially formed Bay Steamship Company, these were to transport such munitions, food stuffs, raw materials and manufactured goods, as had been purchased by the Hudson's Bay Company on France's behalf, originally for the Army, and later for civilian needs. The agreement negotiated in 1915 between the Company and the French

Commerce and War Departments gave the Company a blank credit on the French Treasury, and came about as a result of an initiative by a Monsieur Jean Monnet. This young brandy merchant had traded for several years with the Hudson's Bay Company. 'We needed furs; the trappers liked cognac,' he was to write years later in his published memoirs. At the age of eighteen, in 1906, he stayed at Lower Fort Garry on the Red River near Winnipeg as the guest of the Company. At the very beginning of the Great War in August 1914, Monnet suggested to the London directors that they should become the purchasing agents for the French Government. Accustomed to international trade, he also proposed to the French Premier that France and Great Britain should co-operate during the war regarding supplies and shipping, with the result that his scheme was endorsed by both nations. Monnet was to build on this experience in later years and eventually became the architect of the European Common Market after the Second World War.[2] Thus it was through Monnet's efforts and initiative that the venerable Hudson's Bay Company came to play a hazardous and crucial role with regard to Allied shipping and supplies, during the four years of the First World War.

The Company 'signed approximately 6,600 separate contracts with various agencies of the French Government. Additional agreements were entered into with the Roumanian, Russian and Belgian governments. In the carrying out of these agreements, the Company employed some 145 agents in various countries around the world. A merchant fleet consisting of several hundred ships was organised. Some of these ships were purchased, many were chartered and a number of others were managed for the various allied governments. Over 13,000,000 tons of goods were transported, as well as a substantial number of soldiers, refugees and escaped prisoners of war. During this time, the Company lost 110 vessels, primarily to enemy submarine action.'[3]

The Governor of the Hudson's Bay Company, Robert (later Lord) Kindersley, called in Charles Vincent Sale (later to become the 29th Governor of the Company) to run this far-flung network. Born in 1868 into the world of big business through the family shipping concern, Sale & Co., he had a distinguished career, and was decorated with orders by Japan, Belgium, France and Denmark.[4] A tireless and meticulous worker, he was yet far-sighted, eager after the war to bring in modern methods and to broaden the Company's ventures. These changes in the old ways did not endear him to the long-serving wintering partners or fur traders in the field. Historians and scientists have reason to be grateful to him for centralising the Company's archives, calling in to London journals and records from trading posts all over the north. Conventional in appearance, Sale was to some extent a visionary, 'an impressive man, with much longer views than the Company's staff', wrote one who knew him well.[5] 'It was largely owing to his ability', read a tribute in *The Times* after his death on 22 June 1943, 'that the company functioned so successfully as the purchasing agent for the French Government all over the world.'[6]

The *Discovery* became part of this great enterprise in 1915, the year described by Winston Churchill as 'disastrous to the cause of the Allies and to the whole world. By the mistakes of this year the opportunity was lost of confining the conflagration within limits which though enormous were not uncontrolled. Thereafter the fire roared on till it burnt itself out. . . . But in January 1915, the terrific affair was still not unmanageable. It could have been grasped in human hands and brought to rest in righteous and fruitful victory before the world was exhausted, before the nations were broken, before the empires were shattered to pieces, before Europe was ruined.'[7] The lost opportunity in Churchill's opinion was not to have used British supremacy at sea to relieve the isolation of Russia by forcing the Belts into the Baltic, or Dardanelles into the Black Sea. This was the background to the *Discovery*'s voyages to north Russia later in 1915 and to the Russian Black Sea ports in 1919–20.

## TRANSATLANTIC VOYAGE TO NEW YORK, 1915

After four years laid up, the barque needed refitting. She was assisted in the spring of the year from her lying-up berth in the West India Dock into dry dock and was re-rigged by A. Berry, Rigger of 709 Commercial Road, in the London docks for £55 11s. 0d.,[8] an inconsiderable sum. The boats were repaired and equipped to Board of Trade regulations by Messrs Leslie and Hamblin of Poplar, while medical items were bought from Messrs George B. Hatfield, Shipping and Export Chemists of Limehouse.[9] Provisions were taken on board, fresh, dried, pickled and preserved, including 3 dozen live fowls. The letter-headings of the invoices for these and for the ship's stores almost bring to life a dockland business world of suppliers and manufacturers, Dickensian in its variety.[10]

In their letter of 17 April, the Company trusted that the *Discovery* had been 'sorted and fitted out satisfactorily' and told her master, Captain Williams, to 'look to Mr N. H. Bacon', the Fur Trade Commissioner, on arrival in New York. They wished him 'a speedy voyage and a safe return' and felt sure that, bearing in mind his 'excellent performance on the *Fort York*', this would be accomplished.[11] The *Discovery* sailed in ballast. She was forced to put back into Falmouth on 25 April 1915, because of a bad leak in the rudder truck.[12] She had a rough transatlantic passage, suffering twenty-seven days of strong headwinds, and arrived in New York on 9 June 1915, after having to put into Halifax for coal, with only eight tons left in her bunkers. The Company agent, writing from the Empire Building, Broadway, on 15 June 1915, reported to London that practically the whole of the foremast rigging would have to be renewed, while work on the lower rigging was already in hand. The decks were in a very bad state and would have to be recaulked in a number of places, before her cargo could be properly carried. The engine-room also required some repairs. 'It would appear', he wrote, 'that the ship was sent away very hurriedly from London and a good many of her fittings had been removed to the S.S. *Pelican*.' Despite several enquiries, he had been unable to sell the *Discovery* and asked as to the very lowest figure the Board would accept. He hoped to despatch her on 16 June with a full cargo of caustic soda, bags and corduroy.[13]

The *Discovery* sailed from New York on 21 June 1915 for La Pallice, the outer port of La Rochelle. She arrived there with a cargo of some 415 tons of caustic soda, over 22,000 yards of corduroy and 360,000 empty bags.[14] Captain Williams wrote from La Pallice confirming his arrival there in a letter received in London on 20 July 1915. The first few days of the passage had been fine, but after five days at sea she had sprung a bad leak. Provision stores were destroyed, rooms and cabins were flooded for four days and 35 tons of coal were lost off the deck in a heavy gale. He reported that the ship was still leaking badly and that he had to keep the deck pumps going every watch, fearing damage to the lower part of the cargo. He thought it a big mistake that 'she never had a caulking iron put into her, inside or out, when in dry-dock in London', after being laid up for four years. He would require 'two new truss bands for fore and main lower topsail yards'. The fore was gone altogether and he had the yard slung now with chains.[15]

Having discharged her cargo, the *Discovery* sailed from La Pallice for Falmouth, where she arrived on 30 July and awaited orders. There Captain Williams resigned and was succeeded for the passage to Swansea by the Chief Officer, G. F. Bush.[16] Captain Williams stated on 17 August 1915 that neither the decks nor the outside of the ship had been touched in London before her departure for New York. It was possible 'to drop a caulking iron right through [some of the seams]—and the outside of the ship, after taking off the outside thread of caulking, was in much the same state'. Certain parts were suffering from dry rot and Captain Williams thought that much would have to be taken up, especially aft. He considered the ship had been damaged under the stern, possibly by a big lighter bumping up against it, so that one plank was entirely out of position. This had caused such a leak that she had had to put into Falmouth on the outward voyage, as the crew refused to continue. The repairs were not completed satisfactorily in Falmouth because of pressure applied from London and she had sailed for New York with the plank still out of position. On arrival there, it was found impossible to get near it, because the vessel was too low in the water by the stern. During the return voyage, another leak had developed in the centre of the provision store. The engineers had been unable to carry out all the work usually expected of them during the voyage, because there were insufficient tools on board. There was neither evaporator nor condenser, so that salt water had to be used in the boilers all the time, with the result that they had to be scaled out in New York.[17]

On 4 February 1915, when the *Discovery* was still in dock, before her outward transatlantic voyage, the German Admiralty had declared the waters surrounding Great Britain and Ireland, including the whole of the English Channel, as a war zone, and that from 18 February 'every enemy merchant vessel found within this war zone' would be destroyed 'without its always being possible to avoid danger to the crews and passengers'.[18] This first unrestricted U-boat campaign began as stipulated, but failed initially to disrupt British trade; the German submarine attacks did not begin to bite hard until 1917. On her first wartime voyage, the *Discovery* at any rate would seem to have been in far greater danger of foundering owing to the tempests of the deep than from enemy action. The log of her transatlantic passage does not appear to have survived, but in the correspondence there is no mention of an escort or of danger from U-boats. Attention must have been given to improve her state of repair in Swansea during August 1915, whence she departed for Manchester under Captain William James Bartley, arriving on 7 September. Captain Bartley was to be her master during her next two voyages, the first to Archangel and the second to the Atlantic ports of France.


## VOYAGE TO ARCHANGEL, 1915


The Russian Empire was part of the old order destroyed by the Great War. The Imperial Russia of Tsar Nicholas II found herself almost sealed off from the rest of the world, not by an Iron Curtain, but by the accident of geography. Peter the Great's famous 'window to the west' in the Baltic was closed by German naval supremacy, and the south Russian ports on the Black Sea by the entry of Turkey into the war on the German side.

Before the First World War, Russia had paid for her imports of farm machinery and manufactured goods by the export of wheat, eggs, other foodstuffs and raw materials. But when the Bosporus became blocked by Turkey, and the Baltic by Germany, neither exports nor imports could move. The only remaining large port was Vladivostok on the Pacific Ocean, linked with Petrograd over vast distances by the Trans-Siberian railway. This left Archangel on the White Sea as the main port of entry for vital munitions and equipment for the Russian army, for coal and general goods, and as the export terminal for Russian butter, grain, wood-alcohol, hemp, flax, timber, tow and other products. (Wood-alcohol was used in the manufacture of explosives, hemp and flax by the British navy.)

Archangel had many drawbacks: it was frozen during the winter months and it had extremely limited facilities for handling the goods which began to pour into it after the outbreak of war. The author of the official history of sea-borne trade during the war, C. E. Fayle, has described the situation that arose at the port during the latter months of 1914 and the spring of 1915, particularly as regards the distribution of imports. The quays were too small, the warehousing space was insufficient and the railway station was on the wrong side of the river Dvina. Only a single line of narrow gauge without adequate rolling stock ran from Archangel to Vologda where goods had to be rehandled.[19] In happier days, thousands of pilgrims embarked at Archangel for one of the holiest places in Russia, the mediaeval monastic fortress on the island of Solovets in the south-western corner of the White Sea. The community owned the grey steamers 'that not merely flew the monastery flag, but bore a golden cross at the mainmast and were manned by monks'.[20]

The main pre-war trade of the other White Sea ports of Soroka, Kem and Kandalaksha had been the export of timber, floated down river to the sea. Neither these ports nor the ice-free ones of Kola and Aleksandrovsk on the Murman coast were connected to the interior by rail; they were consequently unable to relieve congestion at Archangel to any

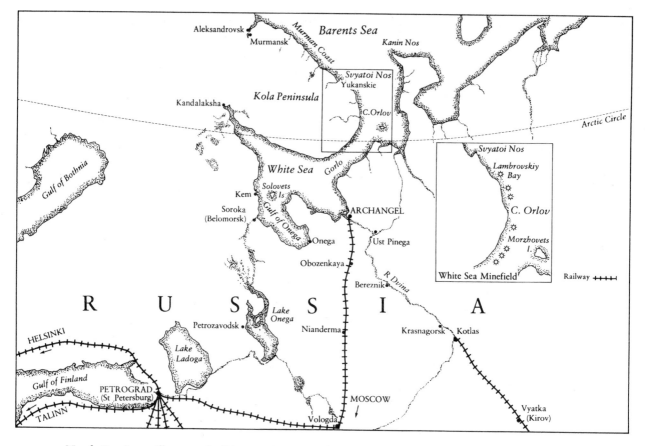

North Russia, to illustrate the *Discovery*'s voyage through the White Sea to Archangel in 1915, based on the maps in C. E. Fayle, *Seaborne Trade,* John Murray, London, 1923-4, and on Henry Newbolt, *Naval Operations*, Vol. V, Longmans, London 1931

real extent until the Murman railway was built. Nevertheless, some efforts were made and reindeer carried light ammunition across snow-bound country during the winter.

Unfortunately, and perhaps surprisingly, as Professor William Barr has pointed out, there was not a single first-class icebreaker stationed in the White Sea and although Russia had the world's most powerful icebreaker, *Yermak* (10,000 hp), this was imprisoned in the Baltic.[21] The Russian authorities therefore negotiated the purchase of a number of Canadian icebreakers, including the fine-lined *Earl Grey* which was renamed *Canada* on her arrival in Archangel in October 1914. Orders for new icebreakers from British yards were also placed, Britain at that time being not only pre-eminent at sea through her merchant fleet and navy, but also ashore in shipbuilding and repair.

Ice was not the only enemy to be faced by merchant ships; the Germans recognised the importance of the White Sea route to the Russian war effort and despatched the auxiliary cruiser, *Meteor*, escorted by a submarine, to lay 285 mines in early June 1915. Between June and September, ten vessels (British, Russian, and neutral) were damaged or lost to mines. A mine-sweeping expedition of six trawlers and two supply ships was sent by the Admiralty from Lowestoft, and reached Aleksandrovsk on the Kola Inlet, north Russia, in early July. By mid-October they had destroyed 150 mines between there and Archangel, finding the mines cleverly laid off headlands and along the courses taken by shipping. A few were destroyed by the Russians, who had no fishing fleet to call on in the White Sea. Mine-sweeping stopped in November 1915 at the onset of a particularly severe winter.[22]

The White Sea or Arctic Squadron of the Royal Navy operated in these waters, its Commodore being senior naval officer in north Russia at Archangel. A second senior officer was stationed at Murmansk in command of the old battleship *Albemarle* and of the cruisers and smaller vessels within his jurisdiction. He also dealt daily with Russian officials in the vicinity. A third senior naval officer was stationed at Yukanskie, a 'rock strewn anchorage' under the lee of Cape Svyatoi Nos, at the northern entrance to the narrow Gorlo or gullet leading to the Gulf of Archangel. It was the duty of the Arctic Squadron and particularly of the British mine-sweeping trawlers to keep a safe channel swept for shipping sailing inward and outward. This third SNO commanded in 1916 HMS *Intrepid*, her sister ship HMS *Iphigenia*, four armed boarding steamers, two yachts, sixteen trawlers, as well as colliers and smaller vessels.[23]

The captain of HMS *Intrepid* and SNO at Yukanskie, 1916–17, Captain Gwatkin-Williams, has written a vivid and often humorous account of the operations of his section of the Arctic Squadron, in which the situation in north Russia during the early part of the war is well explained.

> To Yukanskie, during the period each year that Arkhangel was free from ice, the whole sea-borne trade of Russia converged fanwise. It was there that ships received their orders, and were swept or convoyed to Arkhangel and the other White Sea ports. Day and night the shipping came and went during those short golden summer months, and was boarded, searched, questioned and instructed. . . . Many hundreds of ships passed through each season, laden for the most part with coal, guns, munitions and every species of warlike stores; many whose single cargoes were valued as being worth £2,000,000 each. It was only the old *Intrepid* and the other units of the British Arctic Squadron who made this traffic possible, for, by keeping open the mouth of Arkhangel by which Russia received her war food, they enabled her still to keep going as a combatant.[24]

Further south, the Tenth Cruiser Squadron Northern Patrol was engaged in the blockade of Germany. They operated without intermission on the high seas in all weathers, despite the presence of submarines, intercepting and examining neutral and Allied shipping in an area of 220,000 square miles. This area of the North Atlantic formed a rough triangle between Iceland, Norway and Scotland. The lines of patrol in the autumn of 1915 stretched from the Hebrides to Denmark Strait (to the north-west of Iceland), northward from the Faeroes and to the south-west of the Lofotens. Over three thousand vessels had been intercepted by the end of 1915, of which more than seven hundred were sent to British ports because they carried contraband or suspicious cargoes. In command of the Tenth Cruiser Squadron was Rear Admiral Dudley de Chair, whose flagship was the *Alsatian*. Her record of being at sea for 262 days of the year 1915, steaming 71,500 miles and using over 40,000 tons of coal was typical of the work of each ship of the squadron.[25]

These were the seas through which the *Discovery*'s voyage to north Russia would take her in the autumn of 1915. Under Captain William James Bartley, she departed from Manchester on 8 September 1915, calling at Nantes and Bordeaux before berthing at Brest. Here, from 1915 to 1917, *matériel* from French factories and American ports was piled up on the once sleepy commercial quays of the naval base, for shipment to Russia. The manifest which would have provided a detailed list of the *Discovery*'s cargo on this voyage appears not to have survived. Her freight account shows that she carried a cargo of munitions from Brest to Archangel, arriving on 22 October 1915. A typical cargo of munitions for Russia included a battery of four guns, cartridges, fuses, tubes for firing guns, pistons for Renault engines, Gnome Rhone aero engines (the standard Allied engine in its various forms), acetylene bottles, spare parts for Fiat aircraft engines, units for producing oxygen, bottles of oxygen, Nieuport aeroplanes, radio gear, Renault lorries, De la Haye lorries, machine tools and accessories, antimony, ferro-chrome, ferro-tungsten, tyres, locomotive spares, clothing, oxygen valves, steel tow ropes, pinions, electrical apparatus, pitch and varnish, steel cables, surgical instruments, steel plates, electrical motors and accessories, optical glasses, bronze carburettors, boric acid, aircraft parts, rough cast parts, bolts, screws and sockets.[26]

The *Discovery*'s exact route is uncertain as the log for this voyage is missing, but she must have sailed north from Brest, navigating the area patrolled by the Tenth Cruiser Squadron and then rounded the North Cape of Norway, probably at some distance from the coast, where it was thought there was less danger from submarines. She would then have been escorted by mine-sweepers from Yukanskie with other cargo ships to the Gulf of Archangel, next entering the mouth of the Dvina River, some thirty miles downstream from Archangel itself.

The Hudson's Bay Company (still her owners) had appointed a representative, Mr C. Fuog, in Archangel in May 1915. He travelled to north Russia with Monsieur G. Eybert, the French Vice-Consul, with whom he was to work closely (not without difficulties) in implementing the agreement with the French Government to transport wheat from Archangel to the French ports. The Hudson's Bay Company was to supply the steamers, but the responsibility for finding the cargo and the labour was that of the French Government. Mr Fuog and his assistant, Mr Guthrie, were there 'to smoothe the way'.[27]

*Right:* Sir Clements Markham (1830-1916), who initiated the National Antarctic Expedition, 1901-4, for which the *Discovery* was built. The painting was done in 1913 by George Henry, ARA. To Markham's right is the silver sledge, now in the National Maritime Museum, presented to him on the expedition's return by the officers of the *Discovery* and *Morning*. The portrait hangs in the house of the Royal Geographical Society

*Below:* 'The departure of the *Discovery* from Cowes', 6 August 1901. Oil by Gerald M. Burn. The picture hangs in Dulwich College, London, where Ernest Shackleton (Third Officer) was a pupil, 1887-90

*Right:* The *Discovery* in winter quarters, McMurdo Sound, during the National Antarctic Expedition, 1901-4. By Dr Edward Adrian Wilson, junior surgeon of the *Discovery.* From the Duncan Collection, Dundee Museums. The watercolour was the prize awarded to James Duncan, AB, during the King's birthday sports, 9 November 1903

*Below:* Menu for the farewell dinner in the wardroom of the *Morning,* 1 March 1903, signed by the sixteen officers and scientists of the *Discovery* and the *Morning*

*Bottom right:* Emperor penguins at Cape Crozier, Ross Island, by Dr E. A. Wilson. Body colour

*Above:* Mount Erebus, Ross Island, by Dr E. A. Wilson. Watercolour

*Left:* Castle Rock, near *Discovery's* winter quarters, by Dr E. A. Wilson. Watercolour

SOUTH POLAR TIMES VOL.2.

*Right:* Badge of the
National Antarctic
Expedition, 1901-4

*Top left:* The *Discovery* ice-
bound in winter quarters:
frontispiece to Vol. 2 of the
*South Polar Times*, newspaper
of the National Antarctic
Expedition, 1901-4,
subsequently published in
London (1907)

*Above:* The *Discovery* seen
with parhelia, under sail in
the pack, by Dr E. A.
Wilson. Indian ink and grey
wash heightened with white.
Scott Polar Research
Institute, Wilson Collection

*Left:* Departure of the
*Morning*, 2 March 1903,
from the *South Polar Times*

*Above:* The *Discovery* in 1911, when owned by the Hudson's Bay Company. Oil by Thomas G. Purvis, in the possession of the Hudson's Bay Company

*Below:* 'York Factory, the Hayes, 1981'. Oil by Albert Hochbaum

*Bottom right:* Coat of arms of the Hudson's Bay Company

*Above:* 'Convent of Solovetsk in the Frozen Sea', the name given to the White Sea by the sailors and sealers of the time: frontispiece to *Free Russia* by W. H. Dixon (London, 1870)

*Below:* General view of Novorossiysk on the Black Sea, from an undated old Russian postcard

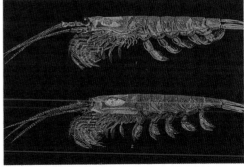

*Top:* Parhelion effect (mock suns), seen off Graham Land, March 1927, during the *Discovery* (Oceanographic) Expedition, 1925-7. Watercolour by Sir Alister Hardy

*Above: Euphausia superba* (krill), drawn by Hélene Bargmann for *Discovery Reports*, Vol. xiv, 1937. Male specimen above, female below

*Left:* Pyrosoma in the phosphorescent wake of the *Discovery*, 11 November 1925, near Ascension Island, South Atlantic Ocean. Watercolour by Sir Alister Hardy

*Left:* Mount Paget, South Georgia, lit by a low full moon, with King Edward Cove still in shade, 14 February 1927. A passing whale catcher is seen on the right. Watercolour by E. R. Gunther

*Above:* Bouvet Island seen from the *Discovery*, ten miles off shore on 17 November 1926. Watercolour by E. R. Gunther

*Right:* 'The *Discovery* at Falmouth, 1927' on return from her oceanographic voyage, by H. S. Tuke RA

Monsieur Eybert got upset at times if the vessels he required were not available. Fuog reported in July that he found it difficult to make the French Vice-Consul listen to reason. 'He is of course a functionary, doesn't see things from the practical business point of view and cannot understand that steamers cannot in these times be at his disposal with the precision of a train service.'[28] German mines and poorly charted waters made it impossible to keep to schedule; other complications were lack of adequate port facilities, a shortage of labour, and winter ice. As regards the HBC's agency in Archangel, it is worth noting that 'for over four years under various forms of Russian Government, including Bolshevic', the Company maintained an agency in Archangel, 'which was only abandoned when the British Government ordered the removal of all British subjects. During that period, all the munitions from France for Russia and Roumania were transported under the Company's flag, in effect, if not always, to Archangel; on the return voyages, over 350,000 tons of wheat, transported by rail and river from Siberia, together with timber, ore, flax, hemp, beetroot seeds and other cargo, were taken to French ports . . . .'[29]

Steamer No. 141 (the *Discovery*) on time charter[30] discharged her 500 tons of cargo at the Russian government berth of Bakaritsya. The munitions were packed in very large cases, which could be unloaded only through the main hatchway. During the voyage, bad weather had caused the ship to labour and strain heavily. The decks were rotten in parts and had leaked a lot, making a great deal of water in the bottom. Thirty-five tons of coal had been lost in a storm at sea and, afraid that some of the cargo might have been damaged, Captain Bartley extended a legal Protest against the weather encountered on the passage, referring any of the receivers of the cargo to Mr J. Schmidt, the ship's broker at Archangel.[31] The ship's company was paid a war bonus for this voyage, a monthly £5 extra for Captain Bartley, £3 for the Engineer and Mate, and £1 for the firemen and sailors.[32] There was much to do in port: manoeuvring the vessel for discharge and loading, taking on coal for the return voyage, dealing with various officials and getting the *Discovery* swung in the ice to ascertain the deviation of her compass at 'Moses Island' whence she was towed by a tug.[33] There must have been opportunities to go ashore too and visit Archangel, a city of gleaming domes and log houses, each with a geranium, fuchsia or oleander at its window.

One of the Petty Officers from the mine-sweeping trawler *Ganton*, Alfred Kneale, kept a diary and went ashore at Archangel a few weeks before the *Discovery* arrived.

A long strangling place on the left bank of the river. There are enormous timber yards going at least $^1/_2$ mile back from the river front . . . It was 14 miles to the city and nearly all timber yards . . . They have enormous barges at least 300 feet long. Some they knock together up country just to bring the timber down. The place was not much to go ashore in. Had a walk around through the market. Great people for fish. Saw plenty of fresh vegetables and potatoes etc. Could not get any to speak English. As a rule you can hear it in any hole in the world. Trade is very busy here.

The steamers are unloading munitions of war, but they can't get it away as their is only a single track line not completed yet. So it will be a long time before the troops can get it. The boating seems to be done by the women, some with 8 oars and they pull like a bit of machinery.[34]

He found that the men handled the timber very cleverly, but that the women otherwise did all the work. They washed their linen in the river. No liquor was to be had in town. Kneale's diary is of great interest in other ways, with its tally of mines destroyed (63 by the end of August), its account of merchantmen blown up by mines or wrecked on lee shores, its description of convoy duties—some vessels trying to avoid the convoy and slip past (these had shots fired across their bows), together with the passengers who flit through its pages—the English lady going home, the Scottish lassies—Red Cross nurses *en route* for the Russian Front, Admiral Phillimore in his yacht being escorted through a minefield on his way to the Tsar's court in Petrograd as Chief of the British Naval Mission to Russia, 1915–16, and lastly the vigorous and abrasive Captain T. W. Kemp, and staff, whose headquarters as Senior Naval Officer in the White Sea were at Archangel. After describing the wooden town, another wartime visitor observed of its people:

Half an hour in Archangel will make you realise two things: first, that you are very far north, among a population which has a whiff of the Arctic Seas—a hard-looking people accustomed to leading a hard life, much of it spent warring with a harsh, inhospitable, uncomfortable climate; the second, that the bulk of the population are concerned mainly with two occupations, the one of the sea and the commerce of the sea, the other of the forest and all that the forest can be made to produce when converted to man's use.[35]

The *Discovery* loaded 557 barrels of spirit (wood-alcohol) of which 364 were iron drums and 193 wooden barrels. These were delivered by the Russian Alcohol Administration and consigned to the order of a Mr Helussan at Brest.[36] The loading and stowage proved difficult because only one hatch was big enough to take in cargo and the drums had to be rolled the length of the ship. She was fortunate to depart for Le Havre before conditions became more and more difficult owing to the freezing of the Dvina and the White Sea, even with the help of icebreakers *Canada*, *Bruce*, *Lintrose* and *J. T. Horne*, which had arrived from Canada and Newfoundland, having been purchased by the Russian Government earlier in the war.[37] One eyewitness described the situation in the port itself, in early December: delays caused by the ice, a lack of cranes, the fact that much work ashore with Government goods was done by slow, spasmodic and unmethodical soldiers and also that the Customs and Port authorities were often at loggerheads with each other. About a thousand motor cars lay unprotected in the snow, 'together with some other cargoes, including machinery and apparently no care being taken as to their condition and no arrangements for goods being moved to the interior'.[38]

Captain Bartley duly discharged his cargo of wood-alcohol in northern France, thus contributing to the Allied war effort. He was instructed to take the East Coast route home and to call at Dundee for orders. From there he wrote to London on 19 November (before leaving for Le Havre) to report that the top tier of barrels had come adrift when the between deck stanchions gave way in a heavy northerly gale and that he was having them restowed. He suggested that the addition of 'Bilge pieces' to the hull would stop the vessel labouring so much and that with a four-bladed propeller she would do an ordinary tramp speed. The construction of a fore hatchway for delivering and taking in cargo would save much in labour.[39] The fitting of bilge keels ten years later did greatly improve the ship.

The *Discovery* was both lucky to escape being frozen in at Archangel (unlike a number of other much-needed merchant ships that winter) and to miss a violent storm with dense snow squalls and a tremendous sea in the North Atlantic on 24 December 1915; the old Scottish whaler *Active* (which had preceded the *Discovery* to the Antarctic in 1892–3) and the brave little *Morning*, her first relief ship, were both lost then. They were carrying munitions to Russia and had also been chartered to the French Government by the Hudson's Bay Company. The Company had bought them for this purpose (together with the *Scotia*) from Robert Kinnes of Dundee. All but two lives were lost.[40] The story of the PQ17 and other convoys to Russia in the Second World War is deservedly well known. Perhaps this account of the *Discovery*'s voyage to north Russia in 1915 will help to draw attention to the ships and men of both Royal Navy and Merchant Navy who may be considered their predecessors in the Great War.

CHAPTER

# TWELVE

## THE SEARCH FOR SHACKLETON, 1916

### THE DEMISE OF THE *ENDURANCE*

LIEUT. ERNEST SHACKLETON, RNR, had been a member of the National Antarctic Expedition, 1901–4, but was invalided home in the *Morning* at the end of the first year, to his own intense disappointment and to the regret of his friends. Having drunk these bitter dregs, his roving and adventurous spirit would not let him rest until he had returned to the Antarctic, this time as leader of the *Nimrod* expedition of 1907–9. He sledged with three companions to within 97 miles of the South Pole, ascending the great Beardmore Glacier (named after his patron) and discovering some five hundred miles of new mountain ranges bordering the Ross Ice Shelf. The following years saw the attainment of the South Pole by the Norwegian explorer Roald Amundsen, and the deaths of Captain Scott and the British Pole party during the *Terra Nova* expedition of 1910–13.

Shackleton next set himself the heroic task of crossing the Antarctic continent from the Weddell Sea to the Ross Sea, as leader of the Imperial Trans-Antarctic Expedition, which was financed very largely by the great Dundee jute manufacturer, Sir James Caird. Its Weddell Sea party in the *Endurance* sailed from London on 1 August 1914, only three days before the outbreak of war. Shackleton offered to place the ship, crew and stores at the nation's disposal, but received a telegram from the First Lord of the Admiralty, Mr Winston Churchill, which read 'Proceed.' After consulting HM King George V and his benefactors, Shackleton resolved to carry on.

The *Endurance* sailed south and became beset in the ice at the head of the Weddell Sea. The dog teams trained for the crossing of Antarctica never set foot on the continent. They remained with the ship, which drifted north until she was crushed and sank on 21 November 1915 some 200 miles east of the Antarctic Peninsula, south of the Antarctic Circle in the north-west quadrant of the Weddell Sea. The party camped on the floes, which continued to drift northwards. Reaching the open sea at last, three ship's boats were launched and after great privations suffered by their crews, beached safely on desolate Elephant Island, to the north of the Antarctic Peninsula. Meanwhile, the other half of the Imperial Trans-Antarctic Expedition, known as the Ross Sea party, on the opposite side of the continent, had been landed from the *Aurora*. Their duty was to lay depots to the southward that could be picked up by the crossing party on the second half of their traverse, from the South Pole towards Mount Erebus and McMurdo Sound.

Shackleton's men from the *Endurance* continued to live in grime and squalor under two of the upturned boats on a grey beach above high water, below the cliffs of Elephant Island surviving on a diet largely consisting of penguins, other birds, seals and shellfish. News of their plight reached the world from the Falklands. Transported by the small whaler *Southern Sky*, Shackleton had gone ashore at Port Stanley from South Georgia, which he reached at the end of his epic voyage from Elephant Island in the third of the *Endurance*'s boats, the *James Caird*. His telegrams reached England late on 31 May 1916, claiming public attention before news started coming in of the Battle of Jutland, between the British and German fleets in the North Sea. Elephant Island is well north of the Antarctic Circle and does not suffer from winter darkness, but it can become ice-bound. Shackleton was anxious to rescue his men before they had to endure much more of the winter. His first attempt in the *Southern Sky* was unsuccessful because of the sea ice.

Despite the exigencies of war, a Shackleton Relief Advisory Committee had been set up by the Admiralty in London, *before* any news came from Shackleton. Its chairman was Admiral Sir Lewis Beaumont, who had served as a young naval officer during the Arctic expedition under Sir George Nares. Two of the other committee members with far greater and more recent experience in the polar regions were Dr W. S. Bruce, leader of the Scottish National Antarctic Expedition of 1902–4, and Sir Douglas Mawson, leader of the Australasian Antarctic Expedition of 1911–14 (who was waiting to go to north Russia). The Hydrographer of the Navy and his Civil Assistant plus representatives of the Treasury, the Board of Trade, the Royal Geographical Society and Shackleton's attorneys made up the rest. The Government approved the Relief Committee's report of 19 May 1916. This recommended the despatch of the *Discovery* to examine the shores of the Weddell Sea, having been equipped with dogs, tents, and sledges and provisioned for two years.[1]

The arrival of Shackleton in the Falkland Islands at the end of May ended the need to search for him and the work of the Committee stopped briefly, since it was thought a rescue vessel would be found there. However, no such ship suitable for use in ice appeared available in South America or at the Cape. Shackleton urged the despatch of a relief expedition from England, asking either for a wooden steam whaler, the *Discovery* or a sea-going icebreaker. The Advisory Committee therefore, while realising there was still a possibility that rescue could be effected locally if the sea ice should clear, recommended on 10 July 1916 that a vessel should be acquired, equipped for six months and sent south in charge of an experienced Ice Master, but with an ordinary crew. This was accepted by the British Government, to whom the Hudson's Bay Company offered to lend the *Discovery* free of charge.[2] The Committee also recommended that on arrival, the relief ship 'should be placed at the disposal and under the orders of Sir Ernest Shackleton'. The *Discovery* was accordingly ordered to Devonport, where she was 'manned and equipped . . . with great dispatch owing to the zeal and goodwill of the Officers and men of His Majesty's Dockyard . . .'. Photographs taken at the time show her square-rigged on the foremast only and minus her topgallant masts,[3] probably about to secure to a buoy for further rigging. She was ready to sail by 5 August, but did not do so for five days because of 'war delays' to the collier which was to tow her south.

The man chosen to command her was Captain James Fairweather, aged 63, whom the Secretary to the Admiralty described as 'an Ice Master and seaman of proved experience and ability'. A native of Dundee and living then in Newport, Fife, he had been master of the whaler *Aurora* in the northern whale fishery for the whole of the 1880s. His brother, Captain Alexander Fairweather, had commanded the *Balaena* during the Antarctic whaling reconnaissance from Dundee of 1892–3.[4] According to an obituary, he was a man of genial personality, with a great fund of Scottish humour.[5] He was short and stocky, with a pointed beard, and in the photographs taken on departure, he is seen holding a black cat. During the Great War, before and after the Shackleton relief voyage, he was Chief Examination Officer, Tay.[6] Captain Fairweather was granted a temporary commission as Lieut.-Com., Royal Naval Reserve, while Dr Gerald Martin was made an acting surgeon, RN. The rest of the ship's company consisted of First, Second and Third Mates, First, Second and Third Engineers, a Purser and Steward, Second Steward, Cook, Second Cook, Carpenter and ten Able Seamen. A uniform allowance of £7 was given to the officers and engineers and one of £5 to the purser and steward, second steward, both cooks and the carpenter.

Lieut.-Com. Fairweather's sailing orders were dated 2 August 1916. When the SS *Discovery* was 'in all respects ready for sea', he should leave Devonport in tow of the collier *Polesley*, for the Falkland Islands. If Sir Ernest Shackleton was at Port Stanley, the Elephant Island rescue should be thought out with him, in the light of the Admiralty's letter to the explorer enclosed for information. This letter would inform Sir Ernest that the *Discovery*,

> under your command is placed at his disposal, and that, subject to the safety and welfare of the Officers and men committed to your charge and to the risk to the ship inseparable from such service, you are to take him [Shackleton] on board and carry out his wishes as far as possible in regard to all measures he may advise to rescue the party.

Sir Ernest's advice concerning the treatment of those rescued, perhaps helpless and disabled, should be followed. Any graves should be marked; no bodies should be embarked. Captain Fairweather should use his discretion as to a further search, if the party had left Elephant Island. A record of his visit should be placed in a cairn or on a conspicuous point on the island. On their return to Port Stanley, the rescued men should be landed and transferred to the charge of Sir Ernest Shackleton. However, a passage home in the *Discovery* might be offered to those willing to accept the accommodation and certified fit to undergo the long voyage. Supposing Sir Ernest were not at Port Stanley, or unable to accompany him, Captain Fairweather should proceed with the rescue to the best of his ability.[7] The letter addressed to Shackleton repeated that Captain Fairweather was to take him aboard and to carry out his wishes as far as possible to effect the rescue of his men. In contrast to the Advisory Committee's recommendation, it stated that 'the command of the ship and all who may be on board as well as the responsibility for the action he takes, must belong in [Captain Fairweather's] hands'. A copy of the Admiralty's orders to Fairweather was enclosed for Shackleton.

## THE VOYAGE SOUTH

The *Discovery* began her voyage in the early evening of 10 August 1916. A hawser from SS *Polesley*, the collier which was ordered to tow her to the Falklands, was shackled on in Plymouth Sound. An armed trawler escorted her on each bow for the first hundred miles towards the Cape Verde Islands. A motor launch was carried on deck and barrels of salt pork stowed in the fore peak. The potatoes quickly began to go bad at the start of the voyage. More than two hundred miles were covered each 24 hours—much farther than the *Discovery*'s unaided power would have allowed. The *Discovery*'s log does not record any difficulties with the tow, despite a great deal of rough weather, even in low latitudes. In the tropics on 1 September, the upper main topmast staysail was carried away, while two days later, in a 'confused southerly swell', the ship was 'diving and jumping heavily'.[8]

After 20 days' passage from the Cape Verdes, the two vessels arrived at Montevideo on 11 September. Here the hawser was slipped from the *Discovery*'s chain bridle and she proceeded with the *Polesley* to the anchorage. The crew were employed scrubbing the *Discovery*'s side 'between wind and water where grass had grown along the sides and barnacles under the stern'. The barnacles may have been surprised by her speed but they had hung on.

Shackleton meanwhile had been far from idle, organising further rescue attempts in various South American craft. The last of these in the *Yelcho*, a small Chilean naval vessel, was successful. On 30 August 1916, with their bay free of ice, the Elephant Island party, ably led during the months spent there by Frank Wild, embarked by boat from their beach in less than an hour, for fear the sea ice should return. Shackleton's delight at finding them all well was equalled by theirs at seeing him. The *Yelcho* returned in triumph to Punta Arenas, with Shackleton immensely pleased that he had managed to organise the rescue himself, without the Admiralty.[9] He appears to have resented their Lordships' stipulation that Captain Fairweather, and not he, should command the *Discovery* after her arrival in Port Stanley. It is stated in the Advisory Committee's Final Report that the Admiralty only heard of his success through the newspapers.

At Montevideo the purpose of the *Discovery*'s voyage was negated as the marooned men had been rescued. The Surgeon, Dr G. M. Martin, was 'paid off and discharged by mutual consent, as he wanted to get home'.[10] Fresh-water tanks were refitted and some painting done, while waiting for orders. The crew were allowed liberty ashore one day with a steam-launch to take them there and back. The *Discovery* was next piloted to Buenos Aires to take on a cargo of grain. Bad weather plagued them *en route* and on arrival, when they had to be towed into harbour on 21 September.

Next day, Flynn the Second Cook was arrested on Captain Fairweather's orders and taken to gaol, no reason being given. 100 tons of coal were landed. The sails were loosed, dried and furled, while a squad of caulkers worked on the vessel's seams. The holds were cleaned for cargo, as were the decks. On 28 September, after a squad of carpenters had made ready the hold, the wheat was loaded in bags. On 30 September, the *Discovery* departed from Buenos Aires, under her own steam, homeward bound. The deck log records that on 11 October, engines were stopped 'to see how the ship would act under canvas, the breeze being satisfactory for such a purpose'. However, the trial proved a failure: 'no sooner the engine stopped than the helm had to be put Hard up'. Even with the helm hard over, 'the ship came to the wind and so remained as if Hove to and as if the helm had been Hard a lea'. Full speed was then rung.

On 16 October, the *Discovery* berthed at Pernambuco, where water and coal were taken on and the cargo shifted. Bad weather still harassed them in the lower latitudes and she berthed on 31 October at St Vincent, Cape Verde Islands, in a gale, causing the bunkering lighter to bump heavily against the ship's side. On 3 November, Captain Fairweather (in the words of the log) 'called the crew together and explained to them that he had been invalided Home and that the chief officer would now become Master and he trusted that the ship's work would go on satisfactorily to all concerned'. At 1.45 p.m. he left ship for home, an elderly man, perhaps tired out by the responsibilities (and the disappointment maybe) of the voyage. The new master was J. Cumming and his replacement as mate, H. Moar. They left St Vincent on 8 November, all fore- and aft-sails being set. More gales were encountered on passage. The decks, the engine-room and the officers' cabins were all flooded as the *Discovery* rolled, shipping heavy seas. On 28 November, the Eddystone Light was abeam and the vessel anchored later in Plymouth Sound, entering the basin next day.

# THIRTEEN

## IN CONVOY TO FRENCH AND SPANISH PORTS, 1916–18, LAST VOYAGE TO HUDSON BAY, 1918–19, COASTING THE FRENCH ATLANTIC PORTS AND THE LOW COUNTRIES, 1919

THE ADMIRALTY HANDED BACK THE *DISCOVERY* to the Hudson's Bay Company—then operating the Bay Steamship Company—at Devonport on 18 December 1916. Her new master was Captain L. Hiles. After coaling and signing on crew, she crossed the English Channel to Lorient on the south coast of Brittany, where she became one of several vessels in the extensive coasting service organised by the Company for transporting grain and other supplies from incoming ocean steamers to the smaller ports of France. Most of the *Discovery*'s logs for these wartime voyages, kept by her chief officers, have survived in the Bay Steamship Company series of the Hudson's Bay Company archives, from which this narrative is largely written.[1] A system of convoys was in operation to combat the menace of German submarines.[2]

## FRENCH ATLANTIC PORTS, DECEMBER 1916–JULY 1917

In Lorient, she discharged the 5,943 bags of South American wheat taken on in Buenos Aires and departed towards Bordeaux on 12 January 1917. At Pauillac, a small port on the south bank of the Gironde to seaward of Bordeaux, she loaded 350 tons of wheat, which were discharged at Bayonne, about 150 miles to the south near Biarritz, from 23 to 26 January. There was an embargo on at Bayonne, as there had been at Pauillac, and the ship was not allowed to proceed until 28 January, with a pilot aboard. At Rochefort she moored alongside the French ship *Laennec* on 31 January 1917 and took on 350 tons of wheat, which she discharged at Bayonne. Here she loaded a cargo of zinc plates (presumably for batteries) and departed for Nantes, escorted by a French gunboat. She anchored off La Pallice, following 'Admiralty instructions' on 12 February, and proceeded under convoy next day for Saint Nazaire. Here the *Discovery* received permission to proceed up river to Nantes, where the zinc plates were unloaded.

After the zinc had been unloaded at Nantes, she took on 300 tons of sugar and 30 tons of bunker coal. On 19 February, all navigation in the River Loire stopped because of dense fog and, a day later, she was still unable to proceed to sea on account, ironically, of the 'large quantity of drift ice' in the river. The next day, she proceeded down stream, anchoring off Saint-Nazaire, 'according to Admiralty instructions'. At 6.15 on the morning of 22 February, she hove up anchor and proceeded 'on her own passage' towards Brest. For the greater part of the afternoon she remained anchored inside Belle Ile, awaiting the right to proceed. At 7 p.m. she hove up anchor and proceeded under convoy, following various courses 'according to Admiralty instructions', towards Brest where she discharged 3,700 bags of sugar and coaled again from 24 to 28 February. At 10 p.m. on 13 March, having taken aboard 853 bags of wheat, the *Discovery* received orders from the French Admiralty to sail at 7 a.m.

Under convoy from Brest she proceeded to Lorient, where she discharged from 18 to 22 March. From there she continued in squalls of snow towards Nantes, where she again loaded wheat in bags, by day and night, finishing on 26 March, having taken aboard 512 tons. She proceeded on her own passage from Saint-Nazaire towards Rochefort, awaiting a convoy under Belle Ile to go south to Rochefort, where she discharged and loaded coal day and night, which was in its turn discharged at Nantes from 10 to 14 April. At Saint-Nazaire, another cargo (illegible in the log) was taken on and discharged at Bordeaux on 30 April and 1 May. Here Captain F. Gray became her master. The vessel next loaded sugar, which she had discharged at Bayonne by 15 May, before taking on a general cargo at Bordeaux and proceeding under convoy towards Nantes. Having discharged there, she loaded sugar again and proceeded, at times under convoy, to Bayonne, where the cargo was discharged. On 12 June, she steamed down to St-Jean-de-Luz and anchored inside the breakwater, awaiting a north-going convoy.

While proceeding towards Bordeaux under convoy, a shock was felt in the after part of the ship, which appeared to have been struck by some sunken wreckage. By midnight on 13 June, water was rising in the engine-room bilges and pumps were used to keep it under control. Anchoring in Verdon roads at the mouth of the Gironde, orders came to proceed to Brest under convoy. On 21 June 1917, the *Discovery* steamed into harbour and was shifted with three tugs first to the military dock and then to the dry dock. Once this was pumped dry, the workmen began the repair work. Mr Nicholls, the owners' superintendent, visited the ship and found several treenails loose and the ship's bottom leaking badly. Repairs and the caulking of her bottom took several days, but she eventually left the dry dock for Commerce Dock, assisted by tugs. Here grain was loaded in bulk. She proceeded under south-going convoy and discharged 677 tons of wheat at Bayonne in mid-July.

The *Discovery* again awaited a north-going convoy at St-Jean-de-Luz (having coaled as usual at Boucau, down river from Bayonne). She proceeded under convoy to La Pallice, the outer port of La Rochelle, and anchored, again awaiting a north-going convoy. This departed on 23 July and on 24 July, the *Discovery* anchored in Quiberon Bay, once more to await convoy. She anchored in Cherbourg harbour, again awaiting convoy, which proceeded on 26 July. On Sunday 29 July, having rounded the Lizard the day before, the vessel steamed up to Barry Dock and moored to the buoys. The first log of this wartime series was kept by G. Pearce, Chief Officer.[3]

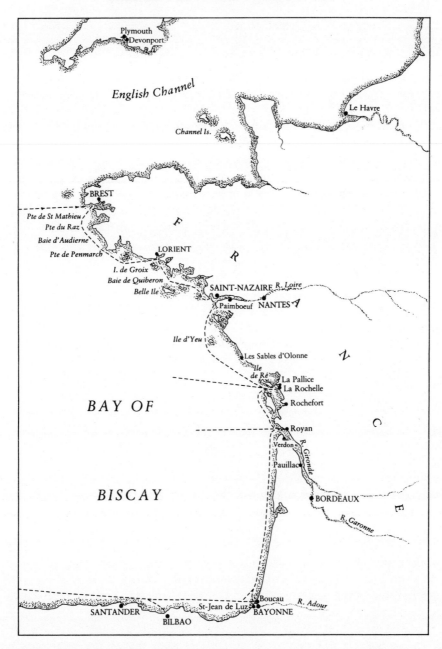

Convoy routes in the Bay of Biscay, 1917-18, adapted from a map in H. Wickliffe Rose, *Brittany Patrol*, W. W. Norton, New York 1937

## BARRY TO MADEIRA AND BORDEAUX, AUGUST–NOVEMBER 1917

Captain Gray continued as master of the *Discovery* with Pearce as mate during this voyage to Madeira. A larger quantity of coal than usual was taken on (144 tons) for bunkering and a cargo of coal amounting to 569 tons. The embargo in force at Barry was lifted on 31 August when the vessel proceeded down the Bristol Channel under Admiralty instructions. She awaited permission to leave at Milford Haven for several days, proceeding as instructed on 6 September, and arrived in Funchal on 15 September. By 18 September, the coal had been discharged and the hold washed out. A general cargo which included heavy guns was loaded between 20 and 27 September,[4] when she departed towards Bordeaux. Fresh gales and heavy seas caused her to strain severely during the return voyage. She put in to Bilbao for bunkers in early October, finally arriving alongside the quay at Bordeaux on 16 October. She discharged between 18 and 22 October, when it was found that several casks were broken in No. 1 hold. She loaded again at Pauillac and proceeded, again under Admiralty instructions, through occasional gales and heavy seas towards Barry. She sheltered in Mousehole Bay and anchored in early November, arriving first at Barry and then Cardiff, discharging there on 10 November 1917. A new mate by the name of A. J. Bills took over then, and he concluded the log[5] on 15 November, as the holds were swept clean.

## FRENCH ATLANTIC PORTS, NOVEMBER 1917–APRIL 1918

The *Discovery* departed from Cardiff on 19 November 1917 and returned there on 1 February 1918, having called at Saint-Nazaire, Nantes and Bayonne, her master being Captain Gray again.[6] The next and last of these French coastal voyages commenced at Cardiff on 23 February 1918 and terminated there on 25 April 1918. Captain Gray was again master, and A. J. Bills mate, and her ports of call were Bayonne, Bordeaux, Nantes and Bayonne again. The various 'legs' of these voyages took place under naval escort in convoy as before. While the *Discovery* lay at anchor in Brest Bay awaiting convoy on 28 February 1918, a destroyer patrolling the harbour, in the words of the log, 'collided with our steamer's port bow, doing damage to same'. While the vessel lay alongside the wharf at Bayonne on 12 March, ready to get under the cranes, the pilot came aboard at 3.45 a.m. to shift her. However, the crew would not turn out to move the steamer to the discharging berth, as they were all drunk. Captain Gray had to engage five men from a Spanish vessel to move ship on the next tide, as five of the *Discovery*'s seamen had gone ashore without leave.[7] Unloading began in the afternoon. At 3 p.m., in the words of the log, 'H.B.M. Consul being on board was asked to speak to the seamen about their behaviour, when one of them (D. Adamtzevitch) began using abusive language, also throwing buckets and toureens about. This man was put under arrest and taken on shore to gaol.' This same seaman was brought back to the ship from prison three days later, as she was about to sail to Bordeaux. One of the seamen (O. Bergstrom) was there taken to hospital, while the *Discovery* loaded timber. The doctor came aboard to visit Seaman Adamtzevitch, who was off duty, sick.[8] The timber cargo was unloaded at Nantes at the end of March 1918. The crew cleaned the holds and the vessel was towed down river by two steam tugs. She moored alongside a Brazilian steamer from which flour was unloaded into No. 2 hatch. Seaman Adamtzevitch refused to come on deck to work and was off duty on several days in early April. He was eventually paid off in Bayonne, where the cargo was unloaded on 10 and 11 April. The *Discovery* steamed north under escort by the usual route and on 25 April 1918 moored under two cranes at Cardiff docks ready to unload the cargo taken on at Boucau, near Bayonne.[9]

She appears to have spent the next few weeks in port, perhaps being repaired and refitted for her next voyage, which was across the Atlantic to Montreal, then north to Hudson Bay.

## LAST VOYAGE TO HUDSON BAY, 1918–19

The *Discovery*'s voyage of 1918 to Hudson Bay was not only her last to the north, but her last wartime voyage. Her master was Captain G. H. Mead of Cardiff,[10] who was making his first voyage as master to the Bay. He was later to command the well-known *Nascopie* on the same route, which vessel had been operating in the service of the Hudson's Bay Company following the *Discovery*'s withdrawal in 1911.

The *Discovery* sailed under the flag of Sale and Company, which firm provided a gun and two gunners for the Atlantic crossing. She left Cardiff on 6 June 1918 carrying 304 tons of coal for her bunkers and some 400 as cargo and arrived safely in Montreal on 30 June, after what Captain Mead called 'a very good passage out, being twenty two days from Pilot to Pilot'. The *Discovery* provisioned for twelve months on the advice of Captain Mack, who had 'long experience in the Company's service' and whom Captain Mead had been asked to consult for information regarding the navigation to Hudson Bay. A bonus of an extra month's wages was to be paid to all who completed the Bay voyage satisfactorily.[11]

The *Discovery* departed from Montreal for Charlton Island on 13 July 1918, with a cargo of Welsh coal, plus Canadian goods comprising flour, pork, fats and eighteen canoes, altogether some 700 tons. She was equipped with a motor boat.[12] The *Nascopie* steamed northwards too as usual in 1918; she had also been on the Archangel run and had been commended by the Admiralty after an encounter with an enemy submarine. News of the war was scanty in the north and came mostly in the form of rumour. There was always the fear that the supply ship might not come at all.[13] The original purpose of the *Discovery*'s voyage was to land cargo at Charlton Island only and to return in ballast. However, it was later decided that she should bring the Charlton 'returns' as far as St John's, Newfoundland. Special stowage and dunnage (packing and wedges) were necessary to protect her cargo from leaks. Captain Mead received his instructions for the voyage from the Fur Trade Commissioner of the Hudson's Bay Company in Montreal, Mr N. H. Bacon. 'As you are aware', read one paragraph of these, 'it is a matter of the most vital importance that you should succeed in completing your voyage out and home, and I am to request that you will take every precaution in navigating the 'Discovery' to ensure the safety of the vessel, and, above all, make proper use of the lead, so as to avoid as far as possible any untoward misfortune to the ship.'[14]

The vessel had a long and difficult passage of Hudson Strait, probably because of Captain Mead's lack of experience. He failed to enter the Strait close to Resolution Island and thus to take advantage of the current flowing west along the north shore. On 26 July 1918, his diary records that his ship was set in towards Cape Chidley, at the southern entrance to the Strait. Cape Chidley is dangerous for shipping owing to the convergence of the southbound Labrador current and the current flowing east along the south shore of Hudson Strait, both carrying masses of ice. Fast in the ice and right under the cliff 'heading inshore, end of jibboom about 100 feet off', she was only half a ship's length from destruction. If the cliffs had not been steep-to and the ship had taken the ground, she would have been lost. Fortunately, the ice eased up and they were able to work clear before she was again beset.[15]

Chief officer J. A. Dernier's log recorded ice-inflicted damage to rudder and steering gear on 28 July,[16] but the *Discovery* was soon freed again, and worked to the northward, sighting Resolution Island on 6 August and then entering Hudson Strait with the help of the west-going current. Nearly a week later, after a period of fog and heavy snow falls, the *Discovery* was again caught in an awkward situation at the western end of the Strait, to the north of Salisbury Island (when she should have been south of it) and trapped by the heavy ice from Foxe Basin flowing to the east towards Charles Island. The ice loosened and the *Discovery* was worked eventually into Hudson Bay, where she still encountered ice and fog off the islands near the eastern shore.[17] James Bay was found clear of ice and the *Discovery* anchored at last at Charlton Island on 10 September, when the schooners *Fort George* and *Eskimo* began taking off her cargo.[18] Captain Mead sent aloft a topgallant mast and yard at Charlton Island. The mast was cut there, but he had to buy the yard from the Hudson's Bay Company post, as he could not find a tree large enough to make it.[19]

They departed from Charlton Island on 24 September, reaching St John's, Newfoundland, on 13 October, where the damage caused by the ice to rudder and stem was found to be not very great. In a letter written at St John's, on 24 October,[20] Captain Mead reported this and suggested to his owners that the vessel should remain in eastern Canada for the seal fishery in the spring and for voyages to Hudson Bay. The repairs were carried out satisfactorily in St John's, where the shipwrights were accustomed to working on wooden ships. The world-wide epidemic of Spanish influenza attacked a number of the crew in both St John's and Halifax, Nova Scotia, including the engineer, who had already been twice torpedoed in Bay ships and whom it was found difficult to replace.[21]

Meanwhile the Great War had ended with the signing of the Armistice on 11 November 1918. The *Discovery* sailed at last for England from Halifax on Christmas Eve, bound for Liverpool. She carried a cargo of some 2,000 cases of canned goods, 113 cases of bronze powder, 1,035 kegs of nails and a sample case of fish.[22] Very bad weather plagued them during the Atlantic passage, straining the decks. The pumps had to be kept going continually to keep the leaks under control. Captain Mead was forced to put into Queenstown (Dun Laoghaire), Ireland, for bunkers and to get the ship on an even keel again.[23] This long-drawn-out last northern voyage terminated in Liverpool on 16 January 1919. Captain Mead saw fit to send an abstract of his diary to the Royal Geographical Society, from which a note was published in the *Geographical Journal*, summarising the voyage and observing that the *Discovery* was still afloat and earning her keep.[24]

## COASTING THE FRENCH ATLANTIC PORTS AND THE LOW COUNTRIES, 1919

The voyage to Hudson Bay was followed by two coasting voyages to France and the Low Countries during the first half of 1919. There was a shortage of shipping immediately after the war, and the *Discovery* continued to act as a small cargo vessel, presumably very largely under steam.

The first of these, again under Captain G. H. Mead, commenced in Liverpool and terminated in Kingston-upon-Hull. Her ports of call were Antwerp, London, Antwerp and King's Lynn. She left Liverpool on 20 February, sighting a floating mine in the North Sea *en route* for Antwerp, where her cargo was discharged at the Old Dock. She proceeded by way of Orfordness (south of Aldeburgh) on both outward and return passages. She next steamed up the London River to Blackwall. Here she began loading barrels of petroleum from lighters and bunkering, the cargo amounting to 2,059 casks in the hold, and 1,341 cases of fish on deck. This oil was safely discharged at the Continental Petroleum Company's wharf, Antwerp, as was the fish, on 16 and 17 March. The *Discovery* then crossed the North Sea again, taking on a pilot off Orfordness, as usual, and a sea pilot at King's Lynn for Hull on 21 March. Strong gales and heavy snow squalls prolonged the voyage, which ended in King George Dock, Kingston-upon-Hull, on the evening of 22 March 1919.[25]

During her second coasting voyage of 1919, the vessel's master was Captain D. D. Richards. This began and ended at Hull, with two calls at Bordeaux, three at Rotterdam, one at Dunkerque and two at Le Havre. She loaded a cargo of 224 tons of potatoes (8,389 bags) in Hull and departed on 30 March for Bordeaux, where the cargo was discharged on 6 and 7 April. At the entrance to Sables d'Olonne, she anchored while the crew prepared the hold for cargo. She then proceeded towards Bordeaux, where a cargo of palm nuts was loaded between 12 and 17 April. During the passage to Rotterdam, a strong wind and a 'rough high head sea' caused the *Discovery* to 'plunge'. She put in to

Dartmouth, perhaps for shelter and certainly to coal, and proceeded via Orfordness to Rotterdam, where a tug helped her to dock on 26 April. Here the cargo was discharged into lighters at the rate of about 200 tons per day. Another log ended on 29 April 1919.[26]

From Rotterdam, the little SS *Discovery*, assisted by a tug at first, proceeded towards the Hook of Holland, in the early morning of 30 April, but had to turn back, 'unable to stem the tide, wind and head on sea'. She crossed the North Sea once more to Orfordness next day, and anchored in the Downs off Deal early on 3 May in dense fog, entering the dock at Dunkerque later that day to wait for orders and to bunker.

From Dunkerque she was sent to Le Havre to load cases of bacon. The crew were employed scraping and painting meanwhile. Unfortunately, many of the cases were broken to pieces as they were handled and stowed, causing the bacon to fall out. Bunker coal was taken on from the SS *Marie Thérèse*. On 19 May, assisted at first by two tugs and a pilot, she proceeded towards Rotterdam once more, by way of Deal and Orfordness. The bacon was discharged on 21 and 22 May, while the crew scraped and painted the funnel and scraped the ship outside.

She returned from Rotterdam to Le Havre, departing on 23 May via Orfordness and Deal, docking on 25 May. Here a second cargo of bacon was taken on board and some of the cases were again badly damaged while being handled in the holds. The crew continued the job of scraping and painting the ship outside. The stevedores completed loading on 28 May and the *Discovery* departed for Rotterdam next morning via Deal and Orfordness. The cargo of bacon was discharged in Rotterdam on 2, 3 and 4 June, while the crew were employed painting the bulwarks, masts and funnel.

On the afternoon of 4 June, the vessel proceeded towards the dry dock, assisted by a pilot and tugs. The crew swept and washed out the holds. Once in the dry dock, workmen started repairs to the deck and engine-room. The crew took the anchor cable out of the locker, pumped water out of the forepeak, cleaned out the chain locker, cleaned the cable chain and white-washed the holds. No work was done on Sunday 8 June and Whit Monday, 9 June. Repairs to the deck, caulking the ship's bottom, overhauling the cable chain, putting in deck planks and replacing the ceiling in the hold were among the jobs completed by the tradesmen. On 14 June 1919, the cable chains were taken on board, the chief officer being on duty for nine hours and the carpenter for eight, while this was done. The crew were next employed painting the funnel, white-washing the 'tween decks and cleaning out the holds. The *Discovery* was ready for sea on 18 June when she departed from Rotterdam for Hull, where the voyage officially terminated on 7 July 1919.[27]

# FOURTEEN

## SOUTH RUSSIAN VENTURE: THE BLACK SEA, 1919–20, LAID UP IN LONDON, 1920–3

### *The Black Sea, 1919–20*

> Not with the plough is our dear, glorious earth furrowed;
> Our earth is furrowed with the hoofs of horses,
> And our dear, glorious earth is sown with the heads of Cossacks.
> Our gentle Don is adorned with youthful widows;
> Our gentle father Don is blossomed with orphans;
> The waves of the gentle Don are rich with fathers' and mothers' tears.
> O thou, our father, gentle Don!
> Oh why dost thou, gentle Don, flow so troubledly?
> From my depths, the depths of the Don, the cold springs beat;
> Amid me, the gentle Don, the white fish leap.
> Old Cossack song, quoted in<br>Mikhail Sholokhov's And Quiet Flows the Don<br>(Putnam, London, 1935)

IN THE SUMMER OF 1919 two elderly square-rigged vessels might have been observed slowly sailing and steaming from Yorkshire through the Mediterranean, Bosporus and Black Sea towards a Russia torn apart by civil war and bloodshed following the Revolution of 1917. One of these vessels was of course the *Discovery*, while the other was the *Pelican*, both chartered from the Hudson's Bay Company by the Merchant Trading Company of London.[1]

In the years before the First World War, the wheat exports of Imperial Russia were harvested in vast quantities in the Ukraine and on the Don, and exported from all the south Russian ports. At that time there existed what was known as the 'coal out and grain home' trade from the British Isles. Because most steamers were coal burners, a network of coaling stations had been established throughout the world where ships could replenish their bunkers. A large number of bulk carriers delivered Welsh coal from the Bristol Channel ports to these coaling stations—one of the most important being Port Said at the entrance to the Suez Canal—and returned with Russian grain when available. Between early summer and late autumn, after discharging her coal cargo at Port Said, a steamer would proceed via the Dardanelles to Constantinople (now Istanbul), cleaning her holds *en route*. Orders at Constantinople would await her stating to which south Russian port she was consigned. The Russian grain was eventually distributed throughout northern Europe from Antwerp, Rotterdam or Hamburg. This lucrative trade came to an abrupt end with the Great War and the alliance of Turkey with Germany. The bloody Gallipoli campaign originated with Churchill's idea of forcing the Dardanelles, so that Russian grain (and oil) could be brought out and armaments taken in.[2] Before the war, Russia had provided Great Britain with huge quantities of raw materials and food, including one-eighth of British imports of grain.[3]

Firing ceased on the long Eastern Front between Russia and the Central Powers on 2 December 1917, nearly a year before the Armistice of 11 November 1918 silenced the guns along the Western Front and the Great War came to an end. The Treaty of Brest–Litovsk, signed on 3 March 1918, bought revolutionary Russia peace with Germany and Austria–Hungary at a price: the western provinces of the old Tsarist Empire, Poland, Finland, Lithuania, Estonia, the Ukraine and parts of the Caucasus.

It was the collapse of Russia and not anti-Bolshevism in the first instance that brought about armed Allied intervention to the north, east and south of the small new Soviet state. What began as an effort to reconstruct the Eastern Front against the Germans became thoroughly bound up with the White Russian cause, partly because of an unwillingness to desert (through a sense of obligation) the forces that had continued the fight after Brest–Litovsk. Added to this was the fear of the spread of Bolshevism at a time when Germany, in defeat, and much of central Europe, seemed to be turning Bolshevik too.[4] John Silverlight, in *The Victors' Dilemma*, has recounted the story of Allied intervention in the Russian Civil War, its origins and the course it ran before it petered out, making up 'one of the most confused yet fascinating episodes in the history of this century'. The struggle in south Russia forms the background to the Black Sea trading voyages of the *Discovery* and *Pelican* in the autumn of 1919. Although it cannot be said that the two vessels took any major part in events, the fact that they were present is notable enough. For it was during those two years of civil war in 1919 and 1920, that the destiny of Russia was settled, in what was truly the aftermath to the Great War.

A small Volunteer Army gradually and painfully came into being in south Russia, harassed not only by the Red Army but also by insurgent peasants led by local brigands comprising the 'Green Army'. The Allies had divided south Russia into sectors of interest and both the British and French navies were active in the Black Sea. Rear-Admiral Culme Seymour commanding the Black Sea Squadron sent regular reports on the situation in south Russia to the Admiralty in London. Some of them emphasised the importance of trade, especially in the wake of the advancing White armies.[5] 'If the liberated people are well looked after and the Bolsheviks realise that people in the country occupied by the Volunteer Army are much better off than they themselves, they will in all probability begin to desert in large numbers. The present is a very critical moment in the Anti-Bolshevik campaign, and it is much to be regretted that British trade is so un-enterprising, and so far behind other nations.'[6] An enclosure in these 'Letters of proceedings' at about the time of the departure of the *Discovery* and *Pelican* reported that most of the original peacetime businessmen had left, but that a Minister of Shipping and Trade had been appointed. However, until reliable agents and land communications were re-established, the discharge of imports and distribution of cargo would remain difficult. The need was for manufactured goods, cloth, boots and shoes, agricultural implements and general cargoes. 'It must be realised that for some time to come, the people of Russia will have no money and nothing with which to trade and merchants will have to combine business with charity if they hope to start a connection with this part of the world.'[7]

It may be that it was as a result of these observations (perhaps released to the British press or in the City of London) that a Lieut. Gurland put forward his proposal to the Merchant Trading Company for 'an expedition to the Black Sea for an exchange of goods' in June 1919. The chairman of the Merchant Trading Company, founded in 1915, was Charles Vincent Sale, and Gurland's proposal met his approval and then that of the Board on 3 June 1919. The Hudson's Bay Company agreed to charter the *Discovery* and the *Pelican*, and to take a 20 per cent stake in the venture. No doubt the Hudson's Bay Company was pleased to have the two vessels profitably employed, although the serious loss of merchant ships during the war would in any case almost certainly have guaranteed a use even for two such old-fashioned auxiliary barques. The *Discovery* and *Pelican* thus became two of eleven merchant ships (Norwegian, Swedish, American, Italian and six British) in Novorossiysk in late September 1919.[8] Fortunately, the logs of both survive in the Company archives.[9]

The *Pelican*, a former naval gunboat of the Osprey and Doterel class, was built at Devonport and launched in 1877. She had been in the service of the Hudson's Bay Company since 1901, generally on the annual supply run from London to the Bay. She was built of wood and was a slow sailer, of the same class as the surveying vessel *Penguin*, well known in the Admiralty Hydrographic Service for her 'clumbunginess' at sea.[10] The master of the *Pelican* for this Russian voyage was A. Borras, while that of the *Discovery* was George Wetherill. The two ships did not sail in company, but met in the south Russian port of Novorossiysk, on the north-east coast of the Black Sea. They followed a roughly similar course outward and homeward, the *Pelican* departing from Hull on 6 July and the *Discovery* on the 25th, both having first loaded coal and general cargo. The *Pelican* fired at and sank a floating mine off the Aegean island of Lemnos on 28 July. They must have been among the first British merchant ships to pass through the Dardanelles and Bosporus since the 1914-18 war, as harbingers of the renewal of commerce in the Black Sea, only to be properly resumed in the mid-1920s after a trade agreement had been signed between Britain and Soviet Russia.[11] Their officers and crew must have been both curious to see the site of the Allied campaign and evacuation of 1915 and sad to remember the many lost in action there. The *Pelican* and *Discovery* anchored off Constantinople in early and late August respectively.

The *Pelican* took on water and embarked passengers at Batoum[12] (now Batumi,

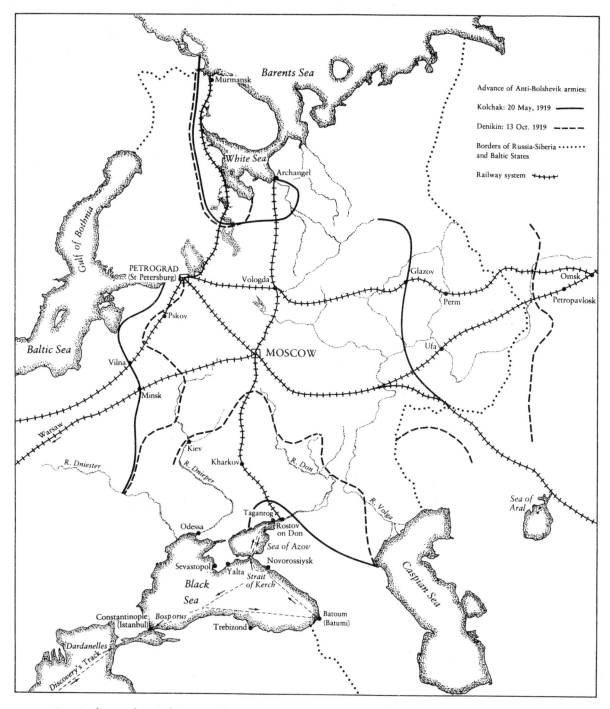

Russia during the Civil War, 1919, to illustrate the *Discovery*'s Black Sea voyage (South Russian venture), 1919-20. From a map in W. S. Churchill, *The Aftermath*, Macmillan, London 1929

important as the terminal of the oil pipeline from Baku) on the east coast of the Black Sea. She awaited orders there between 5 and 23 August and three days later entered Novorossiysk harbour. She berthed on 30 August and began discharging cargo next day. The *Discovery* joined her from Constantinople the day after that. 'Novorossiysk is a very pleasant port', writes Captain A. R. Williamson, who was there in 1907, 'situated about 60 miles east of the Strait of Kerch, the entrance to the Sea of Azov. The port is situated at the foot of well wooded hills, from the summit of which there are extensive views eastward towards the Caucasus Mountains.'[13] A year before the arrival of the *Discovery* and *Pelican*, in June 1918, the port of Novorossiysk had witnessed the dramatic scuttling by the Bolsheviks of the battleship *Svobdnaya Rossiya* and some eleven destroyers of the Russian Black Sea fleet, to prevent their falling into German hands. The affair was organised at Lenin's request by Sub-Lieut. F. F. Ilyin ('Raskolnikov') and has been movingly described by him.[14]

The *Discovery* and the *Pelican* were in the vicinity from late August to November 1919, the critical three months that saw the advance of the White Army, under General Denikin, to within 250 miles of Moscow. By the end of the year, the Red Army had counter-attacked and rolled back Denikin's armies, defeating them in a ghostly civil war.

> During the year 1919 there was fought over the whole of Russia a strange war; a war in areas so vast that considerable armies, armies indeed of hundreds of thousands of men, were lost—dispersed, melted, evaporated; a war in which there were no real battles, only raids and affrays and massacres, as the result of which countries as large as England or France changed hands to and fro; a war of flags on the map, of picket lines, of cavalry screens advancing or receding by hundreds of miles without solid cause or durable consequence; a war with little valour and no mercy. Whoever could advance found it easy to continue; whoever was forced to retire found it difficult to stop . . . a thin, cold, insubstantial conflict in the Realms of Dis . . . When the moment came the Bolsheviks lying in the centre [in Moscow] . . . gave a prick or a punch at this point or that. Thereupon the balloon burst and all the flags moved back and the cities changed hands and found it convenient to change opinions . . . Mighty natural or strategic barriers, like the line of the Volga River or the line of the Ural Mountains, were found to be no resting places; no strategic consequences followed from their loss or gain. A war of few casualties and unnumbered executions. The tragedy of each Russian city, of loyal families, of countless humble households might fill libraries of dreary volumes.[15]

One of the last signs of the sway of the old regime in what Churchill called 'the wreckage of the Empire of the Czars' can be seen on the pages of the official log of the *Discovery*, the Imperial two-headed eagle stamped by the port authorities of Novorossiysk.

On 4 September 1919, stevedores began discharging cargo from the *Pelican* into the *Discovery*. A superintendent and six labourers had already shifted cargo from the

*Discovery*'s 'tween decks to her lower hold the previous day, while the crew were employed painting the lifeboats and the donkey winch, which was in use. Working cargo during the period that the two vessels were at the quay seems to have been somewhat intermittent. No reason is given for this in the logs, but it must have been because of the general disruption and shortage of labour. An officer from the British Military Mission to the Don Cossacks, who arrived in Novorossiysk in the early summer of 1919 and kept a diary, found the grey town wallowing in mud, 'beneath the onion-shaped domes of the churches', for few of the roads had been surfaced, apart from one or two cobbled avenues in the centre, bordered by 'shabby public buildings and a few large dwelling houses'. The place was vastly overcrowded with troops and its streets were 'full of penniless refugees and indescribable beggars'.

> A great many of the Russians in Novorossiisk and the spas of the south had fled from cities of the north like Petrograd and Moscow and formerly wealthy people were living in appalling conditions, crowding into tiny rooms cluttered with their belongings and smelling of the creosote they used to try to discourage the wild life. They stood bed and chair legs in little pans of the stuff in an attempt to keep lice from getting into their clothing and on to their bodies. It wasn't easy, however. Everywhere in South Russia seemed to be so crowded at this time, it wasn't difficult to pick up any disease you could mention, from smallpox and diphtheria to typhus and cholera.
>
> Though the Bolsheviks were actually nowhere near at the time, the people were still in a highly nervous state. Many of them had lived through the horror of the Revolution . . . and for safety they had headed for the cities of the Black Sea . . .
>
> When the Red Army, following them south, had reached Caucasia, they had been persecuted in every conceivable way, but it was when the Whites had approached that the real terror had begun. Then the Bolsheviks shot hundreds of them and almost everyone we met had lost a husband, brother, son or father, and most of their worldly possessions. Great numbers were still terrified the Reds would return.[16]

The crews were employed at various jobs, including setting up the *Discovery*'s topmast rigging and painting the ship outside. By 27 September, when she departed for Constantinople, the *Pelican* had discharged 100 tons of boots, clothing, drugs and woollen garments, while by the time she left on 4 October, the *Discovery* had discharged the same amount of boots, clothing and linen goods.[17] The Russian entries in the *Discovery*'s official log reveal that 1,688 roubles and 81 kopeks were paid in quarantine and customs dues on 21 September, when the ship was authorised to depart for Rostov with a foreign cargo of 23 pieces, duty paid.[18]

The commercial and industrial centre of Rostov-on-Don had grown up in the nineteenth century at the mouth of the Don, one of the great rivers of Russia. The river flows through the Russian steppe, the country of the Don Cossacks. Cossacks had originally settled the wilder areas of the Russian Empire to the south and east in pursuit of freedom, but during the nineteenth century they became the instrument of the Tsarist state, each horseman having to leave home and serve twenty years with the colours in return for a plot of land. The changes brought about in the region by the boom in industry based on coal and iron resulted in the rise of Rostov. It overtook the Don capital of Novocherchassk, and divided the population into the obstinately rural Cossacks, leading the life their fathers had led, and the 15,000 workers in the 400 factories in the province, producing millions of roubles' worth of goods per annum by the end of the century. The world demand for grain in the later nineteenth century encouraged the Cossacks to turn pasture into arable land, bringing almost ninety per cent of land under cultivation. Although grapes and tobacco increased in importance, grain production rose even more, resulting by 1898 in a surplus per head of population of nine bushels; this further stimulated the growth of Rostov, at the north-east corner of the shallow inland Sea of Azov, as a port of wheat exportation.[19]

The rise in the price of land led to discontent among the Don Cossacks and the call for a separate Don assembly in 1913, at a time when the Tsar's rule was still absolute. The non-Cossack peasants were also hungry for land and the workers of the industrial towns of Rostov and Taganrog were becoming militant. The war of 1914–17 and its aftermath brought all these conflicts to a head and devastated both communities and countryside. What the Great War and the civil war meant to the Don Cossacks can be read in the pages of Sholokhov's novels. Some supported the White Volunteer Army and some the Red. The result was chaos and ruin. Stalinism, and later, technology, were to spell the end of Cossackdom.[20]

The *Discovery*'s log records that she proceeded with a pilot towards Taganrog roads, after receiving *pratique* (permission to continue) presumably from the British warship stationed in the narrow Strait of Kerch, the gateway to the Sea of Azov. She met strong head winds and sea next day on 6 October, the vessel pitching heavily and shipping much water aboard as she progressed past navigation lights and markers. She came to anchor at Taganrog roads in 17 feet of water at 6.30 on the fine clear morning of 7 October. Only shallow draft vessels were able to reach Rostov at the mouth of the Don: those with a deeper draft had to anchor off Taganrog, some forty miles away. Here their cargo was transferred to lighters and transported up river to its destination.

The *Discovery* lay at anchor all that day and the next in fine weather, waiting for a lighter to receive her cargo. The morning of 9 October was overcast with a north-east wind. At 6.30 a.m. the steam lighter *Nichole* No. 973 came alongside to take on cargo and her labourers came aboard. By 4.30 p.m. they had discharged all cargo. In happier days, before the cataclysm, the *Discovery* would have loaded a consignment of grain from lighters sent out from Taganrog, but now she had to wait five days for orders. The crew were employed shifting coal from the lower hold to the bunkers. On 15 October at 5.30 a.m. she hove up anchor and proceeded towards Novorossiysk, in dense fog, with a pilot in charge, her whistle blowing and keeping a sharp look-out until the fog cleared in the later afternoon. She came to anchor in Kerch Strait, no doubt to drop the pilot, on 16 October and continued to her destination against a strong breeze and head sea. She arrived there at 10 a.m. on 17 October 1919 and came to anchor to wait for orders. At 2 p.m. the pilot came aboard, the anchor was hove up and she proceeded to the quay berth, moved alongside and moored. The *Pelican* joined her five days later.

The stevedores commenced work on 27 October, with interruptions due to a shortage of wagons, heavy rain and strong north-easterly or south-easterly gales. During the bad weather, fenders had to be continually renewed as a nasty swell set in and caused the *Pelican* to be badly chafed against the wharf on the port side and the *Discovery* on the starboard side. On 7 November, the *Discovery* continually rolled against the *Pelican*, causing her to strike the wharf, damaging both wharf and vessel. Wind and sea being very bad, extra springs were put out fore and aft. The *Pelican*'s log recorded 'a considerable amount of minor damage'.

After nearly three weeks awaiting orders, the *Discovery* proceeded on 8 November with the pilot and moored in the loading berth alongside the Cement Wharf. Between 10 and 14 November, stevedores and labourers loaded a full cargo of cement in 3,936 barrels. The *Pelican* also loaded a cement cargo in 3,000 barrels, between 15 and 21 November, having bunkered 25 tons of coal from the *Discovery*, despite the rolling and bumping caused by a moderate south-easterly wind. A letter survives written in Novorossiysk from Messrs William Jacobs, Owen and Company, agents for the Levant Company, dated 29/11 February 1920 addressed to Messrs Sale and Company, London. It gave news of the *Pelican* and described the general situation in Novorossiysk.

> There is perfect chaos in this port just now, and it is extremely difficult to get cargo alongside, as all waggons are requisitioned by the Military Authorities for their requirements. Hundreds of waggons are being used as dwelling places by refugees from Rostoff, and this contributes considerably to the difficulty in arranging transport.
>
> The S.S. 'Grodno' has been in port 40 days, and we are just today receiving waggons to complete her discharging. The 'Southgate' was lying in the roads 28 days waiting for a berth, and sailed without discharging any cargo at all.
>
> The military position is improving slightly in the Don district, and with the sailing of several steamers in the course of the next few days, we hope the general position will show signs of improvement shortly, as the delay to steamers is most ruinous.[21]

The improvement never came. The situation in Novorossiysk worsened until it seemed, in the words of Major Williamson of the British Military Mission, 'the nearest thing to purgatory one could ever expect to see'. Thousands of men, women and children (including whole train loads) died from typhus or from exposure. From the bay, the British and French warships, *Empress of India* and *Waldeck Rousseau*, shelled the approach roads to the city to slow down the advancing Red cavalry. The evacuation to the Allied ships was limited mainly to White troops and their families, while the waterfront, the foreshore and the streets were thick with other people, as well as camels, horses, perambulators, wagons and hand-carts. Some prayed for help on their knees.

If the other towns and cities to the north had been disasters, Novorossiisk was the worst of the lot as the wreckage of a whole nation funnelled down to the sea and the only remaining seaport in the area. It came into the town from all sides, the flotsam from the defeats at Kharkov and Rostov and Novocherkassk and Tikho-ryetsk and everywhere else where the Whites had been flung back. Pity was an emotion no one could any longer feel. Things had gone beyond compassion and the people had stumbled on without thoughts or feelings, watching their friends and relations fall and leaving them, eating secret scraps of food and looking at the clothes of the men and women in front and thinking 'If you were dead, those would be mine'.[22]

The *Discovery* departed for Constantinople with her cargo of cement from Novorossiysk in mid-November 1919, having paid the requisite dues and taxes. She arrived at the Piraeus on 1 December, where the cement was eventually unloaded, in late December and early January. The crew were fumigated on arrival, while the vessel was in quarantine. On Christmas Day, Able Seaman Cloudsdale, being drunk, started fighting another seaman, causing a disturbance aboard the ship. 'Being a dangerous man', reads the log, 'we put him in irons and called the Police of the Greek man o war', to which warship he was taken in charge as a prisoner. After all the cement had been discharged on 6 January, the fumigating boat came alongside and pumped liquid sulphur down the holds.

At Constantinople between 26 January and 8 February, the *Discovery* loaded a general cargo for London. This comprised nearly 2,000 bags of nuts, more than 1,000 bags of linseed, 15 cases of gum, 213 bales of rugs, 62 casks of copper, 52 casks of caviar, 43 barrels of mohair, 8 bales of carpets and over 800 cases of other cargo.[23] Snowstorms and rough weather delayed departure for three days. The pilot came aboard during the morning of 11 February and the *Discovery* proceeded towards London, having anchored in the Bosporus the same day for clearance by the Examination Officer. She coaled in Malta on 18 February, received *pratique* and bunkered at Gibraltar on 27 and 28 February, and with fresh water on board progressed, rolling and pitching heavily in the March gales, towards the Channel. She stopped off Dungeness to receive the London pilot on board. At Gravesend on 11 March, where *pratique* was received, the sea pilot was discharged and the river pilot took charge of the run up the Thames to the East India Dock. The crew signed off the same day. The cargo was discharged between 12 and 16 March, when it was found that the contents of nearly a whole barrel and two cases of caviar had been stolen.

The summary of the voyage accounts can be found in the archives of the Hudson's

Bay Company, headed 'South Russian account. Venture No. 1'.[24] There were, one presumes, no more south Russian ventures, owing to the conditions at the time. No doubt the *Discovery*'s and *Pelican*'s cargoes of boots, clothes, drugs and linen goods were of great value to the individuals who were able to buy them but they and other trade goods made no difference to the course of the Civil War. In Churchill's words

> It was not the want of material means, but of comradeship, will power and rugged steadfastness that lost the struggle. Bravery and devotion shone in individuals, ruthlessness was never absent, but the qualities which enable scores of thousands of men to combine and to act for a common purpose even when isolated, were not to be found in the wreckage of the Empire of the Czars.[25]

W. R. Colbeck, son of Captain Colbeck of the *Morning* (later to serve in the *Discovery* during her BANZARE voyages of 1919–31), was in one of the earliest merchant vessels to reach south Russia under the trade agreement signed by the two nations when trade between Great Britain and the new Soviet state started in the early 1920s. He was in Novorossiysk during April and May 1922 and found the port derelict and the people starving.

> We took out a cargo of oil-tank wagons, the tanks and chassis being loaded in Hamburg and the bogies, wheels etc. and pipes and other parts from England to Novorossisk. The port was almost derelict. The 'Morocco' was an old ship and the derricks were only good for a safe working load of 4 T 10c and the tanks, I think, 60 in number weighed about 9 T and we had been assured that cranage was available but the only crane in working order would only lift 3 T so we had a good exercise in seamanship, in 'fishing' three of our derricks together and staying the mast to handle these loads. As this rig could only be used at one hatch at a time we were there for some 5 weeks.
>
> We were only the third ship under the red regime and were told to go ashore only in uniform. The captain of the ship before us had been mugged when ashore in plain clothes and later 4 men were hung from lamp posts in the vicinity.
>
> When we arrived all cameras, newspapers and magazines were collected and sealed under bond for the duration of our stay. Two Red soldiers were on the gangway the whole time. The people were starving—a crowd of 30 or 40 would wait for the cook to bring down the galley swill to the bins on the quay and the crowd of both sexes would fight over it.
>
> There were two restaurants and pleasure gardens mainly patronised by Red Army officers and their friends where you could get a decent meal. The rate of exchange was 13 million roubles to the £1. The first visit four of us made to the restaurant we paid with a £1 note and our change came piled on a tray, some notes and some postage stamps without adhesive and overprinted for use as money.

While we were there another British ship came in with a cargo of bulk grain and I went over to visit them. The grain was being filled into sacks which were then carried on men's backs across the quay to a line of rail wagons about 100 yards away, this operation being watched by a large crowd, some 300/400, kept back by a ring of soldiers. While we were watching this from the deck of the ship, one of the carriers stumbled and dropped his bag which burst spilling about 90 lbs. of wheat over the cobbles. This was too much for the spectators who madly rushed and started to pick up the grain into hats etc. The guards yelled and shouted and then opened fire and when the crowd was finally pushed back there were 3 bodies, a young girl and two men who were thrown on to a hand cart and taken away.

One afternoon when discharge was nearing completion, work suddenly stopped and we found the dockers searching the bilges. The previous voyage the cargo had been copra and as the cargo was to be steel, the hold had not been carefully cleaned and quite a lot had been left behind the stringers and in the bilges. One of them must have found it was edible and work was not resumed until every scrap had been removed.[26]

## LAID UP IN LONDON, 1920-3

On the apparent failure of a coal charter in mid-June 1920 after the *Discovery*'s return from south Russia, the Bay Steamship Company had to consider whether she should be laid up. A press cutting was pinned to a memorandum to this effect of 14 June, addressed to C. V. Sale, the managing director. The press cutting was headed, 'The Discovery in the Thames'. Its writer observed that the decline in the shipping boom was shown by the fact that the 'little Discovery' had been lying at a buoy off Deptford for some weeks, waiting for a charterer. She was 'normally used as a whaler, for trading in ice for furs', continued the cutting, 'or for polar exploration work', which was 'sending her name down to history, linked with those of Scott and Shackleton'. 'But recently', concluded the article, 'the circumstances have been anything but normal and in spite of her design, she has been earning large profits as a food carrier. Her last was to Constantinople.'

A formal proposal to lay her up at a buoy berth in the South West India Dock was made to C. V. Sale on 23 June. The costs of this (some £800) would include dock dues of £450 16s. 1d. per annum, a salary of £260 p.a. to a watchman (an elderly Master) living on board, the cost of shifting to the berth, pumping out the water, additional dismantling, emptying and drying boilers, and greasing the engines. Details of the dismantling were as follows: the vessel to be moored with chain and wire (no ropes to be left out); sails, running gear, life-jackets, navigating lamps, flags and all movable gear would be stored on shore. All navigating gear—charts, compasses, books, sounding gear, clocks, barometers, etc., except the lamps—would be handed over to Messrs Kelvin, White and Hutton. All ropes should be unrove and all brass work covered over with white lead. A complete inventory would have to be taken of all gear landed or left on board. All hands would be paid off.[27]

This indeed is what happened to the SS *Discovery*, a vessel of peculiar design, limited cargo capacity and speed, unable to compete in the 1920s with modern merchant ships. However, she did not remain entirely deserted. Early in 1922, through the kindness of the Hudson's Bay Company, the barque became the temporary headquarters of the 16th Stepney Sea Scout troop. Perhaps this precedent influenced the decision to hand her over to the Boy Scouts Association, once her seagoing had come to an end some ten years later.[28]

# PART IV

# THE *DISCOVERY* (OCEANOGRAPHIC) EXPEDITION, 1925–7

# FIFTEEN

## Origins of the *Discovery* (Oceanographic) Expedition, Whales and Whaling, Sale to Crown Agents and Refit by Vospers, Voyage to the Cape, 1925

### THE *DISCOVERY* EXPEDITION, 1925–7

THE FRIENDS OF THE EARTH, Greenpeace, the World Wide Fund for Nature (formerly the World Wildlife Fund) and other conservation societies have been very effective in publicising the plight of many of the great whales, whose numbers have been reduced, through over-fishing, to a very low level. The conservation movement has grown considerably in the later decades of the twentieth century, yet its practical beginnings (as far as southern whales are concerned) go back to the years before the First World War, when a government committee on whaling and the protection of whales was established in London to collect statistical and other information (some provided by the whaling stations in the Antarctic), and a biologist despatched to study whaling operations in South Georgia, during the 1913–14 season.

Whales had been hunted for some three hundred years in the northern hemisphere from small boats operated from sailing (later steam) ships until the early twentieth century. Only certain species could be caught using the prevailing methods: the slow Right whale and the Sperm whale, neither of which sank on being killed by harpoons and lances thrown from the small boats. It was not until the Norwegian, Svend Foyn of Tønsberg, on the Oslofjord, invented an explosive harpoon which could be fired from the bows of a ship (as opposed to a boat) in 1864, that the faster, larger Rorquals and Humpbacks could be attacked; they were inflated on capture so that they did not sink, having been played (until they died a terrible death) on the immensely strong lines linking the harpoon and the whale catcher.

The northern whale fishery has not gone unsung in the literature of the sea. Many accounts of whaling voyages (often fraught with dangers from scurvy or from the ships being crushed in the ice) were written in the nineteenth century. The most authoritative work was William Scoresby's *Arctic Regions* published in 1820, of which the second volume has still some claim to be the standard work on the Greenland Right whale. Scoresby's interests extended beyond whales and whaling to the environment, and in his studies and observations of the sea he is acknowledged as a pioneer in the science of oceanography. The small steam vessel which would be specially built to complement the work of the *Discovery* and later research ships, was named after him.

When it was clear that northern waters were almost depleted of whales, attention turned to the south, where fast whale catchers with explosive harpoons caught vast numbers of Humpback and then the larger Fin and Blue whales. The Compania Argentina de Pesca was formed by Norwegian and Argentine interests in 1904 to operate in the Antarctic, and was soon followed by other companies, also operating in the Dependencies of the Falkland Islands, between the meridians of 20°W and 80°W. The Norwegians recognised British sovereignty (consolidated by Letters Patent in 1908) within this area and paid for licences to set up shore whaling stations on the islands of South Georgia and the South Shetlands; the number of whale catchers they could use was limited in order to reduce the slaughter. These and later taxes on whale oil processed in the Dependencies allowed the Falkland Islands government to build up a substantial research and development fund. The prosperity of the industry may be gauged by the statement in the 1920 report that in 1917 'the actual receipts from the Dependencies amounted to £15,366, while the purely local expenditure amounted to only £776 (plus a share of the cost of central administration)'. This money paid for the purchase of the *Discovery* in 1923 and her refit as an oceanographic research vessel.

The Norwegian historians, Tønnessen and Johnsen, have drawn attention in their *History of Modern Whaling* to the influence of J. A. Mörch, the Norwegian chemical engineer, on the whaling industry and the conservation of the great whales. The archives of the British Museum (Natural History) preserve the brief but important correspondence between him and Dr (later Sir) Sidney Harmer, then Keeper of Zoology in 1910 and 1911. Mörch had visited various whaling grounds during the previous four years and his eyes had been opened to the lack of scientific knowledge of the Blue, Fin and Humpback whales and to their rapid decline in Bransfield Strait, Antarctica, since southern whaling had begun earlier in the century. He felt that it would be of interest to collect records from the whaling grounds that were already under British jurisdiction. Mörch suggested to Harmer in a letter dated 7 June 1910 how this might be organised.

> Each whaling steamer under the licence of the British government should be furnished with a journal wherein should be noted down every whale killed, place where killed, species and sex; for females also if with calf. Also presence of plankton.

He thought that meteorological observations (including water temperatures) might be taken by the whalers in certain localities. The data from the journals could be presented on large-scale maps and sent to 'some British scientific institution', which would thus obtain a 'graphic view' of the situation each year. Mörch went on to point out that the catch from a single 'floating factory' (a converted liner) at Deception Island was valued at nearly £50,000, while the cost of the licence was only £200 for the factory ship itself and its three whaling steamers. He suggested that a proportion of each licence fee should be put aside for scientific research. He followed this with a further letter of 28 July 1910, saying that 'The question which in my humble opinion ought to be considered by the British authorities is to limit the licences so that there might not be run the risk of a depletion in any one locality.' He emphasised that his previous suggestion had been made as much from a commercial as from a scientific point of view and continued, 'By making up maps as mentioned in my former letter for instance for every month during the season, such maps would show not only the number of whales killed, where killed, but also furnish a graphic view of the trek of the various sorts of whales during the different parts of the season.' It would also be educational to furnish the gunners with the opportunity to make such observations.[1]

Dr Harmer was encouraging in his replies, saying that he was hopeful something might be done on the lines indicated by Mörch, given that the Government was sympathetic towards efforts that had been made to protect rare animal species. He acted on Mörch's suggestions and recommended that as much as possible be done to prevent the extermination of the whales.[2] One immediate result was the compilation of the first of a series of Whale Reports to his Trustees in November 1910.[3] The possibility of convening an international conference to consider the question of the protection and preservation of whales was discussed in 1912.[4] Measurements and other statistics would be collected at the whaling stations and sent via the Colonial Office to the British Museum (Natural History) where they appear to have formed the basis for Harmer's reports.

A practical step taken by the Colonial Office on behalf of the committee had been the despatch to South Georgia of the Irish zoologist, Major G. E. H. Barrett-Hamilton, in October 1913. His mission was to investigate the whaling and sealing carried on there, as well as to report on the fauna of the island and to collect for the British Museum (Natural History). He was well qualified for this task, having been one of two British commissioners on the Bering Sea Fur Seal Commission working on the Pribilof Islands in 1896 and 1897. The Commission's recommendations had resulted in the conservation and management of the herds there. Barrett-Hamilton had been a friend and fellow student of Edward Wilson's at Cambridge and both were candidates to the scientific staff of the 1901 expedition. At the time of Wilson's death in the Antarctic with Scott on the return from the South Pole in 1912, the joint production of the two men of *The History of British Mammals*, one as author and the other as artist, was in course of serial publication. Barrett-Hamilton began his investigations at Leith Harbour in South Georgia, measuring his first whale on 15 November 1913. He continued to work until his sudden death on 17 January 1914. His body was brought home in the whaler *Orwell*.[5]

The Interdepartmental Committee on Whaling and the Protection of Whales (the Whaling Committee) sat on 10 December 1913 in London. The purpose of its enquiry was summarised in one of the minutes of evidence (No. 498) as being 'to consider the question whether whales need protection owing to the present rate of fishing, and whether, if so, one can find a method by which they can be protected'. The chairman was H. G. Maurice[6] of the Board of Agriculture and Fisheries. Other officials represented the Colonial Office, the Foreign Office, the Board of Trade, the Department of Agriculture and Technical Instruction for Ireland and the Scottish Office. The enquiry continued until 7 May 1914, a further four sessions having been held.

Eight witnesses gave evidence. Of these, the first three were scientists: Dr Sidney Harmer, MA, FRS, Stanley T. Burfield, BA, experienced in whaling from Ireland, and D. G. Lillie, MA, who reported his observations of whaling off New Zealand while ship's biologist on Scott's *Terra Nova* expedition, 1910–13. The Governor of the Falkland Islands, Mr W. L. Allardyce, CMG, after whom the Allardyce mountains in South Georgia are named, was the fourth witness. Appointed Governor in 1904, he had already instituted a licensing system for whalers based in the Falkland Islands Dependencies (chiefly on South Georgia and Deception Island) in order to limit their catch, envisaged the utilisation of the whole carcass, and forbidden the killing of whale calves and their mothers.[7]

Captain L. Bruun, managing director of the Whaling Station at Belmullet, Co. Mayo in Ireland, and also owner of a whaling station in Portuguese West Africa, gave evidence as to the breeding migrations along the coast of Africa, among other things. The director of the Southern Whaling and Sealing Company of North Shields, in northern England, Mr C. O. Johnson, also spoke from practical experience. His company was then whaling in South Georgia, Port Alexander (West Africa) and Durban (South Africa). He referred to the 'Humpback trek' going north along the African coast at the beginning of the southern winter. He believed that these whales migrated due north from the ice in the Antarctic following, as closely as possible, the same routes north (and south) that they had taken with their parents when young. Perhaps the most authoritative statements were made by Dr Hjort, the Norwegian oceanographer and marine biologist, then Director of Fisheries in Bergen. He spoke from scientific observation, from his experience of the Norwegian whaling industry and from his work on whaling logs.

The odd man out among these witnesses was a Mr Holman Kingdon, MA, the managing director of Joseph Crosfield & Sons Ltd of Warrington, Lancashire, soap and chemical manufacturers. His interest was the market value of whale oil, especially since the discovery, eight years previously, of a process for hydrogenating or 'hardening' oils, which enabled its use in the soap manufacturing industry, thereby revolutionising it. He hinted at the possibility, after more research, of 'hardened' oil being made into an 'edible product', which of course we know now as margarine. Whale oil had been used until then only for lighting, tanning and lubricating, not in soap and certainly not as food.

A confidential report (Miscellaneous 298) was printed for the Colonial Office and issued by the Whaling Committee in October 1915. This consisted of the questions and answers of evidence, all verbatim. The first five appendices (following the evidence) comprised letters to the Committee from Norwegian and British whaling companies and a useful résumé on the 'Distribution of whales in the waters about the Antarctic continent' by Dr Johan Hjort. The remaining two appendices by Martin A. C. Hinton of the British Museum reported on the 'Papers left by the late Major Barrett-Hamilton relating to the whales of South Georgia'. A careful reading of the minutes of the report and of the first five appendices reveals that although a considerable body of knowledge existed, largely due to the whaling industry, scientists actually knew relatively little about the growth, reproduction, feeding habits and general behaviour of whales, their species identity, breeding grounds, migrations and seasonal distributions, and in particular whether the same stock might be hunted both off the southern continents and near the ice. The views of the whalers, as to over-fishing, licensing, the utilisation of the whole carcass, close seasons, the prohibition of attacks on mother and calf, and the enforcement of regulations were also recorded.

M. A. C. Hinton's second appendix constituted an extensive report on Barrett-Hamilton's papers.[8] He admirably presented and analysed the data amassed by Barrett-Hamilton regarding the 294 large whales (of four species) measured and examined on the flensing platform at Leith Harbour. He also collated the work of other mainly Norwegian observers and carried the field work to a proper conclusion, along the lines which the distinguished naturalist might have followed, had he lived. The first part dealt with the whales (principally Humpbacks, Fin and Blue whales), while the second dealt with the state of the whaling industry in South Georgia and the South Atlantic. The threatened extinction of the species chiefly hunted by the whalers, the Humpback, was fully discussed and a number of suggestions made for the future regulation of the industry and the direction of further research, particularly off the coast of Africa. Hinton concluded that 'On its present scale, and with its present wasteful and indiscriminate methods, whaling is an industry which, by destroying its own resources, must soon expire.'

These words may have a familiar ring to modern ears but they were written in 1915, not very long after the start of whaling in the Antarctic. The outbreak of the Great War frustrated an Anglo-Swedish Antarctic Expedition, which was scheduled to run from 1915 until 1920. One of the principal objects of its intended biological station would have been research on whales, leading to their protection from extermination. The scheme was drawn up by Dr Otto Nordenskjöld (who had led the Swedish Antarctic Expedition) in consultation with Professor J. Gunnar Andersson, the geologist. The proposals were communicated in the latter half of 1912 to Dr Harmer, at the British Museum (Natural History) and actively taken up by the Museum's Trustees and by the Royal Society of London. The Colonial Office was also consulted.[9]

The first Interdepartmental Committee on Whaling and the Protection of Whales had suspended its sittings during the war and was eventually replaced by the Interdepartmental Committee on Research and Development in the Dependencies of the Falkland Islands, which had a wider brief. It is remarkable that this second committee had its genesis during some of the worst months of the First World War. On 3 February 1917, the geographer, Dr Robert Neal Rudmose Brown (who had been botanist in the *Scotia* during the Scottish National Antarctic Expedition of 1902–4), proposed to the Colonial Office that there should be a post-war research expedition to investigate whaling in the Falkland Islands Dependencies. Rowland Darnley of the Colonial Office discussed these proposals privately with Dr Harmer who welcomed them.

The Colonial Office wrote to the Admiralty on 1 August 1917 promoting the suggestion of an expedition and Harmer reported to his Trustees the receipt of papers relating to a proposed Whaling Research Expedition, saying that these were of great interest and importance and that (with certain reservations) they should be given a cordial reception. On the last day of 1917, the Secretary of the British Museum (Natural History) wrote to the Under-Secretary of State for the Colonies warmly commending the proposals and saying that he would (at last) cancel arrangements for an Anglo-Swedish scientific station on Graham Land. Despite its heavy responsibilities for the war at sea, the Admiralty too indicated its approval of the scheme.[10]

A second advisory interdepartmental committee called the Committee for the Dependencies of the Falkland Islands was set up

> To consider what can now be done to facilitate prompt action at the conclusion of the War in regard to the preservation of the whaling industry and to the development of other industries in the Dependencies of the Falkland Islands; and to consider not only the economic questions above referred to and the scheme for the employment of a research vessel, but also what purely scientific investigations are most required in connexion with these regions, and whether any preliminary inquiries by experts in this country should be instituted.

The reason for the search for other industries was the decline of Port Stanley's extensive ship repair business following the demise of the windjammer and the opening of the Panama Canal.

The members of the Committee (chaired by Mr P. C. Lyon of the Department of Scientific and Industrial Research) represented the Board of Agriculture and Fisheries, the Colonial Office, the British Museum (Natural History), and the Admiralty. Its Secretary was Mr H. T. Allen of the Colonial Office.[11]

This second interdepartmental committee appears to have begun its meetings early in 1918. It met twenty-one times before publishing its report (Cmd. 657) in April 1920. Its plan of operation was to obtain memoranda from 'acknowledged experts on the principal subjects of inquiry' and then to discuss these with their authors. The assistance of Dr W. S. Bruce, leader of the Scottish National Antarctic Expedition of 1902–4, was sought first of all; Captain C. A. Larsen (who had initiated whaling in South Georgia) and Captain Thoralf Sörlle represented the Norwegian Union of Whaling Companies; others consulted included Lord Rothschild, Sir Napier Shaw, Sir Frank Dyson, Dr G. H. Fowler, Dr S. Chapman, Dr Rudmose Brown, Mr T. E. Salvesen, Mr Holman Kingdon, Dr J. W. Evans, Mr J. F. N. Green, Sir Charles Close, Mr Einar Lea and Mr R. C. Mossman.

Some of the evidence from the earlier committee was either reprinted (Hjort) or summarised (Hinton). The broader brief of the second committee is reflected in the 1920 report with its reviews of whales and whaling (from 1909 when regulations were first imposed), seals and sealing, potential fisheries, and even penguins and reindeer. The sciences of hydrography, meteorology, geology, botany and magnetism were considered in relation to the Dependencies. The phenomenal rise in the use of whale oil during the war for the production of glycerine (for explosives) was recorded. The steep decline in the catch of Humpback whales at South Georgia and the subsequent concentration of the whalers initially on Fin and then Blue whales was also noted and the relevant statistics provided. Some of the wartime shipping losses of the whaling industry were also given.

The Committee's interviews and investigations resulted in the publication in 1920 of what one of its members (Rowland Darnley of the Colonial Office) called a 'Blue Book with a soul', Parliamentary Report (Cmd. 657).[12] The Committee was convinced of the need to study the whole environment of the whale, as well as the question of its biology, in order to provide a scientific basis for regulating the numbers taken during each season. There was at that time no question of abolishing whaling because of its cruelty.

An Executive Committee was appointed in 1924 by the Secretary of State for the Colonies, chaired by E. R. Darnley of the Colonial Office, to carry out the report's recommendations. Other members were: Sir Sidney Harmer (British Museum, Natural History); Sir Fortescue Flannery, Bt. (consulting naval architect); Mr H. T. Allen (Colonial Office); Mr J. O. Borley (Ministry of Agriculture and Fisheries); Captain J. D. Nares (Admiralty); and Mr (later Sir) James Wordie (Royal Geographical Society); Mr H. Horsburgh (technical assistant); Mr E. W. Baynes (Secretary). The committee became known as the *Discovery* Committee. Nares was the son of Admiral Sir George Nares, who had led the Arctic expedition of 1875–6 in the old *Discovery*, and Wordie had been with Shackleton in the *Endurance*.

The Ship's Sub-Committee proposed the employment of two vessels, both wooden three-masted topsail schooners, with steam power and wireless. One vessel should be of some 700 tons net and her consort would be just over 200 tons, similar in size to the old *Scotia*, the ship of the Scottish National Antarctic Expedition. The two should work in close co-operation, the larger being somewhat ice-strengthened, the other more fully protected for work in heavy ice. Besides cabin accommodation, each should have two laboratories, a chart-room (also serving as a study and scientific library) and a dark-room for photography. Motor boats of a speed of nine to twelve knots should be provided for each vessel for the marking of whales. Suitable weapons for doing this, with other items of equipment such as portable huts, double tents and sledges, should be carried. It was decided that the proposal to make one of the ships non-magnetic could not be carried out, in view of expense. The use of an aeroplane was considered but dismissed as premature. Three-masted topsail schooners (rather than barques) were recommended by the Ship's Sub-Committee 'in view of the difficulty of obtaining crews accustomed to square rigs . . . since a vessel with the former rig has the advantage that it can be sailed as a fore and aft vessel until the crew gain experience of square sails.[13] In the event the *Discovery*, a barque, was purchased and converted. Her tender, the *William Scoresby*, was designed as a small fully powered steam ship with a foresail, jib and spanker, for use when these would help to drive or steady the vessel. She was built at a cost of £33,000 to assist in the oceanographic research, to mark whales and to make exploratory trawls off the Falkland Islands.[14]

## SALE TO THE CROWN AGENTS AND REFIT BY VOSPERS

After completing her Black Sea voyage of 1919–20, the *Discovery* was moved from the East India Dock to the West India Dock. On 18 October 1922, an agreement was drawn up between the Hudson's Bay Company and the Crown Agents for her sale at a price of £5,000. This was subject to the inspection, in dry dock, of hull and engines by the purchasers, while the Company was allowed the first option to buy her back, so as to forestall any rivals in the fur trade.[15] From London she transferred to Portsmouth, where she required a very great deal of reconditioning by Messrs Vosper to turn her from a cargo ship into a research vessel. The work was under the direction of Sir Fortescue Flannery (known to the irreverent as 'Flannel bags') and Partners, naval architects.

Captain Scott's criticisms of the *Discovery*'s sailing qualities were taken into careful consideration in the drawing up of the specifications for her reconditioning (in fact virtual rebuilding). Extensive alterations were made in her masting and in the general sailing plan. Barquentine rig was found unsuitable: the chief objection was that a boom mainsail could not be carried, owing to the funnel and other obstructions between the main and mizzen masts. In addition, in order to carry sufficient handy canvas, if square-rigged on the foremast only, the vessel would have had to be rigged as a four-masted barquentine. The foremast was in fact placed four feet further forward and the mainmast, eight feet. More headsail would be carried to meet Scott's objections to the old rigging, while the overall sail area was increased by over 20 per cent. It was intended that she should thus carry an easy helm and be a much improved sailer.[16] The single topgallant was split into upper and lower topgallants for easier handling. The hull was re-planked inside and out, while new decks were laid and new deckhouses fitted.

A wardroom was provided once again, with cabins for the officers and scientists. Accommodation for the rest of the crew was in the crew space on the maindeck. A chemical and a biological laboratory were built. She was provided with a large trawl winch and three powered reels for use with vertical nets and waterbottles. Waterbottles, sounding machines, outboard platforms, and other oceanographic equipment fitted the *Discovery* for her new life as a Royal Research Ship[17] in the Southern Ocean. Her port of registry, since she was owned by the Government of the Falkland Islands, was changed from London to Port Stanley. The vessel was to fly the Blue Ensign emblazoned with the Arms of the Falkland Islands.

The *Hampshire Telegraph* of 8 May 1925 carried an article headed 'Ready for research work: Scott's Discovery as she is today'. The writer pointed out that the art of wooden shipbuilding was passing, 'but that it has not already passed is proved by the condition of the Discovery today'. He described numerous features of the reconstruction, including the replacement of the larger part of the keel. The search for timber of sufficient length for this had recourse in the end to Quebec oak, after five trees from north Somerset had been sawn up and found wanting. The masts had been made of pine from Oregon and were longer than before, while the yards and rigging had been renewed and the engines practically rebuilt. The total cost of the purchase and reconstruction of the *Discovery* excluding scientific equipment was nearly £114,000.[18]

On 2 July 1924, Dr Stanley Kemp (1882–1945) had been appointed leader of the *Discovery* Expedition and Director of Research by the *Discovery* Committee. One of his first duties was to sanction the design of the *Discovery*'s badge, which combined a whale, the ship's name, the Imperial Crown and the waves of the sea.[19] A man of great physical stature, Kemp was modest, beloved of his staff, whom he was able to inspire (and sometimes exasperate) through his own devotion to the task, in often trying conditions, on board the ever-rolling ship. As a young man he had gained experience of the methods of deep-sea oceanography through fishery research off the coast of Ireland. He subsequently spent over a decade in the service of the Zoological Survey of India. Thereafter, until 1936, when he resigned from what had by then become known as *Discovery* Investigations, Kemp 'was occupied in planning, organising and carrying out one of the most comprehensive schemes of oceanographical research ever undertaken by any country in the world'.[20] One reason for the *Discovery* Expedition's being comparatively little known was that its leader (and the Committee) shunned publicity: Kemp was a scientist first and foremost, strictly concerned with routine traverses of the ocean from which data could be obtained, the raw material of research. Sir Alister Hardy, chief zoologist of the expedition, afterwards praised Kemp's breadth of view, his grasp of detail and the tireless industry with which the whole undertaking was directed.[21]

Before leaving England, Kemp informed the scientific world, through an article in *Nature*,[22] about the forthcoming oceanographical expedition of the RRS *Discovery*. In another article,[23] he was at pains to point out that the *Discovery* Expedition of 1925–7 differed from the perilous exploring expeditions of previous years, even though it was carried out in Scott's old ship. He emphasised that it would pursue the 'solution of a particular economic problem . . . a biological one, occasioned by the rapid expansion of the southern whaling industry in recent years'. The main purpose of the expedition was biological and not geographical. Kemp's outline of the *Discovery*'s scientific programme is in the first volume of *Discovery Reports*.[24]

The new master of the *Discovery* was, in contrast to Kemp, a burly sea-dog and romantic from the heroic age of Antarctic exploration. Commander Joseph Russell Stenhouse, DSO, DSC, OBE, Croix de Guerre, RD, RNR, came from a family of shipbuilders in Dumbarton, famous for their clipper ships. Born in 1887, he had seen service in the Antarctic as Captain of Shackleton's *Aurora*, 1914–17, and was well acquainted with the perils of navigation under sail in high southern latitudes. On return from the Antarctic towards the end of the Great War, he had served in 'Q' ships (armed merchant vessels), including HMS *Ianthe* (a sailing ship) which he had commanded. His

DSO was awarded for ramming and sinking a German submarine with the patrol boat PC61, commanded by Frank Worsley, in September 1917. He next served under Shackleton with other old polar comrades in the North Russia Expeditionary Force of 1918–19 and was in charge of organising the winter transport of troops by horse sledge between Murmansk and Archangel. He also organised, equipped and commanded the first Lake Onega flotilla of armed motorboats. He was demobilised in 1920 and served for a time as Salvage Officer in the Dardanelles and Aegean Sea.[25]

Stenhouse was appointed nautical advisor to the *Discovery* Committee in 1923. His old shipmate, Frank Worsley of *Endurance* fame, called him 'one of the most efficient seamen of this century, having sailing ships in his blood and a wide and varied sea experience'. Duty was said to be his watchword.[26] The relationship between the captain of an expedition ship and the scientists he carries is not an easy one.[27] This was true of Kemp and Stenhouse. Kemp, the dedicated scientist, was not the man (thought Hardy) to give Stenhouse the assurance that he would have liked—that he was taking part in something great.[28] The other scientific staff were A. C. Hardy, J. E. Hamilton, N. A. Mackintosh, J. F. G. Wheeler and E. R. Gunther (zoologists), H. F. P. Herdman and A. J. Clowes (hydrologists). They were later joined by D. D. John, F. C. Fraser and L. Harrison Matthews. The marine staff included W. H. O'Connor (Chief Officer); Lieut.-Com. J. M. Chaplin (second officer and surveyor); Eng.-Lieut. W. A. Horton (Chief Engineer) and Lieut.-Col. E. H. Marshall (surgeon).

A. C. (later Sir Alister) Hardy had previous experience of marine biological research as Assistant Naturalist at the Fisheries Laboratory, Lowestoft. Between 1921 and 1924, as a young graduate, he had studied the North Sea herring and its food, especially in relation to plankton, both from the Laboratory's research vessel and from the drifters of the herring fleet. While engaged on this work, he had invented what he called a plankton indicator to provide a continuous record of the plankton when towed for many miles astern of a ship. He first heard of the *Discovery* Expedition in 1923 when he read the article by Rowland Darnley entitled 'A new Antarctic expedition'. Decades later, he could still recapture the excitement which the article had given him long ago.[29] He joined the expedition in May 1924.

Before the *Discovery* set sail, Hardy had been invited by Professor Johan Hjort to join him aboard the *Michael Sars* which was to make the very first whale-marking cruise. The Norwegians would fire a shoulder gun and Hardy would try out the cumbersome crossbow, designed by Professor C. V. Boys, the Cambridge physicist and friend of Sir Sidney Harmer. Sir Sidney, by then Director of the British Museum (Natural History) and Vice-Chairman of the *Discovery* Committee, had taken a particular interest in this. Years later, Sir Alister Hardy recollected Harmer's 'supervising the first experiments with a large cross-bow that was designed to fire whale-marks noiselessly so that the whales should not be scared by the sound of a gun ... At one time he had a large oil-cloth model whale behind the Museum and I seem to remember him in morning coat, striped trousers and bowler hat, excitedly watching the first shots, which I believe I fired, with this very barbarous-looking mediaeval weapon.'[30] The contraption failed to work effectively and caused some hilarity on board. The three weeks' cruise in the North Atlantic was meant as a preliminary to Hjort's major investigations of the stocks of northern whales. Hardy obtained valuable insight into the equipment and methods of this famous oceanographic research vessel, and was especially interested in the large nets that could be closed at the end of their tow in different depths of water, *before* being brought to the surface. This ensured that the catch represented the marine life at a particular depth only. It was agreed that the *Discovery*'s plankton nets would be made to the same design as Hjort's, so that results from either end of the earth could be compared. However, it transpired that Hjort was unable to carry out his project and the idea of co-operation sadly came to nothing in the end.

No full-length account of the 1925–7 *Discovery* (Oceanographic) Expedition appeared until the publication in 1967 of Sir Alister Hardy's book *Great waters*, which is not only a narrative of the expedition (written from his diary and beautifully illustrated with his

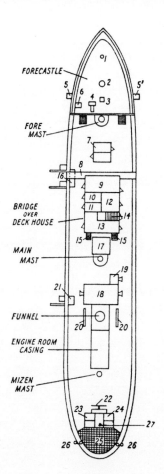

Outline plan of the upper deck and forecastle of the RRS *Discovery*

1. Anchor davit
2. Capstan
3. Searchlight
4. Deepwater hydrographic reel
5. Sounding platforms
6. Lucas sounding machine
7. Companion ways to galley and crew's quarters
8. Wing of bridge (above deck house)
9. Chart room
10. Survey store
11. Wireless cabin
12. Deck cabin
13. Upper deck laboratory
14. Companion way to ward room
15. Stairways up to bridge
16. Two shallow water hydrographic and plankton reels (with outboard platforms)
17. Wardroom skylight
18. Main winch house
19. Auxiliary winch drum
20. Accumulator springs for use with towing warps
21. Deepwater plankton winch (with outboard platform)
22. Auxiliary steering wheel
23. Officers' lavatories
24. Armoury and lamp store
25. Grating platform
26. Stern fair-leads for the warps from the main winch
27. Kelvin sounding machine

own watercolours and sketches) but a commentary on events and scientific work in the light of subsequent voyages and research.[31] This chapter relies heavily on *Great waters*, which is highly recommended to the reader wishing to learn more. A detailed description of the general arrangement and equipment of RRS *Discovery*, can be found in *Great waters*. Hardy guides the reader over the ship, beginning at the forecastle head, where 'there are the most glorious views of the sea imaginable; we have a feeling of soaring up over the waves like a bird, whilst behind us are the great towers of sails, filled with the breeze and brilliant in the sun, like outstretched wings'. Hardy also writes of the joy of 'seeing—and *hearing*—square rig sails set' to the chorus of an old sea shanty sung by the crew many of whom were experienced in sail. The number of each item refers to the sketch plan on the previous page.

On the centre line forward is the wide swinging anchor davit (1) which not only lifts the anchor over the side but also serves for working the deep-water sampling bottles; for this latter purpose a fine-stranded steel wire runs round blocks to the davit from a small steam-winch (4) carrying $3^{1}/_{2}$ miles (3,500 fathoms) of it. Also on the centre line is the capstan (2), geared to a steam windlass on the deck below, and farther aft still is a powerful searchlight (3) which, when we get south, will be invaluable for navigating among icebergs at night.

On either side of the forecastle, jutting out beyond the rail are small platforms (5) from which a sounding with the lead can be taken in shallow water; and, against that on the port side, is the Lucas steam sounding machine (6), capable of plumbing the greatest depths with its fine piano wire.

Coming down from the forecastle to the upper deck (the main deck being that of the cabins below) and proceeding aft we pass the companion-ways (7) leading down to the galley and the crew's quarters and come to the bridge (8). This is most spacious for it covers a large deck house which contains a number of cabins. These include the chart room (9) facing for'ard and spanning the whole width of the house, with a survey store (10) and the wireless cabin (11) on the port side, a spare cabin, used as a sick bay if needs be (12) on the starboard side and, at the after end, the large main laboratory (13); then between the last two items is the companion-way (14) down to the ward room below. The laboratory we shall see in more detail later on. The bridge, gained by two stairways (15) up from the deck aft, is entirely open giving a view of all the rigging and sails; at its forward end it spans the full beam of the ship so that the officer of the watch can look out from either side and see the whole length of the vessel's flank from stem to stern.

Opposite the chart room on the port side is a small steam engine (16) driving two winch drums, each holding 1,000 fathoms of stranded wire; they are for vertical plankton nets and water sampling at moderate depths, and against each a short boom carries the wire out from the side of the ship, where there are also small outboard platforms for working the gear.

Going farther aft, past the skylights of the wardroom (17) and the main mast we come to the steel house (18) which gives protection to the great steam winch. This is truly a magnificent affair, with two huge drums like the winch of a trawler, but with one five times the width of the other. The smaller, on the port side, holds a mile of thick steel rope ($1^5/_8$ths inches circumference) for trawling with a beam trawl; the other carries 5 miles of a special steel rope which tapers in thickness from $1^3/_4$ inches circumference at the inboard end to $1^1/_2$ inches at the outboard end. This latter rope is for letting down and towing very big nets to fish for the strange pelagic life in the great ocean depths; as more and more of the heavy cable is let out, it gradually increases in thickness, and so in strength, to take the strain of the gradually increasing weight in addition to that of pulling the net. Such a tapering warp is very difficult to construct and so very costly. The drums of such a winch have to be immensely strong to withstand the accumulating pressure due to winding on such a great length of cable under high tension.

Outside the house, on the starboard side, but geared to the engine within, is a smaller auxiliary drum (19) carrying 3 miles (3,000 fathoms) of thinner cable for pulling plankton nets at lesser depths. Immediately behind the winch house, on either side, are two long and powerful springs (20); these, when large nets are used in rough weather, are linked by clamps to the cables so that any uneven pull due to the ship's pitching may be damped down by their expansion and contraction and so reduce oscillations in the forward motion of the net.

Slightly abaft the winch house on the port side is yet another small steam engine and winch drum (21) for operating the deep-water vertical plankton nets; this unit is equipped with a similar outward platform and boom to that of the 'shallow-water' unit farther forward, but here the winch drum carries 3,500 fathoms of fine stranded wire. When we come to work a full scale plankton and hydrographic station over deep water, we shall be using all four small winches on the port side at the same time; water-sampling bottles and nets are sent to the great depths by the two winches farthest apart (to avoid entangling the wires) while at the same time samples are taken from the lesser depths by the double unit amidships. Above the engine room casing are the lifeboats, and abaft the mizzen mast are two small houses, one on either side (23, 24) containing an armoury, a lamp store and officers' lavatories. Then at the very stern is a slightly raised platform, a wooden grating (25), on which the large tow-nets will be received as they are pulled in over the port or starboard quarters; here in the rail are placed the 'fairleads' (26) for the cables running aft from the main winch. It is on this platform that we may expect some of our great moments; here we eagerly watch the large nets come in to see what they may have caught after being towed for several hours in the dark depths of some two miles down. Massive wooden bulwarks, breast high, limit our domain on either side, but here and there, both port and starboard, are lengths of step enabling us to jump up and lean over the side, when in the tropics beautiful jellyfish go drifting by and the ship may be slowed down to allow us to catch them with hand nets and other devices.[32]

## VOYAGE TO THE CAPE, 1925

The voyage started badly. The reconstruction of the ship in Portsmouth by Vospers had taken far longer than anticipated and towards the end, the job was very hurried. The original intention had been to reach the South Atlantic by the beginning of the Antarctic whaling season in November. In July 1925, the *Discovery* sailed from Portsmouth for the Bay of Biscay to try out experimental echo-sounding gear developed by the Admiralty scientists who were on board. In the event, she did not leave the Channel. Vospers' workmanship was tested—and found wanting—by a long and violent storm (too rough for the apparatus and for its chief inventor, B. S. Smith) which caused the ship to put into Dartmouth, where she lay for two months while extensive repairs were made. Here the expedition scientists, under Kemp's expert guidance, worked in teak to produce racks for test-tubes and bottles, and shelves for books and other loose items, so that these would remain in place when the ship rolled. Despite the severity of the gale and the damage it caused, it was as well that the ship's weaknesses were identified at the beginning of the voyage and not somewhere far from home.

On the evening of 24 September 1925, the *Discovery* steamed slowly down the river Dart towards the sea and the voyage really began. She put into Falmouth, not for orders, as had so many of her predecessors in sail, but to land the Admiralty scientists, J. A. McGeachy and Bradbury, after a successful trial of their apparatus in deep water on 29 September. The fine old clipper ship, *Cutty Sark* (now preserved at Greenwich), lay in port and the *Discovery* anchored nearby, departing finally for the south on 5 October 1925.

The early chapters of *Great waters* recount the scientist's delight in sailing or steaming slowly southwards through the waters of the Atlantic, examining the creatures of the sea. Hardy's descriptions are so vivid as almost to make them come alive. He writes of tropical nights with a shining wake of phosphorescent *Pyrosoma* near Ascension Island and daytime rides in a bosun's chair beneath the bowsprit 'fishing out treasure after treasure' from the gently swelling sea, of King Neptune and his company being welcomed on board and the mysteries of the old-time sailing ships 'crossing the Line' at the Equator.

Things were different in the engine-room. Young George Gourlay had been appointed junior engineer and the rolling and pitching of the ship made him very sea-sick.

My chief worry was that I should get drowsy and miss attending to some part of the machinery. Left alone in the engine room I felt everything was going to go wrong at once.

The water level was flying up and down in the gauge glasses on the boilers. The circulating pump was slowing down & the Vacuum was falling back. The Air pump was worked off rockers in the main engines & if the Vacuum dropped much below 26" the low pressure piston would hammer through water collecting in the cylinder. I had been taught that this was always very dangerous. So beware, thought I. . . .

The heat of the Tropics was almost unbearable. I only wore a pair of pyjama trousers in the Engine room & the sweat poured off me & I wrang out the trousers and rinsed them after each watch. The $CO_2$ freezer compressor failed. The store room bulkhead opened up with the heat & we had to dump all our fresh meat. Thinking to raise the standard, the Authorities had engaged an hotel chef instead of a sea cook & although a very nice fellow, he couldn't keep the yeast in the hot temperature, so we had no bread—no bread!

The old Bosun used to say 'Come and have some salt beef or salt pork, George' but the stuff had been in the barrels for 2 years. 'Still good', they said & the old salts really enjoyed it. But I could not bear the smell of it even. Tins of sardines and ships biscuits kept me going, but I got as thin as a rail.[33]

The youngest of the three cadets on board, John Bentley (aged 15), had joined the ship from the training ship HMS *Worcester*. What struck him at first was the maze of ropes and rigging, brails, halliards, buntlines, sheets and braces, to mention only a few. Of the voyage south, he wrote home in schoolboy fashion,

You have no idea how beautiful a tropical moonlight night can be with the flying fish jumping right out of the water and some of them landing on board. What a welcome addition they are to our diet, they are delicious fried! It is difficult to describe what it is like being at sea in a sailing ship—sailing quietly without engine power. There is the creaking of the wooden hull, the sound of the wind in the rigging and the rushing of the water swishing past the hull. Lying in one's bunk with just a thickness of wood between one and the sea beyond, one can imagine that the ship is actually carrying on a conversation with the sea. Up aloft, it is even more marvellous looking down from perhaps the topgallant yardarm into a midnight sea, illuminated by masses of plankton drifting by, giving out their luminous and mysterious light.[34]

Another young member of the expedition, E. R. Gunther, found the crow's nest, high up on the mainmast, a refuge from the tuneless singing or whistling of some of his shipmates. His diary,[35] with its regular daily entries, provides many glimpses of these same shipmates as he came to know them on this first leg of the voyage. He particularly liked O'Connor, the whimsical Irish mate, whose seamanship he wrote about and much admired. He described him busy splicing on deck one morning as the $4^1/_2$-metre net was prepared for use—'and as he spliced away now hammering the stiff rope into shape with his fid, now prising the strands apart with the other end, he kept on talking and muttering—*Plenty of grease*, he said as he dipped the end of the fid into the pot: *Plenty of tar and grease is what the sailor-man wants*—more splicing—*and the full moon*—splicing continues—*and a good cook*'.[36]

The young scientist also wrote down his first impressions of the master of the *Discovery*, Captain Stenhouse.

> I am a bit surprised by the culture of our Captain. True his knowledge is superficial, but he takes an interest in almost everything and uses the general library more than anybody. He is an authority on horses: today he told us a lot about harness and how it varied in different parts of the country: he knows a trifle about pictures, is always interested in old customs, Archaeology, Botany and Natural History. As in the development of any Captain, he is convinced that a sailor's idea of a bird is the truth . . . when a man has to live with the bird for months on end, what right has an old fossil at home to call it something else?[37]

Gunther came from a family of 'old fossils'. His grandfather, Albert Günther, had been Keeper of Zoology at the British Museum, while his father, R. T. Gunther, founded the Old Ashmolean Museum of the History of Science at Oxford.

Gunther's cabin, like those of the other scientists, opened off the wardroom and allowed him to overhear their conversation over dinner if he did not eat with them.

> . . . pleasant is the word to express the smoothness with which the expedition is running and the harmony that exists among the members thereof . . . All their voices are pleasing: they talk softly, some of them steadily: seldom are more than three talking at the same time. Every remark is given a full hearing and . . . in the course of dinner every man made his contribution to the issue, and all repartees, jokes, ragging, chaffing, sarcasm and other jists of the conversation preserved a top line tone & furthermore, as for malice, there was none.[38]

He generally preferred to spend the evenings after work in the wardroom or in his cabin, devouring some of the books from the library. He was surprised 'how very much addicted' Dr Kemp was to his 'shop', having 'never a thought or a pause' for anything that was 'not connected with the expedition' and usually passing the evening in the laboratory. Herdman and Hamilton would play bridge with the engineers below.[39]

The *Discovery* called to bunker at Ascension Island. As the scientists went ashore in the whaler, they were surprised to see how much the ship was rolling. The hydrologist, H. F. P. Herdman, who was to return to the Antarctic time and again, found the ship a good cure for sea-sickness since she rolled 'even in the calmest weather'. Writing to a friend from near the Equator, he described his daytime rig of a 'boiler suit, topee and sandals'. The other 'miscellaneous rigs', he thought were 'wonderful—everyone can wear what they like—ships' officers included—the results are lovely!'[40] In fact uniform regulations for colder weather and more formal occasions (including special cap badges and buttons) had been drawn up by the Committee, modified by the Admiralty and approved by the King. Kits were issued free to officers and men, but not to cadets.[41]

Trials of the experimental echo-sounder designed by the Admiralty scientists continued during the passage south. Echo-sounders of both shallow and deep-water patterns were fitted in the *Discovery* (and later in the *Discovery* II). The invention enabled the ocean bed to be charted not only with greater accuracy, but while the vessel was under way. This resulted in an enormous saving of time when compared with the old-fashioned method that required the stationary lowering and raising of the sounding lead on thousands of feet of wire. Deep-water echo-sounding was in fact pioneered more extensively at this time by the *Meteor* during the German Atlantic Expedition of 1925–7. Soundings were made every twenty minutes as the *Meteor* carried out her traverses of the ocean.[42] Hardy described the Admiralty instrument as complicated although based on a simple principle. 'A sharp sound, that of a hammer striking a metal drum is made below the surface of the sea and its echo, sent back from the ocean floor, is picked up by a microphone placed in the bottom of the ship; by timing this echo exactly by electrical means, and knowing the speed of sound in sea water, the depth can be measured and recorded to the nearest foot.'[43] Trials were also made of the oceanographic gear including the very large deep-water tow-nets, fifteen feet in diameter.

The westerly winds were picked up at last some eight hundred miles from Cape Town, resulting in good progress under sail, so that the *Discovery* entered Table Bay on 20 December 1925, in time for Christmas and Christmas mail. The passage from England had taken nearly five weeks and towards the end, water had to be rationed. Because time was short, investigations off the coast of Africa were left for the homeward voyage.

# SIXTEEN

## OUTWARD VOYAGE TO SOUTH GEORGIA, 1925–6, AND ON TO THE FALKLANDS

### THE FIRST SOUTHERN VOYAGE, JANUARY–JUNE 1926

ALTERATIONS WERE COMPLETED to the winches at the Cape, coal was taken on and the *Discovery* finally sailed for South Georgia via the lonely Atlantic island of Tristan da Cunha on 17 January 1926. She carried some fifteen tons of supplies, parcels and mail for the islanders, the first for over two years. Tristan da Cunha was sighted early on 30 January and the anchor dropped off the tiny settlement of thatched stone cottages, overlooked by the great volcanic peak, a spur of which in 1961 was to erupt and cause the evacuation of the populace,[1] which numbered about one hundred and forty at the time of the *Discovery*'s visit. Two of the islands' frail but seaworthy long boats (shells of oiled canvas stretched on a wooden frame) approached the ship and the boats' crews came aboard wearing a variety of old clothes,

> a check cap, an engine-driver's hat, ragged sweaters, patched trousers, bursting shoes or island moccasins laced with knotted string, and some with socks only, so full of holes that the toes protruded—the men rather surprisingly were shaved. They spoke queerly—not only with an eccentric vocabulary, but also in a high-pitched voice such as the deaf are sometimes wont to use. With kit-bags slung over their shoulders, they were ready to barter furs, skins, moccasins and socks for any clothes, food and soap. But their principal object was to beg. Certain articles of commerce are necessary to them: but they are unable to pay and rely upon charity for these, as they do for a missioner . . .[2]

The women (ashore) wore rather old-fashioned long skirts and blouses, with brightly coloured plaid head scarves and shawls. Dr E. H. Marshall, the *Discovery*'s surgeon, landed with Dr Kemp and made a medical examination of the islanders.[3] Some time later, everyone gathered outside the little church to hear Captain Stenhouse (in uniform) read a message from King George V and a proclamation from the British Government in answer to the islanders' petition for a regular steam mail service. He also presented a portrait of the Duke of Edinburgh from the Queen of Romania. It was after her father,

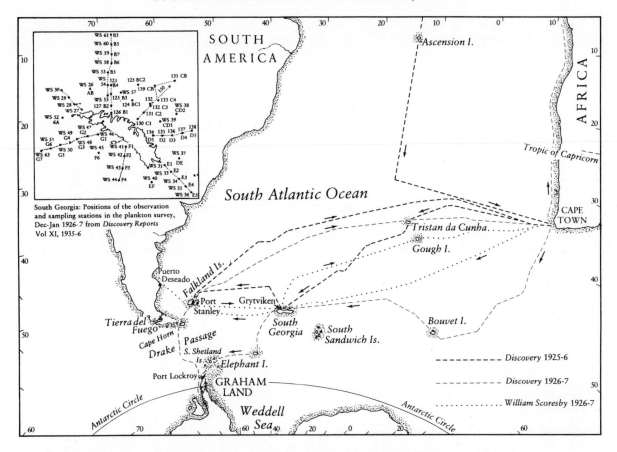

South Georgia: Positions of the observation and sampling stations in the plankton survey, Dec-Jan 1926-7 from *Discovery Reports* Vol XI, 1935-6

South Atlantic and Southern Oceans, showing the tracks of RRS *Discovery* and RS *William Scoresby*, 1925-6 and 1926-7. Based on maps in the *Geographical Journal*, vol. XXII, 1928, p. 226 and *Discovery Investigations. Second Annual Report*, HMSO 1929

the Duke, that the settlement had been named. Formalities ended with the singing of the National Anthem, the islanders continuing each line long after their visitors had finished.[4]

The anchor was weighed on 1 February, but not before much biological work had been done: fronds of giant kelp were examined, many fish and other sea creatures caught and either preserved or eaten. One of the fish, *Decapterus longimanus*, and two shrimps, *Paramoera tristanensis* and *Portogeneia tristanensis*, were new to science.[5] They were pickled for posterity; another particularly rare fish, keenly sought by the British Museum, was eaten for supper by mistake.[6] A breathtaking collection of tree-like corals was taken in the dredge, looking like branches torn from trees, laden with spring blossom of many different colours.[7]

The main oceanographic work of the expedition began with a series of 'standard vertical stations' on passage bound for the sub-Antarctic island of South Georgia. 'The exploration of the sea', wrote Hardy after his return (in the days before modern submersibles), 'so different from that of the land, has a fascination of its own. . . . I would liken the exploration of a wide stretch of ocean to the crossing of a continent on a road in the dark and trying to build up an idea of the country travelled from the samples of minerals, plant, and animal life clutched and groped for a little way to right and left when stopping at intervals.'[8] The tools or instruments with which to take these samples had been devised and modified over the previous century. The Nansen–Pettersson waterbottle was used for sampling water down to a hundred meters and the Ekman reversing bottle at greater depths. Each measured the temperature of the sea at the moment the sample was taken. Samples of plankton were collected by conical nets resembling giant stockings without heels terminating in small 'buckets'; these were similar to those used by the famous oceanographers Hjort and Murray in the North Atlantic. Vertical stations punctuated the ship's passage regularly.

> As soon as we arrive on position the captain turns the head of the ship into the wind and endeavours to keep her stationary with an occasional use of the engine; it is, of course, impossible to anchor the ship in so great a depth of water. Today there was a heavy south-westerly swell and a wind of 'force 4' which made working difficult. The heavy rigging of the *Discovery* offers almost as much resistance to the wind as if we still had some sail up, and so makes the task of keeping our position peculiarly hard. If we should drive before the wind, then the wires carrying our water bottles and nets would no longer be vertical and it would be next to impossible to determine exactly the depth at which we were sampling; to prevent this we often have to steam against the wind, but to keep the ship's head facing into it, when we are making no passage through the water, is by no means easy. Immediately the ship has stopped, the sounding party send away the lead . . . on the fine piano wire from the Lucas machine on the forecastle; the thousands of metres of wire go running out, but the little sounding machine is so designed that it will automatically stop as soon as the lead strikes the bottom and takes the tension off the line. While the sounding is being taken we begin to collect water samples from the shallower depths by using the engine amidships and to make plankton net hauls with the engine aft. The routine temperature readings and water samples are taken at the surface and the following depths: 5, 10, 20, 30, 40, 50, 75, 100, 200, 300, 400, 500, 1,000, 2,000 and 3,000 metres or as deep as the sounding will allow. The vertical plankton net hauls will usually be taken in six stages: from 50 metres to the surface, from 100 to 50 metres, from 250 to 100 metres, from 500 to 250, from 750 to 500, and from 1,000 to 750 metres, and sometimes even deeper.[9]

These long sessions of 'fishing for knowledge in this deep-water world we cannot see'[10] would last for six hours or more. Station No. 10 described above in lat. 46°11′30″S.

long. 22°27′30″W. yielded the first ocean-bottom sample of Radiolarian ooze, taken at 4,402 metres depth by the 'snapper' lead at the end of the sounding wire. It was different from the usual Globigerina ooze, and more characteristic of the Indian and Pacific Oceans, never before recorded from the Atlantic. These oozes on the ocean floors are made of microscopic shells rained down from the surface of the sea over aeons of time on the deaths of their planktonic owners.[11]

The first iceberg of the expedition was sighted at dawn the following Thursday (16 February 1926), a flat-topped tabular iceberg typical of the Southern Ocean, broken off from an ice shelf on the coast of the Antarctic. 'Its sides were beautifully sculptured', wrote Hardy, 'and there were deep caverns and clefts in them; in these was seen that most remarkable, almost luminous, ice-blue; so different from the blue of the sea or the sky.' The sea round about was dotted with pieces of ice broken from the sides of the iceberg. The captain steered the ship among these bergy bits 'to give us for the first time the sound of broken ice upon her bows and sides; a musical scrunching sound, a little like the shovelling of broken glass'.[12] Just as the *Discovery* came directly opposite, the berg calved with a thunderous noise. A flat portion broke off to go its separate way, eventually melting (like its parent), in the warmer waters to the north.

At Station No. 11, a few miles past the iceberg, in lat. 50°26′ S. long. 30°27′ W., a cold layer of water at a depth of 100 to 200 metres between two warmer layers, showed that they were in Antarctic surface water, where, in summer, there is a temperature minimum between sun-warmed Antarctic water at the surface and underlying warmer, more saline, deep water, whose southward movement counteracts the overall cooling and dilution resulting from the Antarctic climate. The temperature minimum marks the limit, generally 100 to 150 metres down, of surface warming, where there may be a movement of colder water from higher latitudes. The Antarctic Convergence at about 50°S. in the Atlantic Ocean (and farther south in the Pacific), where the Antarctic water sinks below warmer sub-Antarctic water in a sharp frontal zone, is of great significance in the lives of some plankton animals and plants which make vertical migrations between the cold and warm waters.[13] Otto Pettersson had predicted just such a system in 1905 from his studies in the Arctic; its existence in the south was revealed independently by two oceanographic expeditions working in the South Atlantic in the same years, our own *Discovery* and the *Meteor* (Captain Z. S. F. Spiess), carrying the German Atlantic Expedition.[14] Sometimes known as the Meinardus Line, the Antarctic Convergence had in fact earlier been deduced by Wilhelm Meinardus from the data collected by the German South Polar Expedition of 1901–4, led by Erich von Drygalski and published in Vol. III of the expedition results, 1923.

## SOUTH GEORGIA, FEBRUARY–APRIL 1926

South Georgia (where Sir Ernest Shackleton had been buried only four years earlier, after his death on board the *Quest*) was sighted from the *Discovery* on 20 February 1926. It had not been explored until surveyed by Captain Cook, who had landed and taken formal possession for the British Crown in January 1775.[15] Almost due east of Cape Horn, and to the south-west of the Cape of Good Hope, the island is over one hundred miles long and twenty miles wide. Its spine of high mountains is covered in perpetual snow and intersected by glaciers. The coast is deeply indented, many of the bays being bordered by ice cliffs, from which large pieces break off and float out to sea. The biggest glacier is the Nordenskjöld (over two miles wide, with a snout some 70 feet high) at the head of East Cumberland Bay. Thousands of elephant seals haul out on the beaches in summer to bear and bring up their young, and later to wallow and moult in glorious mud between clumps of tussock grass. Four species of penguin as well as albatrosses, petrels, cormorants, sheath-bills, gulls, terns and skuas nest there. The Fur seals (very scarce in 1926 through near-extermination in the nineteenth century) have now partly recovered their former numbers. Imported reindeer flourish on a diet mainly of tussock grass.

South Georgia was well in view from the *Discovery* by 7.30 on the morning of 20 February 1926. The mountains were most impressive and many small whalers could be seen.[16] The sea appeared greener and greener as they drew nearer to land. Masses of feathers and straws floated on its surface, this being the moulting season. As they entered Cumberland Bay, members of the shore station came out in motor boats and circled the *Discovery*. She dropped anchor in King Edward Cove, East Cumberland Bay. A great reunion took place there with colleagues of the Marine Station, who had sailed from England in the autumn of 1924. The staff of the shore laboratory were an integral part of the *Discovery* Expedition. Their prefabricated single-storey wooden building had been completed in February 1925 and had withstood the fiercest gales. Its clean, polished and draught-free laboratory (which, above all, did not roll), its comfortable quarters and its conservatory full of geraniums and nasturtiums were the envy of the ship's party.[17]

The shore staff's task was to investigate the whales towed to the station of the Compania Argentina de Pesca, a short boat ride away at the head of the cove at Grytviken. Here, on the flensing platform, the biologists examined the gigantic corpses which had been hauled up for dismemberment before being rendered down into oil and meal. Messrs Mackintosh and Wheeler, and for a time, Mr Hamilton, working surrounded by the blood, stench and slime of the 'plan', had made detailed measurements of 738 whales by April 1926. Analysis of the data accumulated on the great whales revealed their breeding times, the period of gestation, the calves' rate of growth and their age at maturity. Important investigations of their food and a study of the elephant seals and birds were made by Mr Harrison Matthews. The hydrologist, Mr Clowes, analysed the chemical composition of the water samples landed from the ships to build up the physical background to the picture. (The shore party also worked, between South Georgia whaling seasons, at the South African whaling station of Saldanha Bay, where information complementing that obtained in South Georgia was especially valuable as far as the migration and stocks of the whales was concerned.)

The morning after her arrival, the *Discovery* reberthed alongside the wooden wharf at the whaling station to obtain fresh water and coal. Here the stench from the factory could be almost felt and the ship rode in the diluted blood of the slaughtered whales. Hardy's watercolour in *Great waters* vividly depicts the scene that he also describes.

From our deck we look right over the factory. Before us is the flensing platform or 'plan': a scene of great activity for the fishing just now is exceptionally heavy. Floating in the water, belly upwards, are many fin and blue whales, blown up like balloons, waiting to be dealt with. They appear like this for two reasons; firstly, when killed, they have compressed air pumped into their body-cavities to make them float, but then if, as now, the fishing is heavy, there may be some delay before they can be dealt with, so that the gases of decomposition add to their internal pressure. It is a fantastic scene. The water in which the whales float, and on which we too are riding, is blood red. On the platform itself there are whales in all stages of dismemberment. Little figures, busy with long-handled knives like hockey sticks, look like flies as they work upon the huge carcasses; and from time to time these massive remains are pulled about the platform by steel cables or chains working round bollards from steam winches in the background. Then there are the factory buildings themselves, ejecting clouds of steam, and, sheer above it all, is a mountain peak of dark rock splashed with brilliant sunlit snow towering against a clear blue sky. This blue of the sky reflects on the blood-red water below us to give a curious lilac tint; on the quay-side to the right are the rows and rows of oil drums awaiting shipment: the produce of the factory . . .

All around the fjord rise the mountains, giving, on calm days such as this, superb reflections in the water. And the water itself is remarkable for its range of colour: far out towards the entrance, where small icebergs float, it is a pure blue; it then becomes a vivid turquoise and passes into green . . . Finally the green passes through brown to a rich red near the flensing platform where it receives the crimson streams from this gargantuan butchery. We must now add to the scene the sight and clamour of at least ten thousand birds. Near the factory the water is alive with Cape pigeons screaming and fighting over scraps of floating offal, and there are some giant petrels too, a little farther out. In contrast to these scavengers of somewhat revolting habits, are many delicate little black and white birds, Wilson's petrels, which flutter over its surface like butterflies with just their toes touching the water; they snap up morsels from the surface as they hover and only settle farther out in the cleaner water.[18]

Cadet Bentley found the permeating smell frightful although there were compensations in that the ship's company was able to live very well on whale steak, fried whale and boiled whale, which tasted like beef when properly cooked. Fortunately the new cook engaged in Cape Town had served in whalers and knew all the tricks of the trade. Watching the flensing of the whales one day, Bentley was saddened to see unborn youngsters, each about fourteen feet long, taken from the bellies of two females. He was told that this was quite a common occurrence.[19] Pre-1914 regulations laid down by the Falkland Islands Government had forbidden the shooting of whale calves and cows accompanied by calves but failed to protect pregnant cows because they could not be recognised at sea. In practice, this is still the same today. The collection of whaling statistics, the biological examination of carcasses, studies of migration, growth, breeding habits and other research begun by the *Discovery* Expedition at Grytviken and at whaling stations in South Africa during the winter, have none the less enabled the formulation of regulations to safeguard whales, including the unborn calf and its mother, more effectively.

Soon after the *Discovery*'s arrival in South Georgia, Rolfe Gunther, the zoologist, rose early to watch Mackintosh and Wheeler of the Shore Station at their work on the whaling platform. He described the whales in his diary:

> Those towed in by the whalers are Blue Whales and Fin Whales about 60 feet in length and of such colossal bulk that their blood must weigh several tons itself. Their maximum girth is not far short of a railway carriage and yet in spite of these gigantic dimensions the animal does not look large, so beautifully is it proportioned.[20]

The whales were probably much longer, more like 80 feet in fact. A warp would be shackled round the tail flukes and the whale hauled out of the gory water and up the gently sloping planks. 'The platform has water trickling over it in many places', Gunther continued, 'but apart from this there is so much blood, blubber, oils, dripping, and fats and tissues of other kinds, that anything slides easily.' Wooden-soled boots were essential; rubber ones would have been a disaster.

Once the whale's head emerged from the water, the size of its jaws could be appreciated, some six feet long and fringed with a sieve of hairs along the edge of the whalebone. Some of the flensers stood on the whale itself to cut into the blubber, their spiky boots enabling them to keep their feet on the monster's body, while others cut from the ground. After the cuts were made, the blubber was stripped off by the winch, the warp being attached near the animal's mouth and the operation appearing no more difficult than peeling a banana. The strip of blubber would then be dragged up the platform like a long very thick carpet to be cut into small pieces by more men with flensing knives and fed into the slicing machine. From there it was conveyed in a continuous line of buckets into the plant, where the blubber would be rendered down into oil. Gunther noted the rapidity with which the flensing of the next whale began while the earlier one was further processed, the entrails being removed, the meat separated and the bones converted into manure. He further reflected on the pathetic sight the platform offered, contrasting the glad harvesting of hay and crops with the reduction to mineral products of this, the largest creature on earth, created over many ages and 'here being massacred for some men's pockets'. After breakfast, rigged in overalls and clogs, he helped the shore biologists, each equipped with knife and tape measure, to measure the animals. They looked out specially for parasites in the gut and measured the genitalia, occasionally taking sections of these.

The workers at Grytviken were all Norwegians. At first they had been highly suspicious of the shore biologists, fearing these would try to stop the whaling. They did not disguise their resentment,[21] and would sabotage the scientists' efforts by burying interesting organs under tons of carcass or conniving at the disappearance of organs extricated with difficulty which had been put aside for further examination by the scientists. When 'stepping warily across a slimy mass of flesh or strip of blubber, we would be suddenly sent sprawling by someone deliberately heaving on it'. Then the whalers would roar with laughter, most of all when the scientists were covered with the stinking contents of some swollen stomach or intestine. The Norwegians later overcame their suspicions and went out of their way to help. One of the station managers, Hansen, of Leith, was particularly helpful in shipping whale skeletons. These were prepared by L. Harrison Matthews, one of the shore scientists. Specimens of flippers and tails were also carried, pickled in salt, in one of the holds of the transport vessel. They were all destined for the British Museum (Natural History) in London, whose whales gallery is so well known. Dr Kemp considered Hansen 'a wonderful man, prepared to undertake any job, however formidable'.[22]

Away from Grytviken whaling station, young Gunther found South Georgia a beautiful island, the high snow-bound ridge of the Allardyce Range dominated by Mount Paget, whose broad shoulders contrasted with the needle-shaped peaks of the other mountains. An abundance of grasses and flowering plants carpeted the lower ground, above which were rough pavements of rock or steep slopes of scree. Its greatest beauty lay in the colours of the landscape and some of the bays were so warm and calm that they reminded Gunther of Swiss or Italian lakes.[23] Hardy's diary entry for 16 April records one of his more sobering experiences from a trip in a whale catcher while he was in South Georgia.

. . . We are now drawing closer to the whales. There are many, for their 'puffs of steam' appear in all directions, but two together are right ahead of us. We get closer and closer. Then up they come right below the bows; I can see them as clearly as before coming up through the water, but this time so close that they seem almost to graze our stem. They are two large blue whales. Bang! . . . Away goes the line. It seemed a good shot, but he is far from being dead and is pulling away in front. He blows every now and again and is bleeding hard. His companion or mate does not fly off like a scared whale, but swims bravely and pathetically beside him, as if offering sympathy and encouragement . . . Clouds of Cape pigeons circle round and keep settling and rising again over the bloody water.

The gun is quickly got ready again and after playing him for about a quarter of an hour—winding him in and letting him out again—we tire him out. He does not go far below the surface and gradually we wind him slowly in—or wind ourselves up to him, which is it? He is a huge whale, he appears almost as big as our ship. Panting, tugging, blowing, there he goes just ahead with the harpoon in his side clearly visible. We are gaining on him a few feet at a time. Next time he comes up we shall get him; the line is almost in. The captain is ready; his one hand is on the trigger and the other signals to the helmsman who turns the bows a little this way or a little that as required. Up the monster comes again. Bang! Over he turns, his ribbed belly gleaming in the sun. His flipper gives one last flap in the air and he spouts a jet of deep crimson. His huge mouth opens and closes, and he is dead. The ship has stopped and he lies across the bows. His companion is now nowhere to be seen. The cable is wound in to keep him at the surface. At once all is activity; every man quickly but without flurry does his job. To a long pole is fixed a hollow lance which is connected to a rubber hose-pipe coming from an air compressor in the engine-room; the lance is now driven deep into his body cavity and he is inflated to make him float. Whilst this is being done a chain is passed round his tail flukes and he is securely fastened to the ship. As soon as the lance is withdrawn, one of the hands standing on the carcass plugs the hole with a wad of tow. The harpoon lines are cut and the gun is being reloaded. The whale is now brought along and secured to one side of the vessel, the starboard side on this occasion, for towing with the tail pointing forwards. In another few minutes the tail flukes are cut away with a flensing knife for they have little oil value and not only impede the ship by their extra water resistance but tend to make steering difficult.

We are off again. Whales are everywhere. In a moment, a tall staff, with the flag of the company flying from it, is driven into our dead whale, and it is cast adrift. Already we are getting close to our next whale. . . . It is a barbarous business. These creatures are mammals like ourselves and I have no doubt that they feel pain. . . . Perhaps as often as not the whale is killed almost at once, as it should be if the explosive shell reaches the proper target: the main thoracic cavity; but as we have seen it may not. It would never be allowed if it took place on land. Think what an outcry there would be if we hunted elephants with explosive harpoons fired from the cannon of a tank and then played the wounded beasts upon a line! Each time you eat margarine, or wash with soap for that matter, you are quite likely to be using the products of this chase. . . . It is indeed a paradox: I have already emphasised the kind-heartedness of the whaling folk to their fellows. It is amazing how blind and unfeeling man, the carnivorous hunter, can be.[24]

E. R. Gunther also wrote an account of his trip in a whale catcher. He found the whales 'too beautiful for words', seeming 'to raise their knowing heads, be it ever so slightly, and to eye the vessel that pursues them'.[25]

The *Discovery* remained for two months at South Georgia. During that time she carried out the first provisional biological and hydrographical survey of the whaling grounds. The Shore Station biologists, Mackintosh and Wheeler, had already found that of over five hundred Blue and Fin whales examined, the great majority had been feeding on what the Norwegian whalers called krill (*Euphausia superba*), small shrimp-like crustaceans. The biologists at sea were particularly concerned with the swarms of live krill and 'the whole pelagic community of which it forms a part'.[26] By studying the plankton of the whaling grounds (and the conditions that favour its development) they hoped to learn why the whales came in such numbers to South Georgia.

The delayed departure from England, the slow passage to Cape Town and the call at Tristan da Cunha (scheduled by the Colonial Office and favoured by the King) curtailed the amount of work that the scientists could accomplish during their first visit to the South Georgia whaling grounds. They missed most of the finer weather and carried out only a fraction of the scientific programme. The biologists were nevertheless kept very busy examining the dredge hauls from Cumberland Bay and the station material taken at sea. This all had to be sorted, labelled and preserved, ready for later identification if need be. Some specimens were painted by Hardy and Gunther (particularly the fish) before their colour faded. Gunther wrote home a little tartly that

> The very fact that during the whole of March I only got ashore twice—each for a few hours, shows that we were overworked. *Kemp* is a craftsman to his finger tips and is content to work for hours on end without any exercise—life in India has doubtless helped this condition. Unfortunately, he does not realise that others cannot do it—and latterly I have definitely closed down work at five o'clock to go ashore for a run round. Of course we have added considerably to the fauna list of South Georgia and we have gained an insight into whale food: but we have contributed nothing of value to the problems we are trying to solve.[27]

There was a great deal of extra work aboard the ship. Cadet Bentley found the weekly cruises at this time 'interesting, but very tiring for the crew, constantly setting and hauling nets'.

By March, the southern winter was approaching and on several occasions the *Discovery* had to steer through light pack-ice. She hit the wharf hard in King Edward Cove in a fierce storm on 5 April but did not suffer any serious damage. A succession of gales hindered the work of sampling and netting during the first visit to South Georgia, but the groundwork had been done for the more comprehensive survey that would follow next season.[28] The limitations of the *Discovery*, as an oceanographic research vessel, became particularly apparent during these attempts to work nets and waterbottles in howling north-westerly gales and to examine plankton samples at sea. The main disadvantages were her rolling and her tendency to be blown off course owing to the heavy rigging and the engine's limited auxiliary power.[29]

## TO THE FALKLANDS AND BACK TO CAPE TOWN

The *Discovery* sailed from South Georgia on 17 April 1926. The Shore Station was closed for the winter and its inhabitants (apart from Hamilton and Matthews) left to work in South Africa. A line of stations was made *en route* for the Falklands Islands, off which trawling, dredging and additional stations were to be undertaken. The wind had strengthened as she neared the Falklands and at nine knots 'with all her canvas bellied to starboard' she seemed to skim the waters more swiftly than ever before. The low, flat windswept moorland contrasted strikingly with the ice-bound mountains of South Georgia, creating a feeling of wildness and freedom.[30] Stanley had a population of about eight hundred. It reminded Gunther of a Cornish village, and on Sunday 25 April 'the sound of church bells and the peat-smoke of cottage fires were wafted across the Sound and brought to mind our own Islands, 7,000 odd miles away'. Later that day, he made for the wilds and enjoyed a misty walk across the bluff downs to the rocks of Wickham Heights. There he was content to talk to the tame island thrushes, as they bathed in a small pool and fed on moorland berries.[31] A rich harvest of mussels, sponges and other marine animals and plants was raked from the sides of the old hulks at Port Stanley. One of these was Brunel's colossal *Great Britain*, then being used as a wool store, but now returned to Bristol. The motorboat which took a party to the *Great Britain* was lent by Captain Roberts of the gunboat *Afterglow*, whose duty it was to safeguard the seals of the Falklands.[32]

The Governor and his wife, Sir John and Lady Middleton, made an official visit to the ship, then owned by the Falkland Islands and registered in Port Stanley. Members of the *Discovery* Expedition much enjoyed various parties and dances in Stanley, while a small group rode over to Fitzroy, thirty miles away, for a weekend. Gunther found the unshod ponies canny but stubborn. Rivers had to be forded and large ditches crossed, while the way wound round and about, avoiding bogs and other obstacles. The visitors found that Fitzroy was similar to most houses in the Falklands, unpretentious and with bow windows, and reminded them of suburban England.[33] They learned that from here the farmer's wife and her maid had sighted the German cruisers *Scharnhorst* and *Gneisenau* after their victory at Coronel in the Great War.[34] More than half a century later the British landing ship, *Sir Galahad*, was to be blasted in sight of the same farm by Argentine Skyhawks during the Falklands War.

The *Discovery* sailed for Cape Town on 20 May 1926. For the next five weeks and five days, she made a winter passage of the South Atlantic, navigating well to the north of Tristan da Cunha. Sometimes she suffered the turmoil of head winds and heavy seas; at other times she was becalmed almost or would run before the westerlies under a full stretch of canvas. During this long traverse, nine full stations were worked, while the large plankton nets were towed during the intervals between. This was the passage that would have been compared with one planned for the *Michael Sars* across the North Atlantic. Mainly black or red creatures were brought up from the ocean depths, including ten which proved to be new species. The weather would make a great difference to the joys or sorrows of a station, but with practice the operators worked more surely and with greater speed. Gunther found working a station during a rough swell 'unspeakably nasty', especially after a sleepless night being tossed about in his bunk. Directly he clambered over the gunwhale of the rolling ship to take his place on the outboard platform in charge of the nets, his seaboots would fill with icy water as the waves swept by and his feet would feel more and more like 'limp pancakes'.[35] However, a good catch, especially one containing undamaged specimens, compensated for the discomfort of being unable to change for several hours.

When the wind blew strongly on the beam, life on board the *Discovery* became quite topsy-turvy. Green seas came cascading over the side, hitting the deck with tremendous force and making anyone below, in stuffy wardroom or cabin, wonder how much the ship could stand. Pots and jars would be hurled out of fiddles, crashing into pieces on the floor. Water would get into the biology laboratory, creating a damp and soggy atmosphere, which worsened when a dish of formalin was upset. The general fug thickened when soup and gravy were spilt. This state of confusion generally lasted no more than twelve hours, for the wind would either lessen or veer, so that more canvas could be spread.

After five weeks at sea, the immensity of the Atlantic Ocean was impressed upon the scientists. Midway during the voyage, Chief Officer O'Connor demonstrated an old sailor's trick by catching a Wandering albatross with a bait of salt pork towed on a line. The bird, with its ten-foot wing span, did not enjoy standing on the rolling deck. When placed on the poop rail, it took off easily and continued to circle the *Discovery*.[36] Nearing the African coast, the radio operator made contact with Walfvis Bay. They entered Table Bay on 29 June 1926, the officers in spruce uniforms and the scientists still in shirt-sleeves, finishing the laboratory work. Apprehensive as they approached Cape Town with its noise and bustle, they soon adapted to life in port and played football against the *Windsor Castle*.

# SEVENTEEN

## SECOND SEASON IN THE ANTARCTIC, 1926–7,
## VOYAGE HOME, EXPEDITION RESULTS

### THE SECOND ANTARCTIC VOYAGE, OCTOBER 1926–JUNE 1927

THE *DISCOVERY* SPENT THREE MONTHS in dry dock at the naval base in Simonstown while anti-rolling 'sister' (bilge) keels were fitted to the hull and the upper topgallant yards were struck down. This was in order to lessen her rolling and wind resistance. The first annual report summarised the scientific work done in South Africa meanwhile, including detailed studies of *Euphausia superba* and analysis of the *Discovery*'s water samples, the fat content of blubber, and the composition of the South Georgia plankton. Twenty-one whales were measured at the Union Company's whaling station at Durban. Some very early embryos were obtained, the smallest (a Sei whale) stated to be only 2–3 mm long.[1]

The oceanographic gear was overhauled and plans laid for the next season's cruise. At that time Simonstown was a Royal Dockyard of the British Navy and while the *Discovery* was there, her men were well entertained on board the naval ships of the fleet (South African Station) and by the whole of the South African navy which then consisted of two armed trawlers.[2] Mr O'Connor left the *Discovery* at the Cape and Lieut.-Com. Chaplin was promoted Chief Officer in his place. Chaplin was in charge of hydrographic surveying during the expedition (having been lent by the Admiralty).

During the stay in South Africa, the event that caused most stir was the arrival of the Research Steam Ship (later RRS) *William Scoresby* in Simonstown on 1 August 1926. Built for the *Discovery* Committee in 1925, to complement the work of the *Discovery*, the *William Scoresby* was designed for speed on the lines of a whale catcher and constructed in Beverley, Yorkshire, by a famous trawler building firm, Messrs Cook, Welton and Gemmell, for £33,000. She had a displacement of about 370 tons and was 125 feet long at the water-line. She carried two scientific officers, David Dilwyn John and Francis Fraser, both zoologists. Her master was Lieut.-Com. G. Mercer, DSC, RD, RNR (who had come from the great liner *Mauretania*), and her remaining complement consisted of two deck officers (Irving and Lester), two engineer officers (Ridley and Brabender), six petty officers, five seamen and three stokers. Hardy described her as

a compromise to satisfy three distinct purposes: whale hunter, trawler and research ship. She has the whaler's look-out barrel at the masthead, her built-up bow (for firing marking darts instead of harpoons) and a good turn of speed (12 knots). On her port side she is a trawler with the typical steel gallows fore and aft for handling the otter boards of a full-sized commercial trawl; and she is equipped, of course, with the necessary powerful winch. On her starboard side she is the research ship with the small winches and davits similar to those on the *Discovery* for operating water sampling bottles and plankton nets, but without the outboard platforms which are not necessary. Although small, she is a strong and powerful vessel which promises well for the battles ahead, and I was well pleased with all I saw.[3]

The *Discovery* made two short cruises north from the Cape, one over the whaling grounds off Saldanha Bay for a fortnight and the other for a few days to take a series of hauls with large nets. The scientists found the bilge keels greatly improved the ship, reducing her rolling, prolonging its period and doing away with the lurch at the end of the roll, thus enabling them to work in quite rough weather. The donkey boiler, weighing five or six tons, was removed from the starboard side of the forecastle. This lowered her centre of gravity and stiffened her.

## FROM THE CAPE TO SOUTH GEORGIA, OCTOBER–DECEMBER 1926

The *Discovery* sailed from Simonstown for South Georgia to a good send-off from the Navy on 27 October 1926, taking a more southerly route than before in an effort to avoid the westerly winds, while the *William Scoresby* (with greater power) took a direct one. The roaring forties lived up to their name, but nets were towed and stations worked whenever possible. An improvement in method was the designation of a duty scientific officer each day whose task was to see that the nets and other apparatus were in order and ready to hand before a station took place. It grew colder as they drew away from the shores of Africa and out came winter clothing again. No heaters were allowed, so as to save coal. Working in the laboratory, the biologists felt the full blast of the untamed winds of ocean each time the door opened. Gunther could not keep warm despite wearing a 'thick woollen vest, guernsey, shirt, tan jumper, Jaeger pull-over and beaver-cloth pilot jacket'.[4] A furious gale on 10 November put a stop to scientific work. 'Huge waves', wrote Gunther, 'advanced upon the weather beam, their surfaces chiselled into a thousand faces, their edges torn to spindrift.' The *Discovery* plunged, rolled, slid and slithered among these grey mountains.

Eventually one, seemingly mightier than the waters of which it is composed, outgrows itself and its comb, bending before the wind, curls upon itself and breaks: then follow white horses! Sorry would be the plight of a small ship amongst these: but only the mightiest of the mighty can lash its power upon the *Discovery*'s decks.[5]

Armistice Day on 11 November was observed (as it was then ashore) with two minutes' silence. Gunther's diary for the following day reveals that the H.B. (Hardy's Baby, the Continuous Plankton Recorder) had worked particularly well as it was towed astern of the ship, browsing its way through green pastures of diatoms. The samples from the nets revealed that the small plants and animals of the plankton lived in different layers of the sea by day and by night. Gunther thought that this variation in distribution would probably have a bearing on the habits of whales and that its explanation would need a lot of work.[6]

Pack-ice appeared on 14 November in lat. 53°S., after a number of icebergs had been sighted during the previous two days. Gales, followed by fog and poor visibility, prevented sights being taken and when the sun appeared at last, the ship had been driven 90 miles south-east of Bouvet Island (now Bouvetøya) amid thick pack-ice. The small supply of coal and the possibility of meeting even heavier ice made it too risky to continue farther south; the ship altered course to the north-west and emerged from the pack near Bouvet, a tiny ice-capped island, difficult of access, whose 'Cape Circumcision' had been thought by its discoverer, the Frenchman Bouvet de Lozier in the early eighteenth century, to be the tip of a great southern continent. Working the ship in such conditions[7] was not easy, with pack-ice and icebergs providing constant hazards. The *Discovery* came perilously close to hitting a rolling iceberg on 17 November and only just managed to break through the constraining pack-ice at speed to escape by yards. 'The *Discovery* proved herself mistress of the ice', concluded Hardy.[8]

The scientists found it bitterly cold working a station in an incessant snow storm off ice-capped low-lying featureless Bouvet Island. Handling the nets, on which the sea water froze soon after coming up, was no fun in bitter cold on icy decks. Gunther observed that the doctor's toaster (converted from medical apparatus) became a great feature of tea in the wardroom at this time. Buttered toast, and magazines like the *Illustrated London News*, made life worth living.[9] Growing anxieties over contrary winds in these latitudes, the 'frightful fifties', and a shortage of coal forced the oceanographic work to be cut to a minimum, using only towed nets. It was clearly impossible to effect long passages and work stations at the same time in the *Discovery*. Dr Kemp's official report[10] shows that the ship was within an ace of returning to Cape Town. 'From Bouvet onwards', he wrote privately to a colleague, 'over a stretch of ocean of the greatest interest to us, we could do literally nothing. Our average speed for the passage was 3.26 knots.' He had become thoroughly disillusioned with his ship and pointed out to the *Discovery* Committee that attempts to carry out a scientific programme on three ocean passages had completely failed. He continued, to the same colleague, saying that

> Square rigged vessels of the Antarctic type are quite unsuitable for the work we are engaged on and the 'Discovery', as I have proved, is worse than any other vessel of her class. Her sailing qualities are inferior, her speed less, her coal consumption greater and her bunker capacity little more than half.[11]

Despite the unpleasantness he knew would result, Kemp felt obliged to tell the Committee that a new ship was crucial to the necessarily wide-ranging programme of whale research. Fortunately, in the end, strong fair winds blew for four days, while they neared South Georgia, whose approaches were guarded by countless icebergs of every shape and size. The *Discovery* was met by the *William Scoresby* and entered Cumberland Bay on 15 December 1926, with enough coal in hand for two days' steaming. She had just avoided the ignominy of being towed, and secured at the buoy in Grytviken harbour to bunker. The scientists meanwhile worked on the collections (particularly the plankton) gathered by both the *William Scoresby* and the *Discovery* during their voyages from Cape Town. A chart illustrating the results appeared later.[12]

## SECOND SEASON AT SOUTH GEORGIA, DECEMBER 1926–FEBRUARY 1927

During the previous season at South Georgia, Lieut.-Com. John Chaplin, RN, had camped for six days at Undine Harbour, the north-west point of the island. This second season, his party of three were able to complete the survey of the harbour and subsequently worked at Larsen Harbour, at the extreme south-west. Here the elephant seals took exception to a tide gauge erected in their favourite wallow, pushing it over night after night.[13] Having established the latitudes and longitudes of South Georgia's geographical extremities, Chaplin charted Leith Harbour and Stromness Bay. He was also able to fix Cape Buller and Cape Saunders. The importance of the survey work lay in the fact that all the whalers had to use harbours in course of their business. In addition, the catchers in search of whales traversed large areas of uncharted sea and were occasionally compelled to take refuge in the nearest known harbour during heavy weather. Their captains were handicapped by the fact that even large islands and lands were at that time charted in many instances as much as fifteen miles out, and adjacent lands in 'opposite directions'. Chaplin's aim, set out by the Hydrographer of the Navy, was to get as many good geographical positions as he could.[14]

As soon as the *Discovery* arrived in South Georgia, preparations began for the important oceanographic survey of the whaling grounds by both vessels. Five extremely hectic days were spent in completing this, apart from the western side, which was left till later. With the island at their centre, the seven main lines of completed observations and sampling stations stretched out over the sea like the spokes of a cart-wheel. This period of intensive work (with the *Discovery* and *William Scoresby* in friendly rivalry) was a major achievement. Writing 35 years after the completion of this plankton and hydrological programme, Sir Alister Hardy doubted if it had ever been equalled. In $5^1/_2$ days, 29 stations were worked over some 10,000 square miles of sea, yielding 370 water samples and 307 plankton net hauls. Every man on each ship did his utmost to make it a great success. Kemp considered this survey to be 'a really very decent piece of work', and noted that 'More than half the programme was carried out by rush tactics during five days before Christmas, when the weather happened to be mainly fine, and during the five days I don't think any member of my staff got 8 hours sleep. It was just solid, never-ending drudgery the whole time and I almost wept with joy at the cheerful way they stuck it. I am most extraordinarily proud of them.' He concluded that they had obtained data from which much could be learned and now had a standard for comparison with results from future seasons.[15]

Christmas came two days after the end of the survey. A punch-bowl party was held at the Marine Station and the whole expedition (sailors and scientists) spent Christmas Eve in songs, games, high jinks and general jollification. On Christmas morning after a special treat of bacon and eggs for breakfast, a simple service aboard the *Discovery* was held with the old Christmas hymns, followed by Christmas dinner amid all the decorations, and presents all round. The magistrate, Mr Binnie, brought a fine rose and some sweet peas from his greenhouse as a centre piece for the table. John Bentley, the cadet, remembers tinned turkey and all the trimmings, Christmas pudding with flaming rum and brandy butter. After the two main toasts had been drunk to 'The King!' and 'Sweethearts and Wives', he was obliged, as the youngest member, to propose the health of the expedition. At midnight on New Year's Eve, he also had to strike sixteen bells on the *Discovery*'s forecastle bell, eight for the old year and eight for the new. After this the two ships gave a searchlight display.[16]

January 1927 was spent in completing the plankton survey of the waters surrounding South Georgia. The *William Scoresby* worked largely off the rugged and little-known west coast and the *Discovery* to the east. The limits of the continental shelf were ascertained, the patchiness of the krill (swarming like underwater bees) observed, currents measured and plankton analysed. During this month, the *Discovery* ran aground on gravel off Sappho Point, East Bay, but escaped without damage. Gales were followed by fine weather, which enabled the scientists on board the *Scoresby* to complete thirteen stations in just over three days, working without rest from Friday 7 to Sunday 10 January. Perhaps because they were over-tired, the first vertical net on the Monday was lowered too soon and fouled the propeller. Fortunately, the captain and one of the hands, in a dangerous position, eventually cleared it.

The *William Scoresby* found herself in an even more awkward and potentially dangerous situation, when the first trial was made of the big commercial-sized 90-foot otter-trawl, again to the west of the island. One of the thick steel warps from the trawl wrapped itself round the propeller, bringing the main engine abruptly to a halt. Steam was shut off and the stokers, bathed in sweat, worked like supermen to turn the shaft by hand.[17] After two hours' vain effort, with the *William Scoresby* drifting out of control off a rocky lee shore, a whale catcher came to the rescue. Still towing four whales as well as the *Scoresby*, she brought the ship into safe anchorage in Undine Harbour. Here a diver was sent for, who eventually freed the propeller. Hardy, Gunther and Wheeler went ashore to see the Wandering albatrosses, enthroned on their nests and temporarily earth-bound.

While the *William Scoresby* had been completing the western survey under Hardy's scientific direction, Dr Kemp in the *Discovery* had been trawling and dredging in Cumberland Bay, having been often prevented by bad weather from working further out to sea. *Great waters* describes Kemp the enthusiastic collector, getting the utmost from a trawler dredge, searching (when all else had been dealt with) for small burrowing forms of life in rock fragments, coral and kelp roots. His willing colleagues, covered in mud and looking like pirates, were compelled by his example to keep on. If they stopped to relax, Kemp persisted in working, sometimes until the morning hours.[18]

Towards the end of this second southern season, Kemp wrote of the krill that

> *E. superba* is an abominable organism. It lives in small patches of great density at almost any level and even with our best endeavours we have not got any reasonably exact idea of its abundance. A series of surface nets, towed continuously for 25 miles ($^1/_2$ a mile per net) gave astounding results: 10,000 in one haul and 50 in the next—that sort of thing all the way.[19]

It was only after many years of work by *Discovery* Investigations in the Southern Ocean that attempts could be made first to chart and then to explain the curious patchiness of the krill. This appears to depend on surface, shallow and deep-water currents. The results of this survey by the *Discovery* and the *William Scoresby* of the whaling grounds of South Georgia were published in full by A. C. Hardy and E. R. Gunther as 'The plankton of the South Georgia whaling grounds and adjacent waters, 1926–27' in Volume XI (1935) of the *Discovery Reports*. From 1929 to 1980, these reports presented the work of scientists in describing and analysing the collections and data brought back by the *Discovery*, her successors *Discovery II* and the later RRS *Discovery*, and the *William Scoresby*.

The results of the South Georgia survey of 1926–7 are summarised and discussed in *Great waters*. Sir Alister Hardy dedicated his book to Kemp and Stenhouse and paid tribute not only to the *Discovery* and the *William Scoresby* in their 'contest with the tempestuous South Georgia seas', but to the 'work and devotion to the expedition's programme' of all officers and ratings 'which made the harvest possible'. It is not easy to précis the results in even shorter form, but it is possible to say that full identification and analyses of all the data collected eventually yielded a very detailed picture of the whole living community of the whaling grounds and its physical and chemical background, thus linking the tiny plants and animals of the plankton, through its predator the krill, with the great whales themselves.

## THE SOUTH ORKNEYS AND SOUTH SHETLANDS

The ships went their separate ways at the beginning of February, the *Discovery* to the South Orkneys and South Shetlands and the *William Scoresby* to the Falkland Islands, where until the end of April she marked whales and carried out an extensive trawling survey between the Falklands and the mainland of South America.[20] The marking of fish had for some years provided information about migration, rate of growth, stocks and the effects of fishing on stock levels. The application of a marking system to whales was not easy. A marker, similar to a large drawing pin and shot from a shoulder gun, was devised for the *Discovery* Expedition. A great many of these were fired into whales during the later 'twenties from the *William Scoresby*, which was fast enough to approach Blue and Fin whales. This pioneering work proved abortive because the whales were able to rid themselves of the $2^{1}/_{2}$-inch markers. It was not until a longer version, rather like a pencil, was designed that results were obtained. Probably the most important was the marking of a Fin whale calf in the Southern Ocean, which was killed two and a half years later, off the coast of South Africa. This proved the definite link between the South African and Antarctic whale stocks, which up till then had only been assumed from strong circumstantial evidence.[21] The same stocks therefore were being depleted in the Antarctic and warmer waters.

The *Discovery* departed from Grytviken on 4 February 1927, sailing north of South Georgia and making a station in only 177 metres between Shag Rocks and Bird Island, thus proving the existence of a connecting ridge. A particularly fine collection of 'soft corals' came up in the dredge, beautifully described in *Great waters*.[22] Strong winds on the morning of 9 February resulted in the ship flying along at $8^{1}/_{2}$ knots, an achievement for the old *Discovery*. By the afternoon a full gale was blowing and sail had to be taken in. Hardy describes the glory of the old ship, which he loved, despite all her faults, and wrote the day after the gale of the sailors and the ship in their element.

In the afternoon we saw the stuff our seamen were made of. It is difficult today to get a good square-rig sailing crew together, but we have got them; it was a magnificent display. The sky darkened and the wind increased with startling suddenness to full gale. 'All hands take in sail!' ordered the captain from the bridge—and it was echoed below for'ard. At once the whole crew were on deck. The wind was abaft the starboard beam so that the ship, apart from rolling as much as the spread of canvas would allow, was heeling well to port. In a moment or two the huge sheet of the foresail was loosened by some, while others hauled on the ropes that clewed it up; how it tugged on the ropes as it lost its firm contour. Then the topsails followed, fore and main, and now the supreme work of the sailor begins. As soon as the canvas was reduced, the ship, of course, had full scope for her rolling, and the height of the waves appeared to be mounting at every moment. Up aloft go the sailors, as calmly as if the ship had been in port, and out upon the swaying yards which are describing great arcs through the roaring air. Each time a wave breaks against the ship the bridge is blotted out with spray. Filled with admiration, who cannot wish that he had the nerve to stand on the chains which run below the yards, with nothing else for support, and the strength to pull with all one's might at the wet and heavy sail? First the topsail, then the foresail, are methodically tucked away: a smaller party of four are simultaneously at work on the main topsail. All is done in little more time than it takes to write it down.[23]

The mountainous South Orkney Islands (some 500 miles south of South Georgia and therefore colder and more desolate) were reached on 16 February, where the whale factory ships *Sevilla* and *Orwell* were anchored in Paul Harbour and Borge Bay respectively, Coronation Island. The *Discovery* tied up alongside the *Orwell*, whose captain and officers proved most hospitable. The *Orwell* was the type of factory ship common at this time before the stern slipway was generally adopted. The whales were flensed not on deck (as later), but alongside the ship from a raft. First the strips of blubber and then parts of the carcass were pulled up to the deck of the ship by hooks and cables from the great derricks at the masts. 'It is a grotesque sight', wrote Hardy in his diary, 'to see a huge piece, dripping blood, sometimes with a whole flipper complete, go swinging up through space on to the lofty deck of the factory.'[24] The *Discovery* coaled again here and Lieut.-Com. Chaplin took advantage of a sunny day to 'move' the island some 15 miles east.[25] Proceeding towards the Bransfield Strait, a huge tabular iceberg was encountered, over thirty miles long. The *Discovery* sailed past Clarence Island and then Elephant Island, both islands black, white, bleak and forbidding. Rich and intriguing dredges and hauls continued to be made, their contents all to be carefully sorted, labelled and stored. Lieut.-Com. Chaplin corrected the position of Clarence Island and others of the group by many miles.

The next call was at Deception Island from 26 February to 2 March, in the South Shetland group just off the Antarctic Peninsula, the long tail of the continent, separated from the tip of South America by Drake Passage, named after Sir Francis Drake, who was blown to the south of Cape Horn in the *Golden Hind*, during his famous voyage round the world. Deception Island is a dormant volcano, whose central crater has been invaded by the sea to form a sheltered harbour, entered through a narrow channel between high overhanging cliffs, which dwarfed the masts of the *Discovery*. The central lagoon, known as Port Foster, is some four miles across and one hundred fathoms deep. The extraordinary sight of eight former crack ocean liners lying in a small desolate bay, greeted the *Discovery*, reminding the astonished junior engineer of bustling Cardiff docks. One was a famous P. & O. ship, another the old *Albany Castle*, the joy of the Union Castle Line at the time of the Boer War. They had been refitted as factory ships and each of them was serviced by its own whale catchers operating in the Bransfield Strait.

The *Discovery* had some difficulty, after anchoring between two factory ships, in securing to cables ashore in a near hurricane. Six ships' motor boats could not bring her up to the cables, because of the wind resistance of her heavy rigging. In the end two whale catchers, one on either side, succeeded.[26] That evening the expedition was royally entertained on board the *Falk* by Norwegians representing all the ships in the bay. The scientists explored the island while the barque took on coal, finding the black beach warm and steam rising from the water's edge, while on the upper slopes lay ice and snow. The water temperature was measured in Port Foster and was found to fall steadily with depth to 29.3°F at the bottom.[27] One of the whaling captains vividly recounted the earthquake and underwater eruption that had taken place earlier in the 'twenties, a terrifying experience when, 'powerless to move', the steamers' fires having been let out for the season, they found themselves 'anchored in a cauldron of boiling water'.[28]

The ship departed from Deception Island on 2 March to sail south along the western shore of the Antarctic Peninsula, anchoring in Melchior Harbour a week later, of which a rough plan was made with the help of Captain Leif Andersen of the whale factory ship *Saragossa*. The region was at that time poorly charted and one of the *Discovery*'s tasks was to check the reported position of the Kendall Rocks and the Austin Rocks. Their positions on the chart were corrected, as were those of Hoseason, Snow and Smith Islands by Lieut.-Com. Chaplin. A running survey was completed of Schollaert Channel, Gerlache Strait and Neumayer Channel, as well as a rough plan of Discovery Sound, and a new island was named after the ship.[29] Fog and blizzards delayed progress southwards, but the hauls made with dredge, trawl and tow-net were most rewarding; a purple octopus, new to science, was an especially valuable prize. The more interesting specimens were often painted in watercolour by Hardy or photographed with great patience by the surgeon, Lieut.-Col. E. H. Marshall, who described a particularly memorable day on 17 March sailing south from Melchior Harbour to Port Lockroy.

> We entered the Channel and it was like going into fairyland as the view began to show itself. The Channel is about half to one mile wide, and the land on either side is precipitous, the mountains rising to about 2000 ft. in places, with numerous glaciers. The Channel was well open, there being only a little brash ice about. We steamed down this fairyland channel with its various turns disclosing more beautiful scenery. I doubt if there is a more beautiful spot in the whole world than this in fine weather. We passed one mountain side which was precipitous, showing its exposed face blue green with copper. About 4 p.m. we came to Port Lockroy where Charcot wintered his first year. This spot has been used by whalers on and off since 1913 and we found all their moorings intact and several boats, water boats, left on the rocks.[30]

Herdman, the hydrologist, found things less peaceful. In a letter to a friend, he wrote:

> The glaciers keep breaking off all the time, and especially during the night—the noise seems tremendous at first, but one soon gets accustomed to it and misses it afterwards. That noise and the noise of the Cape Pigeons fighting day and night over the 'graks' (or refuse from the whaling station—appalling muck—absolutely indescribable except by the above Norwegian word!) are two that I shall never forget—they both seem to be part and parcel of the place.[31]

The *Discovery* later sheltered from rough weather on 21 and 22 March. On the 24th, the ship steamed through the Peltier Channel to take a full station and put down a dredge off Cape Renard on the mainland. That same afternoon mock suns were seen, a well-known Antarctic phenomenon. The day stood out for Hardy, who was both zoologist and artist, as one of the highlights of the voyage. He recorded how the colours of the mountains, sky and sea changed as the ship steamed back to Port Lockroy.

> . . . everywhere we looked in the narrow channel was lit with coloured light, broad sweeps of pure colour passed either by gentle gradations, or sometimes by sharp contrasts, into different hues. In the sun the snow on the steep ranges high above us was a vivid rose pink with the rocks warmed to a rich apricot shade; the sky behind was violet-blue merging lower down to that rich translucent turquoise now so familiar to us, and the shadows in the snow were of the same pure violet-blue so that high up it almost appeared as if you were looking right through the mountain side to the sky beyond. The water in the channel ahead was as glass perfectly reflecting every detail of colour above, but then, as we approached the mirror became alive; it was fascinating to watch the inverted ice and mountain scene being drawn first into distortion as the surface curved and lifted, and then violently stirred into frantic rippling coloured light. It was as if we were steaming in a giant kaleidoscope.[32]

With autumn approaching, the *Discovery* turned north through Gerlache Strait to King George Island, taking two stations on the way. The doctor recorded that the need for fresh meat and vegetables was beginning to be felt, some not wanting to touch the seal meat that he had procured.[33]

A further station near Deception Island was particularly rewarding in that a quantity of young krill were collected, which could be fitted into the emerging pattern of their life history. 'Each one had only a single light-organ developed', wrote Hardy, 'but there were enough of them to make the end of the tow-net glow brilliantly with blue-green light as it came up to the surface; as we undid the bucket at its end and looked in, the little creatures were milling around, turning this way and that, and flashing in every direction, so that it appeared as if we had uncorked some magic mixture effervescent with fire.'[34]

Lines of stations were worked across the krill nursery in Bransfield Strait during cold frosty weather and further valuable material was collected. At the end of the series, the ship re-entered Port Foster, Deception Island, where she both sheltered from a storm and coaled, until 15 April 1927 before the next leg of the voyage. A series of stations was planned across Drake Passage from the South Shetlands to Cape Horn, where the Atlantic and Pacific meet and just to the west of the whaling area being studied by the *Discovery* Expedition.

The first station was at 5 a.m. on 15 April 1927 in good weather, between Snow Island and Smith Island, in the South Shetlands. With great good fortune and interrupted by only one gale in this notoriously stormy region, the series of stations was completed, but not without the loss of several water-bottles and great lengths of wire cable, much to the chagrin of Herdman, the hydrologist. Nevertheless, a splendid section of the ocean traverse resulted, showing the Antarctic current system and the varying temperature and salinity of the sea. Hardy's invention, the plankton recorder, now came into its own. This was an instrument with a hollow cylindrical body (not unlike a horizontal vacuum cleaner) through which water passed as it was towed at some depth astern of the ship. Any plankton in the water was sieved and retained on a continuous silk roll, which wound onto a storage roller immersed in a preserving fluid. The apparatus had been used before during the voyage, but this time, without a hitch, it provided a complete and continuous record along this important line.[35]

The sixth and last station was completed some miles off Cape Horn in clear weather amid the great waves sweeping towards the massive headland of grey black and white rock. The ship anchored afterwards in St Martin's Cove on the east coast of Hermite Island (known to Fitzroy and Darwin in the *Beagle* as Wigwam Bay, after the tents of the natives of Tierra del Fuego). Both Dr Marshall and Hardy record the joy of seeing trees again after seven months of nothing but sea, snow and ice.[36]

After the storm, the plankton and water samples were packed away and the ship made shipshape. A course was then set (on 27 April) for the Falkland Islands by way of the difficult, shallow waters of Le Maire Strait, which separates Staten Island from the tip of Tierra del Fuego. The *Discovery*'s passage through this strait, where there is a strong tide of four knots or more, was not plain sailing.

With a contrary wind it was a race to get through the channel before two o'clock when the tide would also turn against us. At first, in spite of the head wind, we seemed to make excellent progress with the engines full out and a strong tide to help us; before long, however, the wind increased in violence and, against the tide, produced a most curious and fierce sea. The old ship battled into this clash of elements and pitched as never before, putting down her head and lifting it as if purposely throwing sheets of white spray over her back. Time crept on and with it went the certainty of getting through. Two o'clock came and now it seemed that the turn of the tide must surely carry us back, when suddenly the wind changed from direct ahead to the port bow. There was just room to alter course and bring it abeam with the chance that with all sail we might clear the island. The cry of *All hands on deck* brought everyone to the ropes and in a very short time, to the chorus of *Ranzo, boys, Ranzo!*, *Blow the Man Down* and other shanties, upper and lower topsails were set on both the fore and main, and then fore and main sheets [i.e. courses] with stay-sails and spankers. The ship heeled over to the wind and never have I seen her look finer; she was showing off against the magnificent background of the jagged mountains of Staten Island, standing up like a row of savage teeth. With sails filled and engines at full blast we pushed into the heavy sea at some nine or ten knots—and before long we were through.[37]

Six stations were worked with difficulty during the voyage to Port Stanley in the Falkland Islands, where the ship anchored on 6 May 1927. The two scientists (Herdman and Fraser) standing on the outboard platforms had to be secured with lifelines, since at times they were up to the waist in sea water, as the waves swept by. The *William Scoresby* was already in harbour, back from her trawling survey between the Falklands and South America. She had also made a line of stations from South Georgia to the Falklands and from the Falklands to the mainland of South America at Puerto Deseado (Port Desire).[38] The two ships separated again at the Falklands and each made lines of tow-net stations across the Southern Ocean to Cape Town. The *Discovery* proceeded by way of Tristan da Cunha and the *William Scoresby* by way of South Georgia and Gough Island, a small uninhabited island south-east of Tristan. Full stations were worked near the islands to be compared with those previously made.[39]

From the Cape the *William Scoresby* returned direct to England for alterations while the *Discovery* travelled up the west coast of Africa into the Gulf of Guinea to investigate the whales' breeding grounds and to pick up pertinent information from the different coastal whaling stations.[40] She berthed in Falmouth on 29 September 1927 at the end of what Sir Sidney Harmer called 'the largest and most important scientific expedition that has left our shores since the time of the *Challenger*'.[41]

John Bentley's overall impression of the expedition was more immediate.

One hears of the roaring forties, the howling fifties and the shrieking sixties, but unless one has actually sailed in these latitudes, it is difficult to appreciate the strength of the winds, unfettered by any land mass, or the mountainous waves that they produce. Suffice it to say that when one is standing on an open bridge, with one's only protection from the elements a small canvas dodger around the perimeter of the bridge rails, seeing the ship on the crest of one of these huge waves before diving into the trough of another and always with the possibility of being pooped, one realises as never before how vast is nature and how puny man is in comparison.[42]

And yet this puny man has all but swept the oceans of the great leviathan, evolved over millions of years and cruelly destroyed in a few hundred. The great whales may yet stage a triumphant recovery and the all-important krill may yet be sensibly harvested, partly as a result of the knowledge gained from the scientific work of the *Discovery* and of *Discovery* Investigations.

What is it that goes on in a whale's poor agonised brain when he has been struck by the explosive harpoon; and as he weakens and knows his time has come and he cannot escape? As he hopes desperately in his whale way for the agony to end, do his thoughts go back to the happy days when he swam with his mother? Does he not speak for the whole animal kingdom, including man, when his being, cared for by the Creator through it all, sends out the message again to the world: *Forgive them for they know not what they do?*[43]

There is no whale product for which there is not an economic alternative; therefore there is no reason, apart from man's greed, that this cruelty should continue and why the whales should not live out their days in peace in what Sir Alister Hardy named 'The kingdom of the krill'.

# PART V

# THE BANZARE (BRITISH, AUSTRALIAN AND NEW ZEALAND ANTARCTIC RESEARCH EXPEDITION), 1929–31

# EIGHTEEN

## ORIGINS OF THE BANZARE AND OUTWARD VOYAGE TO THE CAPE

### THE FIRST BANZARE VOYAGE, 1929–30

'BY GOD, I'M GOING IN HER', determined Second Mate K. N. MacKenzie, the moment he saw the *Discovery* in the summer of 1929. The stern of his ship, the *City of Valencia* (one of the ships of the City Line of Glasgow on the mail and passenger service to South Africa), was swinging round into the main basin on her return to London from a voyage to South Africa. The sight of the *Discovery* preparing for her next voyage excited MacKenzie so much[1] that he saw her Master, Captain John King Davis, the next day, and only five days later and despite his lack of experience in sail, received a letter confirming his appointment as Chief Officer of the *Discovery* on her first British, Australian and New Zealand Antarctic Research Expedition (BANZARE) voyage. He was soon deep in her bowels, preparing her for the voyage, choosing the crew, ordering and stowing two years' supplies and equipment in separate lots, so that everything could be located promptly at sea or in the ice, and all this despite a constant flow of visitors, sightseers and reporters, for whom he had very little time.[2]

Antarctica, from an Australian point of view, is hardly remote: it is closer to Sydney than either Singapore or Jakarta.[3] The Australasian Antarctic Expedition of 1911–14, the first to be led by Mawson (who would command the *Discovery* on her BANZARE voyages), made a very considerable contribution towards the exploration of the great arc of Antarctic coastline that faces Australia across the Southern Ocean. Mawson had already ventured to delineate the hypothetical topography of Antarctica in two maps of the south polar regions, published in 1911.[4] After the Great War, calls for the continuation of the work of the Australasian Antarctic Expedition came from Frank Debenham in 1920[5] and then from Captain Davis who had been appointed Commonwealth Director of Navigation in 1920, a post that he held until 1949. Mawson outlined the geographical and scientific tasks still to be accomplished[6] observing that 'more than half the circumference of the globe' remained to be charted in high southern latitudes. This would be the principal geographical objective of the BANZARE. The political side to the expedition, which was very important, was the subject of extensive behind-the-scenes negotiations between the Commonwealth Government in Canberra and the British

Government in London. 'A great Antarctic region lying southward of Australia is, by its geographical situation, a heritage for Australians. There, a stupendous land mass lies nearer to the Commonwealth than the distance between the east and west coasts of our own continent'—so declared Mawson in 1932 after the return of the BANZARE Expedition.[7]

The Antarctic whaling industry had established itself and then expanded rapidly in the early decades of the twentieth century. In 1923, a British Order in Council established the Ross Dependency between longs. 160°E. and 150°W. Following this, a number of whaling regulations were promulgated, which at first affected the Norwegians, the foremost whalers, who began operating in the Ross Sea in 1923. Decrees protecting French interests in Terre Adélie, on the Antarctic continent, discovered by Dumont d'Urville in 1840, and Iles Kerguelen, discovered by a French navigator in the eighteenth century, came a year later. It was obvious that Norwegian whaling (perhaps followed by annexations of land) would extend to that part of Greater (East) Antarctica facing Australia and explored by Mawson in 1911–14.

The BANZARE venture constituted the partial implementation of a more coherent British imperial policy regarding Antarctica that developed from decisions taken in 1919–20.[8] L. S. Amery, then Under-Secretary of State at the Colonial Office, was one of those primarily responsible for the formulation of British policy in this area. He thought it desirable for the British Government to establish sovereignty over the whole continent, one reason being the conservation of the whales and the whaling industry. Another reason, according to Peter Beck, was the growing appreciation of the strategic importance of Antarctic coasts and waters and of (for instance) Antarctic meteorology, in the southern hemisphere's weather system. By January 1920, the British Government apparently favoured a policy of gradual extension of imperial control over the whole of the continent; the policy would have to be discreetly and delicately managed to avoid international differences and counter claims. The adoption of this policy represented, in Beck's words 'a personal triumph for Amery'.

The Imperial Conference of 1926 further defined British policy in the Antarctic. At its meeting on 19 October 1926, the Conference had appointed a committee under Amery's chairmanship, as Secretary of State for Dominion Affairs, to consider the question of British policy in the Antarctic, a subject that remained on the agenda of successive Imperial Conferences. It reported on 19 November 1926, and pointed out that at that time only two areas in the Antarctic were formally part of the Empire, the Falkland Islands Dependencies (1908) and the Ross Dependency (1923) administered by New Zealand. The committee recommended that formal title should be asserted to seven other areas to which a British title already existed by virtue of discovery. These were listed as (i) The outlying part of Coats Land, viz., the portion not comprised within the Falkland Islands Dependencies (ii) Enderby Land (iii) Kemp Land (iv) Queen Mary Land (v) The area which lies to the west of Adélie Land and which on its discovery by the Australian (*sic*) Antarctic Expedition in 1912 was denominated Wilkes Land (vi) King George V Land

and (vii) Oates Land. The first of these should become part of the Falkland Islands Dependencies and the other six should be placed under Australian control with the agreement of the Commonwealth Government. It was recognised that the French had a valid title to some territory in Adélie Land. The Antarctic Committee's report stressed the importance of gradual and cautious progress in bringing the Antarctic regions under British sovereignty and expressed the hope that 'practically complete British domination' might eventually be established.

The legal status of the Antarctic (excluding the Ross Dependency and the Falkland Islands Dependencies) as *res nullius* was touched upon, title to which could 'only be acquired by occupation'. It was suggested that control need not be continuous to be effective, the best way being to send ships to the Antarctic, whose officers would be authorised to act in the Government's name. Discovery and exploration could also be pursued. The committee recommended that the assertion of British control in the Antarctic be divided into three phases:

> The first should be an intimation to the world at large, through the publication of the Summary of Proceedings at the Imperial Conference, of the special British interest in the seven areas mentioned above. All these areas may be treated as British by discovery, and such discovery should be regarded as having conferred an inchoate British title.
>
> The second should be a formal local taking possession by an officer authorised for the purpose of such of these areas as are not known to have been so taken possession of at the time of discovery.
>
> The third should be the issue of Letters Patent annexing the area and making provision for its government.

The report observed that the second stage would 'render desirable the despatch of an expedition to the Antarctic. The date and area of operation of such an expedition would have to be decided in the future.

The Antarctic Committee's report was adopted at the penultimate meeting of the Imperial Conference held at 10 Downing Street on 19 November 1926.[9] Its adoption was moved by the British prime minister, Mr Stanley Baldwin, and it was circulated to the Dominions the following year. The Australian Government consulted Captain Davis, who suggested that the Australian National Research Council (of which he and Mawson were members) should be asked for advice as to the best means of carrying out stage two.[10] On 25 July 1927, the Council recommended establishing claims to the regions lying within the Australian sector by means of an expedition sent from Australia to be controlled, financed and equipped by the Commonwealth Government. They thought that every effort should be made to induce the Imperial (i.e. British) Government to recognise officially Sir Douglas Mawson's acts of taking possession during the Australasian Antarctic Expedition. They further recommended that every effort should be made to obtain the loan of the *Discovery*, the 'only existing vessel suitably constructed for this purpose', for a period of two years.[11]

In January 1928, Major R. G. (later Lord) Casey, the Australian political liaison officer in London, copied part of a confidential letter he had received from Dr W. Henderson, Director of the Australian Department of External Affairs to the Dominions Office. It revealed an Australian cabinet committee's refusal to spend any money at all on an expedition and its failure to understand why the British Government could not proceed immediately to stage three recommended by the Antarctic Committee, and issue Letters Patent formally annexing the discoveries already made.[12]

Nor was the Chancellor of the Exchequer in London any more anxious to contribute towards an Antarctic expedition. The Australian prime minister Mr S. M. (later Viscount) Bruce proposed to the British Government on 26 July 1928 that a joint British expedition should be sent to the Antarctic to complete the second stage of the recommendations of the 1926 Imperial Conference. Scientific investigations into whaling and sealing could also be made. Mr Bruce suggested that Sir Douglas Mawson should lead the expedition in the *Discovery* and that in addition to contributions by Australia and Great Britain of £7,500 each, plus one from New Zealand of £2,500, a public appeal should provide the balance of funds.[13]

In early August 1928, an Interdepartmental Committee consisting of representatives from the Foreign Office, the Treasury, the Dominions Office, the Colonial Office, the Admiralty and the Ministry of Agriculture and Fisheries, plus representatives of the Australian and New Zealand governments met in London to consider these proposals. They concluded firstly that a public appeal might meet with little success and would in any case attract too much foreign attention to the expedition; secondly that the need for the expedition was now acute given the increasing activity of foreign powers, particularly Norway and the United States of America; and thirdly that a South African firm then planning a whaling expedition to the Antarctic might co-operate. This firm was Messrs Irvin and Johnson, which intended to operate off Enderby Land.[14] It was agreed that the possibility of the *Discovery*'s being made available should be brought up at a forthcoming meeting of the *Discovery* Committee. One member of the Interdepartmental Committee mentioned that some feeling might be aroused in Norway if funds—raised largely from the surplus of the revenue of the Falkland Islands Dependencies, four-fifths of which was derived from an export duty on whale oil, mainly paid by the Norwegians and intended to finance whaling research of real benefit to the Norwegian industry—were diverted to pay for a *Discovery* expedition whose primary object would be to preclude Norwegian claims to Antarctic territory.[15]

The second meeting of the Interdepartmental Committee took place on 16 August. Mr Darnley reported on the meeting of the *Discovery* Committee the previous afternoon, which Committee felt qualified to consider the matter only from the scientific point of view and not the political. The *Discovery* was not to be used by them during the 1928–9 season, and certain alterations were to be made to her before she resumed the Committee's work during the 1929–30 season. If Mr Amery decided that she should be released to the Commonwealth Government for an expedition, the *Discovery* Committee would require a new ship for 1929–30; in any event, they did not want to part with the *Discovery* for good. Further consultation with the *Discovery* Committee revealed that their obligations precluded them from lending the vessel free of charge, but that she could be provided at 'the exceptionally low rate of £8,000 per annum'.[16]

Mr Bruce, in the light of these considerations, telegraphed on 8 December 1928 the Commonwealth Government's offer to finance an expedition during the season of 1929–30 on condition either that the *Discovery* be lent free of charge, or that his government should have the chance to buy her for no more than £10,000.[17] The idea of buying the *Discovery* appears to have come from Sir Douglas Mawson and was expressed in a letter written in London to Major Casey on 5 July 1928. The Australian National Research Council had understood, when drawing up its proposals for the Australian prime minister, that the *Discovery* was the property of the Dominions Office in London and had only been lent to the Falkland Islands and Dependencies. Aware of the British Government's interest in the Antarctic, the members of the Council naturally expected that the vessel would be readily lent to the Australian Commonwealth when available.

He had since found that the ship was 'nominally the property of the Falkland Islands and Dependencies'. However, they would not be needing her for the next year or so. Mawson anticipated that the owners would ask a rent for the vessel's loan, but that the British Government, if diplomatically approached, might meet this and lend the *Discovery* without charge to Australia. Mawson even intimated that it might be possible to purchase the ship 'for a small sum' and was sure that she would 'be a very attractive acquisition for the Australian Government'.[18]

The Dominions Office thought the Australian offer to purchase the *Discovery* for some £10,000 impractical, the figure being much less than her true value. However, the Interdepartmental Committee strongly recommended the acceptance of Mr Bruce's proposal and of his first condition, in view of the need for action because 'the activity of foreign powers is threatening the British position in the Antarctic'.[19] The Lords Commissioners of His Majesty's Treasury threw cold water on the proposal. Their memorandum of 2 January 1929 observed (among other things) that such an expedition was 'a matter for the Dominions whose territories border the Antarctic, viz. Australia, New Zealand and South Africa; and that the demand on the United Kingdom for financial assistance' was 'contrary to the now accepted constitutional principle of the Empire as a Commonwealth of Nations. . . . We do not dream of asking Australasia and South Africa to contribute to the maintenance of the Empire's prestige in (say) North America and the Arctic; and there is no reason why the British taxpayer should be asked to contribute towards this expedition.'[20]

Major Casey expressed his regret on hearing of the Treasury's reaction and said that Mr Bruce's proposals 'were definitely conditional on a contribution [i.e. the loan of the *Discovery*] from His Majesty's Government'. Mr Bruce, he maintained, was 'not asking for charity; his object was that the Expedition should be an Imperial one'. Telegrams that Casey had received from the Australian prime minister made it appear that there was very little chance of the expedition proceeding.[21]

Norway raised the flag on Bouvet Island in the Antarctic from the *Norvegia*, a vessel owned by the whaling magnate, Consul Lars Christensen. The island, to which Great Britain also had a claim, was formally annexed on 1 December 1927 by Captain Horntvedt. The Norwegian Government notified London on 19 January 1928 about the annexation of Bouvet and after much diplomatic activity, Great Britain relinquished her claim, Norway agreeing in return not to annex the territories mentioned in the 1926 Conference.[22] However, the future Mac.Robertson and Princess Elizabeth Lands, between longs. 60°E. and 86°E., remained unprotected and the Interdepartmental Committee observed 'that the Norwegian undertaking only applies to those areas to which a public assertion of British title has been made, and that there is nothing to prevent them from occupying any lands or islands which the Imperial Conference was anxious to bring under British control'. A Norwegian expedition was planned for the 1929–30 Antarctic season which might establish a base on the mainland. Commander Byrd's expedition had aroused interest in the United States which might result in further American activity in the Antarctic. The French and Germans too might step in and the whaling industry would always attract foreign vessels. The Foreign Office thought it doubtful whether diplomacy alone could preserve the British title even to the areas specified by the Imperial Conference.[23]

All these arguments were put forward to the Treasury by the Dominions Office in a letter dated 23 January 1929, which summarised the Interdepartmental Committee's view that since the Antarctic had been discussed at the Imperial Conference on the agenda of Imperial policy, measures taken to put such policy into effect could be 'a matter for Imperial co-operation'. The Australian offer was generous and should be accepted as a chance to consolidate the work of previous British and other Imperial explorers. In addition, whaling grounds might be discovered and valuable scientific work undertaken, although the expedition would be 'primarily territorial in object'.[24] In a separate letter also dated 23 January 1929, the Dominions Office requested the sanction of the Treasury for the inclusion in the 1930 Estimate for the Vote for Dominion Services of £8,000 as the first instalment of a proposed contribution of £16,000 towards the expedition.[25]

## BANZARE CONFIRMED

Sir Douglas Mawson put considerable personal effort into the inception and financing of the BANZARE. On 18 January 1928, in Hobart, he was reported as having independently made a forceful statement as to the need for British annexation of the Antarctic.[26] Later that year he visited London to do more work on the expedition being planned for late the following year.[27] On 30 January 1929 Major Casey wrote to Mawson from the office of the High Commissioner for Australia telling him that all was well and that the British Government had decided to lend the *Discovery* without charge for the next two Antarctic seasons and that its offer had been accepted by the Commonwealth Government. A new ship would be designed for the *Discovery* Committee.[28] Arrangements for the expedition would now be set in hand. No publicity at all should be given for obvious reasons. The letter was directed to Mawson at Naples, who was *en route* for England aboard the SS *Orama*.[29]

Mawson continued with preparations for the expedition in London during February and March from the Royal Societies Club, St James's Street. He found it slow work to begin with, especially getting possession of the *Discovery*.[30] He was able to tell Dr H. R. Mill, on 3 February that he had 'requisitioned for J. K. Davis', who would be lent for the job and come to England in June to organise the ship. He anticipated sailing from London towards the end of August.[31] As if to spur Mawson's efforts, on 2 February 1929, Captain Nils Larsen of the *Norvegia* landed and took possession of Peter I Island, discovered in the early nineteenth century by the Russian navigator, Captain Bellingshausen.[32] Sir Douglas Mawson was officially appointed leader of the British Australian and New Zealand Antarctic Research Expedition on 4 February 1929.[33] He found that although the *Discovery* was being lent free of charge, the insurance would cost almost £15,000, a heavy expense. Mill had told him that Charcot's *Pourquoi Pas?* might be available. Mawson was of course committed to the *Discovery*, which, he explained to Mill, would better carry Moth aeroplanes, being a larger vessel.[34] He told the same correspondent, who was of course very well known in the geographical and especially the polar world, that plans were being kept fairly secret, so that neither the French nor the Norwegians might pre-empt them. Dr Mill may have guessed what was in the wind from Mawson's intention to establish a base on either Kerguelen or Heard Island. Mawson strongly suspected that there was 'an embayment between Kemp Land and Gauss Berg', a view that Mill evidently also shared and would be shown to be true. Donations of stores were coming in quite well.[35] Sir Douglas was to find himself doing much of the fund-raising too, despite the official origins of the expedition.

Meanwhile in Australia, following a statement on the expedition in the Commonwealth Parliament by the prime minister on 21 February 1929 an Antarctic Expedition Committee had been formed. This held its first meeting in Melbourne on 12 March, with Sir George Pearce in the chair. Also present were Rear Admiral Napier, Sir David Orme Masson, Dr A. C. D. Rivett, Chief Executive of the Department of Scientific and Industrial Research, Dr W. Henderson, Director of the Department of External Affairs, and Captain J. K. Davis, Commonwealth Director of Navigation. In the light of subsequent events, it is interesting to read in the minutes the gist of Captain Davis's remarks.[36] He thought it preferable, from the point of view of navigation, not to begin in Cape Town (as Mawson had suggested), but in Australia and then work from east to west, starting with King George V Land and finishing at Enderby Land. Advantage would thus be taken of the prevailing easterly winds and more work would be done. Davis also stated that navigation approaching Enderby Land would be less difficult at the end of the season. The Committee agreed with Davis, particularly since it would be more appropriate for a predominantly Australian expedition to set off from Australia, despite the pressing need to plant the British flag on Enderby Land.

Captain Davis felt that the deck crew must have had sailing experience, effectively ruling out volunteers from the Royal Australian Navy. He was doubtful about the *Discovery*'s capacity to carry an aeroplane and also pointed out that the amount of coal that the vessel could bunker would be the main factor governing the area the expedition could cover. He reckoned that 55 sailing days would consume coal at the rate of 6 tons per day and another 30 days with banked fires $1^1/_2$ tons per day, allowing for a voyage of 85 days. The subject of coal was to become a very thorny one during the expedition.

Mawson's Instructions[37] were signed by the prime minister of the Dominion of Australia on 12 September 1929. As Grenfell Price has remarked, both Instructions and Royal Commission 'explain clearly that territorial acquisition was a chief objective of the voyage'. The Royal Commission[38] from King George V was signed and sealed on 29 July 1929. It authorised Mawson to take possession of such lands as he should discover and of those others listed in the document, by reason of earlier British discovery.

The first of two articles by Mawson, outlining the plans and hopes of the expedition, appeared in *The Times* of 12 October 1929. He wrote almost lyrically of Antarctica, that great frozen continent 'withdrawn from the society of other lands, still veiled in secrecy and of unblemished white', explaining that although something was known already of the coastline for upwards of 150 degrees of longitude, the land in rather more than half the circumference of the globe in those latitudes had still to be outlined. He fancied the ship's destination as a southern Eldorado with scientific treasures instead of gold. Mawson mentioned the interest of New Zealand, Australia and South Africa in the mainland whose coastline would almost certainly prove continuous near the Antarctic Circle, the likely topography of undiscovered Antarctica and the fabulous mineral wealth it hid, and the prospects for its future exploitation. The roles of the various governments, committees and individuals, and especially the generosity of Mr Macpherson Robertson (better known in Australia as 'MacRobertson') among many private benefactors, in the financial and other aspects of the organisation were set out. Sir Douglas also summarised the route that the *Discovery* would take from Cape Town, the oceanographic, meteorological and other scientific work to be undertaken on the voyage and the intention to survey islands and the Antarctic coast and investigate their biology and geology. He predicted that the *Discovery* would arrive back in Australia in April 1930 unless she became stuck fast in the ice for the winter, for which eventuality they were well prepared.[39]

The second of Mawson's articles for *The Times* was devoted to the *Discovery*, describing her construction, her operation under sail and steam and her earlier research work. He explained that the rock salt, packed into the spaces between the frames and contained between the inner lining and the outer skins, needed to be renewed every three years. It was there to pickle the wood and prevent dry rot and other forms of decay in the timbers. Only 200 tons of coal could be stowed and an additional amount would be carried as deck cargo and in odd areas all over the ship. The coal being used was in high-quality briquettes, of 25 lbs each, from Cardiff, which would afford a high mileage per ton.

The ship's company comprised the 'navigating captain', John King Davis, second-in-command of the expedition, and a crew of 25 officers and men: three navigating officers, two engineer officers, boatswain, carpenter, sailmaker, eight able seamen, donkeyman, three stokers, radio officer, chief steward, assistant steward, cook and assistant cook. Captain Davis described them in his diary as 'an excellent ship's company and a credit to the Merchant Service', continuing perhaps a little piously that 'We have a stiff task ahead of us, but I am sure the crew of the "Discovery" will make good and I hope I shall prove worthy of the fine body of men who serve under me in this ship by leading them to success.'[40]

## THE VOYAGE TO THE CAPE

The *Discovery* departed from the East India Dock on 1 August 1929, a day of gusty winds and pouring rain, enlivened by the cheers of a small crowd at the docks and by the whistles, sirens, hooters and shouts from passing steamers, as she passed down the Thames to the sea. The ship and her mission were 'certainly well known to all the seafarers—liners and tramps, tugs and barques, even the meanest crew had a shout which rang with good cheer and good luck', and flags and ensigns dipped ashore and afloat; in the outer estuary so many '*bon voyage*' signals were run up that the 'thank you' signal had to remain bent on, ready to hoist as required.[41] *The Times* reported that she was flying the Union Jack at her forepeak, the white Antarctic flag at the foremast and the Australian flag at the stern.[42] At a reception beforehand, some three hundred guests had been received on board by Captain Davis and his officers. They included Vice Admiral Skelton of her first voyage and Sir Hubert Wilkins, the well-known Australian polar explorer and aviator.[43] Another newspaper commented on the Gypsy Moth aeroplane, well secured on deck with wire ropes. It was also reported that the bosun, Mr William Simpson, an old whaler, was hoping to get some good weather in the south. Perhaps he was pulling the reporter's leg on remarking 'You can slip into your sleeping bag, lie down on the ice and have a nice comfortable snooze. You don't want any rum. It is warm enough without that.'[44] An *Evening Standard* reporter described the departure. 'A trim, small sailing ship nosed her way eagerly out of East India Dock into the Thames Basin today, behind an even smaller tug. In comparison with the great liners she passed, the ship was but a rowing boat.'[45]

When asked whether he was pleased with the ship, Captain Davis replied, 'Pleased? If *she* sinks, nothing will float on the seas for which we are bound.' He also spoke proudly of his men, none said to be over thirty years old.[46] On inspecting the *Discovery*, a reporter found 'Everything from the largest packing case to the cook's frying pan, was all spick and span, snugly put away in its proper place and workmanlike.'[47] On passage from London to Cardiff, Davis took with him Captain Hamilton Blair, a veteran of Antarctic seas, as his right-hand man, since none of his three officers, MacKenzie, Colbeck and Child, had any deep-sea sail experience. They 'exercised sail handling from dawn to dusk each day, tacking and wearing ship, reefing and setting sail again. As most of the seamen were sail experienced, several from the Hudson's Bay Company, things went pretty well.'[48] Blair had served his time in the Loch Line of sailing ships and as Chief Officer under Davis in the *Aurora* during her voyage to relieve Mawson at Cape Denison, 1913–14.

Some 350 tons of coal were loaded in four days at Roath Dock, where a reporter from the *South Wales Echo* found men bustling about, 'men who would attract attention anywhere. Men with great firm jaws and the glint of steel in their eyes . . . who knew the danger of ice pack and snow drift . . . who answer unswervingly to the call of great white spaces.'[49] These very men would no doubt have been highly amused to hear themselves so described. However, the reporter was correct in maintaining that some of them were already familiar with the perils of the Southern Ocean in wooden sailing ships.

Captain Davis had been allowed leave from his post as Commonwealth Director of Navigation, to command the *Discovery*. He, Hurley and Marr had very considerable past experience in Antarctic expeditions led by Shackleton and Mawson. Besides MacKenzie as First Officer, the following were appointed to sail from London:

Second Officer:     William R. Colbeck (son of Captain Colbeck of the *Morning*)
Third Officer:      John Bonus Child (P. & O. Steam Navigation Company)
Chief Engineer:     W. J. Griggs (P. & O. Steam Navigation Company)
Second Engineer:    F. B. Welch
Wireless Officer:   Petty Officer A. J. Williams (lent by the Admiralty)

The first of the expedition's scientists to join the ship was J. W. S. Marr ('Scout Marr' of the Shackleton–Rowett Antarctic Expedition, 1921–2, in the *Quest*), who sailed from Britain as 'Planktology Expert' in charge of oceanography, seconded to BANZARE by the *Discovery* Committee.[50] The photographer, Captain Frank Hurley, had taken part in Mawson's earlier expedition, the Australasian Antarctic Expedition, 1911–14, in the *Aurora* and also in Shackleton's Trans-Antarctic Expedition, 1914–17, in the *Endurance*.[51] MacKenzie found these two men 'worth a watch in themselves', ever ready to lend a hand at shifting coal or making fast sail, in both of which they were more experienced than any of the crew. He described Marr as firm, very helpful and unassuming, and Hurley as extraordinary and well worth knowing, helping to keep everyone cheerful with their boyish pranks and buoyant spirits. He also observed that if the remaining scientists (to be embarked at Cape Town) were anything like as good, the expedition must succeed.[52]

The master of the *Discovery*, Captain John King Davis, and the leader of the BANZAR Expedition, Sir Douglas Mawson (who was to join the ship at Cape Town), were old shipmates from *Nimrod* days, when Davis was Chief Officer and Mawson a young geologist, during Shackleton's British Antarctic Expedition of 1907–9. Sir Raymond Priestley has left us an impression of Davis at that time in the preface to Davis's autobiography *High Latitude*.[53] The young Priestley had joined Shackleton's auxiliary barquentine, the *Nimrod*, at Lyttelton, New Zealand, 'to be greeted at the gangway by a tall, hard-bitten seaman who, to my untutored imagination, had all the outward appearance of the "bucko mate" of the more lurid Victorian tales of the sea. He proved to be one of the most gentle men I have ever known, though fearsomely efficient at his own job, and very determined to have his own way in things connected with it.'

Born in London in 1884, Davis spent the early years of his seafaring career in sail and by the age of twenty-two, having passed for First Mate, he began through experience, he tells us, to perceive 'the nature of the qualities that make a true Master Mariner: judgement, a never ceasing sense of responsibility, a constant awareness of all the forces of nature affecting or likely to affect the ship'.[54] He was writing after years in sail and went on to explain the irrelevance of wind and current to modern vessels but that they were everything to the sailing ship, in which the handling of the sails was crucial.[55]

Appointed Chief Officer of the *Nimrod* at the age of 23, Davis took the ship home at the end of the expedition, when Shackleton returned to Europe to be lionised after sledging to within 97 miles of the South Pole. 'For the next thirteen years', wrote Phillip Law (Director of the Australian National Antarctic Research Expeditions, 1949–66), on Davis's death in 1967,[56] 'he was to build a reputation as one of the great navigators of Antarctic history.' His greatest work was accomplished as master of the *Aurora* and second-in-command of Mawson's Australasian Antarctic Expedition of 1911–14. During the 1914–18 War, Davis commanded the *Aurora* again, as leader of the relief expedition that rescued the Ross Sea party of Shackleton's Trans-Antarctic Expedition of 1914–17. In 1922, he had drawn attention to the desirability of charting the Antarctic coastline to the east and west of Enderby Land, unvisited since its discovery by Biscoe in 1831. Captain Davis had advocated the use of an aircraft to determine the nature of the coastline, a wintering party of twelve men and a ship to survey the coast and to carry out oceanographical work during the navigating season.[57]

On 10 August 1929, David Dilwyn John (of the *Discovery* Expedition, 1925–7) and the bride he had married a month before stood on high ground near the village of Wick, in the Vale of Glamorgan. 'Young, in a world which seemed better then than it does now', they gazed out to sea watching the *Discovery* sail down the Bristol Channel. Dr John now feels that Thomas Hardy, who has become his favourite poet, could have written a poem about those two beginnings.[58] The ship was searched for stowaways that day. A boy of fourteen was found by Hurley in the port boat No. 2. He was taken ashore in tears at midday by the pilot.[59]

Once the great Welsh coal terminal at Cardiff and the Bristol Channel were cleared, topsails were hoisted, fore- and mainsails set. The *Discovery* coaled again at St Vincent (Cape Verde Islands) and then laid a course for Cape Town, where Sir Douglas Mawson (leader and organiser of the expedition) and the remaining scientific staff were to be embarked. The young third officer, J. B. Child, found himself 'loving the ship more and more' and (like the others) treating the many discomforts (such as water on his mattress) as a joke. On passage to Cape Town, he wrote:

> I really enjoy going on watch at night because there is so much to think about. 'Look astern and see what you have gone through! Look ahead and see what is before you! And look aloft and thank God you have got so far!' I don't know what old sailor said this, but I often think of it at quiet moments. It seems wonderful to think that 'God willing' I shall be setting foot on and seeing land never seen before, and there is the honour of being in a party to strike 'The King's flag' on the land we claim for Great Britain.[60]

Many of MacKenzie's off-duty hours were spent devouring a manual of seamanship and learning what he could 'of the way of a man with a sailing ship', while his watch passed in the thousand and one deck duties of First Mate, especially since the ship had been laid up for two years. He learned 'one thing which had for long been a mystery and puzzle—of the wondrous beauty, the charm and fascination, the attraction and lasting glory of a *tall ship and a star to steer her by*, glancing aloft at the billowing canvas and feeling her heel to the freshening breeze'.[61] Great efforts were made to smarten the ship up after her long lay in London and by early October she was looking much better. Rust inches thick and old paint were attended to and a lot of new painting done.

Long hot days in the doldrums—and even longer nights—found MacKenzie in the stuffy cabins designed primarily for polar work. The breeze came at last and on 5 September, the barque crossed the Equator in long. 27°W. and followed this, the windjammer track, down the South American coast, passing only 200 miles off its easterly point. When strong winds and rough seas caused the *Discovery* to sail close-hauled (for her, 7 to 8 points into the wind), Davis and the ship often fell out and the officers took the brunt of his annoyance. 'I never again want to sail close-hauled', wrote the Mate, 'after many days of *Full and by*',[62] on 19 September, forty days out from Cardiff, in contrast to his earlier feelings about the joys of a sailing vessel.

> Up half a point and she flapped—away half a point and the old man flapped up saying we were losing way. If it wasn't one flap it was another. One eye on the truck, one on the compass, one on the helmsman, one to windward, one ahead, one to the bridge ladder. We were all eyes—'Lee fore brace', 'Flatten aft that sheet.' Let go staysails halyards up topgallants, down topgallants—it was a constant nightmare—of course the Discovery was no sailer—never made to sail—and because JK was made to beat records he and the ship often fell out—we the officers took

the brunt of it all—so again damn—damn, damn, Full & By . . . I will content myself by simply setting forth in one sentence the true and unadorned mood which today has been good enough to induce—Damn sailing ships and again damn them—we've pulled and hauled—cursed and groaned and still JK has a grouse—nothing is right because the wind has gone to the southward and left us aback—But oh well—bless our little souls we've got tomorrow to come—may it bring the westerlies.[63]

Captain Davis's diary tells the other side of the story. None of his three officers had experience in sail. He wrote of them at this time that

The third mate is the most promising officer on board and will make a seaman before this voyage is over. He is keen to learn and energetic and does not mind doing a job himself. Colbeck, the second, is young, but has promise. He is navigator and does his job well when guided. He also will make a sailor in time as he is keen to learn and comes of seafaring stock which helps him no doubt. MacKenzie is willing and should have done better. He seems uncertain as to what the mate's job is and has not the quickness which a young man of 31 should have. I do not like to jump on him, as he tries, but when he is on deck he does nothing and seems in a dream instead of bustling around and doing any job he sees wants looking to. I suppose in steamers they do not learn much about the general management of a ship of this kind, but I sometimes feel how much one needs a man like Fletcher or Blair on board the 'Discovery'.[64]

The westerlies did come and by 1 October in a strong gale and high full sea, they were carrying all sail and flying along at speeds of up to ten knots, fast indeed for the *Discovery*.[65] On 5 October 1929, they dropped anchor in Table Bay at 1 a.m. after a passage of fifty-five days, three less than on her maiden voyage under Captain Scott.

Sir Douglas Mawson, the two airmen and the scientists from Australia and New Zealand came aboard in Cape Town. A fortnight of feverish activity followed when the ship was daily invaded (through the goodwill of the South African Government) by carpenters, shipwrights, steel-workers, blacksmiths, painters, caulkers, riggers, gold-braided firemen, port officers and officials. A new motor boat was shipped and a whaler landed in place on a specially constructed platform.[66] All the main yards were sent down and landed without mishap, while the 40-foot fore topgallant yards were lashed on deck. The main yards were left in the charge of the Port Authority. Davis's intention in striking the yards off the mainmast was to make the vessel easier to handle with a small crew and to reduce wind resistance aloft when under steam. Her spars and canvas were very heavy, ideal (as Captain W. R. Colbeck has pointed out) for her original purpose to go south and possibly winter, but less suitable for many changes of course sailing in the pack and the consequent work for the crew.[67] During the passage to Cape Town, Captain

Davis had also expressed his worries about being short-handed for a vessel of such a rig, especially in the higher latitudes.[68]

The leader and organiser of the British, Australian and New Zealand Antarctic Research Expedition, Sir Douglas Mawson, FRS, was already famous as an explorer and scientist in the Antarctic. Born in 1882 at Shipley, near Bradford, Yorkshire, he had emigrated when a boy with his parents to Australia, and in 1901 graduated from the University of Sydney. Here he had come under the influence of Professor (later Sir) T. W. Edgeworth David, with whom Mawson sailed as physicist on Shackleton's *Nimrod* expedition of 1907–9 to the Ross Sea area of the Antarctic. Mawson and he were associated with the ascent and geological examination of the active volcanic cone of Mount Erebus (13,350 feet) on Ross Island, and a tough sledge journey of nearly 1,300 miles to reach the South Magnetic Pole.[69]

Mawson had returned to the Antarctic as leader of the Australasian Antarctic Expedition in the *Aurora* (Captain J. K. Davis), 1911–14, which landed three survey and scientific wintering parties. These were in King George V Land, Queen Mary Land and on Macquarie Island, all to the south and south-west of Australia and hundreds of miles apart. King George V Land and Queen Mary Land were both discovered and explored during this expedition and claimed for the British Crown.[70] Mawson made a notable sledging journey of some 300 miles outward from the main base at Cape Denison, Commonwealth Bay, with Dr Xavier Mertz and Lieut. B. E. S. Ninnis, Royal Fusiliers. These two died from accident or illness and Mawson struggled back alone in extreme privation for the hundred miles to base, where a second winter was spent in scientific work. The Australasian Antarctic Expedition of 1911–14 was remarkable for its geographical and scientific results, and also because it was the first to use wireless telegraphy in the Antarctic. Mawson's narrative, *The home of the blizzard*,[71] remains a polar classic. He was knighted on his return to Australia in 1914 and after the outbreak of the First World War was commissioned as a Staff Officer, one of his assignments taking him to Russia, where he was concerned with supplying munitions to the Eastern Front.[72]

In 1920, Mawson had been appointed Professor of Geology and Mineralogy in Adelaide (a post that he held until 1952), where he devoted his energy to the preparation and publication of the Antarctic scientific reports and to geological investigations in South Australia. He was awarded the Founder's Medal of the Royal Geographical Society and was elected a Fellow of the Royal Society. A friendly man of great modesty and striking appearance, he had a lusty and infectious sense of humour,[73] as well as tremendous determination and grit.[74] 'Mawson was, above everything, an intellectual leader', wrote Eric Webb, magnetician of the Australasian Antarctic Expedition, 'with utter motivation and selfless dedication to his objective, which he handed out to all of us in his party so that, by common consent, it became accepted and promoted as the policy of the expedition. Thus when we saw how he was completely committed, so each of us became committed to his own particular discipline. Mawson's dedication to scientific objectives infused a like spirit into us with the determination to emulate and excel the results of our peers. Other factors of great importance in this regard were his thorough and effective planning, his organisation and his contagious enthusiasm.'[75] Frank Debenham, fellow Australian and geologist of the 'heroic era' in the Antarctic, wrote of him: 'As a sledger Mawson was supreme, as leader he was wise, original and entirely practical both in his objectives and his methods of obtaining them ... His tall, spare figure and in particular his uplifted eyebrows over piercing eyes were a familiar sight in Australia ...'[76]

The other scientific staff who boarded at Cape Town were Professor Harvey Johnston (Chief Biologist), Harold Fletcher (Assistant Biologist), Robert Falla (Ornithologist), Commander Morton Henry Moyes, RAN (Survey Officer), Dr William Wilson Ingram (Medical Officer and Biologist), Ritchie Simmers (Meteorologist), Alfred Howard (Hydrologist). The two airmen, who also came on board here, were Flt. Lieut. S. A. C. Campbell and Air Pilot E. Douglas, both of the Royal Australian Air Force.

The meteorologist, Ritchie Simmers, had travelled from London to Cape Town by liner, arriving earlier than Sir Douglas Mawson and party from Australia. His twenty-six cases of gear caused consternation among the officers, as did later that brought aboard by the other scientists. He 'drifted into the wardroom' on 7 October 1929, recording afterwards in his diary, in his irrepressible style,

> What a feeling to be on the old bus at last. How clean and spic she looks in comparison with her appearance in London ... And aren't the officers all of them as young and excited as I, keen and satisfied with her. The spirit of adventure finds a very fertile field well cultivated and often watered in that wardroom.[77]

Tea was laid on a table-cloth; he wondered how long this would last. The following Sunday saw the arrival of Sir Douglas Mawson, of whom Simmers wrote 'he'll do me as a leader and from wardroom remarks he'll do the rest. Now I understand better that historic walk of his. In a few minutes of his arrival he had control, or to me, seemed to have control.'[78]

# NINETEEN

## First Season in the Antarctic, 1929–30, and the Voyage Home

### THE VOYAGE TO ANTARCTICA

THE *DISCOVERY* WAS GIVEN an enthusiastic send-off at Cape Town when she left Table Bay on Saturday 19 October 1929 to the cheers of the crowd and the shrill blasts from the sirens of all the ships in harbour. His Majesty King George V sent a message to Sir Douglas Mawson wishing the expedition success and a safe journey. The Mayor of Cape Town bade farewell with a large basket of oranges, an addition to the quantity of fruit already embarked. Sailing in the *Discovery* for the first time, young Simmers found that she rolled considerably even in an almost oily sea. 'But it was grand', he wrote in his diary, 'and I must say I enjoyed the creaking of timbers which I'm afraid will get into my blood: if creaking can get into one's blood.'[1]

A Reuters report headlined the rivalry between a Norwegian expedition already in the south and the British expedition in their efforts to discover new lands and mineral resources, both being equipped with aeroplanes for reconnaissance. The memory of Anglo-Norwegian rivalry personified in Scott and Amundsen would still have been vivid in 1929.

A course was set for the Crozets (Iles Crozet), a group of volcanic sub-Antarctic islands. The fifteen sheep (and many men) found it tough-going aboard ship in gale-force winds, with icy water awash everywhere. On 29 October 1929, ten days out of Cape Town, with the *Discovery* 'belting along under fore and lower topsails only'. MacKenzie wrote in his journal that the

> Albatross, the great and beautiful birds of southern latitudes, are as numerous as seagulls—flying round and swooping down in the never-tiring and never-ending flights. Two were caught yesterday and are now on the lab table—every particle under Professor Johnston's microscope. A big drop in temperature has caused us all to feel the icy blasts and to realise that we are at last getting down to lonely seas.[2]

Next day proved wild and tempestuous and he resolved to don warm clothing. He had so far managed in the grey bags, cricket shirt and woollen jersey that he had worn in Cape Town, hardly the apparel for 'hard hail and snow squalls and a towering sea—our decks constantly under water, and our lee and weather bulwarks scooping up tons of icy sea at every roll— and these to 35°!'[3] The cook did well—each meal better than the last. The mate found Sir Douglas 'very sociable and spins good yarns—friendly with everyone and treats all alike ever seeing to the comfort and care of his staff', while Captain Davis was 'much aloof and as distant as a master can be', both being firm but very different leaders.[4]

Simmers made some interesting remarks about Davis and Mawson. Early in November, he had 'a good hour with J.K. talking over the programme of met. obs.' On this occasion he found the skipper

> jolly decent, quite different from the gruff, surly, taciturn detached piece of granite that he can be—in fact he explained to me rather humanly that he didn't want me to come near him in bad weather as he got but little sleep, was worried and likely to be nasty. His great slogan is 'Safety of the ship' and he really does live up to it. Never for a minute does he let anything interfere with his task of 'Master' and I would sooner have him on the bridge in bad weather than anyone else. One sleeps better for his presence.[5]

Next day, he remarked, 'I am feeling positively perky—having had another long talk with J.K. on a whole range of subjects . . . The skipper is very stimulating meteorologically and is a keen and careful observer.'[6] His pen portrait of Sir Douglas Mawson is similarly percipient.

> Sir Douglas's conversation is always interesting and in it he lets drop continually little items of interest, which indicate in what wide fields he is interested, and being interested has a thorough knowledge of the facts and problems. In particular, anything remotely connected with polar regions on and in land, sea or air has been studied or remembered. In every branch of scientific research of polar type he knows enough to talk and work intelligently and what he knows of biology and chemistry and magnetism in addition to his own geology is amazing. But he's not absolutely the best organiser—beforehand, yes, as, for instance, in the minute detail in which we have been equipped—but in carrying out things, oh no. If he tells one man some arrangement re programme that seems to suffice to his mind, for the whole group. And so far it hasn't. All the same I wouldn't rather have a different leader for any money as he is so capable himself, looks after everyone, and is such a continual cheerful inspiration.[7]

On 2 November the *Discovery* anchored in American Bay, Possession Island, one of the Crozet group, finding the sealer SS *Kilfinora* of Cape Town at anchor inshore, a big surprise. MacKenzie was reminded of the north coast of Mull in winter. The scientists landed, using motor boat and dinghy, and found themselves witnesses to the slaughter of the sea elephants.

> The whole length of the beach was thronged with these huge harmless beasts and the whalers, starting at one end, were carrying out a systematic slaughter of everything—bulls, cows and pups. An absolute outrage the whole business and one that for sure will be shown up later . . . Bull killing is all right, but when a whole beach is murdered it is time things are made public and Hurley intends to get a cinematograph of the whole ghastly business tomorrow. It seems queer that after so many years of newspaper talk about seal and whale extermination that something isn't done. French . . . policy doesn't seem to run to energetic moves down this far—no control over sealing or whaling and a castaways hut which hasn't been tended for thirty or more years and at present is only a bit of rusty iron.[8]

They observed other rich wildlife for two days ashore, including penguins and other birds which were quite unafraid of man. Extensive collections were made, which were afterwards spread out, sorted and classified on the wardroom table, or preserved in the laboratory. Not only sorting and pickling of specimens went on after the call at the Crozets. Colbeck and Child struggled with their first survey; they knew that the existing chart was wrong and Davis concurred, but they found it difficult to prove.[9] The trip ashore made the members of the wardroom appreciate the splendid variety and quantity of food provided for their healthy appetites which rather contradicted Simmers's idea of polar discomfort.[10]

A westerly gale swept the *Discovery* eastward from the Crozets under bare poles, while 'a blinding snow and sleet blizzard, which lasted for sixty hours, shut out all—all the world but the white breaking sea'.[11] Simmers was exhilarated by the storm, as the decks were continually awash with one or two feet of water 'rushing from side to side making quite a musical gurgle and swish'. However, these cascades sounded less pleasant below as 'each has so much weight and force that the whole place shakes as if it had run into a brick wall'.[12] She was able to beat back to Kerguelen[13] (Iles Kerguelen) by 12 November, steaming all that day up Royal Sound, 'through a very wonderful snow covered country—bays, inlets and deep fjords—wild birds and strange sea animals—one strange and peculiar long stringy seaweed floating for miles—a wonderful island cut off from the world by thousands of wild sea miles'. The *Discovery* moored to the rickety old jetty of a deserted whaling station (Port Jeanne d'Arc), overlooked by four lonely graves marked with white crosses on the hillside.[14] Here coal was embarked, left there for the expedition by the South African whaling and sealing company, Messrs Irvin and Johnson, whose subsidiary, the Kerguelen Sealing and Whaling Company, operated from the islands between 1921 and 1925.

Scientific and survey work was carried out by motor launch along one of the longest fjords, the Bras de Bossière. Mawson contrasted the verdure of the small islands in these waterways with the bareness of the mainland, unfortunately devastated by rabbits. The seals had been decimated by man. Wild dogs were a further calamity, having become like wolves and a real menace to all life on the islands, although many kinds of sea bird still survived on the islets.[15] Altogether 213 tons of coal were loaded with the help of the scientists (including Mawson) and the crew of the whaler SS *Kilfinora*, which took away the expedition's mail.[16]

The *Discovery* departed from Kerguelen on 24 November for Heard Island, further to the south-east and far more desolate, owing to its position within the Antarctic Convergence. One of Sir Douglas Mawson's articles[17] emphasised the importance of the expedition's investigations into the marine life of the Southern Ocean, undertaken particularly by A. Howard, the hydrologist, and J. W. S. Marr, seconded to the expedition by the *Discovery* Committee. They were carrying three different instruments to measure the depth of the ocean: a Kelvin sounding machine for use in shallow water, which was also particularly valuable for navigation when steaming close to land; a Lucas-type machine for use in deeper water (this and the Kelvin apparatus could both take samples from the ocean bed); and a newly fitted echo-sounding installation (the previous one had been of limited value) capable of measuring depths of several thousand fathoms in a few seconds. These three devices together provided information on the contours and nature of the sea floor. The temperature, salinity, current movements and biology of the sea were studied too. Water was sampled with Nansen–Pettersson waterbottles (down to 300 fathoms) and Ekman reversing waterbottles (at greater depths) and its chloride content (a measure of salinity), carbon dioxide, oxygen, nitrogen, phosphorus and hydrogen ion concentrations measured. This information was of real practical interest; Dr Kemp had shown that abundant nitrogen and phosphorus in the waters off South Georgia fertilise plant life (just as they do on land) on which small crustaceans—the principal food of the southern whales—feed. Nitrogen- and phosphorus-rich waters are therefore potential whaling grounds. Lastly, Mawson dealt with the living contents of the waters, the benthic life on the sea bottom, and the life of the surface and intermediate waters consisting of smaller drifting individuals (plankton) and larger swimming organisms (nekton). The contribution of J. W. S. Marr was vital. 'There would have been no, or little oceanography on the first voyage', maintained Sir George Deacon, 'if J. W. S. Marr had not rigged all the equipment, bought missing items with his own money in Cape Town, showed them how to use it and worked all hours of the day and night.'[18]

A fair passage from Kerguelen of some 290 miles kept the forty tons of deck coal safely on board. Heard Island was sighted at dawn on 26 November 1929. This sub-Antarctic island (roughly 27 miles long and 13 wide) is situated in lat. 53°S. long. 73°E. amid very stormy seas where a fierce wind blows almost constantly. It is heavily glaciated and there are no secure anchorages. The *Discovery* lay in Corinthian Bay until she was forced out to sea on 30 November. A shore party of nine, including Mawson, landed in Atlas Cove (later to be the site of an Australian research station from 1947 to 1954) where the motor

237

launch was moored. They were able to sleep in a hexagonal sealers' hut, after first removing three inches of ice from the floor.[19] On the day of their arrival, the weather was fine and briefly revealed the rare sight of Big Ben, a magnificent ice-clad volcanic dome (about 9,000 feet high), down whose sides flow glaciers, many of which end in the sea. Numerous birds (including thousands of penguins) were nesting, while sea elephants lay like logs along the beach, shedding their winter coats. The shore party found life on Heard Island 'most entertaining after the long sea voyage in the ever-rolling *Discovery*.[20]

A full scientific programme was carried out ashore each day in snow and rain after which it was 'a relief to retire within the tiny Norwegian hut where sodden clothes are dried and a hot meal prepared'. The stove was 'kept roaring with an ample application of seal blubber until the pipe, which passes through the crown of the roof, glows a dull red'.[21] Eight men slept in bunks, while the ninth on the floor had anxious moments on two occasions when woken by sea elephants pushing through the door into the hut.[22] The scientists enjoyed some splendid omelettes cooked with prion, skua and Dominican gull eggs. Wreckage on the south shore (including large uprooted driftwood trees) provided ample fuel. On Heard Island nest a legion of birds, which invaded both the hut ashore and the ship at anchor. One morning, Captain Davis (who remained on board the *Discovery*) when 'putting his foot into his long sea boots, discovered to his surprise a burrowing petrel well down in the toe, evidently pleased with its ready-made nest'.[23]

Bad weather caused Davis and his officers much anxiety, the barometer remaining just over 28 inches for several days. The *Discovery* eventually returned to anchor in Corinthian Bay. 'Semaphoring from a cliff we ascertained that Captain Davis was anxious for the shore party to embark and allow the ship to quit these dangerous shores. There was, also, this fact, that delay at the island was eating into our very meagre coal supply, upon which the future of our Antarctic programme depends. We consequently decided to make a trial trip with the launch from Atlas Cove to the ship's anchorage in Corinthian Bay. Towards evening, loaded with our scientific collection, Douglas, Marr, Johnston and myself [Mawson] embarked in considerable seas, which proved ugly along the line of the reef, and on the headland we nearly lost the boat but finally boarded the *Discovery*.'[24]

They decided to wait until morning before making an effort to bring off the remainder of the party and equipment. After an early breakfast, Mawson and Douglas set out in the launch back to Atlas Cove, as the wind rose and the barometer fell rapidly. They safely negotiated the heavy seas off the reef, but were almost wrecked when the engine stopped under the basalt cliffs of Rogers Head against which big seas were breaking. Luckily they managed to get an anchor to hold, while the petrol pipe was unblocked.

The remainder of the party was picked up from shore and after an anxious 90 minutes' run in driving snow and even stronger wind, the launch reached the anchorage in Corinthian Bay. This was none too soon, for the barometer had fallen half an inch during their absence and the *Discovery*'s engines were heavily taxed to stop her from being driven out to sea.[25] The crew were surprised to hear a shout from the bridge 'stand by for motor boat', little thinking that it would have put to sea in the north-westerly gale. However, 'out of the snow and spray she appeared—diving and pitching and giving all a good soak, the stout little pram in tow laden with all manner of birds—penguins dead, penguins alive'. Somehow within two hours the boats were hoisted, swung in and landed in place. One moment the launch rose, 'her fenders crashing our [topmost?] rail, another down—down in the troughs . . . but only to return with all the force of the breaking seas'. Hooking and handling the anchor proved as hazardous, as up it came while the ship plunged and pitched in a wild breaking sea. Black squalls of snow and sleet swept round the headland, while the wind increased to a terrifying roar. Two hours passed before the two-ton mass was landed and secured on deck by many heavy lashings. Not for the first time did the mate admire the 'hardy pluck and endurance and the magnificent and splendid spirit' of his watch—Matheson, Martin, Ayres and Tomlinson.[26] Captain Davis thought they were fortunate to have got the whole party safely on board and that it was 'sheer folly to allow inexperienced people to be fooling about in such places'. He did not want to go through another such week again.[27]

They departed from Heard Island on 4 December 1929, setting a course approximately east-south-east. Three days of continuous gales made the *Discovery* roll and roll, straining the ship and making every rope and wire chafe. It was hoped, by sounding, to ascertain how far the Kerguelen–Heard Island submarine ridge extended towards the Antarctic continent. The soundings were determined by the new Admiralty echo-sounding gear, which worked well, and agreed with the Lucas machine. They found the shallow, later named Banzare Rise, had a depth of 350 fathoms at about lat. 59°S. long. 78°E., in marked contrast to the 2,000 fathoms on either side. The coal on deck and in the winch-house had by then been consumed and the space cleared, allowing the paying out and rewinding of 3,000 fathoms of dredge cable, in preparation for the full oceanographic programme.

Captain Davis felt it unwise to have put over the trawl rope in shallow water, with a falling barometer and many icebergs around. He was evidently already feeling the strain of the voyage and while the doctor had given him some medicine, what he really needed was rest. This was impossible to get in bad weather, while during fine spells, jobs 'like the present one' were 'impulsively undertaken without proper forethought'. He had to be 'always on the alert that they do not do something to jeopardize the safety of the ship. Playing about with wire 3 miles long without any experience is risky . . . but there is little use saying anything. M[awson] regards all advice tending to regularize our operations as in some way trying to put off doing anything at all.' He himself liked 'to do things quietly and with due preparation as is usual on board ship', while Mawson always wished 'to rush at them'.[28]

By 8 December, icebergs of all shapes and sizes dotted a calm and sunlit sea as far as the eye could reach. Steaming at full speed seemed at first to the mate to be asking for trouble, but he soon realised 'that with care one very soon fell into the art of dodging in and out finding lanes here and openings there . . . and since a miss is as good as a mile, we came through in splendid style'.[29] They nosed slowly into the pack on 11 December, observing the life there which included Blue whales and Crabeater seals. Emperor penguins stood on the floes 'looking at the world in general ... with the appearance of nothing better to do'. There were birds of many species, the Antarctic petrel 'a snow-white, dove-like creature being particularly beautiful'.[30] A King penguin, taken aboard at Heard Island, strutted the deck, making friends with all; even Nigger, the ship's cat, seemed prepared to tolerate him.[31]

By noon on 9 December 1929, a full set of oceanographical stations had been nearly completed. Captain Davis felt this was quite a good effort, considering that Marr was the only person used to such work. However, he also felt that these activities added to his responsibilities and prolonged his waking hours.

I have been feeling very much off colour today, and suppose it is due to the life one leads in the circumstances. The master of a ship like this does not get an easy time—he must be always on watch if he does his job and while I do not spend my time on the bridge, I have not had my clothes off since leaving Cape Town. The most difficult part to play is to appear cheerful and good tempered when thoroughly worn out and met with complete lack of understanding. M. has no idea of what it means. He works hard himself and then goes to bed quite satisfied that I shall get them through somehow and as long as I can keep going so I will D.V. [Deo volente] but one has a limit and one feels the cumulative effect of it.[32]

By 13 December, the *Discovery* was fast in the pack-ice, a novel sight to the friendly seals and penguins which came to view her, while she lay 'at rest in the frozen sea'.[33] A blizzard later clothed the ship in fine dry snow and when it cleared, a vain attempt was made to break out of the pack. 'The old ship tried her hardest to force a passage, full-ahead—and up she would come after only a few feet to a full and sudden stop. Then full astern and when a free run had been obtained she'd come on again—but only to meet with a similar rebuff.'[34] The boiler fires were let out to economise on coal. The ship was firmly beset. The leader of the expedition and the master of the ship differed on the best action to take, Mawson being anxious of course to break a way through to the south.[35] 'There is a decided feeling in the ship', wrote one of the seamen, 'that the Old Man [Davis] is not the Pusher he used to be.'[36]

Third Officer Child recorded how on 18 December during his night-watch, he went at full speed regardless of the heavy falling snow. Twice a huge berg loomed up under the bow, which he seemed to clear only by a few feet. Having left the bridge, he took a shot at whale marking, which was unsuccessful, as had been all the attempts to date.[37] The *Discovery* edged up towards the Antarctic Circle in long. 73°30′ E. after traversing the immense area of heavy and continuous pack-ice to the south of Heard Island in fog and snow. Although Mawson announced to the Press that the Circle had been crossed (despatch transmitted 20 December 1929), his diary for the same day[38] makes it clear

*Top left:* Badge of the *Discovery* (Oceanographic) Expedition, 1925-7

*Above:* The extensive refit of the ship for the *Discovery* (Oceanographic) Expedition, 1925-7

*Left:* Ship's company, with Dr Stanley Kemp, scientific director and Captain J. R. Stenhouse, Master, *Discovery* (Oceanographic) Expedition, 1925-7

*Below:* Research Steamship (later RRS) *William Scoresby.* Plate XIV of *Discovery Reports* Vol. 1, 1929, pp.141-232

*Left:* King Edward Cove, South Georgia, *Discovery* in foreground, 1925

*Below:* Whaling station, Grytviken, *c* 1925

*Bottom left:* Old liners converted to whale factories, Deception Island, 1927

*Bottom right:* The *Discovery* at Port Lockroy, Wiencke Island, (Palmer Archipelago), March 1927

*Left:* Rigging one of the vertical nets preparatory to lowering

*Above:* Large (4½ metre) net, *Discovery* (Oceanographic) Expedition, 1925-7

*Below:* Shooting Hardy's continuous plankton recorder during the *Discovery* (Oceanographic) Expedition, 1925-7

*Facing page, top:* BANZAR Expedition 1929-31. The *Discovery* in Cape Town, October 1929

*Facing page, bottom:* The *Norvegia* seen from the *Discovery* in the Antarctic, off the coast of Enderby Land, 14 January 1930

*Above left:* First Mate K. N. MacKenzie in the bows of the *Discovery* during the first BANZARE voyage, 1929-30

*Above:* The *Discovery* under sail, *c* 1930

*Left:* Sir Douglas Mawson aboard the *Discovery* during the BANZAR Expedition, 1929-31

*Above:* The peaks of Enderby Land seen from the *Discovery*, January 1930

*Left:* Hurley filming aboard the *Discovery*, watched by Sir Douglas Mawson during the BANZAR Expedition 1929-31

*Below:* The Gypsy Moth plane during the BANZAR Expedition 1929-31

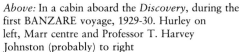

*Above:* In a cabin aboard the *Discovery*, during the
first BANZARE voyage, 1929-30. Hurley on
left, Marr centre and Professor T. Harvey
Johnston (probably) to right

*Top right:* Murray Monolith, Antarctic coast,
13 February 1931, BANZAR Expedition 1929-31

*Right:* Ceremony of taking possession, King
George V Land, during the BANZAR Expedition,
1929-31

*Below:* Mawson's old huts, Commonwealth Bay,
Australian Antarctic Expedition, 1911-14, visited
during BANZARE

*Above:* In the *Discovery*'s galley, BANZARE

*Top right: (left to right)* Captain K. N. MacKenzie, Mr MacPherson Robertson and Captain J. K. Davis on the *Discovery*'s return from the second BANZARE voyage, 1930-1

*Far right:* Sea Scouts being instructed in splicing aboard the *Discovery* in the Thames, *c* 1950

*Right:* Lady Houston, who came to the rescue of the *Discovery* in the 1930s

*Below:* The *Discovery*, cradled aboard the *Happy Mariner*, entering the River Tay at the end of her voyage from London to Dundee in the spring of 1986. Two Phantom fighters from RAF Leuchars fly over in a welcoming salute

that the ship was still three miles to the north, but expected to reach it in a couple of hours. However, such was the apparent state of the ice that the farthest south reckoned that day was 66°31′ 1/2S. at 11 p.m.[39] The ship appears to have drifted over in fact at midnight.[40] One of the crew observed that day that 'We, ie. the sailors, believe the O.M. has lost his nerve. He seems to be afraid of getting caught in the ice for the winter. When following leads in the ice he always follows those leading to the Norrard rather than those to the southard. Also he steams round and round in circles apparently to waste time and coal rather than go south. There is no drive in him at all and everyone is disgusted and fed up.'[41] Not least 'fed up' was Sir Douglas Mawson, whose diary for the voyage is full of his difficulties with Davis,[42] as was that of Davis with Mawson.

Campbell and Douglas meanwhile unpacked and assembled the bright lemon yellow Gypsy Moth sea-plane to make it available for scouting operations. The *Discovery* pushed south on 19 December and there was little doubt in Davis's mind that they were within a hundred miles of land, the soundings shallowing to 1,481 fathoms.[43]

Both Davis and Child saw what they believed to be an island on Christmas Eve.[44] Christmas Day was spent 'far within icefields, never before traversed and upon the margin of unknown land' and given over to festivities.

> On our breakfast table were bundles of wireless messages of good cheer. Dinner was made gay and full of fun by personal presents and table decorations from Australia. On our elaborate menu figured products of famous manufacturing firms of Great Britain and Australia but the principal item was a strictly local production—namely an emperor penguin, which was voted by all quite equal to grouse. Indeed the dinner was so successful that Dr Ingram is now attending several of the ship's company, who dined well though not wisely.[45]

Mawson spent part of Christmas Day writing letters to friends. Between Christmas and the New Year (when the health of the expedition's chief benefactor, Mr MacPherson Robertson, was drunk 'in good Yalumba wine'), the *Discovery* was able to make a tortuous track within the pack-ice. Dredging brought up quantities of granite and other rocks showing that land of continental proportions must be near by. This belief was strengthened by an appearance of land and a coastal mirage. The water shoaled to 261 fathoms by 26 December.

MacKenzie's diary indicates more than an appearance of land. On 26 December, he was on watch in the crow's nest and at 7.20 p.m., while the ship moved slowly south-east in the pack, he saw land: 'Land ho! Land ho!—for thirty golden minutes the great Antarctic continent revealed itself standing out about 20 miles off. With my usual good luck I was busy on watch—the first to sight the hitherto unknown and unsighted land. Great is the excitement on board . . . there was a wild rush for the rigging and a heavy demand on field glasses. I myself could not get down from the nest quick enough to call J.K. who is delighted and in high spirits. I feel much elated at being the first man to set eyes on what God has been pleased to hide from human eyes till now.' He vowed he would never forget the day.[46] Captain Davis thought the land to be about thirty miles off, looking just like Queen Mary Land, 'cold and cheerless', he wrote, 'the new land might well have remained undiscovered, it is the most desolate spot I have been in. Even the seals are not able to live here. I have only seen one in this area.' The fast ice between ship and land prevented any closer approach.[47]

Next day in clear visibility this land could not be seen. It must have been a mirage induced by refraction, a phenomenon not uncommon in these latitudes. No more time and coal could be spared to investigate this promising area, decided Sir Douglas Mawson, much to Davis's regret.[48] By the evening of 28 December, they were in more open water in lat. 66°S. long. 71°E., proceeding towards Enderby Land, the expedition's main goal. Child spent an anxious two hours on the bridge of the *Discovery* during the evening of 29 December, navigating her through close pack and at one point only just managed to avoid two huge icebergs and a piece of floating ice 15 feet high and half a mile long. He called the captain up to the bridge after a particularly bad moment and concluded that only Providence had saved them.[49]

Wind and cloud prevented the plane from taking off until 31 December, when Flt. Lieut. Campbell and Air Pilot Douglas taxied from an ice-free pool within the pack. At 5,000 feet up, they sighted what appeared to be low, hilly, ice-covered land about fifty miles to the south, forty of them unbroken pack and the other ten coastal water. Grenfell Price has discussed the controversy that later arose over this flight.[50] MacKenzie's diary (not available to Price) reads 'Rising to 5,000 feet, they had a wonderful bird's eye view of the pack but as there was a slight haze on the distant surface, they could see nothing of terra firma, which must have been a matter of only 30 miles off.'[51] Davis's diary (also not available to Price) reports too that the aeroplane climbed to 5,000 feet. The aviators found the fast floe extending about twenty miles south of the ship, beyond which there were ten miles of open water and further still either ice or land: they were unable to say which. Davis thought they did well, considering this was a first flight, but was sorry not to have been able to record a definite sighting of land. The same day Simmers' meteorological balloon rose to 53,200 feet in 76 minutes. Despite the open water seen from the plane, the ice blink to the south remained dazzling from the ship, there being no sign of a water line in the sky.[52] Mawson's report to the Commonwealth Parliament of 1930 stated that the airmen 'observed land to the south beyond the ice floe; also islets to the south-west embedded in the floe'.[53]

More oceanographic work was done during this period and on one occasion a thirty-foot trawl brought to the surface full 'with an amazingly rich catch, the weight of which was so great that our powerful derrick, which is worked from the mizzen mast and is designed for hoisting the catch inboard, crashed to the deck. Several members of staff narrowly escaped severe injury.'[54] In contrast, the plane was safely hoisted out and back again on to the skid deck, much to the satisfaction of MacKenzie who had been worrying about it for months.[55]

At midnight on 31 December 1929, Child ordered 16 bells to be struck to 'send out the old and ring in the New Year'.[56] A radio message was received on 2 January reporting the discovery by the *Norvegia* of land between Coats Land and Enderby Land. Captain Davis was disenchanted with the perpetual struggle with the ice. Mawson did his best to cheer and humour him, but their conversations remained depressing to Mawson.

> It is quite impossible for him to be cheerful or see anything in a cheerful light. He is the world's super pessimist, without any doubt whatever. The fact that the first thing he bought for the expedition equipment was 2 pairs of handcuffs illustrates this.[57]

Captain Davis recorded the noon position as lat. 66°35' S. long. 61°19' E. on 4 January 1930. This was the day on which Kemp Land, discovered in 1833 by the British sealer Captain Kemp, was confirmed. 'Land was sighted during the morning watch', wrote Davis in his diary, 'two volcanic peaks showing bare rocky faces on one side, and a stretch of what appears to be mainland to the South of them.' This was about 30 miles east of the charted position of Kemp Land. 'One feels glad', continued Davis, 'to have confirmed the discovery of Kemp, who must have been a stout hearted old buffer to have pushed in so far in 1833 and one would like to know more of him.' At 7 p.m. the sky cleared to the south and Davis was able to see much more of the land from the masthead, although he was unable to establish that both peaks were definitely on the mainland until later that evening.[58]

Piloted by Campbell next day, Mawson was able to examine from the air the magnificent panorama of new land spread out below. It was seen to the SSW by J. B. Child from the main truck as 'a long low coast, interrupted by three high peaks'.[59] The press report transmitted on 5 January described the expedition's discoveries.

> The coastline at the point of ascent, Longitude 61 deg. East, extends approximately along Latitude 67 deg. I traced its outline for 50 miles to the east and for 80 miles to the west, beyond Kemp Land, to new land heading towards Enderby Land. It is clear that these latter adjacent territories are portions of the continuous coastline of the Antarctic Continent. Before us are the rising slopes of the continental plateau, and along the shore are frequent stretches of rock, which are in many places fringed with 10 or more miles of fast ice. A few miles back from the coast are some striking ranges of black, rocky mountains several thousand feet in elevation, the most extensive being south-east of the ship. Rocky outcrops and ice packs extend as far as they can be seen to the east and west, while the plateau summit, fading in the dim distance to the south, is relieved at intervals by striking, sharp protruding peaks.

The great area of heavy pack through which the *Discovery* had battled for weeks could also be seen from the air. The British sealers John Biscoe and Peter Kemp, despatched from London by Messrs Enderby and Bennett respectively, had found similar conditions in the area a century before. The BANZARE voyage confirmed their discoveries. Biscoe's ships were the *Tula* and *Lively*, and Kemp's was the *Magnet*.[60] While the *Discovery* was hove to for the flight, Simmers followed the drift of a meteorological balloon to a height of 40,000 feet and the other scientists made oceanographical observations at a depth of 1,100 fathoms.

During the following clear calm evening, the close pack gave way to more open water, through which the ship was able to steam south-west towards the coast. Mawson's press report transmitted on 7 January 1930 spoke of the gorgeous spectacle presented at midnight by the 'fantastic ice rafts, glowing with every hue and mirrored in the placid waters'. However, within a few hours, this idyllic scene was transformed to chaos by a blizzard of extraordinary ferocity. 'The wind is just howling and whistling past us', wrote Child on 6 January, 'cursing us for seeing these sights and seeing the land here, which it has hitherto kept from man or beast . . . '. The *Discovery* headed for open water, fortunately not far away. 'Never did a more sturdy seaworthy little craft put to sea', wrote Child that same day, 'and with Providence guiding us, we will ride out this cruel storm.' The wind velocity averaged 50 m.p.h., gusting to 70. The plane had a bad buffeting and looked to Davis as if it might go overboard at times. Steering the ship was made more difficult because 'with all these wind obstructions high up, the vessel blows bodily to leeward'.[61]

Great blocks of falling ice from the rigging, like a bombardment of heavy shrapnel, punctured the aeroplane in many places. 'Bless me, Sir, this is worse than the Dardanelles. What you want is a steel helmet, Sir,' said his fellow sufferer on the bridge to MacKenzie. Flt. Lieut. Campbell watched with horror as 'in about a minute, gaping tears began to appear all over the mainplanes and tail . . . One long sliver about six feet long' went 'straight through both upper and lower port mainplanes.' He rushed to the chart-room and grabbed the matting from under Colbeck's feet. His struggle to lay this over the plane was unsuccessful: just as he had it half-laid, the ship rolled viciously and the mat slid off and over the side. Ten minutes of this bombardment resulted in 60 tears in the fabric and ten ribs stove in and flattened.[62] The work of patching the aircraft afterwards took ten days.

Coming south again the following day in thick weather, the *Discovery* met a field of heavy ice in water shoaling to 279 fathoms. With visibility down to three miles and a considerable north-north-westerly swell, Captain Davis considered this an unpleasant position, when the trend of the land was unknown. This led him to comment somewhat sourly in his diary on Sir Douglas Mawson's leadership, contrasting him with Amundsen, who had obtained his Master's ticket to avoid the friction between captain and commander.

With a scientific man as leader of an Expedition, the master of the exploring vessel is constantly pressed to engage in risky adventures which if successful are hailed as

244

great evidence of the leader's capacity, but if in the end they finish in disaster then your scientific head disclaims all responsibility. It is *impossible* to obtain the best results with a layman in charge of a marine expedition.[63]

The next day (8 January 1930), in lat. 66°13' S. long. 58°13' E., was the third spent 'dodging about unable to see anything or do anything', wrote Davis. They had to 'play patience' in what was evidently a windy locality—'old Biscoe had worse troubles and didn't moan about them'.[64] On 9 January more news came through by cable from the Australian Department of External Affairs about Norwegian activities in the Antarctic. After the trouble he had taken to inform them of BANZARE plans, Sir Douglas was exasperated to learn of their having made a claim to land between Kemp Land and Enderby Land. 'This sort of thing is not helpful to science', he wrote in his diary, 'for it means that to compete with such "explorers" an expedition should not arrange any organised programme of detailed scientific work but just rush to most likely points of coast to make landings and raise flags.'[65] 'Today we heard Norwegians had landed on and claimed some land, apparently Enderby Land, Kemp Land and the rest of the places we were going to claim', recorded Seaman Martin. Rumours made it hard to know what to believe, he wrote, 'but all feel we have been fooling around and wasting time when we ought to have been getting down to business. Capt. Davis and Sir Douglas do not seem to get on at all well together and even now after news such as we have had today, we are still hanging about, apparently just wasting coal.'[66]

The reason for the delay was Mawson's hope that a landing could be made thereabouts and the flag raised, particularly in view of the Norwegian claim. The *Discovery* was able to stand to the south on 11 January until she came up to a field of compacted sea ice, with nothing visible to southward. Davis was glad that this heavy pack was at least convincing enough to demonstrate that the ship could not be forced through and that after five days poking about in the hope of getting in to Kemp Land, it had actually been proved impossible. The position on 11 January 1930 was given by Davis as lat. 66°34' S. long. 60°13' E. The coal was down to 186 tons.[67] Mawson's press report dated 10 January 1930[68] announced the proposal to call new land discovered east of Kemp Land, MacRobertson Land [*sic*] to commemorate their benefactor.[69] This land is now considered to extend from the meridian of 60°E. (where it joins Kemp Land) to that of 73°E. (where it joins Princess Elizabeth Land). Bird and animal life abounded offshore. Two rare Ross seals were observed on 11 January, as well as many Emperor and Adélie penguins.

It proved impossible for the ship to approach the coast, nor was it possible to fly. In view of this and because coal was rapidly being consumed, Mawson decided that they could no longer wait, but must press on westward following the edge of the heavy pack and look for an opening to the land. The presence of the Norwegians somewhere nearby trying to claim territory was a crucial factor in this decision.[70] On 12 January 1930 the *Discovery* passed through lines of icebergs stranded on shoals, thought to be the submarine moraines of former glaciers. That afternoon, the weather cleared to reveal 'a series of rocky peaks several thousand feet high, rising from the land ice dome. Rock patches here also broke the monotony of the ubiquitous ice cliffs, which range in height between 60 ft. and 130 ft. . . . This evening the peaks of Enderby Land were visible from the ship.'[71]

Enderby Land (now considered to extend between the meridians of 45°E. and 55°E.) had been discovered on 28 February 1831 by the English sealer John Biscoe in the brig *Tula*, owned by Messrs Enderby of London, after whom it was named.[72] It was not sighted again for almost a century, when in December 1929 the distinguished Norwegian aviator and explorer Captain Hjalmar Riiser-Larsen, accompanied by Commander F. Lützow-Holm of the Norwegian Naval Air Service, flew from the *Norvegia* some ninety miles distant and landed on the coast. The Norwegian flag was hoisted on a skerry near Biscoe's Cape Ann and the land claimed for Norway. The ship was owned and the (third *Norvegia*) expedition was financed and organised by the whaling entrepreneur Consul Lars Christensen of Sandefjord, near Oslo. The *Norvegia* coaled from the whale factory ship *Thorshammer* on 4 January 1930, after which Riiser-Larsen was able to return to Enderby Land and chart its western coast from the air.[73]

Meanwhile the *Discovery* was also nearing Enderby Land on 12 January 1930. Child spotted land soon after midday to the south and south-west of the ship and could hardly contain his excitement as he made his report to the captain after lunch on the bridge. Davis called for Mawson to come up and he too was very pleased. Captain Davis's diary for 12 January gives an account of these discoveries. At noon, they were passing close to the outer berg of a long line of bergs at a depth of 125 fathoms. At one o'clock, Child, the Third Mate, sighted land to the southward and when the weather cleared they saw

> . . . snow covered slopes with eight rocky tops which emerged from the snow slope, the highest I should estimate being 3000 feet. We stood into the South in a wide bay, the land being visible from S.84W. to S.23E. True, distant about 25 miles.

Close pack and a number of grounded bergs prevented an approach to the land. At 8.25 p.m., open water stretched right up to the ice cliffs, off which they were steaming about five miles out. At 10 p.m. an island or mountain peak was sighted ahead, quite clear of snow, and the ship continued to steam westward, still five to seven miles off the land, inside a line of large grounded bergs, the island being 'miraged up' about twenty-five miles distant.[74]

Sir Douglas's diary for 13 January 1930, which is available verbatim in *The winning of Australian Antarctica*, and in the more recently published *Mawson's Antarctic diaries*, recounts the events of the next day, when the flag was raised on Child's discovery and it was named Proclamation Island.[75] The entry is like a number of others in showing the difference of opinion that arose between him and Davis, who made it clear to Mawson that the ship could not stay long in those waters, there being no suitable bottom for anchorage, and asked him to 'Get ashore as quickly as possible, get the flag up and come off—we can't stop here.' Seaman Martin's diary for this first BANZARE voyage consistently bears out Davis's unwillingness to allow anyone to land. This lack of time ashore was naturally disappointing to the scientists and frustrating, even maddening, to Sir Douglas Mawson as far as the making of territorial claims was concerned.

Captain Davis had the anchor over, ready to drop in order to hold the ship, but when the *Discovery* touched rock between two ice-capped islands, he gave up the idea. The weather was calm, but if a wind sprang up, he thought, they would be in a tight corner. He watched the shore party climb to the summit and hoist the flag. They had taken no food or gear, seeming to trust to Providence entirely. 'I hope he will be good to them and us', wrote Davis when they had been away for four hours.[76] MacKenzie had fewer misgivings.

Weather conditions were ideal, in fact yesterday and today have been exquisite— bright sun clear sky and no wind, result bright spirits, clear minds and no growling. No longer time than necessary was spent on the island and by 4pm we were pushing our way out of the pack to the ice berg sea and away westwards. The coast of Enderby Land was in full view—perfectly glorious. Twenty sharp mighty peaks and long white slopes shone in the great clear rays of summer—Antarctic sun which is unlike any other, a strong and bright ball filling every heart with life and the joy of living, for after all our fight and struggle our objective has been achieved . . . so no wonder our hearts are glad, glad and full—full of thankfulness to God for this day. 'Things obtained disappear, but things done last for ever.'[77]

The text of the proclamation ran

In the name of His Majesty King George the Fifth, King of Great Britain, Ireland, and the British Dominions beyond the Seas, Emperor of India.

Whereas I have it in command from His Majesty King George the Fifth to assert the sovereign rights of His Majesty over British land discoveries met with in Antarctica. Now, therefore, I Sir Douglas Mawson do hereby proclaim and declare to all men that, from and after the date of these presents, the full sovereignty of the territory of Enderby Land, Kemp Land, Mac. Robertson Land together with off-lying Islands as located in our charts constituting a sector of the Antarctic regions lying between Longitude 73°E. of Greenwich and 47°E. of Greenwich and South of Latitude 65°, rests in His Majesty King George the Fifth, his Heirs and Successors for ever. Given under my hand on board the exploring vessel 'Discovery', now lying off the coast of this annexed land, in Latitude 65°50′ S. Longitude 53°30′ E. The thirteenth day of January, 1930.

It was witnessed by J. K. Davis, 'Master SY *Discovery*', and signed by Douglas Mawson, 'Commanding Antarctic Expedition',[78] Heading away from Proclamation Island, Mawson noted a 'fine group of peaks rising through the ice cap in locality of Mt. Codrington of Biscoe', as well as an Adélie penguin rookery of some 4,000 birds.[79] Continuing westwards in fine weather in order to complete the chart of Enderby Land, on 14 January a prominent rock was passed in the vicinity of Biscoe's Cape Ann. Mawson believed this to be Cape Ann, mainly because of Biscoe's repeated sightings of it from various positions.[80] Davis however disagreed and marked it on the survey as Point Biscoe. An examination of Biscoe's diary makes it appear that Mawson was right. After this, 'We continued to the West outside the pack', wrote Davis, 'with the land clearly visible in beautiful clear weather, with numerous peaks showing out of the ice cap. One of these I called Mount Tula and I should judge to have been 4,000 feet high, a black rugged summit with several smaller peaks in the vicinity.' MacKenzie found the Enderby Land coast unreal and awe-inspiring, and at times uncanny. By 8 p.m. the land had disappeared bearing south-east-by-south true.[81]

Mawson records the dramatic meeting of the two exploring ships, Norwegian and British, that took place on the evening of 14 January 1930.

The officer on watch [J. B. Child] reported steamship (8.30pm) ahead in early evening. As it had two masts and was small we assumed it to be the 'Norvegia'. She turned around and later came towards us. Was afterwards ascertained that she had been stopped for sounding when she sighted us. Then came on again. She approached us to pass on our port side—very deep in water—only about 2 ft. freeboard—had two large aeroplanes on board—one in well deck the other at stern lengthways with ship. We learnt afterwards that when she rolled the aeroplane wings dipped in sea—certainly she was very precariously loaded—they told us later that they had to hug the pack edge and dive in at times of rough weather. They had just been delayed by 8 days of bad weather. They were loaded down with coal—on deck and in every space—had just been coaled in pack by mother ship of whaling fleet: they told us that 2 whales had been lashed between themselves as a fender during coaling.

We slowed down and finally stopped as they approached, they had got past abreast of us still continuing E. when I asked Davis to run up friendly message, so flags for 'Wish you a pleasant voyage', run up. We had already both dipped flags—they did so first. Then they replied 'Thank you'. Shortly after they began to swing around and turned until nearly abreast of us, they called out through megaphone that Capt. Riiser-Larsen would like to meet me. 'Might he come on board?' We replied 'Yes'. They said they would lower a boat. Later on the boat arrived alongside.[82]

Davis received Riiser-Larsen at the gangway, and they and Mawson talked in the chart-room and Davis's cabin. Riiser-Larsen told them what he had been doing and that he had been warned from Norway not to do anything that might be resented by Great

Britain. Mawson judged that he had been instructed not to raise the Norwegian flag on Enderby Land or Kemp Land and discreetly neglected to ask him exactly what they had done, preferring just to listen. In return he told Riiser-Larsen that the *Discovery* had mapped the coast from about long. 73°E. to their present position but that their progress farther east had been prevented by pack-ice, and a hurricane off Kemp Land. Mawson also said that they had been sorry to hear, in Cape Town, that a Norwegian expedition might overlap with them, but that the *Discovery* expedition was a bona fide project with a scientific programme and had informed Norway that they would stay east of long. 40°E. They hoped the Norwegian Expedition would stay west of that line. Mawson expressed his belief that there was enough room for several expeditions and that overlap was undesirable for every reason. He learned that the *Norvegia* had been commissioned to circumnavigate the Antarctic and asked to work with the whaling fleet south of Bouvet Island, but that the job was too big for them and that they had been instructed from Norway to give up the circumnavigation that year. Riiser-Larsen and Mawson told each other of their likely plans for the following season: the *Discovery* would work farther to the east while the *Norvegia* would operate in the Pacific. Mawson liked Riiser-Larsen and showed him over the *Discovery*. Davis had been very favourably impressed too. He felt sorry nevertheless that the *Discovery* had not been first to plant the flag in this area at the beginning of the season, but he recognised that the BANZAR Expedition had its scientific side and had probably achieved more by not leaving 'the Cape solely to raise the flag'.[83] Davis had also talked to the Norwegian First Mate and other members of staff had cross-questioned him in the wardroom. The *Discovery* gave three cheers for the *Norvegia* as the Norwegians left and then steamed west as the others departed in the opposite direction.

The *Norvegia* had been sent to the Antarctic by Consul Lars Christensen (1884–1965), the Norwegian whaling magnate and shipowner, a very significant figure in both Antarctic whaling and exploration and the 'chief architect of Norwegian territorial claims in the Antarctic'.[84] Besides sending the *Norvegia* in 1927–8, 1928–9, 1929–30, 1930–1, he despatched the *Odd I* (1926–7), the *Thorshavn* (1932–3, 1933–4, 1934–5) and the *Thorshammer* (1936–7). These expeditions were all organised at his own expense; as a comparatively young man he had inherited the extensive shipping concerns of his father, Chr. Christensen, and of his father-in-law, Thor Dahl, at Sandefjord. These Antarctic voyages were made in order to collect information on new whaling grounds and to safeguard Norwegian whaling interests.

Brian Roberts writes that Lars Christensen 'had strongly urged Norwegian territorial claims to counteract the extension of British claims' and planned to bring all the lands between longs. 20°W. and 60°E. under Norwegian sovereignty. The Norwegian Untenriksdepartementet (Foreign Office) supported Christensen whose expeditions focused on the sector between Enderby Land and Coats Land so as to avoid conflicts over sovereignty with other powers.[85] The results of the expeditions were later published in Oslo.[86] Christensen's book, *Such is the Antarctic*,[87] tells the story of the expeditions and of how he bought the *Norvegia* in January 1927 on the return of the *Odd I* from Antarctica. A wooden sealer of 250 tons, built in 1919, her name was changed from *Vesleper*. She had a small auxiliary engine of 350 hp. In between her four Antarctic voyages, she would winter and refit in Cape Town, her 'white hull and upper works, tall mast with the little crow's nest perched 50 feet up' being a familiar sight at the docks. A quite unfamiliar sight were the two seaplanes carried on deck in the Antarctic during the 1929–30 cruise. Transported as far as the ice on the flensing platform of the *Thorshammer* whale factory ship, these were a Lockheed Vega monoplane (in fact never used on the expedition) and a Norwegian-built Hansa-Brandenburg reconnaissance plane, lent by the Norwegian Navy, which was flown several times. Christensen remarks on the *Norvegia*'s strange appearance in the Antarctic, her 'greyish-white hull bristling with great wings fore and aft', this despite a length of only 114 feet.

Riiser-Larsen recorded that he had hailed the *Discovery* in order to speak to Sir Douglas Mawson and Captain John King Davis because he wanted to meet the two famous Antarctic explorers and because he had heard of the unfavourable British press reports on his expedition. 'I therefore came straight to the point and told Sir Douglas and Captain King Davies [sic] that our programme had been made public as far back as 1927, and was being carried out accurately at the present time; that we were not invading other people's territories.' He enjoyed his time, and tour, aboard, and was envious of the *Discovery*'s superior fitness for the job. He was also delighted by the three cheers called for the *Norvegia* as he returned to her.[88]

Mawson described the encounter quite fully in his diary, but fairly briefly in his press report dated 15 January 1930.[89] Riiser-Larsen's own report (published in *The Times* of 18 January 1930) said that he had met with the utmost courtesy from Sir Douglas Mawson, that no misunderstandings remained between them and that Sir Douglas gave it as his private opinion that no difficulties would arise from the fact that the Norwegian flag had been hoisted on 22 December 1929 on newly discovered land between Enderby Land and Kemp Land (i.e. on a skerry off Enderby Land). In fact Lars Christensen on 10 January 1930, after congratulating Riiser-Larsen on this flag-hoisting, asked him by telegram in future not to occupy any more land east of 45°E. or west of 15°W. since Norway had agreed to the resolutions of the Imperial Conference of 1926 concerning British rights of discovery in certain Antarctic territories.[90]

As Grenfell Price remarks,[91] this must have been a great disappointment for Riiser-Larsen, since he had returned to the *Norvegia* on 22 December exclaiming 'Now Enderby Land is Norwegian', annexed in the same way as Bouvetøya (a French discovery) and Peter I Øy (a Russian one). However, Riiser-Larsen went on soon afterwards to discover and explore from the air Kronprins Olav Kyst in mid-January 1930 and Kronprinsesse Märtha Kyst in February. After further explorations, the territory from 45°E. (the western boundary of Enderby Land) to 20°W. (the eastern boundary of Coats Land) was claimed by Norway in a Royal Decree of 14 January 1939. It is now known as Dronning (Queen) Maud Land.[92]

The day after the meeting with the *Norvegia*, a joke, recorded by Simmers, was played on the engine-room staff of the *Discovery*.

> Tonight there has been the most priceless rag—Stew [Campbell] and Cherub [Fletcher] who have both had particularly forestlike beards had a shave which so transformed them that they were almost unrecognisable and Stew when he put a hat on quite unrecognisable. The growing of the beards simply must have changed their facial contours as they didn't look a bit like their Capetown selves . . . Anyway, after making most of us roar at their appearance, they climbed into flying togs and went to the engine room where they were introduced as two Norwegians completely taking the chief in and being shown round the engines like important personages.

The ship's cat, according to MacKenzie's diary for 18 January, had a less enjoyable encounter. 'Nigger' slipped off the icy fore topgallant mast during a pronounced roll of the ship. AB Martin immediately leapt into the water to rescue the cat, but had to return to the ship, unable to reach it. Fortunately Nigger turned back towards the ship too and was pulled out of the water by Tomlinson, suspended on a bowline. 'To grasp the miserable half drowned cat', wrote MacKenzie, 'the individual (one of the scientific party) let go the line from which the rescuer was hanging and the fact of having done so was only realised on hearing a splash below. But enough, both men and the cat are now well—well dried and well able to join in and laugh at an episode well worth avoiding in these waters.' The black cat had been a gift from the RRS *William Scoresby* in Cape Town. Martin was unaffected by the diversion, but the waterlogged cat only recovered after many hours heating in the engine-room.[93] Martin presented one of Nigger's kittens to Lady Mawson at the end of the BANZAR expedition. She records that the kitten 'not knowing how to behave on land, kept crawling up anything that resembled a rope or furled sail, including my father's legs, to his great surprise!'[94]

Educated at Harrow, James Holland Martin had held a commission in the Grenadier Guards from 1917 to 1919. He then served before the mast in the *Garthpool*, the last of the British square riggers in the Australian grain trade. After BANZARE he worked in Norwegian sealers and learned dog driving in northern Canada, with the idea of organising an expedition to the Antarctic. Setting aside his own plans, he joined the *Penola* as mate, during the British Graham Land Expedition of 1934–7, of whose members he was the 'most universally respected'.[95] He was lost at sea in 1940 when the 'Q' ship, HMS *Williamette Valley*, was torpedoed. She was commanded by Captain R. E. D. Ryder, who had been master of the *Penola* and who had sought Martin out to join him as one of the officers of the *Williamette Valley*. 'There was always something new to discover about him', wrote Captain Ryder. 'He was a veritable "Jekyll and Hyde", being a dapper Guards officer one moment and a proper Cape Horn shellback the next, with his heavily repaired denims, cloth cap, beard and Meerschaum pipe—with a fly button pressed into the bowl to improve the draught. . . . Apart from his first-class ability as a seaman, he was a most charming companion with a delightful sense of humour.' The *Williamette Valley* rolled over and sank after the third torpedo. 'The last I saw of James', wrote Ryder, 'he was going down below into the 'tween decks to make sure everyone was on deck.' Apart from those who got away in the lifeboat, only two were picked up.[96]

The *Discovery* was now forced to run for some 150 miles before a north-easterly gale (vividly described in MacKenzie's diary) to her furthest west on 20 January in lat. 66°25' S. long. 43°05' E. (noon position). Captain Davis wondered how the *Norvegia* was faring in the gale. Of his own ship, he remarked that she was 'a good sea boat', but that 'she must have room, as with her lack of power it is impossible to thrash her off'. Not knowing where the ice was, he felt the *Discovery* to be safer away from the lee shore presented by the pack-ice, even in a big sea.[97] Mawson noted in his diary of the previous day how splendidly she rode out the storm.[98] Child, too, praised the vessel as a marvel, believing that others would have foundered, although there were 'many anxious moments' when she was thrown into a trough.[99] One 'cold, wild day' was enlivened for the crew by the discovery of Seaman Martin's mitten 'patched with an old sock' at the bottom of the soup cauldron, when the soup was finished.[100]

There was little sign of a change in the weather on the third day of the gale (20 January). It was very wet and unpleasant on deck and all hands were miserable, noted Davis. The vessel was becoming unwieldy as the coal was consumed and she became lighter. Captain Davis's diary also records that he told Sir Douglas that 120 tons of coal was the smallest amount with which the ship should leave the Antarctic, and that it would be necessary to compress as much work as possible into the next fine spell. Mawson evidently thought there would be no difficulty in reaching Kerguelen and disagreed with Davis as to the amount. Davis noted his duty to those on board as

> to consider and provide against unnecessary folly and to arrive off Kerguelen with no coal in the ship on the assumption we should meet fine weather is not a 'daring act' but a 'foolish one'. M. says we are here to take risks, but this appears to me to be right only when they are unavoidable.[101]

This disagreement over coal remained a point of major contention between the two men. The *Discovery* was able to make some headway under steam towards the east when the wind and sea moderated. Captain Davis made Commander Moyes promise to fix the position of 'Point Biscoe' and hoped that Mawson 'would leave biologising' until then. During the early morning watch of 22 January, Chief Officer MacKenzie observed a loom of land to the south, which Mawson considered to be a south-westerly extension of that sighted by Biscoe in 1831. 'Again, the existence of one of the world's finest mountain ranges was brought to light', wrote the chief officer that day, 'and never will I forget the sight beheld from the [crow's] nest, as those mighty black peaks with their ice worn and torn sides pierced the sky above. Range followed range and never were mountains more wonderful, for never had they been beheld by human eye. The distant ranges were ascertained to be from 5,000 feet upwards, and the number of peaks were beyond our count.'[102]

A massive ice tongue, with cliffs of between 130 and 200 feet high, was sighted extending from the land on 22 January, as the ship steamed north-east along the edge of the pack-ice. The next day, the *Discovery* passed within a dozen miles of the conspicuous high rock that Captain Davis called 'Point Biscoe' and may well have been Biscoe's Cape Ann. An immense number of grounded icebergs were held in the sea ice surrounding the cape. 'We were able to see that Point Biscoe consists of two rocky peaks, quite bare of snow', wrote Davis, 'with another rocky outcrop higher up the snow slope behind the two coastal points, between which a glacier descends to the sea, ending in an ice wall about 50 feet high.'[103] Mawson described it as rising from the sea front to a height of 1,500 feet, most of its northerly face (otherwise black) being coloured from the guano of countless nesting sea birds. Antarctic petrels sped out in clouds to investigate the *Discovery*.[104] Child continued sketching and charting, being praised by Davis for this work, who remarked on its being 'all the more unique, because *no one* has been so close to the land, in fact were doubtful whether it was or not *land*'.[105]

The previous day (22 January 1930), Seaman Martin had recorded an extraordinary entry relating to Captain Davis in his diary.

> With regard to the O.M. and his curious behaviour, Sir. D.M. addressed the starboard watch this p.m. and said he considered the O.M. was too old for his job. That he was scared to take chances, all he would do now was to growl and curse and that our best plan was to get to Melbourne as soon as possible and find another man. Also that the O.M. was too used to a soft shore job and that when it came to the point he wanted to get out of it.

The crew must have heard the two leaders arguing. In Mawson's diary, it appears that the boot was on the other foot. It records that after Mawson had left the bridge, where he had been enquiring about the sighting of new land, Davis was heard 'to address all and sundry . . . in a loud voice, saying derogatory things about me before the Wheelman and other sailors. A nice sort of thing for a Second-in-command to be doing.' A few days earlier (on 18 January) Sir Douglas had delivered a schedule to Captain Davis setting out the work still to be completed. He was particularly anxious to reach Enderby Land to make a further proclamation, this time on the mainland.[106]

On 23 January, which was fine, cold and bright, Martin described the preparations for the landing, 'Flag. Proclamation. Plane. Motorboat, etc. etc. . . . Everyone rather excited but sceptical.' Then at about 10 p.m., 'the O.M. said to Sir D.M., "Launch the plane we may, but go in there", pointing to the land, "we can't" and that was that. So to everyone's disappointment, we go on with any work and steam aimlessly along the coast. We always seem to be trying to get somewhere and when we get there, go on somewhere else.' Davis had hoped that the gale would have blown the sea ice away making it easier to get into the coast. The swell proved in fact too great for the plane to be launched near the cape.[107] They arrived at Proclamation Island again on 24 January, on which day, directed by Marr, who deserved great credit, thought Davis, a good catch of specimens was obtained from the otter-trawl. Davis had feared the loss of the trawl during this 'difficult operation', being done for the first time, but was 'glad to have been proved wrong'.[108]

Flights were made from open water in the vicinity of Proclamation Island on 25 January, during which Hurley shot both still and motion pictures. It was too risky for the plane to come down on the open water near the shore, because small pieces of loose ice were floating on the surface. Mawson therefore dropped a flag on the ice sheet from the air at 3,000 feet, some two miles inland, retaining the Proclamation, which included claims to the newly discovered land to the west. He remarked in his diary for that day that all members of staff were broken-hearted that Captain Davis would not steam the two miles necessary through apparently loose pack-ice to set foot upon the mainland of Enderby Land.

'Captain D's attitude now and always on this expedition', observed Mawson ruefully, 'has been that of one in charge of a passenger steamer in regular service. On no account will he take what may be even a slight risk. It is evident that he should not be sailing an exploring expedition.' Mawson was struck by the irony of some of the sailors volunteering to take risks, this being what they had expected when they signed on. Their willingness contrasted with the captain's over-protective attitude, 'constantly referring to the searching enquiry that would be made on return to Australia should anybody be hurt or killed'.[109] More flights to over 4,000 feet were made the next day (26 January 1930), from which height some 73 nunataks (mountain peaks) projecting above the ice sheet were observed, some estimated as reaching 7,000 feet.[110] Captain Davis gave his reason in his diary for not entering the pack-ice.

> I explained to him [Mawson] that such a course would be fatal to all on board, if the ship got on the rocks on her way in past the islands. The pack would simply shove her over and from what we have seen of its rapid movement here, it would shove her over pretty quickly. To approach a point of land between islands with a boat ahead sounding is a dangerous business in uncharted waters, but to push into pack in such circumstances could not be justified on any grounds whatever.

Nevertheless, he admitted that 'it is unpleasant to have to decline to meet the wishes of the leader of the expedition'.[111]

'Hereabouts', remarked Mawson,[112] 'the land ice slopes are generally of the nature of glistening ice to a height of 2,000 feet, above which level they are composed of hard compressed névé and thus offer the best possible surface for sledging. The whole area is most attractive for land operations.' He went on to describe other activities during the fine weather. These included observations by Simmers of test balloons and marine collections from the continental shelf by Professor Johnston, using both Monégasque and other trawls. Irritating and invisible glassy spines from certain sponges constantly reminded the biologists and their enthusiastic assistants of these dredgings every time they bent or sat down. Saturday 25 January was their last full day off the Antarctic coast. The following day, 'true to the Skipper's word', the *Discovery* turned north, towards Kerguelen as her captain had said she would. In his Report to the Commonwealth Parliament presented in May and printed in June 1930, Sir Douglas Mawson confirmed that 'On the evening of 26th January Captain Davis informed me that having reached the limit of 120 tons of coal he would carry on no longer in Antarctic waters and was about to set a course for Kerguelen.'

In a letter written in Melbourne on 27 May 1930 to the expedition's Secretary and in a memorandum of 16 November 1962, both of which can be found copied in his personal papers, Captain Davis expressed the view that Mawson's statement was 'not a fair presentation of the facts', since his advice 'as to the amount of coal needed to reach Australia if unable to make Kerguelen was accepted by the leader of the expedition at the time'. He pointed out that Mawson's letter to him of 26 January 1930 made this clear and that it was omitted (with the rest of Davis's Report) from *The winning of Australian Antarctica*. He also considered that Mawson's reference to him in the Report with regard to the possibility of coaling from the whaler *Radioleine* was unfair, in that her master endorsed his own opinion as to this being risky in the open sea.

While the *Discovery* steamed north on 28 January, leaving the Antarctic behind, Captain Davis wrote in his diary:

> I think we have done everything possible. One would like to have landed the party on the mainland, but it is no use putting a ship on the rocks for this purpose and the danger of going into the moving coastal pack for this purpose is obvious. It will be a relief to get out of the ice again as the continuous strain and the bad weather are very wearing to the master in a ship like this. I have been fortunate in my officers and crew. The officers and Engineers are a very fine type and have really done very well indeed. I have not heard a single moan from any of them and with the crowd we have on board this ship, things are pretty uncomfortable for them. Each of the deck officers has done his allotted job well . . . For the engine room department I cannot say enough. They have responded to every call made upon them and one knows what a small staff the Chief has.[113]

Mawson's press report of the same date spoke again of the marine biological survey (and of whales and icebergs).

> For several days past we have been busy running a marine section in full detail northward from the coast of Enderby Land into the deep basin of the Southern

255

Ocean, which necessitated conducting a number of stations successively further from the land. Today in lat. 63deg 50min South, long. 54deg 16min East, the operations were conducted in water 5,354 metres (18,500ft.) deep.

A special feature has been the richness in nekton (small animal life) of waters at 1,000 metres (3,280ft.) below the surface, from which a large variety of fish has been netted, some of quite extraordinary form. Among other curiosities are examples both of fish and small cephalopoda, which are quite colourless and transparent, except their glowing eyes and silvery stomach sack.

Today blue whales were abundant, and one performed in a remarkable manner, breaking clean out of the sea and on one occasion shooting vertically almost its full length from the water. As we could not observe any attacking foe, we concluded that it was possibly a case of pure 'joie de vivre' arising out of the glorious calm and sunshine of the day.

Icebergs were plentiful even at this distance from the coast, but, whereas they are compact and tabular in the waters of the continental shelf, here in somewhat warmer waters they show every evidence of decadence, being reduced to spired and turreted forms, often of striking grandeur. We have just passed such a berg the measured height of which proved to be 250 feet.

Although Mawson mentioned a shortage of coal in his press report of 27 January, he did not announce the consequent retreat from the Antarctic until early February. His diary for 26 January 1930 expressed his great regret at having to leave the Antarctic coast at Davis's wish, once coal stocks were down to 120 tons. Another week, thought Mawson, would have completed the aerial survey of Mac.Robertson Land and would also have added detail of the Scott Mountains (the nunataks of Enderby Land, named after Captain R. F. Scott). However, despite being Commander of the expedition, Mawson felt obliged to bow to Davis's advice, as master of the ship; he himself would not have left until stocks were down to 80 tons.[114] It is difficult to judge who was right. Davis had been ashore in administration for over a decade and all his previous experience had taught him the dangers of Antarctic ice. The press reports show that Mawson was prepared to winter in the pack if necessary, the *Discovery* being constructed to withstand ice pressure and the expedition well supplied with equipment and food. Drygalski's *Gauss* (also specially built) wintered involuntarily in the pack well to the east of Enderby Land and Kemp Land in 1902–3, a fact that may have encouraged Mawson and discouraged Davis. Enough coal could have been left to manoeuvre in the ice, giving the *Discovery* an immense advantage over the early navigators in the area, Biscoe and Kemp, who relied on sail alone. Even if (as Davis feared) she were blown past Kerguelen where the remainder of her coal depot was waiting, could she not have sailed the Great Circle route to Australia, taken by so many ships of the nineteenth century relying on wind alone? Davis must have been quite aware of this option, as in addition to his very considerable experience in the Antarctic, he had served in clipper ships earlier in his career.

## THE VOYAGE HOME

The *Discovery* turned north on 26 January 1930, a date which could be considered far too early in the navigation season. Even Biscoe in his small brig *Tula* (150 tons) was still off the coast of Enderby Land in March 1831. In recent times, the navigation season has extended generally to the end of February. It is interesting to read and to compare the ANARE voyages of the *Thala Dan* (Captain Hans Chr. Petersen) off Enderby Land and Kemp Land in 1961 and 1962, with that of the *Discovery* in 1929–30. In 1961, the *Thala Dan* left the vicinity of White Island and Dingle Dome on 29 February; in 1962, she left Mawson research station on 2 March.[115] However, there is a vast difference between a modern ice-strengthened ship with powerful engines, effective radio, radar and ample fuel and the old *Discovery*. A further factor that must have stiffened Davis's resolve to leave was the chief engineer's announcement on 25 January that the boilers could only continue for a further three weeks without cleaning.[116]

Captain A. R. Williamson, who had sailed aboard the *Discovery* in 1911 as a seaman has commented pertinently that

Davis, being a sail-trained man, must have realised that by striking down all the square yards in Cape Town, he was converting a barque-rigged efficient sailing vessel, with an auxiliary engine, into a low-powered steamer with small bunker capacity and a few fore and aft sails. Thus the safety of the vessel depended on the amount of coal in the bunkers. The diminishing amount seems to have given him 'coal fever' in January, which was the reason for proceeding north a month earlier than would have been necessary if the square yards had been aloft and the barque's full sailing potential available in case of necessity.[117]

Williamson is mistaken in thinking that Davis struck down *all* the square yards. Those on the foremast were retained. When asked his opinion of the matter, the only surviving officer of the 1929–30 voyage, Captain W. R. Colbeck (Second Officer), wrote

I feel one factor in Davis' mind was the fact that his three officers—Mac, myself and Child—did not have any deep sea sail experience. I know there were discussions and arguments between Mawson and Davis and later MacKenzie, to which I was not, as a junior officer, a party, but in the later stages of both voyages, they concerned what some called 'coal fever'. I was very junior—I was the youngest on board at 23—but as most brash youngsters, had strong views. I still consider, as I did at the time, that we left Enderby Land for home far too early. I had a possibly presumptuous argument with MacKenzie on the grounds that we could have let our coal stocks go down by many tons to carry out more work in the area and rely on sail to get back to Australia from the pack . . . We had sufficient stores and above all we had wireless communication which earlier expeditions did not have.

Our position and situation would be known and *in extremis* some vessel—whaler?—could have picked us up. We did achieve quite a lot, but another fortnight could have provided a considerable improvement in our survey work.[118]

On 31 January, Martin noted that Captain Davis was 'far more cheerful now we are homeward bound'.[119] That day, Davis's own diary noted that one of the firemen had a poisoned foot and that the other two had to go on to six-hour watches as a result. They received a noggin of whisky at the end of each watch instead of overtime. The following day, all sail was set and he felt it good to see the canvas on the ship again. On 3 February, with 79 tons of coal remaining, the *Discovery* was hove to for an oceanographic station. Captain Davis considered she should have been pressing on for Kerguelen, while the weather was fine. One of his fears was that the lighter her trim (as coal was consumed), the greater the likelihood of her being blown past the islands in a storm.

> It is just this difficulty which keeps on cropping up in a show with two heads. If I say no and we get to Kerguelen all right, then M has a moan that I have prevented him doing all he might have done. If I say yes and we get into a mess, he simply says, oh Captain Davis said it was O.K. With an ordinary man one can reason, but M is only guided by an idea that ships are just like buildings on shore and there you are.

Some 'unfortunate sea birds' were shot and a boat sent to retrieve them. He wished he could 'prohibit killing these poor harmless creatures', it being a 'weakness of certain types that they must kill!' He does not say whether the birds were taken as scientific specimens or shot only for sport.[120]

Between leaving Enderby Land and arriving in Royal Sound, Kerguelen, on 8 February, Mawson despatched two press reports summarising the work accomplished by the expedition in Antarctic waters. The coastline had been outlined between long. 44°E. and 66°E., and the continental margin between 66°E. and 90°E. also roughly indicated; the topography of the coast and islets had been described and compared to those in other parts of the Antarctic; several mountain ranges had been charted and main peaks located; the occurrence and variable nature of continental-type rocks had been established. All the evidence demonstrated conclusively that the land sighted was continuous with the continent located between long. 90°E. and 180°E., thus negating Morrell's claim.[121] Other data collected related to the movements of air and wind over land and sea at heights up to 50,000 feet, the effects of the winds and currents on the pack-ice, the character and limits of the continental shelf and the depth and nature of the water and the sea bed. A vast amount of information on the biology of the sea—especially the plankton—and of the air had also been obtained.

The narrative and results of the first BANZARE voyage (including the sub-Antarctic biology) were more fully set out in Mawson's official report to the Commonwealth

Parliament presented on 21 May 1930 and in the *Geographical Review* of October 1930. The outstanding achievements were the charting or location of the edge of the Antarctic continent between 45°E. and 73°E. (and the claim to all this land and offshore islands for the Crown) and the discovery of the whale fishery off Enderby Land.[122]

The *Discovery* arrived at Kerguelen on 8 February 1930. She secured again to the old jetty of Port Jeanne d'Arc and coaled 190 tons in ten days. Meanwhile the engine-room staff chipped her boilers. More survey flights were carried out.[123] Scientific collections were made by parties using the launch. MacKenzie found the island (no longer snow-clad) much like the wild and rugged coast of Skye.[124] The manager's hut at the abandoned whaling station was turned into the *Discovery* Club, making a cosy place for an evening's entertainment. 'The fire and lamp, the gramophone and sing-song is indeed a pleasant change', wrote MacKenzie, 'and it does me good to relax after the severe ordeal of ship life in polar seas.'[125] Captain Davis too was glad to get ashore, especially as earlier in the voyage he had complained of the impossibility of getting exercise on the *Discovery*'s crowded decks. 'A passage perilous maketh a port pleasant', he remarked in his diary.[126] A day was spent surveying among the islands of Royal Sound. An entry in the official log records the discovery and reporting of 'Green Rocks' in the Sound,[127] not marked on Admiralty chart No. 799 and 'constituting a danger to navigation'.[128] Some white Samoyed dogs 'in fine fettle and quite wild' were frequently seen during excursions, perhaps the descendants of those left by the *Gauss* expedition of 1901-3. Mawson noted how destructive they were of birds and seals. The sites of the British 'Transit of Venus' expedition of 1874-5 and the *Gauss* expedition were visited. At the latter, Simmers redetermined the magnetic elements for comparison with the values taken 29 years earlier.[129]

The sudden descent of wintry weather with severe gales forced Mawson to abandon his plans for a flag-raising visit to Queen Mary Land in the Antarctic and even a cruise as far as Heard Island.[130] However, the enforced stay gave the chief officer a chance to get all secured and shipshape and he left 'feeling confident that my foot ropes and stirrups at least wouldn't carry away and pitch a man headlong into the seas of the roaring forties.[131] A course was set on 2 March for Albany in Western Australia and the voyage proceeded with what MacKenzie called 'the everlasting trawling and dredging', plus stations and other scientific work done *en route*.[132] Grenfell Price tells us that a rather dull month was enlivened with occasional bright patches, such as when Professor Harvey Johnston 'thought he had a new worm from the intestine of a molly mawk', only to find that it was 'a piece of macaroni from yesterday's tea'.[133]

Mawson considered it wiser to proceed to Adelaide rather than Albany, for the sake of the projected second Antarctic voyage, and had the course altered towards South Australia. The coast was sighted on 30 March 1930 and on 1 April the *Discovery* berthed in Port Adelaide to a welcome from Lord Stonehaven, the Governor-General of Australia, and the Antarctic Committee. Civic receptions were later given in Adelaide and in Melbourne in honour of the expedition. The *Discovery* went into dock in Melbourne for an overhaul. Twelve English seamen were paid off and given free passage home by the P. & O. steamer *Bendigo*, and a maintenance crew only retained.[134]

Captain Davis returned to his post as Director of Commonwealth Navigation. By 15 June 1930, his BANZARE commitments had come to an end. On that day, he wrote, 'I have just completed my work in connection with the "Discovery" and feel that I am released from a very thankless task, but such must always be the case in a marine expedition under the leadership of a layman. It will not work.'[135] There may be a hint here by Davis that *he* should have commanded the expedition. Mawson's diary is full of his battles with the master of the *Discovery*. 'I have had no troubles or trials on this expedition, *only Davis*', he wrote on 17 March 1931, and three days later: 'His attitude has always been that he is the virtual leader of the expedition . . . that he is the only one who knows anything about most matters . . .'.[136] The two men did not let these differences ruin their life-long friendship.[137] However, Sir Douglas Mawson considered that much more could have been done and therefore sought Mr MacPherson Robertson's help again. The £6,000 that he promised assured a second BANZARE voyage.

CHAPTER

# TWENTY

## SECOND BANZARE VOYAGE, 1930–1,
## HOMEWARD VOYAGE, EXPEDITION RESULTS

On arrival in Australia I was faced with the serious position of Australia's recent financial troubles, and the change of Government from Liberal to Labour raised difficulties in obtaining continued Government support for our Expedition. As you know, my plans were for two summer cruises. Only in this way could we expect to cover the entire range from 45°E of Greenwich and 90°E of Greenwich. On my arrival in Australia and on discovery that the Australian Government proposed to do nothing further to help the undertaking, I had to get very busy throughout the length and breadth of the country to secure a reversed feeling in this matter. For various reasons Capt. J. K. Davis was not with me in this endeavour, so that the matter was made even more difficult.[1]

MAWSON OUTLINED HIS DIFFICULTIES in a letter written to Dr H. R. Mill from Adelaide in June 1930. It was (and is) not easy to obtain money during an economic recession but the Australian Government sanctioned a second voyage to the Antarctic as early as 22 May 1930 mainly because of Norwegian competition and the importance to Australia of those parts of Antarctica nearest to her. The British Government made the *Discovery* available without charge for a second year and Mawson was reappointed leader. Many British and Australian firms helped the expedition materially and the proceeds from press news and photographs also contributed to the expedition's finances.

Later that year, on the eve of the Imperial Conference, the Australian Liaison Officer in London wrote privately and confidentially to his prime minister stressing the importance of furthering Australian claims in the Antarctic. 'Australia has made a good beginning,' he wrote, 'in the shape of the "Discovery" Expedition, towards the cementing of our claim to the Enderby Land–Ross Sea area, and the work of the "Discovery" in the coming Antarctic summer is likely again to forward our interests;' Norway, in the shape of the *Norvegia* Expedition, was their most formidable competitor.[2]

Captain Davis did not apply to command the *Discovery* for another season, nor did Mawson invite him to do so. Davis wrote from Melbourne on 15 November 1930 to K. N. MacKenzie, formerly first officer, who had been appointed master of the *Discovery* for the second cruise on his recommendation.

It was with very mixed feelings I said Good Bye to you all some months ago, on relinquishing my association with the Expedition, as I could not have wished for a better team of officers and men.

Whatever hesitation I had in recommending you as my successor was due to my knowledge of what a difficult and responsible job you would have as a young man in your first command. Your fitness in every other respect was manifest . . .

Well, the Torch has been handed on to you and you may be sure that it will be with the greatest interest and understanding that I shall follow your fortunes.

While you have some difficult times ahead of you I feel confident that loyally assisted by those with you they will be successfully overcome. You know my views, do what you believe to be right and trust your own judgement.

I was very much touched by your letter and thank you for it, as I am still very much interested in you all and do not forget you never let me down, so I feel that the old ship is in good hands.

God Speed, Good Bye and may Good Fortune attend you all.[3]

Born in Oban on the west coast of Scotland in 1897, the son of a procurator-fiscal, MacKenzie spent his childhood on the island of Tiree. For his secondary education, he went to Kingussie on the Scottish mainland. Here he lived in term time with his uncle, the minister, and became a true son of the manse. The diary that he kept during the BANZARE voyages manifests his great faith in God. Although only sixteen, he volunteered for service on the outbreak of the Great War in 1914 and served as piper, private and lance-corporal, with the Argyll and Sutherland Highlanders. He was invalided out from the trenches of the Somme in 1916 and was honourably discharged as 'permanently unfit' a year later; his health never really recovered. He next qualified as a wireless operator (first class) in the Merchant Navy, but after two years at sea, decided there was no future in this. He then sailed before the mast for five years and eventually gained his Master's ticket in 1929.[4]

There were other changes of personnel. The new mate was A. M. Stanton. 'Lofty' Martin became bosun and Lieut. K. Oom, RAN, replaced Commander Moyes as hydrographic surveyor. Ill-health had caused J. W. S. Marr to return to the United Kingdom. In his stead joined A. L. Kennedy, who had been a magnetician during Mawson's earlier Antarctic expedition. The Sailing Orders issued to Sir Douglas Mawson for the second BANZARE voyage, dated 30 October 1930, were succinct. When the *Discovery* was in all respects ready for sea, she should leave Hobart on 22 November 1930 and proceed to Macquarie Island on a course 'best calculated to provide new scientific information from observations made during the voyage'. A course should then be set to the south, and oceanographic investigations should be made in the neighbourhood of the Balleny Isles and to the north of King George V Land. This work should be carried out until approximately 25 December 1930, when the *Sir James Clark Ross* should be located, from which vessel coal should be taken on. Then the *Discovery* should work steadily westward around the Antarctic continent, making every effort to map its coastline, filling in other details and collecting scientific information of every kind, as time might permit. Operations should be concentrated principally between Adélie Land and Queen Mary Land.

On such lands or islands within the area specified in the preceding paragraphs, you will plant the British flag whenever you find this practicable and in doing so, you will read the proclamation of annexation . . . attach a copy of the proclamation to the flagstaff, and place a second copy of the proclamation in a tin at the foot of the flagstaff. You will keep a record of each such act of annexation . . . During the course of the expedition, you will carry out to the best of your ability all scientific work and investigations which may be practicable . . . within the competence of the scientific staff . . . comprising amongst other things, meteorological and oceanographic observations and investigations concerning fauna, notably whales and seals, of seas and lands visited by you, and all matters connected therewith which may assist in future economic exploration of such fauna . . . On arrival in Australia, you will furnish the Commonwealth Government with a full report . . .

Signed Jno. J. Daly, for the Acting Prime Minister,
30 October 1930[5]

Mawson reported that since the last expedition, the aeroplane and the *Discovery* had both been thoroughly overhauled and the *Discovery*'s scientific equipment, wireless and cameras modified and improved. He announced their intention to complete the survey, begun by the 1911–14 expedition, of the land due south of Australia after calling at Macquarie Island, by then a sanctuary for sub-Antarctic life. The earlier expedition's winter quarters in Adélie Land would be visited and the coastline (first reported by Balleny in 1839 and then by the American, Admiral Wilkes, a year later, running 800 miles west to Queen Mary Land) and Queen Mary Land itself would be surveyed and explored as thoroughly as coal and ice would allow.[6]

On a brilliantly fine day and watched by Lady Mawson, and many hundreds of spectators, the *Discovery* cast off from the Queen's Pier, Hobart, on Saturday 22 November 1930, flying the white flag at her foremast. In addition to the stores and fuel she brought from Melbourne, a further 73 tons of coal, over one thousand pounds of meat (some in barrels), 20 sheep (penned on the roof of the main winch-house), 650 dozen eggs, 6 tons of potatoes, a ton of sheep fodder, half a ton of onions, half a ton of other vegetables, 6 cases of lemons, 20 cases of oranges, 36 cases of apples, as well as butter, tinned fruit and fresh water had been loaded. Well down in the water, the ship was drawing 17 feet forward and 19 feet at the stern. Her large deck cargo consisted chiefly of coal briquettes from Cardiff. A telegram of good wishes was received from Rear Admiral E. R. G. R. Evans of the *Broke*, who had sailed and sledged with Scott. A portable gramophone and records had been presented. Mawson was said to have been busy dictating letters to two typists at the Tasmanian Museum, half an hour before their departure. He admitted to the reporter from the *Hobart Mercury*, from whom these details come, that he was very tired and would welcome a few days' rest. Mawson deeply appreciated the help and hospitality that had been generously given in Tasmania, as had Sir James Clark Ross a century earlier. While Hurley filmed and as 'the historic little vessel drew away with three short blasts from her syren, bedecked with streamers, the crowd gave three cheers. Captain MacKenzie from his bridge led the reply. Coo-ees from some of the Australian members of the expedition, who had climbed the rigging of the mainmast, brought an immediate and delighted response from the crowds on the wharf.' From the bows, in sports jacket and cap, Sir Douglas called for 'a final hurrah' from the ship's company for the people of Hobart.

Mawson expected to return to Australia in April 1931, but in case the ship were forced to winter in the south, sledges, skis, tents and special woollen clothing were taken.[7] The first of a series of marine stations from the Australian continental shelf to the coastal waters of the Antarctic was worked on 23 November. A northerly gale sent the *Discovery* at a decent speed through the seas south of Tasmania and a course was set to enable the western margin of Mill Rise, a large underwater shoal, to be delineated by the echo-sounder. Abundant marine life was hauled from the depth (to 2,000 metres) during the second station on 25 November. 'Though our progress is gratifying', reported Mawson on 10 December 1930, 'the ship's motion is downright aggravating . . . we have become exasperated participants in sea-going rodeo. To be bucked from one's bunk, to say nothing of the capering of viands on the table at meals, or the incessant swamping of sea-boots on submerged decks—these are but a few of the caprices of the playful "Roaring Forties".' The scientific staff, most of them retained from the previous year's expedition, were experienced, and happily helped and worked with the sailors whatever the job, emulating Drake's famous dictum: 'I must have the gentleman to hale and draw with the mariner, and the mariner with the gentleman.'

On 27 November a chain was put over and run under the keel in an attempt to clear the ship's bottom of weed.[8] A third marine station was successfully conducted in 2,100 fathoms on 29 November 1930 in lat. 52°12′ S. long. 152°26′ E., and that evening the ship sailed over a volcanic ridge only fourteen miles wide rising to more than 6,000 feet above the generally uniform sea floor. The temperature of the sea water dropped suddenly the next day and the first iceberg was sighted in lat. 53°23′ S. More were sighted on 1 December, an unusual occurrence so far to the north. In the afternoon, Macquarie Island appeared close at hand through the fog. The *Discovery* anchored in Buckles Bay.[9]

Three members of BANZARE, Mawson, Hurley and Kennedy, were no strangers to the long, green and treeless island. They had called there nearly twenty years earlier during the Australasian Antarctic Expedition. As one of the three areas of operation during that expedition, a scientific and meteorological station, equipped with wireless, had been established there in December 1911 and was maintained until 1915.[10] Mawson had taken a conspicuous part in the campaign to make the island a sanctuary for the penguins, sea elephants and other wildlife, but it was not until 17 May 1933 that it was officially proclaimed a sanctuary with respect to animals and birds generally, by the Lieutenant-Governor of Tasmania, which it has remained ever since. Grenfell Price has published Mawson's diary fragment describing the BANZARE visit of December 1930[11] and there is an interesting account taken from Simmers's diary in Dr Cumpston's history of the island.[12] Mawson comments in his press report from Macquarie Island of 12 December 1930 on the island's ignoble past as a station for the boiling down of penguins and sea elephants for oil, and on the evident but gradual recovery of those animals since the industry had ceased there. He noted the decay of the factory and ironically that 'Penguins now haunt its ruins and sea elephants snore away peacefully amid the perished oil barrels.'

The penguins, filmed by Hurley, Campbell and Douglas, were the stars of the island and were 'evidently anxious to have their say in the "talkies".' Meanwhile Ingram and Fletcher collected life from the island's inland lakes, and alpine plants. Specimens of rare birds were taken and magnetic observations made. The twelve men ashore slept in four tents, badly because of the gale and the noisy activities of the sea elephants. One sea elephant 'tried to enter a tent but found the occupants over hostile'; Mawson's diary makes it clear that it had been diverted there on purpose in order to persuade the laggardly occupants to rise. The old huts and former wireless station were derelict and the shore party returned to the *Discovery* that evening. The ship then continued to Lusitania Bay, a stronghold of the King penguin, where another landing was made. Mawson's report continued:

It was obvious that the landing would be an exciting one, for a considerable swell was running and was breaking in white foam over the reefs and surging through the kelp, thrashing menacingly the 60-foot tentacle-like thongs of this giant subantarctic growth. It needed some deftness in handling the boat to prevent an entanglement with a propeller. All were relieved when, eventually, they were borne thrillingly on to the beach.

Among several millions of subjects at Macquarie, the King Penguin is every inch a king. Standing about 31 inches in height, these splendid birds are the most handsome of the penguin species . . . They enjoy promenading along the sea-front, or strutting about the neighbourhood of their homes in long single files, heads erect, and chests swelling, proud as the ostentatious walk-past of a crack regiment. The queens are sitting, or rather standing, incubating eggs. One egg only is laid, and is kept pressed by the upper sides of the feet in a small feather pouch just above them. The birds make no nest, which leaves them free to move about, clinging to the egg, in a slow, awkward shuffle. The bird may be lifted without releasing the egg. It is gratifying to record that the population has increased since the island was proclaimed a sanctuary, the King Penguin population amounting to about 4000. In this portion of the island, rabbits brought to the island years ago by sealers, have become very abundant, but may eventually prove a serious menace.

The Bishop and Clerk Rocks to the south of Macquarie Island had been closely observed and soundings made on 5 December 1930, the day the expedition departed. This was a hazardous matter in fitful fog and uncharted waters. Captain MacKenzie's diary reveals that they were at one point, in 18 fathoms, obliged to go astern. He got little sleep because of the difficult navigating conditions. 'It is only four days since my last entry—and yet it seems like four weeks—four long days and four longer nights. I have not had my clothes off since leaving Macquarie and my bed has been undisturbed for three nights—fitful snatches of restless sleep on my settee.' He was, as Davis had been before him, suffering from the strain, and had to use all his experience to find a way through the icebergs and rocks.

... The position was a nasty one and I realized that somehow I was in a tight corner with no clear way out. Ice showed up ahead and the sound of breakers seemed to be all round. To get out the boats would only cause panic and in any case no launching could ever be made in those breakers. I stopped and waited and hoped that the fog might lift, but it only came in thicker and the sudden swell, causing us to roll heavily, indicated that I was clear of the lee of either the rock or a big berg. So I slowly made S.E. and suddenly got into 50 fms. and then into deeper water, but kept on this course at slow for three hours—and then got on to our direct track of S.S.E. At 3 pm the fog cleared right up and revealed the Bishop and four gigantic bergs aground to the west—those being responsible for the fog. The 2/O [Second Officer W. R. Colbeck] got a fix and running back, we worked out with a previous alt.[itude] the approximate position of the Island and found, as I had guessed, that it lay 1½ miles south and at least ½ mile east of where charted. Anyway I at the time cared little for I knew only too well how easily we might have been lost and how truly wonderful had been our deliverance.

For some days after this, the *Discovery* laboured in a gale through heavy seas, among many icebergs, with flooded decks, chaotic cabins and rolling frantically. On 6 December all sails were taken in except staysails, 'for the topgallant masts were bending to a nasty angle, and the stays singing like harp strings'.[13] By 8 December, wind and sea had moderated enough for the scientists to continue skinning or pickling the specimens from Macquarie Island and for the captain to undress for a night's sleep. On 13 December the remaining sheep were killed and hung in the rigging to freeze.

Mawson had arranged to bunker from a whaler when approaching the Antarctic in order to make up for the *Discovery*'s limited coal capacity, which had so cut short the exploring season of 1929–30. He was exasperated to find (since his objective was westward) that the *Sir James Clark Ross* was not near the Balleny Islands (to the SSE of Macquarie Island) where a rendezvous had been anticipated, but four days' steaming further east, near Scott Island at the entrance to the Ross Sea. She had moved east with her catchers in search of whales. The ships eventually met on 15 December 1930, the whaler's altered position costing the expedition sixty tons of coal and ten days extra time.[14] Named after the British naval officer who had discovered the Ross Sea and had observed many whales there in the early 1840s, the *Sir James Clark Ross* (built on Tees-side by the Furness Shipbuilding Company in 1930) was the second Norwegian whale factory ship of the name. Her predecessor (formerly the ex-Brocklebank cargo liner *Mahronda*) had pioneered whaling in the Ross Sea. The vessel from which the *Discovery* was to coal was on her maiden voyage, the first large factory ship to be diesel propelled and the pride of Johan Rasmussen's whaling fleet at Sandefjord, south of Oslo.[15]

With a dead whale between them as a fender, it was truly a meeting of old and new, the *Discovery* now effectively devoted to the conservation of the whale while the great factory ship represented the latest development in whaling on the high seas. While the coal was being transferred, MacKenzie and Mawson were entertained on board the *Sir James Ross Clark* by her master, Captain Nilsen, who showed them round 'his great factory, another of man's present day feats of ingenuity—wonderful, marvellous, beyond description . . . The captain's cabin was similar to the suite of a New York hotel . . .'[16] They lunched well with Nilsen and hugely enjoyed the unexpected luxury of a hot bath. One hundred tons of coal were taken on board in five hours (some bags had to be stowed on deck) and twenty-five tons of fresh water were pumped into the tanks. 'It was a hard day for some of the men who worked straight through from 4 a.m. to 8 p.m. thoroughly earning their double issue of whisky.'[17] All hands were allowed to climb up the rope ladder afterwards to visit the giant alongside. One of the scientists, Harold Fletcher, described what he saw.

My first view of the flensing deck, the ship's centre of activity, left me bewildered by its scene of carnage. It was running boot deep in blood and grease, the scuppers spouting continual streams of blood and filth into the sea. Men working like demons were removing blubber in long strips from a large blue whale, which shortly before my appearance had been winched up the slipway or ramp at the ship's stern to its present position. Two other carcasses being similarly treated were already in the late stages of disintegration.

Cranes on an overhead gantry assisted flensers by lifting strips of 15-centimetre-thick blubber, slowly rolling them back, while flensers, with their razor-sharp, long-handled knives, cut the blubber from the flesh. The resulting long strips were then cut into chunks as the crane lowered them to the deck. Stripped of its blubber, men waded knee deep among the one and a half tonnes of bulging intestines and removed the meat. Finally, buzzing steam saws cut the bones of the remaining skeleton into small sections.

Blubber, meat and bones were continually being dragged by other workers over the blood-covered deck and thrown down their respective chutes to the factory below decks. Blubber went to the steam boilers where the oil was extracted; meat went to a refrigerating plant for cutting, dehydrating and canning, and crushing

267

machines converted bones into fertiliser. The intestines, having no value, were thrown overboard, providing an endless supply of food for birds and killer whales. Work continued in 24-hour shifts each day when whales were plentiful.

The products obtained from a blue whale about 27 metres long were: 26 tonnes of blubber, which would yield about 13 tonnes of oil; 57 tonnes of meat and 22 tonnes of fertiliser. It took just over an hour to process a whale.

Proceeding below decks I inspected the factory working at full pressure and creating an incredible confusion of deafening noises. An interesting interlude was a visit to the ship's piggery where 20 well-fed pigs looked the picture of contentment and good health. I stayed there for some time as the pigsty smell was heavenly in comparison with the pervading stench of whale.[18]

Simmers wrote in his diary:

The whale starts its brief one-hour life on the factory ship by being dragged up through the stern skidway, which leads through an opening 18 feet wide by 13 feet deep up on to the main or cleansing deck. The whales are dragged up slowly by about 2"–3" steel hawsers and to lubricate the skidway water is sprayed on the boards the friction of the great monster causing it to rise in clouds of steam . . . As the whale slowly proceeds tail first up the slope, the first batch of flensers are on its back and walking rapidly to the head making as they go clean cuts through the blubber, laying the body clear from tail to head. These flensing knives must be exceptionally keen, as a flenser walks along unhesitatingly anything up to 80 feet, cutting the whole way. By the time the monster is on the huge open after deck it is criss-crossed with cuts and almost before it is stopped the winches are hooked on and are tearing off long strips of blubber. On this deck all the blubber is stripped and in a few minutes he ceases to be a whale. This blubber is rapidly cut into square chunks about 18" square and lifted with hand hooks into the mouths of the digesters which line the deck along both sides. Once the blubber is clear the harpoon is freed and the huge carcass is dragged bodily on to the fore part of this deck. The head is detached and goes to the left, half the body to the right and the tail and entrails right forward. This part of the whale is all meat and bone, and to cut it up it is lifted in long strips on derricks and cut into small chunks as it hangs down. To make the bony parts small enough, they are cut up by long automatic saws which are very flexible and which can cut even when the blade is bent. This deck is even bloodier than the blubber deck and the men need their long iron heel spikes to prevent slipping—a danger with so many keen knives about. These knives are so keen that they can cut up the tail with them—not using the saw.

In 45 minutes the whale carcass is disposed of and the next is on its way and nowhere is there any sign of bustle, each man going methodically about his own job. What struck me as much as anything was the great use made of winches. All round are wires, hooks and leads and they have become most adept at moving large chunks about in short time.

On the factory deck there is little to see, the whole place being filled with these large digesters. In the after areas the blubber is pure and the oil is run straight into tanks, while in the forward ones the oil, which is extracted from the meat and bone, is run off to centrifuges, where it is purified. An endless belt carries away the residue of bone and meat, carrying it in a slow stream over the side.

What is interesting is the maze of pipes there being without exaggeration scores of miles of them. All the time they are adding new ones as required or found convenient and the engineers think nothing of running a few hundred feet of new.

. . . But think of the decimation of these huge mammals. A big blue weighs up to 100 tons, is upwards of 100 ft. long and is all disposed of in 45 minutes. Humpbacks and fin whales which are smaller scale only about half as much. A humpback was alongside and it was interesting to see him—white underneath with white flippers on which are huge gnarled bumps. The blue whales are smooth and dark on the back, with dark bellies seamed with rubberlike longitudinal grooves.

Simmers wrote of his visit that it was one of the highlights of interest in the last eighteen months of new experiences.[19] Mawson also found the ship a revelation. He ascertained that she would hold 20,000 tons of whale oil when fully loaded. Four whales could be flensed simultaneously, but two at a time was more usual, after being pulled up from the stern in a great channel (the stern slipway) by winches on overhead gantries. One of the winches had been pulled clean out and broken, while lifting a large whale up the slipway during a heavy swell. Captain Nilsen had tea on board the *Discovery* and gave Sir Douglas two bottles of Swedish punch on parting. A case of brandy and one of 'Discovery' port were presented to him.[20] The factory ship gave the expedition some whale meat and liver, which were not popular eating, according to Fletcher.

The swell had steadily increased during the day, causing the *Discovery* to snap free of her mooring wire and to bump heavily against the side of the *Sir James Clark Ross*. MacKenzie had to order everyone back on board and cast off at 7.30 p.m. Carpenter Williams, still shell-shocked from the war, was left on the factory ship to return home. One of the airmen, Flt. Lieut. Douglas, was accidentally left aboard too. Child sculled over from where the *Discovery* lay, some two miles off, in a rising sea to fetch him, only to find that he had departed in a whale catcher with Hurley. The photographer had been detailed by Mawson to film operations on board the whale catcher (or 'chaser'). This unauthorised second trip delayed the expedition for 24 hours and the culprits received a severe reprimand from Sir Douglas on climbing aboard from the chaser *Star X* at 8 p.m. the next day. The captain told them that they would next time be left to their fates, whether on board a whaler or on an ice floe. A full vertical station (No. 85) was carried out while waiting for Hurley. Falla, the BANZARE ornithologist, shot a number of bird specimens from the dinghy.[21] Mawson sent letters by the *Sir James Clark Ross*, including one dated 15 December headed 'Antarctic Circle. Entrance Ross Sea', to the Secretary of the Royal Geographical Society, A. R. Hinks. He remarked in this letter how splendidly Captain MacKenzie was doing 'in charge of crew and navigation and a great improvement on our old friend J. K. Davis whose good seamanship is discounted by his morose and quarrelsome temperament'.[22] Martin remarked early in this voyage that things were going 'fairly smoothly between the two heads, I think'. The remainder of his diary makes no reference to quarrels between Mawson and MacKenzie.[23]

The ship at last got under way with topsail set and fore and aft hoisting. The ensign was dipped to bid farewell to the hardy Norsemen and a course set westward with a fair wind for Adélie Land.[24] Mawson described their passage in sunshine through

a crystal sea of bobbing ice . . . broken by wave action into countless fanciful forms . . . A chill wind is blowing, but the thermometers seem more susceptible to the fall in the temperature than ourselves. We scarcely heed the meteorologist's warning that the temperature on deck is 25 degrees (that is, seven below zero); likewise, the knowledge that the temperature in our cabins and wardroom lurks at a wintry 32 'leaves us cold'. It only promotes sleep and stimulates appetite. Frost appears to have quickened the growth of our beards and whiskers, and most members are exhibiting fine forward crops.[25]

The cold weather may have rendered attention to personal hygiene less conscientious on board. Martin found the mate dropping hints to him about washing. 'I wash my face every second night and my hands every night,' he protested to his diary. 'His own ears are none too clean!'[26]

A subsequent press report (22 December 1930) expressed Mawson's belief that this was an abnormally heavy year for ice, the indications being 'that the pack hereabouts extends at least over a million square miles more ocean than normally'. One hundred and eleven 'majestic bergs, sculptured in every variety of form' had been counted from the foretop the day before. Navigation for several days was made difficult by thick mist, snow and gales. A good run of 142 miles was made nevertheless, as the ice cleared the ship of her barnacles.

The airmen began assembling the Moth sea-plane on 21 December, but the weather stopped this, and instead, sledge harnesses were made under Hurley's instruction, for use after landing in Commonwealth Bay. By 23 December, attempts to reach the Balleny Islands had to be abandoned, owing to the ice. In lat. 64°15′S. long. 154°45′E., krill was taken in the nets, while four Blue and three Fin whales were seen. The last of the deck coal was struck down.[27] Christmas Day 1930 was celebrated at Divine Service, conducted by the captain in the mess at 11 a.m., when all crew except those on watch were present and the engineer's band 'excelled itself in the rendering of sacred and other music'.[28] Gifts were distributed and an excellent dinner enjoyed in festive surroundings.[29] Radiograms, parcels and letters from family, friends, schoolchildren and the Royal

Geographical Society of South Australia, were opened with great pleasure. The steering gear of the *Discovery* was overhauled and the chains set taut on Boxing Day. That same day in lat. 65°17' S. long. 147°32' E., a resolute attempt was made to break through to the south, but next morning, in heavy floes and dense icefields, they could get no heading at all.[30] To make matters worse, the compasses had become erratic and almost useless, a faint sun and wind being the only guide. The occasional Emperor and more numerous Adélie penguins, plus Crabeater seals, were to be seen on the ice floes.[31] By 28 December better progress towards the west was being made, but thick ice (north of that found by the *Aurora*, 1911–14) prevented the ship from getting much further south than 64°57' on the 145th meridian of longitude. That day several whales were observed, including a stinking carcass on which multitudes of birds were feeding, which indicated the presence of whalers.[32]

The wireless officer (A. J. Williams) located a whaler, which proved to be the *Kosmos* of Sandefjord. Captain Andraesen kindly offered the expedition the remaining fifty tons of loose coal carried south to refuel the *Norvegia* during her fourth Antarctic voyage (a circumnavigation) of 1930–1.[33] Mawson went on board the *Kosmos* next day (29 December 1930) at 11 a.m. and accepted the offer. This 'gigantic whaling motor ship, with a total capacity of 22,000 tons', reported Mawson,[34] was similar to and slightly larger than the *Sir James Clark Ross*. She had nine auxiliary chasers, which had already secured 'a fabulously valuable cargo' that season. The *Discovery* found herself 'suddenly amongst a fleet of ships and a hive of industry'. By 4 p.m. the yards were cockbilled, the sides cleared, the port boats hoisted in starboard davits, the plane covered and the ship ready to take coal on board by chute. Captain MacKenzie had secured her alongside the *Kosmos*, while both vessels were steaming very slowly into the long ocean swell with a couple of whales lashed between them as efficient fenders. The *Discovery* was however slightly damaged above the water-line on the port side in securing. Captain MacKenzie was heard to remark at the end of the operation that 'he wouldn't go alongside a 20,000 tonner again in such a swell for 50 tons of gold, let alone coal'.[35]

The *Kosmos* had a capacity of 200,000 barrels of oil and had recently created a record for a day's work, in flensing and rendering down forty-eight whales.[36] Captain MacKenzie and Sir Douglas Mawson were given a good dinner by the captain and officers of the *Kosmos*, who drank to the expedition's success. On board they also met the Norwegian Government Inspector, Captain Dingsør of the Royal Norwegian Navy, who was responsible for seeing that the whole carcass of the whale was used. Coaling was completed by 8 p.m. and after being given some whale meat and fresh water, the *Discovery* lay off to hoist her boats. By this time, the oil tanker *C. G. Brøvig* (14,000 tons) had hove in sight and was standing by to take on board 60,000 barrels of oil, the catch to date, and proceed direct to New York.[37] The *Discovery* got under way at 9.45 p.m., continuing her course to the south, passing at midnight one of the whale catchers with four whales in tow, yet apparently still steaming at over ten knots. The end of the day also saw the Moth sea-plane 'on the skids, completely assembled and ready for flying'.[38]

South-easterly gales, force 8 to 10, plagued the *Discovery* in heavy ice off Adélie Land, between 30 December 1930 and 3 January 1931. In his diary Captain MacKenzie recorded the events of a New Year's Eve he would never forget.

. . . At 2 am the call came. The 2nd Officer found that the increasing gale had caused a heavy swell in the close pack in which we lay—the movements of the heavy floes were becoming dangerous. So we got out and made before the wind through the inner drifting ice, hoping to find more shelter. . . .

I cleared the acre of bergs and finding the pack close to, made to clear it. But the wind had increased to force 11 and without the shelter of the berg area, we could do nothing. Before I knew it we were blown into the wild storm tossed pack—great hard round pieces of ice and in a moment we were broadside on and well into it, pieces as big as the ship and some higher than our bridge, with a dense mass of very hard blue ice in between. The heavy sea dashing all together and the swell causing us to lift and roll over hard down on the hard ice. A terrible jumbling warring mass and our little ship like a piece of drift wood. Everyone rushed on deck, everyone thought that we'd be crushed and smashed in five minutes, and I thought of our rudder and propeller, and just wondered how long it would all last. In we went broadside on and as we got in, the ice got bigger—great flat pieces as big as a floating dock, and all pressed as tight as the gale and sea could make.

I immediately sent word below to stop whenever a hit was felt on the shafting—the 3/O [Third Officer J. B. Child] aft to uncover rudder trunk and report position continuously—word being passed by string of the scientific party stationed along the deck. 2/O [Second Officer W. R. Colbeck] on forecastle head to report on ice under stem and all got in readiness for whatever might happen. The time was then 10 am and I hadn't been off the bridge since 2 o'clock. Each hour grew more serious and more full of anxiety. We bumped and bumped, rolled and smashed, crashed into ice that looked like rock—indeed it just might have been floating rock. It was just as hard and our timbers groaned and strained and still the smashing went on and on, as we were drawn into heavier and heavier pack. But . . . we were still afloat and the distance slowly increasing between us and the fierce pack edge.

All again turned to smile, for the little ship had withstood a test which must have sunk any other vessel . . . when suddenly a cry and someone pointed to a great white line in the air just astern. We could not make out what it was, till its slow approach became evident—a great iceberg closing down on top of us, the white line being the berg smoke or snow drift flying from its top . . . I called all hands and even in the teeth of the blizzard ordered them aloft to set sail—for we must get out. Up they went. God how they fought . . . the sheets manned, and away the topsails blew—I thought they'd go altogether—staysails, storm spanker . . . tackles tight . . . on all gear. All hands keep handy. We watched the monster draw closer—closer and watched our ship drive hard against the great ice flow—now we edged a way through this, working engines and rudder whenever possible. It was a great fight and one I felt many doubts about. At 1 pm we had got through and were again in open water. Saved, saved by God's hand saved!

. . . while avoiding a berg, we got caught between an eddy off one corner of it and the pack swept round and rapidly began to close in ahead of us . . . Suddenly we found ourselves between two oncoming streams, which swept round the big berg and in less than five minutes, we were surrounded by heavy pressure ice closing in fast against it. Great big sharp pieces and heavy irregular shaped and massive flows hurled their mighty weight against us. I thought—then surely this is the end now . . .? I wondered why we'd been spared and not taken this morning. God oh God help us now, for we need Thy aid I prayed. Again sail was set and again I took fresh courage, and thought that God would ever more see us through. But it was terrible and I just dug my nails into my glove and snapped out orders to everyone and everyone jumped to obey. Some I cursed and some I damned, but they all did wonders and by 11 o'clock we were again clear and again into open water.[39]

MacKenzie came off the bridge and remained in his heavy wet and frozen clothes till 8 in the morning when, after 30 hours of intense stress, he fell fast asleep and did not wake up till lunch on New Year's Day 1931.

Martin described New Year's Eve 1930 as 'a beauty'. During the previous night, those asleep below deck were 'wakened several times by the most fearful crashes, as the ship was driven almost out of control on to various big pieces of ice. She shook and shuddered. I feel sure any ordinary ship and most whaling ships would have been broken up.'[40] The log (quoted by Grenfell Price) recorded this fight with the elements both concisely and soberly. In contrast, Mawson's press release of 5 January 1931 was even more dramatic than the master's personal diary. He stressed that the pack was of no ordinary nature and that these 'conquering ice warriors' were the size of Atlantic icebergs, 'evil in intent'. The gale continued and great care had to be taken to avoid damage to rudder and propeller, when the *Discovery* became once more enclosed in broad, heavy ice. The propeller struck three times, once so violently that all hands were woken, including Sir Douglas, who came up on deck in his pyjamas, exclaiming 'Has the propeller gone?' MacKenzie did not answer, but went below to interview the second engineer and returned, thankful for the excellent make of its two blades. The captain had then been in his clothes for eighty hours and recorded in his diary that he was finding the responsibility heavier than he had ever thought it could be.[41] To the scientific staff he seemed a different person from the man they knew on the first voyage 'even allowing for necessary restraints because of his increased status'.[42] He rarely spoke to them and appeared worried and withdrawn. MacKenzie was conscious of the gulf that existed between their position and his own. Their sometimes boyish high spirits contrasted with his increasing solemnity and his heavy responsibility; they were free as a rule to curl up in their bunks during the storms and hurricanes, while he and his officers faced the elements on deck.

Twenty years earlier, Mawson had established winter quarters in this particularly windswept area of East or Greater Antarctica (the 'home of the blizzard'), while leader of the Australasian Antarctic Expedition. Captain J. K. Davis was then master of the *Aurora* and second-in-command of the expedition that discovered, explored and named King George V Land and Queen Mary Land. The main party (under Mawson) had wintered at Cape Denison, Commonweath Bay, an area that Mawson then called part of Adélie Land.[43] This is now in Australian Antarctic Territory. The other shore station had been situated over one thousand miles to the west, on the Shackleton Ice Shelf in Queen Mary Land. This purely scientific expedition made the first land explorations in the great span of Antarctica between Cape Adare, lying to the south of New Zealand, and Gaussberg (discovered by Drygalski in the *Gauss*), lying south of the Indian Ocean.[44] A third group spent 23 months on Macquarie Island. A great part had been played by Captain Davis in the *Aurora* whom Mawson had described as 'lion-hearted'.[45]

The *Discovery* was able to anchor off Cape Denison in King George V Land on 4 January 1931 after having real difficulty in finding good holding ground in the force 9 to 10 gale. On approaching Commonwealth Bay, MacKenzie had asked Sir Douglas to help with his local knowledge. However, looking round with the binoculars, Mawson declared MacKenzie to be 'running into some terrible place . . . nowhere near our old base', and told the captain the only course was to 'steam out to sea and get a longitude'. At this, MacKenzie, unable to contain himself, asked him to leave the bridge. He had himself obtained a fix ascertaining their position only the day before and carried on. Sir Douglas went off, but returned to ask MacKenzie to put about, fearing the ship would be lost. Again the captain refused and at 7 a.m. 'was rewarded by sighting the rocky patch on our port bow'. The wind by then had increased again to force 9. Icy spray from the wave tips of a fiercely running short sea lashed the *Discovery*, so that she became thickly coated in ice, adding much extra weight to an already heavy ship. She just made a half to one knot, the chief engineer (Griggs) having nobly got the engines turning at 90 revolutions (the normal being 66).[46]

The port anchor was eventually dropped in 13 fathoms and 80 fathoms of cable payed out. Precautions were taken in case icebergs drifted towards the vessel, making it necessary to let go. Mawson's old huts could be seen, but there was no possibility of launching the boat in such a sea. Everyone was itching to go ashore, wrote Simmers, and all the old hands were picking out familiar landmarks with their binoculars. Despite the gale, he managed a balloon flight, which revealed an almost flat calm at 500 feet, 'quite a significant discovery', he reckoned.[47] It blew all night, while the *Discovery* strained at her cable and even with a hand at the wheel, 'shoved about in a nasty and dangerous manner'.[48]

By mid-morning on 5 January, a brilliant sun shone in a cloudless sky. The scientific party left in the launch for the shore followed later by MacKenzie and Child. On a similarly rare fine day in January 1912, a boat from the *Aurora* had landed Mawson and members of the Australasian Antarctic Expedition from the land-locked miniature harbour just discovered onto a 'charming ice quay', making them the first to set foot on the Antarctic continent between Cape Adare and Gaussberg, a distance of about two thousand miles.[49] Frank Hurley had been official photographer at the main base and A. L. Kennedy magnetician at the Queen Mary Land Station from 1912 to 1913 during this first expedition led by Mawson. Cape Denison and its huts held memories for all three of them, but particularly for Sir Douglas, who had struggled back there in January and February 1913, with his cut-down sledge, after the deaths of his two companions during a lengthy sledging journey across King George V Land, one of the epics of polar exploration. It was here a year later that Mawson and his wintering party had watched the *Aurora* arrive to take them home; thinking that the boat would come ashore later in better weather, they had turned in for a short rest after being up all night. Just as they were dozing off, in came Captain Davis, 'breezy, buoyant, brave and true', as Mawson described him, his 'cheery familiar voice' singing through the hut and rousing the sleepers.[50]

Before the hut was abandoned on 23 December 1913, the windows had been battened down, the chimney stuffed with bagging and the verandah entrance boarded up. On the table inside, Mawson had left a message inviting anyone who followed to make full use of the hut and indicating whence the *Aurora* was bound in case of disaster. Nearly twenty years later, this message was still there and everything was just as it had been left including chocolate (greatly enjoyed by the BANZARE men) and a tin of tobacco, which Mawson was said to have smoked with great relish.[51] Because snow and ice were banked against the walls, entry had to be forced through a skylight in the roof, where a silver spoon from the 1911 expedition was wedged. This was taken by Sir Douglas as a souvenir. The violent winds had eroded some of the exposed timbers more than half an inch.[52] Simmers described how all the wood was deeply grooved with weird knots and hard grains standing as much as an inch above the surface of the softer eroded portions.[53] Among the various items removed from the old base was a sledge which must have been Mawson's well-known 'half sledge', 'no doubt a relic of interest', observed MacKenzie, 'in the Australian National Museum in days to come'.[54]

The few lines that Mawson devoted to describe his return to the old living hut are very matter-of-fact.[55] MacKenzie wrote of it with more emotion:

The hut was filled with snow and ice and not till after much labour was a passage forced and entrance made through the roof to the four snow free spaces—but the food and gear all stood just as they had been left 17 years ago and it was with a feeling of nervousness and awe that we explored and handled the few articles that were not definitely and firmly sealed in ice. Books, bottles and beds, cases, clothing, cans all ice bound and from the beams and spars hung the most wonderful and most picturesque ice crystals and sparkling shapely icicles.

Kennedy made observations over a period of 18 hours in the old magnetic hut (last occupied by 'Azi', Eric Webb, once the ice inside had been hacked out. These showed that 'the south magnetic pole had, in the interval, steadily moved to the north-west and was now probably not more than 250 miles distant from Cape Denison.[56] Variation was also determined. This work was of the greatest interest to MacKenzie as a mariner, the compass being erratic and unreliable in this area, owing to its relative closeness to the magnetic pole. He enjoyed a day off on 5 January watching the scientists at work and occasionally singing out to hurry the men who were icing ship.

At noon that day a Proclamation was read by Sir Douglas Mawson. This had been done during the earlier expedition, but was repeated on this more official occasion. The flag was hoisted by Captain MacKenzie with great pride and a sense of honour as he remembered their struggles to get there. He also witnessed Mawson's signature.[57] References to the site of Mawson's old winter quarters would have to change in future. From that day, by the act of proclamation, the whole area around Commonwealth Bay was included in George V Land, whose boundary with Adélie Land was designated as 142°E. The spot became well and truly red on the map, as Simmers had given his thumb a bad gash with a knife.[58]

The National Anthem was sung after the ceremony of proclamation by the small group of expedition members whose voices to Hurley sounded 'strange and puny in the great spaces of these solitudes'. One arm of the cross that had been erected by Mawson in 1913 to the memory of his lost companions had been broken off by the extremely high winds.[59] Mawson and some of the scientists spent a sleepless night ashore in tents, finding the reindeer-skin sleeping bags much too small. 'Getting Dux [Mawson] out of his bag was I believe reminiscent of skinning a rabbit', wrote Simmers, with his talent for the *mot juste*. In a more serious vein, he summarised the considerable amount of work done at Commonwealth Bay during two still warm days there.[60]

The *Discovery* got under way in the early evening of 6 January after a second calm, warm day off Cape Denison. Proceeding westward along the coast of Adélie Land, the positions of several capes were found to be in error to the tune of several miles. Station No. 89 was carried out and good catches taken with the dredge. In the evening of 7 January, the sea-plane reconnoitred the extensive area of pack-ice off the coast. New land was later seen extending west from Cape Bickerton towards the eastern extremity of that sighted in the *Aurora* in 1912 (named Wilkes Land by Mawson, in honour of the commander of the United States Exploring Expedition 1838–42). The great ice tongue reported by Wilkes and the French explorer Dumont d'Urville in 1840 some ninety years previously was no longer there. Mawson concluded that the 'Clarie Land' seen by d'Urville and Wilkes 'was evidently an immense iceberg aground on the outer end of the shoal'.[61] The pack-ice forced the *Discovery* to push her way north for the whole of 8 January, a day warm enough for Nigger's four kittens to play on deck. Once on the outer edge of the pack, it was possible to progress westward again, making the extraordinary speed of nine knots and running before a strong breeze 'with square sails like drumming balloons and every string singing a different tune'.[62] A 'sound cine' concert of the voyage was given by Hurley and party on 13 January. The same day the *Discovery*'s dolphin striker (below the bowsprit) was found to be badly bent, the result of the force 10 winds and towering seas. This was unshipped on the 15th for repair by Hurley, at the forge rigged forward of the bridge.[63]

Flights were made on 15 and 16 January to 8,000 feet and on 18 January to 3,000 feet in low cloud, when 'Banzare Land' (now Banzare Coast) was sighted about a hundred miles from the ship and named after the expedition. The land reported by the sealer Balleny in 1830 may also have been sighted at this time. It was named Sabrina Land (now Coast) after his ship. The edge of the dense pack itself, 'for all the world like a solid shore with its bays and promontories and small loose tongues like reefs',[64] prevented the *Discovery* even attempting to reach the channel of ice-free water along the coast.[65] The sea-plane was badly shaken and its wing tips torn and bent, while being hoisted on board in the prevailing swell on 15 January. The ship's rudder received a couple of heavy blows in the pack, causing MacKenzie considerable anxiety.[66]

Scientific work continued and on 21 January, Falla captured a black-breasted Adélie penguin. Bagging this curiosity of the bird world cannot have equalled the excitement of finding Arctic terns in the Antarctic. Specimens taken from the *Discovery* in January 1931 proved that these small, delicate-looking birds migrate almost from Pole to Pole, covering immense distances on the wing. Simmers reports that they 'passed many terns, 5 of which were shot and safely bagged. Doubt is now cleared regarding their origin, as one in full plumage is undoubtedly the Arctic tern.'[67]

Frequent tests throughout the voyage by A. L. Kennedy with the Geiger Muller Ultra-Gamma radiation apparatus failed to discover any appreciable variation in the concentration of cosmic rays near the South Magnetic Pole. His Geiger-Muller Counter, as it is now called, had only been invented in 1928. Mawson's press release reported that the apparatus was always a source of interest on board. Its 'registering tube' was said to be embedded in a 'very massive block of lead, sufficiently thick to cut off all Röntgen [i.e. X-] rays', but not to deter 'those recently discovered penetrating rays which reach the earth from outer space'. The apparatus had been constructed for the expedition by Professor Kerr Grant. These were early days for such studies and they were probably the first conducted in high southern latitudes. Although cosmic rays had been discovered by Victor Hess in 1912, the subject did not really advance until the mid-1930s. Kennedy's problem must have been caused by the local radioactivity, which would have masked the small increase in cosmic rays since observed on proceeding towards the South Magnetic Pole; his apparatus was just not sophisticated enough.[68]

Oceanographic work also continued and many varieties of fish as well as a multitude of invertebrates were taken from the sea at about 500 fathoms. 'While one of the nets was being hauled in', wrote Mawson in his press report of 26 January 1931, 'two blue whales became interested in the operation. After examining the steel wire of the hauling cable at the stern of the ship, one of the whales followed the cable down towards the net. For a time we contemplated with anxiety the possibility of securing this undesirably large and embarrassing catch, but the monster evidently lost interest before reaching the net.' Bad weather for several days prevented the plane being flown to confirm indications of land to the south, much to everyone's disappointment. Martin's diary of 25 January 1931 recorded his own disappointment at their not making land. 'Last trip, chance seemed to offer quite often', he wrote, 'and we appeared not to accept. This trip, chance is not nearly so free and we have to struggle for every inch.'[69]

No land was found in the charted position of the American explorer Wilkes's 'Budd Land'. In somewhat better weather, Douglas piloted Mawson on 27 January to 6,000 feet in a gallant effort to confirm Wilkes's Knox Land, in which direction what appeared to be undulating land ice was seen. The small sea-plane had only just managed to take off in a smother of foam from the long ocean swell. It was nearly wrecked and sunk while being hoisted aboard at the end of the flight, Sir Douglas being apparently more concerned with saving the plane than himself.[70] MacKenzie had feared that the machine would burst into flames alongside the *Discovery*, for the petrol tank was badly dented and 16 gallons of fuel poured into the sea. Seaman Matheson was afterwards sent in a boat to rescue life-buoys and other gear that had floated from the plane. Two great Blue whales rose on either side and actually soaked him as they spouted, refusing to be frightened while he wildly beat the water with the oars from his cockleshell.[71] By 6 p.m. the *Discovery* was again heading westwards, 'having at least a new landfall to her credit', wrote MacKenzie that night. 'A great day', he called it, 'for which we thank God for his mercies—on we go and still on.'

The ship steamed or sailed along the pack edge westwards in the next few days towards the Shackleton Ice Shelf, discovering a domed and ice-covered offshore island on 28 January 1931. This was named Bowman Island after the director of the American Geographical Society, who had secured £8,500 from the American Press for the expedition.[72] In this region the *Discovery* was traversing completely unknown seas in lat. 64°50′ S., the pack having receded to the south-west. A fierce gale next day drove the ship from this interesting area. Grenfell Price records that MacKenzie again suffered great worries[73] and the captain's account confirms his preoccupations.

... I without doubt or hestitation give Him all praise and credit for allowing me [to] write again and record, so that in future years I may remember how He guided and how my beloved Mother sent messages of assurance, when in the critical times I heard her say 'All is well Ken and I am with you'.

The night of the 28th when the gale was fast gathering its demon-like force, we were some five miles off the main pack, running westerly in water no vessel had ever before sailed and which, keen to take advantage of every new feature, I deemed it prudent to stand off till anyway daylight. At midnight the pack was out of sight and the blink abaft the port beam and still standing off. Child, the 3/O ventured to ask me if I was going to continue so, as we now had a clear water sky from the port beam to away round to Std quarter. 'Yes Mr Child, we will continue so', &

at 1 a.m. I had such an extraordinary sense of some new danger ahead that, without hesitation, I altered course further to the northward. I record this fact, for it is one of the most remarkable experiences of my life and one I will ever remember. No more direct impress from our great Protector could have been made manifest and even the 2/O, although not questioning my orders, repeated the new course with definite surprise. . . . At 4 am, having gone below to rest on settee, the 2/O called me to intimate that some thirty large bergs and closer pack were showing through the snow fury close abeam. I jumped up. Yes, sure enough, there was the old danger and we were on their course just clearing it . . . for had I continued on former course, it would have been into a Cul de sac and one from which, in that gale, our little ship had little chance of ever emerging.[74]

MacKenzie continued to navigate the *Discovery*, at times almost by intuition alone, in fearsome conditions through all the hazards, concerned now not to collide with the factory ship *Nielsen Alonso* which had promised to provide them with more coal. They released gallons of oil to reduce the swell and help them turn, eventually reaching open sea.

The 'Termination Ice Tongue', some sixty miles long and named in 1912 by Captain Davis after Wilkes's supposed 'Termination Land', was found on 30 January 1931 to have broken away from the Shackleton Ice Shelf. About a hundred big grounded bergs remained, which MacKenzie described as 'standing out against the sky line like so many New York sky- scrapers'.[75] The breakup of the protective ice tongue allowed the sea ice into the coast, making landing difficult.

The pack therefore proved very heavy off Queen Mary Land which had been discovered and charted by Mawson's Australasian Antarctic Expedition, 1911–14. The *Discovery* could only approach to within fifty-five miles of the coast, much to the scientists' regret at not being able to visit the old hut of the Western party (supposing it were still standing) and the Emperor penguin rookeries on Masson and Haswell Islands. Although anxious to carry out his instructions to raise the flag on Queen Mary Land, Mawson decided to conserve coal for the exploration of the unknown coast of what was later called Princess Elizabeth Land (which he re-sighted from the air on 9 February 1931) and far eastern Mac.Robertson Land, particularly the MacKenzie Sea, which was discovered during the expedition and named after the master of the *Discovery*.

Grenfell Price covers this period of 1 to 19 February 1931, the expedition's last two weeks in the far south, in some detail, not only describing BANZARE activities, but relating these to Norwegian discoveries and claims in the same area, a somewhat complicated undertaking. As he remarks, 'The presence of a great fleet of British and Norwegian whaling vessels off the Eastern Antarctic shores had important effects on Antarctic discovery and nomenclature.'[76] The captain of the *Falk*, who later came aboard the *Discovery*, told Mawson that 40 factory ships and 240 chasers were operating in the Antarctic during the 1930–1 season. Captain MacKenzie surmised that there must have been at least a dozen factory ships in the area and that 'no more is the Antarctic the lonely deserted place it is supposed to be'.[77] Martin found these vessels made it 'quite like the [English] Channel'.[78] On 6 February, the *Discovery* was able to receive sixteen tons of coal from the SS *Lestris*, a Swedish collier, which had been coaling the SS *Falk* (5,000 tons), a Norwegian factory ship of the older type which flensed whales over the side. The carcass of a Blue whale acted as a fender. Sir Douglas took the opportunity to write home to his wife and observed that the expedition had been disappointing, largely because of bad weather and heavy ice.[79] He also wrote in the same vein to Dr H. R. Mill, although in more detail.[80]

The sea-plane was miraculously repaired, and a flight was made to 1,000 feet, after parting with the *Falk* and *Lestris*, which showed solid irregular pack to the west. The flight on 9 February (in the lee of a one-mile-long iceberg) revealed an appearance of land some ninety miles to the south-west.[81] At the beginning of the month, the *Discovery* had been close to the position of the German exploring ship *Gauss*, when beset for some fourteen months in the early years of the century. Captain MacKenzie was well aware of this and anxious not to share her plight.[82] Mawson went on board the whaler *New Sevilla*, a converted cargo oil burner flying the Red Ensign and making her maiden whaling voyage, on 10 February 1931. He gained news of ice conditions to the south-west, but no coal. By 4 p.m. the southernmost point for both BANZARE voyages was reached in lat. 67°16′ S. long. 74°E. Another flight was made that day, an appearance of land to the south-west again being reported.[83]

The next day, 11 February 1931, was the 'Day of Great Discoveries' in MacKenzie's words.

> Vessel was kept at full speed throughout night and at daylight we were able to make SSW in open waters. A great array of massive grounded bergs were sighted at 4 am and on approach, the number was such and [such was] the closeness of the lines, that it was found quite impossible to count or even form any approximate figure, for as far as could be seen from aloft, hundreds upon hundreds stretched far ahead to abaft the star-board beam.
>
> The sight was one which filled us with amazement and we marvelled anew at God's handiwork ... At 9.05 am Child reported land ahead and by 11 o'clock the bare white slopes of the continent rising from 2000 to 3000 feet ... Passing within 40 feet of a massive tabular berg, whose height was found to be 220 feet, we obtained a most unique impression of relative size. Our little ship seemed like a mere tug besides this wonderful mountain of ice, which reared above us and for the time shut out sun and sky. Rounding this outpost we came to the edge of the pack. Behold to our utter astonishment clear ice free water stretching away to the south as far as the eye could see. An hour's hard steaming and we had entered this new and unknown sea and had left the pack and the guarding ice bergs behind.
>
> On we steamed and still on, each minute revealing new stretches of land, till at length it seemed as if it and the open water went on for ever. Great excitement

prevailed and everyone in high spirits for this is a discovery which beats anything which our wildest hopes may have conjured up. A discovery almost as good as that of the great Ross Sea. Wonderful, wonderful and still more wonderful! I fail to express our feelings tonight. But let us not be carried away, let us not be entering into the Antarctic trap, for if an easterly gale sets in, our gateway . . . closes tight for a year, possibly for ever . . .

They continued nearly parallel to and only ten miles off the coast all day, and that night celebrated their discovery and the further sightings by the sea-plane with a couple of bottles of champagne in the wardroom and three of port for the crew. The plane dropped the flag over the land that MacKenzie wanted to name Princess Elizabeth Land after 'our popular little Scottish Princess'; it was in fact Mac.Robertson Land, not the present Princess Elizabeth Land. Mawson was at first anxious 'to name something important after the ruling members of [the] present day Australian government', but apparently adopted the captain's suggestion and named the new land to the east of Mac.Robertson Land after HRH Princess Elizabeth, now Her Majesty Queen Elizabeth II, with the permission of her grandfather HM King George V. The great Amery Ice Shelf, lying to the south of MacKenzie Bay, was not claimed as a BANZARE discovery, 'but it seems', wrote Grenfell Price, 'that Oom mistook the coast of this shelf for land ice and charted it as running eastwards for some fifty miles just south of the 69th parallel and then northwards to what Mawson named Cape Amery',[84] the name of which was later transferred to the ice shelf. Grenfell Price has also pointed out that BANZARE did not discover MacKenzie Bay, since this had been passed a month earlier by the Norwegian whale catcher *Seksern*.[85]

After discussing the evidence provided by the journals, sketch maps of the flights of 9 and 11 February and other documentation, Grenfell Price concluded that 'It is indisputable that on 9th February Mawson and Campbell saw the icy slopes of Princess Elizabeth Land from the air and that the leader had every right to name his discovery. It is also indisputable that on 11th February, the party discovered from the ship the far eastern and southward-running coast of Mac.Robertson Land, together with the high land in the vicinity of Cape Darnley—land which they had seen from a remote distance in 1929. Finally the aviators discovered on that day the eastern shores of Mac.Robertson Land stretching farther to the south than could be seen from the ship, while to the east they again saw Princess Elizabeth Land, this time in the vicinity of the Munro–Kerr Mountains.'[86] Mawson called the great bay MacKenzie Sea, after the master of the *Discovery*. This is divided on modern Australian maps into MacKenzie Bay to the west and Prydz Bay to the east. The Norwegians named it Thorshavnbukta and the mountains the Mikkelsen group. The cape marking the western margin of MacKenzie Bay was later named Cape Darnley, after E. R. Darnley of the *Discovery* Committee. A compromise regarding place-names in Australian Antarctic Territory was eventually agreed between Norway and Australia.[87] A prominent peak in the Tula Range of mountains in Enderby

Land had been generously named Mount Riiser-Larsen as early as 1930 by Mawson, after the commander of the *Norvegia* expeditions.

Clear calm weather enabled the ship to continue steaming through the night of 11 February, one that Captain MacKenzie would always remember.

> A clear sky and moon in last quarter allowed us to continue making good speed and we rattled along at 6 knots in a breathless calm. Never shall I forget the impression of those hours spent winding in and out between those great bergs, which strange to say were almost entirely free from pack. Ahead astern and all round they loomed up, shutting out horizon and at times half the sky, throwing great weird shadows and in the moonlight their pale ghostly appearance much accentuated, gave one a fantastic idea of sailing through a graveyard of lost souls. At 2 o'clock I began to wonder if we would ever emerge in the open sea and it was with no little satisfaction that 3 am found us suddenly come through the last mighty gateway.

On Friday the 13th a striking and impressive mass of black rock came into view, rising straight from the sea to over one thousand feet. It was later named Murray Monolith, after Sir George Murray of Adelaide. A landing from the launch proved impracticable and the flag and proclamation had to be thrown ashore, as the boat touched bottom. Despite the steepness of the rock face, the area was found to be a nesting ground for Adélie penguins, snow petrels, fulmars and Antarctic petrels.[88] A rich catch resulted from dredging in the shallow waters off shore. A party was able to land from the launch at an adjacent rocky bay, formed by the lower slopes of a crescent-shaped nunatak nearly 2,000 feet high. This was named Scullin Monolith after the Australian prime minister. The flag was raised and the proclamation read, during this first landing on Mac.Robertson Land.[89] Grenfell Price[90] has quoted Simmers's vivid account of this important day, which in the meteorologist's opinion 'saved the name of the expedition, as we have landed and raised the flag at last'.

The accounts of the *Discovery*'s passage along this stretch of the Antarctic coast by MacKenzie and Mawson corroborate each other well in their descriptions of the dangers, principally hidden rocks and shoals, that they had to negotiate. Martin's diary for 14 February noted that

> . . . for the past two days we have been threading and feeling our way through rocks and reefs. It is often hard to distinguish them from bergs. At times we have a look-out in the crow's nest, one on the forecastle head, an officer on the bridge and an officer taking soundings with the Kelvin machine; last night we had a sounding of 5 fathoms.[91]

MacKenzie, his hands full handling the ship, watched the launch party vainly trying to effect a landing on the rock, angry with himself for having let them go in such a wind.

He saw the flag, proclamation tin and brass tablet being thrown on the rock, and the latter two, and very soon the third, washed away immediately. He planned a second attempt at landing to raise the flag, but before anything could be done, the *Discovery* was suddenly swept out to sea in a violent but short squall.[92] Another chance of landing beckoned and the effort was successful this time. MacKenzie appears to have been almost mesmerised by what he saw on 14 February.

At 6.30 am we were in sight of what appeared to all who beheld, the 8th wonder of the world. Land, why there was no end to it. Four mighty mountain ranges (5000 feet high), with a thousand rugged peaks, ran from the coast inland as far as the eye could see and black rock stretched for miles on the ice free water front. Numerous islands, some nearly a mile long, were dotted all over the sea within 8 miles of the shore. What a harvest for explorers, what a place to explore! We called all hands to witness a sight that even our wildest dreams could have not revealed, fearing lest it was all a strange vision which was going to pass away, or that in reality the indications of snow, which were very strong, would bring a blizzard and shut out all for ever from our gaze. Along we crept . . . and I suddenly realised that I was in a channel between unknown islands, unknown water, along an unknown land. 'Stop her Sir', I said and as if the order had been actually put into my mouth, the call of 2 Officer set my heart thumping—'10 fms. Sir', '7 fms.'—then '5 fms. Sir'. Full astern and we within ten minutes were into a 100 fms. deep. The ocean bed was like the moon . . . from 150 to 5 fm. and only God kept us from bringing the good ship up on the sharp peninsulas and there must have been many just within a few feet of the surface.

Breaker ahead again caused us to turn slowly round and retrace our steps . . . and it looked from the rocks and islands then in view, that it was madness to put back and yet madness to go on. . . . I ordered all boats be made ready and in my mind had fully decided what we would do in the event of suddenly having our bottom ripped open. . . . when again without any warning came that dreaded cry '5 fms. Sir'. It was as much as any man could stand and only by God's greatness did we pass on and out to deep water. No more, no more never again, no, not for all the new lands. Sir D came up on finding that we were heading north. 'Yes', I said, 'North it is going to be, till I find that we are really in safe waters. My life is nothing and I care less for yours', I said, 'but my ship is everything and she must be saved'. Noon found us some fifteen miles off. I then altered course again, but the weather had been showing signs of change and I felt sure that we were in for another blow.[93]

Fine hauls of fish and invertebrates were obtained on 16 and 17 February, with the result that the biologists were tremendously rushed to process the catch. Simmers, Hurley and Oom struggled for much of 17 February to clear out nine tons of coal from the sail locker, which in fact grew to twenty-five, seeming to prove that the captain had additional supplies up his sleeve.[94] A day later, the coal was officially down to one hundred tons, the amount that both leader and captain agreed was the minimum for the *Discovery*'s return voyage of 4,000 miles to Australia.[95] It is evident from MacKenzie's diary that Mawson only agreed with reluctance to this, being anxious to return to Queen Mary Land, on which he had been instructed to raise the flag. The captain refused to consider the idea on account of limited coal and wrote of Mawson that 'He completes his efforts and cares not how or when the ship gets back. I continue my efforts and am responsible for return and safe return and on completion of this, my efforts end.'[96]

This last day off the Antarctic coast proved notable for a further landing in Mac.Robertson Land at Cape Bruce, where Colbeck located an excellent boat harbour, and for some valuable scientific investigations. A large party went ashore. Mawson described the interesting features of the landscape, whose rocks were Pre-cambrian, the most ancient on earth, the occurrence of freshwater algae, moss and lichens, and his impression that the area merited further exploration. A 'cairn was erected, the flag hoisted, and a document relating to our discoveries was duly deposited. The occasion was enlivened by a libation of champagne and was concluded with three rousing cheers for the King.'[97] At the end of that day, MacKenzie was the proud owner of a duplicate brass tablet of the one 'firmly secured on our New Land', which read 'The British Flag was hoisted and British Sovereignty Asserted on the 18th Day of February 1931'. His decision to take the *Discovery* close enough to land to send the launch off had not been an easy one for him to make. The rocky coast could only be reached by very careful navigation past 'wave-washed islets and big, sharp-peaked islands'. The lead was sounded continuously, the look-outs were doubled and the engines kept at half speed.

On we went and suddenly before us there [was] revealed a long and we hoped a deep harbour, a harbour formed by two bold capes, the easterly one rising in places to 1000 feet and coming down to the water in great sheer cliffs. The inside or head was formed by a mile or so of glacier, from which enormous 40 foot high bergs had entered and two lay in mid stream, the outer one caught on some shallow, as we found on approach. The western cape was low and straggled off into a number of islands, between which lay large bergy bits and some fast ice. The entrance to this world's fairy-land harbour, with its little white and crystal gondolas, floating up and down in the shape of boatlike pieces of sparkling ice, was guarded by one flat-topped iceberg on the east and a low island on the west. Between these we gradually felt our way and I was relieved to find that 30 fms. was our lowest sounding . . . It was then about 2.30 pm.

Inside, I put her at full speed and with lead showing a steady no bottom at 100 fms. I knew that the valley between the capes was a safe and sound one, at least till we had reached to within a mile or so of the glacier. A good four mile run and we were up and in sheltered waters, with a bright sun and clearing sky. I felt well rewarded as I sent off the launch and saw the new Union Jack, flying on one of the thwarts, all ready to be set up on shore.

Simmers, who was in the shore party, gave a lively personal account of the day.[98]

*Wednesday, 18th February.* It was on a beautiful night like this that we left the Antarctic last year, so now for the second time we are leaving these shores when they are doing their utmost to beckon us to stay. It seems hard, after cruising so many months and waiting patiently the last three days, to be vouchsafed a much grudged two to three hours when we do get to the land, especially after the trouble we had this morning getting in. As intended last night, we left at 3.30 this morning in worse weather than we had had for twenty four hours, but as we worked south the day improved and with the echo sounder working continuously, we got well into the land by about three p.m. without meeting any of the dangers over which the skipper is worrying so much. What's the *Discovery* for if she can't navigate dangerous waters? . . .

As we were supposed to be two hours away from the ship, Mac wanting to be away clear of the coastal shoals before dark, we hurried ashore, only to find that what we had landed on was only an island separated from the mainland by a stretch of drift ice, too scattered to cross on foot, yet too thick to navigate in the motorboat. . . .

After 10 to 20 minutes ashore, we piled into the launch, reluctantly leaving our little harbour and ran west, wasting a precious half hour skirting unpromising coast, before turning and running east round the outside of the island, which forms the boat harbour, to a sheltered landing place which had been seen when we were first ashore. . . . Conditions here were even more perfect than in the former landing place and we slid quietly, through a glassy sea on to a low rocky beach, which gave on to a little valley between two steep rocky bluffs.

Dux [Sir Douglas Mawson] jumped ashore and ran up the valley waving a flag and looking as pleased as punch—and so he was, because at last we were in a position to make a legal, complete and entire observance of claiming land, which we forthwith proceeded to do . . . In all other attempts (except, of course, that at Cape Denison) there had been some little thing wrong—'Proclamation' was only an island; the first proclamation on the 13th floated out to sea and the second on the 13th had no board or proclamation, but this time things have been done properly—mainland, cairn, board, proclamation, several people, lusty singing—lusty because in the confined space of the valley our voices seemed very loud and cheerful compared with previous efforts, which have been on the tops of hills, where the voices seem thin and are easily lost in space. The ceremony over, it was made doubly correct by the pouring of a little champagne over the cairn, only a little as we wanted to (and did) drink the rest and the hoisting of several other flags . . .

The flag raising over and done, Frank Hurley, Alf [Howard] and I started off up one of the higher knolls armed with a battery of cameras. . . . The climb was hard, the bare rock being steep and the sun hot, but the view from the top amply repaid the effort. From this eminence of about 500 feet we could see far inland and away to the east and west, obtaining a fine panoramic view of this interesting area. Inland are many peaks separated from our knoll by a large ice lake up about 200 feet from the sea, while to the E. and W. are two prominent capes, with numerous off-lying islands. Between our position and the eastern cape is an extensive ice tongue, all cracked into bergs, which still contiguous, are just waiting to drift away. Coming to our own knoll, it consists, as does much of the rest of the rock about, of gneiss simply loaded with garnets. Evidence of copper and iron are noticeable. The basic rock is the same as that at Proclamation Island.

On the southern sides of all the knolls are some most remarkable examples of weathering, the rock being honeycombed with holes about an inch and a half across and up to three inches deep, as if there had been a plague of mammoth worms. I brought back two large ultra pitted examples, which looked almost like dingy coral . . .

Both on the way up and down the knoll I collected rocks till my rucksac, pockets and arms were overflowing and I was hardly able to stagger along having, in addition, two small cameras and a large one of Hurley's. I was a trifle ambitious in my carrying capacity, as though I could manage the load alright on good going, on some of the more difficult places on the descent I had trouble, having in one case to come down a 40 foot ice slope on my behind, knowing only too well of the existence of innumerable sharp ice spikes. Then down this I reached the higher parts of the valley we landed in and had to cross two small fresh water lakes, breaking the ice crust on one and coming a cropper on the other breaking one of my precious specimens. I was well and truly last back, Dux thinking I had slipped and hurt myself.

Well pleased with ourselves we made our way back to the ship a mere hour overdue and ran into a ramping and surly skipper, who immediately got the ship underway . . .

By the time he came to write his diary, the 'hopping mad captain' (MacKenzie) had calmed down[99] sufficiently to record that 'At 6.15 the party returned—what followed is best left unwritten—but I was more than annoyed for I had clearly ordered that an hour was all the time I could give. This on account of getting out before darkness set in, for knowing the reefs 15 miles to seaward I had no intention of passing them at night. As it was, we found a five fathom pool below us while waiting and that upset all love and affection for the new found harbour.'[100] He had steamed close in at 5.30 p.m. to call the party back with the ship's whistle and still felt that the over-eager scientists cared little for the safety of the ship. 'Gales come and they turn in and remain in their bunks day and night till the return of fine weather. Darkness amongst icebergs, islands and breakers is no concern of theirs and none of them realize or appreciate the dangers, just because up to date all has gone well. From now on they will, as passengers, be a damn nuisance and only fit for childish pranks and the general disturbance of the ship's discipline.'[101] One cannot help sympathising with both captain and scientists. A reading of Harold Fletcher's book shows that he at least was conscious of the dangers to the ship. The scientists did share watches on some of the worst occasions.[102] However, on departure, *all* on board were thrilled to witness the capsize of the large iceberg guarding the entrance to the harbour near Cape Bruce. 'The Antarctic turned on a good show as we left', wrote Simmers. 'A berg we were passing turning turtle—a most rare sight. It slowly rolled completely over, then kept rolling round in the water for at least upwards of twenty minutes, by which time we were well away. It was a great spectacle, especially as it was one of the green and white striped bergs of which there are numbers around here.'

## THE VOYAGE HOME

On 19 February 1931 and for several days afterwards, preparations were made for the long homeward voyage to Australia. In the lee of a large tabular iceberg, the topgallant yards were sent up and crossed on the foremast of the *Discovery*. They had been housed on deck while the ship was working in the ice, but were needed to carry more sail during the ocean passage. This was no easy job in the swell and backwash from the berg and for its accomplishment, the chief officer (Max Stanton) and his men deserved credit, considered MacKenzie.[103] All movable gear was stowed below, as near the keel as possible, and sacks of ashes from the boiler, damped with sea water, were used as ballast to replace the coal that had been consumed. This had been the practice for some time as coal stocks became depleted. Fletcher records how the doctor, the meteorologist and he bagged and stowed some two tons of ash off Wilkes Land on 22 January. He states that one ton of ash was usually left after burning five tons of coal.[104]

The call of *Homeward bound!* ran throughout the ship, wrote Captain MacKenzie 'and great was the joy, for our long struggle had been completed and completed in a manner which excelled our wildest dreams'. He recalled the number and greatness of BANZARE discoveries and adventures and thanked God 'for His mercy and for His guidance and care of our little craft'. MacKenzie felt a big burden to have been lifted off his shoulders, a responsibility that he would never come south again to undertake, the worry having been 'enough to last a lifetime—but with God's help we will continue to keep going and in His good time bring our ship and party safely back to civilisation and home'. Shanty songs and choruses showed how glad everyone was to be homeward bound, even though, the captain asserted, no murmurs, grumblings or cries of dissatisfaction had ever been heard throughout the voyage.[105]

Nevertheless, his troubles were by no means over. It took a whole week to get north of 60°, using forty of the last precious hundred tons of coal, against a north-east wind in mist and darkness that seemed to hold 'all the icebergs in Antarctic waters'.[106] Strong sou'westerly gales followed, the seas sometimes filling the waist from bulwark to bulwark, as the *Discovery* plunged and rolled. 'This splendid vessel,' wrote Mawson on the homeward run, 'when well handled and given a reasonable amount of ballast, is safe enough in any storm.' Fortunately, she was able to run the gauntlet of invisible icebergs, 'flying before the gale in the night hours, rendered impenetrably dark by driving sleet and a pall of cloud overhead'.[107] What these 'hellish nights' meant to her master can be read in MacKenzie's diary. On 2 March, she was doing $5^1/_2$ knots under two square sails only. Frank Hurley must have considered the rough weather an excellent opportunity to shoot some exciting film. No doubt anxious about his antics, Captain MacKenzie had him sign this disclaimer.

> To Capt. K. MacKenzie                                   1st March 1931
>   Dear Sir,
>   Any risks I may take to secure Kinema films for the expedition, aloft or on the decks of the Discovery, I do so entirely of my own accord. Your judgement informs me that:- owing to the state of the seas running, it would not be possible to effect a rescue should any person go overside. I quite understand the situation and I accept it; entirely exonerating you from any blame should such an accident occur to me.
>                         Yours faithfully,
>                         Frank Hurley[108]

The next day saw the height of the 'worst gale that this ship has ever come through, having to endure forces only known south of 50°'.

> Yesterday saw the height of its might and our run today is a record for our or indeed any vessel under the same conditions. With only foresail and lower topsail and no steam power, we did 183 miles. At times driving down the slope of a tremendous arc, we swept along at $8^1/_2$ knots. Down down down, sea and sky gone from view, then in a mass of seething, breaking waters we would struggle to free ourselves of the seas which swept our decks from stem to stern—over the bridge, into the wardroom, down to the engine room, bulwarks under and at times only the top of main fife rail showing, but still we lurch. Once I got caught entering the lee chart room door and for a minute thought my life was being crushed out. The door opened, I gained a grip inside and eventually got myself in. But oh, what a foaming sea flooded chart room and my own cabin! That at the time worried me little, all my thoughts were whether the foresail would hang out and keep us before it. Double reeved wire sheets, rigged the previous night, sang like harp strings, the fore yard actually bending in the braces and the sail like a steel sheet. Wonderful, wonderful gear! Nothing but the best, the very best would have withstood such a

storm and none but the best of crews would have answered as did my men. The scientific staff were put into watches and gave all assistance. Two hands being kept at the wheel and the others to help the watch on deck.[109]

MacKenzie concluded the day's diary with an affectionate tribute to the *Discovery* herself, 'My wonderful little ship, you are indeed a credit to your name and history. I'll bring you safe back to Old Father Thames, before many months are out.'[110] One of the scientists, Harold Fletcher, described the colossal size of the seas, wave crests almost 400 metres apart being separated by great valleys—an unbelievable sight.

Several of us made our way to the ship's stern, he wrote, to watch her negotiate the mighty seas. Descending the steep side of a following wave she had little more than 30 centimetres of freeboard at the stern. Towering above was a great wall of water almost vertical, with every appearance of threatening to collapse and overwhelm the ship at any moment. Standing at the ship's stern railing, the sheer wall of the wave could almost be touched with outstretched arms. In the troughs we were deluged by heavy falls of spray whipped by the wind from the wave crests. Sails idly flapped with the loss of wind and it rested with the engines to drive the ship up the towering wall of the sea fronting her. The masts, 34 metres high, were well below the height of the waves. Ascending the wave, we estimated that the ship's length of 52 metres would fit at least twice in between its base and crest. The seas were by far the highest we had experienced on both voyages of the expedition.[111]

Fine weather followed, with good steady westerlies, enabling the vessel to make better runs under sail than with engines. She logged 121 miles on 5 March, 139 on the 6th, 140 on the 7th and on the 8th, with a nor'westerly gale, 170 miles. Nearing the end of the voyage, the ship's company and scientists alike delighted in the 'wonderful rugged scenery of Tasmania's little-known south-western coast' and 'the glorious scent of forest and verdant meadow'.[112] After much washing of persons and shearing of beards, the BANZAR Expedition arrived in Hobart on 19 March 1931. They had been away for 117 days and the *Discovery* had covered a distance of 10,557 miles.[113]

Reflecting upon the expedition while homeward bound, Mawson made some interesting remarks about the feverish activity of the many whaling vessels observed in the far south and forecast the decline of the whale.[114]

To one who has known the Antarctic before the recent invasion of the whalers, by far the most outstanding feature of the voyage has been . . . the intensity of the present whaling campaign . . . With an increase in the number of craft operating, these have pushed out into new areas to such an extent, that our experience has shown that henceforth pelagic factory ships may be met with anywhere along the margin of the pack.

. . . Reminiscent of the days of the historic gold rushes, a feverish activity is being directed to the Antarctic seas in an effort to participate in the golden opportunity presented by these fabulously rich fisheries. Vessels of many nations . . . are all embodied in this ruthless competition.

We learned from reliable sources about the ships that there are no less than forty-two mother factory vessels in Antarctic waters this season and associated with them, an aggregate of some 250 chasers, which have collectively employed about 10,000 Norwegians alone. The annual value of the catch has recently risen to the neighbourhood of eight million pounds. The whale is paying for all this. In these days of high taxation, the whale holds the unenviable record of being the most highly taxed creature on earth. There is a form of taxation even more ruthless than that imposed upon John Citizen of our own suffering communities, for these colossal creatures, fat and thin, male and female, all go into the melting pot and appear as margarine and fertilizer or other lifeless commodities of world trade.

So with such a concentration of activity in quest of these leviathans, it will not be surprising if they should soon become rare.

Mawson followed this news report some days later with another equally interesting, which summed up the achievements of the 1930–1 season:[115]

Shortly summarising the achievements of this season's operations, a notable feature is the wide sector of Antarctic pack-ice region, through which our observations have been pursued. Beginning now in the 180th meridian and ranging west to the 60th degree east longitude, the field of work extended through one-third of the circuit of the Antarctic regions. During the first month spent in the pack-ice zone our operations were pre-controlled by the fundamental necessity of replenishing our coal supplies, which succeeded through kind negotiations with the whalers *Clark Ross* and *Kosmos*.

During this period, the general scientific programme of meteorology, hydrology, and zoology made good progress, but it was not till after the New Year that our geographical work on the coastline commenced. Thenceforth, through 60 degrees of longitude, very notable additions have been made to geographical knowledge. First of all, in passing Adelie Land to our sphere of operations to the west, some additional features were added to the coastline of that territory, and an extension has been made to the coastline designated Wilkes Land by our former 1911 expedition.

In the region still further west, as far as Queen Mary Land, sufficient evidence has now been accumulated to state that land does not exist to latitudes assigned for either North's High Land, Totten's High Land, or Budd's Land, which have appeared on some published maps. In the case of Knox Land, however, ice-covered land does exist in the neighbourhood of the position assigned to it by Wilkes. In this segment, however, new land has been discovered, sighted from our aeroplane. It exists to the northwest from a well defined cape, situated near the juncture of the 66th parallel and extending east and west of the 122nd meridian. This new land has been charted as Banzare Land, after the title of our expedition.

Westward of 120th meridian, soundings and distribution of pack suggest that the coastline trends somewhat to the north. Between 115th and 116th meridian, at about 66th parallel, an ice surface resembling ice-covered land was observed at a distance from the plane. From this landfall, with a view to commemorating Balleny's exploits in this sector in the year 1839, it is proposed to retain the title 'Sabrina Land' which has appeared in diverse locations in several Antarctic charts.

Both the soundings and distribution of pack indicate that westward of 116th meridian, the coast recedes rapidly to the south; but as it goes west beyond meridian of 109°30', it again trends northward to join Knox Land. The Termination Land of Wilkes, like Clarie Land of D'Urville, is an ice jam in shoal waters, where grounded bergs hold up the pack ice and develop stable conditions, conducive to an extension of shelf ice from the ice cap of the adjacent continent. In this region, however, is an ice island about 1300 feet high, quite impossible to have been seen from Wilkes's ships. This we have charted as Bowman Island, after the director of the American Geographical Society.

West of Queen Mary Land, coast was again sighted at a distance from the aeroplane. This landfall commences at 80th. meridian on 76th parallel of latitude, and extends south and west in a great sweep to Cape Amery in latitude 78°21' and longitude 72°20'. Mindful of the interest taken in our work by the Duke and Duchess of York, who visited the *Discovery* before her departure from London, we have had the honour and pleasure of naming this new territory, Princess Elizabeth Land.

Westward of Cape Amery, in the deeply indented territory of MacRobertson Land, is a great sea extending beyond 69th. parallel; but the coast comes north again to Cape Darnley, which is a sharp turn in the coast in latitude 67°20', longitude 69°25'. The coast then follows west and north to join with Kemp Land, as reported last year.

The MacRobertson Land coast has now been mapped in considerable detail, so that all its salient features are charted and named. It is of a most interesting character, being diversified with mountain peaks, islands and other features of note. When MacRobertson Land was discovered last year, it was beset with heavy pack ice, so that portions of coastline were located from the aeroplane at a distance. We now find that in most cases distances to the coast were underestimated owing to the clarity of air and the wonderful visibility in these regions.

From the foregoing, it is to be noted that so far as our operations this season refer to the location and survey of coastline, they have resulted in the discovery of new land, totalling 16 degrees of longitude, and further detailed charting through

13 degrees of longitude of territory discovered last year. Regarded on the broadest geographical basis, the great feature is that sufficient data are now at hand definitely to assert the continuity of an Antarctic continental coastline, through a great arc, nowhere far removed from the Antarctic Circle and extending from Cape Adare to Enderby Land.

The geographical results, however, are only part of the story, for other departments of observation have been equally fortunate. Until a few days ago, when the echo-sounder developed a malady, soundings have been taken at frequent intervals each day, throughout the cruise, detecting submarine banks and otherwise delineating the floor of the sea and the margin of coastline. Opportunity has been found for a considerable number of vertical marine stations, and data thus obtained have been extended by regular daily nettings for marine life, and by chemical examination of waters traversed. This distribution of plankton and its bearing on the whale-feeding areas has been given due attention throughout a wide sweep of Antarctic seas.

Dr. Ingram, one of the most active members of the expedition, besides helping with routine biological work, has conducted investigations on bacteria in the sea water, with interesting results, particularly in regard to their role as denitrifiers.

Mr Simmers (meteorologist), besides maintaining a two-hourly record of observations, has been very successful in pilot balloon work investigations in upper air currents. A feature of general interest, that has now been elucidated, is his demonstration that the violent winds of the plateau and coastal slopes of some parts of the Antarctic, such as Adelie Land, are in large measure, at least, surface winds ascending only to 500 or 1000 feet above ground level.

Useful data in other departments of physical investigations have been made, namely, in magnetics and solar radiation; also observations on cosmic penetration and radiation by a Geiger Muller electron counting apparatus, kindly constructed for the expedition by Professor Kerr Grant. Finally, glaciology, geology, and ornithology have all reaped a harvest in this virgin field.

On several occasions during the cruise, the flag was flown on these friendly lands. This demonstration was effected with special ceremony at Cape Denison, Scullin Monolith and Cape Bruce.

R. A. Falla gives an overall impression of the second BANZARE voyage from the scientist's point of view in a cheerful personal letter to James Marr, written while he was homeward bound to Auckland after the expedition's return. He mentioned that 'Harvey did his best to keep the Dux up to a programme, but there was the same old precedence given to land discovery and curiously enough, an exact repetition of the friction between D.M. and the Skipper . . .'. Falla agreed with Marr that the scientific programme had been 'too extensive to make a first-class show in any department', but thought that the results would be 'voluminous and valuable enough', once put together. Although Marr had been much missed, better organisation had enabled them 'to carry on after a fashion. Matheson was invaluable, Doc. [Dr W. W. Ingram, surgeon and biologist] took his duties as dredging-master seriously right through, and Harvey put in long hours in the lab.'[116] Some years after the expedition's return, Mawson summarised the geographical results:

> The work conducted in Antarctic waters through the two summer seasons 1929–30 and 1930–31 resulted in the amassing of an immense amount of data regarding the region lying south of Australia and the Indian Ocean, between the forty-fifth and the one hundred and eightieth meridians of east longitude. Long stretches of new coast line were discovered. There have been added to the map Mac-Robertson Land, Princess Elizabeth Land, Banzare Land, and Lars Christensen Land; also Kemp Land and Enderby Land were rediscovered and mapped. The approximate coastline thus entered upon the chart extends through about 40° of longitude. Furthermore the existence of Wilkes' Knox Land was confirmed, and an appearance of land was recorded near where Balleny's Sabrina Land has appeared on the map. By means of an echo sounder installed in the keel of the ship, an elaborate record of sea-floor depths was obtained, sufficient to establish the limit of a continental shelf throughout the sector. Thus perhaps the most important outcome of the expedition is that, in conjunction with the discoveries made on the former Australasian Expedition to the same sector, and observations by British and other expeditions elsewhere, the presence of a real continent within the ice has been finally established, with its main bulk towards the Indian Ocean, as prognosticated by Captain James Cook 160 years ago.[117]

The scientific results were eventually published in a series of volumes between 1937 and 1975, with the help of the Federal Government, and the geographical results largely in geographical society periodicals.[118] It was not until 1962 that the *Geographical Report* appeared, edited from Mawson's papers by Sir Archibald Grenfell Price, as *The winning of Australian Antarctica*, the work much cited in this chapter. Mawson tried to write the 'popular story of the cruises', but did not because of the pressure of other work.[119] Finance was still a problem for Mawson after the return of the expedition.[120] He had intended that the proceeds of Hurley's 'talkie' film, *Southward-Ho! with Mawson*, should help with the publication of the scientific results. It was released in the end as the Commonwealth Government's official record, at little profit, presumably, to the expedition. Press reports indicate its showing in London after BANZARE's return.[121]

As to the political results of the expedition, a British Order in Council of 7 February 1933 eventually affirmed the sovereign rights of the Crown over the Antarctic lands (other than the French Terre Adélie) south of lat. 60°S. and between longs. 45°E. and 160°E., about one third of the coastline of the continent. The territory was placed under the authority of the Commonwealth of Australia, after the necessary legislation had been passed.[122] Such claims have been 'frozen' under the Antarctic Treaty of 1959 and other nations besides Australia have established scientific stations in the wide arc of Australian Antarctic Territory since the International Geophysical Year of 1957–8, a special year of scientific co-operation and successor to the International Polar Years of 1882 and 1932.

A link between BANZARE and the post-war Australian National Antarctic Research Expeditions exists through Flt. Lieut. (later Group Captain) Stuart Campbell, RAAF, one of the pilots of the Gypsy Moth, 1929–31. In 1947, he was appointed to organise and lead the first of these government expeditions to the Antarctic that have continued to the present day. Stations have been established on Macquarie Island, Heard Island and on the mainland of Antarctica. Mawson was the first to urge the post-war Australian Government to resume scientific research and exploration in the Antarctic, and later acted as adviser to the Executive Committee on Exploration and Exploitation, which first met in January 1947.[123] He also influenced the choice of the site of the present Mawson Station in Mac.Robertson Land, set up by Dr P. G. Law (director of the Antarctic Division from 1949 to 1966) in 1954. The captain of HMAS *Wyatt Earp*, ship of the first ANARE Antarctic voyage in 1947–8, was Commander Karl Oom, RAN, cartographer of the 1930–1 BANZARE voyage. In 1957, a second Australian station (on the coast of Princess Elizabeth Land) was set up under the leadership of Dr P. G. Law and named after Captain J. K. Davis.

## THE RETURN TO LONDON

Sir Douglas Mawson and the scientists left ship in Australia—all bar Simmers, who continued to take meteorological observations for some 1,500 miles across the Tasman Sea between Melbourne and Wellington from 18 April to 2 May. Lieut. C. Reid, RAN, joined the ship as fourth officer in Melbourne at his own request and with the agreement of the Australian authorities, and it is largely from his log that the following details of the home-ward voyage come.[124] The *Discovery* made some good days' runs proceeding towards Cape Horn. The echo-sounder was out of commission until 20 May, from which date daily soundings were obtained. A search in the charted latitude of the 'Dogherty Islands' was again unsuccessful, as the islands do not exist. A hurricane blew the vessel away northwards from this vicinity, oil bags being streamed from both bows. Captain MacKenzie, who kept only the briefest of diaries during the home-ward voyage, described this 'tempest of unbelieveable force and fury' in a news release for Australia House.[125]

On the evening of 1 June, Cape Horn was abeam in clear fine weather with a following wind, the full moon lighting the high land during the night. Le Maire Strait was entered on 2 June and many soundings were made with the Kelvin machine where none had been previously charted. A particularly large number of Wandering albatrosses were observed here, as well as cormorants and Black-browed albatrosses. The *Discovery* must have been one of the last British square riggers to round the Horn. On 5 June, the longest day's run was made of 217 miles, the noon position being lat. 47°46′ S. long. 61°46′ W. Next day the decks remained dry, for the first time on passage from New Zealand. Hourly soundings were taken with the Kelvin machine over an area in the South Atlantic showing no charted depths. The *Discovery* arrived in Montevideo on 10 June where the British Vice-Consul, ship agents and reporters came aboard. A column in the Montevideo *Sun* summarised the expedition's achievements and referred to a box of Bryant and May's matches and half a tin of Wills' tobacco 'as fresh as if it had just been opened', which had been brought away by Captain MacKenzie after twenty years in Mawson's old hut.[126]

The number of birds in company quickly diminished as the ship proceeded in the warmer weather and waters of the tropics. On 17 June, the Cape pigeon that had followed the *Discovery* from the Tasman Sea made its last appearance, while flying fish and porpoises were seen for the first time in lat. 29°S. long. 45°04′ W. The south-east Trade Winds were picked up in about lat. 14°30′ S., the ship making good speed under all canvas. Painting and cleaning began. An unsuccessful search was made at the Admiralty's request for some islands reported near the Equator. St Paul's Rocks were sighted on 3 July. Two days later, the echo-sounder was declared beyond repair some three degrees north of the Equator and 2,968 miles out of Montevideo. Flying fish were observed for the last time on 20 July in lat. 37°42′ N. and on the next day, the first North Atlantic Stormy petrel. On 30 July 1931, a beautiful summer's day, the *Discovery* made up the English Channel. The Channel pilot boarded at Dungeness and the river pilot took charge in Gravesend. Square sails were set in the lower reaches of the Thames. Several vessels 'in passing down river dipped their Ensign in salute or gave a greeting by sounding the whistle'. The ship made fast in the East India Dock in the late afternoon of 1 August 1931, just two years to the day from her departure.

The *Discovery*'s arrival and achievements during the BANZARE voyages were reported in the London papers. Several bearded members of the crew pulled reporters' legs again, saying they had eaten frozen whisky to keep out the cold. From Melbourne she had come 14,449 miles in 105 days at an average speed of 5³/₄ knots.

'Captain MacKenzie will have arrived with the "Discovery" in London ere this letter reaches you', wrote Mawson to H. R. Mill from Adelaide, at the end of July. 'He proved to be a very fine fellow of good temperament for any expedition work. The second voyage of the "Discovery" was an exceedingly happy and harmonious one. The ship's officers all proved excellent fellows and we accomplished far more than was the case on the first voyage.'[127] As Sir Douglas Mawson was full of praise for him, so Captain MacKenzie was full of praise for his little ship. He had brought her back safely at last to Old Father Thames.[128]

# PART VI

# SEA SCOUTS AND AFTER

CHAPTER

# TWENTY-ONE

LAID UP IN LONDON, 'SAVED FOR THE NATION',
TRANSFER TO THE SEA SCOUTS, 1937, THE SECOND
WORLD WAR AND AFTER, TRANSFER TO THE
MARITIME TRUST, 1979

### 'GINO' WATKINS'S PROPOSED TRANS-ANTARCTIC EXPEDITION, *c.1932*

ANOTHER ANTARCTIC EXPEDITION WAS MOOTED but never sailed. The *Discovery* Committee generously offered to charter the *Discovery* to H. G. Watkins, a young Englishman who made a reputation for himself as leader of small private expeditions to the Arctic in the late 1920s, at a nominal charge, with the expedition paying only the running costs (some £12,000 per annum) and insurance. A little later, still anxious to help and conscious that British prestige would be strengthened by such an expedition, the Committee offered the vessel free of charter. Watkins would have gladly accepted, had he been able, but decided instead (because of the running costs of the *Discovery*) to charter a small sealer, the *Quest*. In the event, and despite the support of an eminent expedition committee, no substantial sums of money were forthcoming. As his biographer put it, 'In the depths of the Depression, private finance was more surely frozen than the ice of the Antarctic.' Watkins abandoned the scheme and organised an expedition to Greenland, during which he died.[1] The British Arctic Air Route Expedition of 1930–1, which he had led, carried out meteorological and exploratory work in Greenland, pioneering what has become the polar route used by airlines since the 1950s. After this success, he had been persuaded to attempt what Shackleton had failed to do: the crossing of the Antarctic to ascertain whether the Ross Sea and the Weddell Sea were joined to form a great channel dividing the continent into two. It was also planned to map the south-west coast of the Weddell Sea.

In the years immediately after the BANZARE, 1932–6, the *Discovery* was laid up in the London docks, but regularly inspected and maintained by Messrs Flannery, Baggalley and Johnson, a section of whose final report on 31 December 1936 read 'The main and auxiliary machinery has been turned periodically and all bright parts oiled down, and the engine room kept clean and tidy. Both main boilers are dry and well ventilated and fresh lime is maintained inside to absorb moisture.' On sounding the bilges, the usual slight gain of water had been revealed.[2] It had become obvious that the vessel had outlived her usefulness. The *Discovery* Committee was well served in the prosecution of *Discovery* Investigations by the steel-hulled, custom-built *Discovery II* and by the *William Scoresby*, whose bows had been raised to render her less like a submarine in heavy seas. Two members of the Committee's staff heard that the *Discovery* might be sold by the Crown Agents. They took the initiative of starting to collect funds to secure her for the National Maritime Museum at Greenwich (which had been founded in 1927 to illustrate Great Britain's maritime heritage), and to pay for her upkeep. These two, B. M. Borley and Miss W. J. Hope, described the ship as having 'not only an historic value', but as 'the finest in existence for use in ice'. She was a 'national asset and should be preserved for the Nation'.[3]

## HEADQUARTERS OF THE SEA SCOUTS, 1937–54, AND A MEMORIAL TO SCOTT AND SHACKLETON

The *Discovery* was eventually offered in October 1936 to the Boy Scouts Association as a training ship for Sea Scouts and as a memorial to Captain Scott and his comrades. 'The acceptance of this wonderful offer was contingent', in the words of Lord Hampton, then Chief Commissioner, on three main factors: 'firstly, the co-operation of the Government of the Falkland Islands, to whom the ship still belonged; secondly, the raising of a sum of money sufficient to ensure her proper upkeep; and thirdly, the consent of the Port of London Authority to allot her moorings in a spot easily accessible to the boys who were to use her'.[4] The offer delighted Lord Baden-Powell, founder of the Boy Scouts Association and Chief Scout. He was 'stumped', however, when practical people at headquarters asked how he was going to pay for her upkeep. An old Sea Scout, Dr John Nash, relates what happened next.

> Not being one to remain 'stumped', B-P wrote to Lady Houston, D.B.E. (who had financed Britain's entry to the Schneider Trophy competition). With typical art, B-P sent her a sketch of the barque and playing on her love for horses, added the comment, 'She's going to the knacker's yard unless you care to save her.' The result was a substantial trust fund for expenses.[5]

Lady Houston was an extraordinary character, somewhat larger than life, whose three husbands had left her several million pounds. She gave generously to many causes and her support of the British team in the 1931 Schneider Trophy race would help to win the Battle of Britain in 1940, since Spitfires and Hurricanes were directly descended from the plane competing in the 1931 race. It may be that Lord Baden-Powell remembered that she had offered to pay for the salvage and refit of the great four-masted Finnish barque *Herzogin Cecilie* in the spring of 1936. This vessel had been wrecked on Bolt Head in south Devon, and Lady Houston, for whom the romance of the sailing ship was said to have a special appeal, wished the barque to become a sail training ship for naval cadets.[6] The Admiralty refused her offer and she was perhaps therefore gratified to find her wish fulfilled in a different way. Her gift to the Scouts of £30,000 was made anonymously under the pseudonym of 'A Patriot', patriotism being one of her greatest characteristics.[7] One of her two addresses in *Who's Who*, incidentally, was the SY *Liberty*.

The agreement drawn up between Lady Houston and the Boy Scouts Association specified that the *Discovery* would be used for the following purposes:

(a) A living memorial to Scott, Oates, Shackleton and other heroes of Antarctic exploration
(b) Headquarters for the Sea Scout Branch of the Boy Scouts Association
(c) A training centre for Sea Scouts and their officers
(d) A training centre for poor and unemployed Scouts where possible
(e) A rendezvous for Deep Sea Scouts of the Royal Navy and Mercantile Marine
(f) A hostel for Sea Scouts from overseas.[8]

A committee chaired by the Chief Sea Scout, Admiral A. V. Campbell, CB, was to administer the fund and to implement the agreement. 'Thus', in the words of Lord Baden-Powell, when writing to Lady Houston in November 1936, 'will be kept alive the tradition of the ship and the example of those heroic adventurers who sailed in her, to inspire the oncoming generation with a like spirit of manliness, self sacrifice, and loyalty to the King, which is so badly needed in these days.'[9] Sadly, Lady Houston died before the handing-over ceremony which took place on board ship on 9 October 1937.

The RRS *Discovery* by then lay at her moorings in King's Reach alongside the Thames Embankment above Blackfriars Bridge, the berth allocated by the Port of London Authority that she was to occupy for the next forty years. During that time she became one of the landmarks of London. The Pilgrim Trust supplied funds to build the pier connecting the ship with the shore, while the Jubilee Trust contributed £1,000. A small museum was set up on board, with the help of Professor Frank Debenham of the Scott Polar Research Institute, Cambridge, who had been one of the geologists during Scott's last expedition. This was to further the Scott memorial condition of the Houston fund. Exhibits for the museum were collected by Lady Kennet, Mrs Irving-Bell, Mrs Wilson, Miss Shackleton, Mrs Bolus and others. The London Zoo provided a husky dog as a mascot.[10]

Sir Herbert Henniker-Heaton, Governor of the Falkland Islands, handed over the *Discovery* to the Duke of Kent, Commodore of Sea Scouts and Deep Sea Scouts (ex-Scouts serving in the Royal or Merchant navies). Attending the ceremony were the Colonial Secretary, six members of the first Antarctic expedition, and a distinguished company. The prayer of Dedication offered by the ship's chaplain, the Reverend Leonard Spiller, read

In the Name of the Father, and of the Son, and of the Holy Spirit, we dedicate this ship anew to the glory of the Eternal Father, and in proud memory of Robert Falcon Scott and of all others who at any time have served on board her in the Antarctic Seas. May their courage in the face of constant danger, their fortitude in hardships and distress, and their faith and trust in Thy perpetual providence be ever here remembered. With no less pride we dedicate this ship to the service of our Empire's Youth and Boyhood. May her story inspire the Scouts who visit her to discover in their Scouting new opportunities for service and high endeavour as citizens in the glorious Kingdom of Jesus Christ our Lord. Amen.[11]

'I went to Con's old ship, the "Discovery", on the Embankment', wrote the former Kathleen Scott, by then a well-known sculptor, in her diary for 9 October 1937. When the Duke of Kent asked her after the ceremony if she were glad about what was happening to the ship, she replied, 'Yes, I thought it was perfect.'[12]

The *Discovery* was used by Sea Scouts from 1937 to 1954, as a training ship and as a hostel for Scouts visiting London. She became the national centre for training Sea Scouts in all branches of seamanship and thousands of Scouts came from all over the country for week-long and weekend courses. Sea Scout leaders attended instruction courses and many local troops kept their boats on the *Discovery*'s moorings or used her boats. She had a small full-time crew and a Rover Service Crew to run the courses and do much of the work in the ship. The Australian Government presented Mawson's standard compass (left behind in Australia) to the Sea Scouts.[13]

The *Discovery* was re-rigged as a barque, i.e. with yards crossed on fore and main masts and the mizzen fore and aft rigged. The two 25-foot carvel-built whalers remained unused in their chocks on either side of the bridge, as they were reputed to be rotten. 'Below decks, the vessel still had her two boilers and triple expansion engine, complete with all the auxiliaries. The engine was unusual because each cylinder was a separate "pot", lagged with teak staves over asbestos',[14] remembers one pre-war Deep Sea Scout who also described her berth.

Discovery lay to moorings fore and aft in the strong tide that ran on the outside of the bend of the river, bringing with it more than a fair proportion of debris and worse. A timber jetty had been built to provide access from the embankment. This had two levels and steps between. A short gangway had to be constantly adjusted every hour and transferred from upper to lower level and back again with each tide. From time to time the jetty would shudder and threaten to collapse as the vessel sheered with the tide and threw its weight against the piles. A short section of the ship's bulwarks had been removed to accept the gangway and a step ladder mastered the embankment wall.

Downstream of the jetty were three sets of buoyed moorings on which were kept two 27 ft. Montague whalers which were in constant use. The ship's accommodation ladder was rigged just forward of the funnel casing on the starboard side and gave easy access to these boats via a dinghy.

An ex-Rover Sea Scout recollected that there was a pre-war paid crew of three, master, chief engineer and bosun. The bosun's name was Joe Miller. He had been ship keeper while she was laid up in the London docks.

> Bosun Miller was most skilled in the arts of sea sailing life and in particular standing and running rigging . . . He insisted on us making hammocks from old sail cloth —little did we know then that most of us would end up in naval hammocks! The last member of the crew (other than the eternal ship's cat) was a Husky dog, who did not find our summer weather to his liking. Therefore, when we were scrubbing decks (barefooted, scrubbers and hose), he would expect to be cooled down.[15]

The master in the pre-war days, a retired Master Mariner, was apparently 'very much a figure head, with little comprehension of Scouting'. Both he and the bosun had cabins, on the port side of the mess-deck and the starboard side of the deckhouse, under the bridge, respectively. The Rover Service Crew gathered at weekends to help in running the courses and with the maintenance of the vessel. They were 'also responsible for assisting the more adventurous visitors to climb the rigging, the goal being the crow's nest on the mainmast. No-one ever fell, which perhaps was as well, since there were no safety nets . . .'

> Those attending were sometimes land scouters and commissioners of some eminence, learning the nautical arts of sea scouting. . . . Star performer of the service crew for the benefit of Sunday afternoon strollers on the Embankment was the smallest member, who would . . . sit on the main truck with the spike of the lightning conductor between his legs. . . . But in real life, he earnt a living as a rivetter's mate, catching red hot rivets in a bucket of sand, while standing on a high girder.[16]

Only two years after the *Discovery* had assumed the new role of training ship came the outbreak of the Second World War. She survived the Blitz in spite of being berthed in the heart of London. It was at this time, however, that her yards and the engine were removed. The story goes that the trailing cable of a wandering barrage balloon collided with one of the yards, which, on further inspection, was found to be rotten. All were therefore struck down and she lost much of her beauty,[17] remaining a de-rigged barque for several decades. The fine triple expansion engine and boilers were cut up into pieces during the later war years and sent, like many railings from the London squares, for scrap. The engine was an embarrassment to A. E. (Alec) Mackenzie, 'a strong personality who left his imprint', and who, as master, ran intensive and rigorous courses for Sea Scout troops, with great energy, until taken to hospital in 1945 with tuberculosis. Dr John Nash (a Sea Scout instructor on seamanship, who lived aboard from 1943 to 1945) tells of the engine's fate.

> Mackenzie had a crew of boys and an old seaman as bosun/cook, which were too few hands to keep the engine room in the sparkling condition, which no doubt

existed when there was a full engine room crew. Complaints from the public about its neglected state were frequent (but none offered to take an oily rag and some polish). The engine and boilers took up space badly needed for the operation of courses, as classrooms and accommodation. Scrap metal was much in demand as the war continued. Accordingly, it was decided to remove the engine and boilers . . . I was aboard at the time and witnessed their cutting up . . . into movable pieces for scrap.[18]

Another former Sea Scout takes up the story after the removal of the engine, boilers and other machinery.

The Sail Locker was extended over the Engine Room to form the After Mess Deck. This provided badly wanted extra space for trainees, and a Carpenter's Shop below, after the bilges had been filled with ballast and concrete. One piece of the engine—a lump of iron and brass—was left under the ballast, perhaps by someone with a sentimental heart. The Boiler Room bilges were filled with shingle as ballast, and a composition floor laid to form a gymnasium. The propeller truck was also filled with shingle ballast, but became a source of rot.[19]

During the early years of the war, the *Discovery* became the headquarters of the River Emergency Service, a river ambulance service, with twenty-two stations between Chelsea and the Nore. She acted as HQ and Training Establishment for the Sea Scout signalmen manning this service, who were boys of over sixteen years of age. It is recorded that despite the air raids, no Sea Scout failed to report at his station for his eight-hour watch. This operation was taken over by the Navy in 1941. For the rest of the war the ship was a Parachute Mine Station; Sea Scouts kept a round-the-clock watch for falling parachute mines and at once telephoned a compass bearing through to a Navy HQ in the docks.[20] Pre-Naval Entry courses held on board during this period were attended by some two and a half thousand Sea Scouts, and one in four boys gained a commission.[21] A former instructor in seamanship recalls the life there.

The programme of instruction laid down by the Master, A. E. Mackenzie, was intensive, starting with a run along the Embankment at an early hour after which no moment was wasted until pipe down. Some boys must have wondered what they had let themselves in for, but I am sure all benefitted from the rigours imposed . . . Instruction was among other things in signalling by semaphore, the alphabet being inculcated to the tune of 'Teddy Bears' Picnic' . . . There were theoretical matters taught, such as the causes of tides (some lads from inland troops needed convincing that it was not the Embankment that rose and fell twice daily.)

Small boatwork in whalers and other boats provided by the Navy occupied much of the day. I devised a 'passing-out' ceremonial for my crews. Discovery was moored fore and aft, heavy chains forming a 'bridge' at the stern. It was possible to take a whaler under the counter and these chains, but somewhat hazardous when a tide was running strongly. When I judged a crew was competent to work together, I would set them pulling fast across the tide and at the order 'Boat oars!' to dart under the counter with enough way on to swing into the moorings between the ship and Embankment. It gave a crew confidence (if successfully performed) in their ability to work as a team. It may have provided a spectacle of smart boatwork to any spectators on the Embankment, but was potentially embarrassing if it failed. With the keenness of these lads we never suffered this humiliation.[22]

When the war ended in 1945, the *Discovery* returned to her peacetime role as Sea Scout training ship. Weekend and week-long courses were run in all aspects of seamanship and boatwork, setting the standard for Sea Scout training for the whole of the United Kingdom. Scouts wishing to stay in London could find accommodation on board, while the first 'Queen's Scout' presentations were organised from the ship.[23] During 1948 all activities ceased while she underwent a major refit, as a result of which much of the unavoidable deterioration of the war years was arrested and repaired.[24] A Sea Scout of the early 1950s writes that

*Discovery*'s last Master was Capt. E. P. Evans. Under him there was a small paid crew, 'Tiny' Matthews the Chief Officer, Dick Coles the Bosun, Peter Royal the Purser, a cook and a ship's boy. Most of the training and the maintenance was carried out by the 'Discovery Service Crew' of Rover Scouts, many of whom were Scouters, with their own Troops in the Home Counties, or Hampshire. . . . *Discovery* was open to the public on Sundays. If you were in a Wardroom cabin, you had to clear all your gear under the desk, out of sight from the door! When the Festival of Britain was on in 1951, a large exhibition of Antarctic Exploration was mounted in the ship, on both Mess Decks, Boiler Room and the Bunkers. In the Boiler Room there was a complete Antarctic campsite, with people, dressed in appropriate gear, cooking pemican over a Primus, and handing it to the public passing by! *Discovery* had a small fleet of her own and other Sea Scout Troop's boats, which were in continuous use, including a 30 ft. ex-German seaplane launch, 27 ft. whalers, gigs and sailing and pulling dinghies. These boats were kept on trot moorings between the ship and the Embankment, and were a constant source of interest to the public looking over the wall.[25]

## A DRILL SHIP FOR THE RNVR, 1954–79

The cost of the upkeep of the *Discovery* had by the early 1950s proved too much for the Boy Scouts Association. In June 1953, she was offered unconditionally to the

Admiralty by the Chief Scout, Lord Rowallan, following discussions with the Admiral Commanding Reserves, who was seeking more space for the London Division of the Royal Naval Volunteer Reserve. She was to be accepted, subject to survey, as an additional drill ship for the RNVR. Reasonable access for the public was to be ensured by the Board of Admiralty. The Admiralty also undertook to leave the original wardroom and cabins as they were and 'to do what we can to allow facilities for weekend training for Sea Scouts and for mooring their boats'. Mr Peter Scott intervened to protest in September 1954, on hearing of the negotiations in hand. He was anxious to save her from being gutted, to preserve public access and to keep her for youth training. A *Discovery* Trust was formed, with an Appeal Committee, and a Question was asked in Parliament. As a result the Admiralty expressed its willingness to give up its claim in favour of Mr Scott and the Trust. However, in the words of an Admiralty memorandum:

> On 12 May, after a meeting of the DISCOVERY Committee, Mr. Scott wrote to the First Lord accepting his assurances and withdrawing the Committee's claim. His letter says: . . . 'our Committee decided that the preservation of the DISCOVERY as a memorial to my father would be best served by accepting the proposals outlined in your recent letters. The Committee felt that the assurances that active training of boys would take place in the ship would meet the objections which they had previously had to her use for office and storage space. They welcomed the proposals for opening the ship to the public and for the forenoon and week-end facilities to be made available to voluntary organisations.'[26]

On the withdrawal of Mr (later Sir) Peter Scott, the First Lord of the Admiralty wrote to Lord Rowallan on 4 June 1954, telling him that the Admiralty would accept the *Discovery*. On 17 June, the Admiral Commanding Reserves was informed and requested to assume administrative responsibility for the ship. The same Admiralty letter also confirmed that the Sea Scouts could continue to keep their boats at the *Discovery* and that they would be provided with facilities on board; the public should also be permitted to visit the ship.[27] Between 1955 and 1979 most of the vessel's surviving Vosper internal fittings and the echo-sounding gear were removed. Although it had been specified that 'the Wardroom Cabins, Chart Room and two compartments abaft the Chart Room were not to be materially disturbed',[28] the two cabins were done away with and the chart-room table removed. Many other alterations were made.

The announcement of the take-over was made at the Jubilee Review on 12 June 1954. After a year undergoing repairs and alterations in the graving dock at Blackwall, she was commissioned as HMS *Discovery* on 20 July 1955, wearing the flag of the Admiral Commanding Reserves. HMS *President*, which also berthed alongside the Victoria Embankment, was the main drill ship of the RNVR London Division and the *Discovery* took her place from time to time for reserve new entry training, when the *President* was under refit. HMS *Discovery* was used mainly for training those about to begin their

National Service until its abolition in 1960. After that date, her role was reduced, but she continued to fly the flag of the Admiral Commanding Reserves until late 1976, just before that post was abolished. The ship also served for some years as a naval recruiting centre in London. Some Heads of Department were given the use of the wooden cabins leading off the wardroom.[29]

By 1973, the Ministry of Defence (Navy) was considering the future of the *Discovery*. In March 1978, the Press announced that a new owner was being sought in the light of the reductions in the Reserves, of reduced votes for defence expenditure and of her need for an extensive refit. It was at that time that the Maritime Trust and the National Maritime Museum assumed an active interest in her preservation.[30]

## WITH THE MARITIME TRUST, 1979-86

On 2 April 1979, HMS *Discovery* was handed over by the Flag Officer, Medway, on behalf of the Ministry of Defence (Navy), to the Maritime Trust during a ceremony on board ship at the *Discovery*'s mooring in the Thames near Waterloo Bridge. On that day she became once again a Royal Research Ship. Her new owners, the Maritime Trust, agreed to work together with the National Maritime Museum. The Maritime Trust (in London) was to take charge of the ship's structure, while the National Maritime Museum would mount displays and provide warding staff. The Maritime Trust had been established in 1969, in the words of HRH Prince Philip, Duke of Edinburgh, 'to do for historic ships what the National Trust does for buildings'.

The *Discovery* was first towed down river to Sheerness, where a major docking enabled essential underwater repairs to be made. It had been suggested that her whole hull was rotten, but all that was required was for the seams to be recaulked and repayed. The Vosper propeller of 1925 was taken off, the shingle ballast removed and the masts stepped. She returned to a new berth in the picturesque St Katharine's Dock, near the Tower of London, entering the dock on the high spring tide to lie near the Trust's outstanding collection of historic ships. It was decided that she should not return to the Embankment, owing to the difficulty of access and a lack of parking and other facilities for visitors there. It was considered essential for her preservation to keep her wooden hull afloat, and St Mary Overy Dock on the south bank of the Thames was considered seriously for some time as a permanent berth.

During her seven years in St Katharine's Dock, the vessel's port side from water-line to bulwark capping was restored, as were the forward hold and galley. Ten yards and a mizzen spanker boom were made from New Forest trees, vastly improving her looks. Essential maintenance was carried out on the ship's fabric, to reduce the ingress of rain-water and to treat and contain wet and dry rot, then prevalent throughout. More than half a million pounds were raised and spent by the Trust on the *Discovery*. This comprised monies subscribed by many donors, including the (then) Greater London

Council, which matched the other donations. The decision was taken at an early stage to restore her only to her 1925 condition; she would have had to be partly rebuilt to reproduce her original form in Scott's day. There were, besides, a hundred Vosper drawings of her refit and a thousand photographs available to provide every detail of her 1925 state. Another factor in that decision was her active role at sea during the *Discovery* Expedition of 1925–7 and during the BANZARE voyages of 1929–31, as opposed to her more passive one as winter quarters during the National Antarctic Expedition of 1901–4.

Various stages of the vessel's restoration were filmed and temporary displays mounted for the public by a small *Discovery* Project Team at Greenwich. Plans for permanent displays covering all her voyages were made. In the end, owing to her move to Scotland, only those showing her construction and the National Antarctic Expedition were actually mounted in the hold. The *Discovery*'s history was researched (leading to this book), and two symposia were held, attended by old 'Discoverers' and interested individuals and organisations.

It was never the intention that the *Discovery* should remain in St Katharine's Dock, as she warranted star treatment. Various other berths in London were considered, particularly in the Docklands, but either the berth was unsuitable or funding to complete restoration was uncertain. Then came an offer from Scotland, where there was no nationally significant ship on show, whereas London already had two. Thus it was that the *Discovery* came to return to Dundee, where she had been built 85 years before.

# TWENTY-TWO

## 'HOME TO DUNDEE'

'HOME TO DUNDEE' proclaimed the banners as the *Discovery* headed away from her berth in St Katharine's Dock on 27 March 1986. She was nudged and towed gently through the narrow lock and into the Thames at the height of an equinoctial tide of 25 feet, the only one that year and one that fixed immutably her departure from London. Detailed planning for this had begun after the signing, on 29 November 1985, of the Charter Agreement between the Maritime Trust and the main financial backers for her return to Scotland, the Dundee Heritage Trust and the Scottish Development Agency. The merits of such a move in the end won over the Greater London Council and others who had wished to keep the *Discovery* in London. As the Maritime Trust's deputy director put it,

> The ship was to return to a prestigious, cold salt water, custom-built dock; a free berth, funds to complete her restoration and an enthusiastic professional team to finish the work started by the Trust in 1979; a £2.6 million project to place a unique part of our maritime heritage in Scotland . . . in a revitalised tourist area of a famous and historic port.

The barque's displacement and stability had first been checked, showing that, as in Scott's day, she was 'stiff but stable'. Only a year after they had been crossed for the first time since the war, the yards had to be sent down (together with the topgallant masts) in order to reduce the strain on the lower masts and to lessen the top weight for towing. Departure from St Katharine's on a high tide was necessary because both lock gates had to be opened at the same time so as to allow the *Discovery*'s 172 feet out into the river. Work on the vessel was carried out to ensure that she was watertight and pumps were installed and safety equipment embarked, all under the eye of the Salvage Association. The dock had to be dredged and a clear passage provided. A team of volunteers, the *Discovery* Service Crew, manned the ropes and warps with professional skill. They felt a quiver of anticipation in her hull as she entered the Thames, the 'call of the running tide' perhaps reminding the old barque of her many voyages of long ago, down river towards distant lands. The *Discovery* made the 500-mile voyage north as dry cargo in the floating dock ship, *Happy Mariner*, owned by the Dutch shipping company of Mammoet, which operated regularly out of Dundee. The *Discovery* docked safely into the mother vessel above Tower Bridge on Easter Sunday, 30 March 1986, and next morning departed for Dundee, securely cradled for her East Coast voyage, as if making once more for Hudson Bay.

'Home sweet home, for old explorer', read one of the newspaper headlines heralding her arrival two days later in Dundee. As the *Happy Mariner* and her precious cargo approached the River Tay, she was met by the Tay pilot cutter, the lifeboat *Spirit of Tayside* and the *Coral Star*, carrying eager sightseers. Crowds lined the estuary to cheer her, while a fly-past of a wartime Shackleton bomber from Lossiemouth and three RAF Phantom fighters from Leuchars welcomed the *Discovery* home. Thousands of Dundonians lined the banks of the Tay to welcome the old ship back, many of them moved to tears at the sight of her and the memory of her deeds. She had returned to Dundee not to be laid up and forgotten, but to take on a new role as the symbol of regeneration for the city that built her. Her return brought a renewed sense of pride and confidence to people who in comparatively recent times had perhaps known more than their fair share of economic disappointment. Now, imaginations have been fired and Dundee has adopted 'City of Discovery' as her slogan and taken the ship to her heart as evidence of a bright new future. Dundee people and businesses had by the summer of 1991 contributed over half a million pounds for the cost of *Discovery*'s restoration. Voluntary involvement with the ship has been enthusiastically given by Dundonians from all walks of life, determined that *Discovery* will continue to inspire generations to come. The first visitor, once the ship opened to the public, was Mr Bill Heald, son of Able Seaman William Heald, Royal Navy, who sailed to the Antarctic during her first voyage, under Captain Scott, early in the century.

The *Discovery*'s final berthing was dramatic: she became jammed in the hold of the *Happy Mariner* and finally, after some delay, reached the Victoria Dock on the midnight tide of 3/4 April, by which time the crowds had gone. 'Only a few romantics were left', read one newspaper report, 'to see her safely back to the place where her lifetime's voyaging began.' The lock swung open to allow her access to the inner Victoria Dock where an RNR piper aboard the old wooden fighting ship, the frigate *Unicorn*, saluted her arrival as a neighbour.

Suddenly a piper appeared on her deck and the *Discovery* slipped home to her final haven to the sound of Scotland's music ringing out across the water of the dock. The wind sent her flags and pennants snapping as she rocked against the harbour wall and the pipe band on the quayside played songs of welcome. The journey was over. The tugs cast off their lines and sounded their sirens. All the work, all the money, all the time invested in the project had been rewarded. *Discovery* was home at last.

# CHRONOLOGY OF THE *DISCOVERY*

### National Antarctic Expedition 1901–4

Leader: Commander R. F. Scott, RN

| | | |
|---|---|---|
| 1900 | March | Keel laid on the Tay at the old Stephen's (Panmure) Shipyard by the Dundee Shipbuilders Company. |
| 1901 | 21 March | Launched into the waters of the Tay, christened by Lady Markham, wife of Sir Clements Markham, President of the Royal Geographical Society. |
| | | Owners: Royal Geographical Society (Registered managing owner, Sir Clements Markham). |
| | 1 August | Anchored at Spithead to swing ship. |
| | 5 August | Secured to a buoy in Cowes Harbour during Cowes Week. Visited by King Edward VII and Queen Alexandra in the morning. Open to the public in the afternoon. |
| | 6 August | Sailed from Cowes via South Trinidad for the Cape, arriving 3 October. |
| | 24 December | Left Lyttelton, New Zealand, for the Antarctic. |
| 1902 | 3 January | Crossed Antarctic Circle. |
| | 4 January | Entered the pack-ice of the Ross Sea. |
| | 8 January | Out into the open sea. First sight of Antarctica. |
| | 30 January | Sailed along Ross Ice Front and discovered Edward VII Land. |
| | 8 February | Found winter quarters near Mount Erebus, Ross Island, McMurdo Sound. Hut erected (at Hut Point). Other work done. Ship made ready for wintering. |
| | 21 June | Midwinter celebrations. |
| | 2 September | First spring sledge journey (Scott). |
| | October | Record deposited by Royds and party at Cape Crozier. Skelton discovered Emperor penguin rookery there. |
| | 2 November | Scott, Shackleton and Wilson left on southern journey. |
| | November | Royds and party re-visited Emperor penguin rookery at Cape Crozier. Egg found. |
| | 29 November | Armitage and party left on western journey. Ascended Ferrar Glacier to reach plateau of Victoria Land. |
| | 30 December | Southern party reached farthest south latitude 82°16′ S. |
| 1903 | 19 January | Western party returned. |
| | 24 January | Relief ship *Morning* (Captain William Colbeck) arrived McMurdo Sound. |
| | 3 February | Southern party returned. |
| | 2 March | *Morning* departed. |
| | April–August | Second wintering. |
| | September | Wilson visisted Cape Crozier (Emperor penguin rookery). |

|  |  |  |
|---|---|---|
|  | 12 October–<br>1 January 1904 | Scott's western sledge journey to inland plateau. Other spring sledging journeys. |
| 1904 | 5 January | Relief ships *Morning* (Captain Colbeck) and *Terra Nova* (Captain H. MacKay) entered McMurdo Sound. |
|  | 14 February | Reached *Discovery*. |
|  | 16 February | *Discovery* at last freed from ice. |
|  | 17 February | Left winter quarters. Blown ashore at Hut Point; aground 8 hours. |
|  | 24 February | Rudder replaced off Cape Adare. |
|  | 2 March | Sighted Balleny Islands. Sailed over part of 'Wilkes Land'. |
|  | 5 March | Re-crossed Antarctic Circle. |
|  | 15 March | Reached Ross Harbour, Auckland Islands. |
|  | 19 March | *Terra Nova* arrived Auckland Islands. |
|  | 20 March | *Morning* arrived Auckland Islands. |
|  | 2 April | Three vessels reached Lyttelton, New Zealand. |
|  | 15 May | *Terra Nova* sailed for Falkland Islands and home, arriving Sheerness 18 August. |
|  | 8 June | *Morning* departed Lyttelton, arriving Plymouth 18 October. |
|  | 8 June | *Discovery* departed Lyttelton. |
|  | June | Made first soundings in high latitudes of South Pacific. Searched for 'Dogherty Islands' (non-existent). |
|  | July | Through Magellan Straits to Falkland Islands, where coal was replenished and last magnetic observations made. |
|  | 9 September | Arrived in the Channel. |
|  | 10 September | Arrived Portsmouth. |
|  | 15 September | Berthed East India Dock, London. |
|  | November | Exhibition of watercolours and photographs at Bruton Galleries, London. |
|  | 7 November | Captain Scott gave lecture on the expedition at the Royal Albert Hall. |

**Hudson's Bay Company: Voyages to Hudson Bay 1905–11**

|  |  |  |
|---|---|---|
| 1905 | January | Bought by the Hudson's Bay Company. Adapted by the ship's husbands Messrs Williams and Sage (London, EC) as a merchant vessel. |
| 1905 | *Voyage* | Master: Alexander Gray |
|  | 15 June | Departed West India Dock. |
|  | 21 June | Arrived Aberdeen. |
|  | 22 June | Departed. |
|  | 27 August | Arrived Charlton Island, James Bay. Discharging and loading at Charlton Island. |
|  | 8 September | Departed. |
|  | 3 November | Arrived West India Dock. |
| 1906 | *Voyage* | Master: John G. Ford |
|  | 14 June | Departed West India Dock. |

| | | |
|---|---|---|
| | 10 August | Arrived Charlton Island. |
| | 24 August | Departed. |
| | 5 October | Arrived West India Dock. |
| 1907 | *Voyage* | Master: John G. Ford |
| | 20 June | Departed West India Dock. |
| | 8 August | Arrived Charlton Island. |
| | 27 August | Departed. |
| | 27 September | Arrived West India Dock. |
| 1908 | *Voyage* | Master: John G. Ford |
| | 13 June | Departed West India Dock. |
| | 19 August | Arrived Charlton Island. |
| | 3 September | Departed. |
| | 7 October | Arrived West India Dock. |
| 1909 | *Voyage* | Master: John G. Ford |
| | 19 June | Departed West India Dock. |
| | 12 August | Arrived Charlton Island. |
| | 25 August | Departed. |
| | 2 October | Arrived West India Dock. |
| 1910 | *Voyage* | Master: John G. Ford |
| | 21 June | Departed West India Dock. |
| | 3 August | Arrived Charlton Island. |
| | 28 August | Departed. |
| | 6 September | Arrived York Road. |
| | 24 September | Departed. |
| | 5 November | Arrived West India Dock. |
| 1911 | *Voyage* | Master: John G. Ford |
| | 17 June | Departed West India Dock. |
| | 4 August | Arrived York Road. |
| | 8 August | Departed. |
| | 14 August | Arrived Charlton Island. |
| | 13 September | Departed. |
| | 29 October | Arrived West India Dock. |
| 1912–15 | | Laid up in London. |
| 1915 | *Voyages* | Master: J. H. Williams |
| | 16 April | Departed London. |
| | | Ports of call: Falmouth, Halifax, New York, La Pallice, La Rochelle. |
| | 30 July | Arrived Falmouth. |
| | | Master: G. F. Bush |
| | | Departed Falmouth. |
| | 6 August | Arrived Swansea. |
| | | Master: William James Bartley |
| | | Departed Swansea. |

313

| | 7 September | Arrived Manchester. |
|---|---|---|
| | | Master: William James Bartley |
| | September | Departed Manchester. |
| | | Ports of call: Nantes, Bordeaux, Brest, Archangel, Dundee, Le Havre, Plymouth. |
| | 10 December | Arrived Swansea. |
| 1916 | *Voyages* | Master: William James Bartley |
| | 28 January | Departed Swansea. |
| | | Port of call: Cardiff. |
| | 3 February | Arrived Bristol. |
| | | Master: William James Bartley |
| | 5 February | Departed Bristol. |
| | | Ports of call: Bordeaux, Nantes, Brest, Nantes, Lorient, Nantes, Lorient, Nantes, Boulogne. |
| | 29 May | Arrived Plymouth. |
| | | Refitted at Devonport Royal Naval Dockyard by the Admiralty and sent south to rescue Shackleton's party marooned on Elephant Island. |
| | | Master: James Fairweather |
| | 31 July | Departed Plymouth 'on a voyage to Elephant Island in the Antartic [*sic*] Ocean' (Official log BT.100/305). |
| | | Ports of call: St Vincent (Cape Verde Islands), Montevideo, Buenos Aires, Pernambuco, St Vincent, where master invalided home and succeeded by John Cumming, Chief Officer. |
| | 29 November | Arrived Plymouth. |
| 1916–17 | *Voyages* | Master: L. Hiles |
| | 20 December | Departed Plymouth. |
| | | Ports of call: Lorient, Pauillac, Bayonne, Rochefort, Bayonne, Nantes, Brest, Lorient, Nantes, Rochefort, Nantes, St-Nazaire, Bordeaux, Bayonne, Bordeaux, Nantes, Bayonne, Bordeaux, Brest, Bayonne (17 July). |
| | 28 July | Arrived Barry. |
| | | Master: F. Gray |
| | 27 August | Departed Barry. |
| | | Ports of call: Funchal, Bilbao, Bordeaux, Pauillac. |
| | 9 November | Arrived Cardiff. |
| 1917–18 | *Voyages* | Master: F. Gray |
| | 19 November | Departed Cardiff. |
| | | Ports of call: St-Nazaire, Nantes, Bayonne. |
| | 1 February | Arrived Cardiff. |
| | | Master: F. Gray |
| | 14 February | Departed Cardiff. |

|            |              | Ports of call: Bayonne, Bordeaux, Nantes, Bayonne. |
|------------|--------------|---|
|            | 25 April     | Arrived Cardiff. |
| 1918–19    | *Voyage*     | Master: G. H. Mead |
|            | 30 May       | Departed Cardiff. |
|            | 30 June      | Arrived Montreal. |
|            | 12 July      | Departed. |
|            | 9 September  | Arrived Charlton Island. |
|            | 23 September | Departed. |
|            | 13 October   | Arrived St John's, Newfoundland. |
|            | 3 December   | Departed. |
|            | 11 December  | Arrived Halifax. |
|            | 24 December  | Departed. |
|            | 16 January   | Arrived Liverpool. |
| 1919       | *Voyage*     | Master G. H. Mead |
|            | 31 January   | Departed Liverpool. |
|            |              | Ports of call: Antwerp, London, Antwerp, King's Lynn. |
|            | 22 March     | Arrived Hull. |
| 1919–20    | *Voyages*    | Master: G. H. Mead (later D. D. Richards) |
|            | 25 March     | Departed Hull. |
|            |              | Ports of call: Bordeaux (twice), Rotterdam (3 times), Dunkirk, Le Havre (twice). |
|            | 7 July       | Arrived Hull. |
|            |              | Master: George L. Weatherill |
|            |              | Owners: Messrs Sale & Co. |
|            | 25 July      | Departed Hull. |
|            |              | Ports of call: Constantinople, Novorossysk, Taganrog roads, Piraeus, Malta. |
|            | 11 March     | Arrived London. |
| 1922       | February     | Hudson's Bay Company granted ship as temporary headquarters to 16th Stepney Sea Scout Troop. |

### The *Discovery* (Oceanographic) Expedition, 1925–7

Director of Research: Dr Stanley Kemp (appointed June 1924).
Master: Commander J. R. Stenhouse, DSO, OBE, RNR (appointed June 1923)

| 1923 |       | Bought by the Crown Agents for the Colonies for the purpose of 'scientific research in the South Seas'. |
|------|-------|---|
|      | March | *Discovery* Committee appointed by the Secretary of State for the Colonies to make a serious attempt to place the whaling industry on a scientific basis. Other aims: to render service to navigation, to ascertain fishery resources and to add to the scientific knowledge of the sea. |

| | | |
|---|---|---|
| 1923–4 | | Refitted by Messrs Vosper. Foremast moved forward one space, mainmast two spaces. Place of registration changed from London to Port Stanley, Falkland Islands. Designated a Royal Research Ship. |
| 1925 | February | *Discovery* Committee's Marine Biological Station on South Georgia set up. Work began under N. A. Mackintosh (and continued with periodical changes of staff until 1931). Examined 181 whales by April 1925, 738 by April 1926 and 1,680 by April 1927. Similar work at Saldanha Bay (South Africa) whaling station was carried out May 1925–October 1926. |
| | 5 October | Sailed south from Falmouth, calling at the Canaries and Ascension Island. |
| | 20 December | Arrived Cape Town. |
| | 31 December | Whale marking and research vessel *William Scoresby* launched. Ready for sea, June 1926. |
| 1926 | 17 January | Left Cape Town. |
| | 30 January | Arrived Tristan da Cunha. Left mail, read message from King, investigated marine fauna. |
| | 1 February | Left Tristan da Cunha. Made five deep-water stations on passage. |
| | 20 February | Arrived South Georgia. Carried out observations on whaling grounds and undertook survey work. |
| | 17 April | Left South Georgia. |
| | 25 April | Arrived Port Stanley, Falkland Islands. Cruised to northern end of Falkland Sound. |
| | 20 May | Left Port Stanley. Made nine full stations on passage. Large plankton nets towed. |
| | 29 June | Arrived Cape Town. Into dry dock at Simonstown to be fitted with bilge keels, the ship's heavy rolling having proved a serious hindrance to the proper operation of the scientific gear. Scientific staff fully employed on laboratory work and on visits to South African whaling stations to measure and examine whales. Some very early embryos found. |
| | 21 September | Left Simonstown and made two short cruises off the African coast. |
| | 27 October | Left Africa for South Georgia meeting heavy ice. Sighted Bouvetøya. |
| | 5 December | Arrived South Georgia and resumed survey of whaling grounds. |
| 1927 | January | Made observations on hydrology, plankton and fish round South Georgia. |
| | 4 February | Sailed for South Orkneys and carried out observations in this archipelago, in the South Shetlands, Palmer Archipelago, Bismarck and Gerlache Straits. Met many icebergs, one 35 miles long. Made hydrographic surveys. Proceeded to Cape Horn, carrying out a series of observations across Drake Passage. |
| | 6 May | Reached Port Stanley, Falkland Islands, and soon afterwards sailed for Cape Town. |
| | June | Spent three weeks at Cape Town in dock. |

| | | |
|---|---|---|
| | July–August | Homeward voyage to England, calling at West African whaling stations. |
| | 29 September | Arrived home, having traversed 37,000 miles and made 299 stations from her decks. The *William Scoresby* had returned to England in August, having made a whale marking and oceanographical cruise off South Georgia and a trawling survey off the Falkland Islands. |

### British, Australian and New Zealand Antarctic Research Expedition (BANZARE) 1929–31

Leader: Sir Douglas Mawson
Master: Captain John King Davis (1929–30); Captain K. N. MacKenzie (1930–1)
The *Discovery* was lent to the expedition by the British Government as Britain's contribution. Two southern summer voyages to the Antarctic were made in 1929–30 and 1930–1.

| | | |
|---|---|---|
| 1929 | August | Left London. |
| | October | Arrived Cape Town. Took on stores. Joined by Mawson and scientific staff. Square rigging removed from mainmast. |
| | 19 October | Left Cape Town for south. |
| | 2–4 November | At Iles Crozet, surveying and carrying out scientific work. |
| | 12–24 November | At Iles Kerguelen, coaling and carrying out surveys and scientific work. |
| | 26 November–3 December | At Heard Island. |
| | 31 December–26 January 1930 | Antarctic continent. Discovered Mac.Robertson Land from the Gipsy Moth aeroplane; visited Kemp and Enderby Lands, proving them to be connected. Position of coastline from long. 45°E. to 75°E. roughly charted from ship and aircraft; met *Norvegia* (Hjalmar Riiser-Larsen) of Norway, near Cape Ann on 14 January 1930, when the leaders of the two expeditions agreed on long. 45°E. as the boundary line between British and Norwegian activities. Landed on Proclamation Island (Enderby Land) on 13 January and asserted sovereignty of King George V to Antarctic sector between 73°E. and 47°E. |
| 1930 | 8 February–2 March | At Kerguelen, coaling, surveying etc. |
| | 1 April | Arrived Port Adelaide. |
| | 22 November | Departed Hobart for the south. |
| | 2–4 December | At Macquarie Island. |
| | 15 December | Coaled from whale factory ship *Sir James Clark Ross* (Captain Nilsen) in lat. 65°41′ S. long. 178°29.5′ E. |
| | 29 December | Coaled from whale factory ship *Kosmos* (Captain Andraesen) in lat. 65°03.5′ S. long. 142°21′ E. |
| 1931 | 4 January | Anchored off Cape Denison, King George V Land. Landing made. 1911–14 hut examined. Proclamation made. |

| | |
|---|---|
| 7 January | Off Terre Adélie. Plane flown. |
| 15/16 January | Plane flown. 'Banzare Land' and Cape Goodenough discovered. |
| 18 January | Plane flown. 'Sabrina Land' named in poor weather. |
| 27 January | Plane flown in bad weather, sighting probable land in vicinity of Wilkes's Knox Land. Plane damaged on being hoisted aboard. |
| 28 January | Bowman Island discovered. |
| 29–31 January | Off remains of previously charted Termination Ice Tongue. Passed whaler *Nielsen Alonso* in 64°S. 98°E. (her reported position). |
| 1–11 February | Largely steaming west in ice. Closed SS *Lestris* and *Falk*. Coaled from *Lestris* on 6 February. Flights on 9, 10 and 11. Discovered Princess Elizabeth Land. |
| 12 February | Cape Darnley sighted from ship. |
| 13 February | Murray Monolith approached. Landed near Scullin Monolith and proclamation made. |
| 14 February | Sighted David, Casey, Masson and other ranges, from ship (discovered 1930). Continued examination of Mac.Robertson Land. |
| 18 February | Landed at Cape Bruce. Proclamation made. Steamed northward. |
| 19 March | Arrived Hobart. |
| 18 April | Departed Melbourne. |
| 2 May | Arrived Wellington. |
| May–July | Homeward voyage via Cape Horn and Montevideo. |
| 1 August | Arrived London. |

### Sea Scouts and After

| | |
|---|---|
| 1931–6 | Laid up in London (East India Dock). |
| 1936 | Member of *Discovery* Committee called at HQ of Boy Scouts Association and suggested that the Scouts should take her over as a training ship for Sea Scouts and as a memorial to Captain Scott and his comrades. Acceptance of this 'wonderful offer' (Lord Hampton) depended on the co-operation of the Government of the Falkland Islands, to whom the ship still belonged, the raising of a sum of money sufficient to ensure her proper upkeep, and the consent of the Port of London Authority to allot her moorings in a spot easily accessible to the boys who were to use her. Lady Houston (who had ensured British participation in the Schneider Trophy air race) contributed generously to the *Discovery* Trust Fund. |
| 1936–7 | Accepted on behalf of Boy Scouts Association by HRH the Duke of Kent, Commodore of Sea Scouts, from Sir Herbert Henniker-Heaton, Governor of the Falkland Islands. The ceremony took place in the presence of the Chief Scout, the Colonial Secretary and a distinguished company, including six members who had sailed on her first voyage. Ship moored alongside Thames Embankment in King's Reach. |

The *Discovery* was used by Sea Scouts from 1936 to 1955 as a training ship and as a hostel for Scouts visiting London. She was the national centre for training Sea Scouts in all branches of seamanship. Thousands of Scouts came from all over the country for week-long and weekend courses. Sea Scout leaders came for instruction courses and many local troops kept their boats on *Discovery*'s moorings or used her boats. She had a small full-time crew and a Rover Service Crew to run the courses and do much of the work in the ship.

| | |
|---|---|
| 1939–45 | Special Admiralty courses were run on board the *Discovery* for men about to enter the Royal Navy. She was also the headquarters of the River Emergency Service. During the war, her engine and machinery were taken out and broken up for scrap. The *Discovery* was undamaged during the Blitz but the cable of a barrage balloon that had broken adrift is said to have fouled and damaged the main lower yard. The yard was found to be rotten, and all the yards were sent down for safety. |
| 1946–55 | Continued in use by Sea Scouts, under ownership of Boy Scouts Association. |
| 1955–79 | Transferred to the Admiralty for use by the Royal Naval Reserve and the Royal Naval Auxiliary Service as an additional drill ship, but also used by Sea Scouts. Many of her surviving 1925 Vosper internal fittings removed. |
| 1979 | Handed over to Maritime Trust by Ministry of Defence (Navy). Restoration began. Research and displays by National Maritime Museum, Greenwich. |
| 1986 | Transfer and voyage to Dundee. |

# NOTES AND REFERENCES

## PART I.
## THE NATIONAL ANTARCTIC EXPEDITION, 1901–4

### Chapter One. The Origins of the National Antarctic Expedition and the Building of the *Discovery*

1 Sir John Murray, 'The renewal of Antarctic exploration', *Geographical Journal*, vol. iii, no. 1, 1894, pp. 1–42, map p. 80. See also Murray's earlier paper, 'The Exploration of the Antarctic regions', *Scottish Geographical Magazine*, vol. ii, 1886, pp. 527–48.

2 For Markham's life, see A. H. Markham, *The Life of Sir Clements Markham* (John Murray, London, 1917).

3 See the summary of Ommanney's paper to the British Association for the Advancement of Science, which 'drew attention to the neglect of the Antarctic regions as a field for exploration' in *Proceedings of the Royal Geographical Society*, vol. vii, 1885, pp. 758–9. On the Australian efforts, see R. A. Swan, *Australia in the Antarctic* (Melbourne University Press, 1961).

4 Captain R. F. Scott, *The Voyage of the 'Discovery'* (Smith, Elder, London, 1905), vol. i, p. 47.

5 *Report of the Sixth Geographical Congress* (John Murray, London, 1896), pp. 109–67.

6 Ibid., p. 780.

7 *Proceedings of the Royal Society of London*, vol. lxii, 1898, pp. 424–51.

8 Markham, op. cit., p. 317.

9 I am indebted to the Archivist, Mrs C. Kelly, for a copy of this letter and the following one—Markham's reply. RGS Archives, AA 1/3/1.

10 Draft letter from Sir Clements Markham to Mr Goschen, First Lord of the Admiralty, 11 November 1895. RGS Archives, AA 1/3/2.

11 N. A. M. Rodger, 'The dark ages of the Admiralty, 1869–95', *Mariner's Mirror*, 1976, vol. lxii, no. 1, p. 36.

12 N. A. M. Rodger, *The Admiralty* (Dalton, Lavenham, 1979), p. 114.

13 Ibid., p. 115.

14 See Ann Savours 'The British Admiralty and the Arctic, 1773–1876' in *Pôle Nord 1983/North Pole 1983 . . . Actes du 10ᵉ colloque international du Centre d'Etudes Arctiques/Proceedings*

*of 10th international Colloquy of the Centre d'Etudes Arctiques, Paris . . . novembre 1983* (Paris, Editions du Centre National de la Recherche Scientifique, 1987), pp. 153–67.

15 Markham later privately called this a 'fatal error'. He had hoped that the name of the Royal Society would bring in funds. In the event he found the coalition 'a source of worry, delays, friction and danger; and no good whatever'. Sir Clements Markham, 'The starting of the Antarctic expedition . . . 1893–1903', p. 21. Scott Polar Research Institute, Cambridge, MS. 1453/2. Much of this was due to the size of the Joint Committee. See the archives of the two societies for both sides of the question and the published version of Markham's account, *Antarctic obsession . . .*, edited and introduced by Clive Holland (Bluntisham Books/Erskine Press, 1986).

16 Sir Clements Markham, *The lands of silence* (Cambridge University Press, 1921), p. 445.

17 Undated press cutting in Longstaff's notebook begun in 1892. In private hands.

18 Obituary in the *Wimbledon Borough News*, 23 November 1916. His grandfather, Henry Blundell, founded Blundell, Spence & Co. (now Blundell Permoglaze), in Hull, 1811. See also *The Criterion* (Hull), 15 September 1877, for which reference I am indebted to Mr A. Credland.

19 Sir Clements Markham, *The lands of silence*, p. 445. Scott to Longstaff, 17 October 1905, in the Longstaff papers, in private hands.

20 29 March 1899.

21 *Standard*, 27 April 1899. One of his sons was Tom Longstaff, the climber, whom Scott invited to join the *Terra Nova* Expedition, 1910–13, as surgeon and naturalist. Longstaff had to decline on account of his own Himalayan plans, but said it was the greatest honour ever paid him. See his autobiography, *This my voyage* (John Murray, London, 1950), p. 163. Tom Longstaff described his father as the 'best friend' he ever had, who shared his interests with his children, particularly natural history. 'Speaking French and German fluently,' wrote Tom Longstaff, 'he had visited nearly every country on the continent, including Russia, during the momentous years of the birth of modern Europe. He had spent a year in Frankfort when it was a Free City, garrisoned by Austrian, Prussian and Bavarian troops, all patrolling the town at night to prevent affrays between their different nationalities. He had seen Austrian sentries posted on the stage of the Opera House in Venice; French bayonets holding Rome; Metz and Sedan just fallen to the Germans; and had been caught in the First Commune in Paris.' *This my voyage*, p. 7. I am indebted to Dr G. Hattersley-Smith for this reference.

22 A. H. Markham, op. cit., pp. 337–8.

23 Preface to *The voyage of the 'Scotia'* by R. C. Mossman *et al.* (Blackwood, Edinburgh, 1906), republished Hurst, London, 1978.

24 Sir Clements Markham. Diary entries, February and March 1901. RGS Archives, CRM 1/14.

25 Sir Clements Markham, 'The Starting of the Antarctic expedition . . .' S.P.R.I. MS. 1435/2.

26 Letter from Sir Clements Markham to Admiral A. H. Markham, 11 August 1899. A. H. Markham Collection, National Maritime Museum, Greenwich, MRK/46. Once the imbroglio with the Royal Society had begun, Markham found Gregory to be 'a man of very nervous temperament', still suffering 'from the effects of tropical fevers', with 'neither experience nor qualification for the command of men'. He considered he had 'no head for organisation and that a serious mistake had been made in selecting him'. Sir Clements Markham, 'The starting of the Antarctic expedition . . .', pp. 188–90. S.P.R.I., MS. 1453/2.

27 H. R. Mill, *The record of the Royal Geographical Society, 1830–1930* (RGS, London, 1930), p. 161.

28  See Sir Clements Markham, 'The starting of the Antarctic expedition . . .', S.P.R.I., MS. 1453/2; also Sir Clements Markham, *The lands of silence*, pp. 447–8; Scott's narrative and the biographies of Scott.

29  Sir Clements Markham to Admiral A. H. Markham, 11 August 1899. N.M.M., MRK/46.

30  Sir Clements Markham, 'The starting of the Antarctic expedition . . .', pp. 6–7. S.P.R.I., MS. 1453/2.

31  Markham to Longstaff, 6 April 1900. (Longstaff papers, in private hands.) Captain Egerton of the *Majestic* had served under Captain Sir George Nares on the British Arctic Expedition of 1875–6, as had Royds's uncle Wyatt Rawson, killed at Tel el Kebir.

32  RGS Archives, AA 3/3/34, 1 April 1900.

33  Captain G. le C. Egerton to Sir Leopold McClintock, 11 May 1900. A. H. Markham Collection, N.M.M., MRK/46.

34  Sir Albert H. Markham, *The life of Sir Clements Markham*, p. 324.

35  Report of the Ship Sub-Committee, 29 November 1899. RGS Archives, AA 5/2/19.

36  A preliminary meeting was held at Markham's house, 21 Eccleston Square, on 17 April 1899 and a formal one on 26 April in the Council Room of the RGS. See RGS Archives, AA 5/2/2, a 'Memorandum naming the chief features of the design of the proposed vessel for the forthcoming British Antarctic Expedition', the result of the two meetings. Mr W. E. Smith, the *Discovery*'s architect, refers to that of 26 April in the *Transactions of the Institution of Naval Architects*, vol. xlvii, part 1, 1905.

37  See letters from Hoskins to Markham of 2, 7 and 17 April 1899 in RGS Archives, AA 5/1/5, 5/1/8 and 5/1/11.

38  RGS Archives, AA 5/1/9.

39  RGS Archives, AA 5/1/4.

40  RGS Archives, AA 5/1/6.

41  For the voyage of the *Fram*, see Fridtjof Nansen, *Farthest North* (Constable, Westminster, 1897), and on Colin Archer, see Tor Borch Sannes, *Colin Archer Skipene* (Bokhandlerforlaget, Oslo, 1978).

42  Report of the Ship Sub-Committee, 29 November 1899. RGS Archives, AA 5/2/19.

43  An obituary of Sir William Edward Smith appeared in the *Transactions of the Institution of Naval Architects*, vol. lxxii, 1930, pp. 333–5, giving further details of his career. He was a member of the Institution for some fifty years, being elected Vice-President in 1906 and Hon. Vice-President in 1926. In 1882 he contributed a paper on 'Hogging and sagging strains in a seaway as influenced by wave structure' and in 1905 another on 'The design of the Antarctic exploration vessel *Discovery*'. He died at Herne Bay in September 1930. A curious story relates to his selection in October 1911 as the future Director of Naval Construction and his dismissal by Churchill (then First Lord of the Admiralty) in the succeeding summer after only one day in the post. In the Lilliecrap Collection of the National Maritime Museum, Greenwich, is a memorandum by J. H. Narbeth dated 16 November 1943, marked 'private and confidential' and headed 'Sir William Edward Smith. Director of Naval Construction of a day' (Classmark LCR/12). It reads as follows:

> In an article on British Schools of Naval Architecture published in *Engineering* some years ago, Sir William Smith states that he was appointed Director of Naval Construction by Mr. McKenna when Sir Philip Watts retired. So far as the writer knows, that is the only authoritative pronouncement on the subject.

That appointment never became operative in the Admiralty office. No office acquaint was ever circulated. Sir William Smith never occupied the Director's room No. 81, and it is believed that he never signed a single paper as Director of Naval Construction.

It is, however, a fact that on one unfortunate day in 1912, he accompanied the Admiralty Board on their annual inspection of Portsmouth Dockyard. The circumstantial story of this visit was told to the writer at Portsmouth Dockyard very shortly afterwards. The Board was assembled on the upper deck (forward) on a battle-ship under construction in No. 15 Dock. Mr. Churchill, who was then First Lord, called for the D.N.C. to obtain information. After a while, Sir William was found discussing a job with a workman 50 or 60 yards away. He was hurried up and when questioned replied that that was his first day as D.N.C. and he had not been able to inform himself on the subject. Portsmouth officers said he was shabbily dressed in ancient attire. Mr. Churchill stared at him with a searching glance of great contempt and turned away to the other members of the Board. He soon spotted the Secretary . . . and said in a gruff voice 'Dismiss that man'. The Secretary made sure who the 'man' was, and began some sort of expostulation, which brought forth a still sterner order 'Dismiss that man tonight'. So before the return train had reached London, Sir William Smith was out of a job. It is believed that he did not return to the Admiralty, not even to gather up his belongings, which were sent on to him . . .

The obituary of Smith aforementioned refers to the matter and implies that the change of First Lord from McKenna to Churchill was responsible for Smith's retention as Superintendent of Contract Work. Churchill was said to have placed on record his 'appreciation of the manner in which Sir William had discharged the difficult and important duties entrusted to him' in the House of Commons, June 1912. Smith was knighted in the Coronation honours of 1911.

44  Sir Clements Markham later wrote a biography of McClintock, *Life of Admiral Sir Leopold McClintock* (John Murray, London, 1909).

45  Published in the *Transactions*, vol. xlvii, part 1, 1905, pp. 1–42, folding plans at end. See also R. W. Skelton's note headed 'Antarctic Exploration Vessel *Discovery*', which must have been written either for Smith or Scott on the return of the expedition. S.P.R.I., MS. 342/5/3. See too Ian Fleming, 'Antarctic research vessel *Discovery*', *Model Shipwright*, 31 March 1980, pp. 44–57. The RGS and the N.M.M. own models of SY *Discovery*. There is also a shipwright's notebook in the Ships' Department, N.M.M. There are plans in the S.P.R.I. and the N.M.M.

46  This list differs from that given in Smith's paper (p. 3) and incorporates Markham's alterations in the copy in RGS Archives, *Discovery* AA 5/2/39. His list in *The lands of silence*, p. 446, resurrects Sir John Murray and Field. Scott does not list the Ship Committee, as being too numerous, *The voyage of the 'Discovery'*, vol. i, p. 46.

47  W. E. Smith, 'The design of the Antarctic exploration vessel *Discovery*', *Transactions of the Institution of Naval Architects*, vol. xlvii, part 1, 1905, pp. 3–4.

48  See Alan McGowan, 'Captain Cook's ships', *Mariner's Mirror*, vol. lxv, pp. 109–18, and A. W. H. Pearsall, 'Bomb vessels', *Polar Record*, vol. xvi, no. 105, 1973, pp. 781–8.

49  Sir Robert Seppings's 'round stern' was introduced in 1821 to improve and provide more strength in that part of the vessel's structure. This new system of stern framing did away with

the square counter stern and also saved a great deal of large curved timbers (transoms). I am indebted to Mr Alan Viner for this information.

50 W. E. Smith, op. cit., pp. 7–8. Mr Alan Viner comments, 'Bilge keels are the most troublesome of fittings and it is doubtful whether any sailing vessel behaves any better with them. The worst rolling can be experienced in a situation where, through lack of wind, the vessel lays beam on to a big sea left over from the previous "blow", but this is a condition which occurs infrequently at sea. Only one or two of the big steel barques with their great weight aloft were fitted with the keels to clamp down their rolling, but they were never a complete success. The retractable stabilisers of later years proved to be the answer.' The bilge keels eventually fitted during the 1925–7 expedition do seem to have done some good. They were bolted onto guard plates and could be removed without damaging the hull.

51 Ibid., pp. 9 and 15.

52 R. W. Skelton. Diaries, vol. i, S.P.R.I., MS. 342/1/1.

53 I am indebted to Mr M. R. C. Parr for pointing out these features.

54 RGS Archives, AA 5/2/19.

55 Copies of the original printed specifications, for ship and for hull, of 1899 are in the McClintock Collection, N.M.M., MCL/46, together with notes by W. E. Smith on sails and rigging, 1899 and 1900.

56 RGS Archives, AA 5/2/21.

57 R. F. Scott, *The Voyage of the 'Discovery'*, vol. i, p. 48. Although it is true that the building of large (i.e. over 200-ton) wooden vessels was quite finished, many hundreds of 50- to 200-ton wooden cargo or fishing vessels were yet to be built up to (and for a few years after) the Great War. The only difference in building a big as opposed to a smaller vessel is related to size, not technique. Even today (1985) fishing vessels up to 100 feet in length are being constructed on the same principles. I am indebted to Mr Alan Viner for these remarks.

58 RGS Archives, AA 5/2/22.

59 RGS Archives, AA 52/23–26.

60 W. E. Smith, op. cit., p. 13. The company was formed in 1894 and took over the Panmure Shipyard from Alexander Stephen and Sons. See Fred H. Walker, 'The Panmure Shipyard and *Discovery*', *Mariner's Mirror*, vol. lxvi, no. 3, 1980, p. 258. A series of Valentine photographs shows building work in progress and the launch of the *Discovery*. These are in the University Library of St Andrews, Fife. See also R. F. Scott, *The Voyage of the 'Discovery'*, vol. i, pp. 56–7, for praise of Gourlay's engines and lifting screw. The Engineering Lieutenant, R. W. Skelton, RN, held the opposite opinion from Smith regarding the shipbuilders. He thought they had 'performed their contract in a most scandalous manner'. Although the hull was well constructed of very good materials, he found their iron, steel and metalwork 'perfectly disgraceful'. S.P.R.I., MS. 342/1/1. See too A. G. E. Jones, 'The steam yacht Discovery', *Mariner's Mirror*, 1980, vol. lxvi, no. 1, pp. 68–71.

61 R. F. Scott, *The Voyage of the 'Discovery'*, vol. i, p. 63.

62 Ibid., pp. 63–4.

63 Letter from R. F. Scott to Messrs Baxter, Bros. (name not supplied on the letter), written from the Imperial Hotel, Torquay, 8 December 1904. Duncan Collection, Dundee Museums.

64 Thorvald Nilsen, 'The voyage of the *Fram*' in Roald Amundsen, *The South Pole* (John Murray, London, 1912), vol. ii, p. 355.

65 Erich von Drygalski, *Zum Kontinent des eisigen Südens* (Reimer, Berlin, 1904). English

translation by M. M. Raraty, *The southern ice continent: the German South Polar Expedition aboard the Gauss, 1901–03.* Bluntisham and Erskine Press, 1989, chapter 3.

66  Roald Amundsen, *The South Pole* (John Murray, London, 1912), vol. i, p. 152. The *Fram* rolled and rolled: 'Hellish rolling! The ship is scooping up water over both rails and there is no possibility of sleeping', wrote A. S. Kuchin, Russian oceanographer, in his diary for 27–8 August 1910, in the Bay of Biscay and later on 17 November in the Westerlies, 'The waves are of such a size as I had never imagined. But *Fram* is a good ship and only very rarely do the waves sweep across her decks. But on the other hand, she rolls hellishly! She swings from side to side like a pendulum!' Quoted by William Barr, Aleksandr Stephanovich Kuchin . . . *Polar Record*, vol. xxii, no. 139, 1985, pp. 404 and 406.

67  W. E. Smith to Sir Clements Markham, 17 February 1900. RGS Archives, AA 5/2/28 and 5/2/29.

68  R. F. Scott, *The Voyage of the 'Discovery'*, vol. i, pp. 52–3. In 1985 the N.M.M. commissioned a model of a section through the hull.

69  Sir Clements Markham, *The lands of silence*, p. 447.

70  W. E. Smith to Sir Clements Markham, 25 March 1901. RGS Archives, AA 5/2/38.

71  Sir Clements Markham's diary, RGS Archives, CRM 1/14.

72  Sir Clements Markham's diary, 16 February 1901. RGS Archives, CRM. 1/14.


## Chapter Two. Plans, Preparations, the Outward Voyage to the Ross Sea

1  Wharton's and Nares's plans (dated November 1900) and that of Mr J. Y. Buchanan, FRS (dated December 1900), which also opposed Markham's, can be found in the paper printed presumably for discussion by the Joint Committee in early 1901. This was entitled 'Plans of operations for the National Antarctic Expedition'. It has as its first item the 'Plan of operations recommended by the Antarctic Executive Committee' and ends with Sir Clements Markham's review of the 'several routes which may be taken to reach the unknown region of the South'.

2  In his speech at the launch of the *Discovery*, Markham was reported as saying that what direction to explore was one of the most difficult decisions. 'But there was a very old canon . . . always followed in Arctic exploration—that in going to the unknown, they should start from the known'. *Dundee Advertiser*, 22 March 1901.

3  RGS Archives, AA 1/10/11.

4  R. F. Scott, *The Voyage of the 'Discovery'*, vol. i, pp. 81–3.

5  A letter from Sir Clements Markham to Scott, September 1901, emphasised the importance of sledge travelling. Markham wrote, 'For myself the spring travelling, whether from winter quarters in the unknown eastern region or from Wood Bay is by far the most interesting and important part of the work of the expedition. It will call forth all your powers of organisation, both in planning out the general scheme and seeing to every detail. I would urge upon you to study the questions connected with sledge travelling with great care during the winter. Recollect that no-one has even remotely approached the work done by *man* under McClintock and Mecham in 1853 and 1854, especially Mecham in 1854. You will find details in McDougall's book. You could easily have sledges made during the winter, on McClintock's pattern. Everything in sledge travelling, depends on close attention to weights. Dogs are only of limited

use, when ice is smooth. You remind me of Mecham to an extraordinary degree, not in face but in many characteristics and ways. In face you are just like Sherard Osborn. Combine the two with the tenacity of McClintock and you will be, as I feel confident you will, the greatest of polar explorers. Throw your whole mind and energies into this travelling work. I shall think of all those sledge flags about next October year.' National Antarctic Expedition 1901–04, bound vols of MSS in S.P.R.I., vol. v.

6   RGS Archives, AA 1/10/11. This was not quoted by R. F. Scott in *The Voyage of the 'Discovery'*. On a point of fact, Halley's *Paramore* was built in 1694 for scientific purposes. See *The Three Voyages*, ed. N. J. W. Thrower (Hakluyt Society, London, 1981).

7   R. F. Scott, *The Voyage of the 'Discovery'*, vol. i, pp. 37–8 and 40.

8   Edward Wilson, *Diary of the Discovery Expedition to the Antarctic Regions, 1901–1904* (Blandford, London, 1966), p. 29.

9   Ibid., p. 30.

10  Sir Clements Markham to Llewellyn Longstaff, undated letter from 21 Eccleston Square, in the Longstaff papers.

11  Llewellyn Longstaff to his wife Mary, 5 August 1901. Letters in the Longstaff papers.

12  A. B. Armitage, *Two Years in the Antarctic* (Arnold, London, 1905), p. 9. There had evidently been many other visitors. 'All along', wrote Skelton on departure, 'we have been much troubled with numberless Ladies who have if anything obstructed rather than aided the work. (R. W. Skelton. Diary, 6 August 1901. S.P.R.I., MS. 342/1/1.)

13  RGS Archives, CRM 1/15.

14  Angus Erskine, 'The men of the "Discovery" ', *Naval Review*, vol. lvii, 1969, pp. 309–14. This contains interesting notes on the group photograph taken in 1904. See also R. F. Scott, *The Voyage of the 'Discovery'*, vol. i, pp. 65–77. Biographical notes on members of the expedition can be found in Appendix A to Edward Wilson's *Diary of the Discovery expedition . . .*

15  RGS Archives, AA 12/1/4.

16  Incomplete undated letter. N.M.M., MRK/46.

17  R. F. Scott, *The Voyage of the 'Discovery'*, vol. i, p. 75.

18  L. C. Bernacchi, *Saga of the 'Discovery'* (Blackie, London, 1938), pp. 207–12.

19  Diary fragment of E. H. Shackleton, 14 August–3 October 1901, Mitchell Library, Sydney.

20  Ibid.

21  Armitage's narrative of the expedition was published under the title, *Two Years in the Antarctic*, in 1905 and his autobiography, *From cadet to commodore*, in 1925. See also A. G. E. Jones, 'Second in command', *Antarctic* (New Zealand), vol. vi, no. 7, 1972, and D. W. H. Walton, 'Profile: Albert Borlase Armitage', *Polar Record*, vol. xxii, no. 140, 1985, pp. 511–18.

22  R. F. Scott, *The Voyage of the 'Discovery'*, vol. ii, pp. 193–4. See also L. B. Quartermain, *Antarctica's forgotten men* (Millwood Press, Wellington, N.Z., 1981), pp. 4–41, and A. G. E. Jones, 'Charles Royds . . .', *Fram*, vol. ii, part 1, 1985, pp. 360–3.

23  R. F. Scott, *The Voyage of the 'Discovery'*, vol. ii, pp. 193–4. See also A. G. E. Jones, 'Michael Barne . . .', *Fram*, vol. ii, part 1, 1985, pp. 357–9.

24  R. F. Scott, *The Voyage of the 'Discovery'*, vol. i, p. 69.

25  L. C. Bernacchi, op. cit., p. 219. Three lives of Shackleton have been published, one by H. R. Mill, who knew him and his contemporaries well, in 1923, one by James and Margery Fisher (1957) and the latest by Roland Huntford (1985).

26  L. C. Bernacchi, op. cit., p. 30.

27 Three different studies of Wilson by George Seaver were published in 1933, 1937 and 1948. Wilson's *Diary of the Discovery expedition . . .* was published in 1966 by Blandford (London) and in 1967 by Humanities Press (New York).

28 R. F. Scott, *The Voyage of the 'Discovery'*, vol. i, p. 75.

29 R. F. Scott, Letter of Proceedings, no. 2, 29 September 1901. RGS Archives, AA 12/1/5.

30 A. B. Armitage to Sir Clements Markham, 14 October 1901. RGS Archives, AA 12/1/7.

31 Sir William Wharton to Sir Clements Markham, 14 December 1901. RGS Archives, AA 12/1/8.

32 A small pamphlet entitled, 'Antarctic expedition. List of instruments provided' was printed in 1901 by William Clowes, probably for the Royal Society and the RGS. It includes 'Dredging nets' and 'Sounding gear' and also gives the quantities, e.g. barographs (3), boats compasses (6), Barrow's dip circle (2). Copy in S.P.R.I.

33 Captain E. W. Creak to Sir Clements Markham, 2 November 1901. RGS Archives, AA 12/2/4.

34 R. F. Scott, Letter of Proceedings, no. 3, 28 November 1901. RGS Archives, AA 12/1/13.

35 R. F. Scott to Sir Clements Markham, Madeira, 15 August 1901. RGS Archives, AA 12/1/1.

36 R. W. Skelton, Diary, 27 and 31 October 1901, S.P.R.I, MS. 342/1/1.

37 R. F. Scott, Letter of Proceedings, no. 3, 28 November 1901, off Lyttelton. RGS Archives. AA 12/1/13.

38 R. F. Scott, *The Voyage of the 'Discovery'*, vol. i, p. 100.

39 R. F. Scott, *The Voyage of the 'Discovery'*, vol. i, p. 101–2.

40 J. Duncan, Diary kept during the National Antarctic Expedition, Duncan Collection, Dundee Museums.

41 R. W. Skelton, Diary, 15 to 21 November 1901. S.P.R.I. MS. 342/1/1.

42 See B. W. Taylor, *The Flora, Vegetation and Soils of Macquarie Island* (Antarctic Division, Melbourne, 1955); Mary Gillham, *Sub-Antarctic Sanctuary* (Gollancz, London, 1967), and P. M. Selkirk *et al.*, *Sub-Antarctic Macquarie Island: environment and biology* (Cambridge University Press, 1990).

43 J. S. Cumpston, *Macquarie Island* (Antarctic Division, Department of External Affairs, Melbourne, 1968).

44 R. F. Scott, Diary, 22 November 1901. S.P.R.I., MS. 352/1/1.

45 R. F. Scott, *The Voyage of the 'Discovery'*, vol. i, pp. 105–6.

46 R. F. Scott, Diary, 29 November 1901. S.P.R.I., MS. 352/1/1.

47 Draft in RGS Archives, AA 12/1/9.

48 R. F. Scott, Diary, 3 December 1901. S.P.R.I., MS. 352/1/1.

49 R. F. Scott, Letter of Proceedings, no. 4, 22 December 1901. RGS Archives, AA 12/3/8.

50 R. F. Scott, *The Voyage of the 'Discovery'*, vol. i, p. 110.

51 Letter from W. E. Smith to Sir Clements Markham, 18 March 1902. RGS Archives, AA 5/3/12.

52 See Ann Savours and Anita McConnell, 'The history of the Rossbank Observatory', *Annals of Science*, vol. xxxix, 1982, pp. 527–66.

53 The Societies' Presidents to Coleridge Farr, draft letter of October 1901. RGS Archives, AA 12/1/11.

54 L C. Bernacchi, op. cit., p. 232.

55 J. Duncan, Diary kept during the National Antarctic Expedition, Duncan Collection, Dundee Museums.

56 R. F. Scott, *The Voyage of the 'Discovery'*, vol. i, p. 112. The dogs travelled out to Melbourne

under the charge of AB William Weller. When Scott decided to save time by not putting in there, they went on to Lyttelton.

57  Ibid., p. 113.

58  Ibid., p. 114.

59  R. F. Scott, Letter of Proceedings, no. 5, 24 December 1901. RGS Archives, AA 12/13/10.

60  *Under Scott's command: Lashly's Antarctic diaries*, ed. A. R. Ellis (Gollancz, London, 1969), p. 20. On Lashly, see also L. B. Quartermain, *Antarctica's forgotten men*, pp. 42–62.

61  R. F. Scott, *The Voyage of the 'Discovery'*, vol. i, p. 115.

62  Captain James Cook, Journal, 21 February 1775, ed. J. C. Beaglehole (Hakluyt Society, 1961), p. 646.

63  See C. E. Borchgrevink, *First on the Antarctic Continent* (Newnes, London, 1901), reprinted Hurst, London, 1980; also H. B. Evans, 'The *Southern Cross* expedition, 1898–1900: a personal account', *Polar Record*, vol. xvii, no. 106, 1974, pp. 23–30; also H. B. Evans and A. G. E. Jones, 'A forgotten explorer: Carsten Egeberg Borchgrevink', *Polar Record*, vol. xvii, no. 108, 1974, pp. 221–35.
    See also Louis Bernacchi, *To the south polar regions: expedition of 1898–1900* (Hurst and Blackett, London, 1901).

64  See H. J. Bull, *The Cruise of the 'Antarctic'* (Arnold, London, 1896), reprinted by Paradigm Press, 1984. For a history of exploration, see L. B. Quartermain, *South to the Pole: the early history of the Ross Sea sector, Antarctica* (Oxford University Press, London, 1967). The tracks of the *Erebus* and *Terror* (1841 and 1842), the *Antarctic* (1895), the *Southern Cross* (1899–1900) and the *Discovery* (1902 and 1904, plus sledge tracks 1902–3) are plotted on the Admiralty chart, no. 3206, *Antarctic Ocean*, Sheet VIII, published June 1901, new editions 1906 and 1910. The latter include the *Nimrod* (1908–9). The front of the Ross Ice Shelf is also plotted, as in 1841, 1842, 1900 and 1902.

65  R. F. Scott, *The Voyage of the 'Discovery'*, vol. i, p. 118.

66  Edward Wilson, op. cit., p. 89.

67  R. F. Scott, *The Voyage of the 'Discovery'*, vol. i, p. 120.

68  Armitage was not entirely happy about the way things turned out for him during and after the National Antarctic Expedition. He returned to the P. & O. and rose to be Commodore of its fleet. He wrote a narrative of the expedition, *Two years in the Antarctic* (Arnold, London, 1905), reprinted in 1984 by Paradigm Press. His autobiography, *From Cadet to Commodore*, was published in 1925.

69  A. B. Armitage, *Two years in the Antarctic*, p. 35.

70  Ibid., pp. 45–7.

71  R. F. Scott, *The Voyage of the 'Discovery'*, vol. i, p. 121.

72  R. F. Scott, Diary, 7 January 1902. S.P.R.I., MS. 352/1/1.

73  Edward Wilson drew or painted many birds of the Southern Ocean during the *Discovery* expedition and later in the *Terra Nova*. See the fine volume of reproductions, *Edward Wilson's birds of the Antarctic*, ed. Brian Roberts (Blandford Press, London, 1967).

74  R. F. Scott, *The Voyage of the 'Discovery'*, vol. i, pp. 122–3.

75  A. B. Armitage, *Two years in the Antarctic*, pp. 37–8.

76  R. F. Scott, *The Voyage of the 'Discovery'*, vol. i, p. 137.

77  J. Duncan, Diary, 9 January 1902. Dundee Museums.

78  A. B. Armitage, *Two years in the Antarctic*, pp. 40–1.

79  R. F. Scott, *The Voyage of the 'Discovery'*, vol. i, pp. 145–6.
80  A. B. Armitage, *Two years in the Antarctic*, p. 42.
81  J. Duncan, Diary, 15 January 1902. Dundee Museums.
82  R. F. Scott, *The Voyage of the 'Discovery'*, vol. i, p. 124.
83  Ibid., p. 149.
84  Ibid., pp. 143–4.
85  Ibid., pp. 151–2.
86  Ibid., pp. 161–2.
87  Ibid., p. 167.
88  Ibid., pp. 167–8.
89  Ibid., pp. 170–84.
90  Ibid., p. 185.
91  Edward Wilson, *Diary of the Discovery expedition . . .*, pp. 109–10. It seems that the site of the colony has still not been found. 'It is the old problem of not enough aerial reconnaissance in late winter and early spring', Dr Bernard Stonehouse told the author on 6 June 1992, 'though there might well be good enough satellite coverage now to show where the open water appears off that coast, and that is where I'd expect to find them.'
92  J. Duncan, Diary, 4 February 1902. Dundee Museums. The balloon apparatus had been bought from the War Office at the suggestion of the aged Sir Joseph Hooker, who had sailed with Ross. There are a couple of letters in his correspondence at Kew about it. The *Gauss* also took a balloon and used it for an ascent from the sea near the Gaussberg on 29 March 1902. Wilson felt the whole proceedings to be full of risk. The balloon was not used again and the deck cargo must have been considerably lessened when the cylinders of gas came ashore. There are some interesting photographs taken of the ascents and from the balloon in Scott's *Voyage of the 'Discovery'*, vol. i, between pp. 196 and 200. The balloon was called Eva.
93.  Antarctic Pilot, 2nd ed., Admiralty Hydrographic Department, 1948, p. 340. In 1987, the Bay of Whales disappeared when a massive ice island broke away from the Ross Ice Shelf. (*Polar Record*, vol. xxiv, no. 148, 1988, p. 75.)
94  J. Duncan, Diary, 8 February 1902. Dundee Museums.

## Chapter Three. Winter Quarters, McMurdo Sound, First Wintering, 1902

1  R. F. Scott, *The Voyage of the 'Discovery'*, vol. i, p. 219.
2  Ibid., p. 210.
3  Ibid., p. 214.
4  Edward Wilson, *Diary of the Discovery expedition . . .*, p. 113, entry for 9 February 1902.
5  J. Duncan, Diary, 13 February 1902. Dundee Museums.
6  Edward Wilson, *Diary of the Discovery expedition . . .*, p. 112. He must have been writing retrospectively.
7  Ibid., p. 113, entry for 9 February 1902.
8  Ibid., p. 110. 'Wilkes Land' had been charted by the US Exploring Expedition of 1838–42. Considerable doubts as to Wilkes's discoveries were expressed by Sir James Clark Ross in his narrative of the 1839–43 expedition. He had sailed over some of the positions assigned to the new coast.

9   A. B. Armitage, *Two years in the Antarctic*, p. 64. Bernacchi says it was called 'Gregory Lodge'. See L. C. Bernacchi, *Saga of the 'Discovery'*, p. 37.

10  J. Duncan, Diary, 15–26 February 1902. Dundee Museums. Duncan thought the design too complicated and the pieces too many and different. He favoured the log-cabin style of the *Southern Cross* hut. However, once built, the hut was to stand the test of time and it is now scheduled as an historic monument by the New Zealand Government. See L. B. Quartermain, *Two Huts in the Antarctic* (Government Printer, Wellington, 1963). It served during the National Antarctic Expedition as a store, a theatre and a refuge or staging post for sledging parties.

11  A. B. Armitage, *Two years in the Antarctic*, p. 64. Bernacchi records that these too were unsuitable. They were placed so as to avoid the influence of the ship's magnetic metals on the observations. L. C. Bernacchi, *Saga of the 'Discovery'*, p. 37. One presumes they were at least better than the 'open Lapp tent', in which he took magnetic observations at Cape Adare, 1899–1900, 'with great personal inconvenience, sometimes even at a temperature of −25°C'. See L. C. Bernacchi's appendix on magnetism in C. E. Borchgrevink, *First on the Antarctic Continent*, p. 311.

12  J. Duncan, Diary, 27 February 1902. Dundee Museums.

13  L. C. Bernacchi, *Saga of the 'Discovery'*, p. 37.

14  J. Duncan, Diary, 9 February 1902. Dundee Museums.

15  R. F. Scott, Diary, 13 February 1902. S.P.R.I., MS. 352/1/2.

16  R. F. Scott, Diary, 15 February 1902. S.P.R.I., MS. 352/1/2.

17  Ibid., 13 February 1902.

18  R. F. Scott, Diary, 13 and 15 February 1902. S.P.R.I., MS. 352/1/2.

19  E. A. Wilson, *Diary of the Discovery Expedition . . .*, p. 125, entry for 13 March 1902.

20  J. Duncan, Diary, 14 March 1902. Dundee Museums.

21  R. F. Scott, *The Voyage of the 'Discovery'*, vol. i, p. 253.

22  Frank Wild, 1874–1939, who joined the *Discovery* from HMS *Vernon*, was later associated with Shackleton in the *Nimrod*, *Endurance* and *Quest* expeditions and with Mawson in the *Aurora*, as leader of the Queen Mary Land wintering station during the Australasian Antarctic Expedition, 1911–14. Armitage described him as 'small in appearance', but 'as tough and wiry as a bit of flexible steel wire'. See A. B. Armitage, *Two years in the Antarctic*, p. 126.

23  R. F. Scott, *The Voyage of the 'Discovery'*, vol. i, pp. 264–5.

24  Ibid., p. 268.

25  E. H. Shackleton, 'Life in the Antarctic', *Pearson's Magazine*, 1903, pp. 306–22. This account was written for the general public after his return to England. The editorial introduction to the article states that payment for it would be handed to the Secretary of the expedition to help the 'Discovery Return Fund'.

26  Shackleton was the editor of vol. i of the *South Polar Times*, which was published in facsimile in 1907 by Smith, Elder. Bernacchi edited vol. ii, April–August 1903. A number of the nineteenth- century Arctic expeditions produced winter magazines, some of which were published on their return to England.

27  L. C. Bernacchi, *Saga of the 'Discovery'*, pp. 43–4. There cannot have been much social intercourse at Cape Adare, as Borchgrevink remarks that meals on special occasions took ten minutes and on others only five. He also remarked that 'the sameness of those cold, dark nights attacks the minds of men like a sneaking evil spirit'. See C. E. Borchgrevink, *First on the Antarctic Continent*, p. 153.

28 J. Duncan, Diary, 20 April 1902. Dundee Museums.

29 Ibid., 29 April and 7 June 1902.

30 Ibid., 9 June 1902. The provision of classes in reading and writing was begun in the Arctic during his first wintering of 1819–20 by Sir William Edward Parry, when many sailors were illiterate.

31 R. F. Scott, *The Voyage of the 'Discovery'*, vol. i, p. 299.

32 J. Duncan, Diary, 2 July 1902. Dundee Museums.

33 Ibid., July and August 1902.

34 Ibid., 23 June 1902. He celebrated his thirty-second birthday next day, the third in the *Discovery*, 'as I was Building Her'.

35 Ibid., 22 July 1902. He gives the dimensions as 8ft 6in×3ft 9in and 2$^{1}/_{2}$in thick.

### Chapter Four. Sledge Journeys, 1902–3 Season, Scott's Southern Journey

1 R. F. Scott, *The Voyage of the 'Discovery'*, vol. i, pp. 273–4.

2 Ibid., p. 507.

3 Ibid., p. 533.

4 Ibid., p. 535.

5 Ibid., pp. 541–2.

6 See Edward A. Wilson, 'The medical aspect of the *Discovery*'s voyage to the Antarctic', *British Medical Journal*, 8 July 1905, p. 77. Wilson tells us that on Thursdays during the second winter, the diet was varied with skua gulls. This particular outbreak is discussed by E. J. C. Kendall in 'Scurvy during some British polar expeditions, 1875–1917', *Polar Record*, vol. vii, 1955, pp. 467–85. For general background, see C. C. Lloyd and J. L. S. Coulter, *Medicine and the Navy, 1200–1900* (Livingstone, London, 1963). See also *Starving Sailors: the influence of nutrition upon naval and maritime history* (National Maritime Museum, London, 1981), ed. J. Watt *et al.*, and Kenneth J. Carpenter, *The history of scurvy and vitamin C* (Cambridge University Press, 1986).

7 Dr Koettlitz, the senior surgeon, would have had to eat his words when scurvy broke out. At the end of an article sent from New Zealand during the outward voyage, he had expressed the conviction that because the food had been inspected for freshness before being tinned—and the likelihood of 'fresh game' (seals and penguins), 'we can take it as certain that no scurvy will be heard of in connection with the expedition, however long it may remain in the High South'. See Reginald Koettlitz, 'The British Antarctic expedition: precautions against scurvy in the victualling of the "Discovery" ', *British Medical Journal*, vol. i, 28 June 1902, pp. 342–3. Scott, and later Koettlitz, had been in touch at the outset, with the Treasury's permission, with the Principal Chemist of the Government Laboratory in the Strand about testing the pemmican and condensed milk. (Copies of documents relating to the National Antarctic Expedition 1901–4 in the archives of the Government Chemist kindly supplied by Mr S. D. Robertson, Departmental Records Officer, Department of Trade and Industry.)

8 All the preceding quotations are from the journal kept by R. W. Skelton, vol. v, 1 September to 29 November 1902. S.P.R.I., MS. 342/1/5.

9 Sir Clements Markham, 'The starting of the Antarctic expedition . . .', p. 36. S.P.R.I., MS. 1453/2.

10 Edward Wilson, *Diary of the 'Discovery' expedition . . .*, p. 209.

11  R. F. Scott, *The Voyage of the 'Discovery'*, vol. ii, p. 19.

12  R. F. Scott, Diary, 19 and 29 October 1902. S.P.R.I., MS. 252/1/2.

13  R. F. Scott, *The Voyage of the 'Discovery'*, p. 21.

14  Ibid., vol. i, p. 472. Trontheim had obtained Nansen's dogs from the Ostiaks and Samoyeds in 1893. See W. C. Brögger and Nordahl Rolfsen, *Fridtjof Nansen, 1861–1893 . . .* (Longmans, London, 1896), pp. 325–30, and L. C. Bernacchi, *Saga of the 'Discovery'*, pp. 66–8. Bernacchi wrote of the dogs that their provision was only 'half hearted' in view of the small number taken (23) and that they were inferior West Siberian dogs (rather than East Siberian or Canadian), 'to save time'.

15  The dogs of Scott's second and last expedition in the *Terra Nova* (1910–13) were chosen in Siberia and brought south by Cecil Meares who also drove them in the Antarctic. They kept their Russian names because they were accompanied by two Russians, Anton Omelchenko and Dmitri Gerov, one of whom looked after the Siberian ponies.

16  R. F. Scott, *The Voyage of the 'Discovery'*, vol. i, pp. 470–3.

17  Ibid., vol. ii, p. 12 *et seq*. There is an appealing photograph of 'Joe', happy on an English lawn, facing p. 279 of his master's book. Louis C. Bernacchi, *To the South Polar Regions . .*

18  E. H. Shackleton, 'Life in the Antarctic', *Pearson's Magazine*, 1903, pp. 306–22.

19  R. F. Scott, *The Voyage of the 'Discovery'*, vol. ii, pp. 31–2.

20  Ibid., pp. 33–4.

21  Ibid., pp. 35–6.

22  Ibid., pp. 40–1.

23  Ibid., p. 53.

24  E. A. Wilson, *Diary of the Discovery Expedition . . .*, p. 229.

25  R. F. Scott, Southern journey diary, 10 and 14 December 1902. S.P.R.I., MS. 1464/4.

26  E. A. Wilson, Ibid., p. 228. It appears as Christmas Mountain on Mulock's map of 1905.

27  R. F. Scott, *The Voyage of the 'Discovery'*, vol. ii, pp. 74–7. R. F. Scott, Southern journey diary, 27 December 1902. S.P.R.I., MS. 1464/4.

28  R. F. Scott, *The Voyage of the 'Discovery'*, vol. ii, pp. 74–7.

29  Ibid., vol. i, pp. 466–7.

30  See ibid., vol. ii, pp. 28–9, and vol. i, pp. 463–8, on the pros and cons of using dogs for sledging, where he remarks that the experience of the southern party was probably an exceptionally sad one, but 'it left in each one of our small party an unconquerable aversion to the employment of dogs in this ruthless fashion', literally driving them to death. In these pages occurs the often-quoted passage about the greater nobility and splendour of conquest won by man-hauling. This is followed by a lesser known paragraph, which observes that 'few expeditions can command the numerical strength to perform extended journeys with men alone' and that a large party of men is 'not only a great responsibility, but a great expense; the dog gives little anxiety, requires no housing and draws no wages'. It was the 'dog-eat-dog' method that brought Amundsen triumphantly back from the South Pole in 1912. Dogs had been used for extensive journeys during the nineteenth-century British naval expeditions in the Arctic. Concentrated modern food has enabled long journeys to be made without sacrificing the dogs. The British Antarctic Survey used dogs until 1975, when the cost of their food made their general use uneconomic. *Polar Record* contains numerous articles on sledge dogs, for example, 'The breeding and maintenance of sledge dogs', by R. J. F. Taylor, *Polar Record*,

vol. viii, no. 56, 1957, pp. 429–40. The French explorer, Paul-Emile Victor, provides a 'petit manuel du parfait conducteur de traineau de chiens', a series of appendices on dogs and dog driving to his popular book, *Chiens du traineau, compagnons du risque* (Flammarion, Paris, 1974).

31 R. F. Scott, *The Voyage of the 'Discovery'*, vol. ii, p. 85.

32 Ibid., p. 92.

33 E. H. Shackleton, 'Life in the Antarctic', *Pearson's Magazine*, 1903, pp. 306–22.

34 R. F. Scott, *The Voyage of the 'Discovery'*, vol. ii, p. 104.

35 Edward Wilson, *Diary of the Discovery Expedition . . .*, p. 244.

36 R. F. Scott, *The Voyage of the 'Discovery'*, vol. ii, p. 124.

37 Gerald Doorly, *The Voyages of the 'Morning'* (Smith, Elder, London, 1916), pp. 109–10.

38 R. F. Scott, Southern journey diary, 9 February 1903. S.P.R.I., MS. 1464/4.

39 R. F. Scott, *The Voyage of the 'Discovery'*, vol. ii, p. 125.

40 Wilson made this point in his diary for 28 December 1902, published in his *Discovery Diary*, p. 229. Even when reduced for publication with the expedition's scientific results, Wilson's panoramic sketches extended to over 100 feet, covering as well as the southern journey, the coast south of Cape Adare, 'an astonishing record of his perseverance in the face of difficulties'. See *Edward Wilson's birds of the Antarctic*, ed. Brian Roberts, p. 18.

41 R. F. Scott, *The Voyage of the 'Discovery'*, vol. ii, p. 145.

42 Charles W. R. Royds, Sledging diary, 8 November 1902. S.P.R.I., MS. 641/1/2. Microfilm. Edward Wilson called this 'The first authentic egg' in his Appendix (No. 2) on Antarctic fauna in R. F. Scott, *The Voyage of the 'Discovery'*, vol. ii, p. 490. Brian Roberts makes the same assertion in *Edward Wilson's birds of the Antarctic*, p. 18. In fact the first Emperor penguin egg collected anywhere appears to be the 'Drayton egg' discovered on the sea ice by a member of the French expedition of 1838–42 commanded by J. S. C. Dumont d'Urville. From Paris, it passed into the hands of a private collector and was kept at Drayton House near Norwich and then in the Norwich Museum, which presented it to the S.P.R.I. I am indebted to Dr B. Stonehouse for this information.

43 J. Duncan, Diary entry and sports programme, 8 November 1902. The watercolour is kept with his diary. Dundee Museums.

44 A. B. Armitage, *Two years in the Antarctic*, pp. 149–51. Diary, concert and sports programmes in the Duncan papers, Dundee Museums. The flag had been presented by Admiral Nares and the officers of the Arctic expedition of 1875–6.

## Chapter Five. First Relief Expedition of the Morning, 1902–3

1 Sir Clements Markham's diary, 2 December 1901. RGS Archives, CRM 1/15.

2 Sir Clements Markham's diary, September and October 1901. RGS Archives, CRM 1/15.

3 RGS Archives, AA 19/3/3. There is a deck plan of the *Morgenen* among the Colbeck papers on microfilm in N.M.M. This gives the length as 148 feet and breadth 27 ft. 6 in.

4 Sir Clements Markham's diary, 20 November 1901. RGS Archives, CRM 1/15.

5 C. E. Borchgrevink, *First on the Antarctic Continent*, pp. 14–15. See also A. G. E. Jones, 'Captain William Colbeck', *Fram*, Winter 1984, pp. 177–85, and L. B. Quartermain, *Antarctica's Forgotten Men*, pp. 63–84.

6 Quoted in C. R. Markham's 'History of the Morning', p. 63. RGS Archives, AA 19/3/3.

7 Sir Clements Markham's diary, 12 April 1902. RGS Archives, CRM 1/15.

8 G. S. Doorly, *The Voyages of the 'Morning'*, p. 20. Doorly's journal is in the Mitchell Library, Sydney.

9 Ibid., p. 33. This instrument proved too large to be taken below decks and for this reason had its 'keys unshipped'; the rest of it was cut into sections by the ship's carpenter and put together again. That it was well used for over two years is shown in Doorly's booklet of words and music, *The Songs of the 'Morning'* (Bread and Cheese Club, Melbourne, 1943). Doorly's journal is in the Mitchell Library, Sydney.

10 Captain William Colbeck, letter to his fiancée, March 1903. Microfilm in N.M.M., MSS. MRF/178. Quotations are from this unless otherwise indicated.
See also A. G. E. Jones, 'Scott Island and its discovery', *Antarctic* (Wellington), vol. vi, no. 12, 1973, pp. 437–40. The log of the *Morning*, 1902–3, is in the S.P.R.I., MS. 366/9.

11 Undated memo by R. F. Scott, headed 'Officers and men discharged from "Discovery" to "Morning" '. RGS Archives, AA 12/4/1.
See also E. A. Wilson, 'The medical aspect of the *Discovery*'s voyage', *British Medical Journal*, 8 July 1905, pp. 79–80. Wilson stated that Shackleton's throat and breathing passages had been affected and that his attacks of dyspnoea, cough and blood spitting were regularly induced by the approach of a southerly blizzard, making it inadvisable for him to risk a second winter.

12 RGS Archives, AA 12/4/2.

13 R. F. Scott to Admiral Markham. N.M.M., MRK/46.

14 R. F. Scott, *The Voyage of the 'Discovery'*, vol. ii, pp. 171–2.

## Chapter Six. Second Wintering, 1903, Sledge Journeys, 1903–4 Season, Scott's Western Journey

1 R. F. Scott, *The Voyage of the 'Discovery'*, vol. ii, pp. 176–7.

2 Ibid., p. 177.

3 Ibid., pp. 192–3.

4 George F. A. Mulock, *The Charts of the 'Discovery' Antarctic Expedition* (Royal Geographical Society, London, 1908). L. C. Bernacchi believed that the 'Parry Mountains' were a mirage of what Scott named the Royal Society Range. See *Saga of the 'Discovery'*, pp. 32–3. The matter is discussed by M. J. Ross in *Ross in the Antarctic* (Caedmon of Whitby, Whitby, 1982), pp. 256–8.

5 E. A. Wilson, *Discovery Diary*, pp. 277–8.

6 Ibid., pp. 260–1.

7 Ibid., p. 267.

8 Ibid., pp. 268–9, 1 July 1903.

9 A. B. Armitage, *Two Years in the Antarctic*, p. 217.

10 R. F. Scott, *The Voyage of the 'Discovery'*, vol. ii, p. 196.

11 Ibid., p. 199.

12 E. A. Wilson, *Discovery Diary*, p. 283.

13 Ibid., pp. 283–4.

14 R. F. Scott, *The Voyage of the 'Discovery'*, pp. 200–1.

15  Ibid., p. 203.

16  Ibid., pp. 204–12.

17  E. A. Wilson, *Discovery Diary*, pp. 293–4, 13 September 1903.

18  Ibid., pp. 294–5, 13 September 1903.

19  Ibid., p. 297, 16 and 17 September 1903.

20  Ibid., pp. 300–1, 28 September 1903.

21  Ibid., pp. 306 and 310, 18 and 29 October 1903.

22  R. F. Scott, *The Voyage of the 'Discovery'*, vol. ii, p. 220. This was corroborated by Frank Debenham, geologist on Scott's *Terra Nova* Expedition, 1910–13 and Founder-Director of the S.P.R.I., when discussing the question of man-hauling vs dogs. He pointed out that dogs provide food supply as well as energy and concluded, 'As to rate of travel on a long journey, there is not a great deal of difference. Few dog parties, working under plateau conditions, have ever exceeded Scott's best, when on foot, he and Evans and Lashly made an average of over 14 miles a day in 50 sledging days, when returning from their plateau journey of 1903.' *Polar Record*, vol. v, nos. 37/38, 1949, p. 316.

    Debenham is not quite correct here and really refers to the second sledge journey as a whole. Scott gives the average over 50 marching days as 14.5 miles. Over the whole 81 days' absence (i.e. taking in the false start when the party had to return to the ship to repair the sledges) he found that Evans, Lashly and himself 'had covered 1,098 miles at an average of 15.4 miles a day'. They had also climbed heights totalling 19,800 feet, 'not including minor undulations', in a polar climate at great altitude. R. F. Scott, *The Voyage of the 'Discovery'*, vol. ii, p. 296.

23  R. F. Scott, *The Voyage of the 'Discovery'*, vol. ii, p. 144.

24  Ibid., vol. ii, p. 145.

25  See H. G. R. King, *The Antarctic* (Blandford, London, 1969) for an informed survey for the general reader of geography, natural history, exploration and science in the Antarctic, the adjoining islands, the Sub-Antarctic and the Southern Ocean.

26  Born in 1879, Ferrar had taken the Natural Science Tripos shortly before the expedition sailed. His report on field geology was published among the expedition's scientific results in 1907. He made his later career largely in the Middle East and New Zealand, where he died in 1932. His Antarctic diaries are in S.P.R.I.

27  R. F. Scott, *The Voyage of the 'Discovery'*, vol. ii, p. 220.

28  Ibid., vol. ii, pp. 222–3.

29  Ibid., vol. ii, pp. 223–4.

30  Ibid., vol. ii, pp. 229–32. Scott points out that Ferrar's party broke the record for one day in achieving 37 miles on 21 October 1903.

31  Ibid., vol. ii, pp. 239–40.

32  Ibid., vol. ii, p. 245.

33  Ibid., vol. ii, pp. 252–3.

34  Ibid., vol. ii, p. 254.

35  Ibid., vol. ii, pp. 260–2.

36  Ibid., vol. ii, pp. 258–9.

37  *Under Scott's command: Lashly's Antarctic Diaries* (Gollancz, London, 1969), pp. 73–4.

38  R. F. Scott, *The Voyage of the 'Discovery'*, vol. ii, pp. 264–5.

39  Ibid., vol. ii, p. 265.

40  Ibid., vol. ii, p. 266.

41 Ibid., pp. 268–9.

42 Ibid., vol. ii, pp. 277–80.

43 *Under Scott's command: Lashly's Antarctic Diaries*, p. 81, 14 December 1903.

44 R. F. Scott, *The Voyage of the 'Discovery'*, vol. ii, pp. 283–5.

45 Ibid., vol. ii, p. 286.

46 Ibid., vol. ii, pp. 290–2.

47 Ibid., vol. ii, p. 293.

48 See H. G. R. King, *The Antarctic*, p. 56. Of the reason for the dry valleys, H. G. R. King writes that the most probable explanation is 'that the katabatic, or downward-falling winds from the Antarctic plateau, compress and therefore raise the temperature of the bottom air of the valleys; coupled with this is the fact that large areas of exposed rock will absorb more solar radiation and thus help to raise the average temperature'. Mr King also observes that the simplest explanation of the mummified seals found many miles inland is that 'at some time in the past they must have wandered inland from their native beaches and then somehow lost their sense of direction and died of starvation'. He also remarks that the 'unique features of these unique valleys are the saline lakes, Lake Vanda in the Wright Valley and Lake Bonney in the Taylor Dry Valley'.

49 R. F. Scott, *The Voyage of the 'Discovery'*, vol. ii, p. 295. Scott remarked that 'few watches have done greater service' and 'for the benefit of future explorers', he pointed out 'the importance of the manner in which a watch is carried on such a journey', in his case sewn to his inner vest, where the harness could not touch it. He held it in the palm of his hand when taking sights.

50 Many of Skelton's (and others') plates survive in the RGS's photographic collection.

51 See H. G. R. King, op. cit., pp. 62–3. The geological results were published in the scientific reports of the expedition. Ferrar's 'Summary of the geological observations made during the cruise of the SS *Discovery*, 1901–1904' was published as Appendix 1 to Scott's narrative, vol. ii, pp. 437–68. He also contributed a paper entitled 'Notes on the physical geography of the Antarctic', published in the *Geographical Journal*, vol. xxv, April 1905, pp. 373–86, in which the discussion afterwards was reported. W. N. Edwards established the interest of Ferrar's specimens by splitting open a large block of shale, in which were found the fossils mentioned. See his paper, 'The occurrence of *Glossopteris* in the Beacon Sandstone of Ferrar Glacier, South Victoria Land', *Geological Magazine*, vol. lxv, 1928, pp. 323–7.

52 L. C. Bernacchi, *Saga of the 'Discovery'*, pp. 100–1.

53 Ibid., pp. 103–4.

54 See Edward Wilson, *Discovery Diary*, pp. 304–17.

55 R. F. Scott, *The Voyage of the 'Discovery'*, vol. ii, p. 305.

## Chapter Seven. Second Relief Expedition of the *Morning* with the *Terra Nova*, 1903–4, Release of the *Discovery* from the Ice

1 R. F. Scott, *The Voyage of the 'Discovery'*, vol. ii, pp. 306–13.

2 An ice saw and tripod from the Nares Arctic expedition of 1875–6 are in the N.M.M. Scott describes the apparatus and its use in *The Voyage of the 'Discovery'*, vol. ii, pp. 314–15.

3 R. F. Scott, *The Voyage of the 'Discovery'*, vol. ii, pp. 317–20.

4 Edward Wilson to Charles W. R. Royds, 5 January 1903 [*sic* 1904]. In private hands.

5 Edward Wilson, *Diary of the 'Discovery' expedition . . .*, p. 332.

6 See A. G. E. Jones, 'Harry MacKay, Master of the *Terra Nova*', *Antarctic* (Wellington, N.Z.), vol. vi, no. 9, 1973, pp. 316–21.

7 E. A. Wilson, *Discovery Diary*, p. 332.

8 R. F. Scott, *The Voyage of the 'Discovery'*, vol. ii, pp. 325–6. See also A. G. E. Jones, 'The Voyage of the *Terra Nova* 1903–1904', *Geographical Journal*, vol. xxxviii, part 3, 1972, pp. 309–15.

9 W. Colbeck, letter to Edith, 3 March 1904. Colbeck papers, in private hands.

10 Ibid., quoting his diary for 11 January 1904.

11 R. F. Scott to W. Colbeck, 13 January 1904. N.M.M., MS. 79/123.

12 Nearly all the men were to go in the *Terra Nova*, with Scott and the majority of the officers. Armitage, Dailey, Ford and the scientists were to go in the *Morning*. The latter was to leave no later than 27 February and would wait in the open sea for the more powerful *Terra Nova*, which would depart in March. N.M.M., MS. 79/123.

13 R. F. Scott, *The Voyage of the 'Discovery'*, vol. ii, pp. 347–9. It is interesting that Captain Colbeck considered it doubtful whether the ship would have got out without the explosives.

14 Ibid., vol. ii, p. 352.

15 Ibid.

16 Ibid., vol. ii, pp. 355–6.

## Chapter Eight. Homeward Voyage, Homecoming, Expedition Results

1 R. F. Scott, *The Voyage of the 'Discovery'*, vol. ii, p. 359. The ship's log for 17 February 1904 contains a little diagram of the *Discovery* showing 'Soundings in fathoms when grounded off Hut Point'. RGS Archives, AA 21/4.

2 Scott later remarked that, 'whilst it is certain that we must reject Wilkes Land to the eastward of Adélie Land, Wilkes' soundings still remain as a guide to the limit of the continental plateau in this region. Our own uniform soundings of 250 fathoms to the south, together with his, show that there is a considerable extent of shallow sea, limited more or less by the track of Wilkes' ships.' *Geographical Journal*, vol. xxv, 1905, p. 370.

  Sir Douglas Mawson in 1912 named the coast of Antarctica between longs. 130° and 136°E. after Wilkes. Sir A. Grenfell Price, *The winning of Australian Antarctica* (Angus and Robertson, Sydney, 1962), p. 192.

3 E. A. Wilson, *Discovery Diary*, p. 346, 6 March 1904.

4 Ibid., p. 387, 17 July 1904.

5 Ibid., pp. 389–90.

6 R. F. Scott, *The Voyage of the 'Discovery'*, vol. ii, p. 334. The heat in the stokehold perhaps proved too much for Leading Stoker Whitfield. In the *Discovery*'s log for the return voyage can be found two loose sheets signed by Captain Scott and dated 1 August 1904. They list the precautions to be taken regarding Whitfield, so that his 'whereabouts and occupations' were known. The 'general idea' was that he 'should be given as much freedom and as much fresh air as possible, but that he should be watched sufficiently carefully to prevent harm or to detect any new phase in his disease and for this the officer of the watch must be mainly responsible'. Dr Koettlitz was to be informed by Whitfield's messmates about his habits, meals

etc. 'Should any fresh symptoms be noticed', Captain Scott himself should be told immediately. RGS Archives, AA 21/3. Scott's diary reveals that Whitfield had been 'acting oddly since the arrival of the mail, when he seems to have received bad news'. R. F. Scott, Diary, 24 January 1904. S.P.R.I., MS. 352/1/3.

7 Sir Clements Markham, Diary, 1901–5. RGS Archives, CRM 1/15.

8 This sledge was bought by the National Maritime Museum at Sotheby's in December 1984. An exhibition of watercolours, photographs and 'articles of interest used in the South Polar Regions' was held at the Bruton Galleries in Bond Street in November 1904. Its catalogue lists 464 items and contains interesting photographs, advertisements and biographies of the expedition's officers, scientists and men.

9 L. C. Bernacchi, *Saga of the 'Discovery'*, pp. 113–14. Bernacchi goes on to remark that no funds were available to enable the expedition's scientists to analyse and publish their results themselves and that 'this comprehensive and important work had to be undertaken chiefly by scientists in Government departments'. Today, in contrast, the British Antarctic Survey is an official body whose continuity enables work in the field to be evaluated and published. Bernacchi records on p. 114 (after mentioning the polar medals) that Captain Scott was awarded the CVO by King Edward VII and 'a special gold medal by the Royal Geographical Society, of which officers and crew received silver replicas'. He ends with the rueful remark that 'Like Llewellyn Longstaff, who had contributed in all £30,000 to make the great expedition possible, *Discovery*'s scientists received an expression of thanks from the Learned Societies and a niche in polar history.'

Details of the silver and bronze polar medals and lists of their recipients from the *Discovery*, *Morning* and *Terra Nova* can be found in Neville W. Poulsom, *The White Ribbon: a medallic record of British polar expeditions* (Seaby, London, 1968).

10 R. F. Scott, *The Voyage of the 'Discovery'*, vol. i, p. 22.

11 Sir Raymond Priestley, 'Twentieth-century man against Antarctica', *Advancement of Science*, vol. xiii, no. 50, 1956, p. 4.

12 *Geographical Journal*, vol. xxv, 1905, p. 370.

# PART II.
## VOYAGES TO HUDSON BAY, 1905–11

### Chapter Nine. Purchase by the Hudson's Bay Company, 1905, Voyages 1905 and 1906

1 The Right Honourable Sir Winston Churchill, Grand Seigneur of the Governor and Company of Adventurers of England trading into Hudson Bay in his foreword, written at Chartwell, September 1957, to Professor E. E. Rich's history of the company, 1670–1870, cited in reference 3, below.

2 It was to be held in free and common socage, on the same terms as the Manor of East Greenwich, 'the standard prototype of such tenure paying yearly to the Crown two elks and two black beaver, whenever the King, his heirs and successors, should enter the territories so

granted'. E. E. Rich, *Hudson's Bay Company* (Macmillan, New York, 1961), pp. 53–4.

3  A brief history of the Hudson's Bay Company, published by the Company c.1980, p. 8. For voyages through the Strait and into the Bay, see A. H. Markham, 'Hudson's Bay and Hudson's Strait as a navigable channel', *Proceedings of the Royal Geographical Society*, no. 9, 1885, pp. 549–67, map; also A. H. Markham, 'Hudson's Bay and Strait', *Royal Geographical Society Supplementary Papers*, vol. ii, part 4, 1889, pp. 617–60. More general works are (among others): E. E. Rich, *Hudson's Bay Company 1670–1870* (Hudson's Bay Record Society, London, 1958–9) and (Macmillan, New York, 1961); Douglas MacKay, *A History of the Hudson's Bay Company* (McClelland and Stewart, Toronto, 1936, and later editions); Glyndwr Williams, 'The Hudson's Bay Company and the fur trade, 1670–1870', *The Beaver* (Winnipeg), Autumn 1983; Peter C. Newman, *Empire of the Bay . . .*, Toronto, Viking/Madison, 1989.

4  HBC Booklet, c.1980, p. 20.

5  E. E. Rich, *Hudson's Bay Company* (1960/1), vol. iii, p. 405.

6  HBC Booklet, c.1980, p. 22.

7  Ibid., p. 26.

8  Ibid., p. 34.

9  Philip Godsell, *Arctic trader*, London, 1935. New edition, 1951, pp. 305–6. 'In retrospect, the northern natives were better off with the company than with government bureaucrats', observes Arthur J. Ray. *The Canadian fur trade in the industrial age* (University of Toronto Press, 1990), p. 227. See also George Binney, 'Hudson Bay in 1928', *Geographical Journal*, vol. lxxiv, no. 1, 1929.

10  *Morning Post*, 19 January 1905. Cutting in the Koettlitz Collection, Dover Museum.

11  Ibid.

12  Book of ships' movements, Hudson's Bay Company Archives, Provincial Archives of Manitoba.

13  In the event of being unable to do so, it was suggested that the *Morning* and the *Scotia* (of the Scottish National Antarctic Expedition) might both be bought. These would together be capable of carrying the largest cargo needing to be sent.

14  HBC Archives, A10/168.

15  Ibid. Mr M. R. C. Parr points out that the *Discovery* did *not* have a banjo frame.

16  Ibid., A10/168–9.

17  Ibid., A10/169. Letter dated 18 April 1905.

18  Captain A. R. Williamson, verbal communication; *Discovery Reports*, vol. i, 1929, pp. 153–4. *Moccasin Telegraph*, December 1953, p. 9.

19  L. C. Bernacchi, *Saga of the 'Discovery'*, p. 119.

20  Reference number C.4/1.

21  He had previously been master of the Hudson's Bay Company's ships *Labrador* (1872–82), the *Erik* (1890–9) and the *Pelican* (1900–5): Book of ships' movements, HBC Archives.

22  Book of ships' movements, HBC Archives; letters from Williams and Sage, A10/169.

23  Book of ships' movements, HBC Archives; Public Record Office, Board of Trade records. Official log and crew list.

24  Alan Cooke and Clive Holland, *The exploration of northern Canada* (Arctic History Press, Toronto, 1978).

25  Philip Godsell, *Arctic trader* (2nd ed., Hale, London, 1951), p. 20.

26  PRO. Board of Trade Records. A ship's Articles form a legal contract signed by master and seamen embodying the conditions of service on board.

27 Book of ships' movements, HBC Archives; Moose Factory journal, 28 September 1903.

28 Philip Godsell, op. cit., 2nd ed., p. 22.

29 Ibid., p. 26.

30 Introduction to *The strange and dangerous voyage of Capt. Thomas James. Edited and annotated by W. A. Kenyon* (Royal Ontario Museum, Toronto, 1975), pp. 1–2.

31 P. G. Downes, *The Sleeping Island* (Jenkins, London, *c*.1941).

32 Thomas James, *The strange and dangerous voyage . . .* (London, 1633), pp. 112–20. A modern edition of James's gripping narrative was published in 1975 by the Royal Ontario Museum, Toronto, edited and annotated with modern photographs by W. A. Kenyon from the text of the Hakluyt Society edition of 1894.

33 See W. A. Kenyon, 'Charlton Island', *The Beaver*, Summer 1974.

34 See E. E. Rich, *Hudson's Bay Company* (Macmillan, New York, 1961), vol. ii, pp. 218 and 257–9.

35 See ibid., p. 272.

36 See ibid., vol. iii, p. 494.

37 HBC Archives, B 135/e/33. Report on transport, James Bay District.

38 W. A. Kenyon, 'Charlton Island', *The Beaver*, Summer 1974, p. 27.

39 HBC Archives, B 135/e/33.

40 Ibid., A/12/FT/313/1, 1905–18, folios 37 and 39.

41 Book of ships' movements, HBC Archives.

## Chapter Ten. Voyages, 1907–11

1 It must be remembered that the *Discovery* had a bridge open to all the elements, unlike those well-glazed strongholds of merchant ships today.

2 The *Stork*, which had left London five days later than the *Discovery*, did not reach Charlton until 7 September, doubtless because of the ice. She left Charlton on 5 October, but owing to the lateness of the season, turned back to winter at Charlton Island. She took ground on the night of the 10th and was abandoned on 11 October. Book of ships' movements, HBC Archives.

3 Philip Godsell, *Arctic trader* (Hale, London, 1951), p. 27.

4 Ibid., p. 27.

5 Ibid., pp. 29–30.

6 See Eric W. Morse, *Fur trade routes of Canada, then and now* (2nd ed., University of Toronto Press, Toronto, 1979), for a fascinating account of the natural inland waterways of Canada paddled, sailed or tracked by the 'voyageurs', both French Canadians and Orkneymen.

7 These must have come from the great hall of the North West Company at Fort William on Lake Superior, where they are hung once again. See Bryan Eddington, 'The great hall at old Fort William', *The Beaver*, Summer 1981. Outfit 312:1.

8 All the preceding quotations are from Philip Godsell, *Arctic trader*, 1951 ed. The cannon have been silent now for many decades. The post was abandoned in 1957, after the completion of the railway from the south to Churchill, the grain- and ore-exporting port, the site of another old HBC post some 200 miles north of York Factory, on the western shore of Hudson Bay. The Federal Government acquired the site in 1968. Goose hunters, according to E. W. Morse writing in 1978, until recently tore off its boards to burn on the barren marshy flats. Parks

Canada is preparing a management plan for this historic site and has issued *York Factory Newsletters*, since 1983. Its *Research Bulletins*, no. 70, 1977; no. 114, 1979; no. 115, 1979; no. 151, 1981; no. 157, 1981; no. 167, 1981; no. 173, 1982; no. 184, 1983; no. 196, 1983 describe field work and historical research relating to these most historic buidings. A *Management plan summary* was published in 1988 by Parks Canada. For an account of everyday life at York Factory see Michael Payne, *The most respectable place in the Territory* (Canadian Parks Service, Ottawa, 1989).

9  Sir John Franklin, *Narrative of a journey to the shores of the polar sea in the years 1819–20–21–22* (3rd ed., John Murray, London, 1824).

10  E. W. Morse, op. cit., pp. 93–4.

11  It was replaced as the main distribution centre by Fort Garry, but York Factory continued as a company post until 1957, a life-span of some 275 years. The last York Boat can be seen at Lower Fort Garry, the 'Stone Fort', near Winnipeg. This former HBC post on the Red River was built in the 1830s on the orders of Sir George Simpson. It is now a historic monument, open to the public in the summer months and housing many relics of the fur trade of years gone by. The full-size replica of the *Nonsuch* as well as a replica of a York Boat, are in the Museum of Man and Nature, Winnipeg.

12  Books of ships' movements, HBC Archives. The *Beothic* was sold to the Russian Government in 1915 and was renamed the *Georgiy Sedov*. As such she had an interesting career. See William Barr, 'The role of Canadian and Newfoundland ships in the development of the Soviet Arctic', *Aspects* (St Johns, NF), vol. ix, nos. 1 and 2, 1977.

13  A. R. Williamson, 'Voyage of the "Discovery" 1911', *The Beaver*, Spring 1983, pp. 12–23, and Summer 1983, pp. 20–9.

14  *The Beaver*, Spring and Summer 1983. The seaman mentioned in this paragraph was R. M. Clifford, aged 22, born in Maidstone, whose previous ship was the *Kilmeng*: Crew list for 1911. Public Record Office (Kew). Board of Trade records.

15  *The Beaver*, Spring and Summer 1983.

16  A. R. Williamson. Unpublished ending to article in *The Beaver*, Summer 1983.

# PART III.
## THE FIRST WORLD WAR AND ITS AFTERMATH, 1915–20

### Chapter Eleven. To New York and Archangel, 1915

1  Provincial Archives of Manitoba. Hudson's Bay Company Archives, classes A1, A5 and A10. I am indebted to Ms Anne Morton for providing information from these files. See also A. G. E. Jones, 'The 1914 Stackhouse expedition', *Fram*, vol. ii, part 1, 1985, pp. 344–8.

2  For general background, see Jean Monnet, *Memoirs . . .*, trans. from the French by Richard Mayne (Collins, London, 1978); Lord Salter, *Memoirs of a public servant* (Faber and Faber, London, 1961); J. A. Salter (later Lord Salter), *Allied shipping control: an experiment in*

*international administration* (Clarendon Press, Oxford, 1921). The minutes of a post-war HBC committee meeting record that after the company's appointment in 1915 'Monnet's actions and influence were essential to the safety and success of the operations': independent of both the French Government and the company, he never claimed expenses from either. The same minutes record that the HBC 'made from the French business very large profits totalling over one million pounds', much of this accruing after the war. When, in 1922, the family firm had fallen on hard times, Monnet's request for a large loan from the company was granted (and later repaid in full) because of the HBC's 'very considerable obligation' to him: he had 'entirely neglected his own personal interests, both during and after the War, leaving them in the hands of others'. Hudson's Bay Company Committee meeting, London, 28 March 1922. HBCA A.1/165, pp. 212–13. I am indebted to Mrs Shirlee Anne Smith for this reference.

3  Alex Ross, then Head of Twentieth-Century Records, speaking at a symposium in Winnipeg, 28 May 1984. Quotation from typescript in the author's possession.

4  Who was Who, 1941–1950 (Black, London, 1967).

5  Charles Elton, personal communication, 1985. See also Anne Morton, Charles Elton, . . . *The Beaver*, spring, 1985, p. 24, and Philip H. Godsell, *Arctic trader*, 1951 ed., pp. 165 and 296–7.

6  Sir Edward Crowe in *The Times*, 29 June 1943.

7  Winston Churchill, *The world crisis 1915* (Thornton Butterworth, London, 1923), p. 17.

8  HBC Archives, A12/FT/313/1. fos. 104–6.

9  Invoices. HBC Archives, A12/FT/313/1, fos. 112–16.

10  HBC Archives, A12/313/1, *Discovery*.

11  HBC Archives, A5/116, fo. 64.

12  Official log book for the New York voyage. PRO, Board of Trade series. Copy in N.M.M.

13  HBC Archives, A12/FT/313/1, *Discovery*, fos. 59–60.

14  Ibid., AFG/3/6/1.

15  Ibid., AFG/5/2273.

16  Ibid., AFG/5/2542.

17  Ibid., AFG/5/2273.

18  Quoted in Winston Churchill, *The world crisis, 1915*, p. 283.

19  C. E. Fayle, *Seaborne trade* (John Murray, London, 1923), vol. ii, pp. 122–3. The river frontage was however developed later in the war, with new jetties, quays, big floating docks in mid-stream and an enormous crane transported from the United Kingdom. See E. P. Stebbing, 'The forest region of north-east Russia . . .', *Geographical Journal*, June 1918, pp. 361–2.

20  William Hepworth Dixon, *Free Russia* (Hurst and Blackett, London, 1870), p. 33. From Archangel, this English traveller visited the great monastery of Solovets, whose daily life he describes in detail. He remarks of Archangel itself that, whereas to Western eyes the city was a storehouse of oats, tar, planks and skins (its principal trade), in native eyes it was 'the Archangel's house, the port of Solovetsk, and the gate of God' (p. 38).

21  William Barr, unpublished manuscript on the Canadian and Newfoundland ships sold to Russia during the First World War.

22  Archibald Hurd, *The Merchant Navy* (John Murray, London, 1924), vol. ii, pp. 67–9.

23  R. S. Gwatkin-Williams, *Under the black ensign* (Hutchinson, London, c.1925).

24  Ibid., p. 51.

25  Archibald Hurd, op. cit., pp. 146–8, maps p. 156 and at end. See also E. Keble Chatterton, *The big blockade* (Hurst and Blackett, London, 1932).

26 Manifest of the cargo of the *Romney*, signed by Captain Richardson at Brest 13 September 1917. HBC Archives, AFG/3/50. Mr Alex Ross, Head of Twentieth-Century Records, HBC Archives, kindly produced this manifest as being typical of such cargoes in the absence of the *Discovery*'s own. The original is in French. For Brest and Archangel see F. Menez, 'Brest pendant la guerre', *Revue maritime*, 1935, pp. 27–30.

27 HBCA French Government Archives, AFG/5/984. 'Notes regarding Archangel for Mr. Fuog'.

28 HBC Archives, AFG/5/986.

29 Sir William Schooling, *The Hudson's Bay Company 1670–1920*, London, 1920.

30 The file copy of this time charter between the Company and the French Government stated (among other things) that the vessel could carry 721 tons dead-weight cargo and bunkers, exclusive of stores and water. The last clause in the agreement overruled all others and stipulated that 'Should the steamer meet with an accident during the voyage, either by perils of the sea or by mines or acts of the enemy or from any other cause whatsoever, or should she be detained by ice, the hire is under all circumstances to be paid to the Owners in full without deduction until the steamer be fully repaired and re-delivered to Owners at a port in France or in the United Kingdom.' HBC Archives, AFG/26/4/47.

31 HBC Archives, AFG/5/2451.

32 Ibid., AFG/5/2451.

33 Ibid., AFG/5/987.

34 Alfred Kneale, diary kept in HM Trawler *Ganton*, minesweeper no. 1524, Expeditionary White Sea Squadron, 10 August 1915. N.M.M., JOD/131.

35 E. P. Stebbing, 'The forest region of north-east Russia', *Geographical Journal*, June 1918, p. 361.

36 HBC Archives, AFG/5/987. Copy of bill of lading dated 21/3 October 1915 (Old and New Style dates).

37 For the story of these and other ships for use in ice sold to the Russians, see William Barr, 'The role of Canadian and Newfoundland ships in the development of the Soviet Arctic', *Aspects: Journal of the Newfoundland Historical Society*, vol. ix, no. 1, 1977, pp. 19–26; no. 2, pp. 17–23.

38 HBC Archives, AFG/5/987, 5 December 1915: situation at Archangel when Mr Jenner left.

39 HBC Archives, AFG/5/2451.

40 Ibid., AFG/8/5/1–5; AFG/8/5/193. Basil Lubbock, the writer on maritime history, maintained that these last two ships of the Dundee whaling fleet sank during the gale because 'they were never meant to carry heavy deadweight cargoes'. As a result, they 'strained so badly that their seams opened and they gradually filled and sank'. See Basil Lubbock, *The Arctic Whalers* (Brown, Son & Ferguson, Glasgow, 1955), p. 451.

## Chapter Twelve. The Search for Shackleton, 1916

1 Captain John King Davis was to command this relief expedition, PRO. Shackleton Relief Advisory Committee, Final Report, Adm. 1/8483/60 on which much of this section is based. See also A. G. E. Jones, 'The relief of the Elephant Island party, 1916', *Fram*, vol. ii, part 1, 1985, pp. 349–56; also Ann Savours, *Polar Record*, vol. 29, 1993, p. 343.

2 HBC Archives, Provincial Archives of Manitoba: Reports and Proceedings, 2 August 1916, p. 12.

3  It is curious that the Advisory Committee's proposals of 19 May 1916, recommending the *Discovery* as relief ship, stated that her topmasts, yards, sails and rigging were reported to be at Dundee, in good condition.

4  Information from Mr David Henderson, Dundee Museums. Captain Fairweather wrote a series of articles in the *Scots Magazine*, vol. ix, 1928, pp. 348–59 and 426–34; vol. x, 1928, pp. 50–61, 137–45 and 231–40. These were privately reprinted in 1928 as a book. I am grateful to Miss P. Mugliston for supplying copies of the *Scots Magazine*, also to Nancy Rycroft, Captain Fairweather's granddaughter, for comments on the draft.

5  Dundee Advertiser, 24 March 1933.

6  *Discovery* Crew List, 1916. PRO, Board of Trade series. Copy in N.M.M. Fairweather family papers.

7  Shackleton Relief Advisory Committee, Final Report, 12 October 1916, PRO, Adm. 1/8483/60. The text of the Admiralty letter to Shackleton is given in the same report.

8  This and subsequent quotations concerning the voyage come from the deck logs of the *Discovery* in the PRO, Adm. 53/39960 (4 August to 14 November 1916) and Adm. 53/39961 (15–29 November 1916).

9  Telegram from Shackleton to his wife, 3 September 1916, quoted in Margery and James Fisher, *Shackleton* (Barrie, London, 1957), p. 395, and in Roland Huntford, *Shackleton* (Hodder and Stoughton, London, 1985), p. 614.

10  PRO, Board of Trade, Official Log, *Discovery* 1916. Copy in N.M.M.

## Chapter Thirteen. In Convoy to French and Spanish Ports, 1916–18, Last Voyage to Hudson Bay, 1918–19, Coasting the French Atlantic Ports and the Low Countries, 1919

1  HBC Archives, Bay Steamship Company records, Series 18/1294–/1298, soft green covers overprinted 'Sale and Company, 21 Old Broad Street, London E.C.'.

2  None of the escorts is mentioned by name in the logs. The phrase 'as per Admiralty instructions' quite often occurs, but presumably the French rather than the British authorities are generally implied. For background to these coasting voyages, see C. E. Fayle, *Seaborne trade* (John Murray, London, 1923–4), vols. ii and iii. The British Admiralty was only converted whole-heartedly to convoys in April 1917. For a war correspondent's account of the French patrols out of Brest, see Marcel Nadaud, *Les patrouilleurs de la mer* (Albin Michel, Paris, c.1917). The United States joined the French in protecting merchant ships after entering the war in 1917. See H. Wickliffe Rose, *Brittany patrol* (W. W. Norton, New York, 1937).

3  Ibid., Series 18/1294.

4  HBC Archives, AFG/5/2451. The cannons appear to have been consigned to one Henri Ferrière at Bordeaux, who paid 7,478.05 francs to the HBC for their freight from Madeira.

5  HBC Archives, Bay Steamship Company records, Series 18/1295.

6  Official log, PRO, Public Record Office, Board of Trade series. Copy in N.M.M. The ship's (mate's) log does not appear to have survived in the HBC's Archives for this voyage.

7  HBC Archives, AFG/5/2451.

8  HBC Archives, Bay Steamship Company records, Series 18/1296. This log ends on 20 March 1918 with the *Discovery* at Quiberon Bay awaiting orders.

9   Ibid., Series 18/1298. This log, kept by A. J. Bills, First Officer, ends here.

10  Crew list and official log, 30 May 1918 to 16 January 1919. PRO, Board of Trade series. Copy in N.M.M.

11  HBC Archives, Provincial Archives of Manitoba, Sale & Company records, S.19 and S.20.

12  HBC Archives, A12/FT 313/1.

13  For an account of life at the posts in wartime, see William Ashley Anderson, *Angel of Hudson Bay* (Evans, London, 1961).

14  HBC Archives, A12/FT 313/1.

15  G. H. Mead, 'Copy of Master's diary. Hudson's Bay Company's auxiliary barque *Discovery*. Montreal to Hudson Bay'. Typescript in the archives of the RGS. 4 p. I am indebted to Captain A. R. Williamson for comments on Captain Mead's seamanship and other nautical aspects of the voyage.

16  J. A. Dernier, Chief Officer's log, 28 July 1918. HBC Archives, C.1/274. The remaining logs are also in the HBC Archives as follows: Bay Steamship Company records, RG4, Series 18, no. 1299, Cardiff to Montreal; HBC records, C.1/275 and C.1/276.

17  Chief Officer's log, August 1918. HBC Archives, C.1/274 and C.1/275. Captain Mead's diary extract, RGS.

18  Chief Officer's log, 10 and 12 September 1918. HBC Archives, C.1/275.

19  HBC Archives. Sale & Company records, S.21.

20  Ibid., S.20.

21  Ibid., S.20 and S.21.

22  Ibid., S.22.

23  Ibid.

24  *Geographical Journal*, vol. lv, no. 4, 1920, p. 326.

25  Log kept by A. J. Booth, Mate, 6 February 1919 to 6 March 1919; 7 to 9 March by J. W. Jones, Second Mate; 10 to 23 March by J. Weatherhead, Mate. HBC Archives, unclassified documents.

26  Log kept by J. Weatherhead, Chief Officer, 24 March to 29 April 1919. HBC Archives, unclassified documents.

27  Log kept by J. Weatherhead, Chief Officer, 30 April to 18 June 1919. HBC Archives, unclassified documents.

### Chapter Fourteen. South Russian Venture: the Black Sea, 1919–20, Laid Up in London, 1920–3

1   This phase of the *Discovery*'s career appears to have been unwritten until now. I am much indebted to Mr S. D. Robertson, Archivist of the Department of Trade and Industry, for the provision of copies of the official log which brought it to my notice.

2   I am much indebted to Captain A. R. Williamson, DSC, for his account of this forgotten trade (which I have quoted verbatim to a large extent) in which he served in 1907 and 1908–9 and of which voyages he has given me a vivid personal narrative. Letters to the author of 15 February and 17 March 1985.

3   Sir Robert Horne, President of the Board of Trade in the House of Commons, 22 December 1920. Quoted in Stephen White, *Britain and the Bolshevik Revolution ...* (Macmillan, London, 1979), p. 23.

4 During the first months of the peace conference in Paris, Allied statesmen 'were haunted by nightmares of Bolshevik hordes, German and Russian, sweeping westwards across Europe'. John Silverlight, *The Victors' Dilemma* (Barrie & Jenkins, London, 1970), pp. ix. There was even talk (ironically, the day before the Armistice was signed) at a British Cabinet meeting of having to build up the German Army 'for fear of the spread of Bolshevism'. Winston Churchill, quoted by Silverlight, ibid., p. 1.

5 PRO, Adm. 137/1741, 27 May–2 June 1919.

6 PRO, Adm. 137/1741, 27 May–2 June 1919.

7 PRO, Adm. 137/1741, Black Sea Letter of proceedings, 8–14 July, enclosure dated 18 July.

8 Merchant Trading Company (now Metco). Board minute, 3 June 1919; PRO, Adm. 137/1743. Black Sea Proceedings, no. 26, 19 September–2 October 1919. Since only the records of Board meetings of the Merchant Trading Company in its early years appear to have survived, it has not so far proved possible to identify Lieut. Gurland.

9 HBC Archives, C1/649–657 (*Pelican*) kept by John Benson, Mate, and HBC Archives, Bay Steamship Co. records, Series 18/1303–1309 (*Discovery*), kept by Jo. Parry, Mate.

10 See Admiral Boyle Somerville, *The chart-makers* (Blackwood, Edinburgh, 1928), for an amusing account of survey work in the *Penguin*. An outline of the *Pelican*'s service with the HBC appears in *Beaver*, Outfit 260, no. 1, 1929, p. 215. She is believed to have been scuttled in 1953, says Mr A. W. H. Pearsall of Greenwich, where there is in the N.M.M. a model (1879–1) of the *Miranda* of the same class. The *Gannet*, last survivor of the class, is at Chatham Historic Dockyard, Kent.

11 See Stephen White, *Britain and the Bolshevik Revolution . . . 1920–1924* (Macmillan, London, 1979).

12 See Konstantin Paustovsky, *Southern adventure*, trans. Kyril FitzLyon (Harvill Press, London, 1969), pp. 82–3. A less romantic picture of the town and port during the Revolution is given in James Colquhoun, *Adventures in Red Russia* (John Murray, London, 1926).

13 Captain A. R. Williamson. Letter to the author, 15 February 1985.

14 See F. F. Raskolnikor, *Tales of Sub-Lieutenant Ilyin. Translated . . . by Brian Pearce*. London, New York Publications, 1982.

15 W. S. Churchill, *The aftermath* (Macmillan, London, 1944), p. 232.

16 H. N. H. Williamson, *Farewell to the Don: the journal of Brigadier H. N. H. Williamson*, ed. John Harris (Collins, London, 1970), pp. 27–9.

17 PRO, Adm. 137/1743. Black Sea Proceedings, no. 26, 19 September–2 October 1919.

18 I am indebted to Mrs Valentina Ward for the translation of these. The originals are in the PRO, Board of Trade series. There are copies in the N.M.M.

19 My source for most of the preceding paragraph was Philip Longworth's *The Cossacks* (Constable, London, 1969), chapter 10. Alexander Solzhenitsyn refers to Rostov in his *August 1914*, trans. Michael Glenny (Bodley Head, London, 1971), p. 45.

20 See Philip Longworth, op. cit., chapters 10 and 11, and John Silverlight, op. cit.

21 HBC Archives, unclassified documents. Letter included in some Sale and Company files, apparently transferred to the Archives with the French Government Records. I am indebted to Mr Alex Ross for drawing my attention to this letter.

22 H. N. H. Williamson, op. cit., p. 281.

23 Log of the *Discovery*, HBC Archives, Bay Steamship Co. records, Series 18/1306. Proceeds of some 25 million roubles deposited in three Russian banks were accounted as a loss in view

of the depreciation of the rouble. Some 30 million were invested in the Novo Grozny Tashkala Oil Fields, which combined with another in October 1920 to form the Anglo-Caucasian Oil Company Ltd. Charles V. Sale was its chairman.

24 HBC Archives, 10/189a no. 3.

25 W. S. Churchill, *The aftermath*, p. 275.

26 Captain W. R. Colbeck. Letter to the author, 29 September 1980.

27 HBC Archives, AFG/5/2451. The same file includes a sheet dated 1 June 1920 and headed, 'S.S. Discovery. Cost per day, 23 men'. This analysis of daily costs in pre-decimal pounds, shillings and pence, seems interesting enough to record below:

| | |
|---|---|
| Wages | £15-2-0d. |
| Provisions for 23 men at 4/7d. per day per man | £ 5-5-5d. |
| Stores, approximately | £ 3-6-8d. |
| Insurance | £1-7-10d. |
| Sundries, approximately | £ 3-0-0d. |
| Management and superintendence | £ 1-5-0d. |
| Total: | £29-6-11d. |

Repairs: cannot hope for less expenditure than £2,000 to £3,500 per annum, say, £6 to £10 per day.

28 *Chart and Compass*, February 1922, p. 178. I am indebted to the British Sailors Society and to Mr K. Snowdon for this reference.

# PART IV.
## THE *DISCOVERY* (OCEANOGRAPHIC) EXPEDITION, 1925–7

### Chapter Fifteen. Origins of the Discovery (Oceanographic) Expedition, Whales and Whaling, Sale to Crown Agents and Refit by Vospers, Voyage to the Cape, 1925

1 J. A. Mörch to Dr S. F. Harmer, 7 June and 28 July 1910. British Museum (Natural History) Archives, Keeper of Zoology's letters, Incoming 1909–14. Mörch's paper, 'On the natural history of whalebone whales', *Proceedings of the Zoological Society of London*, no. 47, 1911, pp. 661–70, communicated by Harmer, covers both hemispheres. Despite Harmer's encouragement to do so, he said little about the possibility of measures to protect the whales.

2 Dr S. F. Harmer to J. A. Mörch, 25 July 1910 and 9 January 1911. British Museum (Natural History) Archives, Keeper of Zoology's letters, Outgoing 1910–11, vol. ii.

3 Dr S. F. Harmer to Dr S. W. Kemp, 23 February 1925. British Museum (Natural History) Archives, CP.747/1. Whaling 1922–5.

4 British Museum (Natural History) Archives. File DF/1004/CP/749/3. Whales 1912–14.

5 See the obituaries in *Irish Naturalist*, vol. xxiii, 1914, pp. 81–93, plate, and *British Birds*, March 1914, p. 291. His South Georgia diary is in the Zoological Library of the British Museum (Natural History).

6 Maurice had recently been appointed to the Board. During the next thirty years he was to play an extremely important role in promoting marine science and the cause of conservation of fisheries and whaling in Great Britain and overseas. I am indebted to Miss Margaret Deacon for pointing this out.

7 Henry R. Heyburn, 'William Lamond Allardyce, 1861–1930: pioneer Antarctic conservationist', *Polar Record*, vol. xx, no. 124, 1980, pp. 39–42.

8 Ten years later, in February 1925, Martin Hinton's appendices to the 1915 confidential report were reissued by the Colonial Office 'in view of their scientific value', which had (in the words of the 'Prefatory Note' of 1925) by then 'assumed an additional importance in relation to the proposed investigation into whales and the whaling industry by the *Discovery* Expedition'.

9 British Museum (Natural History), Archives, letter from Professor J. G. Andersson to Dr Sidney Harmer, 19 December 1912, reported to the Trustees 20 January 1913 (both stamped 219). See also *Ymer*, Årg. 34, Häft 1, 1914, pp. 16–33; Häft 3, 1914, p. 284, Årg. 39, Häft 2–3, 1919, pp. 218–19, and *Geographical Journal*, vol. xliii, 1914, pp. 554–8; vol. xliv, 1914, pp. 234–5; vol. xlv, 1915, p. 81. Sir Sidney Harmer referred to this earlier Anglo-Swedish scheme in an article in *Nature*, 21 April 1923, p. 540, entitled 'Scientific investigation of the whaling problem'.

10 British Museum (Natural History) Archives. File DF 1004/CP/749/4. Whales 1916–17. For Rudmose Brown, see the obituary in *Polar Record*, vol. viii, no. 56, 1957, pp. 466–7. This states that during the war he worked in the Intelligence Department of the Naval Staff in London, being largely responsible for Arctic information. He was Dr W. S. Bruce's former colleague and his later biographer.

11 Report of the Interdepartmental Committee on Research and Development in the Dependencies of the Falkland Islands (HMSO, London, 1920).

12 Rowland Darnley, 'A New Antarctic Expedition', *The Nineteenth Century*, May 1923, pp. 718–28.

13 Report of the Interdepartmental Committee, London, 1920.

14 Figure from 'Capital expenditure: appendix to estimates of 1 June 1925 to 31 December 1925', pp. 15–16, kindly supplied by the late Sir George Deacon. For an account of the *Discovery* and the *William Scoresby*, by S. W. Kemp and A. C. Hardy, see *Discovery Reports*, vol. i, 1929.

15 HBC Archives, unclassified material. I am indebted to Ms Anne Morton for drawing my attention to this document.

16 Paraphrased from a letter to the Governor-General of South Africa from the *Discovery* Committee, 29 May 1925. Institute of Oceanographic Sciences, Deacon Laboratory. Library files of *Discovery* papers, file on maintenance and refit, *c*.1925.

17 In July 1925, HM King George V approved the designation of RRS after the Admiralty had indicated that the prefix suggested by the *Discovery* Committee of HMRS (His Majesty's Research Ship) was unacceptable. *Discovery* Committee papers, S.P.R.I.

18 *Discovery* Committee minutes, section 5. S.P.R.I. In contrast, the steel-built new vessel *Discovery II* was built in 1929 for a modest £60,000, complete with all spares and equipment.

19 This was finished by N. A. Macintosh from Harmer's rough sketch. A rorqual was chosen because the expedition would be mainly concerned with these whales (Dr S. F. Harmer to Dr S. W. Kemp, 10 July 1924. British Museum (Natural History) Archives, CP 747/1. Whaling 1922–5). The heraldic description of the badge reads: 'On a plate, in chief on a scroll ensigned

by the Imperial Crown the word "Discovery", in base a whale embowed naiant to the sinister in waves of the sea, all proper'. (Note by Dr D. Dilwyn John.)

20  W. T. Calman, 'Stanley Wells Kemp', *Obituary Notices of Fellows of the Royal Society*, vol. v, March 1947, pp. 467–76.

21  Alister Hardy, *Journal of the Marine Biological Association*, June 1946, pp. 219–34.

22  Stanley W. Kemp, 'The expedition of the RRS *Discovery*', *Nature*, vol. cxv, no. 2903, 20 June 1925, p. 950. See too the earlier announcement by Sir Sidney Harmer, 'Scientic investigation of the whaling problem', *Nature*, vol. cxi, no. 2790, 1923, pp. 540–1.

23  Stanley W. Kemp, 'The "Discovery" Expedition', *Natural History Magazine*, vol. i, no. 6, April 1928, p. 185.

24  *Discovery Reports*, vol. i, 1929, p. 140.

25  Photocopies of Stenhouse's MS summary of his career in the possession of his daughter, Mrs P. Mantell. Obituary in *The Times*, 19 March 1942, p. 7. 'Taffrail', *Endless Story*. Hodder and Stoughton, London, 1932, pp. 273–4.

26  Obituary of Stenhouse, *Polar Record*, vol. iii, no. 24, 1942, pp. 581–2. Stenhouse, the fine seaman and martinet during the Second World War, appears in the pages of L. M. Bates, *The spirit of London's river* (Gresham Books, London, 1949). See also the stirring pages of Stenhouse's *Cracker hash: the story of an apprentice in sail* (Percival Marshall, London, 1955) which covers his youth at sea. A reviewer in *Sea Breezes* commended this as 'one of the best books of its type to have been published in recent years . . . a record of a dying era' of 'unquestioned literary merit and readability'. L. M. Bates, *The Londoner's river* (Muller, London, 1949), pp. 31–6, provides a sketch of his life and character.

27  The General Regulations and Instructions for the *Discovery* Expedition (Colonial Office, May 1925) laid down that the Director of Research was the expedition's leader, who would direct the movements of the ship and instruct the scientific staff. The Captain was to 'use his best endeavours to secure the safety of the ship' and to 'comply with the instructions of the Director of Research in regard to the movements of the ship, except that it shall be his duty to decline to comply with any such instruction if, in his opinion, compliance would involve undue risk to the ship or ship's company'. In such an event, he must report in writing to the *Discovery* Committee. He and the remainder of the ship's company when within the Falkland Islands or Dependencies were subject to the orders of the Governor and Commander-in-Chief.

28  The late Sir Alister Hardy in conversation with the author, 23 August 1983.

29  Sir Alister Hardy, *Great waters*, p. 37. Darnley's article concluded by saying that in the *Discovery*, the expedition would be as safe as possible and would also avoid 'physical adventures' and risks such as those incurred by Scott. 'But it would be hard to overrate the splendour of the opportunity for spiritual adventure which will be afforded to fresh minds eager to penetrate into the unknown, and we can confidently anticipate that it will develop men not unworthy to be mentioned in such company as that of Darwin and Hooker, Ross and Nares, Murray and Bruce.' How right he was! For Hardy's life, see N. B. Marshall's obituary in *Biographical Memoirs of Fellows of the Royal Society*, vol. xxxii, 1986, pp. 223–73.

30  Letter quoted by W. T. Calman in his obituary of Sidney Frederic Harmer, 1862–1950. *Obituary Notices of Fellows of the Royal Society*, vol. vii, November 1951, p. 366.

31  Sir Alister Hardy, *Great waters* (Collins, London, 1967). His lecture on the expedition to the RGS appeared in the *Geographical Journal*, vol. lxxii, no. 3, 1928, pp. 209–34. Articles by Kemp were published in *Nature*, vol. cxv, 1925; vol. cxviii, 1926; and vol. cxxi, 1928.

32  Sir Alister Hardy, *Great waters*, pp. 60–3.

33  George Gourlay, unpublished memoirs, *c*.1977. Copy in the N.M.M. He was to serve the *Discovery* Committee for fourteen years altogether.

34  John Bentley. Talk given at the second *Discovery* symposium, N.M.M., 26 June 1980.

35  Diary kept by E. R. Gunther during the *Discovery* Expedition, in private hands. Together with his letters home (a habit no doubt instilled at Winchester and Gonville and Caius), Gunther's diary provides a remarkably continuous record of the expedition. On its return, he spent a number of years on the detailed analysis of the plankton samples. The results of this were published in collaboration with A. C. Hardy. In 1931, he was charged by the *Discovery* Committee with an examination of the Humboldt or Peru Current in the *William Scoresby*. A distance of 2,500 miles was covered from the Straits of Magellan to Ecuador, a difficult task, faithfully accomplished. He continued to work for the *Discovery* Committee, this time on whale marking in South Georgia waters, and made valuable observations on the habits of whales. He died in 1940, aged thirty-seven, after being shot accidentally, while on active service with a searchlight unit. See the obituaries by Dr Stanley Kemp in the *Geographical Journal*, vol. xcvi, no. 2, 1940, p. 152, and by A. C. Hardy in *Nature*, vol. cxlvi, no. 3691, 1940, p. 123, and the relevant *Discovery Reports*. Kemp praised his 'many fine qualities, among which his enthusiasm, thoroughness, determination and sturdy independence were pre-eminent'. He was an accomplished watercolour artist, ably depicting both the creatures of the deep and scenery ashore.

36  E. R. Gunther. Diary, 7 December 1925.

37  Ibid., 23 November 1925.

38  Ibid., 4 December 1925.

39  E. R. Gunther, letter home, 1 November 1925.

40  H. F. P. Herdman, letter to 'Bill', 1 November 1925. S.P.R.I., MS. 911/1.

41  *Discovery* Committee papers, S.P.R.I., 27th meeting. Item 9, 12 March 1925.

42  See F. Spiess, *The Meteor Expedition . . .*, English trans. ed. William J. Emery (National Science Foundation, Washington, D.C., 1985).

43  Sir Alister Hardy, *Great waters*, p. 64. For background, see Willem Hackmann, *Seek and strike: Sonar, anti-submarine warfare and the Royal Navy 1914–54* (HMSO, London, 1984). Gunther reveals that the bilge keels fitted a year later in Cape Town adversely affected the apparatus because of the 'water sounds' they caused (Gunther papers: letter of 21 September 1926). It is interesting that the RRS *Discovery* should have been instrumental in the successful development of an apparatus which was later used world-wide.

**Chapter Sixteen. Outward Voyage to South Georgia, 1925–6, and on to the Falklands**

1  See Allan Crawford, *Tristan da Cunha and the roaring forties* (Skilton, Edinburgh, 1982).

2  E. R. Gunther, *Notes and sketches made during two years on the 'Discovery' Expedition* (Dragon School, Oxford, 1928), pp. 7–8.

3  Dr Marshall's report is summarised in 'A visit to the island of Tristan da Cunha', *British Medical Journal*, vol. ii, 28 August 1926, pp. 399–400.

4  E. R. Gunther. Diary, 30 January 1926.

5  Sir Alister Hardy, *Great waters*, p. 143.
6  Ibid., pp. 142–3.
7  Ibid., p. 141.
8  *Geographical Journal*, vol. lxxii, no. 3, 1928, p. 218.
9  Sir Alister Hardy, *Great waters*, pp. 145–6.
10  Ibid., p. 146.
11  Ibid., pp. 144–5.
12  Ibid., p. 154.
13  Ibid., p. 317 and pp. 342–50.
14  Die Deutsche Atlantische Expedition, whose scientific director was A. Merz. See F. Spiess, *The 'Meteor' Expedition: scientific results of the German Atlantic Expedition, 1925–1927*, English trans. ed. W. J. Emery (National Science Foundation, Washington, D.C., 1985).
15  For an account of the history, geography, geology, biology, economy and government of the island, see Robert Headland, *The island of South Georgia* (Cambridge University Press, 1984).
16  E. R. Gunther. Diary, 20 February 1926.
17  For an account of the marine biological station by N. A. Mackintosh, see *Discovery Reports*, vol. i, 1929.
18  Diary for 21 February 1926 in *Great waters*, pp. 161–2. A fuller account of the whaling station, for which there is not space here, is given in *Great waters*, pp. 190–5.
19  John Bentley. Talk given at the second *Discovery* symposium, N.M.M. 26 June 1980.
20  E. R. Gunther. Diary, 21 February 1926.
21  Alfred Saunders, *A camera in Antarctica* (Winchester Publications, London, 1950), p. 14.
22  Dr S. W. Kemp, letter to Sir Sidney Harmer, 26 January 1927, in the archives of the British Museum (Natural History).
23  E. R. Gunther, letter home, 3 May 1926.
24  Sir Alister Hardy, *Great waters*, pp. 179–89.
25  E. R. Gunther, *Notes and sketches . . . 1925–27*, p. 31.
26  Sir Alister Hardy, *Great waters*, pp. 65–6.
27  E. R. Gunther, letter home, 3 May 1926.
28  A. C. Hardy, *Geographical Journal*, vol. lxxii, no. 3, 1928, p. 215.
29  Sir Alister Hardy, *Great waters*, p. 173.
30  E. R. Gunther, *Notes and sketches . . . 1925–27*, p. 14.
31  Ibid. and Diary, 25 April 1926.
32  Sir Alister Hardy, *Great waters*, p. 211. E. R. Gunther. Diary, 12 May 1926.
33  E. R. Gunther, *Notes and sketches . . . 1925–27*, p. 15.
34  Ibid.
35  E. R. Gunther. Diary, 5 June 1926.
36  Sir Alister Hardy, *Great waters*, p. 232.

### Chapter Seventeen. Second Season in the Antarctic, 1926–7, Voyage Home, Expedition Results

1  'Discovery Expedition' First Annual Report (HMSO, London, 1927), p. 7.
2  John Bentley. Talk given at the second *Discovery* symposium, N.M.M. 26 June 1980.

3 Sir Alister Hardy, *Great waters*, pp. 245–6.

4 E. R. Gunther. Diary, 6 November 1926.

5 E. R. Gunther, *Notes and sketches . . . 1925–27*, p. 23.

6 E. R. Gunther. Diary, 12 November 1926.

7 John Bentley. Ibid.

8 Sir Alister Hardy, *Great waters*, p. 267. The log entry recording the near miss with the iceberg (written in ink rather than the usual pencil) reads: 'Wind freshened at Noon and Pack ice became close, drove Eastward under influence of wind, ship could not make headway, Position insecure among Berg studded Pack, Altered course to Northward towards open water distant about 4 miles. 1300 Ship setting down in Pack towards small Berg (100 yds. long 30 feet high, approx.) 13.15 Berg capsized when ship was within a 100 yards. 13 30 abm of Berg with Pack driving ship towards Berg under influence strong wind and heavy swell. Set lower Topsails and headsails and cleared danger by about 10 yards. 1400 clear of Berg and heading for open water, heavily hummocked Pack which rolled heavily in swell. 14.45 cleared edge of Pack. Made all sail fast, dull and overcast, strong wind and rough sea, streamed and set log at zero. Ship making NNE.' (Entry for 16 November 1926, afternoon, in one of twelve logbooks, formerly in the possession of Mrs P. Mantell, Stenhouse's daughter, and now in N.M.M., MSS. 84/146.)

9 E. R. Gunther. Diary, 30 November 1926.

10 Quoted by Sir Alister Hardy, *Great waters*, pp. 268–9. The Committee wrote to Kemp on 24 February 1927 saying they had received his account of the *Discovery*'s deficiencies as a research vessel 'with much concern'. They shared his disappointment at the opportunities lost because of her lack of power. They recognised that she could not carry out alone, 'even in the most favourable conditions, the full range of investigations contemplated'. They observed, however, that this to some extent was not unexpected, since financial stringencies had restricted the expedition to a single vessel, despite the Interdepartmental Committee's original recommendation of two. They were now looking carefully at what 'additional or alternative measures' could be adopted to expedite the work within the funds available. (Letter from the *Discovery* Committee, Colonial Office, to Dr S. W. Kemp, 24 February 1927. Institute of Oceanographic Sciences, Deacon Laboratory, Wormley.)

   Darnley had written to Kemp about a month earlier saying that a new ship would cost a great deal 'and from a purely financial standpoint it would no doubt be cheaper to put up with a considerable waste of time'. He was, however, 'apprehensive of the psychological effect on the staff' and appreciative of the 'disgust with which you regard the existing hindrances to scientific work on long passages'. (Letter from E. R. Darnley at the Colonial Office to Dr S. W. Kemp, 31 January 1927. Institute of Oceanographic Sciences, Deacon Laboratory, Wormley.)

11 Dr S. W. Kemp, letter to Dr W. T. Calman, Keeper of Zoology at the British Museum (Natural History), 20 March 1927. Zoology Department Archives, 384/7.

12 In the *Geographical Journal*, vol. lxxii, no. 3, 1928, Fig. 3.

13 Sir Alister Hardy, *Great waters*, p. 301.

14 Abridged from Chaplin's remarks on the hydrographic surveying published in the *Geographical Journal*, vol. lxxii, no. 3, 1928, pp. 231–3.

15 Dr S. W. Kemp, letter to Dr W. T. Calman, 20 March 1927. British Museum (Natural History), Zoology Department Archives, 384/7.

16  John Bentley. Talk given at the second *Discovery* symposium, N.M.M. 26 June 1980.

17  E. R. Gunther. Diary, 21 January 1927.

18  Sir Alister Hardy, *Great waters*, p. 312.

19  Dr S. W. Kemp, letter to Dr W. T. Calman, 20 March 1927. British Museum (Natural History), Zoology Department Archives, 384/7.

20  A. C. Hardy, 'The work of the Royal Research Ship "Discovery" in the Dependencies of the Falkland Islands', *Geographical Journal*, vol. lxxii, no. 3, 1928, pp. 223–4. E. R. Gunther in *Notes and sketches . . . 1925–27*, pp. 33–9, gives a personal account, including a visit to the Jason Islands to survey the protected fur seal colony.

21  See A. C. Hardy, 'Whale-marking in the Southern Ocean', *Geographical Journal*, vol. xcvi, no. 5, 1940, pp. 345–50.

22  Sir Alister Hardy, *Great waters*, pp. 372–4.

23  Ibid., pp. 374–5.

24  Ibid., pp. 380–1.

25  *Geographical Journal*, vol. lxxii, no. 3, 1928, p. 233.

26  Sir Alister Hardy, *Great waters*, p. 389.

27  *Antarctic pilot*, 1948 ed., p. 165.

28  Sir Alister Hardy, *Great waters*, pp. 389–90.

29  Lieut.-Com. Chaplin's remarks on the survey work. *Geographical Journal*, vol. lxxii, no. 3, 1928, p. 233. 'Discovery Island' was named in ignorance of the name given by Charcot, 1905. It is now called Guépratte Island: information kindly supplied by Dr G. Hattersley-Smith.

30  Dr E. H. Marshall. Diary, 1925–7, in private hands.

31  H. F. P. Herdman, letter dated 19 June 1927. Scott Polar Research Institute, MS. 911/4.

32  Sir Alister Hardy, *Great waters*, pp. 404–5.

33  Dr E. H. Marshall. Diary, 27 March 1927.

34  Sir Alister Hardy, *Great waters*, p. 405.

35  For further information on the recorder and its successors, see Sir Alister Hardy, *Great waters*, pp. 414–22, and *Discovery Reports*, vol. xi, June 1936, pp. 457–510. An early model is in the Science Museum, South Kensington.

36  Dr E. H. Marshall. Diary, 22 April 1927; Sir Alister Hardy, *Great waters*, pp. 422–7, where there is a delightful account of the days among the trees, ferns and streams, the haunt of the tiny and endearing 'Happy Larry Bird', as *Oxyurus tupineri* was christened by its new friends.

37  Sir Alister Hardy, *Great waters*, pp. 428–9.

38  *Discovery Investigations, Second Annual Report, 1927–1928* (HMSO, London, 1929), pp. 23–5, and T. John Hart, 'Report on trawling surveys on the Patagonian continental shelf', *Discovery Reports*, vol. xxiii, 1946, pp. 223–408, compiled mainly from manuscripts left by the late E. R. Gunther.

39  A. C. Hardy, 'The work of the RRS *Discovery* . . .', *Geographical Journal*, vol. lxxii, no. 3, 1928, p. 224.

40  *Geographical Journal*, vol. lxxii, no. 3, 1928, p. 227.

41  Sir Sidney Harmer, *Geographical Journal*, vol. lxxii, no. 31, 1928, p. 229.

42  John Bentley, Ibid.

43  Harry R. Lillie, *The path through penguin city* (Benn, London, 1955). The author of this book worked as a doctor with the whaling fleets. Much of it relates to his efforts to introduce a more humane method of killing the whale with an electric harpoon. This has not been adopted.

PART V.
THE BANZARE (BRITISH, AUSTRALIAN AND NEW
ZEALAND ANTARCTIC RESEARCH EXPEDITION),
1929–31

### Chapter Eighteen. Origins of the BANZARE and Outward Voyage to the Cape

1  Captain K. N. MacKenzie. Diary. BANZARE, 1929–31. Microfilm in the N.M.M., MSS. MRF/137.

2  Ibid.

3  Alun Anderson, 'Science in Australasia: Antarctica', *Nature*, vol. cccxvi, 18 July 1985, p. 202.

4  Douglas Mawson, 'The Australasian Antarctic Expedition', *Geographical Journal*, vol. xxxvii, 1911, pp. 609–20, maps (p. 613 and facing p. 700).

5  Frank Debenham, 'The future of polar exploration', *Geographical Journal*, vol. lvii, no. 3, 1921, pp. 182–204.

6  Sir Douglas Mawson, 'Unsolved problems of Antarctic exploration and research'. In: W. L. G. Joerg, ed., *Problems of polar research* (American Geographical Society, New York, 1928), pp. 253–66.

7  Sir Douglas Mawson, 'The B.A.N.Z. Antarctic Research Expedition', *Geographical Journal*, vol. lxxx, no. 2, 1932, p. 101.

8  Peter Beck, 'British Antarctic policy in the early 20th century', *Polar Record*, vol. xxi, no. 134, 1983, pp. 475–83; 'Securing the dominant "place in the wan Antarctic sun" for the British Empire: the policy of extending British control over Antarctica', *Australian Journal of Politics and History*, vol. xxix, no. 3, 1983, pp. 448–61; 'Britain and Antarctica, the historical perspective', *Fram*, vol. i, 1984, pp. 67–82. Beck points out that the head of the Foreign Office's western department admitted in 1928 to the 'fact that we are trying to paint the whole Antarctic red as the result of a deliberate and settled policy'. Whatever the politics, it is true that British expeditions to the Antarctic regions had played a leading part in their exploration, as is borne out in Robert K. Headland, *Chronological list of Antarctic expeditions* (Cambridge University Press, 1989).

9  Stenographic notes of the meeting, classified as secret until 1977. PRO, CAB/32/46. The draft was very slightly revised at the final meeting on 23 November 1926.

10  A. Grenfell Price, *The winning of Australian Antarctica: Mawson's B.A.N.Z.A.R.E. voyages, 1929–31, based on the Mawson papers* (Angus and Robertson, Sydney, for the Mawson Institute for Antarctic Research, 1962), p. 16. BANZ Antarctic Research Expedition Reports, Series A, vol. i, the Geographical Report.

11  PRO, FO 371/13359/1928/W 950/532/50.

12  PRO, FO 371/13359/1928/9 January 1928.

13  PRO, CO 78/183/7.

14  Ibid.

15  PRO, CO 78/181/16.

16  Ibid.

17  PRO, CO 78/183/7.

18  PRO, CO 78/181/16.

**19** PRO, CO 78/183/7.

**20** PRO, FO 371/14086/W240/98/50. Letter from the Chancellor of the Exchequer to L. S. Amery, Dominions Office, 2 January 1929.

**21** PRO, FO 371/14086/W393/98/50. Enclosure in letter from Batterbee of the Dominions Office to Campbell, First Secretary of the Foreign Office, 12 January 1929.

**22** Lars Christensen, *Such is the Antarctic* (Hodder and Stoughton, London, 1935), pp. 142–3. The large volume of correspondence dealing with Bouvet Island at this time is in the PRO, FO 371/13359.

**23** PRO, CO 78/183/7.

**24** Ibid.

**25** Ibid.

**26** R. A. Swan, *Australia in the Antarctic* (Melbourne University Press, 1961), p. 175. This book provides a good general background to BANZARE.

**27** Sir Douglas Mawson to Dr H. R. Mill, 14 September 1929, aboard SS *Mooltan* off India. S.P.R.I., MS. 100/75/8.

**28** Towards the end of 1929, RRS *Discovery II* was commissioned to continue the oceanographic researches in the Southern Ocean begun with the *Discovery* Expedition of 1925–7. Mawson must have been particularly glad to see Scott's *Discovery* operating as a Royal Research Ship. It was in March 1911 nearly twenty years earlier, when organising the Australasian Antarctic Expedition of 1911–14, that he had sent a letter requesting her purchase or charter from the Hudson's Bay Company. He wanted her then because she was a non-magnetic vessel, since the main aim of the 'very important scientific exploring expedition' of which he was in charge, was 'the magnetic charting of the ocean area in the vicinity of the South Magnetic Pole', which he had reached by sledge journey 'as one of three on Shackleton's recent expedition'. He pointed out that the *Discovery* was built as a scientific ship and that it would be a great boon to the scientific community were the company to substitute a sealer for her. However, the Governor and Committee declared themselves unable to accede to his request, since the steamer was required for trading in the coming season. HBC Archives, A.10/187, no. 5 and A.5/104, fo. 100. I am indebted to Ms Anne Morton for drawing my attention to this correspondence.

**29** Major R. G. Casey to Sir Douglas Mawson, 30 January 1929. Mawson Institute, Adelaide.

**30** Sir Douglas Mawson to Dr H. R. Mill, 11 March 1929. S.P.R.I., MS. 100/75/11.

**31** Sir Douglas Mawson to Dr H. R. Mill, 3 February 1929. S.P.R.I., MS. 100/75/9.

**32** Lars Christensen, *Such is the Antarctic*, p. 121.

**33** A. Grenfell Price, op. cit., p. 17.

**34** Sir Douglas Mawson to Dr H. R. Mill, 17 February 1929. S.P.R.I., MS. 100/75/10.

**35** Sir Douglas Mawson to Dr H. R. Mill, 11 March 1929. S.P.R.I., MS. 100/75/11.

**36** Minutes of the first meeting of the Antarctic Expedition Committee, 12 March 1929.

**37** Mawson's Instructions:

> Being in all respects ready for sea, and having embarked all necessary personnel, equipment and stores, you are to leave Cape Town on October 15th or at the earliest possible date thereafter, and proceed to Kerguelen Island, calling at the Crozet Islands at your discretion. Having completed coaling at Kerguelen Island you will proceed to the western extremity of Queen Mary Land (west of Mount Gauss), calling at Heard Island en route if you deem it advisable to do so. From

thence you will cruise westward to Enderby Land following the coast or ice barrier as circumstances permit, to longitude 45° east, and, at your discretion, if conditions are favourable, to 40° east. You will then cruise back along the coast eastward to Kemp Land and then to Queen Mary Land and Knox Land, subject to any change of course which you may find it necessary to make either by reason of coaling requirements or otherwise. When conditions make further cruising in Antarctic regions impracticable you will proceed to Australia, calling first at such port in the Commonwealth as may be most convenient.

You will use your best endeavours to make a hydrographic survey of the coast and its contiguous waters between the western extremity of Queen Mary Land and Enderby Land at 45°/40° east, such survey to comprise the correct location and charting of coasts, islands, rocks and shoals.

On such lands or islands within the area specified in the preceding paragraph you will plant the British flag wherever you find it practicable to do so, and in doing so you will read the proclamation of annexation as set out in Annexure A to these Sailing Orders, attach a copy of the proclamation to the flagstaff, and place a second copy of the proclamation in a tin at the foot of the flagstaff. You will keep a record of each such act of annexation in the form set out in Annexure B.

During the course of the expedition you will carry out to the best of your ability all scientific work and investigations which it is practicable for you to do in respect of all the matters falling within the competence of the scientific staff which has been selected to accompany you, comprising, amongst other things, meteorological and oceanographic observations and investigations concerning the fauna, notably whales and seals, of the seas and lands visited by you, and all matters connected therewith which may assist in the future economic exploitation of such fauna. All written records made, and all specimens of whatever sort taken and preserved, and all negatives and photographs made during the course of the expedition, will be the property of the expedition, and you will be responsible that no improper use is made of them by any member of the expedition.

On your arrival in Australia you will furnish the Commonwealth Government with a full report of the work which you have carried out in respect of each and all of the objects of the expedition as set out above.

[*Signed*] S. M. BRUCE,
Prime Minister

Quoted in A. Grenfell Price, op. cit., pp. 22–3.

**38** Mawson's Royal Commission:

GEORGE R.I.

GEORGE, BY THE GRACE OF GOD, OF GREAT BRITAIN, IRELAND AND THE BRITISH DOMINIONS BEYOND THE SEAS KING, DEFENDER OF THE FAITH, EMPEROR OF INDIA, etc., etc., etc. TO ALL AND SINGULAR TO WHOM THESE PRESENTS SHALL COME, GREETING!

Whereas We have judged it expedient to appoint a fit person to take possession in Our name, during the course of the expedition presently to be conducted to the Antarctic regions by Our Trusty and Well-beloved Sir Douglas Mawson,

Knight Bachelor, Officer of Our Most Excellent Order of the British Empire, commanding the Royal Research Ship 'Discovery', of such territories now unknown as may be discovered in the course of the aforesaid expedition, and further of certain territories not under the sovereignty of any other State which have been discovered in the past by subjects of Our Royal Predecessors or of Ourself, to wit: (i) The outlying part of Coats Land, viz., the portion not comprised within the Falkland Islands Dependencies, (ii) Enderby Land, (iii) Kemp Land, (iv) Queen Mary Land, (v) the area which lies to the west of Adélie Land and which on its discovery by the Australian [sic] Antarctic Expedition in 1912 was denominated Wilkes Land, (vi) King George V Land, (vii) Oates Land;

Now know Ye that We, reposing especial Trust and Confidence in the discretion and faithfulness of Our Trusty and Well-beloved Sir Douglas Mawson, Knight Bachelor, aforesaid, have nominated, constituted and appointed him to be Our Commissioner for the purpose aforesaid; hereby giving and granting him Full Power and Authority to do and perform, during the course of the aforesaid expedition, either himself or through such persons under his direction and authority as he may see fit to designate in writing for the purpose, all and every act and acts, thing and things, which he may lawfully do and perform for the fulfilment of the said purposes; whereof he shall give account to Us in due course.

In witness whereof We have caused Our Great Seal to be affixed to these Presents, which We have signed with Our Royal Hand.

Given at Our Court of Saint James, the Twenty-fifth day of July, in the Year of Our Lord, One Thousand Nine Hundred and Twenty-nine and in the Twentieth Year of Our Reign.

[*Great Seal*]

Ibid., pp. 23–4.

**39** *The Times*, 12 October 1929.

**40** Captain J. K. Davis. Diary 1929–30 (typed), October 1929. State Library of Victoria, Melbourne, classmark 3236/6(a).

**41** Captain K. N. MacKenzie. Diary. BANZARE, 1929–31. Microfilm in the N.M.M., MRF/137.

**42** *The Times*, 29 July 1929. Cutting in J. B. Child album, copy in private hands.

The Australian blue ensign had been hoisted when the expedition took the ship over in the London docks, although she remained registered in Port Stanley, Falkland Islands. This was because Australia was providing most of the finance for the expedition. The warrant to fly the Australian flag must have been obtained by Mawson and Davis early on (Captain W. R. Colbeck, letter to the author, 17 April 1985). There is of course no Antarctic flag. The so-called white flag of Antarctica is now in the N.M.M., presented by Mrs J. B. Child.

**43** *The Times*, ibid.

**44** J. B. Child album of BANZARE press cuttings, copy in private hands.

**45** J. B. Child, ibid.

**46** MacKenzie was in fact over thirty, having been born in November 1897.

**47** J. B. Child, press cuttings album.

**48** Captain W. R. Colbeck, letter to the author, 23 January 1983.

However, these things are not learnt in a day. On 1 October 1929, while on passage to Cape Town, one of the seamen observed, 'The Mates don't know their work and are now beginning to take it out on us in consequence. They often let go wrong ropes and give wrong orders.' That evening the wind changed suddenly and they were 'taken by the lee and the Mate was at a loss what to do. However the O.M. [Davis] arrived and put things in order.' J. H. Martin. Diary of the first BANZARE voyage. S.P.R.I., MS. 429/2/1.

49  J. B. Child, press cuttings album.

50  See the fine obituary of Marr by B. B. Roberts, *Polar Record*, vol. xiii, 1966, pp. 94–7. His *magnum opus*, a far-ranging study of the Antarctic krill, was published in *Discovery Reports*, vol. xxxii, 1962, pp. 33–464.

51  See David P. Millar, *From snowdrift to shellfire. Capt. James Francis (Frank) Hurley 1885–1962* (David Ell, Sydney, 1984), and Lennard Bickel, *In search of Frank Hurley* (Macmillan, Melbourne, 1980). Hurley's magnificent film of the *Endurance* voyage can still be seen today, as can 'Southward Ho! with Mawson', the film of the BANZARE Expedition. Copies of both films are in the N.M.M. According to Bickel, p. 87, Hurley found the *Discovery* slower than the old *Aurora* and a great disappointment as an Antarctic ship.

52  Captain K. N. MacKenzie. Diary. BANZARE, 1929–31. Microfilm in the N.M.M., MRF/137.

53  J. K. Davis, *High latitude* (Melbourne University Press, 1962).

54  Ibid., p. 54.

55  Ibid., p. 55.

56  *Geographical Journal*, vol. cxxxiii, part 3, 1967, pp. 428–9.

57  John King Davis, 'Future exploration of the African quadrant of Antarctica', *Scottish Geographical Magazine*, vol. xxxix, no. 4, 1923, pp. 237–43.

58  Dr D. Dilwyn John. Letter to the author, 3 October 1984.

59  J. B. Child's diary, 10 August 1929, in private hands.

60  Ibid., 1 September 1929.

61  Captain K. N. MacKenzie. Diary. BANZARE, 1929–31. Microfilm in the N.M.M., MRF/137.

62  'Full and by' is 'the condition of a sailing vessel when she is held as close to the wind as possible, with sails full and not shivering. *The Oxford companion to ships and the sea*, ed. Peter Kemp (Oxford University Press, 1976).

63  Captain K. N. MacKenzie, Diary, 19 September 1929.

64  John K. Davis. Diary kept during the first BANZARE voyage, 1929–30, entry for 28 September 1929. Davis papers, State Library of Victoria, Melbourne, classmark 3237/1.

65  Captain K. N. MacKenzie, Diary, 1 October 1929.

66  Ibid., 6 to 18 October 1929.

67  Captain W. R. Colbeck. Letters to the author 23 January and 17 November 1983.

68  John K. Davis. Diary kept during the first BANZARE voyage, 1929–30, entry for 28 September 1929. Davis papers, State Library of Victoria, Melbourne, classmark 3237/1. In the same diary on 16 October 1929, he records writing a letter from Cape Town to R. G. Casey saying that the main yards had been left in the charge of the Port Authority. They must have been transported to London after the return of the *Discovery* to England in 1931 at the end of the expedition.

69  A. R. Alderman and C. E. Tilley, 'Douglas Mawson', *Biographical Memoirs of Fellows of the Royal Society*, vol. v, February 1960, pp. 119–27.

70  One can become confused as to the place-names in this area in that Mawson wrote of Commonwealth Bay (his main base for 1911–14) as being in 'Adelie Land'. He also named the area to the west of the present Terre Adélie 'Wilkes Land' (now Wilkes Coast), in honour

of the nineteenth-century American explorer. During the BANZARE, Commonwealth Bay was proclaimed part of King George V Land. Mawson's term 'Wilkes Land' is now applied to a much larger section of the land mass, between Terre Adélie and Queen Mary Land.

71 London, 1915 and later editions. See also Lennard Bickel, *This accursed land* (Macmillan, Melbourne, 1977), and David Parer and Elizabeth Parer-Cook, *Douglas Mawson, the survivor* (Alella Books, Morwell, Vic., 1983).

72 A. R. Alderman, 'Professor Sir Douglas Mawson . . .', *Transactions of the Royal Society of South Australia*, vol. lxxxii, 1959, 6 pp. Reprint.

73 A. R. Alderman and C. E. Tilley, op. cit.

74 Sir Raymond Priestley's reminiscence of Mawson in *Polar Record*, vol. ix, no. 61, 1959, p. 377.

75 'Eric Webb, An appreciation'. In: Lennard Bickel, *This accursed land* (Melbourne, Macmillan, 1977), pp. 202–3.

76 Obituary in *Geographical Journal*, vol. 124, 1958, pp. 584–5.

77 R. G. Simmers, BANZARE diary. Antarctic manuscripts collection, Canterbury Museum Archives, Christchurch, New Zealand. Copy in Mawson Institute, University of Adelaide.

78 Ibid., 13 October 1929.


## Chapter Nineteen. First Season in the Antarctic, 1929–30, and the Voyage Home

1 Diary kept by Ritchie Simmers, 19 October 1929.

2 Captain K. N. MacKenzie. Diary, 29 October 1929.

3 Ibid., 30 October 1929.

4 Ibid.

5 Diary kept by Ritchie Simmers, 6 November 1929.

6 Ibid., 7 November 1929.

7 Ibid., 8 November 1929.

8 Ibid., 3 November 1929.

9 Ibid., 7 November 1929.

10 Ibid., 8 November 1929.

11 Captain K. N. MacKenzie. Diary, 12 November 1929.

12 Diary kept by Ritchie Simmers, 10 November 1929.

13 For a history of Iles Kerguelen and a life of their eighteenth-century discoverer Yves-Joseph de Kerguelen-Trémarec, see Raymond de Brossard, *Kerguelen, le découvreur et ses îles*, 2 tomes (France-Empire, Paris, 1971). France has claimed sovereignty over the islands since 1924 and they now form part of *Terres Australes et Antarctiques Françaises*.

14 Captain K. N. MacKenzie. Diary, 12 November 1929.

15 Mawson's report for *The Times* despatched 25 November 1929.

16 Captain K. N. MacKenzie. Diary, 21 November 1929.

17 Undated press cutting. J. B. Child album in N.M.M.

18 Sir George Deacon, FRS, letter to the author dated 2 February 1984. Sir George went on to say that the BANZARE scientific reports do little justice to his vital contribution.

    'The difficult conditions of work' experienced by Marr were set out after the first BANZARE voyage in a confidential letter to the *Discovery* Committee of 28 July 1930. He had found on joining ship in London that Captain Davis believed scientists to be a nuisance on board. From earlier experience, Davis 'was firmly convinced . . . that our wires would get foul of the propeller, that we should lose all our gear the first time it went over the side, and that our work would be haphazard and conducted without any definite plan . . .'. At Cape Town, it appeared evident to Marr that Sir Douglas Mawson and Captain Davis were 'as far apart as the stars' and that he would 'have to fill many gaps in the flimsy fabric of organisation', namely 'directing the ship during scientific investigations and the entire rigging, running and repairing of the oceanographic gear'. He found too a lack of experience and of determination among the zoological staff as regards the 'meticulous labour' and long hours needed in the laboratory. They had a 'natural apathy' towards the operation and maintenance of the oceanographic gear, Sir Douglas Mawson himself being an exception and 'on occasion' one of Marr's 'chief A.B.'s'. S.P.R.I., MS. 1403/3/15. Marr's health was affected by having overworked and he did not return for the second voyage; Matheson, a seaman, was instead attached as an assistant to the scientists, which improved matters. That Davis persisted in his belief is borne out by Mawson's diary. Towards the end of the voyage, he wrote of the master's 'peculiar attitude to the staff—treating them as inferiors and practically never speaking to any of them, locking himself in his cabin and glaring into space'. *Mawson's Antarctic diaries*, p. 343, 20 March 1930.

19 *Mawson's Antarctic diaries*, p. 266, 26 November 1929.

20 Mawson's report despatched 13 December, undated press cutting in J. B. Child album.

21 Ibid.

22 Ibid.

23 Mawson's despatch transmitted on 17 December 1929 and published in *The Times* the following day.

24 *The Times*, 18 December 1929.

25 Abridged from Mawson's report in *The Times*, 18 December 1929.

26 Captain K. N. MacKenzie. Diary, 3 December 1929. For a vivid account of a summer of science and mountaineering on the island and a splendid map, see G. M. Budd, *The ANARE 1963 expedition to Heard Island* (Antarctic Division, Department of External Affairs, Melbourne, 1964). The leader of the Atlas Cove party, Nils Lied, recorded the February weather as follows: hail on two days, snow on eight days, mist on nine days, dust storm on one day, fog on nine days, rain on thirteen days, drizzle on six days. To this, he added 'the almost constant gales, the crash of falling ice and the roar of the Southern Ocean pounding the beaches, rocks and ice cliffs'. See also Brian Roberts, 'Historical notes on Heard and McDonald Islands', *Polar Record*, vol. v, no. 40, 1950, pp. 580–4, and A. G. E. Jones, 'Captain Peter Kemp and Kemp Land', *Mariner's Mirror*, vol. liv, no. 3, 1968, pp. 233–43.

27 Captain J. K. Davis. Diary, 3 December 1929. State Library of Victoria, classmark 3236/6a.

28 Captain J. K. Davis. Diary, 8 December 1929. State Library of Victoria, classmark 3236/6a.

29 Captain K. N. MacKenzie. Diary, 8–9 December 1929.

30 Ibid., 11 December 1929.

31 Ibid.

32 Captain J. K. Davis. Diary, 9 December 1929. State Library of Victoria, classmark 3236/6a.

33 Captain K. N. MacKenzie. Diary, 13 December 1929.

34 Ibid., 14 December 1929.

35  Ibid., 15–24 December 1929.

36  J. H. Martin. Diary, 14 December 1929. S.P.R.I., MS. 429/2/1.

37  J. B. Child. Diary, 18 December 1929.

38  A. Grenfell Price, op. cit., p. 48.

39  Ibid.

40  Captain K. N. MacKenzie. Diary, 20 December 1929.

41  J. H. Martin. Diary, 20 December 1929. S.P.R.I., MS. 429/2/1.

42  See *Mawson's Antarctic diaries*, ed. Fred Jacka and Eleanor Jacka (Allen and Unwin, Sydney, 1988).

43  Captain J. K. Davis. Diary, 19 December 1929. State Library of Victoria, classmark 3236/6a.

44  J. B. Child. Diary, 24 December 1929. Seaman Martin again remarked on Davis's conduct in spending 'time steaming round and round an ice lake. It seems the O.M. is determined not to go South and to waste coal steaming about when we might drift or tie up.' J. H. Martin. Diary, 24 December 1929. S.P.R.I., MS. 429/2/1.

45  Despatch to *The Times* transmitted 27 December 1929.

46  Captain K. N. MacKenzie. Diary, 26 December 1929.

47  Captain J. K. Davis. Diary, 26 December 1929.

48  Ibid., 28 December 1929. For a discussion of how much of the continent was seen on 26 and 27 December 1929, see A. Grenfell Price, op. cit., pp. 54–5 and 170–1. See also Davis to Orme Masson, 5 June 1933, in Davis papers.

49  J. B. Child. Diary, 28 December 1929.

50  A. Grenfell Price, op. cit., p. 59.

51  Captain K. N. MacKenzie. Diary, 2 January 1930. Martin remarked 'Airmen do not bring back any very exciting reports of land.' J. H. Martin. Diary, 31 December 1929. S.P.R.I., MS. 429/2/1.

52  Captain J. K. Davis. Diary, 31 December 1929.

53  *Report by Sir Douglas Mawson . . . on the work of the expedition in R.S.S. [sic] 'Discovery' . . . 1929–1930* (Government Printer, June 1930).

54  Mawson's press reports transmitted 27 and 31 December 1929.

55  Captain K. N. MacKenzie. Diary, 2 January 1930.

56  J. B. Child. Diary, 31 December 1929.

57  *Mawson's Antarctic diaries*, p. 304, 3 January 1930.

58  Captain J. K. Davis. Diary, 4 January 1930.

59  J. B. Child. Diary, 4 January 1930. 'The land as I first saw it' is sketched under entry for 5 January 1930.

60  See A. G. E. Jones, 'Captain Peter Kemp and Kemp Land', *Mariner's Mirror*, vol. liv, no. 3, 1968, pp. 233–43. Mr Jones confirms Kemp's sighting of land in the vicinity of Cape Davis, but considers that the name 'Kemp Land' on modern charts has been wrongly applied. We see that Mawson and Davis disagreed as to the identity of Biscoe's Cape Ann. On Biscoe's landfalls, see J. S. Cumpston, 'The Antarctic landfalls of John Biscoe, 1831', *Geographical Journal*, vol. cxxix, 1963, pp. 175–84. For his voyage, see A. G. E. Jones, 'John Biscoe's voyage round the world', *Mariner's Mirror*, vol. lvii, 1971, pp. 41–62, and Ann Savours, 'Who was John Biscoe?', *Geographical Magazine*, vol. xxxvi, 1964, pp. 499–505, in which is reproduced Biscoe's sketch of Enderby Land. See too Douglas Mawson, 'Historical features of the discovery of Enderby and Kemp Lands', *Geographical Journal*, vol. lxxxvi, 1935, pp. 526–30.

61 Captain J. K. Davis. Diary, 6 January 1930.

62 Letter from Group Captain Campbell of 4 June 1962 quoted in John Grierson, *Challenge to the poles* (Foulis, London, 1964), pp. 219–21.

63 Captain J. K. Davis. Diary, 7 January 1930.

64 Ibid., 8 January 1930.

65 *Mawson's Antarctic diaries . . .*, p. 310, 9 January 1930.

66 J. H. Martin. Diary, 9 January 1930. S.P.R.I., MS. 429/2/1.

67 Captain J. K. Davis. Diary, 11 January 1930.

68 Mawson's press report released on 10 January 1930. Captain K. N. MacKenzie. Diary, 7 January 1930.

69 This place-name has been spelt in various ways in the literature and on maps and charts. The official Australian version is now Mac.Robertson Land. In a letter to A. R. Hinks of the Royal Geographical Society, dated 23 December 1931, about his paper for the *Geographical Journal*, Mawson wrote 'It is important to note that, on the authority of Mr. Mac-Robertson himself, Mac-Robertson Land is to be spelt Mac-Robertson.' The letter is among the Mawson correspondence in the RGS archives.

70 *Mawson's Antarctic diaries*, p. 312, January 1930. MacKenzie's diary for 9 January 1930 records the receipt that day from Australia House of a wireless message about the earlier discovery of land by the *Norvegia* between Kemp and Enderby Land, 'the very coast off which we now lie'. Many were depressed by this disappointing news. Mawson's brave smile was noted and admired by MacKenzie.

71 Mawson's press report transmitted on 12 January 1930.

72 See Ann Savours, 'John Biscoe', *Polar Record*, vol. xxi, no. 134, 1987, pp. 485–91.

73 Hj. Riiser-Larsen, 'The *Norvegia* Antarctic Expedition of 1929–30', *Geographical Review*, vol. xx, 1930, pp. 555–73.

74 Captain J. K. Davis. Diary, 12 January 1930.

75 A. Grenfell Price, op. cit., pp. 70–2; *Mawson's Antarctic diaries*, pp. 313–15.

76 Captain J. K. Davis. Diary, 13 January 1930.

77 Captain K. N. MacKenzie. Diary, 14 January 1930.

78 Quoted by A. Grenfell Price, op. cit. p. 71, from the copy in the Mawson papers, Adelaide.

79 *Mawson's Antarctic diaries*, p. 315, 13 January 1930.

80 Ibid., 14 January 1930.

81 Captain J. K. Davis. Diary, 14 January 1930.

82 *Mawson's Antarctic diaries*, pp. 316–18.

83 Captain J. K. Davis. Diary, 15 January 1930.

84 Obituary by Brian Roberts, *Polar Record*, vol. xiii, no. 84, 1966, pp. 353–8, from which the following biographical notes are largely taken.

85 Ibid.

86 *Scientific results of the Norwegian Antarctic expeditions 1927–38 et seq. instituted and financed by Consul Lars Christensen* (Oslo, 1935–61).

87 Lars Christensen, *Such is the Antarctic* (English translation published by Hodder and Stoughton, London, 1935). See also Lars Christensen, 'Recent reconnaissance flights in the Antarctic', *Geographical Journal*, vol. xciv, no. 3, 1939, pp. 192–208, map (at end).

88 Translation, presumably, of Riiser-Larsen's diary, quoted in Lars Christensen, *Such is the Antarctic*, pp. 175–6.

89 A. Grenfell Price, op. cit., pp. 75–6. The 'wireless press message' sent by Mawson via the Admiralty on 15 January was received at the Dominions Office in London on 27 January. It covers a single sheet of paper. PRO, DO/35/152/2 file 6083/3,f10.

90 A. Grenfell Price, op. cit., pp. 16 and 73.

91 Ibid., pp. 73–4.

92 See translation of this decree in *Polar Record*, no. 18, 1939, pp. 169–73, map. See the obituary of Hjalmar Riiser-Larsen in *Polar Record*, vol. xiii, no. 82, 1966, pp. 97–8, and Thor Heyerdahl *et al., Great Norwegian expeditions*, Oslo, 1964. Riiser-Larsen's autobiography, *Femti år for Kongen*, was published in Oslo in 1958 and his narrative of the 1929–30 *Norvegia* expedition, *Mot ukjent land . . .* in Oslo, 1930. He became Chief of the Royal Norwegian Air Force during World War II. The other pilot aboard the *Norvegia*, Commander F. Lützow-Holm, eventually became a Commodore (Kommandør) and head of the Norwegian Fleet Air Arm (Marines flyvevåben).

93 Mawson's press report dated 23 January 1930. J. H. Martin was later First Mate in the *Penola* during the British Graham Land Expedition, 1934–7. See John Rymill, *Southern Lights* (Chatto and Windus, London, 1938). A. R. Hinks, Secretary of the RGS, later questioned the wisdom of Mawson's reporting such trivia. Mawson stoutly defended his account of the cat's rescue by saying in reply that the Hearst Press had paid £8,500 for these reports, which had to be aimed at a popular market. The correspondence is in the RGS's archives. Martin's only diary entry about Nigger's adventure, on 16 January 1930, is 'cat fell overboard at 6pm and was rescued'.

94 Paquita Mawson, *Mawson of the Antarctic* (Longman, London, 1964).

95 B. B. Roberts in the obituary published in *Polar Record*, vol. iii, no. 21, 1941, p. 390.

96 Letter to the author from Captain R. E. D. Ryder, VC, RN. Mr Duncan Carse of the British Graham Land Expedition, in conversation with the author, recollected Martin's height, his attention to detail (for example in his neatly mended clothes) and the pipe of pungent baccy in the bunk above his. Martin's false teeth were put away in his bowler hat at the beginning of the voyage. 'His remarkable qualities of courtesy, patience, and above all loyalty, were combined with an ability to adapt himself to his company', wrote Brian Roberts, 'so that he was as much a part of his surroundings in the fo'c'sle of a sealing ship as in his London clubs. He never expected credit for anything he did, and was always willing to watch others get praise for his work.'

97 Captain J. K. Davis. Diary, 19 January 1930.

98 *Mawson's Antarctic diaries*, p. 322.

99 J. B. Child. Diary, 19 January, 1930.

100 J. H. Martin. Diary, 20 January 1930. S.P.R.I., MS. 429/2/1.

101 Captain J. K. Davis. Diary, 20 January 1930.

102 Captain K. N. MacKenzie. Diary, 22 January 1930.

103 Captain J. K. Davis. Diary, 23 January 1930.

104 Mawson's press report dated 23 January 1930.

105 J. B. Child. Diary, 23–27 January 1930.

106 *Mawson's Antarctic diaries*, pp. 323 and 320–1.

107 Captain J. K. Davis. Diary, 23 January 1930.

108 Ibid., 24 January 1930.

109 *Mawson's Antarctic diaries*, pp. 325–6, 25 January 1930.

110 *Mawson's Antarctic diaries*, p. 326, 26 January 1930, and Mawson's press report of 27 January 1930. Seaman Martin was also disappointed. 'Fine, bright, cold day. Launch plane and Sir D.M. and Capt. Hurley take flights and report open water right up to the Island. So reluctantly the O.M. gets under weigh and by the 1st Dog Watch we are about a mile from the land but there is some light pack ice and the O.M. refuses to drive through it, so we hang about. It seems to me that there is an absolute lack of guts somewhere. We have come miles to get [to] land with men and equipment and now whenever the chance offers we get cold feet.' J. H. Martin. Diary, 25 January 1930. S.P.R.I., MS. 429/2/1.

111 Captain J. K. Davis. Diary, 25 January 1930.

112 Press report, 27 January 1930.

113 Captain J. K. Davis. Diary, 28 January 1930.

114 *Mawson's Antarctic diaries*, p. 327.

115 See D. F. Styles, *Coastal exploration of Kemp and Enderby Lands, Antarctica* (Antarctic Division, Department of External Affairs, Melbourne, 1964).

116 Captain J. K. Davis. Diary, 25 January 1930.

117 Captain A. R. Williamson. Letter to the author, 21 January 1985.

118 Captain W. R. Colbeck. Letter to the author, 23 January 1983.

119 J. H. Martin. Diary, 31 January 1930. S.P.R.I., MS. 429/2/1.

120 Captain J. K. Davis. Diary, 31 January to 3 February 1930 and 26 January 1930.

121 Benjamin Morrell was an American sealer who wrote a book entitled *A narrative of four voyages . . . From the year 1822 to 1832* (New York, 1832). In 1822–3, he made a voyage to the Antarctic in the *Wasp*, together with Robert Johnson in the *Henry* from New York. He visited South Georgia, Bouvetøya, Kerguelen and the South Sandwich Islands and probably penetrated to a high latitude in the Weddell Sea. He reported land he called 'New South Greenland' in about long. 48°W. between lats. 62°S. and 69°S. The foregoing information is largely from B. B. Roberts's *Chronological list of Antarctic expeditions* (S.P.R.I., Cambridge, 1958). See also R. V. Hamilton, 'On Morrell's Antarctic voyage . . .', *Proceedings of the Royal Geographical Society*, First Series, vol. xiv, 1869–70, pp. 145–56.

122 Parliamentary Paper no. 80 of 1930, pp. 93 and 95.

123 The aerial photographs obtained by the two pilots, ground photographs, and surveys by Commander Moyes and Lieut. Colbeck were used as the basis for the map of south-east Kerguelen published in the *Geographical Journal*, vol. lxxxiii, no. 1, 1934. Mawson's 'The Kerguelen archipelago', which provides a summary of what was known about the islands, appears in the same issue, pp. 18–29.

124 Captain K. N. MacKenzie. Diary, 8 February 1930.

125 Ibid., 10 February 1930.

126 Captain J. K. Davis. Diary, 13 February 1930.

127 Ibid., 6 March 1930.

128 PRO, Board of Trade Series. Copy in N.M.M.

129 Mawson's press reports of 18 and 22 February and 3 March. The *Gauss* expedition of 1901–3 was led by Erich von Drygalski. His narrative *Zum Kontinent des eisigen Südens* was published in Berlin by Georg Reimer in 1904, of which an English translation by M. M. Raraty was done in 1989 (Bluntisham Books/Erskine Press). The main party wintered in the pack-ice aboard the *Gauss*, discovering Kaiser Wilhelm II Land. A separate scientific party spent 16 months on Kerguelen, conveyed in the *Tanglin* and *Stassfurt*.

The British 'Transit of Venus' expedition observed the transit of December 1874 at Anse Betsy, Kerguelen. S. J. Perry was the chief astronomer. The vessels carrying the party were HMS *Volage* (Captain Fairfax) and HMS *Supply* (Captain Inglis).

130 A. Grenfell Price, op. cit., p. 92. Martin recorded on 26 February that they were expecting every day to leave for Heard Island, but the departure had been daily postponed. 'Today the O.M. and Sir D. were arguing loudly over something. Think both of opinion too early to return to Australia—one wishes to kill time anchored here, while the other wishes to visit various islands on the way home.' S.P.R.I., MS. 429/2/1.

On 17 March (quite late in the Antarctic season), Davis told Mawson that he had no wish to embark on new schemes after a long voyage of five months, it being unfair to get the men to carry on indefinitely. Mawson could get someone fresh if really necessary. He himself was 'just worn out with the long worry of a voyage such as we have had and this will be evident to anyone reading this journal. I cannot growl to anyone else so I have to growl here and when I read it afterwards it will not please me but it is a safety valve.' Captain J. K. Davis. Diary, 17 March 1930.

131 Captain K. N. MacKenzie. Diary, 6 March 1930.

132 Ibid., 6 March 1930.

133 Diary kept by Ritchie Simmers, 8 March 1930, quoted by A. Grenfell Price, op. cit., p. 92.

134 Reuters report from Melbourne, 14 May 1930.

135 J. K. Davis papers, classmark 3236/6a.

136 *Mawson's Antarctic diaries*, pp. 339 and 343.

137 A. Grenfell Price, op. cit., p. 83.


## Chapter Twenty. Second BANZARE Voyage, 1930–1, Homeward Voyage, Expedition Results

1 Sir Douglas Mawson to Dr H. R. Mill, 18 June 1930. S.P.R.I., MS. 100/75/13.

2 R. G. Casey to J. H. Scullin, 14 August 1930, published in Neville Meaney, *Australia and the World* (Longman Cheshire, Melbourne, 1985), pp. 374–6. The same letter outlined a proposal by the Hudson's Bay Company to set up permanent stations on the continent at which arctic foxes could be farmed, penguins' eggs collected and hair seals exploited, in addition possibly to prosecuting whaling and fishing by pelagic methods.

3 MacKenzie papers. Copy in N.M.M.

4 Not long after leaving the *Discovery*, MacKenzie commanded HEMS *Mabahiss* in the Red Sea, Arabian Sea and Indian Ocean during the John Murray Oceanographic Expedition of 1933–4, led by R. B. Seymour Sewell. MacKenzie finished his sea career with this voyage. Curiously enough, the *Mabahiss* was still afloat in Alexandria some years ago, when there were plans to convert her into an oceanographic museum. He became Assistant Marine Superintendent with the London, Midland and Scottish Railway at Euston, 1935–7, and then Marine Superintendent and Harbour Master at Holyhead. He was a Younger Brother of Trinity House and died of heart trouble in 1951, aged 53. For a fuller biographical sketch by his son, Captain K. M. MacKenzie, see *Deep-sea challenge: the John Murray/'Mabahiss' Expedition to the Indian Ocean 1933–34*, ed. A. L. Rice (Unesco, Paris, 1986), pp. 274–6.

Mawson's verdict on MacKenzie after the expedition's return was most favourable. In a letter to J. W. S. Marr of 21 July 1931, he wrote 'He turned out splendidly as Skipper. It is a pity we had not got someone like him for the first voyage.' S.P.R.I., MS. 1403/3/7.

5  PRO, F.O. 371/15657 (W160/29/50).
6  Undated press release, probably November 1930, J. B. Child album.
7  Undated press report by Mawson, presumably 1930, Child album.
8  Captain K. N. MacKenzie. Diary, 27 November 1930.
9  Mawson's press report of 10 December 1930.
10  See Sir Douglas Mawson, *The home of the blizzard* (London, 1915).
11  A. Grenfell Price, *The winning of Australian Antarctica: Mawson's BANZARE voyages, 1929–31, based on the Mawson papers*, pp. 101–5; *Mawson's Antarctic diaries*, pp. 356–61.
12  J. S. Cumpston, *Macquarie Island* (Antarctic Division, Department of External Affairs, Melbourne, 1968), pp. 325–30.
13  Captain K. N. MacKenzie. Diary, 8 December 1930.
14  A. Grenfell Price, op. cit., p. 108.
15  For an obituary of Rasmussen, see *Polar Record*, vol. xiii, no. 87, 1967, p. 806. A press cutting in Simmers's diary, dated 17 July 1930, gives further details of the ship.
16  Captain K. N. MacKenzie. Diary, 16 December 1930.
17  R. G. Simmers. Diary, 15 December 1930.
18  Harold Fletcher, *Antarctic days with Mawson* (Angus and Robertson, London, 1984), p. 251.
19  R. G. Simmers. Diary, 15 December 1930.
20  Paraphrased from Mawson's description quoted by A. Grenfell Price, op. cit., pp. 108–9 and *Mawson's Antarctic diaries*, pp. 362–3.
21  These were packed in a case and taken aboard the factory ship with a request that they be kept in the freezing chamber and handed over to a representative of the Auckland Museum on arrival at Stewart Island, New Zealand.
22  RGS Archives, Mawson's BANZARE correspondence.
23  J. H. Martin. Diary, 11 December 1930. S.P.R.I., MS. 429/2/2.
24  Captain MacKenzie. Diary, 16 December 1930.
25  Press report, 16 December 1930. Martin thought the beautiful bergs looked like coral islands. J. H. Martin. Diary, 21 December 1930. S.P.R.I., MS. 429/2/2.
26  J. H. Martin. Diary, 18 December 1930. S.P.R.I., MS. 429/2/2.
27  A. Grenfell Price, op. cit., pp. 110–11; Harold Fletcher, op. cit., pp. 254–5.
28  Captain K. N. MacKenzie. Diary, 25 December 1930.
29  A. Grenfell Price, op. cit., p. 111.
30  Captain K. N. MacKenzie. Diary, 27 December 1930.
31  A. Grenfell Price, op. cit., p. 111.
32  Ibid., p. 112; unreferenced press cutting.
33  During this, the *Norvegia* made further discoveries, leading eventually to the Norwegian claim to Dronning Maud Land in 1939.
34  Press report, 30 December 1930.
35  A. Grenfell Price, op. cit., p. 112.
36  Ibid.
37  Ibid., p. 113.
38  Ibid.

39 Captain K. N. MacKenzie. Diary, 1 January 1931. Punctuation, upper and lower cases slightly amended.

40 J. H. Martin. Diary, 31 December 1930. S.P.R.I., MS. 429/2/2.

41 Captain K. N. MacKenzie. Diary, 2 January 1931.

42 Harold Fletcher, op. cit., p. 254.

43 This part of the coast of Greater Antarctica was first sighted by the French explorer J. S. C. Dumont d'Urville in 1840. Terre Adélie now forms the French sector, claimed as part of the 'Terres Australes et Antarctiques Françaises'. A number of modern French expeditions have taken place there since 1948.

44 Paraphrased from Mawson's preface to the 'Black Jacket' edition of *The home of the blizzard*, published by Hodder & Stoughton, 1938. Mawson's diaries of the Australasian Antarctic Expedition, edited by Fred and Eleanor Jacka, were published in *Mawson's Antarctic diaries* (Allen & Unwin, Sydney, 1988).

45 Preface to the 'Popular edition' of *The home of the blizzard* (Hodder & Stoughton, London, 1930). See also Davis's narrative, *With the 'Aurora' in the Antarctic, 1911–14* (Melrose, London, 1919).

46 Paraphrased with some quotations from Captain K. N. MacKenzie, Diary, 6 January 1931.

47 R. G. Simmers. Diary, 4 January 1931.

48 Captain K. N. MacKenzie. Diary, 6 January 1931.

49 Sir Douglas Mawson, *The home of the blizzard* (6th ed. 1938), pp. 59–60.

50 Ibid., pp. 316–19.

51 J. B. Child press cutting album. Undated report from the *Evening News* on the *Discovery*'s return to the East India Dock, London. 1 August 1931.

52 A. Grenfell Price, op. cit., p. 115.

53 R. G. Simmers. Diary, 15 January 1931.

54 Captain K. N. MacKenzie. Diary, 6 January 1931. Mawson in fact presented this sledge to the RGS. Some restoration work on the huts has been carried out in recent years by the Australian Antarctic Division, Department of Science. Archaeological investigations formed part of the work of 'Project Blizzard', 1985–6, a private venture intended to conserve the site. See Jonathan Chester, *Going to extremes* (Doubleday, Sydney, 1986), and Angela McGowan, 'Historical Archaeology at Cape Denison, Commonwealth Bay, Antarctica', *Polar Record*, vol. xxiv, no. 149, 1988, pp. 101–10; also Janet Hughes, 'Mawson's Antarctic huts', Ibid., vol. xxviii, no. 164, 1992, pp. 37–42.

55 A. Grenfell Price, op. cit., p. 115; *Mawson's Antarctic diaries*, p. 366. Mawson kept no full, continuous BANZARE diary 1930–1.

56 A. Grenfell Price, ibid.

57 Captain K. N. MacKenzie. Diary, 6 January 1931. The proclamation was found intact in its container at the base of the flagstaff on 14 January 1974 by members of the Australian National Antarctic Research Expedition. See *Polar Record*, vol. xvii, no. 108, 1974, pp. 307–8, plate.

58 R. G. Simmers. Diary, 5 January 1931.

59 Frank Hurley's diary, quoted in Lennard Bickel, *In search of Frank Hurley* (Macmillan, Melbourne, 1980).

60 R. G. Simmers. Diary, 6 January 1931.

61 A. Grenfell Price, op. cit., p. 118.

62  Captain K. N. MacKenzie. Diary, 12 January 1931.
63  Ibid., 15 January 1931; A. Grenfell Price, op. cit., pp. 118–20; Mawson's press report of 19 January 1931.
64  R. G. Simmers, Diary for 16 January 1931, quoted in A. Grenfell Price, op. cit., p. 123.
65  A. Grenfell Price, op. cit., pp. 121–3.
66  Captain K. N. MacKenzie. Diary, 15 January 1931.
67  R. G. Simmers. Diary, 23 January 1931. Kindly transcribed by Mr David Harrowfield. See R. A. Falla's report on the Arctic tern in *Birds*. BANZ Expedition Committee, Adelaide, 1937, pp. 251–4.
68  Mawson's press report of 21 January 1931; letter to the author from Professor Arnold Wolfendale, 14 June 1988.
69  J. H. Martin. Diary, 25 January 1931. S.P.R.I., MS. 429/2/3.
70  A. Grenfell Price, op. cit., p. 129.
71  Captain K. N. MacKenzie. Diary, 27 January 1931.
72  Mawson to A. R. Hinks, Secretary of the RGS, 3 July 1930. RGS Archives.
73  A. Grenfell Price, op. cit., p. 133.
74  Captain K. N. MacKenzie. Diary, 30 January 1931.
75  Ibid., 31 January 1931.
76  A. Grenfell Price, op. cit., p. 134.
77  Captain K. N. MacKenzie. Diary, 5 February 1931.
78  J. H. Martin. Diary, 8 February 1931. S.P.R.I., MS. 429/2/3.
79  Paquita Mawson, *Mawson of the Antarctic* (Longman, London, 1964), p. 177.
80  Sir Douglas Mawson to Dr H. R. Mill, 6 February 1931. S.P.R.I., MS. 100/75/15.
81  Mawson's press report of 4 February 1931.
82  Captain K. N. MacKenzie. Diary, 2 February 1931.
83  Ibid., 10 February 1931.
84  A. Grenfell Price, op. cit., p. 144.
85  Ibid., p. 170.
86  Ibid., p. 145.
87  See ibid., pp. 146, 172–3. See also the chronological table setting out Mawson's and the Norwegians' explorations in Kemp Land and Mac.Robertson Land in G. W. Rayner's report on the coastal survey by RRS *William Scoresby* in these areas 1935–6. This appears in *Discovery Reports*, vol. xix, 1940, pp. 165–84, where Rayner's view of Kemp Land is reproduced as a colour plate. See also the folding map, 'The course of Antarctic exploration between longitudes 20°W. and 110°E.', which accompanies Lars Christensen's paper, 'Recent reconnaissance flights in the Antarctic', *Geographical Journal*, vol. xciv, no. 3, 1939, pp. 192–203. The map shows the contributions of Norway, Great Britain and others. Notes on the map are on pp. 204–8.
88  A. Grenfell Price, op. cit., pp. 147–151.
89  Ibid.
90  Ibid., pp. 151–3.
91  J. H. Martin. Diary, 14 February 1931. S.P.R.I., MS. 429/2/3.
92  Captain K. N. MacKenzie. Diary, 13 February 1931.
93  Ibid., 14 February 1931.
94  R. G. Simmers. Diary for 17 February 1931, quoted in A. Grenfell Price, op. cit., p. 154.

95  A. Grenfell Price, op. cit., p. 154.

96  Captain K. N. MacKenzie. Diary, 17 February 1931. Mawson records that MacKenzie's anxiety arose in part because this was his first command and its success or failure would affect his career. See *Mawson's Antarctic diaries*, p. 384.

97  Mawson's press report of 20 February 1931.

98  Quoted in A. Grenfell Price, op. cit., pp. 155–7.

99  H. Fletcher, op. cit., p. 302.

100  Captain K. N. MacKenzie. Diary, 18 February 1931.

101  Ibid., 18 February 1931. MacKenzie also felt that the airmen and scientists did not wash enough. See *Mawson's Antarctic diaries*, pp. 383 and 385.

102  H. Fletcher, op. cit., p. 299.

103  Captain K. N. MacKenzie. Diary, 19 February 1931. It is curious that Fletcher, op. cit., p. 303, states that on account of depleted coal stocks the *lower and upper yards on the mainmast* were rigged to increase the sail area and had 'been taken down to lessen wind resistance before leaving Cape Town on the first voyage and had been lashed on deck alongside the bulwarks'. MacKenzie's Master's Report agrees with his diary.

104  H. Fletcher, op. cit., p. 278. Mawson felt that MacKenzie worried unnecessarily about the stability of the ship. See *Mawson's Antarctic diaries*, pp. 383–4.

105  Captain K. N. MacKenzie. Diary, 19 February 1931.

106  Ibid., 26 February 1931.

107  Mawson's press report, 9 March 1931.

108  Document in the MacKenzie papers.

109  Captain K. N. MacKenzie. Diary, 4 March 1931.

110  Ibid.

111  H. Fletcher, op. cit., p. 309.

112  Mawson's press report of 20 March 1931.

113  Captain K. N. MacKenzie, Master's Report, SY *Discovery*. Copy of undated typescript in MacKenzie papers.

114  Mawson's press report of 12 March 1931.

115  Mawson's press report of 16 March 1931. See also Sir Douglas Mawson, 'The unveiling of Antarctica', *Report of the 22nd meeting of the Australian and New Zealand Association for the Advancement of Science* (Melbourne, 1935), pp. 1–37.

116  R. A. Falla to James Marr, 29 March 1931. S.P.R.I., MS. 1403/3/12.

117  Sir Douglas Mawson, 'The unveiling of Antarctica', *Report of the 22nd meeting of the Australian and New Zealand Association for the Advancement of Science* (Melbourne, 1935), p. 28.

118  These are listed in A. Grenfell Price, op. cit., pp. 198–200. In a letter to Dr H. R. Mill of 30 July 1931, Mawson said that his article for the *Geographical Review* of 1930 had been 'rather foolishly hurried off' to Dr Isaiah Bowman 'before all our maps were redrawn and the data worked over' in return for his 'assistance . . . in securing Press subsidies'. S.P.R.I., MS. 100/75/16. Cabled modifications arrived after the map had gone to press. Once the present charts were completed, Mawson intended to contribute a more definitive article for the *Geographical Journal* in London. His correspondence with A. R. Hinks relating to this article is in the archives of the RGS and is of interest from the point of view of place-names and cartography.

119  Sir Douglas Mawson to James Marr, 21 July 1931. S.P.R.I., MS. 1403/3/7.

120  Sir Douglas Mawson. Letter to A. R. Hinks, Secretary of the RGS, 28 March 1934. RGS Archives. In an earlier letter to Dr H. R. Mill of 30 July 1931, he wrote on the same theme. 'The greater part of my time in connection with these "Discovery" cruises has been occupied in begging for money and equipment. I am glad that all that is now done, but there yet remains the provision of a fund for the publication of the scientific results. The present Commonwealth Government do not appear to be at all interested.' Hopes of using the profits from 'the very excellent cinema film' were being dashed by the Government representative on the expedition committee, who 'appears to look upon such assets as a reasonable perquisite for the Government and an offset against expense incurred in the actual work up-to-date'. In fact, he wrote, 'the Commonwealth Government has contributed only a very small sum. Apart from the cost of the charter of the vessel defrayed by the British Government, nearly all the expenditure has been met by private donations and returns from Press articles.' S.P.R.I., MS. 100/75/16. See Grenfell Price, op. cit., pp. 17–19. Price states that the unofficial receipts by mid-1931 amounted to £27,627, while contributions from the British, Australian and New Zealand Governments approximately equalled that sum, the Commonwealth of Australia granting £12,000, the British Government chartering the *Discovery* for £11,714 and the New Zealand Government giving £2,500. This does not appear to agree with Mawson's assertion quoted earlier.

121  There are copies of the film in the Australian National Library, Canberra, and in the N.M.M. In a letter to James Marr of 21 July 1931, Mawson expressed the view that the film was a 'very fine photographical production, but some of us think the talk that goes with it might have been improved. Also Hurley's voice is not the best for such a production.' S.P.R.I., MS. 1403/3/7. In this same letter, he said that the film had been shown in most of the Australian states and that it was to be shown in England. He said too that arrangements for the scientific publications had been waiting for a financial return on the film. The sale of expedition equipment had been disappointing.

122  A. Grenfell Price, op. cit., pp. 162–4.

123  For post-war Australian activities in the Antarctic, see the following: Phillip Law and John Bechervaise, *ANARE* (Oxford University Press, Melbourne, 1957); John Bechervaise, *Antarctica, the last horizon* (Cassel, Australia, 1979); Phillip Law, *Antarctic Odyssey* (Heinemann, Melbourne, 1983). A series of *ANARE Reports* and *Interim Reports* has been issued by the Antarctic Division since 1950. These are mainly scientific, but include some narratives. See also the periodical *Polar Record*.

124  Typescript owned by Captain K. M. MacKenzie. Copy in N.M.M.

125  *The Sun*, 11 June 1931. I am indebted to Mr H. G. R. King for this press cutting.

126  MacKenzie papers. News release received Portishead, 26 May 1931.

127  Sir Douglas Mawson to Dr H. R. Mill, 30 July 1931. S.P.R.I., MS. 100/75/16.

128  A letter from the *Discovery* Committee, Colonial Office, dated 3 September 1931 expressed thanks to Captain Davis and Captain MacKenzie for the 'excellent condition' in which the ship was found on the expiry of the BANZARE Charter. Captain MacKenzie's opinion of the *Discovery* can be found among the papers of the *Discovery* Committee, 109th meeting, together with some statistics of her performance during the 1930–1 voyage. He had found her under-powered and very slow—a defect when pressing through ice or against a head wind. On the whole the barquentine rig had proved very satisfactory. Schooner rig would be

best in the south, but yards could be crossed with advantage on passage to and from the Antarctic. It was not possible, however, to strike down the lower main yards in the south and to house them aboard. In the Antarctic, she had travelled about two thousand miles under sail alone, the best day's run then being 180 miles, and under sail and steam, 217 miles. Her speed might be improved by the use of higher powered engines, oil fuel and the use of a differently bladed propeller. In most respects 'the ship had proved very efficient, and *with sea room*', he 'would feel more safe in her than in any other vessel. The ship improved on acquaintance and responded satisfactorily', although she had insufficient power to charge the ice. 'Note of Captain MacKenzie's remarks on R.R.S. "Discovery".' Typescript in *Discovery* papers. Institute of Oceanographic Sciences, Deacon Laboratory.

# PART VI.
## SEA SCOUTS AND AFTER

**Chapter Twenty-one. Laid Up in London, 'Saved for the Nation', Transfer to the Sea Scouts, 1937, the Second World War and After, Transfer to the Maritime Trust, 1979**

1  J. M. Scott, *Gino Watkins* (Hodder and Stoughton, London, 1935). The continent was crossed overland eventually by the British Commonwealth Trans-Antarctic expedition, 1955–8, led by V. E. (later Sir Vivian) Fuchs. On 20 June 1932, the Hudson's Bay Company, for the sum of £1,250, relinquished its right to repurchase the *Discovery*. This sum was paid by the Crown Agents for the Colonies. The agreement appears to have been concluded in the light of the possibility of Watkins actually buying, rather than merely chartering, the vessel. HBC Archives, A92/Corr./254/3 and Unclassified material: Agreement, HBC and Crown Agents, 20 June 1932.

2  File relating to the *Discovery*'s maintenance and refit in the library of the Institute of Oceanographic Sciences, the Deacon Laboratory, Wormley, near Godalming.

3  File concerning the chartering or disposal of the *Discovery*, post 1931, in the Institute of Oceanographic Sciences: letter to the Earl of Plymouth, PC, dated 23 June 1936, from B. M. Borley and Miss W. J. Hope.

4  Quoted by L. C. Bernacchi in *Saga of the 'Discovery'* (Blackie, London, 1938), p. ix.

5  Dr John Nash, unpublished typescript, 'RRS Discovery and Sea Scouts', written at the author's request, March 1988. This quotation is based on the text of Lord Baden-Powell's speech at the handing-over ceremony on 9 October 1937 in the archives of the Scouts Association, ref. TC/120, kindly provided by the Archivist.

6  Warner Allen, *Lucy Houston, DBE 'One of the Few': a memoir* (Constable, London, 1947), p. 164. See also the entry in the supplement to the *Dictionary of National Biography*, which describes her as a 'philanthropist and eccentric'.

7  Copy of letter from Dame Lucy Houston to Lord Baden-Powell, 13 November 1936, in the archives of the Scouts Association, ref. TC/34.

8  Copy of agreement in the archives of the Scouts Association, undated, ref. TC/120.

9  Copy of a letter from the Chief Scout to Lady Houston, 12 November 1936, in the archives of the Scouts Association, ref. TC/34.

10  Copy of Lord Baden-Powell's speech at the handing-over ceremony in the archives of the Scouts Association, ref. TC/120.

11  Printed programme of the handing-over ceremony in the S.P.R.I.

12  Lady Kennet, *Self-portrait of an artist* (John Murray, London, 1949), p. 318. There is much of polar interest in this delightful and very personal book. She had married Captain Scott in 1908. Her statue of him stands in Waterloo Place, London.

13  Information kindly provided by Mr M. R. C. Parr, MRINA, *c*.1980.

14  Recollections of Sea Scout days kindly supplied by Mr Peter Hollins, RIBA, ACI (Arb.), 22 March 1988.

15  Lieut.-Com. John Dawkins, VRD, RNR, 'The story behind the picture', *Friends of the Maritime Trust Newsletter*, no. 7, Summer 1984, p. 21.

16  Recollections of Sea Scout days kindly supplied by Mr Peter Hollins, RIBA, ACI (Arb.), 22 March 1988.

17  Dr John Nash, unpublished typescript, 'RRS Discovery and Sea Scouts', March 1988. Dr Nash did not witness this 'un-nautical collision with an aerial object'. His correspondent, Mr John Rapley, then liaison official in Scout HQ for matters pertaining to the *Discovery*, maintains that the rot in the yards was found rather as the result of a routine inspection and not in the more dramatic way.

18  Dr John Nash, op. cit. Dr Nash adds that his recollections concerning the engine have been confirmed by Mr John Rapley. The cutting up was done after consultation with the Admiralty and Ministry of Supply. Admiralty engineers decided that the removal of the machinery intact was impractical. It appears that the engine was sacrificed only after careful deliberation.

19  M. R. C. Parr, MRIN, unpublished typescript, 'RRS *Discovery* in Scout ownership 1936–1952', *c*.1986.

20  Booklet, *Royal Research Ship 'Discovery'—the history of Captain Scott's famous vessel* (Scout Association, London, 1951), p. 19. See too A. P. Luscombe White, 'London's River Emergency Service', *Strand Magazine*, September 1940, pp. 392–5 and frontispiece.

21  Ibid.

22  Dr John Nash, op. cit.

23  M. R. C. Parr, op. cit.

24  *Royal Research Ship 'Discovery'—the history of Captain Scott's famous vessel*, p. 19.

25  M. R. C. Parr, op. cit.

26  Undated Admiralty memorandum 'RRS DISCOVERY—Opening to the Public', from RNVR files.

27  Ibid.

28  'Minutes of meeting held on board R.S.S. [*sic*] DISCOVERY at London Graving Dock, 7 July 1954 to discuss alterations and additions necessary for conversion to R.N.V.R. Drill Ship London Division'. Admiralty, Bath, DNE Memorandum no. 743/54, 14 July 1954. An appendix lists the proposed alterations and additions.

29  This paragraph is a summary of information in Gordon Taylor, *London's navy: the story of the Royal Naval Volunteer Reserve* (Quiller Press, London, 1983), pp. 113–15. I am obliged to Mr Robert Baldwin for drawing my attention to the book. It contains two photographs of the *Discovery* at that time.

30  *The Times*, 4 March 1978.

# DISCOVERY: SELECTED READING LIST

This list does not in general cover periodical articles or the series of scientific results published by the National Antarctic Research Expedition, 1901–4, the *Discovery* Committee (*Discovery Reports*) and the British, Australian and New Zealand Antarctic Research Expedition, 1929–31. Sets of these may be found in the Scott Polar Research Institute, Cambridge, analytically catalogued in the G. K. Hall Published SPRI Library Card Catalogue (17 vols).

See also Notes and References for other works of interest.

## General

BERNACCHI, Louis C.
*The saga of the 'Discovery".* London, Blackie, 1938.
[Ship history by member of 1901–4 expedition.]
FOGG, G. E., *and* SMITH, David
*The explorations of Antarctica, the last unspoilt continent.* London, Cassell, 1990.
KIRWAN, L. P.
*The white road: a survey of polar exploration.* London, Hollis & Carter, 1959.
SMITH, *Sir* William Edward
The design of the Antarctic exploration vessel *Discovery*.
*Transactions of the Institution of Naval Architects*, Vol. 47, April 1905.
WALTON, D. W. H. *ed.*
*Antarctic science.* Cambridge University Press, 1987.
[From Captain Cook to 1980s.]

## National Antarctic Expedition, 1901–4

ARMITAGE, Albert B.
*Two years in the Antarctic.* London, 1905.
[Narrative of National Antarctic Expedition, 1901–4, by Scott's second-in-command.]
DOORLY, Gerald S.
*The voyages of the 'Morning'.* London, 1916.

[Narrative of the *Morning*'s Antarctic voyages under Captain William Colbeck to relieve *Discovery*.]

DOORLY, Gerald S.
*Songs of the 'Morning'*. Melbourne, 1943.
[Copy in Mitchell Library, Sydney.]

FISHER, Margery, *and* FISHER, James
*Shackleton*. London, 1957.

HUNTFORD, Roland
*Scott and Amundsen*. London, Hodder and Stoughton, 1979.
[The result of much painstaking research, but extremely biased against Scott. It has been called 'the case for the Prosecution'.]

HUNTFORD, Roland
*Shackleton*. London, Hodder and Stoughton, 1985.
[Monumental biography, the result of much research.]

HUXLEY, Elspeth
*Scott of the Antarctic*. London, 1977.

LASHLY, William
*Under Scott's command: Lashly's Antarctic diaries, edited by A. R. Ellis. With an introduction by Sir Vivian Fuchs*. London, 1969.
[Writer was Leading Stoker, RN, during the National Antarctic Expedition, 1901–4.]

MARKHAM, Sir Clements
*Antarctic obsession: a personal narrative of the origins of the British National Antarctic Expedition 1901–1904*, edited by Clive Holland. Bluntisham Books and Erskine Press, 1986.

MURRAY, George, *ed.*
*The Antarctic manual for the use of the expedition of 1901. With a preface by Sir Clements R. Markham. Presented to the expedition and issued by the Royal Geographical Society*. London, 1901.
[Memoirs and instructions on various scientific subjects by leading authorities of the day. Includes Antarctic bibliography by H. R. Mill and three track charts of explorers.]

QUARTERMAIN, L. B.
*South to the Pole: the early history of the Ross Sea Sector, Antarctica*. London, Oxford University Press, 1967.

QUARTERMAIN, L. B.
*Two huts in the Antarctic*. Wellington, Government Printers, 1963.
[Illustrated booklet describing the condition of huts of the 'heroic age' of Antarctic exploration, Ross Dependency.]

SCOTT, Robert Falcon
*The voyage of the 'Discovery'*. London, 1905 (and later editions).

SCOTT, Robert Falcon
*Scott's last expedition*, edited by Leonard Huxley. London, 1913 (and later editions).

SEAVER, George
*Edward Wilson of the Antarctic*, London, 1933; *Edward Wilson, nature lover*, London, 1937; *The faith of Edward Wilson*, London, 1948.
[Trilogy relating to the surgeon, artist and vertebrate zoologist during the British National Antarctic Expedition, 1901–4.]

*SOUTH POLAR TIMES.* Vols 1 and 2. London, 1907.
[Facsimile edition of the illustrated newspaper produced during the British National Antarctic Expedition, 1901–4.]
WILSON, Edward
*Diary of the 'Discovery' expedition to the Antarctic regions, 1901–4*, edited from the original mss. in the Scott Polar Research Institute by Ann Savours. London, Blandford, 1966; New York, Humanities Press, 1967.
[Includes colour reproductions of his watercolours.]
WILSON, Edward
*Edward Wilson's birds of the Antarctic*, edited by Brian Roberts from the original illustrations in the Scott Polar Research Institute, Cambridge. London, Blandford, 1968.
[Includes bibliography and reproductions in colour.]

## Hudson's Bay Company Voyages, 1905–11

COOKE, Alan, *and* HOLLAND, Clive
*The exploration of northern Canada, 500 to 1920: a chronology.* Toronto, Arctic History Press, 1978.
[Lists *Discovery*'s Hudson Bay voyages 1905–11 and 1918–19.]
MacKAY, Douglas
*The Honourable Company: a history of the Hudson's Bay Company.* Toronto, McClelland & Stewart, 1936.
NEWMAN, Peter C.
*Empire of the Bay: an illustrated history of the Hudson's Bay Company.* Toronto, Viking Studio/Madison Press, 1989.
SCHOOLING, *Sir* William
*The Hudson's Bay Company . . . the Governor and Company of Adventurers of England during two hundred and fifty years 1670–1920.* London, 1920.
WILLIAMSON, A. R.
'Voyage of the "Discovery" 1911', *Beaver* (Winnipeg, Hudson's Bay Company), Spring 1983, pp. 12–23; Summer 1983, pp. 20–9.
[By Able Seaman of voyage to Hudson Bay.]

## *Discovery* (Oceanographic) Expedition, 1925–7

COLEMAN-COOKE, John
*Discovery II in the Antarctic: the story of British research in the southern seas.* London, 1963.
[Continuation by *Discovery* Investigations of work of the *Discovery*, 1925–7.]
HARDY, *Sir* Alister
*Great waters: a voyage of natural history to study whales, plankton and the waters of the Southern Ocean in the old Royal Research Ship 'Discovery', with the results brought up to date by the findings of the RRS 'Discovery II'.* London, 1967.
[Narrative 1924–7 largely from author's diaries, watercolours, photographs and sketches.]

SAUNDERS, Alfred
*A camera in Antarctica.* London, 1950.
[Well-illustrated account by member of staff of *Discovery* Investigations, 1924–30.]


## British, Australian and New Zealand Antarctic Research Expedition (BANZARE)

BICKEL, Lennard
*This accursed land.* London, Macmillan, 1977.
[Life of Sir Douglas Mawson.]
FLETCHER, Harold
*Antarctic days with Mawson: a personal account of the British, Australian and New Zealand Antarctic Research Expedition of 1929–31.* London, Angus & Robertson, 1984.
DAVIS, John King
*High latitude.* Melbourne University Press, 1962.
[Autobiography, but does not cover BANZARE.]
MAWSON, *Sir* Douglas
*Mawson's Antarctic diaries*, edited by Fred Jacka and Eleanor Jacka. Sydney, Allen & Unwin, 1988.
[Includes BANZARE.]
MAWSON, Paquita
*Mawson of the Antarctic: the life of Sir Douglas Mawson, F.R.S. O.B.E.* London, 1964.
[By his widow.]
PRICE, A. Grenfell
*The winning of Australian Antarctica: Mawson's B.A.N.Z.A.R.E. voyages 1929–31. Based on the Mawson papers.* Sydney, Angus and Robertson (for the Mawson Institute for Antarctic Research, University of Adelaide), 1962.
SWAN, R. A.
*Australia in the Antarctic: interest, activity and endeavour.* Melbourne University Press, 1961.
[Historical study.]

# INDEX

INDEX